W9-CIK-025

SILENT MISSIONS

SILENT MISSIONS

Vernon A. Walters

1978

DOUBLEDAY & COMPANY, INC., GARDEN CITY, NEW YORK

No copyright is claimed on United States Government material that appears in Chapter 29, or any other incidental government material in this book.

ISBN: 0-385-13500-9
Library of Congress Catalog Card Number 77–16853
Copyright © 1978 by Vernon A. Walters
All Rights Reserved
Printed in the United States of America
First Edition

To the brave men and women who have laid down their lives
on the invisible battlefield that we might live free.

I wish to acknowledge gratefully the assistance which I have received from several people in the preparation of this book.

My assistant for nine years, Nancy Ouellette, provided me with invaluable advice through her recollection of, and sometimes participation in, events. Her organization of my files and notes combined with her wise counsel greatly facilitated my task in writing this book. My debt to her is very great.

Lieutenant Lee E. Martiny, a young naval officer who teaches English and history at the United States Naval Academy, contributed extremely valuable critical and constructive comments on my manuscript as to form, style and content. He helped bridge a gap that will, I hope, make this book more readable to readers of his generation. I am very much in his debt.

My brother Fred Walters and his wife Virginia, my brother Vincent Walters and his wife Sherry, and my sister Laureen Masini made helpful comments on my manuscript and often reminded me of stories or events that I had told them in past years and which had slipped from my mind. Thanks to them a number of these are included in this book. I am grateful for their encouragement and help. My thanks also to Mrs. Sharon Lannon, who typed a great part of the manuscript.

CONTENTS

I

SILENT MISSIONS

PART I

1. FINDING MYSELF AS A SOLDIER

On the warm summer morning of June 19, 1970, I found myself at the gate of the Chinese Communist Embassy in Neuilly, a suburb of Paris. I was the U. S. Military Attaché to France. For more than twenty-five years the Chinese Communists and Americans lived in an atmosphere of mutual hostility yet almost without contact. Only rarely had there been any contact and then only through third parties. In my pocket I carried a letter to the Chinese Communist government from President Richard Nixon. My orders were to deliver it this morning. In the light of a recent rebuff from them I expected difficulty.

For years at diplomatic parties and on official occasions, Americans and Chinese had studiously ignored one another, never even acknowledging each other's presence. On attaché trips I had taken, when the Chinese attaché had been along we carefully avoided contact and at meals prudently sat well away from one another. Harsh incidents had occurred between our two countries. They had shot down our planes and had issued us innumerable "grave warnings." They had imprisoned some Americans for more than twenty years. Little did I realize that I would someday be actively involved in obtaining the release of those Americans. The Chinese Communists were actively supporting our North Vietnamese enemies in a protracted and bitter war.

A few months earlier I was called back to the United States to see President Nixon in the White House. He directed me to get in touch with the Chinese Communists in Paris without telling anyone in either the Embassy or the Defense Department. I had great difficulty in finding an opportunity to find the Chinese Communist attaché Fang Wen alone so that I could talk to him without drawing attention to our conversation. The contact must be made with the utmost discretion. Finally I saw Fang Wen alone in the courtyard of the Polish Embassy and attempted to deliver my message to him. His surprise at being addressed by me was almost comical. But it quickly changed to alarm. He fled into his car.

Now suddenly I received a specific order to deliver the letter I carried on the morning of the nineteenth of June. I could only surmise that Henry Kissinger had been in touch with them without my knowledge and that this time they might be willing to accept my message. As I stood there just before pushing open the gate of the Embassy I reflected that here I was, a major general in the U. S. Army, standing at the entrance of the residence of the Chinese Communist Ambassador to France. He too was a general but in the People's Liberation Army of Red China.

I had walked from my own house, which was about a mile away. I looked at my watch. It was eight-twenty. In ten minutes the Ambassador would drive out the gate of the residence on his way to his office on Avenue George V in the center of Paris. I pushed open the gate of the fence surrounding the grounds of the Embassy and immediately saw standing before me a youthful Chinese in a Mao jacket and wearing heavy glasses. He did not seem surprised to see me. I said to him slowly in French, "I am the American Military Attaché and I have a message for your government from my President." For a moment I thought that his impassive expression meant that I was about to be rebuffed once again in my efforts to communicate with them. Then he held out his hand and shook mine. He waved me toward the entrance of the building. Side by side we walked across the driveway and I felt the gravel crunch beneath my shoes. I did not know exactly what was going to happen in the next few minutes but as I walked with the young Chinese my mind wandered back to the circumstances and events that brought me to this time and place on such a mission. I was a U. S. Army officer bearing an offer to open talks with those who had regarded us as their sworn enemies for a quarter of a century.

Born in New York in 1917, I lived for ten years (from six to sixteen) in Europe. My parents sent me to French and British Catholic schools and I acquired proficiency in French, Spanish, Italian, and German. Soon after I returned to the United States as a teen-ager my father met with serious business reverses and I found it necessary to quit school and go to work.

My father very much wanted one of his sons to go to work for the insurance company of which he had once been manager. My older brothers had other ideas and all of the paternal pressures fell on me. I started to work for the London Guarantee and Accident Company as an office boy. Thanks to my knowledge of languages I soon moved on to become a claims adjuster and investigator. I dealt with claimants who spoke languages that I could handle and who lived within one hundred miles of New York. This involved a lot of travel by car. I found it interesting and was able to remain proficient in my languages. I knew that this was not what I wanted to do with my life. On the other hand, I was not yet sure what I did want to do.

On the morning of September 3, 1939, I heard on the radio the tired, almost broken voice of British Prime Minister Neville Chamberlain saying, "No such assurances have been received from the German government and now I must tell you that England is at war with Germany." From that point on there was no doubt in my mind that the United States would enter the war sooner or later. We could not escape from history no matter how much our isolationists wished to hide their heads in the sand. I said to my father, who was an old Englishman, "Dad, you know what is going to happen. Surely you don't expect me to just stay here and work in the insurance company?" "No" he said slowly. "I know what is going to happen and you can go into the Army." I have always said that Adolf Hitler did at least one good deed in his life, even though it was completely involuntary and unknown to him. He got me out of my father's insurance company—with his blessing.

On May 2, 1941, I reported to the Flushing Armory in New York with a large number of other young men who were entering the service. We were interviewed by many people, given physical examinations, vaccinated against all sorts of diseases, issued clothing and lectured on venereal diseases and other less gruesome subjects. At one point a master sergeant was very impressed by the fact that I spoke a number of languages. He went and got a major, who was a pretty exalted being in those days, or so it seemed to me. The major came over and asked me many questions about my life in Europe and the languages I spoke. This was a time when large numbers of people were being taken into the Armed Forces, some of them in very high ranks. The president of General Motors, Mr. Knudsen, became a lieutenant general in Transportation. David Sarnoff of RCA became a brigadier general in the Signal Corps. I half suspected that they might offer me a job as a lieutenant colonel in Intelligence. Since I felt that we would soon be in the war and that everybody had to make sacrifices, I decided that if they offered me a majority, I would take it.

We were also interviewed by a psychiatrist. When my turn came he asked me whether I had any great fears. I replied that I did and this visibly titillated him. He brightened visibly and asked me what they were. I replied that I had been given several going-away parties and gifts and that if I were rejected for the service I did not know how I could go back and face these people. He smiled and seemed relieved that this was apparently all that was weighing on my mind. Then he asked me a number of very personal questions relating to my sexual experiences. With some embarrassment I told him that I had never slept with a woman. "Ah," he said, "an honest man." Then he frowned and asked me why not and didn't I like women. I assured him that I did but I had just not slept with any. Again he asked what had stopped me from doing so. I replied that if I were to try and analyze it, I would say that it was due 65 per cent to Catholic religious inhibitions, 30 per cent to opportunities only with girls who did not attract me and 5 per cent to the lack of opportunities with the ones that did. He relaxed, smiled, patted me on the shoulder and said, "You'll be all right. You're in. Good luck."

Relieved, I went down the line and found lots of other young men who were in the same situation as myself examining the paper that had been given to each of us as we went through this processing. They were looking for what they called their M.O.S. (Military Occupational Specialty, that is the code indicating what they would be doing in the Army. I looked at the appropriate place on my own piece of paper and found a number, 0506. I thought that this was the time to use some of the leadership for which I expected to be called upon shortly. I turned to one of the other young men and said, "Go down and find out what 0506 is." It worked like a charm. He practically saluted me. He went off and soon came back and told me that 0506 was a truck driver. I laughed and said, "Someone has made a mistake." Surely, with all my languages and having lived in Europe all that time they weren't going to do that to me. They were.

We were then taken by buses to Camp Upton on Long Island. Here there were further examinations and property and clothing were issued. Unfortunately, they did not have one of the nice-fitting olive Army uniforms for me. All I got were ancient blue fatigues dating back to World War I and a floppy blue hat. At Camp Upton they taught us the rudiments of military courtesy, marching, saluting and personal hygiene. We also had to learn our general orders and become familiar with certain customs and usages of the service.

On the Sunday after my arrival at Camp Upton, my parents and my brothers and sister came out to see me. They were quite stricken to find me dressed in the blue fatigues, which looked like a prisoner's clothing. I was nearly as stricken myself. Later I was finally issued my olive Army uniform and after putting it on and examining myself in the mirror, I was quite pleased with what I perceived to be my military appearance. At this camp we also received further inoculations. Americans of my generation were very reluctant to be stuck with any kind of a needle, and during such inoculations one or two of the soldiers fainted. As we left the dispensary we would say to the incoming soldiers, "Wait till you see the hook they put in you here!"

At this camp I came into contact for the first time with what the Army calls policing up the area. I was particularly indignant because in the course of this policing up I was required to pick up other people's cigarette butts. Since I didn't smoke this seemed a great injustice to me, but my indignation did me no good; I went around picking up other men's cigarette butts.

After three days at Camp Upton we boarded a train and learned that we were on our way to the unit with which we would serve our permanent assignment. I was assigned to the 187th Field Artillery Regiment at Fort Ethan Allen near Burlington, Vermont. It was a long ride. I wrote a letter home giving my impressions of the Army. My mother kept it and I have it to this day. It makes interesting reading in the light of what happened to me thereafter.

We arrived at Fort Ethan Allen in the late evening. We got off the train at the nearest station at a place called Essex Junction. To our surprise we were met by the regimental band of the 187th Field Artillery and by our commanding officer, Colonel William Green, who wished us welcome. We then marched down the road with music to our barracks. These barracks were brand-new. On the north side of the post there was an older post with a large parade ground.

The 187th Field Artillery had actually been a New York National Guard unit called into federal service. As a Guard unit it had been the 14th Infantry but had been federalized as a field artillery regiment. We were quickly integrated and absorbed into this unit. I was in the headquarters battery of the 2nd Battalion of the regiment. We were armed with French World War I 155-mm. guns. My battery commander was a Captain Graver, my platoon leader was a Lieutenant Brennan and my first sergeant, Dominic Volpe, was twenty-three years old. All of them had been with the unit when it was a Guard outfit. We learned about guns, rifles, trucks and fell quickly into the military routine of a unit such as ours. In the course of learning how to handle our weapons we were taught the use of the bayonet. This was a real shocker. We were told to aim for the throat with the bayonet and "when he stumbles hit him in the groin with the rifle butt." This brought war home to us rather vividly. The Army knew that I had driven my car a good deal in the course of my civilian occupation before entering the Army, and on completion of my basic training they assigned me as driver of a two-and-a-half-ton truck that towed a quarter-ton trailer. The truck with the trailer attached was hard to handle and my duties included much maintenance work. I learned how to change the kingpins and bushings, and how to pack the bearings. Curiously, I liked it.

I was somewhat of an odd man in the outfit since I did not come from Brooklyn like almost everyone else. I soon formed close friendships with several other men there—Jim Clark and Sal Baudo from Queens; Sydney Resnick, Knute Friis and Jim Abbaticchio, all from Brooklyn. We all remained very close at Fort Ethan Allen and when we went on maneuvers. Subsequently, Clark, Resnick, Friis and I became officers. Jarvis was the name of another man who was very close to us. He was thirty-two or thirty-three years old and the rest of us never ceased to wonder that an "old man" like this had been taken into the service. In addition to my duties as truck driver, I was also required on occasion to drive for the platoon leader, Lieutenant Brennan. While at Ethan Allen we sometimes went in groups to Montreal, which was less than a hundred miles away. Here we were able to see what a country at war was like. There was no doubt at all in my mind that we would shortly become involved in the war. Jim Clark thought otherwise and was counting the days until he would complete his year of service and return to his job at the J. Walter Thompson advertising agency. This was not to happen. He fell in France in 1944 shortly after the invasion. After we had become fairly proficient in our duties we began to go out on field exercises to the artillery range on Mount Mansfield near Stowe. Here we learned how to put our guns into battery and prepare them to fire. Finally the day came when we actually got to fire them and it was a great thrill. I was amazed at the noise made by the gun when it fired and by the endless cleaning and swabbing that were necessary to keep it in shape.

Time slipped by quickly. I was often used as a messenger. Several times I drove down to Fort Devens in Massachusetts. The month of June found us out on the range at Underhill. On the fourteenth a rumor swept through the outfit that Germany had attacked the Soviet Union. This was strange as they were virtually allies at that time, yet one week later it actually happened. I have often wondered about that rumor. It appears that the British had found out that the attack would take place on the twenty-first of June and had so informed Stalin, who disregarded the warning.

During all this time I had no leave and in the late summer we went down to the Carolinas to take part in large-scale maneuvers which were being held there. My regiment moved in convoy and the trip took several days. I drove my own truck and Syd Resnick, who had become an acting corporal, rode in the front seat with me. While on these maneuvers I was assigned to the supply detail that drew the rations for our battalion. At night we would go to the supply points and draw the rations for our batteries and then deliver them before daybreak. Then we were allowed in theory to sleep all day as we were operating under simulated war conditions and it was not considered wise to do all this driving around in daylight. The maneuvers were quite realistic and blackout was strictly observed. All of the trucks and other vehicles drove at night with their small blue blackout lights, a faint cross barely visible. This was an interesting and exciting time and I enjoyed it much more than the regular garrison duties at Ethan Allen. Sometimes the rations we drew included ice cream and if we could not find the batteries who were to receive it we would have to eat it ourselves before it melted. This happened from time to time.

One night my first sergeant, Dom Volpe, who was nicknamed "The Ball Breaker" because he was very young and thought of himself, correctly, as being very tough, decided to go with us to see how the supply detail operated. He decided to ride with me in my truck and as we were moving along a road in blackout he told me to turn on my headlights. I told him that if I did so we would probably be attacked by an "enemy" aircraft. He said, "God damn it, don't argue with me. Turn on the Goddamned lights." I shrugged and did so. Within minutes we heard an aircraft roar low over us. I turned to him and said, "Sergeant Volpe, you are dead and you just got me killed too, and I don't appreciate it." He was not amused.

These maneuvers were most interesting and I learned a great deal that was to help me in the years ahead—how to live off the countryside and how to move silently and swiftly at night. We were supposed to sleep in pup tents, small two-man tents, but nearly every night I slept illegally on the canvas between the bow supports for the cover of my truck. Many of the soldiers who slept on the ground suffered a variety of insect bites. Sleeping on top of my truck, I escaped both the insect bites and discovery.

Sometimes on weekends we were free, and as I liked to travel, I would take buses or hitchhike to places like Charlotte, North Carolina, or Columbia, South Carolina. The people in the area were very friendly toward the soldiers and it was easy to get a ride. On one occasion, however, a man who had picked me up made a pass at me and I had to switch off his ignition and get out of the car. On occasion some of us would stay behind at the base camp when the battery went out. Once when the battery returned we found that they had all shaved their heads, including the company commander and the platoon leaders. They soon trapped us and shaved our heads too. It took about six months for our hair to grow back.

Late in the year we started back to Fort Ethan Allen. It was a long drive and it took us several days. We stopped in Virginia, Maryland, and at Binghamton, New York. As the convoy of trucks passed through the towns, the people would often throw fruit and candy into the trucks for the soldiers. Syd Resnick asked me what I thought it meant and I replied that I thought it meant that war was very close and that somehow the people sensed this and wanted to show the soldiers how they felt. Late

at night on the sixth of December we reached Fort Ethan Allen.
We busied ourselves unloading the trucks, moving our gear into
the barracks and lighting the furnaces to heat the barracks, as it
was already very cold in Vermont. Exhausted, we fell asleep
about three o'clock in the morning. We were told that the next
day, Sunday, we could sleep late and that there would be church
in the late afternoon. The next thing I remembered was Lieutenant Romano shaking me by the shoulder and saying,
"Walters, get up. We are at war." "With Germany?" I asked
and he replied that we were at war with Japan, who had attacked Pearl Harbor that morning. I was surprised because I
knew that our Navy had been convoying supplies to Britain and
shooting at German submarines on sight, but I had not sensed
the imminence of war in Asia. I had always believed that it was
far more likely that we would become involved with Germany
first.

The outbreak of war led to a great deal of tightening of security at the camp and all of us taking a much more serious view
of our duties. It also greatly reduced the number of men who
could go on leave and a much greater degree of alertness was
maintained in our unit.

In addition to this greater degree of security, I had the misfortune on Christmas Day 1941 to be on kitchen police duty. We
had a number of huge cooking pots that had been used to cook
sweet potatoes that had burned and far into the night I strug-
gled to scrape them clean. There was dirt, heat and ignominy
connected with kitchen police duty. It was very unpopular.

Shortly after New Year's, it was announced that applications
would be received for candidates to go to Officers Candidate
School. In this respect I had a problem. I felt myself educated
enough to go to this school, but my education had been so complicated in France and England that I did not have the equivalent of an American high school diploma. I knew that this
would make things more difficult for me if I applied. I went
ahead anyway and applied. The application was approved by my
first sergeant, my platoon leader and my company commander.
Captain Graver did ask me why I wanted to be an officer. I

replied that my knowledge of Europe, proficiency in languages and background would enable me to make a greater contribution to the war effort as an officer. This satisfied him and my application was approved at battalion and regiment.

Soon after this I was to have my first intelligence assignment. One night in my barracks I woke and found a man standing over my bed with a flashlight. He showed me an FBI badge and asked me if my name was Walters. I replied affirmatively and then rather melodramatically he asked me what I would do for my country, I equally melodramatically replied that I would do anything for it. He motioned for me to follow him, and we went into one of the vacant non-commissioned officers' rooms at the end of the barracks. There he explained that the FBI believed there was a group of German spies operating out of Stowe posing as refugees from the Nazis. It was believed that they had a radio station and were passing information on shipping movements from New York harbor to German submarines at sea. He asked me to ingratiate myself with this group and find out who belonged to it. I had been selected for this task because I was the president of the Fort Ethan Allen Ski Club. Friis, Resnick, Clark, Jarvis, Abbaticchio, Baudo and I used to go skiing nearly every weekend we could get off in the Stowe area and we were known to the other soldiers as the Ski Hooples. Major Hoople at that time was a popular character in the comic strips. I performed this mission to the satisfaction of the FBI. Later they were to send me a cryptically worded letter of commendation. It arrived at the battalion two or three days before I was to leave to go to Officers Candidate School. I thought that it would do me much more good to receive it there than at Fort Ethan Allen and arranged to have it strategically delayed a few weeks. On the night the FBI agent woke me in the barracks I called the battalion adjutant a minute or two after he left. This was not easy to do, as it was late at night. I apologized to the adjutant for calling him so late but he replied that if I had not called to check with him they probably would not have used me. That showed the sort of judgment that they wanted from me.

Shortly before this episode a board came up from the VI

Corps area at Providence to examine the applicants for Officers
Candidate School. It so happened that the only vacancy available was to Military Police School. As I went to face the board I
found myself competing with former New York City policemen,
State Troopers and other men with considerable police experience. I felt that I did not have much chance for that one vacancy. The chief of the board, a Colonel Hamilton, was an enthusiastic skier and when he found out that I was not only a
skier but the president of the ski club and spoke a number of
languages as well, he seemed most interested. Several weeks later
I was notified that I had been selected for the vacancy and
would be going to Officers Candidate School. I would attend
the Infantry School at Fort Benning, Georgia, and upon completion of that course, I would go for a month to a Military
Police course since there was not at that time a Military Police
School per se. Regardless, I was delighted with this news and
the opportunity it represented to get ahead in the Army. I was
beginning to suspect that I wanted to make the Army my career
and that I had found what I was seeking. I was given a couple of
days' leave at home on my way to the Officers Candidate School
at Fort Benning. I then reported in and was assigned to the
22nd Officers Candidate Class. There were to be something like
six hundred classes before the war was over. The school was
tough. They told us that they were going to be hard on us and
that they wanted the people who would break under pressure to
break at the school and not on the battlefield. There was a tremendous amount of spit and polish. Discipline was ironclad. We
had very little time to ourselves, even on weekends. In fact, during the whole three months I was at Fort Benning I only went
to the main post once and to Atlanta twice. The latter trips
were to order my uniforms and Sam Browne belt. I was never to
wear the belt, since it was eliminated as an item of the uniform
just before I graduated.

The training was physically and mentally tough and demanding. Every few weeks we were required to rate all of the other
men in our platoon. I made good friends there with whom I
would remain in touch in the years ahead. As time passed, I felt

more and more confident that I would graduate from the school. The only course which gave me any trouble was the mortar course. This involved some mathematics and parabolas that were beyond my previous experience, but I made it anyway. At that time there were none of the combat assault courses that developed later and which gave the soldier some familiarity with real battlefield conditions. At least he had to crawl under real rifle and machine gun fire. We had none of this and when we encountered the real shock of battle it was a shock indeed. The only artillery fire we saw at the school was sitting on benches in a sort of grandstand and watching at a distance of several miles the exploding shells of 75s, 105s and 155s. This did not give us any real idea of what incoming artillery would be like. We did have considerable practice in firing rifles and machine guns on the range. All bullets were issued on the range and we had to return the expended cases. They kept us on the go from dawn to dusk and there were constant examinations and inspections. Often I had to clean my rifle after lights out. I would sit on my footlocker and disassemble the rifle and clean it in the dark because I had not had time to do it before lights out. There was no leave, no going to town, nothing but training.

It was about halfway through the course that my citation from the FBI arrived. It made a favorable impression on the company commander, even though I could not explain what I had done. One morning, about two weeks before we were to graduate, we were drawn up for a morning formation; a number of names were read out and these men were asked to fall out of the formation. We all knew what this was. This was the selection of the men who were not going to graduate as officers. About 25 per cent of our class was in this group. We marched off promptly to an exercise and when we returned to our company area these men were gone with all of their baggage and equipment. We did not see them again. The rest of us then knew that barring some unusual development, we were going to graduate and be commissioned as officers in the Army. After finishing our exams we were given a weekend off and along with some friends we took a cabin for the weekend at a Georgia state park. We relaxed and went swimming and had a quiet weekend, something we had not had since arriving at Fort Benning.

As the course was drawing to a close we were told that we would have to organize a show. Each successive class had to put on a show before graduation. I was one of the organizers of this show. I wrote a song called "Benning School for Boys." I understand that it is still sung sometimes to the tune of "Far Above Cayuga's Waters." I also wrote a series of verses for the program for the show. This was in the shape of the school's insignia, a blue shield with a bayonet and the motto "Follow Me." This was to be our motto and meant that we were to lead our men from in front, not from the rear.

Graduation was now close at hand and I had heard nothing further about my Military Police assignment. I inquired about this and was told that this was no longer on. "We've got a great shortage of Infantry second lieutenants and you are going to be one." A day or two before graduation I received my orders to my first assignment as a commissioned officer. I was to go to a newly formed division at Camp Shelby, Mississippi. This was the 85th Division that was being activated there. On the May 29, 1942, I was graduated and commissioned as a second lieutenant in Infantry. We had a lunch at the Officers' Club. It was the first time we had been there and in accord with an old Army tradition, we had to give a dollar bill to the first enlisted man who saluted us. I was proud and pleased. I was one of the few graduates who did not have a member of his family present for the graduation. I took the train to New York and spent a few days with my parents, who were even prouder than I was. I felt that it was an achievement and was happy to have successfully completed the tough and competitive course. My mother kept all of my letters and as I read them now I can see how highly charged up I was against the Nazis and the Japanese and how anxious I was to do something against them.

As a second lieutenant I was earning $125 a month and I could have my car with me at my new assignment. I drove from my home in Queens, New York, to Camp Shelby near Hattiesburg, Mississippi. I reported to my new outfit, which was the

Headquarters Company of the 338th Infantry, one of the three regiments that made up the 85th Division. The regimental commander was a small, tough, wiry, effective officer, Colonel Gerow, who was later to become a major general in Europe. There were already three lieutenants in the company to which I was assigned. I was the junior and so got a lot of uninteresting jobs, such as teaching courses in field fortifications, about which I knew very little. I had to bone up on them extensively before I taught. I was in command of a platoon and soon formed a close bond with my men. After I had been there some weeks the battalion commander called me in to his office and asked me how I would feel about becoming his battalion intelligence officer. This position was normally held by a captain or a major and I was still a second lieutenant. To have a job that required a rank at least two grades above the one I then held carried for me a promise of promotion if I performed successfully. I was very interested in intelligence and this kind of work attracted me. I said that I would be very happy to do it. The colonel then asked me whether I did not believe that more duty with troops would be good for me. Reluctantly, but truthfully, I replied, "Yes." "Well," he said, "in that case you are going to do both jobs. You are going to be both the battalion intelligence officer and a platoon leader." So I did both jobs. There was an almost Jekyll and Hyde character to my two jobs. In one I was a lowly platoon leader and in the other I was a member of the powerful battalion staff. On one occasion we had an exercise in the woods. I was a member of the battalion commander's staff. When the problem was over the troops were marching back to the company area, but the staff were riding back in jeeps. I realized that if I did not march back with my weary, sweaty platoon I would never hear the end of it. I went to the battalion commander and asked for permission not to ride back with him, but to march back with my platoon. He understood what was involved and let me do it. It rained all the way.

I organized a number of troop information and education programs. I got records from a radio station in New Orleans and found a Jewish tailor, also in New Orleans, who would make replicas of Nazi insignia so that I could teach the men what German Army uniforms would look like. There was real irony in this—the Jewish tailor making Wehrmacht shoulder straps for me. I was also able to obtain some films and put on some musical programs that were effective and appreciated by my battalion commander.

Suddenly, all of this changed. The regimental commander called me in and told me that he had received a telegram ordering my immediate transfer to the Military Intelligence Training Center at Camp Ritchie, Maryland. He was quite pleased with me and very irritated at having me thus plucked out of his command just when I was beginning to produce to his satisfaction. He told me repeatedly how hard it was for him to organize and train a unit when men were constantly being taken away from him. The telegram came from the War Department and there was nothing he could do about it. A few days later I said good-bye to my men. They gave me a fountain pen, which by today's standards was probably illegal, but it was a token of their feelings and I was proud and happy to get it. I then drove to Camp Ritchie, which was located quite close to Washington.

This was an old National Guard camp. I was somewhat unhappy to see that I was going to have to live in a tent as there were no barracks other than the classrooms. Camp Ritchie contained an extraordinary conglomeration of soldiers and officers, all of whom had some sort of foreign or intelligence background. Rare was the man who spoke English without an accent. Nearly all had lived abroad or were immigrants or refugees and had some sort of linguistic capability. I found that I was assigned to the French section. Thus, a year after I entered the Army it had, without computers, found me a task for which my long years of residence in France had qualified me.

The man who taught us French Army organization was a curious and unusual figure. He was already a distinguished author in French and was later to become a member of the French Academy, the first American ever to be elected to this body, which in France is generally considered as the ultimate goal of an intellectual. His name was Julian Green. Years later he was to write a book about his experiences while a sergeant in the U. S. Army during the war. In this book he was to mention me as having been a young officer who spoke good French and treated him in a fashion of which he approved.

There were many sections at Camp Ritchie. Some were for prisoner-of-war interrogators in German or Italian, some were for Photo interpreters. Some were trained in counterintelligence, some were trained in Arabic for the Middle East. Others were trained in Chinese. All of the specialties of intelligence were taught here. Once again, the training was tough and demanding both physically and mentally. We were in class all day and often spent most of the night on map problems wandering around the Maryland countryside. Many of the farmers in the area had signed pieces of paper authorizing the Army to use or move across their land. Not many of them expected us to move across their land in the middle of the night wearing German uniforms and helmets. More than once we were chased by angry farmers who thought that paratroopers had landed.

One of our primary subjects at this time was learning how to use foreign maps. We would sometimes be given maps of the area with all of the place names changed. We would be told to find our way to a place with a foreign name. We did not know what its real name was so we could not ask the farmers how to get there. They would take us out in a truck at night with the canvas cover on so we could not see where we were going. They would let us out in the middle of a field in groups of two men. My teammate was usually Archie Roosevelt, a grandson of Theodore Roosevelt's. Archie was very shortsighted and did not know much about reading maps. He used to follow me very closely when I moved. The exercise was quite realistic, as there were men playing the enemy on the terrain, and if one struck a light or shone a flashlight one would be shot at, with blanks of course. The only only way I could get oriented was to kneel down on the ground, put a tent shelter half over my head, put the map on the ground and light the flashlight so that it would not show from under the shelter, trying to find some terrain feature that would be a point of reference to find out where I was.

This was difficult, and often I had to walk a long way until I came to a railroad, a power line or a small river that would give me a clue as to where I was. Having located this feature on the map, I would then move to the point which had been indicated as my goal. There were trucks there waiting to take me back to Camp Ritchie. The earlier one got to the goal the more sleep he got that night. Archie and I never came in later than third of the two-man groups. The unlucky ones who got to their goal close to daylight had to be in class shortly afterward, minus sleep.

I liked Camp Ritchie and what I was doing there. I was very interested in the organization and insignia of the German, Italian and French armies. I found this more fascinating than anything else I had done in the Army up to this time. My class, the second at Camp Ritchie, was supposed to graduate around the end of October or early in November. One night we had been out on an all-night problem. Then we were in class until 5 P.M. I was exhausted and said I was going to my tent to sleep. I did not care for any dinner. I lay down on my bunk and it seemed only a minute or two before I was awakened by a great bustle in the camp. I was told that the camp had been sealed off and no one was allowed to leave. All of the phones had been disconnected—something was happening. I was so tired that even this did not excite me. I went back to bed saying, "If I am involved, let me know." I then dozed off again.

In a little while I was awakened and told that I was involved. I got up and packed all of my belongings. Late that evening we assembled in trucks in front of the commandant's office. We sat there having no idea what was happening or where we were going. My car was at Camp Ritchie and I had no way of getting it home. No one was allowed to communicate with his family. The married officers were not allowed to talk to their wives, who lived just off the post in Blue Ridge Summit. As we prepared to drive off, the commandant came out and watched us. I was shocked by the fact that he said nothing to bid us farewell or wish us luck. We were obviously not going to complete the course and were clearly on our way overseas, yet he had no word of encouragement or farewell for us. It was a lack of leadership that I was not to forget soon. Finally, we drove off and rode through the night, still not knowing where we were going except that we were now sure that we were going to the war. As we rode we sang all sorts of songs. Old U.S. songs and the "Marseillaise," the Nazi Horst Wessel song, the Italian Fascist anthem "Giovinezza" and many others. Late that night we arrived at Fort Myer near Washington. Many years later I was to reside there for four years as a lieutenant general and deputy director of the CIA. That night we slept on the floor of the gymnasium. In the morning we were issued combat equipment and the new steel helmets and submachine guns. This made plain to us what was about to happen. At Fort Myer I learned that I was to have a small detachment of men who had been in the French Section. We were going to Fort Bragg, North Carolina, to join the 9th Infantry Division. My detachment was smaller than the others. I was the only officer in my detachment, but we could all pass as Frenchmen.

We left Fort Myer in the morning after breakfast and drove to Fort Bragg near Fayetteville, North Carolina. We arrived in the late afternoon and reported to the G-2 or Intelligence officer of the division. We were told that we were to be assigned to that division as a special Intelligence detachment, with our main job that of interrogating prisoners of war. For cover purposes we were called the Special Missions detachment. This earned us the nickname of "missionaries" and this followed us across the ocean.

When we reported in the G-2 seemed quite surprised to see us and told us that he had not expected us until embarkation at Newport News several days later. He had no place for us and told us that we could go home provided we reported in to Newport News on the 1st of October. He gave us the pier number and the name of our ship, the U.S.S. *Lyon*. We were delighted with this opportunity to go home for a couple of days, but as I look back on it the security, mechanics and legality of the whole thing escape me. We drove back to Washington and I then took a train home to New York. I had a steel helmet and was carrying a Tommy gun, and this greatly impressed the "feather merchants" or civilians on the train. I sat there trying to look grim, secretive and combat-experienced. In the meantime, my car had been driven home from Camp Ritchie and it was delivered to my father and mother, who were told that I was on the high seas. They were absolutely astounded when I walked into the house with the helmet and the gun. I still had no ammunition for the gun and hoped I would get some soon. After two days at home I took leave of my parents. My father was proud and concealed any emotion he felt. My mother was more upset. I promised that I would let her know as soon as I could where I was and what I was doing. I told her not to worry, that the war would soon be over. As I look back on this time, I am surprised at how relatively little fear I felt and how much excitement and desire I had to get on with the war and get it finished. I went to Newport News and reported aboard the *Lyon*. This was the transport that was to take me overseas. It was a small, converted Moore-McCormack ship adapted to troop transport. When I went aboard I felt a real letdown. I found the compartment where I was to sleep with hundreds of other men in five tiers of bunks made of canvas. The thought of being cooped up there for a long period of time was not a happy one. The idea of what it would be like when people got seasick was not pleasant. I also thought about what would happen if the ship were to be torpedoed or bombed and we had to get out of this hold in a hurry. I was young and recovered quite quickly from my disappointment at finding that I was not going to have a stateroom. I fell quickly into the routine of shipboard life. The troops were fed around the clock. I could go and eat any time I wanted and as many times as I wanted. There were so many men on the ship that this continuous feeding was set up rather than the service of separate meals.

We sailed out into Chesapeake Bay and up to Solomons Island. There we scrambled down nets on the side of the ship and onto assault landing craft and stormed the undefended beaches of Solomons Island. This drove home to us the fact that we were undoubtedly going to take part in an assault landing and that, unlike Solomons Island, the beaches would be defended. We were highly excited and there was much speculation as to our real destination. Most of us, knowing that we had many French-speaking men with us (there were also some German-speaking teams aboard as well), felt sure that we were going to Dakar in French West Africa. This city had resisted on behalf of the Vichy government of occupied France the attacks of both the Free French and the British. The capture of Dakar seemed essential for us to operate effectively against the German submarines in the South Atlantic.

In the midst of all of the excitement around me, I had come to the realization that I had found what I had been seeking in the Army, a life where I enjoyed what I was doing and felt that in serving I could also contribute to the things in which I believed very deeply. It is hard to articulate in words thirty-six years later what my feelings were, but there was a sort of quiet comprehension that I had found the path I was seeking. I knew now what I wanted to do with my life. Why and how I came to this realization under these difficult circumstances I cannot explain. I only know that on the eve of setting forth on a dangerous and long journey to an uncertain fate at an unknown place, I realized that I had found my place in life. I was not to lose this conviction in the thirty-four years that were to follow in the Army.

2. TO MOROCCO

In 1942 the war was far from going well for America and her Allies. In the spring the Japanese had continued their sweep forward in the Pacific and in Southeast Asia. In Russia with the coming of the spring, the German armies thrust forward from the Don to the Volga and deep into the Caucasus. In Africa the balance seesawed back and forth between the British and the Germans, but as the year neared its end the Germans had driven forward deep into Egypt and were standing on the El Alamein position. Cairo and Alexandria were both threatened. The Germans still held all of occupied Europe firmly in their grip. At sea, German submarines operating in wolf packs were wreaking havoc on Allied shipping. The United States and Great Britain still did not feel strong enough to invade German-occupied Europe. Yet, it was felt something should be done to ease some of the pressure on the Russians, while contributing to later Allied operations against the Germans. A decision was reached at the top level between President Roosevelt and Prime Minister Churchill to move into French North Africa in a vast seaborne operation. This operation bore the code name "Torch." Careful intelligence preparation made contacts possible with key friendly French officials. Robert Murphy, then a U.S. consul in Algiers, skillfully conducted the political preparation for the coming operations under the guise of his consular position.

An attempt was made to convince the senior French officer, General Maxime Weygand, to come out of France and lead the French forces in North Africa. He refused, saying that he was bound by his oath of loyalty to Marshal Philippe Pétain, the ruler of what was called unoccupied France. An Allied submarine therefore brought out another distinguished French soldier, General Henri Giraud. This was to lead to complications later because of the rivalry between him, General Charles de Gaulle, who headed the Free French in London, and Admiral Jean Darlan, who was Marshal Pétain's deputy, and who was visiting his sick son in Algiers where the invasion surprised him. Seeing the great strength of the Allies he promptly announced that he was joining them. Thus, there were three candidates for the leadership of French forces in North Africa. This posed very thorny problems.

The occupation of these French territories in Algeria, Tunisia and Morocco would open the Mediterranean and relieve the pressure on long-besieged Malta. It would take the Germans in Egypt from the rear and provide a platform for launching further operations against what Churchill called the "soft underbelly of Europe." Those of us who later fought in Italy found it not so soft.

It was also hoped that this would swing other French colonies still loyal to the Pétain government in Vichy over to the Allied cause. Basically, the operation was to be staged from the United Kingdom and the United States. There would be landings in eastern, central and western Algeria at Bône, Algiers and Oran. Outside the Strait of Gibraltar, plans called for landing the Western Task Force on the coast of Morocco at Fedala, Port Lyautey, and in the south at Safi. My mission to Morocco would lead me to take part in the landing at this southernmost point, the second largest port in Morocco after Casablanca.

On October 8, 1942, those of us who departed Newport News aboard the U.S.S. *Lyon* knew nothing of our destination. On several occasions previously we had sailed out, but each time, we turned north and went up into Chesapeake Bay. We did not go out of the Virginia Capes. Finally, in the late afternoon of the eighth of October we pulled away from the pier at Newport News and headed down into the bay. This time we did not turn north into Chesapeake Bay. We headed straight out past the Virginia Capes and we could see a long line of ships stretching as far as the eye could see ahead of us. We could see other ships falling into line behind us. As we went out past Cape Charles, I saw one of the big new battleships which I knew from my *Jane's Fighting Ships* had been under construction; but I did not know it had already been completed.

Late that autumn afternoon we passed Cape Henry and entered the cold dark Atlantic, destination still unknown. Scarcely were we out on the ocean when general quarters sounded. We felt this meant a submarine attack. However, it was simply a drill and after we recovered from it, we went back to our sleeping compartments and fell asleep. The next morning, since the compartment was stuffy and unpleasant, I went up on deck and saw an astonishing sight. Instead of the single line of ships ahead of us and astern of us that I had seen at the fall of darkness, I now saw an entire sea covered with ships in every direction. Three or four ships behind us sailed an aircraft carrier and three or four ships in front of us was another aircraft carrier. As far as I could see in every direction there were ships. I was later to learn there were hundreds of ships in this convoy. This gave me a feeling of great security, as I felt sure that if submarines or wolf packs closed in on us, they would certainly attack the outer fringes of this armada first. Since we were deep on the inside of the armada, I felt quite safe.

Hand grenades and ammunition for our Tommy guns now began to appear in unlimited quantities. We had been accustomed to the strict rationing of ammunition on the various training ranges in the United States. We were astounded to be offered anything we wanted without restriction. Each of us drew a private arsenal sufficient to sustain us for weeks of warfare.

All of my life I have kept diaries and notes. I have my diaries from the time I was ten years old to this date. Aboard the ship I did not depart from my custom. I wrote what I felt and what I believed. On October 20, 1942, I made this entry in my journal:

We are crossing an ocean infested with enemy submarines that are waiting for us like sharks to begin their savage attack. We are on a ship loaded with explosives. We may be the object of offshore bombing. I do not yet know for sure where I am going, and, yet, what I feel is not fear. I have always thought of myself as being somewhat cautious, yet what I feel now is more excitement and curiosity than what I had expected. The morale of my men under the adverse conditions in which they are living is magnificent. Perhaps it is at this well that I draw confidence. Now I know that I am glad to go despite bombs, torpedoes or anything else. I have felt ashamed not to have gone before. Whatever fear I may feel seems drowned by the pride of being part of America's answer in the Atlantic. It is perfectly clear now that we are going to force a landing against a defended shore. Talking with my men, uncommon men, I find that their feelings are much as mine. Where do we find this confidence? In my case the knowledge that I am at peace with my God and ready to face Him if this is my time sustains me extraordinarily. I do not think that death will come for me this time, but if it does, I am ready to face my Creator.

I cannot put in words the relationship between my men and me. It is like an electric current that fills us both with strength for the coming storm. They are my strength and in some measure I am theirs. We all understand our interdependence and that we cannot let one another down. Ever since I became an officer, I have been aware of the strength that I draw from the confidence and respect of the men under my command and from their friendship. Today, sundered as we are from the rest of America, I feel this force stronger and more reassuring than ever. It is not pride; it is something more. Without so saying, my men have given me reason to believe that they feel the same way.

We are now many days at sea. We are passing southeast of Bermuda. The ocean is rough and a strong wind is blow-

ing. The phosphorescent water sparkles miraculously. Now
we know where we are going. As soon as we had been told,
one could hear the buzz of excited and anxious discussions.
I think of the landing with excited curiosity and some anxiety. The manner in which we will be received interests us
all. I am sure it will be with gunfire. We must get the tanks
ashore quickly. That will speed the end of resistance. I
must find the crane operators at their homes and get them
to their cranes as soon as possible after we land so that they
can unload the tank-carrying ships. How will they react
when I come for them?

I think also, mostly at night, about submarines, but the
screen of destroyers is very reassuring. I think vaguely about
the bombing planes that may attack us offshore. This is a
worried curiosity. I will not let myself think of it as fear.
Cut off from all communication with the outside world, rumors fly about the ship. We are, after all, many thousands
packed aboard a small combat-loaded ship. The crowding is
unbelievable. I sleep in a bunk with two other bunks below
me and two above me. The enlisted men live in even more
difficult conditions, but they are terrific. It is really a privilege to be an officer among such men. I am glad that when
my time came to go to battle I would have such comrades
at my side. I have not heard a man aboard this ship lose his
temper. Laughter is frequent and there is a good deal of
gambling and good-natured horseplay. To this moment I
have felt no weakness, no regrets, only pride. Standing on
the deck at night, looking out over the black immensity
that hides both friend and foe, God seems near and eternity close. I am calm, serene and ready.

The long days went by at sea, thirty of them, in fact. On the
third day I received my sealed orders and opened them and
learned to my astonishment that we were going to take part in
an assault landing on the port of Safi in French Morocco. I was
surprised and somewhat shocked, as I felt that Safi was probably
within range of the German submarines and within range of the
German aircraft from bases in the South of France. Therefore,
the landing would be even tougher than at Dakar, where we

would have been out of range of the German submarines or aircraft.

I was asked by the battalion commander aboard, a Major Evans, who was later seriously wounded in Tunisia, to talk to the soldiers on board about the French, about the French Army, about the way the French did things and about what I thought would happen when we went ashore. Now, I had noted that the Vichy French had resisted everywhere—in Madagascar, in Dakar, in Central Africa, in Syria—and I told everyone on the ship that I was sure that as we attempted to land in Morocco, the French would resist and we would have to overcome this resistance. We received very accurate order of battle on the French Army in North Africa and the location of the German armistice commissions. I was somewhat relieved in going through these documents to read that there were no German troops in the area and that we would only be facing the French, or, largely, the French North African troops.

One day at sea the battalion commander, Major Evans, called me down to his cabin. He had on his desk in front of him an open wooden box with a strange pipelike instrument inside. He asked me if I was in Intelligence and I replied that I was. He then said, "Do you know what this is?" I did not realize that I was looking at my first bazooka. I told the major that I did not know what it was and he seemed disappointed. No one else on the ship knew what it was, and there were several hundreds of these loaded aboard. No instructions for their use could be found. The ship, incidentally, was fully combat-loaded. The decks were covered with crates of shells, aerial bombs and ammunition of all sorts, and we all felt uneasily that if the ship were attacked in any way, some of this stuff would explode and cause a lot of damage and difficulty for us.

Eventually, since no one on the ship knew how to use this bazooka, a very tall major on the ship, Major Alva Adams, Jr., who was the son of the adjutant general of the Army, volunteered to try it out. The projectile for it looked like a small shell except that there was a wire leading from the top to the back with a ring on it, and no one quite knew if when you pulled this ring it armed the projectile or detonated the projectile, which clearly fitted inside the pipelike arrangement. Major Adams went up on the bridge, with the reluctant consent and considerable disquiet of the captain. He raised the bazooka in the air and fired it. The flame that came out of the back set fire to canvas around the bridge. The captain was greatly agitated and put it out, but we quickly deduced that the weapon was some sort of a hand-carried piece of artillery. What we did not realize was that it was intended strictly for use against tanks. During the landing we actually used it against snipers and against buildings. On board no one had ever fired one until Major Adams ignited the canvas and the ship's captain.

The crossing was extraordinarily calm. Very few people were seasick. I felt very much at home aboard the ship after a few days. I had my small detachment. My men's morale was tremendously high. They seemed to trust me and I felt I could rely on them. As the time of the landing approached, we could feel the mounting excitement within us. The captain assigned me to monitor the German and Italian radio to determine whether the movements of our vast fleet of ships moving across the ocean remained a secret. I was told that if I heard any mention of it, I was to report only to the captain and no one else. On the twenty-third of October I heard the report of Montgomery's attack at El Alamein, and began to realize what immense pincers were going to close between that attack coming from Egypt and our own landing in North Africa. By this time I understood that there was going to be a landing not just in Morocco but also in Algeria and possibly in Tunisia in a bold attempt to seize the whole of French North Africa to use as a springboard against the Germans in southern France and against the Italian boot.

On the long nights I would often stand on the deck watching the phosphorescent water and the flying fish, looking at the stars, wondering what would happen, how I would behave when I came under fire, whether I would be able to carry out my duties, whether I would not be too distracted by the fire, how my men would behave. I had a great deal more curiosity than fear. I did not yet know exactly what war was going to be like, but I felt an excitement and desire to do something. All of us thought our country had been through a long period of reverses ever since the start of the war. Now, finally, we were going to strike a great blow and, in a sense, it would be the first good news that the American people would have almost since we became involved in the war. The news had nearly always been bad. We had lost the Philippines. We had lost small islands in the Pacific. Pearl Harbor had been bombed. The British had sustained great reverses at sea and on land. The war had been running against us and we felt that now for the first time we were going to be able to strike a powerful blow.

Looking around at the vast armada extending in every direction as far as the eye could see, with the aircraft carriers fore and aft of us, gave us an impression of power and strength. As I looked over my sealed orders and the documents concerning the place where we were going to land at Safi, I was astonished at the detailed information that was provided, at the biographical information concerning the French officers there, at the detailed emplacements of the guns, at the complete information concerning the town of Safi, at the state of morale and at a great many other things.

Our D-day would be on the morning of the eighth of November. As this day drew close, we went through a great sweep down toward Dakar in a feint to lead the Germans to believe that we were going to attack Dakar. Then we turned sharply north. About nine o'clock in the evening of the seventh of November we could see the lights of the African shore. I had long wondered whether or not North Africa was blacked out and it was soon evident that it was not. We were told that initially the ships would lie eight miles offshore and we would then embark in small assault-landing craft and be taken ashore.

My orders called for me to go ashore at H plus 10, that is, ten hours after the landing. However, on the eve of the landing Major Evans came to me and said that he would be commanding the assault landing. He felt very much the need to have someone who could speak French and asked whether I would volunteer with my team. He could not order us to go, but he asked me whether I would volunteer to go ashore with him in the assault rather than wait for H plus 10 as my orders indicated. I agreed and said that I would go ashore with him. He then told me that he had asked two of the other teams if they would do so, and they had said no, that they had to hold to their orders. He was angry at them and pleased with me, not knowing that I had agreed to do what he wanted because I was afraid to say no to a major.

We had been many days at sea and now the fateful hour was at hand. The last hours of November 7, 1942, were ticking inexorably away as the vast armada drew in toward the African coast, still unnoticed by those ashore. The lights of Safi flickered dimly through the rain squalls and the line of cliffs overhanging Safi was not visible. It was a tremendous thrill to realize that our Navy had seen this great fleet across the ocean undetected and that we were about to spring ashore out of the night to deliver America's first great blow in the West. The ships moved silently to their assembly positions some miles from shore. The night was inky black and the expectancy tremendous. Excitement knotted in my throat like a ball. There was still a little time and I reflected on what this day and hour would mean in my life, and I decided to sit down in the wardroom and write down what I felt. I have kept these notes, and, juvenile and trite as they may seem to some today, thirty-five years later, this is what I wrote and this is what I felt:

The Eve of Battle

And now the day has arrived. At eleven last night we pulled in to the coast and saw the lights of Safi through the rain. The secret of our coming has been wonderfully kept. I am writing this at 1:10 A.M. in the wardroom of the U.S.S. *Lyon* as we move into assembly position to launch the assault. The assault boats are being lowered and the loudspeakers are blaring military music, every now and then interspersed with a swing number. It seems incredible that this cannot be heard on shore. Everyone is alert but no one shows visible signs of fear. I feel tremendous excitement but it is not what I expected fear to be like. The men are calling to one another from boat to boat and to the deck of the ship.

All of my life I have secretly wondered how I would feel at this moment of testing of my manhood. In the years to come I will always want to know what it was that I felt at this time. Soon we will be ashore and in the thick of the fighting that will break out as soon as we try to land. The night is dark and there is no moon. Perhaps that is why they chose this night. I am not afraid in the ordinary sense that I expected because I feel certain that I will come through the assault unscathed. This complete confidence makes it difficult for me to feel the kind of fear that I had expected. However, when fire is opened, it may be different, and the road to Berlin and Tokyo is long. Perhaps all the years of my youth will be spent along it. No one has ever tried to kill me before. Soon they will be trying. When they do, will it overwhelm me? Or will I be able to do what I must do and lead my men as they deserve to be led? Being unworthy of them is unthinkable. The methodical planning of this gigantic operation and the clocklike precision with which it is being carried out adds to my feelings of confidence. Nothing has been disregarded or left undone. The excitement which I feel (I would rather call it excitement than fear) is so great that it is difficult for me to sit here in cold blood and write this. I notice that I do not want to be alone. I want people with me. I yawn often and wish I had some candy but I have none. Despite my confidence a sense of realism has made me give the captain my address and parents' names. I felt awkward and embarrassed doing this just as I did when I showed my men where I was carrying the sulfanilamide powder so that they could take it if anything happens to me. But then, I know that nothing will happen to me, not this time anyway.

Now I think I know the answer to a question that has bothered me all of my life: how I would face the test of battle. So far I am pleased but then nothing has really happened yet. I know that there will be danger, great danger, but I pray and hope that it will not keep me from doing what I must do and that whatever I feel will not show in such a way as to shame me. I am puzzled by the certainty I feel that God will sustain me through the storm that is about to break. I am excited, tremendously excited. I feel as though someone had pulled a belt very tightly around my stomach. I feel hungry despite the turkey dinner we had earlier this evening. I wonder if this attack will make the morning papers in New York. There are no afternoon papers on Sunday. I am about to live a moment I shall never know again, my baptism by fire.

It is almost time to move to the boats. I feel throbbing excitement but not fear in the form I had expected, paralyzing fear. In a few moments the fighting will begin. I know the French and I am sure that they will fire when they see us as they did at Dakar and elsewhere. The men are more quiet now. They are determined to smash any resistance. They have not been sharpening those trench knives for days for nothing. They are as tired as I am of the weeks of boredom aboard the ship and they are going ashore no matter what the resistance may be. A strong blow now will save a lot of trouble later. The only way I can account for my lack of fear as fear is that my year and a half in the Army has made me a soldier. God, I am proud of it!

Then I could no longer wait in the wardroom and I went up on deck to prepare for my part in what was to come. We were lined up on the deck of the U.S.S. *Lyon* and heard President Roosevelt announce our landing in North Africa. We were horrified and felt sure that this would alert those on shore to what we were about to do. As it turned out, no one in Safi heard the President's address. Then they played "The Star-Spangled Banner." It was moving beyond words, but we looked at one another and wondered, is this the twentieth century and are we really going to war to the sound of our national anthem? Yet, if one must do it, it is comforting to do it to the sound of martial music. As I climbed down the net to the small craft that was to take us to the landing, I remember wondering idly, "Wouldn't it be a hell of a thing to be killed without ever knowing what it would be like to be with a woman?" Then the enormity of what was about to happen pushed this and everything else aside. As we pulled away from the *Lyon* a Navy ensign called out, "Goodbye, suckers!" The replies were unprintable.

It was pitch-black and as we approached the harbor mouth, we could see the flickering signal light obviously questioning who we were. At this point lights were observed at sea and I remember the immediate rumor that swept us. "It's the *Tirpitz*," the largest battleship in the German Navy. Actually, it was a lost Spanish fishing vessel that was astounded to find itself in the middle of this vast armada. Without answering, two destroyers crept silently into the harbor. Their superstructure had been razed off so they would be lower than the breakwater and would not be observed until they were in the harbor. As we went by the breakwater, a curious thing happened. We saw a figure standing on the end of the breakwater and someone on the ship shouted, "Where did the destroyer go?" A voice answered with a British accent, "It ran aground inside the harbor but the men are getting off." As we went into the harbor, the French opened fire. The whole horizon was lit with gunfire and the ships at sea replied, firing at the batteries.

We ran the boat aground close to a large phosphate warehouse and scrambled ashore. I was astounded to see the great naval shells from the battleship *New York* arching up into the sky and crashing into the enemy's position beyond us. The French coastal batteries, realizing that someone was in the harbor, fired on the harbor. The shells were not really close but they were terrifying. None of us had ever seen shells exploding at such close range before, and the red and black explosion was a truly awesome sight. Now I truly felt fear but it did not paralyze me. I was astounded that there was no small-arms fire in the harbor and later discovered that the machine guns in the harbor area had the wrong ammunition. They had 9-mm. ammunition and 7.6-mm. weapons. This was the kind of disorganization which had contributed to the defeat of the French Army in 1940. The naval fire control party accompanying us radioed the battleship *New York*, corrected the fire, and before the *New York* could fire again, a French battery, known as the "La

Railleuse" battery, fired at us again from the top of the cliff with guns removed a year or two before from a sunken ship. The shells were not close but they thoroughly shook us all up and we looked at one another as if to say, "My God, nobody told us it was going to be like this." Certainly, nothing we had seen in training had led us to expect what was happening.

Again, we saw the great flash of fire at sea as the old battleship launched her giant twelve-inch shells at the battery. The second salvo she fired landed at the foot of the cliff. The battery was on the top. On her third salvo she struck the gun pits and "La Railleuse" never fired again. We cheered the Navy. Meanwhile there was desultory fighting going on all over the town. I set up my command post in the phosphate warehouse. Fighting was going on all around us and soldiers began to bring back toward the dock the prisoners they had taken. My job was to interrogate those prisoners and find out what was happening. I set up my interrogation post on the ground floor of the phosphate warehouse. I had five enlisted men and one officer. It was an odd situation. Since the fighting was going on all around us, the soldiers who captured the prisoners would bring them in themselves and say, "Here, Lieutenant, I caught this son of a bitch shooting at us."

Soon I had about two hundred prisoners, a few of them French, but most of them North Africans, fighting in the French Army. Where to put them became a problem. I decided to have three of my five enlisted men guard them in the upstairs loft of the warehouse. I continued the interrogation of the officers below. The interrogation was fruitful. I learned that the attack had come as a complete surprise. Clearly morale was not good. They said they would resist if it was a commando raid, but if it was clear that it was a large-scale U.S. invasion, they would join us. As a matter of fact, one of the French officers told me that Weygand, the French commander in North Africa, had said, "If the Americans come with five thousand, I will fire upon them. If they come with one hundred and fifty thousand, I will welcome them with open arms." Nonetheless, the welcome was not with open arms. There was shooting going on all over the town.

One of my tasks was to seize the crane operators at their homes and get them back to the docks to operate the cranes at daybreak when the ships came into the harbor. This operation was successful. We picked up all of the crane operators at their homes and brought them down to the docks. They were wholly with us and worked with a will. In the meantime I had some two hundred to three hundred prisoners on my hands. There was fighting and sniping and shooting going on all around the dock, and all of us were concerned that daybreak would bring French planes from the large airfield at Marrakech. All through the night I continued interrogating the prisoners. The battalion commander set up his command post alongside of mine and was continuously asking me what was happening, which units were involved, and so forth. I soon learned that the French order of battle which had been given to me on board the ship was correct and that the units which we had expected to find at Safi were actually those we faced.

I went upstairs to look at the prisoners. I had three of my men standing there with Tommy guns guarding them. They did not appear to be a very combative lot. They seemed to be somewhat quiet, so I decided that in the dim light, provided by one small Coleman lantern on the table, I would mingle with them and see if I could pick up any additional information. I mingled with them, speaking unaccented French, and heard a number of them discussing whether help would be coming from Marrakech, from Mogador or from Agadir, and gleaned what I thought was very valuable information. Quite pleased with myself and the deception that I had practiced by posing as one of them in the half-light, I then came back to where my men were standing and suddenly realized that my pistol was no longer in its holster. I turned and looked at the two or three hundred men in the half-light and thought, "My God, one of them has got that pistol. He could shoot us at any time." I thought about this, not knowing what to do, and finally I came to a decision. I called them together and said that someone had taken my pistol and that I wanted it back. I said I was going to turn out the light for just a few seconds and then I would turn it back on and I wanted the pistol to be on the floor. If the pistol was not on the floor, they would be searched individually, and, not knowing what I could threaten them with, I said, "I feel sorry for whoever has got it." Then I said, "Do not attempt to rush us when the light is turned down. There are four of us standing here with leveled Tommy guns. If you are not interested in your own life, just realize that if anybody tries to rush us, we will fire and the casualties will be very heavy and you will be responsible for them." Then with great misgivings, I turned down the Coleman lantern, waited a few seconds and turned it on again. When I looked at the floor, there were six pistols there, including mine. Even the prisoners laughed. I was later to tell this story over "The Army Hour" in the United States.

Another problem with which I had to deal was that a number of the prisoners wanted to go to the bathroom. Since I only had five men, it was very difficult for me to deal with this problem. The only bathroom was one of those stand-up French jobs on the ground floor. I called the prisoners together and explained the problem to them in French. I said the only way I could see to handle this matter was to send them down in small groups under the escort of one of my men. I said I felt the only fair way to do this was in alphabetical order and since my name began with W and I had suffered enough from alphabetical rosters, we were going to do this one backward. Would all the men whose names began with Z, Y, and X step forward. This system operated successfully as we took them down in reverse alphabetical order.

Prisoners kept coming in. French officers were being brought in and it was upon these that I concentrated my efforts. The more junior ones were very friendly to us and delighted that America was intervening actively in the war and expressed the desire to join us, but all explained somewhat uneasily that they had been obliged to take an oath of allegiance to Marshal Pétain. They felt somewhat bound by this and hoped that the marshal on learning of our massive landings in North Africa would release them from this obligation.

About daybreak a young French officer was brought in. He was quite badly wounded in the face. He had been bandaged but was still bleeding. I was interrogating him when I heard a shattering roar outside and multiple firings of guns of all sorts. Not realizing what had happened, I dived under the table and found myself facing Lieutenant Le Turcq, who had also dived under the table. Then I realized that it had been an aircraft strafing the harbor as the ships came into the harbor at the first light of daybreak. Somewhat sheepish and shamefaced, I got back up on my chair and, feeling that I had lost face with Lieutenant Le Turcq and would not be able to exercise over him the ascendancy and domination that all the manuals said I should, I sent him out and had another French officer brought in, a captain who was a rather tough and defiant type and not particularly friendly. He took his oath of allegiance to Marshal Pétain seriously and regarded us as people who were trying to snatch away poor wounded captive France's remaining colonies in overseas areas. While I was talking to him, I heard the same sound and realized another aircraft was overhead dropping small bombs and firing at the ships in the harbor. This time I had myself under control and I continued my questioning of this captain, feeling extremely pleased that I had not this time shown the panic and agitation that had overtaken me the first time.

I cannot recall whether or not I ate at all during this period. I had field rations with me, but I was so intensely interested in what I was doing that food or rest did not seem important. The pressure for more information from the battalion commander, subsequently from the regimental commander, and later from General Ernest N. Harmon, commander of the 2nd Armored Division, was tremendous. Each of them set up his command post in the immediate vicinity of where I was conducting these interrogations. Clearly, they were getting intelligence from no other source. They were getting it only from these prisoners and they were hanging over my shoulder demanding more and more information. The flow of prisoners was continuing as they were

being brought in from farther out as our troops spread out inland expanding our initial beachhead.

As daybreak came the ships sailed into the harbor. I recall
that one of them was a Chesapeake Bay ferry carrying tanks. I
recall going out and watching General Harmon supervise the
unloading of the tanks ashore. This was important because there
was still sniper fire going on from all over town. I believe that in
the whole operation at Safi we lost fifty-one men. Later in the
morning we had largely secured the whole area around the harbor, but every now and then a sniper in the upper part of the
town would shoot down at the ships and the ping of the bullet
could be heard on the ship's hull. This would produce a storm
of fire from the small arms on the ships, which would fire back
without really seeing what it was that they were firing at. They
just knew they had been shot at and they wanted to fire back. I
recall that one or two of these sniper shots set off a tremendous
barrage from the ships back toward the old quarters of the town.
General Harmon was infuriated by this and ran out screaming
in his high, squeaky voice, "Cease fire! Cease fire! I'll court-martial the first son of a bitch who fires a round." Gradually the
firing died away. But the sniping continued. Clearly it was organized.

Now about this time a couple of soldiers from the 47th Infantry brought in two Arabs in civilian clothes and indignantly told
me that these two "sons of bitches" had been shooting at them
and they ought to be shot because they were firing in civilian
clothes. I made certain that they spoke French. I asked the two
soldiers who brought in the men whether they had searched
them and they said they had. They had not. I found one of
them had a pistol strapped to his leg which I removed. I then
said to these men that under the laws of war they could be shot
for sniping while in civilian clothes but that General Harmon
was a merciful man (he wasn't), and if they would tell us where
the sniping was coming from or who was organizing it, we
would spare their lives. They practically sank to the floor saying
that they had nothing to do with this, that they were poor innocent civilians and were not involved in this in any way. But

upon searching them, I found they had French Army pay books with recent entries and I realized full well that they were soldiers who had simply taken off their uniforms and put on civilian clothes in the hope of losing themselves in the population.

I called Sergeant Philip Toomey, who was my principal noncommissioned officer, a man of extraordinary humor and courage. He later became an officer and a college professor. During the night when all this firing was going on, he had jokingly shown me his service record, across which was stamped in red letters: "Non Combat Service Only." We could not help but laugh under the circumstances, as we were in the middle of the fighting that was going on all around us. I said to him, "Toomey, if we get out of this, I'll do something about it, but right now there is nothing I can do." Toomey, like my other men—Lucien Chiarelli, a little Frenchman; John Major, a quiet French Canadian; Antoine De Paris, a Maltese who had previously worked for the French telephone company and knew all about the telephone exchange when we got there; and a number of others—was just absolutely superb in doing his job in a quiet, efficient way under completely new and strange circumstances of confusion and danger.

I instructed Toomey to take the two Arabs outside and I said to them, "We would be justified in shooting you but we don't want to do it. I want you to go outside and I want you to think about the seriousness of what you've done. In a few minutes I'm going to call you back in here and I'm going to ask you where this sniping is coming from and who is organizing it." They bitterly protested that they had had nothing to do with it as Toomey led them out. A few minutes later Toomey came back and said, "They want to speak to you." The two men came in and confessed that they were soldiers from the 2nd Regiment of Moroccan Riflemen, that their company commander was Captain Paul Vanuxem, who was up at a place on the cliff, the Dar el Bahr, the house of the sea. It was he who was organizing the sniping against the ships in the harbor on the orders of the port commander, a French Navy captain, Captain François Deuve, who was later captured and brought to me.

Immediately upon finding this out I told General Harmon. He gave me two tanks and we went up to the Dar el Bahr, where we were greeted by heavy machine gun and rifle fire. This did not last very long, however, as one of the tanks fired a round, which missed the building. Shortly after that the door opened and a French captain came out with his hands up. I walked up to him and he said, in a rather belligerent voice, "I was ordered to fight to the last cartridge. I have just expended my last cartridge and that is why I am surrendering, for no other reason. You can go into that building and search it, and you will find there is no ammunition left." I did. He told the truth.

Vanuxem later became a general in the French Army. He was a distinguished soldier who fought extremely well in Vietnam. Later he was arrested during the Army plot against de Gaulle. Thirty years later he and I were to meet at the commemoration of the eighth of November, the Allied landings in North Africa, under the Arch of Triumph in Paris. He was then brigadier general in the French Army and I a major general in the United States Army.

I then went back down to my original interrogation point at the phosphate warehouse and found that Captain François Deuve, who was the senior French military officer in Safi, had been captured and brought in. Admiral Darlan had not trusted the Army. He did trust the French Navy more, and he had tried wherever possible to have a Navy officer as the *commandant d'armes*, that is, the senior officer present. Deuve was a convinced Vichyite, blindly loyal to Marshal Pétain and completely hostile to us. He told me that he had been at Oran when the British sank the French fleet and would never forgive them, and so forth and so on. I pointed out to him that they did this to prevent the fleet from falling into the hands of the Germans. Deuve said that Darlan would never have surrendered it to the Germans, that it had been a frightful massacre, that we were the allies of the British and, therefore, he was against us.

About this time General Harmon came in and said, "Who are all these people? What, are all these prisoners?" He had seen the two or three hundred prisoners I had upstairs on the first floor of the warehouse. I explained to him that they were French prisoners. He said, "To hell with that. We're not fighting against the French. Tell them if they promise not to fight against us, we will set them free." I protested that shortly before many of them had been shooting at us. He said, "Nevertheless, you tell them what I say." So I called the prisoners together and I said to them in French that we were fighting to liberate France, we had no quarrel with them, the Germans were landing in Tunisia, we wanted to go to Tunisia and drive out the Germans, and that if they would give us their word that they would not take hostile action against us, we would release them. Before I could do anything, Deuve stood up and said, "I will court-martial the first man who accepts that offer." That complicated the problem and very few of them did accept the offer. I realized then that I had not separated the officers from the enlisted men as I should have, but it was an almost impossible problem for me since I had only five men to handle this large crowd.

By this time I had lost several of my men because captains or majors who were going by and needed someone who spoke French simply requisitioned my men. Some of the other teams had come ashore and were desperately looking around to find some place to settle. One of the officers in particular was not a very impressive guy. He had been very pompous and very filled with the fact that he was a first lieutenant and the rest of us were second lieutenants. He insisted that I help him find an appropriate place in which he could set up his headquarters. I told him I couldn't do it because I was too busy with these people. He went off in a great huff and some of his enlisted men drifted back to ask if they could help me. They were disgusted with wandering around with him and becoming the laughingstock of the soldiers who were involved in the fighting that was going on not far away from where we were. So, as I lost men to some officers more senior that I was, I gained some from these other teams who came and worked for me to the considerable indignation of some of their officers, who were mainly interested in finding quarters for themselves. These officers complained about

this to the G-2 of the 2nd Armored Division, and he spoke to
them extremely harshly, telling them they had been afraid to
come ashore when he wanted them, that he didn't really need
their help, that their enlisted men were working for me and producing results and that he had nothing further to say. I was
quite astonished at the harshness with which he spoke to them.

The evening of the second day arrived and prisoners were still
coming in from outlying places inland from Safi. I had not slept
in more than fifty-five hours. I finally told my men that I would
go aboard one of the ships in the harbor and sleep there. I cannot even remember clearly the circumstances of this. I was so
exhausted. I went aboard one of the ships and was given a bunk
and slept. When I woke in the morning, I was told that I had
slept through an air raid on the ships. The noise of the guns
firing on the deck is deafening when one is belowdecks, yet
somehow I had slept through it. I had gone more than fifty
hours without sleep and was so exhausted that not even the
firing of the guns woke me.

I then went ashore and found a great many more prisoners,
more indications of movement, and soon I realized that we were
going to move north. I learned that Casablanca was still resisting. We had figured that Casablanca would be hard to take and
that was why we had made the surprise commando-style raid at
Safi in order to secure the second-largest harbor in Morocco,
should Casablanca prove difficult to capture. I understood that
movement of the troops toward Casablanca was imminent. I
had been reverted to the control of the 2nd Armored Division
by the division G-2. I left Major Evans and the gallant 3rd Battalion of the 47th Infantry to which I had been attached for the
assault part of the landing. I was told by the intelligence officer
of the 2nd Armored Division that I was to be ready to move in
the early afternoon with my men and my equipment toward
Casablanca. I did not understand how I was going to move since
I had no vehicles or transportation. I approached the division
G-4, or supply officer, who had come ashore. He was a tough,
hard-bitten colonel by the name of Ralph Butchers who later
became a major general. I went to him and informed him that I

was Lieutenant Walters of the Prisoner of War Interrogation Team, that I was to go to Casablanca and that I wished to draw the two jeeps and trailers that my table of organization provided for. He looked at me outraged and said, "Lieutenant, the general has no jeeps, I've got no jeeps, and you want *two* jeeps!" I said, "Sir, how do I get to Casablanca?" He said, "Lieutenant, have you ever heard of initiative?" I said, "Yes, sir." He said, "Well, use yours now and don't bother me any more."

Realizing I was not going to get anything from Colonel Butchers, I walked up into the main square of Safi, where I saw a large bus. I walked up to the bus driver and informed him that I was requisitioning the bus and that he was to fall into the convoy that was forming up to take us toward Casablanca. He protested bitterly but moved into the convoy. It was a charcoal-burning bus which had been converted to charcoal burning since there was little gasoline available in North Africa. To get it started a little gas was required. A Moroccan therefore sat on the fender from Safi to Casablanca periodically priming the carburetor with liquid gasoline.

In the late afternoon we pulled out of Safi and headed toward the first spot where we thought we might find further resistance, Mazagan. The convoy moved slowly through the night. We were expecting an attack all the time, but none came. At daybreak we found ourselves at the town of Mazagan, halfway to Casablanca. And here our intelligence told us we would find a French battalion in garrison. This battalion had moved out of Mazagan, had gone north about ten miles to the Oum er Rbia River and had taken up positions on the north bank of the river to oppose our drive toward Casablanca. When the convoy of the 2nd Armored Division stopped on the side of the road near Mazagan an Englishwoman came up and told me that nearby there was a camp where a number of British sailors who had been torpedoed off the Moroccan coast were being held along with some Poles and other Allied personnel. I notified General Harmon, who sent out a patrol which located these people and liberated them. I asked one of the local French people who this woman was. I did not refer to her as an Englishwoman and he told me that she was a Frenchwoman who had been living there for many years. Clearly, she was British. She had missed little that had taken place in Mazagan.

Reports came in that the French had mined the bridge over the Oum er Rbia and had taken up defensive positions on the north side of the river. General Harmon told me, in his own usual colorful language, that he didn't want to fight the "goddamned French." He then directed me to go and tell that "goddamned colonel" to come back and take up his garrison duties in town while we went on into Tunisia to stop the Germans who were landing there. He said, "You go up there in my halftrack. You stand up in the front seat next to the driver so that they'll see that you're coming on a friendly mission." He said nothing about a flag of truce or white flag. I was appalled at this suggestion but didn't know what I could do about it. I was afraid to say anything for fear he would accuse me of cowardice. I went out and got into the halftrack, looked at the driver, who was a very young soldier, and at this point a first lieutenant from the Signal Corps whose name was Ahbe came up and said to me, "Do you mind if I go with you?" I saluted him and said, "No." He said, "Why are you saluting me?" I said, "I'm being sent on this mission and you're volunteering for it." He got in and sat down in the halftrack. In accord with General Harmon's instructions I stood up in front next to the halftrack driver, expecting a sniper to take a shot at me at any moment.

We moved north out of Mazagan through the little village of Azemmour. In the main square at Azemmour there was a large French flag flying on a pole. Every shutter was closed but I could feel the watching eyes, and as we went by the flag, I gave it a big salute, hoping that any snipers would see this and not fire at me. If there were snipers it worked because no one fired. We drove on through Azemmour and down toward the bridge, I could see the wires leading from the holes in the bridge to the other side and realized that the bridge was mined. The driver stopped the halftrack short of the bridge and looked at me and I looked at him. He said, "What do we do, Lieutenant?" I thought about the alternatives and both of them were bad. Either I cross the bridge and the French blow it up, or I do not cross the bridge and return to General Harmon to explain that the bridge was mined, whereupon he would probably court-martial me for cowardice. I decided that in the case of crossing the bridge I would simply be dead, whereas in the case of refusing to cross the bridge, I would be both dead and dishonored. Not trusting my voice, I pointed across the bridge and looked at the driver. He said, "Shall I go?" I nodded. He looked at me and said, "Do you mean it?" I said, "Yes, I mean it." The young soldier shrugged and drove forward. As we drove onto the bridge, I was convinced that the French were going to blow it up, even though I was standing up in the halftrack and waving my hand.

To my astonishment and unspeakable relief, the French did not blow the bridge. As I reached the other side, two men sprang out of the bushes, pointed Tommy guns at me and announced in French, "You're a prisoner." Enormously relieved at having gotten across the bridge alive, I said sharply, "Stop all this nonsense and take me at once to Colonel Signard." They were quite astonished at the fact that I knew his name, and I said, "I haven't got any time to waste with you. Now get in this vehicle and take me up to Colonel Signard." I wanted a French uniform in the halftrack with me. To my astonishment, they lowered the Tommy guns and climbed into the vehicle. They had not seen anything like it. They took me up the hill to Colonel Signard's command post. Now militarily, this was absurd. They led me in an armored vehicle to the command post of their battalion and nobody fired. We were lucky in that this indicated the confused state of mind of the French. They had not decided whether to resist us or not. Some of them were for us. Others were against us. All knew that we were there in great force. They realized that we had tanks behind us, and these things, I think, militated in favor of their allowing us to cross the bridge and not shooting me when I was standing in the halftrack. But this time I had really felt the grip of fear.

I stepped from the halftrack and walked toward Colonel Signard, who sat at a table with his chin resting on his hands. I stepped up smartly, saluted him and began to explain in French that I had come in the name of the old friendship that had united our countries ever since the days of Lafayette and Rochambeau. He interrupted me roughly and said, "Don't give me that Lafayette sauce. Tell me what it is you want." I said, "Colonel, the Germans are landing in Tunisia. We want to get there and drive them out of Tunisia. We want you to go back into Mazagan and take up your normal garrison duties so we can move on forward through to Tunisia." He looked at me and said, "Don't you realize that I have orders to stop you?" I said to him, "Colonel, whose orders are they?" He snapped at me, "Orders are orders." I replied, "Colonel, if you got orders to spit on the French flag, would you do it or would you look to see whether the orders came from a French authority or a German armistice commission?" He said, "I have my duty to do." I said, "It seems to me that your duty is to occupied, martyred, imprisoned France. I have lived ten years of my life in France. You cannot live that long in a country without feeling something for it, and when I think that the Germans today are marching as masters through the streets of Paris, it shakes me within." I saw the tears start in his eyes and he said, "I am a Frenchman. What do you think it does to me?" I then said to him, waxing lyrical, "Colonel, every soldier you cause to be killed here, whether he be French or American, is one soldier the less to march under the Arch of Triumph when dawns the day of glory of which the 'Marseillaise' speaks." That shook him and I pressed my advantage further. That day the Italians had occupied the Riviera, and I said, "Today the Italians are kicking Frenchmen off the sidewalks in Nice." He banged his fist down on the table and said, "I can't stand it. What is it you want me to do?" I said, "Colonel, I want you to ride back with me to General Harmon and join us in celebrating the second armistice. The eleventh of November is a glorious day for us twice— in the first war and in this war. Return to your barracks in Mazagan and let us move on to drive the Germans out of North Africa." He agreed, came down with me and got into the half-track, by which he was very impressed. I took him back to General Harmon, who was absolutely delighted. He said, "Walters, I'll make you a first lieutenant for this." We then had a great celebration with Colonel Signard and the members of his staff, during the course of which he asked me if it was true that the general had made me a first lieutenant. I said he had. At this point someone brought up a first lieutenant's bar and General Harmon pinned it on me. Colonel Signard asked me for the second lieutenant's insignia. I asked him why he wanted it; without replying he pinned it to his tunic over the left breast pocket. Wine now appeared to celebrate the fact that Frenchmen and Americans were again fighting on the same side. During the afternoon an armistice had been signed and Admiral Darlan announced that the French forces were joining us and re-entering the war against Germany and Italy.

After the wine had time to take effect, I worked up enough courage to ask Colonel Signard why he had pinned my second lieutenant's bar to his breast pocket. Tapping the lower part of his sleeve, where the French then wore their rank, he said, "Down there I'm an old colonel"; and then tapping the second lieutenant's bar over his left breast, he said, "But here beats the heart of a second lieutenant." This was a memorable eleventh of November.

The fighting ceased and we moved on toward Casablanca the next morning. That afternoon a French submarine, the *Medusa*, had escaped from the harbor of Casablanca and run aground off Mazagan. The crew came ashore and joined us, after hearing that the armistice with the French forces in North Africa had been signed. We drove on from Casablanca to Rabat, the capital of Morocco. I pitched my tent with the 2nd Armored Division camped in the forest of the Mamora, but I only slept there for two days. Because of my proficiency in French I was ordered to go into Rabat and take charge of liaison with the French. I moved into a very comfortable room in the Balima Hotel, which was the best hotel in town. I was unquestionably the only first lieutenant in the hotel, but then, I was the only first lieutenant around who spoke French.

In Rabat my duties were manifold. I dealt with everything

from cold storage and barrels of nails to the delicate issue of control of the brothels. The brothels proved to be a particularly sensitive political question. The French feared that the Americans with all their money and chocolates and everything else would monopolize the girls' attention and squeeze the French out completely. A command-level agreement was made. The Americans instituted a ten o'clock curfew for the brothels; the rest of the evening belonged to the French. My virtual and virtuous military governorship was about to end. A U. S. Army colonel, Leonard Nason, a former volunteer in the French Foreign Legion, who spoke excellent French, arrived. He was a decorated veteran of the Riff war. I was sent back to my tent in the forest of the Mamora, but I still retained my duties as he took over my room at the Balima.

On his first evening I took him on an inspection of the various brothels. He approached one in the old city, in the medina. He banged on the door. No answer. He banged again, now angrily. Finally, the door opened and a middle-aged Frenchwoman looked out on us and said, "Ah, the Americans! I worked with them in the First World War." Colonel Nason made it plain to her that if there were any Americans in the establishment after ten o'clock at night, she would be in serious trouble and might have the place closed down. She understood this and said that she agreed and that there would be no trouble with her. We then went on to two other such establishments and finally wound up in one of them which appeared to be a bar/nightclub on the ground floor with the other action taking place on the second floor. This establishment was owned by a very sophisticated, well-dressed Frenchwoman. Fortunately for her, she had received a supply of French liqueurs and drinks of all sorts just before the invasion, and her establishment was one of the few places where you could get crème de menthe, benedictine, Cointreau and so forth in North Africa. Her business thrived.

One of the things that struck me was the tremendous shortage of food in North Africa. The only dessert I ever saw was a tiny orange known as a clementine. I ate with a number of

French families and was surprised at how difficult it was for them to get food.

Around November 14 a large number of people began coming up to declare themselves Gaullists, opposed to negotiating with Marshal Pétain and Admiral Darlan. Some of the young men who had been imprisoned in the hinterland or desert for being Gaullists had escaped and returned to the cities. They were indignant at our dealings with Darlan. So ardently did they declare their loyalty to General de Gaulle and their hostility toward Admiral Darlan that I reported to my superiors threats against Admiral Darlan's life. A little over a month later he was assassinated by a young fanatic in Algiers.

Life in Rabat resumed an element of normalcy for a short period. In the evenings I accompanied Colonel Nason on his rounds, and later returned alone to the three brothels to make sure that the ten o'clock curfew was being observed. This required a room-by-room inspection. Sometimes I would kick a door open only to have it kicked shut. I would then point out to a somewhat aroused American soldier that professional international relations ended at ten o'clock. I cannot remember ever being thanked for this information!

One night when I called at the rather sophisticated establishment, the French owner said to me, "Lieutenant, you always come here on official business. Why don't you pay us a social visit sometime? There won't be any charge." I realized that if I did such a thing, I would be beholden to her and would not be able to exercise the authority that was necessary over the establishment, and I said, "Madame, there is the dignity of the country which I represent." She said, "Lieutenant, that dignity is all very well, but you are only young once." On one occasion she suggested that I look through one of her see-through mirrors. I refused, fearing that if I looked, I might become a customer. She was puzzled but not offended by my refusal. Finally, we agreed that Colonel Nason and I would go to dinner with her at her home, and we did.

We drove out in Colonel Nason's jeep, and found that she lived in a very large and luxurious home with her husband, who was a prosperous French farmer. He owned a large farm. He farmed and his wife ran the brothel as a sideline. We had a splendid dinner. Evidently, there was no shortage of food down on the farm. As we drove back, the jeep broke down. Colonel Nason looked at me and said, "This is a hell of a thing to happen to us. We break down in the goddamned desert in the middle of the night coming back from the home of a whorehouse owner." Fortunately I got the jeep started and we returned without incident.

One day I was told that the thirteen-year-old Crown Prince of Morocco and his seven-year-old brother were coming out to the forest to see the equipment of the division. When they arrived I rode them around, first in a tank and then in a halftrack. Crown Prince Hassan, who was thirteen, behaved with extraordinary aplomb and dignity, even though he was visibly impressed by the equipment. We dressed them in coveralls which were obviously much too long, and we had to roll up the sleeves and legs. Prince Moulay Abdullah, Hassan's brother, found this very amusing. Hassan endured it in the most dignified and stoic way. He asked me many questions. He was clearly very interested. He spoke superb French, as did Moulay Abdullah. They were accompanied by a number of French officers and by a robed vizier. Thus began a friendship which was to endure until the present day with King Hassan II.

I became involved in the political intrigue in North Africa. Various groups schemed continuously to hold or to seize power. I was sent to General Auguste Noguès, who was the French resident general in Morocco, to tell him that no harm must come to General Antoine Béthouart, who had commanded the division at Casablanca. Béthouart had known of the landing and had attempted to prevent French resistance to it. He had been arrested by General Noguès, and sent to Meknes. I was instructed by General Patton in no uncertain terms to tell General Noguès that not only was no harm to come to General Béthouart but he was to be released at once, as were all the other officers who had attempted to join us. This included Colonel Pierre Magnan of the Colonial Infantry Regiment of

Morocco, who on the day of our landing had ordered his regiment to surround the resident general's quarters and to await our arrival. Unfortunately, we did not land at Rabat. He thought he had cut all the telephones from the resident general's house, but he had not. The resident general had been able to summon a battalion of tanks, and Magnan, faced with the fact that he was surrounded by tanks and that we were not landing at Rabat, had been compelled to surrender. He was threatened with execution, and I informed Noguès in respectful but unequivocal terms that Béthouart and Magnan were to be released, and if anything happened to these officers who had been sympathetic to us, we would hold Noguès responsible. I think he was appalled at being told things like this by a first lieutenant, even though I was doing it on orders from General Patton.

During this period I discovered to my consternation that my promotion to first lieutenant was illegal. The colonel who was the adjutant general of the 2nd Armored Division came to me somewhat sheepishly and said, "I have just found out that you are attached to this division, not assigned to it; therefore, the general does not have the power to promote you to first lieutenant. So you now revert to second lieutenant, but I promise you he will get the paper work done and you will be a first lieutenant very shortly." This was a somewhat embarrassing experience. It was the first of the two times that something like this happened to me in the Army. The same thing happened on the occasion of my promotion to captain, on yet another mission in 1943.

I went forward to Tunisia to act as a prisoner-of-war interrogator in a much tougher kind of war than the one we had fought in Morocco. Now we fought the Germans. I went up to a point where I could see Tunis from the II Corps front. Shortly after that, the Germans counterattacked and drove us back. One day, driving between Tebessa and Medjez-el-Bab, I had to leap from a jeep three times to avoid strafing by German aircraft. A soldier learns that under these circumstances he should not look up because the white face provides a target for the aircraft. However, as one lies face down alongside of the road and hears the aircraft coming, an almost irresistible impulse arises to turn one's head to look and see whether the aircraft's fire is in line or not.

I interrogated German and Italian prisoners. The Italians were from the Wolves of Tuscany Division, very tough. The Germans were from the mixed first German/Italian Army and also very tough and cocky. It was hard to get information from them. On one occasion a German major I was questioning took out a cigarette, lit it and blew the smoke in my face. I knocked the cigarette out of his mouth, told him in no uncertain terms that he was my prisoner and that he should behave accordingly. He looked at me and replied, "We have a protecting power, Switzerland, that will prevent you from doing anything." I said, "That protecting power is in Algiers, three hundred miles away, and here you are a prisoner and if you attempt to escape, you will be shot, and you might easily attempt to escape." One of the more effective things I found in dealing with the German prisoners was to quote their German soldier's oath to them. A prisoner is always in a state of shock and somewhat ashamed of his position. If the interrogator struck the right chord, he often received co-operation. For instance, I would ask a German prisoner a question. He would refuse to answer and say that his soldier's duty would not let him answer. I would recite slowly to him the German soldier's oath, which said, "I swear before God and the German people unconditional obedience to my *Führer* Adolf Hitler who has united the German people in National Socialism. I further swear that I will at all times be ready as a gallant soldier to lay down my life in fulfillment of this oath." I would then say to him, "But you didn't lay down your life. You have not fulfilled the oath. Stop talking to me about your soldier's duty." This was harsh but effective. Some broke down and then talked freely. The officers, however, were tough and I soon learned that there was no point in trying to break an officer who refused to talk. Once one of the German officers said to me, "If you were my prisoner, would you answer the questions you are asking me?" Since a sufficient number of soldiers did answer questions, I simply did not have the time to try to get co-operation from the officers.

I received orders to go to Algiers. While there I saw Admiral Darlan at the Palais d'Été. Admiral Darlan, in spite of the fact that I was wearing an American uniform, asked repeatedly whether I was really an American. I was somewhat irritated by this and I said, "Yes, I was born in the United States, and my father is English." The admiral turned away and asked me no further questions. I then flew to Gibraltar with General Béthouart, and at this point he was appointed to be the head of the French Military Mission in the United States. I received orders to return to the United States to teach prisoner-of-war interrogation at Camp Ritchie. I was chosen because I was the only member of the various prisoner-of-war interrogation teams who had interrogated French, Italian and German prisoners. The breadth of experience in three national psychologies was considered valuable for training new interrogators.

My problem now was how to get out of Gibraltar and back to the United States. I knew that by going to Casablanca I could get a ship or possibly aircraft, but I wanted very much to go through England, where I had members of my family. Getting back from England would be a lot easier than getting back from North Africa. I went down to the small U.S. liaison detachment at North Front Airport at Gibraltar and talked to a Colonel G. He explained to me that he did not know when he could get me on an aircraft. I had low priority and he had to deal with a lot of important people. I then asked where I could stay. He informed me that he was not running a hotel for transients and I would simply have to make my own arrangements. This was the only time in the war that anybody in any army ever refused to give me a place to sleep. I left my baggage at the airport and walked into Gibraltar.

By one of those extraordinary and impossible coincidences I met a boy I had gone to boarding school with in England. He was a captain and was the aide to the governor general of Gibraltar. When he learned that I had just come from Tunisia, he felt that Governor General Mason McFarland would be very interested in fresh news from the front. Forthwith he took me up to the governor's palace. I spoke to the governor, an elderly

British general who showed keen interest. I described the tough situation in Tunisia. The Germans and Italians had brought in reinforcements. They had firmly entrenched themselves around Tunis and Bizerta. Farther south along the coast they had reoccupied the Mareth Line facing Libya. A lot of fighting still lay ahead in Tunisia. He asked about the state of French politics in North Africa, and I tried to explain to him how complex they were even though I myself did not fully understand the numerous factions in the struggle for power. Finally, the governor asked me rather kindly where I was staying, and I said I had no place in which to stay yet and that the American liaison officer indicated that there were only two hotels in town, the Bristol which was full, and the Rock which was reserved for VIPs. The governor told his aide, "Take him up to the Rock and get him a room."

The governor's aide took me up to the Rock Hotel, where I was immediately assigned a very comfortable room with a magnificent view over the Bay of Gibraltar toward Algeciras and the Strait. I was absolutely delighted. Nothing like this had happened to me since the war had begun. I sent a telegram from Gibraltar to my parents telling them that I was alive and well. This was the first communication I had been able to send home since the landing. My next problem was how to get out of Gibraltar. Each day I would go down to the airport and look to see if my name was posted on the manifest for the daily plane departures. Day after day my name failed to appear. I met with General Béthouart on a number of occasions during my stay in Gibraltar. I gave him my parents' address and asked him to call them when he got to the United States. He promised to do so. To my astonishment, and to the great delight of my mother, he did. He, in turn, knowing I was going to London, gave me a letter to deliver to General de Gaulle.

I continued my daily vigil at North Front Airport waiting for my name to make the list. I regularly saw Colonel G. dining at the Rock. One day he told me that I would be leaving in a few days. I asked him if there was any way I could get my luggage out to the airport and he replied that he knew of no way and offered no help. I realized that I had a real problem on my hands. I called the governor's aide and he loaned me a jeep so I could take my luggage out the evening before. On the appointed day, I saw Colonel G. at dinner. He confirmed to me that I would be leaving. Next morning I got up at five o'clock and walked to the airport with just a handbag containing my toilet articles. At the terminal an RAF sergeant was manifesting people aboard the aircraft going to the United Kingdom. I stepped up and told him my name was on the manifest. He looked up and down the manifest and said, "I'm sorry, sir. You're not on the manifest." I said, "I must be. Colonel G. told me I was." He repeated, "You're not on the manifest, sir," and showed it to me. Obviously he was right. The sergeant then whispered, "Colonel G. took you off the manifest yesterday at noon when some friend of his came in from Algiers." I was furious! Not at being removed from the passenger manifest—this I could understand if one of Colonel G.'s friends had shown up with a higher priority. His confirmation to me the previous evening could only be interpreted as a petty and malicious deception. Little men take pleasure in little things. For ten more days I waited in Gibraltar. Finally, in desperation I volunteered to go as the waist gunner of a B-17 flying to England. This was an interesting experience.

We took off from Gibraltar in the early morning darkness, climbed out over the Strait and then headed westward. We flew along the Spanish and the Portuguese coasts and could see brilliantly lighted towns and cities. Daylight came as we rounded the southern tip of Portugal, near Sagres Point, where Henry the Navigator planned some of the great Portuguese voyages of exploration. Setúbal and the mouth of the Tagus were visible, though Lisbon itself was hidden by the clouds. At the time I did not realize the role that Portugal and its language would play in my next mission; indeed in my career in the years ahead. We flew northward and then early in the afternoon I dozed a little in my heavy flying suit. The pilot came back to ask me if I wanted to see the French coast, which was visible far away to the right. I was distressed to find that we were close enough to see it and, therefore, close enough to be on the German radar screens. Shortly after lunchtime, the unmistakable fields of England appeared below us and we landed at Portreath in Cornwall.

Here the problem arose as to how to get to London. It was, in wartime, a ten- or twelve-hour trip by rail. However, the pilot suddenly decided that he would fly there, and a two-and-a-half-hour flight brought us to the huge sprawling metropolis that is London. The barrage balloons were a novelty. I had heard a great deal about them, but I had never seen them before. We landed at Bovingdon Airport, and I got my gear out of the aircraft and talked myself into transportation to Watford Underground Station, from where I rode into town to the home of an old friend of my mother's, whom we always called Aunt Pauline. I looked up two of my other aunts, both of whom were in their fifties, and discovered to my amazement that they were both flight sergeants in the Royal Air Force. I went out to see my uncle, who had been a brigadier general in the British Army in World War I and who was now a colonel in the Home Guard. He was very pleased to see me and to know that I was a lieutenant in the United States Army and to learn that I had seen action in North Africa. I was not to see him again. He died a few months later. His serving in the Home Guard and my aunts' service in the RAF drove home to me the total mobilization in England.

I waited in London for several days, and I was debriefed by Intelligence officers at General Eisenhower's headquarters about conditions in North Africa and the complexities of French political maneuvering between the Gaullists, the Giraudists and the Darlanists. Finally, I got orders to return to the United States. While waiting one night I had sat on the roof of my aunt's office building in Leicester Square when her turn came for fire watch.¹ On the night of my departure I took a train out of the blacked-out London station and did not know where I was

_____

¹ It was an eerie experience looking out over the blacked-out city watching the searchlights probing the skies for enemy aircraft that did not come that night.

going. In the morning I arrived at Greenock on the Clyde in
Scotland, boarded the *Queen Elizabeth* and found myself in a
large first-class cabin with about fifteen other officers. Most of
them were pilots who had ferried aircraft to the United Kingdom and were returning to fly more aircraft across the Atlantic.
At dawn on December 18 we nosed out of the Firth of Clyde
and, moving at high speed and without escort, we rounded the
northern tip of Ireland and headed westward. Frequent zigzag-
ging in the course was designed to make interception by a
U-boat difficult. We made the westward crossing in a little over
four days. Once again, much sooner than I expected, I was back
in the United States and about to embark on my next mission.

3. PORTUGAL

After I returned from Europe and Africa in 1943, I was reassigned to the Military Intelligence Training Center at Camp Ritchie, where I was put in charge of the Italian Prisoner of War Interrogation Department. We already knew that we would be moving on from North Africa into Italy. It was imperative that we have a large number of teams trained to interrogate Italian prisoners and trained in matters of intelligence relating to the Italian Armed Forces. I was also required to give each class that went through the Military Intelligence Training Center a three-hour lecture describing how my intelligence team had been organized, how it had functioned in the actual landing in North Africa, how I had functioned in Tunisia and my thoughts about the organization and use of such intelligence teams in the light of the experience I had had. Since I was, at that time, the only officer who had returned from the fighting area, this was a required lecture for all students at the school.

One day in April 1943 I received a telephone call from a colonel at the Pentagon, Colonel Charles Leonard. He worked in Foreign Liaison. He told me that he had discussed the request that he was about to make to me with Colonel Banfill, who was the commandant at Camp Ritchie. Basically, he told me that he wanted me to report to the Pentagon the following morning in order to accompany a group of Portuguese around the United

States. Portugal, though it had a centuries-old alliance with Great Britain, was neutral in the war, at least officially. We were taking three groups of Portuguese officers on an extensive visit in order to impress them with the growing power and determination of the United States and to convince them we would certainly win the war. This was part of a broad campaign to obtain Portuguese agreement to allow us to use the Azores for anti-submarine forces, both surface and air. The Allies were sustaining extremely heavy shipping losses in the North Atlantic at the hands of the German U-boat wolf packs. Colonel Leonard told me he wanted me there the following morning at nine o'clock ready to take this group around. I said to him that I thought there must be some misunderstanding since I did not speak Portuguese. He replied, "No, but you speak Spanish, French, Italian and all of that stuff, and you'll certainly understand what they are saying." I protested and said, "Colonel, I love to hear Carmen Miranda's songs, but I cannot understand what the words mean. I don't understand Portuguese." He then said, "Lieutenant, there is a misunderstanding. You seem to be under the impression that I am *inviting* you to be here tomorrow morning at nine o'clock. I am not. It's an order. See that you are here, and see that you are speaking Portuguese." I checked out with the post adjutant and he told me that Colonel Banfill had agreed to this mission. I set about finding some Portuguese material to try and familiarize myself with the language. I knew that it was closely related to Spanish, and that from past experience I could read it fairly well. I rounded up some issues of *Em Guarda*, a propaganda magazine that the United States was putting out at that time for distribution in Brazil. I perused this magazine and was worried because I could read it so easily. In fact, from Spanish I could understand 90 per cent of what was written in the magazine. Yet, I did know that when I heard Portuguese spoken, I could not understand it nearly as well as I could understand the written words. The spoken language sounded a great deal different to me.

I studied these magazines and whatever other Portuguese books I could lay my hands on for most of that evening. The following morning I reported in Washington to Colonel Leonard's office in the Pentagon. He informed me that I would accompany an Air Force group. There was an Army group, a Navy group, and an Air Force group. A U. S. Navy commander was going with the Navy group, and a U. S. Army lieutenant colonel was going with the Army group. The Pentagon was somewhat embarrassed by the fact that I was a first lieutenant, because the leader of the Portuguese group was a very senior Air Force officer. Nothing, however, could be done for the moment about this problem. The Portuguese group was made up of a number of officers. At that time the head of each particular service mission was a colonel or Navy captain. There were a few field grade officers and some captains and lieutenants. Three of these officers later became chiefs of staff of their service. One of them became minister of the merchant marine. One of them was killed in an airplane accident, and the officer whom I accompanied most closely, Colonel Francisco Craveiro Lopes, subsequently became President of Portugal.

After certain briefings, entertainment and a meeting with General Marshall in Washington, the three parties set out on their respective tours of the United States to visit installations of the greatest interest to them. All three groups crossed the continent to California and back again. The group I had was given a B-15, an old twin-engined airplane, in which to travel, and we set forth on our long journey.

When I saw the itinerary and the things we were going to show them, I could not help but ask Colonel Leonard whether we really should be so free with our information since Portugal was a neutral. These officers, as I understood it, had recently visited the German forces on the Eastern Front; and there were many German Intelligence personnel in Lisbon. I was told the time of hiding was past. We wanted to show them what we had and what we would soon have, and to convince them that we were going to invade Fortress Europe and destroy the Nazi regime.

I was delighted to find early in the trip that through these officers' knowledge of French and Spanish I was able to communicate with them quite easily, and they began helping me to learn Portuguese. Now, this is less complex than first meets the eye since 80 per cent of Portuguese words are completely recognizable in Spanish. As I have mentioned, the Pentagon was a little concerned by the fact that I was only a first lieutenant, whereas a full commander was with the Navy group and a lieutenant colonel with the Army group. When I arrived with the Portuguese in Fort Worth, I received a telegram from Washington saying, "Effective immediately you are promoted to the temporary temporary grade of captain." I regarded the repetition of the word "temporary" as merely being for emphasis. At this time all promotions were temporary and so the wording seemed normal to me. I told the Portuguese and they were delighted and flattered. Colonel Craveiro Lopes pinned on my captain's bars. I was aware that I had not yet served the necessary six months in grade to be considered for promotion, but I thought that the powers in Washington had somehow overcome this obstacle. Needless to say, I wrote my family and friends and told them of my good luck. I had not yet been an officer a full year and here I was a captain. I was highly pleased with myself and did not yet realize how awkward a "temporary temporary promotion" could be.

We flew to Fort Worth, Texas, where we visited the headquarters of the Air Training Command and were very graciously received by the commander, who in his little speech praised the Portuguese as our staunch allies. Since Portugal was a neutral, I eliminated this phrase in my translation into Portuguese, but Colonel Craveiro Lopes mentioned to me later that he had understood what the commander had said to him. In Fort Worth also we viewed a most impressive sight, an enormous factory that looked half a mile long to me. In it B-24 Liberator bombers were being assembled on a visibly moving assembly line. The Portuguese were deeply impressed that so large a piece of equipment could be fabricated so rapidly and in such great quantities. We also toured various other installations in the area such as the Gunnery School at Matagorda and the B-26 School at Del Rio, and then moved on to El Paso and finally to Tucson, Arizona, where we visited Davis-Monthan Airfield. Here, the commander of the base was a member of the crew of the NC-4 flight that had flown right after World War I from the United States to Portugal in one of the very first transatlantic flights. He was very insistent that they go out in the desert near Tucson and see a very old Spanish church at San Xavier del Bac. This was the site of an old Spanish mission and is, in fact, one of the oldest churches in the United States. We had been flying most of the day and our tired guests did not want to go. They knew that anything they would see in America would not be old in terms of Portugal. Nevertheless, the base commander was so insistent that we finally drove out to the church, in which they expressed a polite but limited interest. Finally, they asked me the age of this church, since its great age had been emphasized so much to them. I replied that it was more than two hundred years old. Colonel Craveiro Lopes smiled, looked at me and said, "Walters, a church two hundred years old in Portugal is regarded as contemporary, not ancient."

We flew on to the Los Angeles area, where an amusing incident occurred. We were to visit the divisions training in the desert near Indio, and as we were about to leave Los Angeles, the pilot discovered that there was a cracked cylinder in one of the motors. He refused to go. The commanding general in Los Angeles, who was anxious to get rid of the Portuguese, as he had spent all of his entertainment money, ordered the pilot to go. The pilot, a slow-spoken Southerner, said to him, "General, there are two kinds of pilots—old pilots and bold pilots. There are no old bold pilots, and I intend to be an old pilot." We did not go until the aircraft was repaired. The visit to the forces training in the desert impressed the Portuguese with our equipment, training and determination. There were two armored divisions and one motorized infantry division.

At the Kaiser shipyards, they were simply dumbfounded to see how quickly the ships were built from the date of the keel-laying. In fact, I feel they harbored some idea that we may not have been fully truthful with them since the construction of these ships was going forward, thanks to Henry Kaiser's new methods, with a speed that bore no relation to previous ship construction. We then went on to visit the Portuguese communities in the San Francisco area.

From San Francisco we flew on back to the east. We flew to Chicago and visited a huge steel mill in the Gary, Indiana, area. We then went to Detroit, where we visited another aircraft production factory and a tank arsenal where huge numbers of tanks were being turned out, again, on visibly moving assembly lines. From here we flew to Niagara Falls and then visited the Curtiss-Wright factory at Buffalo. At this factory, again, large numbers of C-46 transport aircraft were being constructed, and here Colonel Craveiro Lopes noted with interest that on the tail of these aircraft was a large hook obviously designed to tow a glider. He turned to me and said, "Now I know that even if you can't get through the Atlantic Wall, you are going to try to go over it." I replied, "Colonel, we are not only going to go over it, but through it as well." At this factory, also, a very curious and extraordinary coincidence took place.

Shortly after the North African landings, a large number of U.S. aircraft traveling between the United Kingdom and North Africa had been forced, either by engine trouble or fuel shortages, to land in Portugal. There the crews were interned for a while and then allowed to return to the United Kingdom or the United States. The aircraft, however, remained in Portugal and were for many years the backbone of the Portuguese Air Force. On one occasion an aircraft of a new type had landed at an airfield some distance from Lisbon. Major Costa Macedo, who was with the Portuguese group I was accompanying, had been designated to fly this aircraft back to Lisbon. However, he found the aircraft totally unfamiliar and asked that the American pilot be brought there to show him how it operated. The pilot came and Costa Macedo asked him to give him his word that he would not attempt to escape if they let him get into the cockpit to show Costa Macedo how to fly the aircraft. The American officer readily gave his word, and climbed up into the cockpit while Costa Macedo stood on the wing and received instruction from the pilot in the peculiarities of the aircraft. The Portuguese had refueled the aircraft and it was ready to go. The pilot proceeded to show Costa Macedo how to start the engine, and when the engine was running and had been running for some time and was fully warmed up, he suddenly leaned forward and pushed Costa Macedo off the wing, forcing him to jump to the ground. The pilot then gunned the plane down onto the runway and took off and flew to North Africa. As we were visiting the Curtiss-Wright factory, we met this officer. He was considerably embarrassed at the meeting since he had given Costa Macedo his word of honor that he would not attempt to escape. Costa Macedo took me aside and told me to tell the American officer not to be too embarrassed because, had he been in his shoes, he would probably have done the same thing. Costa Macedo did say that the matter made a considerable amount of trouble for him. Since his wife was Polish and he was known to be in sympathy with the Allies, there was some suspicion that he had been in collusion with the American pilot in facilitating his escape.

From this area we returned to New York and visited some major installations there as well as the large Portuguese colonies in both New York and Newark. We then went up to New England and visited the Portuguese colonies in New Bedford and Fall River. By this time the Portuguese were talking fairly frankly to me, and they said very plainly that they wanted the Allies to win. But they were fearful that an Allied victory or a German collapse would result in a Russian takeover of a large part of Europe, and since they feared communism very much, they described their position as being one where they would like to see the last German fall dead across the body of the last Russian.

We returned to New York for a few days prior to their departure. Here an amusing incident occurred. We were staying at the Waldorf-Astoria; I had a room adjacent to Colonel Craveiro Lopes' and we shared a common bathroom. Shortly after I got to my room, the phone rang, and a girl's voice was on the phone. She greeted me and asked me how I was. I was somewhat baffled as I did not know who was speaking, and I said,

"Who is this?" She replied, "This is Jean." I thought it was a girl I knew by the name of Jean, and I said, "Oh, hello, Jean. How are you? How is Marie?" (her sister). She said, "I'm afraid I am not that Jean." "Well," I said, "who are you?" She said, "Well, as a matter of fact, you don't actually know me." Still no light dawned on me. Then she said, "Norma told me to call you." And I said, "But I don't know anybody by the name of Norma." And then, seeing that I was so dense that I had not yet understood the nature of the call, she said, "Well, this *is* a rather unusual way to meet you, but we just thought you might want some companionship." At last I understood and said, "Well, that's very kind of you, but I am with a group. No, thanks." "Well," she said, "if you should change your mind, here is my number." I hung up. The door between my room and the bathroom and the one between the bathroom and Colonel Craveiro Lopes' room was open, and a few minutes later I heard his phone ring. He did speak a little English, and I heard this curious conversation: "Who? What? Norma? Who is Norma?" I went into his room laughing and told him to hang up the phone. When he hung up, I explained to him what had happened and he seemed surprised that this kind of proposition could be made in a rather luxurious hotel. I reminded him that it was wartime and that in wartime many of the conventions that normally apply in peacetime are not applied as strictly. He commented that in Portugal these things happened too, but only in cheaper hotels.

I saw the Portuguese off on the Pan American Clipper returning to Lisbon. They were most grateful for my help and they wrote a very warm letter to General Marshall in which they greatly praised my Portuguese, which had improved considerably in the two months I had spent taking them around the United States. In fact, I had effected a very broad conversion from Spanish to Portuguese without actually losing the Spanish. When they arrived in Lisbon, they sent me a personal telegram to tell me that they had arrived safely, which I much appreciated.

After seeing the Protuguese off in New York, I returned to

the Pentagon to report on the trip. As I was walking through the Pentagon concourse, I ran into someone from the Foreign Liaison section, and he said to me, "What a weird promotion that was they gave you—only for the duration of your mission and then you were to revert to first lieutenant." I was aghast and asked him whether he was sure. He replied that he had seen the paper work on it and was sure. I was thunderstruck. How was I going to explain this demotion at a time when the general motion was up? Nevertheless, I stopped in at the uniform store in the concourse and bought and put on a first lieutenant's bar. I had generously given away all my lieutenant's bars to other lieutenants who were hoping for promotion. Thus accoutered, I presented myself to Colonel Leonard. He seemed relieved that I already knew. I accounted to him for the $10,000 in cash he had given me to pay for the expenses of the party and presented to him all of the receipts I had collected to justify these expenses. He then showed me the letter the Portuguese had written about my services and congratulated me. But his words were like ashes in my mouth as I thought about having to explain my demotion. I returned to Camp Ritchie thinking that this was an isolated mission that would not recur and that I would return to my normal teaching function at the Military Intelligence Training Center. Little did I realize that this was not to be the case and that this mission on which I was exposed for the first time to the Portuguese language was to lead to my next mission to the Brazilians and through it to a profound influence on my life.

At Camp Ritchie everyone wanted to know how I had fouled up with the Portuguese to get demoted. Had I gotten them lost, taken them to a whorehouse or revealed secrets? In vain I showed my letters of thanks and commendation. No one believed me. The awkwardness of the matter was increased by the fact that the commandant, Colonel Banfill, always referred to me as Captain Walters, and this made me even more uncomfortable. About two months later when I was just beginning to adjust to the situation, I passed the post adjutant, Captain Julian Zimmerman, and he greeted me as "Captain." I explained to him that I did not find it funny. He laughed and said,

"No, you really are a captain." He then took me to his office and showed me a message from Washington conveying a decision by the Judge Advocate General stating that I was either a captain or a civilian. Since they still needed me for the war, I reverted to captain and received my back pay. I never really felt completely safe until I became a major a year later in Italy.

The whole purpose of our efforts with these Portuguese officers was to convince them that we would win the war. Emotionally they were on our side but they feared that if they allowed us to use the Azores base to fight the submarine menace the Germans might demand passage across Spain to attack Portugal in retaliation for such an action. Whatever these fears were, the Portuguese overcame them, and not long afterward, by invoking their ancient treaty with Great Britain, they authorized the British, and, through the British, the United States, to build and use the Azores bases as we had hoped. This contributed in very great measure to our being able to bring Allied shipping losses down to a manageable figure, and soon the great armadas that were to bring liberation to occupied Europe were moving across the Atlantic in relative safety.

4. BRAZIL

In 1942 as the United States prepared to move against Germany in the Atlantic area, we had to find some way of getting aircraft across the ocean and on to North Africa, to the Middle East and the China-Burma Theater. Distances across the Pacific were prohibitive for all except the largest transport aircraft at that time. Some planes flew via Iceland to England, but even this was beyond the flight range of all but the largest aircraft. In addition, the weather conditions on this northern route posed serious problems for most of the year.

Skillful negotiations with Brazil even before her entry into the war in August 1942 had led to an agreement that established a series of U.S. naval and air bases along the northeastern bulge of Brazil. These reduced the ocean gap to be flown by nearly half. In the middle of the South Atlantic, on the tiny British-owned island of Ascension, U.S. engineers had carved a runway into the side of an extinct volcano, to reduce the ocean gap. The naval bases in Brazil greatly facilitated operations by the U.S. and Brazilian navies against German submarines active in the South Atlantic. The fierceness of these U-boat attacks against Brazilian shipping pushed the Brazilians to seek a more active part in the war against Germany. In keeping with their desire to strike back, and to be something more in the world than a regional South American power, the Brazilians offered to furnish an expeditionary force to fight under U.S. command in the Mediterranean Theater. The Brazilian Navy and Air Force would also participate in operations against the Axis powers. Brazil's immense size, her resources, her strategic position in the South Atlantic made her an attractive partner and ally. It was against this background that my first mission to the Brazilians developed. For political as well as military reasons it was important that the largest nation in South America take an active part in the war against Germany. Brazil itself was anxious to take its first step onto the world scene.

Shortly after concluding my mission with the Portuguese, I returned to Camp Ritchie and the Military Intelligence Training Center. Within a month, however, I was summoned again to go on a similar mission, this time with Brazilian Air Minister Pedro Salgado Filho. At this time the war was not going too well for us and we were wooing the Brazilians in an attempt to get them to increase their assistance beyond the already valuable bases which they called the "Bridge to Victory." Air Minister Salgado Filho arrived in the United States and I presented myself to him in Miami. I was delighted to find Brazilian Portuguese a lot easier for me to understand than that spoken by the European Portuguese. The pronunciation seemed much closer to Spanish and the words were enunciated more clearly.

I accompanied Salgado Filho on a tour rather similar to that of the Portuguese. This time it was confined to Air Corps bases many of them the same training installations I had visited earlier with the Portuguese in Texas. During the Brazilians' visit to the Air Gunnery School at Matagorda, Texas, I bragged to a young pilot that though I had flown a great deal, I had never been airsick. I was in fact certain that I could not become airsick. He smiled and said, "Well, if you want to try, come with me and I'll show you." Having put out this much braggadocio, I could scarcely back out. I reluctantly accompanied him to a training plane, an AT-6. We got into this plane and as I strapped myself in, I began to regret my boast. I considered the possibility that I might eat my words but nothing else for the rest of the day. We climbed to a couple of thousand feet and he

asked me through the intercom, "Are you ready?" I said, "Yes."
He immediately began a series of snap rolls, dropped off on one
wing, then on the other, and then he looped. I was quite
horrified to feel the intense force of gravity at the bottom of the
loop. I did not expect the drag at such low speed and I just
knew I had a brain hemorrhage. As he continued various types
of maneuvers, I could feel nausea begin to creep up on me. Fortunately just as I thought I was actually going to be airsick, he
said, "Well, I guess we had better go back now." To my great
relief, we returned to land at the Matagorda base. I put my head
way down between my legs in an effort to force some color back
to my face. We landed, I got unsteadily out of the airplane and
stood on the ground for a minute, and the pilot looked at me,
shook his head and said, "You know, I am amazed. I was about
to get airsick myself, and you didn't feel anything?" "Well," I
said, "one more maneuver in any sense and there would have
been a cockpit to clean out. That's how close I came." I did not
feel too well, so I went up to my room in the bachelor officers'
quarters and lay down on the bed. I found that I could not close
my eyes because the minute I did, the bed seemed to drop off on
one wing to the right or the left underneath me. So I just lay
there for about half an hour staring at the ceiling until, I guess,
the labyrinths in my ear recovered their normal position and I
ceased to feel this kind of nausea and confusion.

Other than that, the Salgado Filho trip went well. There were
Brazilian cadets training at many installations, and they were
very pleased to see their air minister out to visit them. Salgado
Filho was one of the very few civilian air ministers in Brazil's
history. He was effective and popular. He was close to President
Vargas and like him came from the state of Rio Grande do Sul.
He died in a postwar airplane accident after he insisted that his
pilot take off in spite of adverse weather forecasts. The Salgado
Filho tour ended in Miami, where I put him on the plane to
Brazil.

Once again, I returned to Camp Ritchie and resumed my role
as head of the Italian Prisoner of War Interrogation Department. However, the month with Salgado Filho had greatly im-

proved my Portuguese and given it more of a Brazilian slant. Not long after this came another summons. This time I was told I would be accompanying Brazilian War Minister General Eurico Dutra, who was coming up to visit the United States. Reportedly he was not very friendly to the United States and did admire the Germans. Therefore, this was a very important trip, and it was essential that we make a good impression upon him. In Washington I reported in to the Foreign Liaison section, and was told to meet General Dutra's Chief of Cabinet, a Colonel José Bina Machado, a former Brazilian Military Attaché to the United States who spoke fluent English and knew his way around the United States. I found him in his room at the Shoreham Hotel lying on a bed and talking on the phone to a Chilean colleague. I was shocked at the insults he hurled at the Chilean. I expected a diplomatic incident. I was relieved to learn that they were old friends and joking together.

Colonel Bina Machado was an extraordinarily jovial and friendly man. Rarely did I see him out of good humor. Accompanying General Dutra was Brigadier General Claude "Flap" Adams, a senior U.S. officer who had been sent to Brazil by General Marshall. General Dutra was very fond of General Adams and in later years when he returned to the United States as President of Brazil, he went out to Humboldt, Tennessee, for the sole purpose of seeing his old friend General Adams, credited in Washington with swinging General Dutra to an ever more friendly position toward the United States and its war effort.

In addition to Bina Machado General Dutra's party consisted of his son Captain Antonio Dutra and some six or seven senior Brazilian officers. We set forth, here again on a very extensive trip around the United States, visiting Fort Benning, where General Dutra watched a parachute jump. The general appeared quite ready to jump himself if asked, and he did jump from a free parachute tower. Then we went to Fort Jackson in Columbia, South Carolina, where a massive parade of two complete infantry divisions with all of their equipment was held. We then went to the Armored School at Fort Knox, Kentucky.

We flew on to the Artillery School at Fort Sill, Oklahoma. From there we continued to the West Coast to visit various installations as well as the troops training in the desert at Indio. From there we went on to San Francisco. Then we swung on back through the central United States, again visiting steel plants in Indiana, the Chrysler tank arsenal in Detroit, all installations calculated to impress General Dutra with the seriousness, the determination and the capability of the United States to conduct the war to a victorious conclusion.

At the end of the trip we returned to Washington, where I accompanied General Dutra in his call on President Roosevelt. This was the first time I entered the Oval Office or met a President of the United States. I was to return to that Oval Office with foreign dignitaries during the tenure of every President of the United States from Roosevelt to Ford with the exception of President Kennedy, as I served outside the United States during his entire tenure. At the end of the trip General Dutra awarded me the Brazilian Order of Military Merit.

Toward the end of the trip General Dutra was intrigued with my knowledge of the Portuguese language and surprised to learn that I had never visited Brazil or Portugal. He said to me, "Walters, it is ridiculous for anybody to speak Portuguese as well as you do without ever having been to a Portuguese-speaking country. I want you to come back to Brazil with me." To which I replied, "Mr. Minister, I would be delighted, but the problem is not in my hands. It rests in the hands of my superiors." General Dutra, a notoriously laconic man, said that he would talk to my superiors about the matter. He did speak to my superiors in Washington who decided to send me to Brazil with him for ten days.

We flew to Belém, Brazil, via Miami and Puerto Rico. Belém, a large city with a distinct colonial appearance, had at that time no tall buildings or large hotels. We stayed out at the American base at Val de Cães Airport. We spent the night there and left the following day to go to Rio de Janeiro. Unfortunately, bad weather in Rio compelled us to land at a large Brazilian city of which I had no knowledge, Belo Horizonte. Belo Horizonte was founded around the turn of the century as a new capital for the state of Minas Gerais. It was a surprisingly large and modern city. General Dutra entertained us that evening at a casino near a lake in the vicinity of Belo Horizonte. The casino was known as Pampulha. There was an excellent floor show and a girl sang a number of American songs without a trace of an accent including "Grandfather's Clock." When she came to our table afterward I was amazed to find out that she could not speak a single word of English and that she simply imitated the American singers with no comprehension of the words.

I was simply staggered the next day to see the beauty of Rio de Janeiro, an immense city in the most beautiful location one can imagine on the south shore of the great Guanabara Bay stretching around the entrance of the harbor and along the ocean beaches south of the harbor. I stayed in the splendid Gloria Hotel, as the guest of the Brazilian government. The Gloria is an old-fashioned but very luxurious hotel, one of the largest and most prestigious in Rio de Janeiro. I was greatly impressed by Rio. We arrived early in the morning on a very clear day, and as many times as I have seen Rio in the years since then, I will never forget the impression that this gleaming city made upon me. The extraordinary mixture of white sandy beaches on the open Atlantic, tropical jungle and rugged mountains combined with tall modern buildings is found only in Rio.

On the afternoon of my arrival, I went out for a long walk to try out my Portuguese, and I was delighted to find that everyone understood me. It was a curious feeling to come to a country for the first time and not have any language difficulties.

I was taken sight-seeing to Petrópolis, a resort near Rio de Janeiro, in the mountains, which served the purpose of summer capital before the invention of air conditioning. Subsequently, General Dutra provided me a plane to fly me to the great city of São Paulo, the industrial heart of Brazil, and then on to Curitiba, the capital of the state of Paraná, a large city which was just beginning to grow. A few years later the population of Curitiba would exceed a million inhabitants. We stopped briefly in Santos, the port for São Paulo, and then flew back to Rio. I re-

ceived an invaluable bird's-eye view of Brazil and an introduction to the Brazilians, a warm, friendly, intelligent people,
imbued with a sense of historical destiny and a determination to
do everything they could to hasten the day when Brazil would
become a great power in the world.

The Brazilians were deeply angered by German torpedo attacks upon their shipping. At this time there was neither a highway nor a railroad connecting the northeast of Brazil and the
Rio-São Paulo area; all traffic therefore was by sea. The five
thousand casualties resulting from the German sinkings ultimately led Brazil to declare war on Germany on August 22,
1942. This step took courage because at that time the war was
not going well for the Allies. Allied forces had yet to land in
North Africa or Europe. We were being pushed back throughout the Pacific. The Japanese had taken Singapore, Hong Kong,
the Philippines and Burma, and were threatening Australia and
India.

Food was abundant in Brazil. Only gasoline was rationed.
Most vehicles had been converted to burn charcoal. I stayed in
Rio de Janeiro until the sixth of October when I boarded a U.S.
military aircraft and flew north to Recife. I could have flown
back commercially, but I felt it was wrong to expend government funds for what was essentially a pleasant trip for me. We
spent the night at Recife, a large city in northeastern Brazil, and
then we flew on to Natal. Finally we flew on to Belém, where
we arrived in the very late afternoon. I then returned to the
United States and reported back to Camp Ritchie. However, I
was soon informed that I was to go to Fort Leavenworth, the
Army's Command and General Staff School, and assist a large
group of Brazilian officers through a special course that was
being organized there for the officers who were to serve in the
Expeditionary Force that Brazil was planning to send to Italy.

The Brazilians were anxious to participate actively in the
war. Discussions with U.S. authorities led to a concept under
which Brazil would furnish an Expeditionary Force composed
of three infantry divisions organized along U.S. lines. At one
point before the Portuguese gave permission to use the bases in

the Azores, the Allies contemplated using Portuguese-speaking-Brazilian troops to seize the islands for use against the German submarines. Fortunately, the Portuguese agreed to permit the Allies to use the Azores as a base. Nevertheless, at the time I was in Brazil, it was still expected that the Brazilians would send three divisions to Italy. In fact, they sent one division with replacements, not because of their reluctance to send the three divisions but because we became committed to the cross-Channel landings on the coast of France and this would tie up most of our shipping. When this occurred, Italy and the Mediterranean would become a secondary theater.

As I made the long journey back to the United States, I was greatly intrigued by this tremendous country, but I was still yearning to get back to the war. I knew that my special language qualifications would probably keep me in intelligence and out of a foxhole, and I knew that the most exciting jobs with the greatest promise of advancement were in the Combat theater. I also had a sense of guilt about being absent from the war while many thousands of young men of my age were engaged in deadly combat with the enemies of our country. I was constantly scheming to escape from Camp Ritchie. Colonel Banfill, however, was reluctant to let me go until more people returned from the war with newer and more dramatic adventures to tell than mine. As these veterans began to trickle in, I went to Fort Leavenworth with a small detachment of Portuguese-speaking enlisted men to organize a course for Brazilian officers. Here I met many of the officers who were to become my close friends in Italy in the Brazilian Expeditionary Force. Later on in postwar Brazil a large number of them rose to very significant positions.

At Fort Leavenworth I met and became friends with Lieutenant Colonel Humberto Castelo Branco, the prospective operations officer of the Brazilian division in Italy and years later the President of Brazil. Even though I went through the Command and General Staff Course twice, once in English and once in Portuguese, I never received a diploma qualifying me as having attended. Curiously, the main tactical problem of this

class of Brazilians involved an Allied landing on the coast of
Normandy with three British divisions on the left flank, two
U.S. divisions on the right flank, two U.S. airborne divisions
to be dropped behind the U.S. beaches and one British airborne
division to be dropped across the bridges over the Orne River.
Eighteen months later an almost identical plan was the basis
for Operation "Overlord." We had photographs and maps; we
had all sorts of detailed information on this area of Normandy.
There was also another problem for the class of a similar-type
landing in the Calais area. This landing, of course, never took
place, but the Germans were convinced that it would and this
belief tied down a large number of German troops in the Calais
area during the initial phases of the Normandy landing.

While I was still at Leavenworth, I suddenly received orders
to go to Rio de Janeiro to escort the prospective commander of
the Brazilian Expeditionary Force, on a reconnaissance tour of
the Mediterranean. I flew to Rio de Janeiro in a Douglas C-47.
The trip took three days and was long and rough, especially
flying through the stationary tropical front that normally lies
over the Amazon. I arrived in Rio, met Major General Mascarenhas de Moraes, Colonel Humberto Castelo Branco and a
number of other officers and we left Rio de Janeiro on the seventh of December in a B-24 to fly to Natal. I sat down then and
wrote my reflections. Again, these may seem juvenile and trite to
some, but this is what I wrote on December 7, 1943:

It is two years ago to the day that the Japanese attacked
Pearl Harbor, and here I am on my way to Africa and Italy.
It is thirteen months to the day from the day I first landed
in Africa. At 11:04 P.M. we boarded our B-24 Liberator that
was to carry us across the ocean, and after an explanation as
to how to use our life belts and being told that we were to
wear them until we landed, we took off from the great base.
The heavily loaded plane rose slowly into the air. We
circled the field, the great engines snarling as they tore the
plane loose from the earth. We flew out to sea, climbing
sharply as we did so. In a few moments the lights of Natal
faded into the darkness as the great plane roared out over

the dark Atlantic toward Dakar and the distant African
shore nineteen hundred miles away. All through the hours
of darkness the plane roared on northeastward toward the
African shore. I slept quite a bit, as my chair was not too
uncomfortable even though it was all the way up in the
front of the plane. Looking out of the window I could see
the dull red glare of the exhaust manifold with the little red
flames licking at the tip of the exhaust. Alternately I slept
and watched through the windows the hungry yawning
ocean below. Around two o'clock we flew through a front
of rough weather; then it calmed down again and the stars
shone reassuringly. The tireless throb of the great engines
beat through the night hour after hour grinding away mile
after mile devouring the ocean gaps between the continents. Far ahead a glow began to light the sky, and the
angry red of the exhaust began to fade before the approaching dawn. Daylight broke on the plane ten thousand feet
above the water below. Down there the somber intensity of
the ocean was still wrapped in darkness, and as the sun rose
higher, the ocean too lost its gloom and slowly became very
blue. I became restless as the long hours dragged by and
went and sat in the tail gunner's position in the plane and
gazed out through the big window at the emptiness behind,
broken only by the lazy swaying to and fro of the plane's
aerial riding out behind it with a weight on the end. Then
I felt hungry and ate breakfast, which had been put on the
plane the night before, a cheese sandwich, a peanut butter
sandwich, coffee and a banana. Still restless from the
cramped quarters for so long, I took some pictures of the
cloud formations from the tail gunner's turret.

As I write this we are still five hundred miles out of
Dakar. The weather is clear with some broken clouds here
and there drifting by below, now the open sea, only little
whitecaps on the surface. I've looked for hours for submarines but have seen nothing. The sky is quite clear and
somewhere far ahead still below the horizon lies the bulge
of Africa, only hours away in time but many hundreds of
miles in distance. The air is very steady. The unfaltering
beat of the engines thunders on. As I stepped onto the
plane last night at Natal, my principal worry was not the

distance nor the ocean but the takeoff of the plane heavily
loaded with gasoline for the ocean flight. Once she was
off—and it was a beautiful takeoff—I sat back reassured
and settled down to sleep. The thought of the vast distance
bothered me not at all. After leaving the Brazilian coast, I
saw only the running lights of the plane, not another light
in all the many hundreds of miles flown during the hours of
darkness, and in the hours since daybreak nothing but sea
and sky.

Now it is eight fifty-five in the morning. The sun is shin-
ing brightly and cheerily on the plane. We are in Green-
wich time now. It is wonderful how cheery and friendly the
sun seems after a night on a plane. I went up to the pilot's
cockpit and stood behind him and the co-pilot's chair.
Ahead lay a heavy haze and I waited straining my eyes, and
then like a mysterious shadow in the mist I saw the African
shore come up over the horizon. First it was just a shadow.
Then it was real and vivid and welcome. Swiftly the plane
drew inshore and the white gleam of the houses of Dakar
and the Île Gorée were the first things that I recognized.
The plane lost altitude rapidly and in a few moments thundered in across the shoreline, dropping swiftly over the village of Rufisque down onto the metal runway. The wheels
touched. Then the nosewheel dropped. The plane rolled
swiftly across the field, and I settled back in my chair with
a feeling of gratitude to those four great engines and to the
great plane that in eleven hours had carried us across the
Atlantic and dwarfed the reality of the tremendous distance. Somehow those engines reminded me of the human
heart, beating on unceasingly, sustaining the organism into
which it is built. We are in Africa, less than forty hours'
flying time out of Miami.

We went to our quarters at the airfield where we were to stay
and went into Dakar to see the various sights. Had the "Torch"
landings taken place at Dakar the French were ready. The whole
place was a mass of pillboxes, gun emplacements, barbed-wire
entanglements and the like. We spent the night there. Two
of the Brazilian officers had not gone downtown, so I took

them back again, and we saw the various sights. We also saw the
red-light district along the Rue des Essarts, with the Alhambra,
Aux Parisiens and other local dens of iniquity. I felt an idle curiosity as to what it must be like to go to a place like that, but I
did not satisfy it. We had dinner and went to the Officers' Club.
Some musicians came over and played for us. These included a
New Zealander, who played the violin wonderfully. They were
joined by some entertainers from camp shows who were passing
through Dakar.

The next morning, on the ninth of December at six-thirty we
went out to the field and boarded our plane, the faithful *Gremlin's Castle*, and in a moment we were roaring down the runway
and aloft. We flew north along the coast in brilliantly sunny
weather, passed over St. Louis of Senegal, then swung inland
away from the coast in order to pass behind the Spanish colony
of Río de Oro, leaving behind the green vegetation and passing
out over the rocks and sand of the Sahara. We flew across this
for several hours and then even the rocks vanished and the desert as I have always imagined it appeared below—an endless,
limitless ocean of sand. Only the ripples of the wind in the sand
below broke the vastness. Then, suddenly, out of the desert
sprang a little town with a fort out of *Beau Geste*. We landed
and refueled at the Tindouf airfield. A cold north wind was
blowing down out of the Atlas Mountains carrying clouds of
sand with it. We took off again and flew northwestward. The
weather over the mountains was bad so we flew to Casablanca
instead of to Marrakech. We passed out to sea between Ifni and
Agadir, past Agadir and Mogador, and then in the failing light I
saw Safi, where I had first set foot on the African continent on
the dark morning of November 8, 1942. The sight of it brought
back thoughts of the year before. Bomb craters were visible as
we flew over the Sidi Embarak crossroads. Then we flew north
racing against daylight and passed over Mazagan and the bridge
at Azemmour, which again brought back vivid memories to me.

Almost as soon as we passed Mazagan we could see the white
buildings of Casablanca. The pilot was warned to land with
great care as the field was wet and muddy. In fact, the field was

under water and it looked exactly like a lake. The plane circled
for about fifteen minutes in the fading daylight. The pilot
aborted his first approach, gunning his engine and raising his
landing gear. He circled and came around again. On the second
approach as the wheels touched a torrent of mud struck the window, blinding the view. I settled back in my seat, wiping off the
perspiration, and got ready to get out. We were met by a guard
of honor and Colonel John P. Ratay, the base commander, with
his mustache bristling. We got our baggage off and drove to the
Villa Mast and then I took the Brazilians in to see the town.
We returned to the villa late and very tired.

The next day we flew to Algiers, where for the first time, I
met General Eisenhower. I took the Brazilians to see him. I was
greatly impressed by the man's confidence and by the sense of
power and competence that radiated from him. They also called
on General Giraud, who was then the head of the French government. The interview was somewhat disconcerting to translate
because he always referred to himself in the third person. After
discussions in Algiers concerning the employment of the Brazilian Expeditionary Force, we flew to Naples, Italy, to see General Clark at Fifth Army headquarters.

On arriving in Naples we were appropriately met and taken to
the Parco Hotel, which was a billet for senior Allied officers. It
offered an excellent view over the Naples harbor. The main
Naples hotels right along the waterfront were blown up or destroyed by the Germans before their withdrawal from the city.
Shortly after our arrival we visited the port of Naples installations and the supply base there. It was through this base that
the Brazilian Expeditionary Force would arrive and would be
supplied while fighting in the Fifth Army.

We called upon General Clark at his command post in the
garden behind the palace at Caserta, a former Italian royal palace. Lengthy discussions ensued about the employment of the
1st Brazilian Division. It was now clear that this would probably
be the only Brazilian division that would be employed in Italy
because all available shipping was going to be diverted to support the landings in western Europe. General Clark and General

Mascarenhas, as well as General Euclydes Zenobio, the second-in-command of the Expeditionary Force, hit it off very well, and Clark seemed enthusiastic at the idea of having this division. I believe the decision was made to put the Brazilian division in the Fifth Army because General Clark already had an army composed of contingents from several nations. He introduced the Brazilians to a number of people of diverse nationalities and seemed somewhat intrigued by my ability to speak several European languages. Although he did not say anything to me at the time, I believe he made the decision then to have me assigned as his aide.

The British Eighth Army, which was the other Allied army fighting in Italy, also had forces composed of many nationalities, and, in this sense, the Italian front was an international front into which the addition of a division speaking another language would not create awkward problems. On the contrary, the Brazilian division would reinforce the Italian front at a time when it did not appear this front was likely to get much in the way of reinforcement in either American or British troops since these were being held for the invasion of western Europe.

We toured the front and witnessed an attack preceded by a very heavy artillery barrage. I recall Mascarenhas shaking his head and saying to me, "My, this is a rich man's war." We familiarized ourselves with the various staff chiefs of the Fifth Army and did a little sight-seeing. One of the trips was to take us down to Pompeii, where the Brazilians visited the ruins of that city which was destroyed by a volcanic eruption in A.D. 79. Needless to say we were given the standard tour of the house of the Vetii, with its pornographic murals, and were also taken to a building which had obviously been a brothel. In it were a series of cubicles; on the exterior of each was portrayed rather graphically the sensual specialty offered within. The chief American officer with us, the chairman of the Brazilian-American Defense Board, General James G. Ord, examined these closely through his glasses, shook his head and said, "I'm in my fifties and I never knew there were such things." The Brazilians found them very amusing.

Upon completion of the visit to Italy, we returned to Algiers, and another visit with General Eisenhower. We spent Christmas Day 1943 in Marrakech. I remember going to midnight mass in a small building on the edge of the airfield with the Brazilians. We were all a long way from home and far from the end of the war. The thought occurred to me that all of the years of my youth might be spent in this long war. Next day we flew south, repeating the journey we had made northward, only this time instead of stopping at Tindouf, we stopped at another, similar little Foreign Legion fort called Atar and then flew on to Dakar.

On December 27, 1943, just before two o'clock we drove from our quarters at the airfield to the plane and boarded it. I left my coat and briefcase in the rear left seat, which is where I liked to sit; however, I hardly ever succeeded in getting such a seat. We were then sprayed with insecticide before we taxied down the runway. The great Liberator swept down the runway, the acceleration pushing us back in our seats. I saw the shock absorbers on the landing gear relax and in a moment I felt the gentle swaying motion that told us we were airborne. We flew past the torpedo nets of Dakar in the harbor and then with resolution the great plane turned her nose out to sea, climbing as she flew out into the setting sun. The African shore faded from view within a few moments as we flew through the failing hours of daylight toward the distant Brazilian shore nineteen hundred miles beyond the setting sun. Darkness fell after a long race with the sun which we eventually lost. Most of the Brazilians slept. I slept myself from time to time wrapped in a blanket. I was used to the Mae West life jacket. A little before eleven o'clock at night I saw a flash of light ahead that told me that there lay the Brazilian shore. The searchlight played on us for a moment. It was an uncomfortable feeling coupled with comfort at being over land again. The lights of the airport shone brilliantly in the clear night. We flew down to the end of the runway and landed. I settled back in my seat and a feeling of weary satisfaction swept over me. I had not been exactly afraid, but two thousand miles of water is two thousand miles of water. The Brazilians looked happily at one another and patiently endured the spraying with insecticide until we were allowed out of the plane again and set foot on the American continent. Wearily I got the baggage together, went up to our quarters and fell into bed. It had been a long day.

In Rio the new American Military Attaché, General Hayes Kroner, formerly Chief of Military Intelligence, who was aware of my activities in Safi and in North Africa, had directed that I remain with him rather than return to Camp Ritchie. Since he was a brigadier general and the commandant at Ritchie was a colonel, I stayed. At first I was delighted with the idea of staying in Rio and improving my Portuguese, but as I thought about it, I realized that this job might last the whole war and keep me away from any action. I was young at the time and anxious to return to the war. What I wanted most at that time, I think, was to serve, to get medals, to travel and to be promoted. And it seemed to me that all of these things would be hard to do in Rio. Nevertheless, I was to remain in Rio for four months as aide to General Kroner. General Kroner had low blood pressure, and one of his favorite pastimes was climbing mountains. On one occasion I climbed Sugarloaf with him at the entrance to Rio harbor—a task less difficult than it looks. A footpath leads practically to the top. However, when we reached the top, we ran into a problem. Since all tickets for the cable car were sold at the bottom of the lift for a round trip, we had none. The conductor was reluctant to let us aboard the cable car. After much haggling he relented and we rode down.

In March of 1944 I flew up to Natal to act as aide and interpreter for Mrs. Franklin Delano Roosevelt, who was visiting the great base there. She was a most welcome visitor. Most of the men there, while realizing they were in a fairly safe and comfortable place, nevertheless felt like spectators watching those going to the war and those coming from the war, and it was difficult for them to realize the huge contribution they were making. For in large part the fronts in the China-Burma area, in North Africa and in Italy were supported by this great air bridge from Natal to Dakar. Mrs. Roosevelt went everywhere, talked to everyone, and when she walked into the enlisted men's dayroom, cries of "Hi, Eleanor" greeted her. "Hi, boys," she replied. She was an instant hit. In a short speech she said that the only reason she was allowed to travel was to take messages for the President to places he could not go himself. She told them the President was proud of them and appreciated what they had done. She spoke to them warmly. The boys loved it and many of them were visibly moved. They sang, "For She's a Jolly Good Fellow" and "Pistol Packin' Mama." Mrs. Roosevelt beamed. I must say I harbored some prejudice against her but she quickly won me over. An altogether charming and delightful lady. She impressed me when she told President Vargas' daughter, "I hope when you come to the United States you will visit us. We may not be in the White House but you will always be a welcome guest in our home." I noticed also that before she stepped aboard the plane, she shook hands with every single person standing there regardless of rank. Her visit was certainly a great morale booster for the soldiers. They loved the idea of that old lady flying thousands of miles just to see them.

During this period I was active in working on the preparation of the Brazilian troops at the Vila Militar, a large camp near Rio, where one of the infantry regiments was going to the Expeditionary Force. In addition to this, I was fortunate enough to get a trip to Montevideo, Uruguay, in a military aircraft. As we were there three days, I took the boat across to Buenos Aires. It was a large, impressive and tremendous city, but most impressive to me was the fact that all the lights were on and that food was abundant. Even in Rio, Copacabana Beach was darkened, not to protect the coast, but to avoid silhouetting the ships entering and leaving the harbor for German submarines which might be lying outside. I flew back from this trip to Rio de Janeiro, and shortly thereafter rumors began to reach me that General Clark was endeavoring to have me assigned as his aide in Italy. After a few weeks it was clear that he would be successful.

On April 3, 1944, I jotted a note down called "Return to the Wars":

And now the time has come when for the third time I must return to the war area. I have received notice that I am to go to General Mark Clark, after all, to serve as his aide. I am glad it has gone through. Naturally, there are many reasons why I should not be glad. First, the discomfort and danger of life over there as compared with the pleasant safe life that I am leading here. Secondly, it will probably mean no promotion, whereas if I stayed here, I would get it. But in compensation my conscience is clear. I know that my duty is in Italy, and I hope I shall have the privilege of being present at the fall of Rome. With any luck, at the side of General Clark I should see many historic events. I like medals. There is more chance of getting them there than here. I hope I am able to finagle myself a nice trip on the way over. I am a terrible tourist and I would love to see the Pyramids and other wonders of Egypt as well as Ascension Island and will do my best to arrange my trip to go that way. I do want to go to Italy and carry my share of hardships and danger. I would be ashamed to have to say that I had spent the whole war in Rio de Janeiro. Yet I do not think that the time I have spent here has been entirely wasted. I think that in some measure I have helped the United States here in Brazil. If I have, I am satisfied. If Mother ever knew that I had connived to get out of Rio de Janeiro and go to Italy, she would be furious, but the voice of my conscience is very loud.

Those were my thoughts on April 3 as I received the information that I was to go to Italy. Shortly thereafter, on April 12, 1944, I boarded a C-54 and flew out over the Atlantic. Once again, the lights of Natal faded behind us and I curled up as best I could in the aircraft, a military cargo plane with bucketseats. Aloft I watched the sunrise from the plane and as always it was magnificent. I strained my eyes looking ahead for that tiny volcanic speck in the immensity of the ocean that is Ascension Island. Finally, beneath a cloud I saw the shores of the island, bleak and barren as nothing I have ever seen. We came down very swiftly and were landing on the runway almost before I realized it. I got out of the plane and saw Lieutenant Milner,

whom I knew as Priorities and Traffic Officer in Rio. He also
had that curious affection for the island that so many of its garrison had. I looked at the runway and was duly awed. The runway
was cut like the slash of a giant's knife in the flank of the volcano. It was one of the great achievements of the war. The
bleakness of the island was almost frightening. It had an arctic
desolate quality.

We had a breakfast that was not too good, got back aboard
the plane, taxied down the runway, and once again, the plane
was airborne. It was a strange feeling to see the plane already airborne and yet to see the mountains towering above the wings of
the plane on both sides. The runway was cut deep into the flank
of the mountain. We circled off the end of the island and, looking at it, I wondered again at the instruments that permitted the
crew to find such a speck in the vastness of the night over the
ocean. We gathered speed and altitude and headed for the African coast. All through the long morning hours and early afternoon we roared across the blue sky with the blue sea below. Toward midafternoon with startling suddenness the African coast
sprang above the horizon. We flew along the shore for a while,
until we were over Accra. I was astonished at the vastness of the
airfield and installation there. We circled the field and our steel
bird swooped to a faultless landing three thousand miles from
Natal. I got out and cast a grateful look at the great plane that
so steadily and so faithfully had carried me once more across the
Atlantic vastness. Then the formalities of my arrival—to my displeasure I was given a typhus shot and billeted and so to bed.

The next morning I was awakened at four and told I was leaving at six. I fought my way out of the mosquito net and the
greasy smear of the insect repellent, got dressed and had breakfast and boarded the plane. We flew to Monrovia in Liberia and
then on to Dakar. At Dakar there was a brief interval of a day
during which I went for a wonderful swim and also for a canoe
ride in a native canoe with some Olof natives. At dawn the next
day I left for the remainder of my journey. I flew in a South African C-47 with Humphrey Bogart and his wife. We sat on the
floor of the airplane and played cards. It was a real thrill seeing

someone whom I admired and had seen in the movies and having this close personal relationship under such circumstances. I could not help but marvel that he would take time out to go to Italy and visit the troops, and I felt warmly toward him for it. I flew on to Italy, there to begin my next mission, my mission with General Clark.

5. WITH GENERAL CLARK

While all of Europe except Sweden and Switzerland was still held by the Germans, 1943 had brought some improvement in the situation of the Allies. Naval and air victories in the Pacific had checked, if not rolled back, the Japanese advance there. The Germans had been surrounded at Stalingrad and their Sixth Army had been forced to surrender, but the Germans still occupied vast areas of Russia. The German Navy's submarines still prowled the seas sinking enormous numbers of Allied shipping. Portugal had granted us bases in the Azores to use against the enemy submarines. The Allied armies had swept the Germans completely out of North Africa and had crossed the Mediterranean into the Italian boot. Italy had abandoned the German alliance. Fighting was tough and the advance slow for the Allied forces as they moved up the Italian peninsula through rugged mountainous terrain against grim German resistance. Only in Italy were U.S. forces in actual contact with the German Army. These forces were a part of the Mediterranean Theater of Operations Headquarters. The over-all commander was a British officer, General Henry Maitland Wilson. Under him on the western side of the Italian peninsula was the U. S. Fifth Army commanded by Lieutenant General Mark W. Clark, comprising U.S., French, South African and Italian forces (the latter since Italy after her surrender joined the Allies as a "co-belligerent").

This was the first U.S. army ever to be organized outside the United States. It was activated in Morocco and its shoulder patch bore an outline of a mosque to tell of its Moroccan birthplace. On the eastern part of the front was the famous British Eighth Army, commanded first by General Sir Bernard Montgomery and later by General Sir Oliver Leese. The Eighth Army too was made up of many nationalities. British, Canadians, Poles, Greeks, Indians and a Jewish Brigade. The Allied armies in Italy were a reflection of the multi-national character of the enemies of Hitler's Germany.

In December 1943 I had visited General Mark Clark's headquarters with the advance party for the Brazilian Expeditionary Force, which was later to serve under his command in the Fifth Army. At that time he had noted my command of several languages and had asked that I be assigned to Fifth Army headquarters as his aide-de-camp. It took quite some time for this request to move through the vast bureaucracy of the U. S. Army at war, but eventually the transfer was approved.

General Clark was then the only senior U.S. general commanding forces in combat against the German Army in Europe. The great landings in Normandy were still many months in the future. Clark was a commanding figure. He was six feet three inches tall, slender with a hawklike nose and was an impressive figure of a soldier. He was a first-class professional, who had fought and been wounded in World War I. He always demanded and often obtained the best from those serving under his command. Working for him was to bring a new dimension into my career.

I learned many things while working for General Mark Clark. I had been quite naïve about dealing with high ranking people up until that time, but by virtue of being his aide, I was inevitably thrown into contact with people of all sorts. I remember one rather amusing incident which occurred when we received word that Soviet Ambassador Bogomolov was coming up to Fifth Army headquarters to confer some Soviet decorations on Fifth Army personnel. Naturally, a proper ceremony had to be laid on with national anthems and all the other flourishes and accompaniments. I had some misgivings about the ability of the Fifth Army band to play the recently changed Soviet national anthem. In an effort to ease whatever concern their Anglo-American allies might have, the Soviets had abolished the "Internationale," and had adopted a new, more purely patriotic and Russian national anthem.

I asked the Fifth Army band leader if he knew the Soviet national anthem, and he said that he knew only the "Internationale." General Clark would be highly displeased if the wrong anthem were played or if no anthem were played, so in desperation I finally called up the Soviet Military Mission in Naples. This took considerable perseverance on the telephone of those days. Then I had to find someone who could speak English. I asked him if they had the music of the new national anthem. He said they did not, but he used to listen to it on the radio at night and he could hum it. So I put the band leader on the telephone, and the Russian at the other end hummed the new Soviet national anthem to him. The band leader made his notes, and when the time came and Bogomolov arrived, the band played the new Soviet national anthem and everything seemed to go off smoothly.

During the awarding of the decorations there was some difficulty because Soviet decorations do not have pins in them. They involved small plaques that require a rather large hole in the uniform, and most American uniforms did not have this kind of hole. Bogomolov, who was quite resourceful, unbuttoned the upper shirt pocket, put the decoration through the buttonhole and fastened the screw back on.

I had previously mentioned to General Clark some of the difficulties in getting the proper music, and after the ceremony was over, General Clark had a brief reception for the Soviet Ambassador and the newly decorated officers and men during which he asked Bogomolov (who did not speak English but spoke excellent French; I acted as translator) how well the band had played the Soviet national anthem. Bogomolov smiled somewhat awkwardly and said that he did not know—he himself had never actually heard it played. So it seems that all the effort that we put into this had in a sense been in vain because the man who was supposed to be the judge of how well it had been played had in fact no idea what it should sound like.

Of course, as the aide to the commanding general, I had great facility for getting things. When I called any of the staff sections of the Fifth Army on the telephone and said, "This is the commanding general's aide," whatever I wanted was generally forthcoming without argument. Sometimes, however, there were differences. General Clark, shortly after I reported in as his aide, had told me that he wanted me to wear parachute boots and a green silk scarf as he did. After several fruitless efforts to get the boots, I went to the quartermaster of the army, a rather irascible colonel, and told him I needed a pair of size 11-E parachute boots. He crustily informed me that he didn't have enough parachute boots for the airborne troops assigned to the Fifth Army. I explained that I was General Clark's aide and that I had been directed by the general to wear these boots while accompanying him. He looked at me angrily and said, "Well, why does General Clark change his aides so often?" I replied, "Colonel, that is something you will have to ask General Clark; I don't know the answer." I got the boots and later the answer.

General Clark's aide did not have the easiest task in the word. The general was a difficult man to satisfy. Anything less than a 100 per cent performance aroused considerable comment and irony from him. In retrospect, I am sure I became a good deal more attentive to detail and a good deal more thorough during this period than I had ever been before. I had several lessons in this particular area during the time I served as his aide. He would frequently tell me to have something done, and I would tell the responsible party to do it. Some time afterward, he would say, "Well, was so and so done?" I would say, "Well, I told the Army signal officer [for instance] that you wanted it done." Whereupon he would inquire, "And did they do it?" I would say, "Well, I don't know, sir, but I think so." "In other words, you don't know. When I tell you to get something done, you do it. You check to see that it's been done. When you are convinced that it's been done, recheck that it's been done, and then report to me that it has been done." I was not to forget this lesson. It frequently led to a great deal of work and at times some expense to the taxpayers.

On one occasion, he received a letter from a little boy in Montclair, New Jersey, in which the boy asked General Clark for an autographed photograph and also asked him to transmit a letter he had enclosed to Marshal Tito in Yugoslavia. Frankly, at this time Tito either didn't exist, was a legendary figure, or else was really somebody else called Mihailovich as far as I was concerned. However, the general handed me the letter and said, "Get this to Marshal Tito." This staggered me. I had no idea of how to get it to Marshal Tito, and I looked at him and said, "How, sir?" He said, "That's your problem, not mine; get it to him." So I started inquiring around to see how I could get this letter to Marshal Tito. Eventually I found that the Fifteenth Air Force occasionally ran a supply plane across to Yugoslavia. I went down to see the beautiful WAC captain aide of the commanding general, Constance Flanagan. I always wondered how any girl that pretty could be as efficient as she was. I asked her and she said they had a supply flight once a month, and she would see that the letter was included in the parachute drop to the Yugoslavia partisans on the next plane that went over. I thanked her and came back to the Fifth Army. Two or three months passed and I was visiting one of the divisions with General Clark, had just put him in his light aircraft and was going back to my own to get in when he rapped on the Plexiglas window of his plane. I went back and he said to me, "What about that letter to Marshal Tito?" Well, by this time I had received several hundreds, if not a thousand letters, and I didn't have a very clear memory of it, and I asked him, "What letter to Marshal Tito?" He told me the little boy's name, said that he lived in Montclair and gave me the approximate date. This rang a bell in my mind, and I told him regretfully that I would have to check when I got back to Army headquarters to see what had been done. When I got back, I checked through my files and found that on May 18 I had given this letter to the Fifteenth Air Force for air drop to Marshal Tito, so I quickly returned and told General Clark what I had done. He looked at me ironically and asked, "Well did they deliver it?" I was quite taken aback by this and I said, "Well, I believe so, sir." To this he said, "In other words, you don't know. Find out!" I left his van. He was going off on a two-day trip with one of the other aides. I went down to the flight strip. I got a light aircraft and went to the nearest major airfield in Grosseto. By this time the Fifteenth Air Force had gone into the South of France and was up near Vittel taking part in the campaign there. I told the squadron commander at Grosseto that I had to get to Vittel, the Fifteenth Air Force headquarters, and he quite cheerfully offered to fly me there in a B-25. I left that morning, flew up to Vittel, found the Fifteenth Air Force and Captain Flanagan. She was amazed at my inquiry, but after some checking, she told me that the letter, along with other supplies, had been parachuted to the Yugoslavian partisans at Kragujevac, Yugoslavia, on May 29. Pleased with this, I flew back to Grosseto, flew to the Fifth Army headquarters, and, as I went in to report to the general, I suddenly thought with alarm that he might then require me to proceed to Yugoslavia to find out whether Marshal Tito had actually gotten the letter or not. However, when I told him that it had actually been dropped by the Fifteenth Air Force, this seemed to satisfy him, and I was not ordered to pursue the matter further. It was to be seven years before I met Marshal Tito.

General Clark was very assiduous in his efforts to make me improve my sloppy habits, my forgetfulness, my carelessness and, in general, my efficiency. Sometimes this had a rather wearying and discouraging effect. I had never been as modest as I should be, but during this period of my life, I often lay in my sleeping bag at night reading by flashlight my letters of commendation and citations solely to reassure myself that I was not a complete damn fool and that some people in the world thought I did a fairly good job.

During one particularly frustrating period, I decided to resign as General Clark's aide. I had always heard that this was the one job you could get out of in the Army by asking. It took me some time to work up enough courage to go in to General Clark to tell him that I felt he ought to get another aide. Finally, I did screw up enough gall to do it. I went into his van and said, "General, it's quite obvious to me that I cannot give you the type of service you want [I did not say that I could not do the job because I honestly thought I could and did do it well], and so I think in all fairness to you and to me, it would be better if you got an aide who could." There was a long silence as he looked me up and down from head to toe, and finally, speaking sharply out of the corner of his mouth, he said, "Walters, let's get one thing straight—you don't quit when you feel like it—I fire you when I am ready, and I am *not* ready." Feeling about three inches high, I backed out of his presence. It wasn't until the following day that I realized he had said something relatively pleasant to me. If I really had not been performing to his satisfaction, he would have gotten rid of me long before this. It was a demanding job. I had no leave, no time to myself. I was with General Clark all day long, but fortunately, he used to go to bed quite early.

One problem was that I had to know at all times where every division and corps headquarters was. And this was not "know" in the sense of know on the map; this was "know" in the sense of being able to describe to General Clark what the road was like, where you turned off, how you got into the headquarters. After all, I had inherited the job as his aide because my predecessor had gotten lost while driving into Rome on the day of its liberation while trying to find the Hotel Excelsior. His confusion had cost him his job. We entered Rome on June 5, 1944, and on that day I became the senior aide. The general took over a very handsome suite on the second floor of the Hotel Excelsior and adjacent to this suite was a very nice room for me as senior aide. This was the first time I had slept in a bed in a building in a very long time. On my little night table there was a radio. I recall that during the night I woke up and heard some bombs dropping beyond the northern edge of Rome. Obviously, our columns were moving to the north and one or two German aircraft were dropping some bombs on them. I switched on the radio idly and I heard a German station playing bugle calls, the

sort of trumpeting that normally heralded a special announcement or special bulletin by the German Armed Forces
Command. And so I listened with some interest. We were close
to the time when I felt that the landings on the west coast of
France would occur. In fact, there was a pool on it and I had,
without any knowledge, taken June 10. Suddenly, the trumpeting stopped and the German announcer, in a very serious voice,
said, "In the last half hour very heavy Allied airborne landings
have begun on the Cotentin Peninsula. The invasion fleet is
approaching the Channel coast and the batteries of the Atlantic
Wall have opened fire." That was all. I was greatly excited by
this news and I wondered whether I should wake the general
and tell him what I had heard. I saw nearly everything that he
saw, but he did get some papers to which I did not have access,
and I thought he probably actually knew the date already. So I
decided to wait until the next morning, and at six o'clock I went
into his room and woke him and said, "General, last night the
landings began on the coast of France." He looked at me for an
instant and then he said, "The sons of bitches! They didn't even
let us have the newspaper headlines for the fall of Rome for one
day." The liberation of Rome, which otherwise would have been
sensational headline news, was relegated, by the immensity of
the Channel landings, to an inside page in the newspapers.
These too are the vicissitudes of war.

General Clark lived and worked in a van. I had the responsibility for moving this van when the Army headquarters moved.
The van was built by an ordnance company and properly fitted
out with sleeping accommodations, a desk and all the equipment and conforts an Army commander would require. A continuing source of trouble was an Italian gas icebox which invariably broke down each time the command post changed
location. Generally the general had a ham or turkey or something else that would spoil. Another difficulty with the van was
the flushing toilet and that required a very large cesspool. Usually, this cesspool was dug by a Signal Corps post-hole digger
and normally this was quite adequate, but if we stayed for a very
long time at any one location, the cesspool filled up and some-

times overflowed, a source of great irritation for the general and
great trouble for the aide—me!

During this period, General Charles de Gaulle came to Italy.
I had last seen him in London in 1942, where I had spoken only
French with him. I had been told that he was coming to visit
General Clark and that I should be present to translate for
them. This seemed strange to me, as General de Gaulle had
been in London for four years and I felt sure that he must speak
good English. When I expressed doubt that my services would
be needed, I was shown a copy of a popular American magazine
that carried a long article on General de Gaulle and mentioned
specifically that despite his long residence in London, he did
not speak English. Being young and inexperienced, I believed
everything I read in the papers. He duly arrived. I met him with
General Clark and we went to the general's van for their discussions. He briefly recalled our London meeting a year and a half
before. Our Army headquarters was located at a little village
north of Rome by the name of Roccastrada.

The main subject under discussion was the withdrawal of the
French corps of four divisions that was serving under General
Clark for the impending landings in southern France. I translated into English what General de Gaulle said and into
French what General Clark said. Sometimes when General
Clark would say "no" in answer to a question, General de
Gaulle would ask me what he had said. This and other indications soon confirmed my belief that General de Gaulle neither
spoke nor understood English. Emboldened by this, I began to
add a few comments to what he was saying when I translated it
into English. For instance, I would say, "General de Gaulle says
that he can't do this, but I think if you press him a little he may
agree," or else, "He says that he agrees but I don't think he is
very enthusiastic about it." When the talks concluded and General de Gaulle rose to leave, he turned to General Clark and said
in good but accented English, "General Clark, we have a useful
and interesting talk. It is my devout hope, and I am sure it will
be realized in the near future, that the next time we meet, it will
be on the liberated soil of France." Immediately I realized that

he had evidently understood all of my asides. My confusion was at its peak. I flattened myself against the wall of the van to let him pass. He turned to me with a touch of a smile, tapped me on the shoulder and said in English, "Walters, you did a very good job." Eight years later, he was to recall this incident to me in Paris. It served as a lesson to me never to meddle with what I was translating, and I was guilty of this on only one other occasion later in the war with the Brazilians.

General de Gaulle, despite the fact that he had little actual power, in a military sense, at his command, was an impressive figure—taller than General Clark. Few people were. He carried himself with an immense sense of dignity and assurance. He radiated confidence in himself and his cause. It was my good fortune that at odd times for the next twenty-five years, our paths crossed—in France, in the United States, in Brazil and again in France. While many disagreed with him, it is hard to deny his greatness and steadfast courage.

Once we were just south of Leghorn and General Clark went forward to the front, located about two or three miles north of the Cecina River. We drove forward in the general's jeep, the general sitting in the front seat as usual and I sitting in the back with his helmet. I always had to have the helmet with me but he very rarely wore it. When we reached the north bank of the river, the regimental commander there came up to advise the general against going any farther forward. He said that if we went any closer to the little town of Vada, presently under attack, we would come under enemy observation and probably be fired upon. The general said that he wished to go forward. He wanted to see more of what was going on. The regimental commander got in the back of the jeep with me and the general motioned to Sergeant Adaysh, our driver, to drive north. We drove about a mile and half north to a V-shaped fork in the road where the commander of the battalion which was attacking Vada greeted us and briefed us quickly on the situation. While he was talking, a burst of machine-gun fire struck the wall above our heads and slightly to the rear. General Clark looked at the regimental commander and then said to the driver in a very slow voice, "I guess we are drawing fire on the troops. Sergeant Adaysh, turn this jeep around and let's go on back." Sergeant Adaysh responded with some alacrity and we went on back to the bridge. Here the regimental commander pointed out to General Clark that his observation post was excellent and it was really not necessary for him to go forward. General Clark looked at him and said, "You obviously don't understand. I did not go forward to see; I went forward to be seen." In this he was quite right. Many times I would see tired, weary soldiers, dirty and disheveled and sometimes sleepless for days, lying on the side of the road, and the effect of seeing the Army commander among them was extraordinary, particularly if he went forward to an exposed position. Every soldier has an innate feeling that he is out front risking his skin while the big brass are back where it is safe. But when he sees the big brass up there with him and knows the big brass doesn't have to be there, it gives his morale a real boost. General Clark was fearless and unmoved by danger.

Another amusing episode occurred around this time. I had just come in to Urbe Airport in Rome with General Clark, and riding back to town, I was sitting in the back of his jeep as usual. As we drove across the airfield, there were a number of young airmen working on an aircraft, and they stood up and watched us go by. There were three stars on the front of the jeep, three stars on the general's cap, three stars on my aide's insignia and three stars on the general's pistol holster. A young soldier stared at him without saluting. Barely had we gone by when the general ordered the driver to stop and back up to this soldier. I reached for a little black book, which I kept in my pocket, to record the names of various transgressors the general encountered during his trips around the Fifth Army. If the transgression was serious, he would generally ask me, when we got back to headquarters, for the transgressor's name. If it was not, by common consent, I would not speak of the matter again. The transgressor, of course, would live for a considerable period of time in great concern waiting for some punitive action to be taken against him, and generally this period of stewing was the punitive action in itself. I could not imagine what this young soldier could say. He had obviously looked at the stars on the front of the jeep, he had looked at the general and had seen the stars on his cap. I didn't know what excuse he could possibly give for not having saluted. General Clark said to him in a very stern voice, "Soldier, didn't they teach you to salute in the Air Corps? Don't you salute a general officer? Don't you even salute a lieutenant general?" The soldier, who appeared to be all of seventeen years old, looked the general right in the eye and said in an obviously sincere voice, "General, I never ever saw a lieutenant general before!" Greatly mollified, General Clark said, "Well, son, see that you remember it in the future," and with that, he turned to the driver and said, "Adaysh, drive on." Whether this was presence of mind on the soldier's part or rather, as I was more inclined to believe, the truth, it was the only answer that would have gotten him out of trouble.

Another episode occurred shortly before the fall of Leghorn. I was riding in a jeep along State Highway No. 1 with General Clark. He turned around to me to ask in a rather querulous voice, "May I ask just what, if any, precautions you have taken for my safety against enemy air attack?" Well, at this stage of the war, neither he nor I had seen a German airplane since Salerno. Nevertheless, there was a standard drill which I had inherited from my predecessor and remembered, so I said to him, "General, the military policeman alongside the driver of the jeep in front is scanning the sky to the front, the military policeman alongside the driver of the jeep in the rear is scanning the sky to the rear, and I am covering as much as I can." The general replied scornfully, "Of all the ridiculous, silly, unmilitary, idiotic systems I have heard, this is the worst. My dog Pal could think up a better system than that." I almost said, "Well, General, why don't you ask him to." He then asked, "How are these air-raid wardens of yours going to advise anybody if they see anything?" I said, "That is easy, sir; there is a siren on all three jeeps, and the first person that sees anything sounds the siren on his jeep." He turned to me again scornfully and using several adjectives he had not used before, said, "That is the silliest, most idiotic, theatrical and unmilitary system I have ever heard. It is perfectly obvious to me that you have never been strafed." This irked me and I said, "General, during the landing in North Africa, I saw a man killed by four machine-gun bullets in the chest from a strafing aircraft. In Tuinsia where there *was* a German Air Force [I couldn't resist this piece of impertinence because I knew that at this time he had been in Oudjda in Morocco, feasting and banqueting with the French and organizing the Fifth Army], I was strafed five times in one day on the road from Tebessa to Medjez-el-Bab." Actually I had only been strafed three times, but I was sure there was no way he could check, and I felt quite safe and pleased that I had won the discussion. He turned to me with a triumphant smile on his face. "Is that so? Then it is perfectly obvious to me that you have learned nothing from it." This was about the last time I attempted to argue with the general. Thereafter, when he would berate me for something, I would simply say, "Yes, sir." To this he would say, "That is all you can say, but you never pay the slightest attention to what I am telling you to do."

Life with General Clark was not easy, but I realized how lucky I was to be living in the comfort and safety of an army headquarters, compared to the thousands of men who were out in far more exposed conditions. However, it became increasingly obvious to me that I was not cut out to be General Clark's aide.

Many figures of great importance visited the Fifth Army during this time. General Marshall came and I was fortunate to meet again this great man with whom I had the privilege of serving on a number of occasions after the war. His stepson had been killed at Anzio. I was given the job by General Clark of finding the crew who had been in the tank when his stepson was killed by a sniper. I brought them to General Marshall. Later, I took him to the exact spot where his stepson was killed.

The Army commander had the right to give every decoration except two. The exceptions were the Congressional Medal of Honor, for extraordinary heroism, and the Distinguished Service Medal, which was given to general officers or other senior officers with positions of great responsibility. These had to be approved in Washington. Normally, a recommendation went to

Washington and returned with the medal, the citation and all the other appurtenances. During General Marshall's visit, General Clark gave a lunch for the corps commanders: General Geoffrey Keyes, the II Corps commander; General Willis Crittenberger of the IV Corps; General Lucian K. Truscott, who commanded the VI Corps; and Marshal Alphonse Juin (he was a general at that time), who commanded the French corps. Also invited were several division commanders, particularly the two division commanders of the new draftee divisions, the 85th and 88th, which had been tried in battle for the first time and had performed magnificently. General Paul Kendall commanded the 88th Division and General John Coulter commanded the 85th Division.

Shortly after the luncheon, the general came back into my tent and said to me, "Give me three Distinguished Service Medals." This shook me because I did not have any. I finally found one in a drawer and one in the safe. Then, in desperation, I went to one of the generals in the Fifth Army who had the DSM and asked him to loan me his with the promise that I would replace it. He agreed and I took the three medals to General Clark. General Marshall proceeded to pin them on Generals Coulter, Kendall and Juin. I marveled at the action because I knew these medals could only be awarded by a board in Washington. No recommendations had even been made to the board. Several days later, I saw the recommendations for all three come across my desk on their way to General Clark for approval. I read them through carefully and they were perfectly normal, except for the final paragraph which read, "It is requested that action be expedited on the approval of these medals since they have already been presented by the Chief of Staff." Here again, I learned that many things that theoretically cannot be done can be done by those with great authority. General Marshall certainly had that kind of authority.

A somewhat similar incident occurred when General de Gaulle came, accompanied by the Chief of Staff of the French Army, General Béthouart, and General Juin, to General Clark's headquarters. There was an unusual protocol problem which arose in this connection because General de Gaulle was a two-star general; General Béthouart, the Chief of Staff, was a four-star general; and General Juin, who commanded the corps, was a five-star general. This was an inverse order to their real rank, and when I asked the French liaison officer what we should do, he said we should observe the position they held rather than the number of stars each wore. General de Gaulle brought a plaque of Grand Officer of the Legion of Honor for General Clark, and this decoration was awarded at Fifth Army headquarters. The French, who were not yet in control of France at this time and were actually operating out of Algiers, apparently had great difficulty in finding a Grand Officer's plaque to give General Clark. General Béthouart, whom I had known during the negotiations following the landing in North Africa, had approached me quietly after his arrival and explained that the plaque to be used for the ceremony belonged to a ninety-two-year-old general in Algiers and asked me to use my good offices to get the plaque back for him so they could take it back to Algiers. He said they were having more of these plaques made in Cairo and promised to send one along as soon as they were ready. After the decoration ceremony was over, I discreetly got the plaque back from General Clark and returned it to the French, who took it back to Algiers with them. General Béthouart was as good as his word and a proper plaque arrived later.

I was lucky in that I came to Fifth Army headquarters just before the main attack across the Garigliano River which led to the liberation of Rome. I flew on occasion with the general to the Anzio beachhead. Normally we circled the Circeo mountain, which was held by the Germans, but on one occasion the General ordered the pilot to fly right across the neck of the isthmus, which connected the mountain mass with the Italian mainland, and after we landed, we found one bullet hole in the tail of the aircraft. I recall on one occasion flying to the Anzio beachhead and, as we landed, the airfield came under German artillery fire. After that I did not volunteer to go to Anzio. I waited with the other aides until my turn came along. Anzio, of course, was an extraordinary position where we were holding the

plain and the beachhead around the twin towns of Anzio and
Nettuno against the Germans, who hemmed us in on all sides
and enjoyed extraordinary observation from the Alban Hills and
the mountain of Latium beyond Highway No. 6. They could em-
ploy observed fire on our rear area and generally did. This was
one of the few places during World War II where we sustained
casualties in units as incongruous as the Army laundry and
Army bakery. I believe some sixteen nurses were also killed in
hospitals by enemy artillery fire. The hospitals were as far to the
rear as they could be in the beachhead, but they were still under
enemy artillery fire.

The Fifth Army forward command post was installed in
Anzio in the Borghese Palace and in a tunnel which was dug underneath the palace. The more open parts of the beachhead
were frequently covered during that time by smoke from smoke-
generating machines which afforded some protection from the
ever watchful Germans on the hills around the beachhead.
However, it was always an exhilarating experience to go to the
beachhead. One could not go into this island of Allied strength
behind the German lines without being inspired by the conduct
of the men who defended this position from late January until
the final breakout in late May against every attack the Germans
could bring to bear on it. The situation was tough for the men
who fought there, but they were proud to be there and they
walked straighter and with more of a swagger than most other
men. They had a feeling that they were at an outpost by themselves and that they were fighting better and harder than anyone
else in the Army. This probably wasn't true, but anyway it did
give them a special kind of pride and morale that made it possible for them to withstand the long siege and, when the time
came, to smash out of the beachhead and join up with the main
forces of the Fifth Army thrusting north from the Garigliano toward Rome.

By virtue of my position as aide to the commanding general, I
was aware of the plans for the drive on Rome and, in fact, I
knew the date, hour and place where the attack would begin. It
was at eleven o'clock on the night of May 11 that I stood down

near the Garigliano River bridge with the ruined sphinxes and watched the artillery barrage go off that heralded the Allied attack.

As a young lad, I had read histories of World War I. I had read of these great barrages, but I had never seen one go off. I remember standing waiting in the darkness, looking at my watch and waiting for the minute I knew that this great barrage would be set off. It was curious in a way because thirteen years later I stood on the deck of an aircraft carrier in Eniwetok Lagoon waiting for the detonation of a nuclear weapon and feeling just the same kind of anticipation, feeling my pulse racing as the moment approached that would bring the barrage in one case and the nuclear detonation in another. On this night I waited and suddenly, with a most tremendous roar, the entire front exploded. I stood there and watched the flickering fire run across the horizon, across the mountain tops as far as I could see to the east and down to the water's edge by the mouth of the Garigliano. It was as though hell on earth had broken loose. For an hour the guns fired incessantly and the night sky flickered with the unending lightning of the tons of death that were being hurled on the defending Germans before the hour of the assault came at midnight. At the hour of the assault, the Fifth Army thrust across the Garigliano and headed north for the long-pursued goal of Rome, thrust north beyond the Garigliano, thrust along the mountain ridges in the interior, thrust past long-defended Cassino and up the main valley leading to Rome. Simultaneously with this drive, the forces within the beachhead began to smash their way out of their long encirclement.

Several days later as the forces neared the junction with the Anzio beachhead, I remember General Don Brann, the G-3, Operations Officer of the Army, reported to General Clark that every infantry unit of battalion size in the Fifth Army was committed to battle. Not one infantry unit of battalion size was available as a reserve. The gamble worked and on May 23, I drove up Highway No. 1. I rounded the corner at Terracina and sped into the Pontine Marshes, past the German-held Circeo. I asked Italian peasants whether there were still any Allied troops ahead of me, and when they said there were, I turned off on a small road leading to the west toward the little town of Sabaudia, built by Mussolini. There for the first time I saw men from a unit that was not part of the Fifth Army's main thrust. I stopped and asked who they were and they answered that they were the men of Company B of the 39th Combat Engineers breaking southward out of the beachhead. I then raced back to the Fifth Army and reported to General Clark that physical contact had been established between the troops and the beachhead. This, of course, he knew from other observers, but at least this was someone of his own immediate entourage who reported it to him from his own experience.

I then went back up the highway and drove as far as I could behind the advancing troops, which were well up the road to Cisterna, a town drenched with American blood in the early days of the beachhead when two battalions of rangers were destroyed here by the Germans. Coming back later in the afternoon, I found several of our tanks along the road exchanging fire with the Germans in a little hill town called Sezze, up on the hills overlooking the highway that winds its way through the Pontine Marshes toward Naples. I watched this duel for a while, then drove back to the Army headquarters.

Then the uncontainable surge of the Army moved forward toward the Eternal City, and in the last hours of June 4, I paused by the Rome race track and the Ciampino Airport while the last German resistance was wiped out. During the night the advancing columns of the 85th and 88th divisions began to move into the city. Early in the morning, I drove between the lines of wearily trudging infantrymen into the great square by the Colosseum, up the edge of the Imperial Forums to the square where Mussolini used to harangue the Fascist masses in front of the Tomb of Italy's Unknown Soldier on the steps of the Victor Emmanuel monument. I remember a small German staff car burning in the square. I looked up toward the monument. At this moment, when the Mother City of Western civilization was changing hands, when everything was changing, silent and motionless on either side of the Tomb of the Unknown Soldier stood two carabinieri mounting guard.

I could but think of the picture I had seen as a child of the Roman legionary standing motionless at his post under the falling ashes of Vesuvius because he had not received the orders to move. Everything was changed, but the carabinieri, true to their traditions of duty and discipline, guarded the shrine of their nation while a tremendous convulsion took place around them.

This is one of the lasting impressions I have retained of the day of the fall of Rome. I drove into St. Peter's Square and the square was empty of vehicles. Soon there were many cheering people around us. I drove up to the front of the basilica and I stopped. I didn't want to go armed into the church. I did not want to order my men to stay in the jeep while I went in, so I waited for a little while until another jeep came and I asked them to stay and watch our weapons while we went into this church, which is so fraught with significance to any Catholic. I felt awe as I entered the vast, cool, quiet church. I felt small and insignificant, but grateful to have made it this far. I told God so.

I came out and a very large crowd had gathered and was cheering and putting flowers in the camouflage nets that covered our helmets. One of the soldiers, in a moment of excitement while Italians were waving flags and cheering, grabbed an Italian flag and draped it around his neck as a scarf. A sudden chill fell over the crowd; all of the pent-up enthusiasm fell silent. I grabbed the flag from around his neck, shouted "Viva l'Italia" and gave it back to the crowd, which then began to cheer again. I turned to the soldier and I said, "How would you have felt if you had seen someone do that with an American flag?" He was embarrassed and muttered that he had not realized what he was doing. It was quite obvious that he had not.

By this time we had great difficulty in getting away from the enormous crowd that had gathered in the square, and as we moved back, I met General Clark and General Alfred M. Gruenther riding in a jeep, making their triumphant entry into the city. I fell in ahead of them and led them to the Hotel Excelsior. General Clark then went out onto the balcony on the second floor of the hotel and spoke to a crowd gathered outside and I translated the speech for him into Italian. This was the first time I had ever addressed a large group of people publicly. It was not to be the last. Once, near Leghorn, I was driving along with the general and a large group of Italian partisans was walking along the side of the road. General Clark ordered the driver to drive over to them and he said to me, "Ask these birds if they know who I am." Well, I was taking no chances on their not recognizing him, so I said in Italian, "Do you recognize the commanding general of the Fifth Army?" whereupon they all shouted, "Generale Clark!!" The general beamed and we drove on. Had they not recognized him, the rest of the day might not have been quite so pleasant.

Difficult as these times were, I realized the general was under enormous stress and strain. One night when we had had fairly heavy casualties, he called me up to his van and asked me to have a drink. He knew I didn't drink, but I was so relieved to find him in such a good humor that I took it, and he said, "Sometimes if I appear to be unreasonable, you must remember the burdens I bear are very heavy. The time comes when I have to give orders that will result in the death of a large number of fine young men—and this is a responsibility I cannot share with anybody. I must bear it by myself. So you just see that you remember that when you think I am being unreasonable." I suddenly realized the enormous burden he carried and my many complaints seemed petty indeed.

After the war on one occasion, I took his daughter Anne out to dinner and she asked me, "Were you really Daddy's aide?" I replied that I was. "For how long?" she asked. I replied, "For five months." She then exclaimed, "Oh, you were one of the longest." I said, "No, I *was* the longest." Then she asked, "Was it really very tough being Daddy's aide?" When I asked her why she asked a question like that, she replied, "Well, around the house Daddy always says that the only way to get things done in the headquarters is to grind down the aides." I thought for a moment how to answer, and I said, "Anne, there is one thing you can say for your father; he is a man who lives by his principles."

The Fifth Army was somewhat of a curiosity during this period. An unending stream of visitors came to see General Clark. King George VI came shortly before we reached the Arno, and there were many preparations for his visit. General Clark was particularly anxious that the visit should go well. The Army command post was in a pine forest near Cecina, and there was an adjacent airfield at which the King could land. A careful program was drawn up for the visit and it included a lunch under the trees outside General Clark's van. The other aides and I were discussing how the table should be set up. General Clark normally kept some vitamin tablets on the table and Bob Berenson, the second aide, said that we ought to remove them. I said that we ought to leave them there as that would give them something to talk about. Everyone thought that was a huge joke, but since I was the senior aide, the tablets stayed. The King arrived and, after receiving appropriate honors, was led to General Clark's van for a private talk with the Army commander. He was followed at a respectful distance by a sedate-looking man wearing a bowler hat. As the King started up the steps to the general's van, a very loud explosion was heard. The King paused for an instant without showing any emotion. This was not, however, true of the sedate man in the bowler. Off came the bowler and out came a pistol in the twinkling of an eye. Then, as nothing further happened, he put away the pistol, looking somewhat embarrassed, and the King and the general entered the van for their private discussion. The general asked me to find out what had caused the explosion. On checking I discovered that one of our soldiers had disregarded the "Mines" signs near the beach and had stumbled onto a mine and had been killed. It was a sad note to an otherwise successful visit. The vitamins, by the way, were a prime subject of conversation during the lunch.

Another visitor was Secretary of the Navy James Forrestal, a restless, brooding man. He spent the day with General Clark and had dinner with him. General Clark customarily retired early and at nine o'clock he took Secretary Forrestal to the guest van and bade him good night. Forrestal could not sleep at this early hour and soon wandered down to the aides' tent, where Bob Berenson and I were handling the mail, visit arrangements and other matters, and he began to talk to us about the war in the Pacific, about which we knew so little. Bob and I were fascinated by what he had to say. He spoke of the impact of naval and air power, of the strategic situation in the Pacific and of the fact that the Japanese still had fifty-five divisions in their home islands which had not yet been in combat. Then he asked us for a map of the Pacific, and when we produced it, he showed us the twin drives, one across the mid-Pacific and one up from the south toward the Philippines. He tapped the map at Formosa and said, "This is the whole key to the future in the Pacific. He who controls Formosa can oversee the whole coast of continental Asia. We can never, never let this island be controlled by any power potentially hostile to us. It is from bases here that we must maintain a forward posture in a postwar Asia." Years later I repeated this remark to Chiang Kai-shek's son, Chiang Ching-kuo, and he nodded his approval.

Another impressive visitor was Secretary of War Henry L. Stimson, agile and alert. In Rome I went with the general to call on the Prime Minister of South Africa, the legendary Field Marshal Jan Smuts. His country's 7th South African Armored Division, really a small corps, had distinguished itself greatly during the operations leading to the liberation of Rome. The field marshal wore his insignia on his shoulder tabs, half on the red and half on the khaki. He was at the time more than seventy years old, yet he appeared full of vigor and vitality. In his presence one had the feeling of looking at a man who had been a giant in three wars—the Boer War, World War I and now World War II.

There were lighter and happier days too during this period. On July 14 General Juin called to tell me that he had just approved the award of the Croix de Guerre to me along with a number of other American officers and that he would award them at a ceremony at Siena on July 20. I must quite candidly confess that I have always liked medals and I was delighted with this news. A few weeks before on the Capitoline Hill, in newly liberated Rome, I had received the Italian Bronze Medal for Valor.

Early in the morning on July 20, 1944, those who were to be decorated that day by the French met at the airport adjacent to the forward command post of the Fifth Army at Cecina. The party would go over to Siena in General Clark's aircraft, a C-47. We would land at Melegano Airport and drive from there to Siena's other airport, where the *prise d'armes* or decoration ceremony would take place. In the plane, piloted by Ned Dixon, General Clark's pilot, were many of the section chiefs of the Fifth army and a number of other junior officers, including myself. We took off in fine weather from Cecina and flew uneventfully to Siena. The plane was full, and as the junior officer present, I had no seat and sat on the floor with my back to the radio operator's little cabinet. We arrived over Melegano Airport and circled it. As we circled, I noticed that there were fresh bomb craters on the runway and there was only one runway at the field. At about this time, the ground crew fired a red Very light signaling us not to land. Dixon buzzed the field at a low altitude several times, but still did not get permission to land. We then flew to the other field northwest of Siena. Here we saw that half the field was covered with French troops drawn up for the ceremony and the other half was also cratered. For nearly an hour we flew back and forth between the two fields unable to decide what to do. Some of those aboard said, "To hell with it; let's not break our necks to get medals, we can always get them another day." But the senior officer aboard made it plain that he wanted his medal. He consulted with Dixon, who said that he believed he could set the plane down on the field where the troops were. Dixon then proceeded to execute a masterly landing, putting the C-47 down in the narrow space between the troops in formation and the fresh craters. Apparently during the preceding night the Germans had staged one of their rare air attacks and had cratered both airfields. We stepped out of the plane and were ushered by the French to our places for the ceremony in the midst of a huge square formed by the troops. General Juin appeared and ordered, *"Ouvrez le ban,"* and ruffles and flourishes followed. The general with his aide at his side then advanced to decorate the colors of the units which had distinguished themselves in the thrust north from the Garigliano. Among them, curiously, was the 2nd Regiment of Moroccan Riflemen which had opposed our landing at Safi a year and a half before. It was a great moment for the French. It was their last great effort in Italy before going on to the landings in the South of France. General Juin came down the line of American officers in cotton khakis with ties. I was the last in line and when he reached me, with a twinkle in his eye, he said in French, "Walters, you have worked a lot for me and you have smoothed many problems. This one is a real pleasure for me to award." I told him how honored I felt and meant it. Then the bands massed and thundered out the "Marseillaise," and there were few there who did not feel a thrill at this last action of the French Expeditionary Corps in Italy, where they had, at such a heavy cost in blood, done much to redeem the honor of French arms. The ceremony was followed by a splendid lunch which showed us what miracles French chefs could perform with U.S. field rations.

During this period, as the aide to the commanding general, I had a small one-quarter-ton van in which I had my bed and a chest of drawers, a real advantage for me when the headquarters moved. I had no packing to do.

I was conscious of the comfort and the prestige of being assigned to an Army headquarters and of being the aide to the commanding general. An insignia on my uniform made everybody aware of this fact. Somehow I could not escape a feeling of guilt whenever I went down to see the men who were doing the real fighting. I would come back to the comforts that were inherent in an Army headquarters. I consoled myself by thinking that I had not asked for this assignment. I could not help, at night sometimes when the wind was blowing from the north, watching the horizon flickering with gunfire and occasionally listening to the distant sound of guns, wondering whether this was really my place or whether I should be where I could make a more direct contribution. I was a young officer and I had friends

in the 85th and 88th divisions who had gone to Officers Candidate School with me. It just seemed wrong that they were living
in danger of their lives every hour of every day and night while I
lived in the comfort and prestige of an Army headquarters.
When the time came for me to go to the Brazilian division
when it arrived in Italy, it was almost with a sense of relief that
I went. In the months beyond, when the little town where I was
with the Brazilians was under heavy shellfire, I would often
think, "Why didn't I stay at Army headquarters instead of coming to this?" I knew in my own inner heart that despite the fear
I felt at that moment, this was my place and that if I had
not come forward to that division, I would have never felt
quite right about what I had done in the war. I think that I
would always have had the feeling that I had lost some of the
experience of my generation in that I had not been a real part
of the most significant event that had occurred in my life, and
that I had not shared in the extraordinary experience of so
many millions of young men my age during those years of conflict.

I am often reminded of a sentence which Colonel Castelo
Branco said to me one night while we sat through a heavy
shelling in the town of Porretta. He spoke of an officer who had
behaved quite badly under the shelling:"The men that war does
not kill it leaves completely transparent." By this he meant that
whatever the mask a man may wear in everyday life in peacetime, he cannot maintain it in the horror, danger and weariness
of war, and that in combat every man is seen as he really is—
with all his virtues and all his faults. I sometimes wonder if this
is not one of the subtle and horrible fascinations of war—that we
see ourselves and all those around us as we really are rather than
as we would like others to think we are.

General Patton once wrote a poem in which he said, "I run
rampant through the ranks of men. I bow the heads no other
can for I am fear." I had come far from my first experience at
Safi. I knew now that all men feel fear and that only submission
to fear is truly humiliating. And so, I went to the Brazilians to
begin my next mission.

6. THE BRAZILIAN EXPEDITIONARY FORCE

In 1944 and 1945 the Brazilian Expeditionary Force fought in Italy to give concrete expression to Brazil's outrage over German submarine attacks on Brazilian commercial shipping and to fulfill her desire to take a more active part in the war against the Axis.

The original intent was to send a 100,000-man Army corps to Italy, but difficulties in training and equipping such a force, together with Allied shipping problems, caused a scaling down of this original ambitious plan. The final plan involved an infantry division with supporting troops totaling some 25,000 men. This division was to be organized and equipped according to U. S. Tables of Organization and Equipment. Brazil insisted that this force must serve within a U.S. major command. The U. S. Fifth Army in Italy was already composed of contingents of several nationalities and seemed the natural place for the Brazilians. The Brazilian Air Force also sent a fighter squadron to Italy and the Brazilian Navy escorted the troops as they moved across the ocean and into the Mediterranean.

It required a major effort by Brazil to send this division to Europe and it embodied that country's desire to play a more important role in the world. Brazil was the first South American country ever to send an expeditionary force across the ocean. This division saw 229 days of continuous combat. Operating in a strange land and under weather conditions unknown in Brazil they pulled their weight and performed in a most creditable fashion. They had the satisfaction of receiving the surrender of the first German division to surrender as a unit in Italy. I was their American combat liaison officer.

As I said, I was anxious to go to the Brazilians when they came. On August 5, 1944, I flew down in a light plane to Rome to see General Mascarenhas at the St. Georges Hotel. We discussed the problems the Brazilian troops would face in Italy and he indicated that he would like to have me as a liaison officer. I spoke Portuguese, had been in Italy for some time, and as General Clark's aide was the man to see to get things done in the Fifth Army. He felt this combination would be useful to the Brazilians. Then he paused and said, "But I suppose you are the general's aide." I hastened to assure General Mascarenhas that General Clark could easily get other aides. He decided he would contact General Clark in order to have me assigned to the Brazilian division.

On August 11 I went down to the Brazilian camp at Tarquinia to escort the general and his staff to the Fifth Army headquarters in General Clark's C-47. The group included the division commander, General Mascarenhas; the divisional infantry commander, General Euclydes Zenobio da Costa; the chief of staff, Colonel Floriano Lima Brayner; and the G-4, Colonel João Almeida Freitas. They were received with a guard of honor and were fully briefed on the combat situation at Fifth Army headquarters. They had lunch and then visited the various army staff sections. In the evening we flew back to Tarquinia. I left them at their headquarters and then flew back myself to the Fifth Army.

A few days later across my desk came a letter from General Mascarenhas to General Clark asking that Captain Walters be assigned as combat liaison officer to his division on the basis of his knowledge of Portuguese and his knowledge of conditions in Italy and experience at Fifth Army. He said that this would solve many problems for the Brazilians. During the next few days, I moved back and forth between Fifth Army headquarters and the Brazilian troops, who were still at Tarquinia. On August 21 I actually moved from the Fifth Army to the Brazilian division, after drawing a new jeep and drawing a Coleman lantern and a stove so that I could light myself if we were without electricity and also cook my own rations if need be, since I was not sure that I would always like what the Brazilians were doing to the rations that they drew from the U. S. Army depots. I remained with the Brazilian division for the rest of the war.

On August 19, Prime Minister Churchill came to Vada to make a speech to the American and Brazilian troops. The indomitable old man began his speech by saying, "Brazilian and American comrades in arms." (Nearly twenty years later Churchill was to recall this event to me during his meeting with President Eisenhower at Bermuda. He could not place it but he knew that the meeting had taken place.) The Brazilians, who had not yet fired a shot in anger, were greatly pleased at being thus addressed by the old lion.

The Brazilian troops coming in had been trained in Brazil, but had received very little equipment. Nevertheless, on August 25, Brazilian Army Day and the birthday of their national hero, the Duke of Caxias, they held a parade at Vada near Leghorn. General Clark came and spoke to them and I translated. Then I left all the international activities and drove down to the coast for a swim in the sea. It was great!

I traveled around Italy, attempting to overcome the natural reluctance of any Army unit to issue equipment to another. Eventually the Brazilians were properly equipped. During this period, I accompanied a number of the Brazilian operations and intelligence officers on orientation visits to American divisions. In September we visited troops in the Florence area, then on September 9 we went to IV Corps headquarters to see General Willis D. Crittenberger. The 1st Brazilian Infantry Division was assigned to his command as part of his IV Corps. I spent quite a long time with officers of the IV Corps, explaining the kinds of problems that would arise as the Brazilian troops entered combat with that corps.

The Brazilians, in the meantime, had assembled at a new

camp near Pisa in the old royal hunting preserve at San Rossore. Here they continued their training with combat-experienced American personnel.

On September 20, 1944, the Army commander, General Mark Clark, came to inspect the BEF. At the conclusion of his inspection he spoke to a large group of Brazilians. He spoke of the task that lay ahead and thanked the Brazilians for coming to take part in the common struggle. He would pause from time to time for me to translate. Finally he said, "I have one more thing to do and that is to promote Captain Walters to the rank of major." I was so surprised that I did not repeat what he had said in Portuguese. He said to me in a low voice, "God damn it, Walters, when I say something you translate it." I immediately did so. He then took the gold leaf that was the insignia of a major out of his pocket and pinned it on my shirt collar. He then said some kind words about me and my performance of duty and added that he would be expecting a lot more from me now that I was a major. The whole thing was so completely unexpected that for once I had nothing to say except to thank him and say that I would try and do my best. While I was delighted there was a sort of wistful feeling. Most of the majors I knew were somewhat older and I wondered if this was not the end of my youth. This feeling passed quite quickly. The Brazilians took it as a mark of the interest General Clark had in them. I could hardly believe that in a little more than two years, I had gone from second lieutenant to major.

General Dutra, the War Minister, was given temporary command of a task force in the line. While I was with him, the Brazilian troops brought in three prisoners, two Italian and one German, and I interrogated them on the spot, each in his own language. This made a considerable impression on the Brazilians.

About this time while driving to Florence I got caught in a flood of the Arno River and had to spend the night on the top of my jeep until the waters receded. A little later in October I flew with General Dutra from Rome to Dijon and then drove to Vittel, where we visited General Jacob Devers, previously the commander of the Mediterranean Theater of Operations and now commander of the Sixth Army Group in France. He was decorated by the Brazilians. I then went on with General Dutra to Paris and London. In London the British briefed General Dutra at the London Air Defense Center and spoke to him for the first time about the German V-1 and V-2 rockets that were falling on London and southern England. They described the measures they had taken to parry the V-1, namely firing anti-aircraft artillery barrages east of London and having Typhoon fighters fly alongside the V-1 and tip it over, destabilizing the gyroscope and causing it to crash in the countryside east of London. When General Dutra asked what they were doing about the faster and more sophisticated V-2s, the British replied somewhat wistfully that the only defense they could think of was to try to overrun the launching sites, since the rocket moved at such speed there was nothing that could be done to it while in flight. We saw two V-1s while in London. They were a chilling sight.

On October 15 we flew back to Naples and General Dutra departed for Brazil from there on the eighteenth. I then returned to the Brazilian division. On October 22 General Mascarenhas, in a gesture recalling that performed by many of the crusaders on their way to the Holy Land, had a mass said in Pisa Cathedral and laid his sword on the altar. The 1st Brazilian troops were committed in the Serchio Valley as a regimental combat team under the divisional infantry commander, General Zenobio da Costa, to accustom them gradually to combat. The sector was usually quiet but on one occasion the threat of a German penetration in this area brought forward an Indian division which had been resting in the Fifth Army area. The Germans became aware of this reinforcement and canceled their expected attack in this area.

General Zenobio was a brave and gallant soldier and one of the few men I have known who never showed a trace of fear. On one occasion, I was standing with him on a bridge over the Serchio River when we came under heavy artillery fire. His aide and son-in-law, Captain Rubens Vasconcellos, was with us.

Seemingly oblivious to the artillery falling quite close at hand, Zenobio did send his son-in-law off on a mission in order to get him off the bridge. On this quiet front the Brazilians gradually became accustomed to the Italian winter, to the mountains and to conditions that they had not known in Brazil. They learned patrolling and small-scale combat operations. They liberated the small town of Camaiore.

On November 1, 1944, General Mascarenhas assumed command of all Brazilian troops in the line. On the third I went up into the Reno Valley to Porretta Terme with Colonel Henrique Moraes to see Colonel Lawrence Dewey, who commanded a small task force on that sector of the front. On November 5 Brazilian troops of the 6th Infantry Regiment relieved the 13th Tank Battalion and its task force and assumed responsibility for this sector. This was the first time the Brazilians were really committed to the main front of the war. We quickly found the area to be much tougher than the Serchio Valley. Here the Germans had a complete view of our positions from the high mountains that ringed the valley. Our command post in the small town of Porretta was continuously shelled. The 170-mm. guns proved distracting, nerve-wracking and lethal. On one occasion one of these shells struck near a mess line. This resulted in thirty-two casualties. The Germans were also firing smaller-caliber guns into Porretta.

Field Marshal Harold Alexander came to visit the Brazilian division for the first time on November 8, and we had made elaborate preparations to receive him. The Brazilians planned a lunch for the field marshal preceded by a briefing in the center of town at the Hotel Helvetia. When the Germans evacuated Porretta, they destroyed the entire water system, so we had to build a private latrine for the field marshal in the garden of the Hotel Helvetia. The Brazilians, who at this time still lived a little bit in the world of World War I, drew up an impressive guard of honor in the main square of Porretta. Field Marshal Alexander arrived and reviewed the troops, who then played "God Save the King" and the Brazilian national anthem, which is quite long. In the midst of this ceremony German shells began to fall. They continued throughout the briefing and the lunch.

General Mascarenhas briefed the field marshal on the military situation of the division and I was translating what the Brazilian commander was saying into English. The shelling was quite distracting. Inevitably I listened with one ear to the incoming shells and with the other to General Mascarenhas. Every now and then I would miss his remarks and would have to ask him to repeat what he had just said. At one point he said to me, "Walters, you haven't had this trouble before." I replied in Portuguese, "General, I haven't translated before with these particular sound effects." I did not bother to translate what I had said into English for the field marshal.

Lunch followed the briefing. We were all sitting at a large U-shaped table in the hotel dining room. I was the only person inside the U, facing General Mascarenhas, who had the field marshal on his right and General Crittenberger, the corps commander, on his left. While we were at lunch, twenty-one shells landed in the immediate vicinity of the hotel. One of them scored a direct hit on the field marshal's as yet unused privy. Another shell hit the terrace directly in front of the hotel, killing a Brazilian sentry. Each of us silently counted the bursts. At the end of the lunch, Field Marshal Alexander made a short speech in which he said that the eighth of November would always live in his memory because now it was the dual anniversary of the Allied landings in North Africa in 1942 and of his first visit to the Brazilians in 1944. The Brazilians were, of course, pleased to be in the same category as the Allied landings in North Africa. The field marshal went on to say that while he was very grateful for the twenty-one-gun salute which General Mascarenhas had arranged (obviously Alexander had been counting like the rest of us), as a field marshal he only rated eighteen guns. General Mascarenhas was much amused by the joke and impressed by Alexander's coolness under fire.

Alexander next visited one of the Brazilian regiments in the line, the 6th Infantry Regiment, commanded by Colonel Nelson de Mello. As we left the headquarters, a barrel full of steel helmets for the visitors stood by the door. I picked up one and handed it to General Lyman Lemnitzer, the field marshal's deputy and later the Supreme Allied Commander in Europe of NATO. I said to him, "General Lemnitzer, do you want a helmet?" He looked at me and, in a low voice, said, "Christ, yes. But he won't wear one and if he doesn't wear one, I can't wear one." I returned his helmet to the barrel and put my own on. We always wore our helmets in Porretta even though we thought that they would eventually make us go bald. We were prepared to lose our hair, but not our heads if we could help it. I drove the jeep to Colonel Nelson de Mello's headquarters at Riola. The field marshal was much taken with a small Brazilian musical group which was playing lively Brazilian sambas when we got to the 6th Infantry Regiment. Alexander's visit substantially boosted the Brazilian morale. They felt they had really entered the big league. Alexander was an impressive soldier. He was completely unflappable, forceful, intelligent and gracious in a non-pompous way. He had been Montgomery's commander in chief in the desert at the time of El Alamein. I had come to admire and respect Field Marshal Alexander greatly when I was General Clark's aide. His behavior during his first contact with the Brazilians, and his calm, soldierly conduct during the shelling only served to increase my respect and admiration for this truly great British soldier. He was later to become governor general of Canada and Earl of Tunis.

The winter of 1944–45 was a tough period for the Brazilian Expeditionary Force. First of all, the Brazilians found themselves in very mountainous terrain to which they were unaccustomed. They found themselves facing a grim European winter, colder than anything most of them ever knew in Brazil. Most significantly, they faced the German Army. The Germans occupied positions on the mountains which enabled them to look down our throats in Porretta and they shelled us often. During the time the division had its command post in Porretta, the G-2 section of the Brazilian division counted some fifteen hundred rounds of incoming heavy artillery; that is, 155 millimeters or larger. It seemed like even more.

The Brazilian division was something of a curiosity in the Fifth Army and many visitors to Italy would come up to see it. General Mascarenhas used to say that he was thinking of setting up an extra section in the division headquarters simply to take care of the endless stream of visitors. On one occasion we were visited by Congresswoman Clare Boothe Luce, a brave, handsome and charming woman. The Brazilians were delighted by her visit. She insisted on being taken right up to the front lines. The Brazilians feared that something might happen to her, but were delighted that she wanted to go. She was wearing a chocolate-colored Eisenhower jacket and matching slacks. On the left breast of her jacket she wore a metal plaque. One of the Brazilians asked her whether it was a medal or a piece of jewelry. She replied she had been awarded it by an Asiatic country. It was the Order of Chastity Second Class. With a grin, she added, "I don't know if I have been decorated or insulted." The Brazilians considered her one of their greatest visitors. General Willis Crittenberger, the corps commander, was somewhere in the sector of the Brazilian division almost every day. My diary for November 9 notes that the Germans started to shell us about nine o'clock. The shells fell close to our command post and continued for hours. I slept little that night. It was a very unpleasant experience, but was to be repeated often.

For a time Colonel Castelo Branco, the operations officer and I lived on the top floor of a small hotel in a town continuously under fire. The Germans shelled the town with both medium and heavy artillery. Often such shellings would go on throughout the night. On several occasions when the shelling was heavy and close, I phoned Colonel Castelo Branco, even though his room was on the same floor, to ask whether, perhaps, he thought we should take shelter in the basement. He invariably responded that he was a Brazilian and did not like cold. Snug in his sleeping bag he had no intention of leaving it, shelling or no shelling. I could go if I wanted. Needless to say, I could not have taken shelter without intolerable loss of face, and so I did not, much as I was inclined to do so. One night a shell exploded right outside my window and several fragments embedded themselves in the wooden shutters. The windows had long since been smashed, and the force of the explosion almost threw me off the camp cot on which I had spread my sleeping bag. The next morning at breakfast, Colonel Castelo Branco commented on the explosion and said it must have been quite loud on my side of the building. I confirmed his suspicions and told him about the fragments in the shutters. I went on to wonder if we should not move to another building in town. He laughed and responded with the following story:

> Once upon a time there was a Sultan of Egypt who had a very capable minister. One day this minister rushed into the presence of the Sultan, greatly agitated, and said, "Oh, Sultan, I must leave this place at once. If I have served you faithfully, give me some money so I can go far away." The Sultan, not understanding his minister's agitation, said, "Why do you want to go away?" The minister replied that he had been walking in the bazaar and had met the Angel of Death, who had looked at him so strangely that he felt he must leave at once. The Sultan, seeing that he could not reason with his minister, handed him a bag of gold, saying, "You have been a good minister. When you have recovered, return to be my minister again." He then asked the minister where he was going and the minister replied that he was going far away to Central Asia to the half-mythical city of Samarkand. Several weeks later the Sultan was walking in the gardens of the palace and he met the Angel of Death. The Sultan said to him, "Oh, Angel, why did you so frighten my minister?" The Angel replied, "Oh, Sultan, I did not mean to frighten him, but I could not help showing my surprise seeing him here still in Egypt when I knew that I had an appointment with him tonight in Samarkand."

Chilled, I got his point. I did not move and no other shell came that close again. Under all this shelling, the early unsuccessful operations of the Brazilians, the pressure of U.S. commanders and the envy of some other Brazilian officers, who resented the immense confidence that the division commander

placed in him, Castelo Branco remained unperturbed and deci-
sive. Often we sat talking into the early morning hours with
officers in his operations section about the war and the world.
Without being ostentatiously religious, there was a deep fiber of
spiritual belief in Castelo Branco. In more than a year of daily
contact with the man in the stress of battle, on a few days' leave
in Rome, in contacts with Americans, British or Italians, I never
saw Castelo Branco do a mean thing or heard him say a shame-
ful word. The moral integrity of the man was beyond challenge.
At times of danger, he clearly felt fear as all men do, but the
iron self-discipline he always maintained guaranteed his icy
calm. He demanded it of those about him. About two o'clock
on a snowy night in December, I awakened noting that Brazilian artillery firing in our support was falling not too far from our
command post. Uneasy and anxious, I lay in my sleeping bag reluctant to get up, yet knowing that I must. Finally, I rose, threw
on my clothes, went over to Castelo Branco's room and knocked
on the door. He was not there. I went down to the operations
section and found him (a northern Brazilian used to warmth)
wrapping himself in heavy clothing and obviously getting ready
to go out. I asked him what was happening and he said that he
was not sure but that something peculiar was going on at Sila
Bridge about two miles away. He asked whether I wanted to go
with him, as IV Corps would undoubtedly be calling me soon to
find out what was happening. By this time, I felt sure the Germans must be at Sila Bridge and we would be greeted by them
there. I agreed to go. Trying to hide my six feet three behind his
five feet six, I climbed into the jeep behind him and we drove to
Sila Bridge with the shelling continuing. At the bridge we saw
a group of Brazilian soldiers milling around. Castelo Branco
found the lieutenant in charge and asked him sharply who he
was and what he was doing there. The lieutenant came to attention and answered that his platoon had gone into position early
that night after coming up from the personnel replacement center in the rear area. At about two o'clock in the morning they
had been attacked by the Germans. The lieutenant, greatly excited, said that thousands of huge, blond Germans had swarmed

over his positions shouting, "Heil Hitler." Castelo Branco eyed the lieutenant coldly and said that there were not thousands of Germans facing them and no one had charged shouting, "Heil Hitler," since Tunisia. The lieutenant excitedly said that this was indeed what had happened to him. Castelo Branco said to him sternly, "Did you have orders to leave your position?" "No, sir." "Then go back at once." "Colonel," said the lieutenant, "I don't mind dying for Brazil. But I don't want my child to be an orphan in a hopeless cause." Castelo Branco looked sharply at him and casually reached down and loosened the cover of his holster and said, "Lieutenant, go back at once or your son will really be an orphan before morning." The lieutenant grasped the full portent of his meaning. Impressed by Castelo Branco's cool authority, he clicked his heels, saluted and, followed by his men, moved silently out into the night to resume his position. Six weeks later that same lieutenant was decorated for heroism. Castelo Branco's icy calm had made the lieutenant and his men understand their duty as soldiers of Brazil. Not often is one able to observe a man under such conditions. The true measure of Castelo Branco's courage and calm had been shown to me. At no time did his humor or wit desert him. A brilliant man, he was impatient with incompetence and little disposed to tolerate weakness or lying. He was never afraid to express his opinions in dealing with his superiors or U.S. officers. I never saw him ill at ease, arrogant or servile.

After dark on December 10, a single German airplane flew over Porretta and dropped a bomb close to the headquarters. It completely destroyed a building housing refugees and killed thirty-five people. We were about to sit down to dinner at General Mascarenhas' mess when all the lights went out following the tremendous explosion. I went out to see what had happened. The bomb had fallen through the basement of the building and had exploded there. The entire building collapsed, leaving only a pile of debris. I walked up onto this pile in the dark and experienced an unpleasant sensation. I looked down and realized that I was walking not just on mere debris but on bodies and pieces of human flesh. This German airplane had overflown the headquarters for several evenings previously, but had never before taken any hostile action. No one worried about it that evening.

During the winter we had a number of non-Brazilian units assigned to us. There was a U.S. signal company, commanded by a Captain Bernard Marschner. This company tied in the Brazilian phone and radio network with adjacent U.S. units and with the higher headquarters to our rear. We also had a British anti-aircraft unit equipped with 40-mm. Bofors anti-aircraft guns. The 13th Tank Battalion remained for a while and on other occasions another tank or tank-destroyer battalion usually would provide some sort of armored support for the Brazilians.

On Thanksgiving Day, 1944, I feared that the Brazilians probably would cook our Thanksgiving turkey Brazilian-style. All units were issued turkey for the occasion. I made arrangements to have Thanksgiving lunch with the U.S. tank battalion and Thanksgiving dinner with the U.S. signal company. Both meals were delicious.

I did not smoke but was very fond of candy. Every day we were issued a pack of cigarettes, but only one chocolate bar a week. I tried to swap my cigarettes for chocolate but since people only had one bar a week they were not often willing to swap. My one whiskey bottle a month was more helpful in getting chocolate. Finally, I wrote my mother a letter and asked her to see if she could mail me some chocolate. She could not find any in the stores because of wartime shortages, so she sent my letter to the Hershey Chocolate Corporation, which promptly sent me a case of chocolate bars. I thereupon wrote the Hershey company to say that now I really knew what I was fighting for.

One night in December during one of the shellings, a great many Brazilian installations in Porretta were hit. Each time General Mascarenhas sent a staff officer down to report to him on the damage. This particular evening so many were hit, he ran out of Brazilian staff officers and when the next hit was reported on the neuropsychiatric clearing station, he asked me to go down and find out what had happened. I walked down to the main square in Porretta and found the building in which the clearing station was located on fire. I could not repress the thought that it was a strange location for neuropsychiatric patients—in an area under heavy shellfire. People ran in and out of the blazing building. As I arrived, a very small individual came dashing, wild-eyed, out of the building. I grabbed him, thinking it was one of the patients, and he said, "No, no. I am a doctor." "Oh," said I soothingly, "so am I." At that point, the Brazilian Military Police soldiers tapped me on the shoulder and said, "Major Walters, he really is the doctor in charge of this post." I let him go.

From time to time I would go over to Fifth Army, either by plane or by road, to report to the Army commander, General Lucien King Truscott, who had succeeded Mark Clark. I thought Truscott was perhaps the greatest combat commander I knew in World War II. I must admit that I welcomed these occasions because they gave me the opportunity of getting away from the nightly shellings in Porretta. Sometimes returning down the valley toward Porretta, I would pause just before the railroad tunnel at the southern edge of town and watch a shell explode in the city. Then I would make a dash for the headquarters since there were about four- or five-minute intervals between the large-caliber shells.

In the early part of the Brazilian move into the Porretta area, there was no airstrip on which the division's observation and liaison aircraft could land. The division was entitled to some seven such light aircraft. General Mascarenhas did not use his plane much, but I did. The pilot, initially, was a young American lieutenant by the name of Walter Byron. I would frequently not only use the aircraft but get Byron to show me how to fly it. Finally, after I had used the aircraft from an airfield some ten miles to our rear, the Brazilians decided to bulldoze a small airstrip in the bend of the Reno River across from Porretta. This was done and a revetment or earth wall was constructed around the general's airplane, which was kept there. On one of my trips to Florence I had a fine set of red leather cushions made for the aircraft to give it an even more plush appearance. For some time the Germans took no action against this aircraft or airfield. The

Brazilians then enlarged the airstrip in the bend of the Reno and constructed six more revetments for the other aircraft. For several days nothing happened, even though the planes were clearly visible to the Germans on the heights above the valley.

During this time the German shelling of the roads in the division area was so intense that we had to bring in smoke-generating machines at the various key road junctions to generate smoke all day long to prevent enemy observation of traffic. The smoke was in the air constantly, as well as in eyes, lungs and mouths. One morning I received a phone call telling me that a few shells had fallen in the vicinity of the airstrip. I worried immediately about the red leather cushions in the general's airplane and decided to go get them out of the plane. I jumped in my jeep and drove down to the area directly across from the airstrip. The river was fordable at this point. Just as I reached this point, shelling of the airfield began. I sat down on the bank of the river and watched helplessly, cursing as the Germans shot every one of the aircraft out of the revetments, a catastrophic loss for us as the attack resulted in the destruction of all the light liaison aircraft assigned to the division, not to mention the red leather cushions.

That afternoon General Mascarenhas sent me to Fifth Army to get replacements for these aircraft. I welcomed the opportunity to go to Florence and spend at least one night quietly away from the shelling. I drove down to Florence and went to the Fifth Army flight section, which was in the race track in the Cascine Park just west of the city. I went up to see the major who was on duty there and explained that I was the liaison officer with the 1st Brazilian Infantry Division in the Reno Valley and that we had lost some aircraft in operations and needed replacements. He noted this and said, "Okay. How many did you lose?" I replied, "We lost seven." He looked up at me, startled, and said, "My God, that's every one you had!" I said, "Yes, it is." He asked, incredulously, "How could you lose seven?" At this point I decided that attack was the best form of defense so I said to him, "Major, it may be difficult for you to understand back here in the peace and quiet of Florence, going to dinners, the opera, movies, dances and night clubs every night, but up there in the valley, it is winter, the snow is deep and we are fighting the Germans. They are tough and mean and they know how to shoot. That's how we lost the seven aircraft." He was somewhat taken aback by this and he said, "You mean they hit all of them?" I said, "They shot every single one of them out of their revetments. They are on the mountains all around us and they shoot at us all the time. It's rough up there." He gulped, duly impressed, and without further argument provided the necessary replacements. We did not, however, move them back to this particular airstrip for a very long time, since it really would have been tempting fate and offering too lucrative a target for the Germans. We might not have been lucky enough to get all the aircraft replaced a second time.

The first snow came. It found us high in the Apennine Mountains, an area of heavy snowfall. A couple of days later I was called to investigate what the Brazilians described as a large number of long boards and some pointed sticks with rings on them. Inspection revealed that in the inimitable American fashion a Fifth Army truck had delivered the Brazilian division's allotment of skis and ski poles for the troops who would have to go out on patrol. The snow in many places was so deep that it was impractical for the infantry to try and walk on it. I called Fifth Army and they indicated that they would get a ski instructor down to us fairly soon, but in the meantime, since I knew how to ski, I should start ski classes for the Brazilians. I started the instruction and then had to stop because I found that I would have to invent a whole new Portuguese vocabulary to describe the various maneuvers and movements on skis. This I did and then I asked the three Brazilian regiments to designate men from their patrolling platoons to take this instruction. On the hills behind Porretta I taught basic skiing to freezing Brazilian soldiers. Eventually Fifth Army sent us a ski instructor, a Lieutenant Francis Sargeant, who years later was to become governor of Massachusetts. He was a very good ski instructor. One day early in the period of instruction, we heard an aircraft approaching from the north with its engines desynchronized. This usually was the way the Germans flew for some reason I never understood which was supposed to confuse our air defense. As I watched the aircraft I saw that it was a B-25 with U.S. markings and seemed to be in some difficulty. It circled our area briefly before a number of parachutes appeared out of the door of the aircraft. Suddenly the plane went into a screaming dive, crashed and burned in a rather spectacular fashion in an open field.

I immediately said to my class, "I'm going down to the division command post to see what's happened. Follow me." To my astonishment, they all followed and successfully made it down the hill despite previous protests that they could neither go down hills nor stop. I entered the operations section and found it extremely busy as many of the units in the line were reporting paratroopers dropping on them. Apparently all units were reporting the same five crewmen from the B-25. These airmen were brought into the division command post. They were extremely suspicious of the Brazilians in their green uniforms and speaking a strange language. They did not know that there were Brazilian troops in the line in Italy and refused to give me any information despite my efforts. Finally, after talking about U.S. baseball, football and various typically American things, I was able to overcome their suspicions. The crew said they were flying from a base in Corsica, were hit by anti-aircraft fire over Bologna and found on trying to fly south that they could not fly high enough to clear the high summits of the Apennines. They had, therefore, decided to jump. I got them hot coffee and food, which they wolfed down.

I called the Air Corps headquarters in Florence and explained to a major that I had a crew that had just jumped from an aircraft. He responded, "Oh, you're up on Highway 62. Just put them out on the side of the road and they can hitch a ride." I was mad as hell at this reply for a number of reasons. I said to him, "Major, you have no goddamned business indicating over the telephone where our command post is, and secondly, you don't seem to understand that these men have been on a plane damaged by enemy fire and have just had to parachute out of that aircraft. They landed in deep snow. I don't know what the temperature is like back there in Florence, but up here it's very cold, and before I tell this crew to go out on the road and hitchhike, I will ask the Brazilian general for his sedan to send them back to Florence. I will be embarrassed as an American that my own Air Corps would not take care of these men after the harrowing experience they have just been through. You may be sure, however," I added, "that I will notify the Army commander of your attitude the next time I see him, and I am his personal representative with the Brazilians." The major rethought the problem and sent transportation for the men that night to take them to Florence. Once again, I found that when dealing with people in rear areas, rough talk was the most effective approach. It generally produced rather satisfactory results since they felt somewhat embarrassed about being so far back and so safe. When I was at Fifth Army headquarters and went forward to one of the divisions, I noted the sly cracks about the comfort and safety of the Army headquarters. This feeling is typical in all armies. No matter how far forward you go, the fellow in the next echelon back is always regarded as some sort of draft dodger. This was less accurate in the Brazilian division. The division headquarters received far heavier shelling than any of the regimental or battalion headquarters. The Germans knew exactly where the division headquarters was located and maintained harassing fire on it for a very long period of time. They crowed over this in their propaganda broadcasts to the Brazilians. This program was called "The Green and Gold Hour" (these are the colors of the Brazilian flag). It always gave the daily Brazilian football scores and these were of great interest to the troops. The harassing fire was to lead me to one of the more embarrassing experiences of my translating career.

General Crittenberger, the corps commander, came up to see General Mascarenhas to say that he understood the Brazilian division headquarters had been under heavy artillery fire, which was making it difficult for it to function properly. General Crittenberger indicated that he had no objection to Mascarenhas moving his headquarters back out of this intensive shelling. Not having slept very well for a week, and the only person present who spoke both languages, I must confess that my translation in Portuguese was much more enthusiastically in favor of moving the headquarters out of the shelled area than Crittenberger's original statement. When I had concluded my somewhat slanted translation, General Mascarenhas looked at General Crittenberger and said, "General Crittenberger, you are an American. You have many headquarters in Italy. You can move them forward, sideways or backwards and no one is going to pay any attention. This is the only Brazilian headquarters in Italy and when I move it, it is going to be forward and not backward." I was duly chastened by this reply and really felt quite ashamed of myself for having presented a Portuguese version considerably more favorable to the move than General Crittenberger had expressed in English. My only excuse was the pressure of continuous shelling and lack of rest.

One night during the shellings, I sat reading a newspaper in the lobby of the hotel in which we had our headquarters. A group of about six young Brazilian lieutenants had come forward from the replacement depot in the rear area, and were sitting somewhat nervously near me. They saw that I was an American officer and assumed that I spoke no Portuguese. One of them said to the other, "Look at that American son of a bitch sitting there quietly reading a newspaper while this bloody shelling is going on." I lowered the newspaper and said to him in Portugese, "If you think I'm really quietly reading this newspaper, you are sadly mistaken. I'm just as worried about those shells as you are—in fact, more so because I have been here longer than you and have used up more of the law of averages." The Brazilian lieutenants were greatly amused.

I note in my diary that on December 23 I said, "After supper I went to bed at about ten-thirty. We were shelled all night and I was quite scared." I had come a long way from the landings at Safi when I would not admit to myself that I really was frightened.

The Brazilians held quite a celebration for Christmas. The Brazilian chaplain said and I served midnight mass. We then had an elaborate supper and I went to bed at two o'clock in the morning. On Christmas Day we had more feasting, with steak and turkey. Christmas Day brought no respite in the shelling. I didn't think this was very friendly of the Germans. From Christmas to New Year's we were shelled every single day.

All, however, was not grim. An amusing incident occurred during this period. As I previously explained, the Germans had destroyed the waterworks in Porretta, making it necessary to have jerry cans of water to wash and to flush the toilets. One day in the toilet adjacent to the G-2 section of the division, someone made a mistake in cans and flushed the toilet with gasoline rather than with water. The next occupant threw a cigarette into the toilet bowl, which promptly exploded and caused a minor alarm within the headquarters. Fortunately, there were no casualties other than the toilet bowl. One day the Brazilians brought an unexploded 170-mm. shell into the headquarters and asked me what I thought of it. I replied, as I left the building, I am leaving until you get it out of here. Alarmed, they threw it in the river, but it still did not go off. I then returned to the headquarters.

Colonel Adémar de Queiroz arranged for all of the artillery and mortars in the Brazilian division to fire simultaneously at midnight on December 31. We were having a party at the division headquarters and we listened to the fire of the Brazilian guns and mortars roll out like thunder. Then we toasted 1945, the year of victory. We had set up a fairly elaborate buffet to which I had contributed a large round cheese. As we prepared to attack the buffet, the Germans' answer to our New Year's greeting came crashing down in the vicinity of our headquarters. Once again, I found myself under the table, and I was by no means alone. The building shook with the exploding shells. Then as suddenly as it had started, the shelling stopped. I crawled out from under the table with my Brazilian colleagues. Part of the ceiling had fallen on the buffet table and my cheese was covered with plaster. The operations officer, Colonel Castelo Branco, picked up the ringing phone. It was the operations officer of the divisional artillery, Colonel Adémar. "How did you like that fireworks display we put on?" he asked. "Adémar, never do that again. The whole German answer just landed on us. We're lucky to be here to answer the phone."

On December 12, 1944, the Brazilians conducted their first unsuccessful attack on Monte Castello, a major terrain feature held by the Germans. After the attack failed, they were initially greatly depressed and some acrimonious recriminations were exchanged among themselves and with the Americans. I reminded the Brazilians that this was no disgrace. The Germans had a very good army and further training would be necessary. In all the Brazilians were to attack this mountain three times before they finally took it. It had become a sort of symbol for them and only when they stormed it did they feel that they had overcome the evil spell that had held them back.

The midwinter period was difficult. Ammunition was strictly rationed, the snow lay deep on the mountains, and fierce German resistance continued whenever we probed their positions. Everyone knew that in the spring we would thrust forward and that tough fighting lay ahead.

The relatively grim episode of the failure of the first attack on Monte Castello was relieved by one amusing episode. I watched this attack with General Mascarenhas from his observation post. As it became clear that the attack had failed under a German counterattack the doughty little Brazilian commander's frustration was great. He was greatly irritated with the regimental commander who was conducting the attack. He went, and I went with him, to the regimental command post and severely upbraided the colonel. General Mascarenhas concluded by saying that this had been a disgraceful day for the Brazilian Army. They had been humiliated before their allies. Looking at the colonel he said, "My God, those weren't even Germans, they were Austrians!" (Actually the division facing us was a crack German mountain division made up of Bavarian and Austrian mountaineers.) The colonel looked at the general with a woebegone expression and replied, "General, those Austrians have been in the Germany Army so long that you can't tell the difference any more." Mascarenhas laughed and forgot his initial intention of relieving the colonel, who later fought very well.

The Brazilians took advantage of the relative lull in the fighting to re-equip themselves and to conduct intensive training programs. While the cold was new to the average Brazilian soldier, he generally came from peasant stock and was accustomed to hardships. In contrast to many American divisions, there were almost no cases of trench foot in the Brazilian division. They had fewer cases of respiratory ailments than most American divisions. Through training, patrolling and constant contact with the Germans they gradually improved and acquired self-confidence. Finally, after the second unsuccessful attack they took Monte Castello. This conquest was an enormous boost to their morale. I was with General Mascarenhas in his observation post when we saw the Brazilians reach the top of the mountain. It was a great moment for them. The IV Corps commander, General Crittenberger, arrived a few minutes later to congratulate the Brazilian commander. Though no major follow-up operations were conducted, since we were not yet ready for the major spring offensive, the Brazilians pushed out patrols. Some did not return. Later, as we moved forward, we found in one place three graves with the inscription in German, "Here lie three brave Brazilian soldiers." After the fall of Monte Castello, the Brazilians stormed the heights of Soprasasso, from which the Germans had long overlooked their position at Riola. I watched this attack and saw the desperate German resistance even though we had them surrounded and they knew it. The Brazilians brought me one of the prisoners and I asked him in German if he did not know that his position was surrounded. He said that he did but that his comrades were still there and that "one stays with one's comrades, doesn't one, Herr Major." This was typical of the attitude that made the Germans such formidable opponents.

Finally, on April 14, 1945, the great spring offensive of the Fifth Army began and the Brazilians were in line to play their part. The Brazilians attacked the town of Montese and this attack led to the heaviest fighting in which they were to be involved in Italy. As the Brazilian infantry and the U.S. tank destroyers supporting them drove to the edge of Montese, we could see that there was some hesitancy on the part of both from the observation post where General Mascarenhas and I were watching the battle. The general was anxious to clear Montese before night. He turned to Castelo Branco and said, "Get down there and get those soldiers and the tank destroyers moving." Castelo Branco beckoned to me and I followed him out of the observation post. We got into his jeep behind the crest of the hill and drove to a point halfway to the cemetery at the edge of town. There we had to dismount, as the jeep was too much of a target. We moved forward cautiously past Colonel Machado Lopes' engineers, who were clearing mines, and ran from sheltered spot to sheltered spot until we came to the cemetery at the west edge of Montese. Here we found evident confusion between the Brazilian battalion commander and the U.S. tank destroyer command. Quickly Castelo Branco explained, with me translating, what they were to do—move into Montese at once, secure the city before dark and push on beyond, both west and north. He answered their questions and told them to get going. The Brazilians infantry clambered up onto the huge tank destroyers and together Brazilians and Americans swept Montese clean despite the heavy artillery falling in and around the city. This action was to win Castelo Branco the only Combat Cross First Class awarded to a member of the division staff. That evening, two thirds of all the German artillery falling on the front of the IV Corps fell in and around Montese. As darkness descended, the whole area was illuminated by exploding shells and the roar of the explosions was incessant. On the morning of the fifteenth, the Brazilians drove north beyond Montese up the valley of the Panaro.

On the twentieth while we watched an attack from a Brazilian observation post, a five-gallon gasoline can suddenly exploded, showering me with flaming gasoline. I was able to put out the fire by wrapping myself in an army blanket that had been lying on the floor, but I was painfully burned. I received first aid from Brazilian medical personnel, but the battle was raging and they had more serious cases to handle. I got into my jeep and drove myself to the field hospital north of Porretta. I was in great pain and sat in the tent there watching severely wounded soldiers being brought in. I knew that while I was in great pain, I was not in any danger of life. I sat there gritting my teeth, desperately anxious not to moan or give out any sound that would indicate how much it hurt. Eventually I was given a general anesthetic and operated upon. When I recovered consciousness, the hospital was being shelled and they took me off the bed and laid me in a shallow trench until the shelling stopped. It was almost like being buried alive. Next day I was evacuated to a large hospital on the seashore near Leghorn. I remained there until the end of the war two weeks later. I was desperately anxious to get back to the division and had almost convinced the doctors in the hospital that they were depriving the Fifth Army of a whole division by keeping me there, since no one else could talk to the Brazilians as I could. One morning, one of the doctors walked in, and throwing a *Stars and Stripes* newspaper on my bed, he said, "They are doing better without you than they ever did with you." I looked at the paper and it reported that the Brazilians had captured the first German division to surrender as a unit in Italy. This was the 148th Division. By bad luck, I missed their greatest success.

Besides the division, the Brazilians had a fighter squadron in Italy fighting with the U. S. Air Corps. They carried out many attack missions in northern Italy and even ranged into southern Germany. The Brazilian Navy bore its share in the war against Germany, losing the cruiser *Bahia* with great loss of life. The soldiers of the Brazilian Expeditionary Force justified the faith placed in them. They were in continuous combat for 229 days without relief. They drove northwest from the Florence area to the foothills of the Alps, where they met the French west of Turin. They lost some 550 killed and 2,500 wounded. Forty-one Brazilians were captured by the Germans. They captured some 20,000 Germans, 4,000 vehicles, and even the 170-mm. gun that had shelled us for so long in Porretta. They asked for and received permission to take it with them back to Brazil.

A few days after the end of the war, I was released from the hospital and rejoined the division at Alessandria in northern

Italy. I went briefly with General Mascarenhas to the French Riviera for a few days and then went with the Brazilians to an area at Francolise where they were to await shipment back to Brazil. I then returned to northern Italy and was decorated on the shores of Lake Garda by Lieutenant General Lucian K. Truscott, the army commander.

On July 14, 1945, I flew with General Clark, who had become the army group commander, and General Crittenberger, the corps commander, to Brazil. They had been invited by the Brazilian government to come to Rio to witness the return of the Expeditionary Force and the subsequent victory parade. On the way I developed laryngitis and almost lost my voice. In Recife in northern Brazil where we spent the night before our arrival in Rio, General Clark said to me, "Walters, you will have to do a lot of translation for me. Now you get your voice back, that is an order." I did.

The parade was a tremendous success and Rio overflowed with pride and joy at the return of the first Brazilians ever to go overseas to fight in a distant war. Thus ended my mission to the Brazilian Expeditionary Force. A sometimes difficult but always rewarding mission.

7. TO RIO WITH PRESIDENT TRUMAN

Following the triumphant return of the Brazilian Expeditionary
Force to Rio de Janiero, I received orders assigning me to Brazil
as Assistant Military Attaché at the American Embassy
there. This seemed to be a logical sequence of events, as I had
known so many key figures of the Brazilian Army in Italy. I was,
however, given a period of leave in the United States to go
home and see my parents. I flew from Rio to Miami, arriving
there on the evening of the day the war in Asia ended. Again, in
keeping with my custom, I wrote some notes on this day entitled "The End of the Shooting." I quote them for whatever
value they may have thirty-two years later: they are the thoughts
of my youth.

> Well, I am flying home. In a short while we will be in
> Miami and in the United States once more for the first
> time in several years. I can hardly believe that I am going
> home. The big things like home and the little things like
> milk seem years and miles away. Now suddenly the Florida
> coast lies ahead like a dark shadow in the water. I can feel
> my heart beat faster as I see it. The sight of Miami moves
> me as I have not been moved in a long time. It is the dear
> land that for so long seemed so far. The gleaming buildings
> on the beach shine whitely in the afternoon sun. The bay
> glitters as we cross it and bank down toward the 36th Street

airport. Now the wheels have touched. I ease back in my chair as we roll down the runway and taxi up to the operations building. The plane stops and we peer out at the people waiting outside. The door is opened for an instant and a soldier steps into the plane. Are we to be sprayed with an aerosol bomb or not? There is a short argument and then it is decided we will not be sprayed. The door opens again and the warm smell of American summer fills the plane. Oh, how good it feels. I lie back in the seat and breathe it in. The passengers begin to get out. I feel a peculiar reluctance to get out, almost as though I were afraid to step on the ground. Finally, I get out and stand contentedly on the concrete, smothering the urge to get down on my knees and kiss the hallowed ground. It is all wonderful—the solid concrete, the clean buildings, the American voices, the friendly faces, the pretty little WAC lieutenant, the grim leathery customs inspector. They all look marvelous. "Is the war over?" I ask. "Not yet," they reply. All afternoon on the plane's radio we have been listening to the news. We have been told that Japan's answer will soon be published. After much milling around at the airport, we all get into staff cars and are driven out to Miami Beach. All the way I gaze at the houses, the billboards, the shops and the people as though they were from another world. For years they would have probably seemed perfectly normal to me, but now they look like the suburbs of paradise. The drive through the wonderful American streets makes my heart sing. We arrive at the Dorchester in Miami Beach, where we are to stay, and Sergeant Eichhorn, the desk sergeant, asks if we have heard that the war is over. I listen to the radio. President Truman has already spoken. Then I hear Attlee's voice, strangely like Churchill's, telling the British people that it is all over. There is a lump in my throat and I am not ashamed of it. At least, just short of six years, the war has come to an end. All the long, dark, terrible years are over. A prayer of thanksgiving rises in my heart, "Thank God, thank God, it's finished." The excitement makes me feel like leaping and shouting, but I don't. Outside, the cars are hooting their horns, and the soldiers and sailors in the street are shouting, "Over, over, it's all over." It does not

seem possible. The war has been going on for a great part
of my adult life. Now no more brave kids must be killed or
smashed physically or morally by the war. How far back
seems that morning when Mother woke me to say that she
had heard over the radio that the Germans had marched
into Poland. How sure I was then that we would have to
enter this terrible war that we have now, by God's grace,
won. I washed and cleaned up and went out for a walk.
The crowds are dancing in the streets, climbing on the cars.
The shops are closing and my search for milk is long. Finally, I find a place and, to the utter amazement of the girl
behind the counter, I drink more than two quarts of milk.
God, it's good. The years of waiting make it seem better.
Then to the Officers' Club opposite the Roney Plaza for
dinner. Good steaks and more milk. Then an entertainer
comes out and sits at the piano and begins to sing and tell
stories. The stories were dirty, dirtier than I had heard outside of the barracks. I felt vaguely irritated. This seemed to
be a hell of a way to celebrate the end of the war. There
were waitresses and the hat-check girl present. The stories
were so raw I felt embarrassed. I looked around me. I saw
no other majors, no other higher-ranking officers. I stood up
and said to those at my table, "I'm sorry. I don't go for this
stuff. Excuse me." I yawned ostentatiously and left. I
walked along the beach by myself for a while, still trying to
realize that the war was over. So many memories flocked
back. The beginning of the war, the news of Pearl Harbor,
the Officers Candidate School with its three months of hell
and fun, Camp Shelby, my platoon, Ritchie, the ocean
crossing, back to the States, Brazil, Italy, Clark, the surge
north from the Garigliano, the smell of death in the ruined
Italian villages, the hell of Anzio, the triumph of Rome,
the pursuit north, Pisa, Leghorn and the snipers. The
flights across the German lines in the cub plane, the arrival
of the Brazilians, the long tough winters, the days and
nights of shelling in Porretta, Castello, and Castelnuovo,
the soul-shattering shelling by the Germans in Montese the
night we took it, the explosion, the burn of my hand, the
idle weeks in the hospital, the war's end in Europe, and still
the menace of the Japanese war ever present. And now it is

over. I kept repeating to myself, "It's all over, it's all over," as though I could not convince myself that it really was. I walked back to the hotel and put in a telephone call to my parents. The operator told me there would be a three-hour delay. I said that was all right and went on to my room to bed. It was very hot and I could not sleep. I was too excited at being home, at the end of the war, and, besides, the noise of the merrymakers in the street made sleep almost impossible. That is what I thought until I fell asleep.

I went home the next day. My parents saw me and were very upset because I was so thin. I weighed 151 pounds. They fed me. I had a great month at home and then I flew back to Brazil. Here I found that the Brazilians were preparing to send a group of officers to the airborne school at Fort Benning. I attempted to go with them. I did not get a definite answer but I did get orders telling me to go as far as Fort Benning with them. I flew up with them in a Brazilian Air Force plane to Fort Benning and took the physical examination for airborne training and started the course. On the second day, I got a telephone call from a colonel in the Pentagon. He asked me what I was doing and I said that in compliance with my orders I was going through airborne school with the Brazilians. He answered, "You had no such orders. You had orders only to take them up there and see them into the school." He said, "You must return to Rio at once, where you are required as Assistant Army Attaché." When I protested, he said to me sharply, "Walters, stop playing and go back to work." I realized there was nothing I could do and so, reluctantly, I left the school and returned to Rio.

I had an interesting time during this period. There were many important visitors to Rio. General Eisenhower came in 1946, and this was to be my first close contact with him and with Mrs. Eisenhower. I lived with them in the house which was loaned to them by Roberto Marinho, the owner of Rio's largest afternoon newspaper. Admiral Halsey came. General Spaatz of the Air Force came. I went up to Washington to get him and brought him back. I served at this time under Ambassador Pawley, one of the truly great and patriotic men I have known. He was succeeded by Ambassador Adolf Berle, a brilliant, able man whose wife shared his brilliance and ability. I went with the Air Attaché to an attaché conference in Panama, which gave me the opportunity to fly across the Andes at 19,000 feet, and at that age by sitting quietly I was able to do it without taking oxygen. I got to see Santiago in Chile, Lima in Peru, and on up to Panama. I then returned to Rio and continued my job there until 1947, when the Pan American Conference was to meet in Rio. This was to be a very important occasion and General Marshall, the Secretary of State, was coming down for it. Senators Connally and Vandenberg represented the two great American political parties. President Truman was scheduled to attend and stay for the Brazilian Independence Day celebrations on September 7.

Ambassador Pawley instructed me to hold myself in readiness in case I was needed to translate for any of the senior members of the U.S. delegation. Ambassador Pawley himself spoke absolutely flawless Spanish. General Marshall arrived and had with him a rather senior ambassador who was to serve as his interpreter. As he went around calling on the various foreign ministers, this ambassador, who knew many of the ministers from previous meetings, became involved in lively conversation with them. General Marshall did not like this and I was soon commandeered as General Marshall's interpreter. I was ordered to report to General Carter, his assistant, in a private home in the mountain resort of Petrópolis, where the conference was being held.

I went up one morning and was taken in to see General Carter, who was sitting at the breakfast table having breakfast. He was wearing a bathrobe and on the bathrobe he had pinned his general's stars. This struck me as somewhat strange but I did not say anything. General Carter invited me to sit down and have breakfast with him, which I did. During breakfast he told me what General Marshall liked and did not like, about some of General Marshall's idiosyncrasies, and the way he wanted things done, and emphasized that I must never let him eat shrimp; it made him sick. At the end of the breakfast, I stood up to leave. General Carter said to me, "You didn't ask me why I wear stars on my bathrobe, so I'll tell you. I have never worn a uniform since I became a general, and, by God, I am going to wear these stars on *something*."

Later that day I reported to General Marshall, who remembered me from previous occasions. I then accompanied him on all of his calls on the various foreign ministers of the other American countries. Each morning I would sit on the terrace of his suite at the magnificent Quintandinha Hotel and read the morning papers to him. I recall that on the day of the opening of the conference, I was wearing civilian clothes and I had on a rather bright yellow tie—perhaps a reaction to the long years of wearing a uniform. While I was having breakfast with General Marshall, he looked at me quizzically and said, "Are you going to wear that tie when I make my speech this afternoon?" Not knowing what he was driving at, I replied, "No, sir." He said, "Well, I am very relieved, because when I speak this afternoon, I want to be sure that they are listening to my speech and not looking at that tie." From that day to this, I have had a very conservative taste in ties. That afternoon at the opening of the conference, I translated his speech into both Spanish and Portuguese wearing a somber and conservative tie. No one noticed.

Another highlight of this meeting was that Eva Perón, the wife of Argentina's president and a political power in her own right, was coming to the meeting. I was lucky enough to translate her conversation with General Marshall. She struck me as being much more feminine and much softer than she appeared in her photographs. She was bright and witty, with a certain innate shrewdness and intuition. During the conference, she gave a reception at the Argentine Embassy in Rio to which I was invited. I asked General Marshall's permission to go and he smilingly agreed. At the reception I was talking to someone when I felt a tap on my shoulder. I turned around. It was Mrs. Perón, and I was standing on the long train of her evening dress. I was enormously embarrassed but she was charming and very gracious about it, and inquired where I had learned such fluent Spanish. I liked that.

The conference went well. President Truman was scheduled

to fly down and, in a sense, close the conference and attend Brazilian Independence Day celebrations on September 7. Unknown to me at this time, General Marshall recommended to Mr. Truman that he not bring an interpreter but use me when he arrived. Mr. Truman arrived in Rio and was met at the dock of the Navy Ministry by President Dutra. He landed at Galeão Airport on an island in the bay; at that time there was no bridge to the mainland and one had to come to downtown Rio by launch. He had an extraordinarily enthusiastic and triumphant procession through the streets of Rio to the Embassy, where he was to stay. The city went wild. It was a high point in Brazilian-American relations. I recall being struck by Mr. Truman's simplicity and directness. I translated his speech at the conference. The fact that the President of the United States—at the peak of its power—had come all the way to Rio de Janiero to attend this meeting of the Organization of American States conveyed to the representatives of the other American states a sense of the value we placed on their friendship. When Mr. Truman concluded his speech, he was given a standing ovation. Later, I was also to translate a speech he gave aboard the battleship *Missouri*, on which he returned to the United States. No liquor was served aboard this ship, in accordance with U. S. Navy custom, to the great dismay of the many foreign guests, who had looked forward to champagne at best, whiskey at worst.

One morning during Mr. Truman's stay at the American Embassy, he invited me to have breakfast with him and I happily agreed. He then pointed to the chair on his right and asked me to sit there. I looked uneasily at Admiral William Leahy, who was the senior serving officer in the United States Armed Forces, a five-star admiral. Mr. Truman caught my glance and said, "I see him all the time but I don't see you all the time. You sit down here." Thus, a direct order from the President of the United States settled my protocol problem. During breakfast the question arose of what Mr. Truman would do after he left the White House since the "no third term" amendment had just been passed. Someone said to him—I can't recall who—"What is there in your future, Mr. President, after you leave the White

House? You will still be a young man with many years ahead of you. What is there in your future?" Mr. Truman replied without hesitation, "When you are President, the only future you have is in the memory of the people."

On several occasions in subsequent years, I have repeated the remark to several chiefs of state. Each nodded thoughtfully. They understood what he meant.

On another occasion, Mr. Truman was speaking about the critics of his daughter's singing. This was before he wrote the famous harsh letter to a certain critic. His daughter, Margaret, a truly charming and gracious girl, who was traveling with him, said, "Daddy, whenever you're criticized, Mother and I are furious and you tell us that this is part of politics and we must expect it. If I'm going to be in the entertainment world, you've got to expect criticism of my singing." The President replied, "Maybe, but any son of a bitch who says about you what he did doesn't do any business with the President of the United States."

The Brazilians provided lavish entertainment for the President and his party. There was a fabulous dinner at Itamaratí Palace, the seat of the Brazilian Foreign Office. During this dinner a small episode showed Mr. Truman's human side. As a waiter was approaching carrying a huge tray, he slipped, lost his balance and dropped the tray almost alongside Mr. Truman's chair. The crash was enormous. Conversation at the table stopped; President Dutra, the host, frowned. In the moments of silence that followed the crash, President Truman said to me, "Major Walters, tell President Dutra that that makes me feel right at home. It happens at the White House too." When I translated this into Portuguese, President Dutra smiled happily and the look of relief and gratitude on the face of the crestfallen waiter was beyond description.

Former King Carol of Romania was living in Brazil at this time. The wife of the Brazilian Foreign Minister was a Romanian so King Carol and his wife Princess Helena were invited to all the social occasions. That evening Mr. Truman told me that he did not think highly of King Carol, who had run out on his country. Later, when Carol was introduced to him, President

Truman commented crisply, "That's a great boy you have in
Romania [Carol's son King Michael]. He is doing a good job in
very difficult circumstances." He then turned away from Carol
to speak to the next guest.

Following the dinner, there was further entertainment around
the reflection pool of the Foreign Office. The whole area was lit
by thousands of candles. Beniamino Gigli sang, the Ballet Russe
de Monte Carlo performed and it was truly one of the most brilliant evenings I can recall. As Mr. Truman left me that evening,
he paused to thank me for my help during the day. A gesture
typical of him, but very moving to me as a young officer.

Later at the Embassy the Brazilians presented Mr. Truman
with a large collection of beautifully bound books. I translated
his speech of thanks into Portuguese and it impressed me deeply,
for this is what he said: "I have had very little formal education.
Most of what I know I have gathered from books, and this is
why I am so fond of them."

Mr. Truman's visit had a great impact on Brazilian-American
relations. The Brazilians were happy and proud that the President of the United States had come to see them. Mrs. Truman
and Margaret added greatly to the visit by the warm touch they
gave of a quiet, dignified and devoted American wife and a real,
unspoiled American girl. They made a real hit with the Brazilians. Most of all, Mr. Truman struck them as he did me—a simple man who had grown fully into the tremendous job which
destiny had thrust upon him. I was most happy after the trip
when he sent me an autographed photograph of himself with a
most generous inscription. Mr. Truman won my admiration and
affection by his courage, forthrightness and personal simplicity.
Yet he managed the difficult task of never letting anyone forget
that he was also the President of the most powerful nation on
earth. He did it with dignity but without pomposity.

He got along well with Brazilian President Eurico Dutra. The
two men shared many qualities and their outlook on life was
very similar; there was even a certain physical resemblance between them. A few years later President Dutra was to return
President Truman's visit by traveling to the United States. By

Mr. Truman's order it was once again my privilege to translate for them. My association with President Truman was to extend into the years ahead. In 1948, after his unexpected victory in the elections, I was in Paris with Secretary of State Marshall, attending the United Nations General Assembly. On learning of the election results, General Marshall scribbled a telegram to Mr. Truman on a piece of paper which he asked me to take to the Embassy for transmission. The message simply said, "Congratulations on the greatest one-man victory in American history."

During his stay in Rio, Mr. Truman was most gracious to my mother, who was living there with me following the death of my father. On one occasion, he told her that she had a great son, but that it took a wonderful mother to produce a great son. Needless to say, she remained a faithful and loyal Truman devotee until her death in 1964.

In 1950 I was to serve my only tour of duty in the White House as assistant to Averell Harriman, who was assistant to President Truman.

Still later, I was to see Mr. Truman at Wake Island when he met with General MacArthur, and again in the mid-fifties at Fort Leavenworth when we discussed the fact that General MacArthur had not saluted him on his arrival at Wake Island.

When I saw him at Independence in the late fifties, he greeted me smilingly. "Well, Walters, what do you have to say?" I replied, "Only this, thank you, Mr. President!" He looked serious and said, "I understand and appreciate what you have just said."

The United States was fortunate in finding such a man to fill its highest office at a time when history had catapulted our country into a position of leadership and economic and military strength without parallel in human history. He filled this office with simplicity and dignity, tempered with a human touch and with wisdom and authority. He will always live in the hearts of the American people. I feel fortunate that even though my service to him was brief it enabled me to meet this giant among men.

The Organization of American States, or Pan American Organization, comprises all of the countries of North, Central and South America (except Canada and some British-controlled territories). The Organization holds meetings at the ministerial level every few years at regular intervals. Such a meeting was scheduled to be held in Bogotá, the capital of Colombia, in April 1948. Secretary of State George Marshall attended.

I had served as General Marshall's aide and interpreter at the Rio conference in September 1947, and I was still serving as Assistant Military Attaché at the American Embassy in Rio in March 1948. A telegram came from the Department of the Army saying that General Marshall had requested that I proceed to Bogotá to serve him in the same capacity, namely as aide and interpreter, during the Seventh Pan American Conference, which was to take place in the Colombian capital in April.

The Army, of course, agreed; the orders were issued and I flew from Rio up to Trinidad, where I took another plane westward to Barranquilla in Colombia. Here I met with difficulty getting a plane reservation into Bogotá and had to spend two days in Barranquilla. The Del Prado Hotel on the beach was a good place in which to be marooned and I bore up bravely under the hardship. Finally, I flew into Bogotá and went to the American

Embassy, where preparations were under way for the arrival of General Marshall.

The Embassy informed me that I would be living with him in a private house which had been turned over to the principal members of the U.S. delegation to serve as their residence for the duration of the conference. This was a large, handsome red brick house in the Chapinero district of Bogotá, a very well-to-do residential area which belonged to a wealthy Colombian family named Puyana. The family had moved out to their place in the country and left the housekeeper and servants to take care of the house during the stay of the American delegation. Since Bogotá was quite short of hotels at this time, this generous action had been repeated by other Colombian families for all of the other delegates to the Pan American Conference.

General Marshall arrived in Bogotá with his assistant, Brigadier General Pat Carter, and other members of the U.S. delegation who would be living in the Puyana house with him. They were Secretary of Commerce Averell Harriman, whom I met for the first time and who was later to have a significant influence on my life; Assistant Secretary of State Norman Armour; Federal Reserve Chairman William McChesney Martin; Norman Armour's aide, Cecil Lyon; and Sergeant Clarence "Jim" George, later Colonel George, who was General Marshall's aide. The house was large and spacious and we were all comfortably accommodated in the building.

The Seventh Pan American Conference had been under way in Bogotá for several days. The conference was meeting in the capitol building of the country located on the main square at right angles to the cathedral in what was then the heart of downtown Bogotá. Rumors abounded that there would be violence during the conference. I remember that on one occasion, I called with General Marshall on the Italian Ambassador, who stated that he had positive knowledge that the Communists would attempt to disrupt the Pan American Conference and to embarrass the Organization of American States.

The general pattern of activity each day was that General Marshall would drive down to the American Embassy, two or three blocks from the capitol. I generally rode with him. When the time came for the meetings, he would usually walk from the Embassy to the capitol. His commanding figure was easily recognized by most of the bystanders and people would come up and ask for autographs or simply applaud as he walked by.

On April 7, 1948, while I was in General Marshall's office in the capitol, I received a report that the house where we were residing had been attacked by a mob. I immediately called up the house and spoke with the housekeeper and she assured me that nothing of the sort had happened. This was typical of the sort of rumors that we were getting, indicating that on such and such a day something would happen. Nothing happened until April 9. After the morning session of the conference at the capitol, we drove out to the Puyana house for lunch. General Marshall had decided to invite Ellen Veber, the daughter of one of the officials of the Embassy in Bogotá who had been acting in a supervisory capacity in the house to make sure that everything was comfortable for him. While we were having lunch at the dining room table, General Marshall, Secretary of Commerce Averell Harriman, General Carter, Miss Veber, William McChesney Martin, one or two other people and myself, *Life* magazine photographers came in and took some pictures of the luncheon. I always remember this with interest because these photographs were taken only a few minutes before the shooting started.

After the *Life* photographers left, General Carter was called to the telephone. I had a sense that something was amiss. Earlier that morning I had translated articles from several Bogotá newspapers to General Marshall and had commented on the extreme violence of the language used between liberals and conservatives. The language was so vitriolic that it resembled the things we and the Germans used to say about one another during the war. It was not the language generally used between two parties in a democratic society. General Carter came back from the telephone and, in his usual diffident manner, said, "That was the Embassy. They say that some guy by the name of Gaitán has been shot and killed downtown." I was appalled at this information because I knew that Jorge Eliecer Gaitán was the leader of the liberal opposition and a sort of "man on horse-back" or "knight of hope" of the liberals. I realized at once that if this man had indeed been killed, very serious consequences were to follow. I said to General Carter, "If that is true, there is going to be a revolution or a civil war today." He looked at me disapprovingly and said, "Walters, you shouldn't make extreme statements like that in General Marshall's presence." Almost within minutes of this, we began to hear the first sounds of firing around the house. This firing soon became general throughout the whole area. The only weapon we had in the building was a .38-caliber pistol which belonged to Sergeant George, who had been with General Marshall for many years. We did have a couple of Colombian policemen outside the door in the street, but as soon as the shooting began, they took refuge inside the building. A couple of other policemen from the neighborhood also drifted in and took refuge in our residence.

I was concerned because the radio broadcasts that we could hear and were being heard throughout the city were extremely inflammatory. The rebels against the government had seized all eight of the radio stations in Bogotá and were broadcasting impassioned appeals to revolution, passionate appeals for justice and punishment against those responsible for the death of Gaitán. They attacked the President, Mariano Ospina Perez, and the Americans. They also attacked the conservative leader Laureano Gomes and urged the people to go to the residences of "the guilty" and "do justice." They also gave their addresses, ours included. I therefore called the Ministry of War, where I had a friend in the minister's office, and suggested that they send over some soldiers to protect General Marshall and the U.S. delegation. I told him that as far as I could tell all the radio stations were in the hands of either the Communists or the liberals, and they were sharing time on the air and saying that the assassination of Gaitán was the result of a deliberate plot in which General Marshall and the Americans had taken part.

Shortly after my call, even though the War Ministry itself was also under attack, a young Colombian lieutenant and thirteen men reported at the front door. The lieutenant posted his thir-

teen men in front of the house. He then came in and sat stiffly
on a chair inside the lobby. General Marshall had taken a very
calm view of the whole situation, despite the continuous alarm-
ing telephone calls we were getting. They reported fighting
going on all over the city. The Secretary of State was sitting in
the living room reading a Western novel. He looked out of the
window at the soldiers standing there, and then he turned to me
and said, "I would like to speak to the officer in charge of these
men." I came out into the lobby and told the young lieutenant,
who was sitting there in a most military fashion, that General
Marshall wanted to speak to him. He seemed stunned at the
idea that he was to talk to the American Secretary of State who
had been the Chief of Staff during the stirring days of World
War II. He came into the living room where General Marshall
was, with his helmet under his arm and a loud clicking of heels,
he reported to General Marshall that he was Lieutenant Valen-
cia of the Colombian Army, and was in charge of the detachment protecting the U.S. delegation's residence. This young
officer was later to distinguish himself with the Colombian battalion in Korea, and still later became Chief of Staff of his country's Army.

General Marshall asked, "Lieutenant, how many men do you
have?" I translated the question into Spanish and the lieutenant
replied that he had thirteen men. General Marshall cast a glance
through the window and said, "But they are all at the front
door." The lieutenant nodded and said, "Yes, sir." General
Marshall then said to him, "Well, what are you going to do if
they come to the back door?" The lieutenant said, "I don't
know, sir." General Marshall smiled, probably thinking of the
millions of men he had moved around during World War II, al-
locating them to MacArthur and Eisenhower in the different
theaters of war. He told the young Colombian lieutenant, "If I
remember my small-unit tactics correctly, when you are defending a perimeter, what you do is to garrison that perimeter lightly
and place a large, centrally located, mobile reserve at a point
where it can move rapidly to any threatened point on the perimeter." The lieutenant nodded but looked somewhat confused

and said, "Yes, sir; but what shall I do?" General Marshall smiled and said, "Put one man at the front door, one man at the back door and all the others in the garage, where they can keep warm tonight." (Bogotá is located at 8,000 feet and the nights are extremely cold.) The lieutentant digested this, nodded, clicked his heels, about-faced and went out into the lobby. He went out the front door and carried these measures into effect: he put a small detachment of two men at the front door, sent two men to the back door and put all the others in the large, multi-car garage, where there was plenty of room for them and where they were sheltered from the chill that was falling with the oncoming night.

By this time firing was going on all over the neighborhood and there were two bodies lying in the street about a block up from our house where we were. I saw them when I went out and looked up the street about five o'clock that afternoon. There was also a heavy attack under way against the large Jesuit college up the hill. This mixed liberal and Communist revolution had a considerable anti-clerical bias, a fact which was almost entirely passed over in silence by descriptions of these events.

Later in the evening, after it had become dark, a truck drove up to the front door. In it were a large number of very senior U.S. non-commissioned officers. I asked them what they had in the way of weapons and they replied that they had no weapons since they were clerks and typists. I said, "In that case, I'm sorry, we can't keep you here; we've got forty-six people feeding in this house right now." They looked disappointed and drove on.

Darkness had now fallen over the embattled city and the sounds of firing were audible from all directions. In spite of this, we had an excellent meal prepared by the staff under the stalwart direction of the Puyanas' housekeeper. In the meantime, the problem arose of what to do about Miss Veber, whose parents were calling up and expressing great anxiety concerning her. It was decided that I would take her home since I spoke Spanish. We called her parents and told them we would be leaving shortly in General Marshall's car and that I would bring her to her home. We drove through the darkened streets of the city

—no street lights were lit—and even though the distance was short, it was an eerie trip. As we pulled up to her front door, the door opened and her parents looked out anxiously. I took her to the front door and said good night. I doubt if I have ever said good night to any girl faster than I did to her. I then got back in the car with General Marshall's faithful and undaunted driver Aníbal. He was from Barranquilla and kept repeating over and over, "These people in Bogotá are a bad lot; they're a bad lot. They are an untrustworthy lot." He drove me uneventfully back to the Puyana house and here I found the rest of the U.S. delegation listening anxiously to the radio reports describing what was going on.

One of the strange things about this revolution was that in the first three hours after the assassination of Gaitán, the liberals and the Communists seized all eight radio stations in Bogotá. Some were controlled by the liberals, some by the Communists. In some stations we could hear them quarreling over whose turn it was to broadcast. The curious thing is that either they must have had some foreknowledge of Gaitán's death or else extraordinarily effective contingency plans which they were able to implement at a moment's notice. Their speed and efficiency in doing this were noted and commented upon by Mr. Harriman.

All through the evening hours we heard these stations broadcasting the most inflammatory appeals to revolution, fierce attacks on President Ospina Perez, attacks on the Americans, attacks on the conservatives, the repeated addresses of many of the people they were attacking including ours. The broadcasts urged the people to go to these places and "do justice to the criminals who were guilty of the death of the people's hero, Jorge Eliecer Gaitán."

Nothing happened in the immediate vicinity of our house, and one by one the other members of the U.S. delegation drifted off to their rooms to try and go to sleep. Not so Mr. Harriman, who was intensely interested in the radio broadcasts and pressed me to give him running translations of what was being said. Now, simultaneous interpretation, even under the best of circumstances, is a very tiring job. Doing it under these circum-

IN BOGOTÁ WITH GENERAL MARSHALL 157

stances, in a city torn by fighting from one end to the other, made it even more exhausting. Mr. Harriman was insatiable in his desire for translation of everything that was being broadcast.

One of the great enigmas of this whole extraordinary day was the lack of any indication as to what the Colombian Armed Forces intended to do about these widespread disturbances. Until the fall of night, most of the fighting had been taking place between the city and national police on the one hand and the rebels on the other. There had been no sign of the Army in town at all. About eleven o'clock at night we began to get some indications that the Army had decided to intervene and restore order in Bogotá. This was confirmed in a most dramatic fashion. I was listening with Mr. Harriman to Radio Nacional of Colombia broadcasting torrents of revolutionary rhetoric when there was a sudden sound of firing, a banging of doors, distant shouting and then an agonized voice shouting into the microphone, "My God, my God; the Army is murdering the people! Comrades, come at once to Radio Nacional of Colombia and defend the voice of the people! The Army is murdering the people." There were more sounds of shots, more shouts and banging of doors, and then a quiet voice said, "Ladies and gentlemen, this is Radio Nacional of Colombia. We will now broadcast the communiqué of the Armed Forces concerning the disturbances which have occurred today in the capital of the Republic. These disturbances are being put down by the Armed Forces and order will be restored."

This was the first clear statement that the Armed Forces of Colombia had decided to support the legally constituted government of President Ospina Perez and would intervene actively to put an end to the appalling disorders that were taking place in the city. Between eleven o'clock at night and three o'clock in the morning we heard the other seven radio stations change hands in a similar dramatic fashion. As the last of the radio stations were taken over by the Armed Forces, it was nearly three o'clock in the morning and I asked Mr. Harriman if he did not think we should go to bed. He looked dubious, but finally nodded and said, "I guess there is nothing more we can do now." I went up to my room, lay down and fell quickly to sleep in spite of the fact that there was shooting still going on all over the city.

The next morning a few other members of the American delegation drifted in, including Ambassador Walter Donnelly, the American Ambassador to Venezuela. He was married to a Colombian and had excellent contacts in both Colombian parties. He offered to work with both Colombian parties to seek a means of bringing an end to the disorder and restoring some sort of harmony between the contending factions. At the time we had no idea how difficult this was to be. These disorders were later to degenerate into a sort of endemic civil war that was to go on for many years. It was finally ended by a pact between the liberal and conservative parties agreeing that each four years they would alternate in occupying the presidency. It was only through this pact that the bloody and long-drawn-out hostilities were finally brought to an end. All of this was far in the future and we did not perceive it at the time.

The next day there were many rumors that some of the delegations wanted to leave the city and reconvene the conference elsewhere. A rump session of the U.S. delegates met in our house and decided that U.S. policy should be that we would not allow the Organization of American States to be pushed around by a disorderly band of revolutionaries and that it should be U.S. policy that the conference continue in Bogotá. From contacts with other delegations, however, it was clear that many of them were extremely alarmed and favored moving the conference to some other site such as Lima, Peru.

During the daylight hours of Saturday, there was considerably less shooting and Army troops appeared all over town. However, at nightfall on Saturday, the shooting began again in earnest all over the city. The Army proclaimed a curfew and announced that there would be control of all movement in the streets after dark. In the midafternoon, I had asked to go down to an apartment house in another part of Bogotá to get General Marshall's secretary, Mildred Asbjornson, who lived there, and bring her to the Puyana house, as General Marshall wanted to dictate some telegrams. I brought her to the house and for several hours General Marshall dictated and she typed. Later when it became dark, I was again given the mission, since I spoke Spanish and could talk my way through the curfew, of taking her back to the apartment house where she and other staff members of the U.S. delegation were staying. Again, I did not relish this mission but I could find no way of decently avoiding it. I liked Miss Asbjornson very much and had great respect for her efficiency. I was worried about getting her home, but even more worried that people would realize just how worried I was. So I accepted the task of taking her home, trying my best to look daring or at least unconcerned.

We started back to her apartment and were driving down one of the main streets of Bogotá, Calle Séptima. This means Seventh Avenue. We came to an Army barricade across the street. Now, one of the disturbing things that occurred more or less regularly during these disturbances was that when you were challenged by a Colombian soldier, he pointed the rifle directly at you with the safety catch off. A young Colombian lieutenant stepped up to the car and said, "Who are you and where are you going?" I explained that I was the aide to the chief of the U.S. delegation, that this was his secretary and I was taking her back to her quarters in the Carreras Rojas apartments farther down Calle Séptima. The lieutenant said, "Well, you can't go down Calle Séptima, there are snipers in a number of the buildings who are shooting and we are in the process of cleaning them out." I said, "Yes, but I have to get this young lady home. How can I do it?" He said, "Go down the next street over, all the way down to the back door of Carreras Rojas, and then you can get into the building from the back." I told the driver to do this and as I did, Millie Asbjornson, who did not understand Spanish, asked me, "What did he say?" I replied, "He said that we were not allowed to go down this street and we should go down the next one." She looked worried and said, "That's not what he said, and I'm not coming out after dark again." Fortunately, we were able to get her back safely to her apartment house. She went upstairs and while she was in the living room used by the staff members of the U.S. delegation, a burst of machine-gun

fire came through the window and splattered on the ceiling. I
then returned uneasily to the residence of General Marshall,
being stopped once or twice by Army patrols on the way. Aníbal,
the driver, kept muttering, "*Gente mala, gente mala, estos bogotanos*" (Bad people, bad people, these bogotanos).

The next morning was Sunday, and as daylight came, the
firing died away and the day dawned in relative quiet. I decided
that I would go to church at the cathedral. Cecil Lyon, who was
also a Catholic, decided to go with me. We asked General
Marshall if we could use his car and he said, "Yes, you can; but
be sure you bring it back. I may need it." We set off with Aníbal
for the cathedral, which was located in Capitol Square. We
reached Capitol Square without any difficulties and the car
stopped in front of the cathedral. I went up the steps to the
massive old colonial building and found to my dismay that the
doors were locked. I was greatly disturbed at this. For the doors
of the cathedral to be locked in a South American city on a Sunday morning meant that things were far, far from normal and
that the absence of shooting at that time was not as significant
as I had thought. Cecil Lyon, who spoke excellent Spanish,
seemed quite undaunted by this and said to the driver, "Aníbal,
drive into that square where the Granada Hotel is; there is another church there, maybe it will be open." Muttering under his
breath, Aníbal drove us to the square. As we entered it, we saw
that under the trees in the central part of the square there were
many soldiers who had stacked their rifles and were lying around
on the ground smoking or talking to one another. Just as we
drove into the square, a number of snipers in various buildings
around it opened fire on the soldiers under the trees. The soldiers immediately unstacked their rifles and began firing back at
the invisible snipers in the buildings. This produced pandemo-
nium in the square. Such drivers as there were put their foot
down on the accelerator and their hand down on the horn and
took off in all directions. Aníbal started to do the same. Cecil
leaned forward, tapped him on the shoulder and said, "Aníbal,
stop the car." I asked, somewhat concerned, "Cecil, do you
think this is a good idea?" "Yes," replied Cecil in a very quiet

voice. "People generally shoot at moving cars, very rarely at parked ones." I meditated over the value of this thought while I bent low and examined the carpet on the floor of the car and checked to see if my shoelaces were tied. In a moment I looked over the driver's shoulder into the square; it was entirely empty of people except for the soldiers firing at the building trying to hit the snipers they could not see. I said to Cecil Lyon, "Cecil, don't you think we can go to church now?" Cecil looked calmly around the square and said, "Yes, now we can. Aníbal, drive to the church." We drove over to the church and Cecil, a polished diplomat and very much the so-called "striped-pants diplomat," got out of the car and started up the steps into the church without a backward glance at the fusillade taking place behind us. On about the fourth step he paused and without actually turning around to look at what appeared to him to be a vulgar brawl, he said to the driver, "Aníbal, we'll be in here about forty-five minutes. You can come back for us then." "Oh no, señor," replied Aníbal. "Today I too am going to church." And he dashed past us into the church. The church was an old building with heavy stone walls and actually afforded very considerable protection.

I noticed that as the mass progressed and the sermon began, the priest exhorted the congregation to "get down on your knees; you won't have as far to fall." There were a lot of people praying very hard in the church that morning; not all of them were Colombians! When we came out, the sniping had ended. The soldiers once again were standing around under the trees and quiet seemed to have been restored. We drove back to the Puyana house. We could hear some distant sporadic shooting but nothing intense in our immediate area. I was greatly relieved to arrive back at the Puyana house and hoped that I would not have to go out again that day.

A little later, to my dismay, I saw Mr. Harriman making evident preparations to go to a lunch with President Ospina Perez to which he had been invited several days before. When it was clear he was going, General Marshall asked him, "Harriman, do you have any reason to believe that this lunch is still on?" Harriman replied, "Well, it has not been canceled, and, you know, when the President of a country invites you, it is a command performance. I've got to go." General Marshall said, "Harriman, this could be very dangerous. You heard about the difficulties Walters had this morning." Mr. Harriman replied, "I've been expendable before and I guess I can be expendable now." Turning to me, he said, "Come, Walters, let's go." This, of course, was the actual development I had feared. I had hoped that he would not need me, but he decided that he would. There was no decent way in which I could back out of it, so I climbed into the car with him and we started to drive downtown. I was looking cautiously in all directions and up all the side streets. Mr. Harriman was sitting in the back seat fascinated by a report on the economic production of the province of Cundinamarca and appeared completely unconcerned by what might be going on in the city.

We drove again into the square in front of the capitol and off to one side was the President's palace. In front of the palace there was a single light tank. As we came across the square, the turret traversed, following us. I could not help but wonder if the shell would explode inside the car or whether it would go straight out the back if the tank were to fire. Fortunately for us, the tank did not fire. There was a cluster of five small American flags on the radiator of General Marshall's car. These may have helped. We drove up to the front door of the presidential palace, which was an old colonial building. The sentry box was empty, another disturbing phenomenon. The door of the presidential palace was closed, but there was a huge circular brass knocker on the door. Mr. Harriman looked at me impatiently and said, "Knock." I reached over and knocked heavily three times. Slowly the door half opened. A butler in a white tie stood there holding a Tommy gun in his hand, saying, "Who are you and what do you want?" Mr. Harriman, completely unconcerned, took off his hat and handed it to the butler, who fumbled with the Tommy gun and the hat, not knowing which one to put down first. He then opened the door and we walked into the entrance hall of the presidential palace. We were shown to chairs in the lobby and we sat down and waited. While we were waiting, we saw a number of people come out of side doors or up on a mezzanine which surrounded this hall and look down at us dubiously, nodding and shaking their heads, apparently puzzled at our presence.

After a short wait, we were shown up to the President's office. This was a sort of glass bubble on the top of the old Spanish colonial building. There were several bullet holes in the bubble. The President told us that on Friday and Saturday he had been unable to occupy this office since snipers were shooting at it from adjacent buildings, and it was only in the late hours of Saturday that they had been cleaned out and he had been able to reoccupy his office. The President told Mr. Harriman that he had had nothing to do with the assassination of Gaitán. He was actually out opening a commercial fair when he received the report of the attack on Gaitán, and had been able to make his way back to the presidential palace only with the greatest difficulty.

The President said, "I am the constitutionally elected President of Colombia. They are calling upon me to resign. I had nothing to do with the assassination of Gaitán. I will not resign and, in fact, I will not leave this palace while I am alive, during this emergency. I intend to remain here and exercise my prerogatives as the constitutionally elected President of this country." President Ospina Perez spoke superb English. He had been educated at an American university. He had a lion's mane of white hair and was an extraordinarily dignified and impressive figure. He looked at Mr. Harriman and smiled and said, "Mr. Harriman, I suppose you've come for the lunch to which I invited you." Mr. Harriman said, "Yes, I have." The President said, "You may be interested in knowing that I invited a total of twenty-four people and you are the only ones who have shown up for the lunch. Sit down; we will have lunch."

We sat down around the President's desk and food was brought to us by his wife. In South America when the President's wife is waiting on table, things are grim indeed. I could not help but admire the calm and dignity of President Ospina Perez. And I could not help but feel a certain pride, as an Amer-

ican, in the courage shown by Mr. Harriman and in the fact that
he was the only guest who had shown up for the President's
lunch. I was there too, but I must confess in all truthfulness
that my presence, unlike Mr. Harriman's, was not voluntary.

On our return to the Puyana house, the city was once again
quiet. That evening, however, as soon as darkness fell, firing was
heard from all parts of the city. The snipers came out at night
and this was an infuriating problem for the Army. Nothing is
more frustrating to a soldier than being fired upon by snipers in
a built-up area. It is almost impossible to see where the snipers
are as they move from window to window, and it is very slow
and bloody business to clean them out. It requires that the
buildings be cordoned off and that a room-to-room search be
made. Under these circumstances, it is not infrequent for soldiers, exasperated by the death of one or more of their comrades, to either push the sniper through the window or shoot
him first and then throw his body out of the window as a sort of
lesson to the others. There was some of this in Bogotá.

By Monday, there was enough calm in the daytime to begin
holding meetings of the various delegations. I accompanied
General Marshall on a number of visits to other delegations. He
made it quite plain that it was the United States' desire that the
conference continue. The Argentine Foreign Minister, Juan
Bramuglia, always a great defender of national sovereignty,
suggested that the United States drop the 82nd Airborne Division into Bogotá. General Marshall said that he could not consider such a thing, which would be a violation of Colombian
sovereignty. A number of other, smaller countries also asked
that the United States take some sort of action to restore order,
and they were told quite plainly that the United States would
not do so. This was a Colombian problem and the Colombians
would have to take care of it. Many of the delegations seemed
quite concerned for their safety, others less so.

In the afternoon the former American Ambassador to Brazil,
William Douglas Pawley, asked me to go out to University City,
some five or six miles away, to see if I could locate his pilots and
bring them to him. Mr. Pawley had a DC-3 aircraft which was

his own personal property. It belonged neither to the State Department nor to the Air Force. I said that I would go but that I would wear a uniform as I would have to pass through many barricades held both by rebels and by the Army. I put on my uniform, and after being stopped a number of times, I reached University City, where I found one of Pawley's pilots, Grady Matthews. I picked him up and started back into town. About this time I was stopped by a Colombian lieutenant colonel who asked me who I was. I told him. He said, "I've been out of touch with the War Ministry. I cannot get them on the phone. Would you take a message to the War Ministry for me, telling them what the situation is. We control this area and we also control the airport." I had seen enough red flags flying downtown to know that I was not totally neutral in this battle. I agreed to take the message for him, and on my way back to the Puyana house, I stopped by the War Ministry, where I saw some Colombian officers I knew, and delivered the message from the lieutenant colonel, who was in control of both University City and the airport. The War Ministry was delighted to receive this news, as they had been wondering what was happening at both places.

Mr. Pawley, who was at the U.S. delegation's house even though he actually was living with Mrs. Pawley at another house he had rented, took a roll of banknotes out of his pocket, handed five thousand dollars to Grady Matthews and said, "I want you to fly to Panama. Buy about twenty hams, twenty turkeys, twenty pots of caviar and twenty pots of foie gras." General Marshall asked, "What are you going to do with all this, Pawley?" Pawley replied, "General, these delegations are living on Army rations. They think they are in a state of siege. If I can get them some of the luxuries of life, they will settle back and vote to keep the conference here." I could not help but marvel at his accurate perception of their probable reaction. Matthews flew to Panama, came back later that day with the supplies, and Mr. Pawley went around to each delegation, leaving a turkey, a ham, a pot of foie gras and a pot of caviar. On the following day a rump meeting of the conference met in a schoolhouse, away from the center of town, and voted unanimously to keep the conference in Bogotá. This was a triumph for the United States. It was also a triumph for Mr. Pawley's skill in understanding the Latin American mentality. He had, after all, spent most of his life in contact with them—no American understood them better. To the best of my knowledge, he was never reimbursed from any fund for the five thousand dollars of his own money which he put out. Five thousand dollars in 1948 was a very considerable sum of money. Bill Pawley was a great ambassador, a gallant, dedicated American and a good friend.

As the sessions resumed in this schoolhouse, there was considerable concern about General Marshall's safety, and it was decided that each day he would go to the meetings by a different route. Someone had the idea that it might be a good idea to send me—I looked at some distance something like him—in the big car, and General Marshall would then go in another car. All of this, of course, was unknown to General Marshall. It was explained to him that for some technical reason he would go in the other car. I agreed to, in a sense, be the decoy, but I refused absolutely to carry out one of the suggestions which was made, namely, that I would wear a gray fedora hat like the one General Marshall wore. At this time I was a young man. I had never worn a hat before I came to the Army and I never wore a hat outside of uniform. And I said, "If I'm going to be killed, I'm damned if I'm going to be killed in a gray fedora hat." So I refused to wear it.

The simultaneous-translation equipment which had been available in the capitol had been damaged or destroyed and there was no translation equipment available in the school. I was called upon to translate and as the conference started, I was the only interpreter present because the other interpreters were marooned at University City. It was very tedious since I had to translate whatever was said in Spanish into English, Portuguese and even French for the Haitians. After a few sentences, the Brazilian Foreign Minister, João Neves da Fontoura, said with a smile, "Normally, we insist on the Portuguese language but in view of the emergency conditions and the fact that we Brazilians understand Spanish as well as we understand our own language, I will be happy to dispense with the Portuguese translation." I looked expectantly at the Haitian, hoping that he would make the same offer since he was the only one of all the delegates present who spoke French. He was also the Haitian Ambassador to the United States and spoke excellent English. He still did not waive the French translation. I was therefore compelled to translate in Spanish, English and French throughout these rump sessions for a day or two until the other interpreters, who were out at University City, could be located and brought in to the meetings.

During these events President Truman had been most anxious concerning General Marshall's safety and well-being. Now that the conference had resumed, he was urging General Marshall to return to Washington and leave the technical discussions to other senior members of the U.S. delegation.

One other amusing incident occurred during this conference. One of the difficulties the Colombian Army was having was the lack of coats for the soldiers at night. Most of the soldiers had been flown up to Bogotá from the warm tropical valleys or coast lands elsewhere in Colombia. As I have mentioned previously, the nights were extremely cold in Bogotá, and the soldiers, accustomed to the tropical heat, suffered greatly from the cold. Appeals were made to the U.S. delegation and General Marshall finally sent a message to Panama asking that four thousand raincoats be shipped to Bogotá. This was done and these raincoats were distributed to the soldiers who had restored and were maintaining order in Bogotá. When General Marshall was Secretary of Defense some time later, this bill came to him with the recommendation that the Defense Department not pay it since it was a State Department expense. It was therefore returned to the State Department. Subsequently, the bill went to the American Red Cross at a time when General Marshall was president of the American Red Cross, and he said that when he received the bill for the second time, he felt he really should pay it and did.

General Marshall left Bogotá and I stayed on with the U.S.

delegation until the end of April. The days were quiet but at night there was continuous shooting. The damage and vandalism in the city were beyond belief. Bogotá looked as if it had been through a major air raid. Hollow, burned-out shells of buildings stood all over the downtown area. I went to Bolívar's historic home and found that this too had been set on fire. It was hard to believe that any patriotic Colombian would countenance the burning of the home of the liberator. There was a nihilistic, anarchic character to this revolt. Subsequently, it appeared that Gaitán had been assassinated by a mentally deficient individual not acting from any particular political or economic motivation.

The important thing was that the conference was not intimidated. General Marshall stayed there until all of the daytime violence was over, and the Organization of American States gave an excellent example to the world that it could not be intimidated by this kind of violence. This was one of the early attempts at terrorism; unfortunately such attempts were to recur many times in coming years. Fidel Castro's name came to my attention for the first time in Bogotá. He was reported to have been one of the ringleaders in the disorders.

During these events I had developed a very close association with Mr. Harriman, who was intensely interested in everything that was going on. He had indicated to me that he would shortly be resigning as Secretary of Commerce and going to Europe to help set up the organization of the Marshall Plan, the purpose of which was to help the European countries get back on their feet. Thus they could resist the internal threat of communism arising from the discontent of their peoples, who were still living in extremely difficult conditions three years after the end of the Second World War. He did not at any time say anything to me about wanting me to go to Europe with him. However, when I flew down to Panama at the end of April, I called on my old wartime chief, Lieutenant General Willis D. Crittenberger, under whom I had served in Italy, and he said to me, "Mr. Harriman was very impressed with your actions in Bogotá, and he intends to ask the President to have you assigned to his office in Paris." This came as quite a surprise to me since Mr. Harriman had not discussed this possibility with me.

I flew back to Brazil, stopping in the middle of the night at Belém and meeting my mother there for a few minutes as she was flying up to Panama for some medical care. I flew back to Rio and a few days later I received a phone call from the Department of the Army in Washington. They informed me that Mr. Harriman had asked President Truman to have me assigned as his military assistant in Paris and the President had approved this. They wanted to know when I could leave, and I said, "You're not really asking me a question about accepting, are you?" They replied, "No. Since the President has approved your assignment, it is not really a question of whether you want to go or not. All we want to know is when you can leave." I said, "Well, my mother is in Panama. I have a house, a car, a dog to take care of. I can arrange for their shipment, and can probably leave in a week or ten days." They said, "That won't do. You will leave the day after tomorrow." They were right. Two days later, I left Brazil. Fortunately, friends were able to help me with the move. My mother returned from Panama and carried out the actual move.

On the day I left Rio I was at the airport waiting for my plane when the deputy commander of the Brazilian Expeditionary Force, who now commanded the Rio garrison, showed up at the airport with a guard of honor and a band. I reviewed the guard of honor and the band played "God Bless America." An American passenger who was there turned to me and said, "I don't mean to be offensive, but how come as a major you rate a guard of honor?" I explained to him that I had been the liaison officer with the Brazilian division in Italy during the war, that the present commander of the Rio garrison had been the number-two man in that Expeditionary Force and that we were close friends and this was a gesture from him.

Thus, after three years in Brazil I left for my next mission, the mission to the Marshall Plan.

Six years of war had left all of Europe prostrate. The long German occupation, Allied bombings and the fighting which accompanied liberation had devastated almost all of the Continent and in 1948 there prevailed in Europe an atmosphere of hopelessness and despair. The breakdown of governments, the severe winters and above all, the feeling that they could not get out of this morass by themselves had sapped the will of the Europeans to recover.

The damage to the industrial plant of Europe, the war-fed dispersal of the pool of skilled labor, the machinery, worn out from six years of intensive wartime production and the lack of spare parts, had contributed to the creation of a situation where Europe could not replace its own machine tools, renew its infrastructure or manufacture enough goods to pay for the raw materials that would be required for industrial recovery. There was little capital available for new investment or plant renewal. Most European currencies were either not convertible or convertible at completely artificial rates. Financial restrictions on the movement of money were almost universal. Each nation was attempting to recover on its own without much regard to what its neighbors were doing. Food was still rationed almost everywhere three years after the end of the war. The breakdown of the transportation and distribution systems, the lack of mechanization for agriculture and the shortage of fertilizers all contributed to the generalized loss of productivity of the European economies.

The United States, either directly or through international organizations, had been providing food, goods and money in a somewhat stopgap and disorderly fashion. The prevailing economic distress was also causing political problems in many of the countries. In Greece the Communists were attempting to seize power by force and to establish a Communist government. In this attempt, they were being aided by Greece's Communist neighbors. Turkey was under tremendous pressure from her huge Soviet neighbor to make territorial concessions and take a more friendly attitude toward the U.S.S.R.

It was against this background and in line with a policy to contain Soviet expansion that President Truman went to the Congress to ask for a program to assist Greece and Turkey. These two countries were under some form of military pressure as well as in economic difficulties. Bipartisan support for President Truman's program ensured its approval. It was a time when there was a widespread understanding in the United States of the fact that the threat to human freedom was economic and political as well as military. From that program there developed within the United States government an understanding that if Europe was to recover it would have to be on the basis of a broad program that would envision closer unity among the European nations and their working together for the common good in close collaboration with the United States.

At Harvard University, General George Marshall in 1947 in a speech first proposed the plan that was to bear his name. It provided for a broad framework of co-operation between the United States and those nations of Europe which wished to join to work out an assistance program that would enable our European partners to recover and stand on their own feet again. The free nations of Europe enthusiastically welcomed the idea. The U.S.S.R. prevented its allies from joining. A European organization was set up to work with the U. S. European Recovery Program. The United States established a central office in Paris to work with the Europeans in developing the programming and distribution of U.S. assistance. Averell Harriman, former Ambassador to the U.S.S.R. and Great Britain, as well as former Secretary of Commerce, was named to head this office. He asked that I be assigned to him and I was.

A historic movement was at hand. For the first time in human history, a nation, the United States, was about to finance its competitors back into competition with it. In this context my mission to the Marshall Plan began.

When I arrived in Washington, I found that all the hurry about leaving Rio de Janeiro was unnecessary. As a matter of fact, I was assigned to go to Europe on an Army transport called the *Jarrett N. Huddleston.* The transport was scheduled to take eleven days to reach Bremerhaven. Because of rough seas, it took fifteen days. When I arrived in Bremerhaven, I was appalled at the destruction which I could see everywhere, not only around the dock but everywhere else in the whole city. The war seemed to have ended the day before and not three years earlier. I took the Nord Express, which was one of the few international trains running in Europe at that time, into Paris. On arrival in Paris I stayed at the California Hotel just off the Champs Elysées until I could find a place to live. I left my mother in Rio to close the house, to ship my household goods and the dog and to get back to the United States by herself. Since she was well into her seventies by this time, it was no mean feat for a lady of her age, but she was a very remarkable woman and carried out the whole move successfully. This was in July and she was not to join me in Paris until November.

After arriving in Paris, I reported in to Mr. Harriman and to my new immediate chief, Lieutenant Colonel Charles H. Bonesteel, III, who was the Army Attaché at Large. We both had offices on the second floor of the Hotel Talleyrand on the Place de la Concorde. This is in a sense the corresponding building to the American Embassy on the other side of the square. This historic building had been the home of the famous French Foreign Minister and served as the headquarters for the U.S. recovery program in Europe until it was taken over many years later as a location for the offices of the American consulate general in Paris. It is still used for that purpose.

I began to look for an apartment and finally located a very nice small apartment on Avenue Lannes overlooking the Bois de Boulogne. I then returned to Bremerhaven from Paris to pick up my car and drove it back to Paris. During the long summer days of July 1948, I found Europe still prostrate. The damage and the shock of the war were still visible everywhere and the only ray of light was the manifest determination of the United States to help our European friends get back on their feet and recover their economic stability and to help them offer their people a better life in freedom than anything communism could promise. I worked for Mr. Harriman in many non-military activities. I used to travel with him extensively throughout the countries of the Marshall Plan, frequently translating for him during his discussions with political and labor leaders and with financial experts and other high-level figures in the various countries. This was for me an extraordinarily instructive, interesting and rewarding experience. It broadened my own horizons and brought me into contact with the economic, social and financial problems of the world, with which I previously had very little contact. Sometimes it was embarrassing because I would have to translate some rather complicated financial or currency convertibility matter which I did not fully understand and it is quite impossible to translate adequately into another language something you do not understand yourself. Many people believe that this type of translation is a purely mechanical process. It is quite impossible to convey in another language someone's meaning unless you have fully grasped and understood it in your own. Extensive travels made it possible for me to see Germany, Belgium, Holland, Luxembourg, France, Italy—in fact, all of the countries of Western Europe—at a time when the smoke of war had not fully cleared from the scarred landscape. The cities still lay in ruins, many of the factories lay idle and silent, the machinery damaged or gone. With raw materials unavailable and petroleum products not obtainable, Paris, the city of light, was dark. Only one out of every two street lights was lit and that was lit at half intensity. Not a shop window nor a theater marquee was lit. Belgium was much better. On one occasion I drove from Paris to Brussels. On crossing the border, I was struck by the fact that in the Belgian town of Mons there were bright lights everywhere. I passed in front of a bakery store and, to my amazement, in the windows I saw cakes with whipped cream on the top. I had come from Paris, where bread was rationed and whipped cream was illegal. I went in and asked the Belgian baker cautiously whether any of this was rationed. He said it was not, so I ate one of the whipped cream cakes. It tasted so good I asked for another one. The Belgian looked at me ironically and said to me, "Do you come from France?" I said that I did, thinking he meant where did I just come from. I had forgotten that for many years the Belgians had been the butt of many French jokes which usually revolved around how stupid and what hayseeds the Belgians were. When I replied that I did come from France, the Belgian baker looked at me and said with obvious satisfaction, "Some difference in Belgium, isn't it?" I must admit it was. Later that night I got to Brussels and was astounded to find that in Brussels all the city lights were on. Signs of hard work and recovery were everywhere, and Belgium seemed to be leading Europe out of the postwar morass. I found that nothing was rationed in Belgium, neither food nor soap nor any of the things for which I had grown accustomed to giving ration coupons in Paris. I must say that I found Belgium a welcome island of prosperity and normalcy in an otherwise shadowy and dark Europe. It was later to become the seat of the European Common Market and the heart of the Continent.

Today after many years have passed, large numbers of people have forgotten what conditions were like in 1948. They have forgotten that we then embarked upon an enterprise without precedent in history, that of financing our competitors back into competition with us. Within a few short years of the beginning of the Marshall Plan, the wheels of European industry were turning again, and the dawn of prosperity and a living standard never previously reached in these countries lay ahead for these war-devastated nations of the old world. Both our allies and our enemies received assistance in every field on a scale which has no parallel in all the recorded history of mankind. Human memories are short, but as a participant, I cannot forget that for the freedom and prosperity of Europe we gave first our men in war and then our treasure in peace without counting or measuring the sacrifice. When I say that many have forgotten, this was not true everywhere. There were places where there was understanding and gratitude. But many regarded the whole recovery program as some sort of clever scheme by the United States to create customers. If the Volkswagen factory, the Fiat factory, the Renault factory soon began producing vehicles again in large numbers, it was in no small part due to the assistance that we rendered in machine tools and in the purchase of equipment, which was not then obtainable in Europe, to start production going again.

In Holland I saw a Marshall Plan poster put up by the Dutch government in Dutch bakeries, which said, "One half your daily bread is baked with Marshall help." In Austria installations put up for the tourist industry also credited the Marshall Plan. But by and large no matter how hard we tried, it was difficult to make the average European understand the magnitude of the assistance which we were rendering and the disinterested spirit in which we were rendering it. Yes, we hoped the Europeans would become prosperous and buy things from us, but this was not the chief motivation of the Marshall Plan. The chief motivation was to help our friends and allies and former enemies who were living in dire days, and it was to prevent the advance of communism across a field of human misery.

Rendering the assistance was not always easy. It required extensive planning on the part of the recipient country as well. They had to present to us a program stating what they planned to do with the U.S. currency we would make available to them. At the same time they had to deposit in their own local banks an equivalent sum in the local currency which could then be used, with our consent, for further recovery and improvement programs within the country for uses which did not require foreign currency. In a sense, the money worked twice—once in the form of dollars to get equipment or raw materials from the United States or elsewhere which were not available in Europe, and secondly as local currency within the country. The elaboration of the programs each year was quite difficult for some of the smaller countries. France, the United Kingdom, Germany and Italy were able to do this kind of planning. For the others it required a kind of expertise which they did not always have. In a sense, the Marshall Plan, for many of these nations, was a school in economic planning. It was a school and an experiment to bring the Europeans together. Many Europeans to this day believe that the United States is or was opposed to European unity. During this period, almost all of the assistance we gave was conditioned on steps toward achieving European unity. This was a time of giants in Europe. In France there was Robert Schuman, born in Luxembourg, who had served as a German soldier in World War I and had lived to become Prime Minister and Foreign Minister of France. There was the gigantic figure of Konrad Adenauer, who led Germany out of the ashes of defeat to take her place among the civilized nations of the world. In Italy there was Alcide de Gasperi, who had started his political life as a member of the Austrian parliament representing the Italian minority in the Austrian empire. There were giants in the little countries too, like Paul Henri Spaak of Belgium. With all of these Harriman had an extraordinary close relationship. He was a man who inspired confidence in his grasp of problems, in his integrity and in his ability to make the United States government understand what was needed and more often than not to get it. It was truly a heroic time. There was so much to do, but there were giants and there was a will.

I recall on one occasion going to Essen with Mr. Harriman. I was appalled at the magnitude of the destruction that lay everywhere around us. We went to visit a German family, who lived in a basement. We talked to them briefly and when we left, I said to Mr. Harriman, "Do you think they can ever rebuild this?" He said, "Yes, they can." I said, "What makes you so sure?" He said, "Did you see what was on the table in that basement?" And I replied that on the table I had seen a bowl of flowers. Mr. Harriman said, "That's right, any people who in the midst of this desolation think of putting flowers on the table will rebuild the ruins." I must say that at that time I did not think that even if I lived to be a very old man, I would ever see a Europe prosperous and rebuilt, and yet within ten years one had to look hard for the physical traces of war.

In most of the countries of Europe the principal problem was the paralysis of industry and the negligible production taking place in those countries. In one country, Greece, there was actual military conflict going on. Greece was under attack from her Communist neighbor on the outside, and from the Greek Communist party from within. This Greek civil war was to sap the energies of Greece and slow recovery in that country for a very long time. On New Year's Day, 1949, I went to Athens with Mr. Harriman. He seemed to have a proclivity for traveling on holidays. Almost invariably on Thanksgiving Day, or the Fourth of July, or New Year's Day, we were traveling somewhere with him. He was a tireless man and dedicated. He was passionately devoted to the freedom, unity and recovery of Europe in friendship with us. We flew to Athens and arrived there at a very awkward time. Shortly before we arrived the Minister of the Interior had been assassinated in downtown Athens and heavy security precautions were in effect for us. At this time one could not travel outside Athens in the daytime without a military escort, and one could not travel at night at all outside the cities. Many of the Greek leaders did not speak English, but spoke French, and in this case I was able to be of some assistance to Mr. Harriman in his discussions with them.

In Greece the overwhelming problem was not economic. The overwhelming problem was the attack by the externally supported Communist guerrillas all over the country and the government's consequent needs for military assistance. Mr. Truman had responded in an extraordinarily unselfish fashion to this by sending not only military equipment but a large group of U.S. officers to assist the Greek Armed Forces in facing up to the naked threat to which their country was being subjected at this time. I translated for Mr. Harriman in his discussions with the

Minister of Economic Co-ordination, Mr. Stephanos Stefanopoulos. The latter asked me to come out and see him at the Pentelikon Hotel at Psychiko, not far from Athens, and I agreed to
go. I was sharing a room with another colleague from the
Marshall Plan by the name of Glenn Moorhouse, and shortly
before I was due to go out to this luncheon engagement with
Mr. Stefanopoulos, I suddenly remembered the case of the U.S.
newspaperman who had been murdered in Salonika and was
found floating in the bay with a bullet hole in the back of the
head, and the thought crossed my mind that this invitation
might be some sort of trap. I did have a gun and I decided that I
would take the gun with me, and at least, if I were going, I
would not go like a helpless sheep to the slaughter. I disassembled the gun on my bed and cleaned it. When I started to
put it together again, the final assembly, that is, the insertion of
the barrel into the gun, escaped me. As I saw time running out
on me, I became more and more agitated in my efforts to reas-
semble it. I finally realized that I would not get it reassembled
in time, when a knock came on the door and a soft voice said,
"This is Gheorgios Daskalakis. I have come to take you away." I
said to my roommate, "Take a good look at this guy. It may be
the only clue we will have." And with that I shoved the still
disassembled pistol under the pillow. Mr. Daskalakis took me
downstairs, where I got into a station wagon and sat in the front
seat next to the driver. There were two soldiers in the back seat
and as we drove out into the country, I expected at any moment
to feel the cool circle of a rifle barrel against the base of my
neck. However, none of this happened. I went to the Pentelikon
Hotel and had tea and a long talk with Mr. Stefanopoulos. His
real purpose was to ask me to drive home to Mr. Harriman the
fact that Greece was in a very difficult situation from any of the
other countries in the Marshall Plan in that actual fighting was
going on on her soil and large areas were under the control of
Communist guerrillas. Therefore, this situation was more urgent
and Greece should have a greater priority in receiving assistance
than the other countries, who did not find themselves in a similar situation. A few minutes after I left the hotel, I remembered

the final step in reassembling the gun, but this did me no good as the gun was under the pillow in my hotel room. When I got back to the hotel, Moorhouse told me that the maid had come in to make the bed and he had pointed to my bed for her to make first. Greece was under martial law at this time, and the possession of firearms was theoretically punishable by death. The maid went over to my bed, pulled off the pillow to make the bed, saw the pistol, uttered a piercing scream and ran out of the room. She did not return to make the bed. This may sound somewhat comical at this time, but conditions there were such that it was a very awkward and difficult situation and her agitation was fully justified.

As Mr. Harriman went out to the plane to return from Greece—he had had a number of bodyguards or detectives who had been watching over him during his stay in Greece—he turned to me and muttered, "Lend me something for the cops." I am sure he did not mean this in a derogatory sense. It was the first word that came to him to describe the police. I said, "How much do you want?" "Oh," he said, "I don't know. Give me half a million drachmas." This was $150 at that time. I must say that I felt enormously proud at loaning Mr. Harriman a half million anything. I did get my money back subsequently.

On one of my trips while I was absent from Paris, I was elected president of the European Cooperation Administration's Activities Council. This required a great deal of social organization and contact with the European organization that had been created to receive and channel the Marshall aid, the OECC (Organization for European Economic Cooperation). One of the things we did at this time was to organize a Roosevelt Birthday Ball for the benefit of the infantile paralysis victims in France. It took a considerable amount of searching for us to find such a charitable organization, but we finally did. Then the wives of senior members of the Marshall Plan and senior members themselves went around to various people with whom they did business and asked them to contribute something to be raffled off for this benefit. Schiaparelli gave a dress. Air France gave two airplane tickets, and many other firms contributed different things. We had a meeting to discuss this and at the meeting a French girl who worked for the Marshall Plan said that her father ran an art gallery and she thought she might get a contribution for us. At the next meeting, I asked her whether she had gotten a contribution and she replied affirmatively that she had gotten several. She had gotten paintings by the following artists: Utrillo, Matisse, Segonzac and Dufy. I said, "You mean copies." She said, "No, I have originals." Due to the great value of the paintings by such well-known French artists, we decided that rather than raffle these off we would sell them in an auction sale.

I went to the prefecture of police to get a permit to hold a raffle of this type since this was required by French law. When I got to police headquarters, I was astonished to find a raffle division which handled such matters. I went in and asked the official how I could get a permit. He gave me a form to fill out which required me to indicate who the organizers were. I noted that the president of the Roosevelt Birthday Ball was an American lawyer in Paris by the name of Ambrose Chambers, and that I was the vice-president. The official went out of the room for a few minutes and when he came back, he reminded me that at the age of eight I had been arrested for riding a bicycle without the proper license plate on it. I was amazed that something like eighteen years later, after the German occupation, the liberation, they would still have this kind of information in their files. He also told me that Mr. Chambers' wife, before she married him, once became involved in an altercation with a French policeman and struck him with her handbag. I must say I was greatly impressed at the French ability to collect and retain such information. This official did give me the permit, and, in fact, he was the authority designed to come and watch the drawings. I am happy to be able to report that he won a small door prize with absolutely no prearrangement.

During the years I worked in Paris with Mr. Harriman he often had to go back to Washington to testify at congressional hearings before the various committees which approved the funds for the Marshall Plan. Returning from one such trip with him I went to the Washington airport to fly to New York to take the transatlantic plane. There Mr. Harriman met a young congressman he knew by the name of John Fitzgerald Kennedy. Congressman Kennedy was sitting in the rear of the aircraft and I had a seat next to Mr. Harriman. Seeing that they were extremely interested in talking to one another, I told Congressman Kennedy that he could take my seat next to Mr. Harriman for the trip to New York and I would sit in his seat in the rear of the aircraft. He gratefully accepted. This was the one and only time in my life that I was ever to meet President Kennedy, since during the years when he was President, I served outside the United States.

During this time General Marshall, who was Secretary of State, came to Paris to attend the General Assembly of the United Nations, and since I had known him on previous occasions, Mr. Harriman made me available to him as aide and interpreter. This gave me an opportunity to meet some of the other European leaders, such as Finance Minister Pella of Italy, who had done a yeoman job of restoring stability to the lira; and on many occasions to see Paul Henri Spaak of Belgium. On weekends General Marshall would take Mrs. Marshall to visit the battlefields where he had served as a young colonel and aide to Pershing in World War I. We went out one weekend and spent Saturday night at Rheims. This was a time when there were considerable threats from Jewish terrorists against General Marshall, and either his executive assistant General Carter, whom I had known from Rio, his aide Major George or I took turns sitting outside his door with a loaded pistol. We had dinner at the hotel in Rheims that night and none of us ordered any wine. General Marshall was recognized by many people in the room and at one point a Frenchman with a waxed mustache walked over to the table, placed a bottle of champagne on the table, looked with disgust at the water we were drinking and said in English, "Gentlemen, water rots your boots. Please accept this with my compliments." General Marshall was delighted with the gesture, as it was an excellent vintage of champagne.

On the following day we drove to Metz in eastern France. As we approached the city from the west, General Marshall said, "Around the curve of this road on the right side there are some monuments that were put up after the war of 1870, and if my memory does not fail me, there is a monument to the 17th Brandenburg Infantry Regiment." I was astonished that over a span of thirty years he could remember this kind of detail. We went around the curve and on the right side of the road there was a brown stone monument commemorating the deeds of the 17th Brandenburg Infantry Regiment in 1870. We spent some time in Metz and then went on to Nancy, where when we registered at the Grand Hotel, the woman at the reception desk pulled out the 1918 register of the hotel and showed General Marshall his signature along with that of General Pershing when they had registered at this hotel thirty years earlier. While we were at Nancy (since General Marshall was incognito, the prefect left his card at the hotel but did not attempt to see General Marshall) General Marshall asked me to call in the nearby town of Gondrecourt and find out if a certain Madame Jouatte was still alive. He had been billeted in her house as a colonel in the closing months of World War I. I called the local gendarmerie and ascertained that Madame Jouatte was still alive and lucid, but was more than ninety years old. On the following day, I drove to Gondrecourt with General and Mrs. Marshall. We stopped in front of the house and I went upstairs and rang the doorbell. A very old lady opened the door and I said, "Madame, are you Madame Jouatte?" She said, "Yes, I am." Then she looked at me and she said, "Oh, mon dieu, he is here, isn't he?" She had heard on the radio that General Marshall was in the area but she could hardly believe he had come to see her. I then went down and got General and Mrs. Marshall. He came up the stairs, and Madame Jouatte impulsively kissed him on both cheeks. She was extraordinarily grateful because through some action of General Marshall's, her son, who was a prisoner of war in the First World War, had been liberated well ahead of the time she had expected. She told us an amusing story that General Patton had come to see her when his troops passed through the town during World War II. General Marshall had asked General Patton if he went through Gondrecourt to look up Madame Jouatte and do something for her. Patton's idea of doing something for her was to draw up a two-and-a-half-ton truck full of food, which was very scarce in France at the time, and unload it at Madame Jouatte's. He then had an armored regiment parade by Madame Jouatte's window while he and Madame Jouatte reviewed the parade from the window. Mrs. Marshall was delighted to meet Madame Jouatte, as she had often heard General Marshall speak of the months in which he lived in this house in World War I.

During this same period, I went with General Marshall to visit Italy and Greece. In Italy we saw various members of the Italian government, who were all deeply impressed with General Marshall. I think I have known few people in my life who radiated such presence and such a sense of dignity and integrity as General Marshall. He made a profound impression on all of the statesmen with whom he dealt. In Greece on one occasion he was talking to Prime Minister Maximos, who was then in his eighties. General Marshall kept referring to his own age. He was then in his mid-sixties and this obviously irritated Prime Minister Maximos. After General Marshall's third or fourth reference to the fact of how old he, General Marshall, was, Maximos looked at him and said in French, which I translated, "General Marshall, you keep talking about how old you are. Do you realize that I am old enough to be your father, and I am the Prime Minister of Greece?" I must say this stunned me, as the idea of anybody being old enough to be General Marshall's father seemed well nigh incredible. General Marshall was very vigorous and alert at this time, and we had an interesting visit to Greece. I think the fact that the American Secretary of State had come to Greece at this difficult time in Greek history was of great encouragement to them.

Still later I was to return to Greece again with Paul Hoffman, the administrator of the European Recovery Program in Washington. On this occasion I went to northern Greece and spent a few days with the troops there. I was in a town called Florina with the 2nd Division, which was commanded by a formidable Greek general, about six feet four inches tall with tremendous handlebar mustaches. His name was Papadopoulos (not to be confused with the later dictator of Greece) and his nickname was "Papoose." The city of Florina had been under some form of siege by the guerrillas for nearly three years, and while I was there, the siege was lifted. Large Greek forces entered the city and ended the long siege. At this time the 2nd Division was ordered to drive for the isthmus between great Lake Prespa and small Lake Prespa. I was with these Greek troops when we went down to the isthmus, and the Albanian border lay just beyond. When the Greeks reached the border, the guerrillas were still firing at them and the Greeks continued to advance. I knew that very shortly there would be a call from Athens ordering the Greek troops to stop, but local Greek commanders said that as long as the guerrillas were firing on them from inside Albania, they were going to continue to advance. I went down myself and put both feet inside Albania and then hastily recrossed back into Greece. I believe that I am one of the very few American Army officers who has been in Albania since World War II. The Greek Army's morale was very high at this point. Greece had been at war for nearly ten years and these soldiers realized that at long last, since Yugoslavia had withdrawn its support from the Communist guerrillas, the war was close to coming to an end.

One day I was riding down the road in a jeep with a *Time* correspondent and there was a Greek battalion resting at the side of the road. The *Time* correspondent asked us to stop and we did. He asked, "Is there anyone here who speaks English?" A young Greek soldier said that he did, that he had been to school in the United States and spoke English. The *Time* correspondent asked him what he did in civilian life, and he replied that he was a shoemaker. He did not intend to remain in the Army. When the war was over, he would go back to being a shoemaker. The *Time* correspondent then asked him whether the Greek Army had improved very much since the arrival of the U.S. military mission. The young corporal looked him right in the eye and said, "Sir, the Greek Army has always been a good army. It is the best army in the world." It was this kind of spirit that enabled this Greek Army to drive the guerrillas into Albania and Bulgaria. It was an exciting and exhilarating time. The Greek Army was a singing army and I learned some of the Greek marching songs, "Perna e o stratos" and "Anteki o Grammos," songs that spoke of the reason why the Greek soldier was fighting. The impression made upon me by the Greek Army at this point was an extremely favorable one. It did not look like the army of a small country. It looked like a sophisticated modern army. Greece had been at war almost without interruption since 1940. I came back to Florina one night as the Deputy Prime Minister, Mr. Venizelos, was making a speech announcing the end of the siege. He was enthusiastically received. I then received a telephone call ordering me to return to Athens at once, as I was to accompany Mr. Hoffman in a call on the Greek Prime Minister. I flew back to Athens from the Kastoria airport. I arrived in Athens covered with dust. There was a vehicle waiting for me and I was taken straight to the Prime Minister's office. I was extremely embarrassed as I was dirty, not only my clothes, but my face and hands. I was brought into the Prime Minister's office with Mr. Hoffman and apologized for my appearance. The Prime Minister patted me on the shoulder and said, "There is nothing to be ashamed of or embarrassed about. That is Grammos dust, honorable dust from our second Grammos victory." And so I was forgiven for my undiplomatic appearance on this occasion. (The Grammos Mountains were the scene of a great victory over guerrillas.)

When the Europeans realized that we were serious about ensuring the recovery of Europe, that we showed serious signs of considering the defense of Europe as important to us, a spark caught and the hopelessness that had pervaded Europe in the preceding years began to fade. The European nations took steps to ensure not just their recovery but the defense of their common freedom. France, Great Britain, Belgium, Holland and Luxembourg formed the so-called Western Union to look to their common defense. The initial over-all command was entrusted to Field Marshal Montgomery, the victor of El Alamein, who still wore the aura of that victory around him. For the command of the ground forces the Western Union turned to General Juin, who had commanded the French troops in Italy during the war. Juin, then resident general of France in Morocco, however, declined the command and it was then offered to General Jean de Lattre de Tassigny, who had commanded the French troops in the invasion of southern France and subsequently the First French Army on the extreme right of the Allied army groups as they advanced into Germany. General de Lattre, an extraordinarily brilliant soldier, was to prove his skill and ability again in Indochina a few years later. He was a rather difficult man and had had several clashes with some of his U.S. colleagues and superiors. One day he asked for an appointment with General Marshall during his stay in Paris. I was instructed to be present in order to translate. General de Lattre, who knew General Marshall from the war, came in, shook hands and they sat down in the living room of the U. S. Embassy residence. General de Lattre began the conversation in an extraordinarily direct and almost brutal way. He said to General Marshall that he had been asked to assume the command of the ground forces of the Western Union after Juin had refused it because there were no forces to command. De Lattre felt, however, that someone had to make a beginning and for that reason he was disposed to accept. The British, French, Belgians, Dutch and Luxembourgers had told him that he had their confidence. He knew, however, that he did not have the confidence of the Americans, and since the Americans would sooner or later be involved in the defense of Western Europe, he wanted to know how he could get this confidence. General Marshall seemed somewhat taken aback at this directness, but he answered with equal directness. He said, "There were several incidents during the war that made us wonder about you. I came to your headquarters and you talked to me in a very critical way about some of the U.S. commanders in front of the newspapermen." De Lattre said to him, "No one told me that those men in military uniforms wearing small green tabs on their shoulders were war correspondents. I thought they were staff officers. When I found out later, I was very embarrassed." "Then," said General Marshall, "there was another incident. You crossed the Rhine without orders from higher authority to do so." General de Lattre then replied, "General Marshall, you are a soldier. Can you conceive that after my country had been occupied by the Germans for four years, that at the time when Germany's enemies were battering their way across the Rhine the French Army should not be present at such a crossing?" General Marshall nodded understandingly and finally said, "There was one other item, and that was when you were asked to evacuate Stuttgart. You refused to do so." De Lattre replied, "General, commanding an army within a coalition has always been difficult. Marshal Foch once said that after commanding a coalition, his admiration for Napoleon had decreased considerably." De Lattre continued, "But commanding an army in a coalition under foreign command on the soil of your own country is even more difficult." He then produced a letter from General de Gaulle as chief of the French provisional government ordering him not to evacuate Stuttgart. I translated the letter briefly for General Marshall. He looked at de Lattre, smiled and said, "You have my confidence. Go ahead. Take the command and very shortly we will get congressional authority to give you the equipment for two divisions for the Western Union forces from our stores in Germany." I was later to see de Lattre on a number of occasions. He was a forceful commander and a remarkable man. Had he lived, I do not know how the French war in Vietnam would have finished, but I am sure that it would have finished in a way other than the tragic defeat at Dien Bien Phu.

It was a rewarding and fascinating time to watch the fire begin to burn again in the ashes of war-torn Europe, to see, in a sense, the springtime begin after the long winter, and to understand that we were helping to restore faith and production in Europe. The ancient, but powerful heart of that continent began to beat strongly once again. I think the most important achievement of the Marshall Plan was not so much the material aid it gave as the rekindling of hope, the rekindling of energy and the rekindling of the Europeans' belief that they could not only return to a normal life, but move to an even better life than they had known before the war. The extraordinary vision that proposed the Marshall Plan, the willingness of the United States Congress to finance it, the acceptance by American business of the recovery of its competitors, led many successful American businessmen to serve at Mr. Harriman's call in various parts of the Marshall Plan. Others came from academic and all walks of life and together they produced a team of extraordinary capability and enthusiasm which infected the Europeans. Mr. Harriman's tireless energy and his constant pursuit of the goal of European recovery likewise made a deep impression on the Europeans and marked indelibly in their memory the affection and esteem in which he is held by them to this day. I traveled back and forth around Europe with him, all over Western Europe, Portugal, Scandinavia, as well as many times back to the United States to meet with President Truman or to testify before Congress. It has been said that familiarity breeds contempt. This is often false. As I worked closely with Mr. Harriman, my admiration for him grew, for the courage I had seen in Bogotá and was to see later in Teheran, for the energy and for the dedication which he constantly showed. He was a man of independent wealth who need not have taken part in these strenuous efforts but could have been enjoying the fruits of his wealth; yet he has devoted almost all of his adult life to the service of his country and human freedom. It is a happy nation that is served by public servants such as Averell Harriman.

This was a particularly fruitful and interesting part of my life because it opened for me a whole new political, financial, economic and labor world with which I had not had previous contact. The time I spent at the Marshall Plan was to be of enormous assistance to me in later years and helped in formulating the judgments I was required to make at different times. The visible recovery of Europe was a tremendous reward in itself. Colonel Bonesteel had gone on to a much higher job in London, and at Mr. Harriman's request, I was appointed the Military Attaché at Large. I was a major at this time, and I believe that I was the only major in the attaché system who was an atta-ché himself and not an assistant attaché. I found the job ever more fascinating as we moved into the summer of 1950. I did not realize that this very rewarding and educational period of my life was about to come to a close with the outbreak of the Korean War and that within a few weeks I was to begin a new series of missions of quite a different nature, my mission to Korea with Mr. Harriman and my mission to Wake Island with President Truman. The North Korean attack on the morning of June 25, 1950, signaled the end of my mission to the Marshall Plan and the beginning of those which were to follow.

10. TO MACARTHUR WITH HARRIMAN

On the morning of June 25, 1950, the armies of Communist North Korea invaded South Korea without any warning in an attempt to reunify the country under communism. This took the U.S. forces on the peninsula by surprise. The North Koreans seized Seoul and thrust vigorously southward. Following President Truman's courageous decision to intervene, elements of the U. S. Army in Japan were moved to Korea. They were ill prepared for sudden violent combat and had been living a comfortable life as an occupation force. They were derisively called the "Tatami Army" after the Japanese mats. The North Koreans continued their sweep south, driving the South Koreans and Americans before them into the far southeastern corner of the country around the great port of Pusan. Here, supported by massive Air Force and Navy strikes, the U.S. and South Korean resistance hardened along the edges of the Pusan perimeter. The North Koreans strove to force a re-embarkation of our forces on us: an Asiatic Dunkirk. Reinforcements from the United States and our total air and naval supremacy enabled us to hold the perimeter.

MacArthur as always was thinking of an offensive. President Truman was anxious to know his frank views, plans and needs, so he sent one of his closest aides and advisers, Averell Harriman, to see the general to get the full and complete picture from him. On very short notice Mr. Harriman told me that I would be going with him to the meetings to make notes and to help write the telegrams to the President. So it was that on a day in August my mission to MacArthur with Mr. Harriman began.

On the day the Korean War broke out, June 25, 1950, Mr. Harriman was in London. He called me on the telephone and told me to make arrangements for him to fly back to the United States at once, but not to make the reservations in his own name. This was quite difficult to do. Harriman returned to Paris and I made the arrangements for him to leave through London because his departure for the United States from Paris would be more conspicuous. He had at his disposal a C-47 military airplane and we flew in it to London. Since I had heard the news of the North Korean invasion of South Korea, I was very anxious to know what the United States was going to do. I knew that all the NATO nations would be watching to see whether or not we would really live up to our commitments. Rightly or wrongly we were perceived to be the patrons or the parents of the South Korean state. If we were to abandon the South Koreans, it would certainly have a tremendous impact on the confidence of the Europeans in the military guarantees of the United States.

At this time few doubted our industrial and military superiority over the Soviets. A lurking fear, however, existed and endures a generation later that the United States would be unwilling to use that force for anything short of an attack on the United States. For this reason, I felt it extremely important that we take speedy and forceful action to support the South Korean government.

Mr. Harriman and I took off from London for New York and Washington. Halfway across the ocean, Mr. Harriman revealed to me that he had talked to Mr. Truman earlier in the day by telephone. The President planned to intervene militarily to support the South Korean government. This greatly reassured me. It was still unclear whether the war would be confined to Korea, whether the Russians would openly support the North Koreans and whether the war could be limited to the Korean peninsula.

We arrived in Washington. Mr. Harriman was appointed assistant to the President and needed offices in the White House. He immediately plunged into a series of high-level conferences and left me to take care of the details, i.e. find him a White House office and a suitable house in which to live. He would be returning for permanent assignment to Washington. His instructions to me were amazingly vague, nothing about size, location or cost—"just something appropriate."

The first problem was to find an office in the White House. This proved extremely complicated. All the worthwhile offices were taken and no one appeared in the slightest disposed to giving up any of the space already occupied. By searching diligently, I found that General Pershing's old office in the Executive Office Building directly across the street from the west entrance of the White House was free and available for Mr. Harriman. There was a protocol problem involved since Mr. Harriman was theoretically senior to anyone else in the White House except the President and Vice-President. When I broached the subject to him, I told him I had found an office and he seemed pleased, but when I said it was in the Executive Office Building, he frowned. I explained to him that to get an office in the White House would have required actual physical expulsion of some senior dignitary. The office in the Executive Office Building was a very prestigious office. It had a highly desirable view of the west entrance of the White House and was for many years the office of General John J. Pershing. Mr. Harriman agreed reluctantly to look at it. When he saw its size, much larger than anything he would have gotten in the White House, and its floor plan indicating rooms for secretaries and assistants, he agreed to accept it.

The next problem was to find him a place to live. I attacked this problem through a real estate agent, a very pretty blond woman, who offered a house on Foxhall Road which had belonged previously to Perle Mesta, "the hostess with the mostest." It seemed about right for Mr. Harriman and eventually I got him out to look at it. He was pleased and took it. I asked the real estate woman to see if she could find me a place to live, but she indicated that she did not deal in such small, cheap places. With some difficulty, I found a place in Bethesda.

As the Korean War developed, one of my jobs was to go to the CIA and the Defense Department to obtain the latest information on how the war was progressing and then report back to Mr. Harriman and brief him on what was happening in Korea. I had little of a positive nature to report. We were being inexorably and steadily driven back. The small force we had in Korea was greatly outnumbered. The troops we brought in from Japan had been wallowing in the delights of occupation and were really not ready for a brutal, tough war such as the one the North Koreans were waging. Most of the World War II veterans had returned home. The North Koreans drove us from Seoul, the capital, and we withdrew rapidly south with our South Korean allies and were driven into the Pusan perimeter. We met considerable difficulty in getting the reinforcements needed into the peninsula in quantity, quality, and in time.

One day in August Mr. Harriman told me, confidentially, that Mr. Truman was sending him to see General MacArthur and he was to go to Korea to see exactly what was going on and what would be needed. I was to go with him and I was to get him some summer clothing to wear in Korea. I asked him whether I should take a uniform and he said yes, but to take civilian clothes as well. On August 14 we departed Washington in a Constellation of the United States Air Force. Traveling with us were General Matthew Ridgway, the Deputy Chief of Staff of the Army; General Charles Cabell of the Air Force; General Lauris Norstad, also of the Air Force; and several of their aides. I went along as Mr. Harriman's aide.

We flew from Washington non-stop to Alaska. This was one of the two times in my life I took a sleeping pill. I needed it to sleep on the aircraft as I knew that after Alaska there was another thirteen-hour flight to Tokyo. Both flights went off uneventfully and we arrived in Tokyo tired from the long journey through many time zones. This was my first trip to Japan, my first time in the Far East. General MacArthur met Mr. Harriman at the airport. It was quite a thrill to look out the window of the aircraft as we came to a stop in front of the terminal at Haneda and see that legendary figure clutching his pipe and wearing his crushed fifty-mission cap. MacArthur was already a legend larger than life. He was serving in his third war as a general (World Wars I and II, and now Korea).

We drove to the Embassy guesthouse, where Mr. Harriman stayed as General MacArthur's guest. MacArthur himself resided at the Embassy. In the course of his talks with Harriman MacArthur indicated that if he were given a certain number of reinforcements—and he did not ask for a large force—he would be able to restore the situation in Korea. He did indicate that we were simply short of fighting infantry troops. We had a number of supply units and logistic units, but we were short of actual ground troops to fight. He said that he had been in Korea regularly, that South Korean President Syngman Rhee's spirits were high, and the old man, who was in his eighties, was "indomitable." General MacArthur then suggested that Mr. Harriman go over to Korea and have a look for himself to see what the situation was really like. He should talk to General Walton Walker, the Eighth Army commander, and ascertain what Walker felt his needs were in addition to those perceived by MacArthur. General MacArthur in passing complained of the fact that he was still flying around in his old C-54 aircraft, the *Bataan*. He had used it since the beginning of World War II. He made a strong pitch to Mr. Harriman to appeal to President Truman to get him something more modern like a Constellation or a DC-6. Mr. Harriman agreed to do so. The following morning we went out to Haneda Airport and boarded the *Bataan*. The aircraft, however, would not start. Whether this was part of General MacArthur's demonstration of the fact that he needed a new airplane or not I do not know. We had to transfer to another C-54 belonging to General George Stratemeyer, the commander of the Far East Air Force. MacArthur made his point to Mr. Harriman.

We took off in this aircraft, flew past Mount Fugi and had a great view of it. We flew on to Taegu, the temporary capital of the South Korean government since the fall of Seoul. The front line was close and ran along the Naktong River. At this point our forces were compressed into the smallest beachhead of the Korean War. We were received at the airport by General Walker, the commander of the Eighth Army, and by the commander of the Air Force in Korea. We went to their headquarters in Taegu for a briefing on the situation. General Walker, a tough soldier, exuded confidence in his troops and himself. He was to die tragically not long after our visit in a jeep accident.

It was a curious feeling to come back to a war five years after the end of World War II. With 40-mm. guns in sandbag revetments around the airport and soldiers wearing steel helmets, the general atmosphere of war was totally present. I experienced a strange *déjà vu* feeling. The briefing at Eighth Army was not encouraging. Some Marine reinforcements had recently arrived, but General Walker indicated that nearly all of his infantry units were committed in line and he had almost nothing in reserve. At this point, General Ridgway asked him what he would do if his forces were driven from the Naktong line. General Walker, whose nickname was "Bulldog," said that he would *not* be driven from the Naktong line. General Ridgway pressed his point and said, "That's what you tell the troops, but what will you really do if you are driven from the Naktong line?" General Walker's jaw jutted out. He looked Ridgway straight in the eye and he said, "General, I will *not* be driven from the Naktong line." He never was.

There was a large North Korean build-up in front of the Naktong line and Walker planned shortly to use a heavy Air Force bombing concentration on this build-up. Walker was relying on this air attack to blunt the expected thrust by the North Koreans across the Naktong. Mr. Harriman decided to visit one of the units holding the Naktong line. This was the 1st Cavalry Division commanded by General Hobart Gay. We went to his command post near the Taegu race track. General Gay was a courtly, soldierly figure unshaken by the reverses we had sustained thus far. His division came into Korea across the beaches at Pohang. General Gay seemed quite confident that he could hold the Naktong line. We then drove by jeep up to one of the battalions holding positions right on the river. While we were in the battalion command post, we could see our artillery bursting across the river. General Gay said to me, "Wouldn't it be a terrible thing if I got Averell Harriman killed here." Since we were in a very exposed place, I nodded slowly. Not long thereafter the briefing at the battalion headquarters was terminated and we were driven back to the Taegu airport. On the way, Mr. Harriman called to see Syngman Rhee, who was living in a private home. The old man was unshaken by the reverses he had sustained. He said that if only he were given a little more support, a little more help from the United States, he would smash his way back into Seoul and restore his government to its rightful capital. He was then over eighty years old and his resilience, his determination and his confidence were inspiring to see. He made a considerable impression upon Mr. Harriman. He had not yet begun to be the target for various leftist groups. He was somewhat of a national or international hero at this point. I recall at a later time when I was translating for Secretary of State John Foster Dulles and French Foreign Minister Georges Bidault. Dulles, in his normal blunt way, asked Bidault what he really needed to win the Indochinese war. Bidault replied with a sly smile, "Syngman Rhee instead of Bao Dai," then chief of state of Vietnam.

While in Korea we learned that Winston Churchill's son, Randolph, covering the war as a newspaperman, had been wounded while on patrol with U.S. troops behind the North Korean lines across the Naktong River. Only a few days before, I had met him with Mr. Harriman in Tokyo. At the time I had asked Mr. Harriman what he thought of Randolph Churchill, who was a somewhat controversial figure. Mr. Harriman had replied that Randolph had all of his father's guts and very little of his brains. Upon learning of the circumstances under which Randolph had been wounded, Mr. Harriman reminded me of his earlier comment. Still I could not help but admire Randolph Churchill's courage. Brainy or not, I thought him a worthy son of his father. I recalled how shortly before World War II the

Oxford University debating society had approved a motion that said: "Under no circumstances will this house fight for King or country." Later Randolph and some friends broke in and tore the offending motion from the records. But the harm had been done. The Nazi Ambassador to London reported the approval of the motion to his government, commenting that the young aristocrats who had done so much to win Britain's wars no longer wanted to fight. I am convinced that Hitler saw in this a green light and moved ahead with his plans against Poland confident that Britain would not fight. Many times apparently small incidents have an unexpectedly great impact on history.

We returned to the airport, took off and flew back in the falling darkness to Tokyo. The following morning I went with Mr. Harriman to have breakfast with General MacArthur in the Embassy dining room. I will always remember this breakfast as one of the truly memorable events of my life. General MacArthur handed Mr. Harriman a list of the units he was requesting as reinforcements from the United States. I do remember that among others there was a regimental combat team from Hawaii and another one from Puerto Rico. He also wanted some air units and some support units. MacArthur, speaking in his usual slow, dramatic way, said, "I cannot believe that a great nation such as the United States cannot give me these few paltry reinforcements for which I ask. Tell the President that if he gives them to me, I will, on the rising tide of the fifteenth of September, land at Inchon and between the hammer of this landing and the anvil of the Eighth Army, I will crush and destroy the armies of North Korea." He said it most dramatically and I was quite moved. I could see that Mr. Harriman was also impressed. MacArthur was as good as his word. He got the reinforcements and on that rising tide he did smash the hammer ashore at Inchon which crushed the armies of North Korea and would have put them out of the war had the Chinese not intervened.

I was somewhat surprised, however, that there were Japanese servants in the room at the time MacArthur spoke. He gave both the location of the landing and the day on which it would occur. He must have been very sure of their loyalty and discretion. I was somewhat concerned. However, as subsequent events showed, the secret was well kept and the landing came as a complete surprise to the North Koreans. Mr. Harriman, meanwhile, had been on the phone to Mr. Truman and had secured the promise of a new Constellation aircraft for General MacArthur. General MacArthur's pilot, Colonel Anthony Storey, flew back to the United States with us. General MacArthur came out to the airport to see Mr. Harriman off and the farewell was extremely cordial. He expressed gratitude for Mr. Harriman's visit, gratitude for the support he had received so far and confidence that his government and President Truman would not let him down. Late that afternoon we took off from Haneda Airport at Tokyo for the long flight back to the United States via Attu in the Aleutians.

When we got back to Washington, Mr. Harriman made it clear that now that he had discovered I could do something besides speak languages, I would have to stay with him. His original intent had been that I merely come and help him get settled in the first few days of his assignment to the White House. I said to him that I would have to go back to Paris to bring back my mother, my household goods and my car. He said, "Why don't you send a telegram and have them take care of that?" I replied, "Mr. Harriman, when you send a telegram, a lot of people jump to carry out the order. If I were to send such a telegram, no one would pay any attention." And he said, "Well, you can't go now." It was some weeks later before I was able to get back, close my house in Paris and bring my mother back to Washington and get settled in my assignment to Mr. Harriman in the White House.

This, incidentally, was the only time in my life that I have actually been assigned to the White House. It was during this period that the Puerto Rican terrorists made their attempt on Mr. Truman's life. The White House was being rebuilt and he was living across the street at Blair House. I was working almost directly across the street when it happened. Right after the shooting, which killed a guard, I called my mother, who had not yet heard the news, and told her that she would be hearing something but not to worry—the President was unharmed.

I continued to brief Mr. Harriman and work with him on various military matters that were of his competence as assistant to the President. Shortly after Mr. Harriman returned to the United States, he instructed me to locate Major General John R. Deane, who had been his Military Attaché and Chief of Military Mission in Moscow during World War II. He was very anxious to get General Deane to work for him on matters relating to the National Security Council. I finally found General Deane in California, where he was president of the Roma Wine Company. He made it plain to Mr. Harriman that he could not give up this job where he was earning a very good salary and noted that his Washington pay would not even meet the payments on his house. He did agree, however, to come and work for one month to help Mr. Harriman get started with his duties, and he took a month's leave from the Roma Wine Company and came to Washington to assist Mr. Harriman. When Mr. Harriman realized that General Deane would not stay with him permanently, he then instructed me to find Brigadier General Frank Roberts, who had been his Deputy Chief of Military Mission in Moscow. I finally located General Roberts in California. At the end of the war, Roberts had been reduced to the rank of colonel and was now Professor of Military Science and Tactics at the University of Southern California. I got him on the phone for Mr. Harriman, who instructed me to listen in on the conversation, which I did. He made a strong plea for Colonel Roberts to come and work for him at the White House. Colonel Roberts explained that this would be difficult for him, that at Southern California he was given quarters, was serving a fixed term there, had been married not long before and had a small child, and so forth. Mr. Harriman then said, "Frank, could you come as a general?" I heard the catch in Roberts' voice and I knew that he was hooked. After some hemming and hawing, he finally agreed that as a general he could come but he didn't think Mr. Harriman could get it done. Mr. Harriman assured him he could.

Shortly after this I went with Mr. Harriman to see the Secre-

tary of the Army, Frank Pace, and Mr. Harriman explained to
him that he was very anxious to have a certain Army officer detailed to his staff. Mr. Pace was most co-operative and said,
"Averell, just leave his name outside with my military assistant
and we will issue the orders." Whereupon Mr. Harriman said,
"There is one catch. He is now a colonel and I need him as a
brigadier general." Mr. Pace then explained that such promotions were done by promotion boards and had to follow certain
patterns. Harriman countered by saying that Roberts had already been selected once before as brigadier general and should
never have been reduced. The Secretary replied that he couldn't
do it, that under such circumstances only the President could do
it. Mr. Harriman picked up his hat and said, "Well, Frank, get
ready because he's going to ask you to do it this afternoon." We
then went back to the White House. Later that day, I went in
with Mr. Harriman to see President Truman. Mr. Harriman explained that he needed a general officer to represent him on the
National Security Council, that he had the ideal man, this man
had already been a general but had been reduced at the end of
the war in a blanket measure to the grade of colonel, and he
asked Mr. Truman if he would promote him. Mr. Truman
reached across his desk and pulled out from among his papers a
list of general officers which had been submitted to him for approval. He looked up at Harriman and he said, "What is this
man's name?" Mr. Harriman replied, "Frank Roberts." Mr.
Truman said, "What is his middle initial?" Harriman looked
questioningly at me and I said, "His middle initial is N." Mr.
Truman wrote in ink at the bottom of the list the name Frank
N. Roberts and then signed the list. And so Colonel Roberts
was promoted to brigadier general and did come to work for Mr.
Harriman. This also taught me that if you go high enough you
can get almost anything done.

General Roberts, incidentally, had been on the gunboat
Panay some time before World War II when it was attacked in
the Yangtze River by Japanese aircraft. The commander had
been wounded and Roberts, though an Army officer, had assumed command of the gunboat. For this action he had re-

ceived the Navy Cross, one of the very few Army officers I have
ever known to be awarded this essentially naval decoration. He
was a spendid assistant to Mr. Harriman and went on to be
promoted to major general and wound up his career as Chief of
Staff to the Commander in Chief of Allied Forces, Southern
Europe, six or seven years later.

And so with the establishment of Mr. Harriman's staff, I continued my duties there until the time came in October for my
next mission, the mission to Wake Island with President Truman to meet General MacArthur.

11. TO WAKE ISLAND WITH PRESIDENT TRUMAN

MacArthur executed a masterly landing at Inchon on the west coast of Korea in September, and with the South Koreans we had recaptured Seoul and driven the North Koreans completely out of South Korea and across the 38th parallel, the frontier between the two Koreas before the North Korean aggression began. All along the front MacArthur's troops were moving north toward the borders between North Korea and China and the Soviet Union. The U. S. Administration was somewhat uneasy. It feared that MacArthur wanted to broaden the war. He was talking to the press about bringing in Chinese forces from Taiwan. Many intelligence sources warned that the Chinese Communists would not stand idly by if the U.S. forces reached the Chinese border on the Yalu River. Other intelligence sources reported massive Chinese preparations to intervene openly in the war. Perplexed by MacArthur's attitude and public statements, President Truman sought to consult with him. MacArthur made plain that at this crucial time in the war he could not take time out to fly to Washington. President Truman agreed to meet with him on the tiny mid-Pacific island of Wake, thousands of miles from Washington. Averell Harriman as Mr. Truman's special assistant was to attend and he decided that I would go with him. I was to help in preparing the minutes of this historic meeting, together with others, including a State Department secretary, Vernice Anderson, and General Willis Matthews, who was an assistant to General Omar Bradley.

These minutes were later leaked in Washington and MacArthur stated that he had not known that they would be made. General Bradley took full responsibility for them before Congress. Against this background my mission to this fateful meeting began.

Early in October Mr. Harriman indicated to me that Mr. Truman was very anxious to talk to General MacArthur but that General MacArthur felt strongly that he could not return to the United States with events moving as rapidly in Korea as they were—after the Inchon landing our forces had swept north through Seoul across the 38th parallel, had seized Pyongyang, the North Korean capital, and were pressing northward. In the light of General MacArthur's reluctance to leave his command for any extended time, Mr. Truman, in a gracious gesture, decided to meet General MacArthur at Wake Island in the mid-Pacific, three quarters of the way from Washington to Tokyo. Mr. Harriman indicated that he would be going along and I would be with him as his assistant.

On October 13 we departed in a special military aircraft for Wake Island. We flew first to San Francisco. In Mr. Harriman's party was General Omar Bradley, the chairman of the Joint Chiefs of Staff; Ambassador Philip Jessup; Assistant Secretary for Far Eastern Affairs Dean Rusk; and two assistants to General Bradley, Generals Matthews and Hamblen. We stopped to refuel at San Francisco and then flew on to Honolulu, where we were all quartered at the naval station at Pearl Harbor. I recall getting a great thrill as I walked into my assigned room—there was a bright green flowery Hawaiian sports shirt on the bed, and on it was a card: "To Major Walters with compliments from President Truman." Ever since my experience with General Marshall in Rio I had not been given to loud clothing, but I could not resist the impulse to put on this bright green shirt at once. I have it to this day.

After spending the night at Pearl Harbor and visiting the

wounded at the hospital, we flew off early the next morning on the Constellation to Wake Island. Admiral Arthur Radford, the commander in chief of U.S. forces in the Pacific, joined the President's group. The propeller aircraft trip to Wake Island was a long one—it took all night. Early in the morning, I went up to the pilot's cockpit and was astonished to see the island on radar. The island's physical geography was outlined on the screen, and I could clearly make out the lagoon in the center of the island. We landed just before daybreak. As we got out of the aircraft it was still dark. I was surprised at how cool it was, considering we were in the tropics.

Mr. Harriman looked around and asked, "Where is General MacArthur?" Someone pointed a little distance away and said, "He is sitting over in that jeep." I was a little surprised that he had not come to the aircraft inasmuch as aboard our aircraft was the Secretary of the Army, Frank Pace, and the chairman of the Joint Chiefs of Staff, General Omar Bradley. In my book the Secretary of the Army was the boss of all American soldiers regardless of rank. We walked over to where General MacArthur was sitting, and Mr. Pace and Mr. Harriman had a long talk with him while I stood at a respectful distance and awaited further developments. Pretty soon it was announced that Mr. Truman's aircraft would be arriving shortly. The canard that General MacArthur kept Mr. Truman's plane waiting at Wake Island is simply not true. General MacArthur had arrived the evening before President Truman did and spent the night on the island. Just after daybreak the President landed and his plane taxied up to a point close to where General MacArthur was sitting. Those of us who were standing with General MacArthur walked over to the plane from which Mr. Truman would be emerging shortly. The steps were wheeled up, the door opened and Mr. Truman appeared in the doorway and waved his hat as the two air policemen came down the ladder and stood on each side of the ladder at the bottom. Mr. Truman then slowly descended the ladder. As he did so, General MacArthur got out of his jeep and walked over to meet him. I noticed with some surprise that General MacArthur did not salute President Truman. The United States Constitution makes quite explicit the role of the President as commander in chief of the Armed Forces, and it seemed strange to me that an old soldier like General MacArthur would not salute the President of the United States, whatever might be General MacArthur's political convictions.

Mr. Truman gave no indication of having noticed MacArthur's failure to salute. He shook hands with General MacArthur, who introduced John Muccio, the U. S. Ambassador to Korea. Mr. Truman and General MacArthur got into a pickup truck and went off to an isolated building, where they spent about an hour together alone. What transpired at this meeting only President Truman and General MacArthur know. I never heard Mr. Truman discuss the conversation nor did I ever see any memorandum of conversation covering their talk. In the meantime, the rest of us were taken to a small weather shack which had been set up as a conference room. The shack had a large table in the center with chairs around the table. A few chairs lined the walls for second-level people like myself. There was a small hallway off to one side of the room leading to another room. Vernice Anderson, Mr. Jessup's secretary, sat there to make the necessary minutes of the meeting. Presently, President Truman and General MacArthur appeared, apparently on very cordial terms. Mr. Truman walked to the head of the table, pointed to the chair on his right and said to General MacArthur, "You sit here." Mr. Truman then indicated chairs around the table to the other members of the party. I was one of the junior members so I sat on a chair away from the table and back against the wall. The room, however, was quite small and I clearly heard everything that transpired. Just before the meeting began, I asked Mr. Truman if it would be all right for me to take some moving pictures inside. He laughed and said yes, he had no objection to this. As far as I know, these are the only photographs which were actually taken inside the weather shack.

The meeting then began, with General MacArthur giving a briefing on the situation in Korea. He was extremely optimistic during this briefing and wound it up by saying, "No commander in history has ever received greater support from his government than I have received from mine, and I want you to know, Mr. President, how grateful I am for that." Mr. Truman nodded graciously and then the period of questions began. Mr. Truman said to General MacArthur, "General, all of our intelligence sources indicate that the Chinese Communists are about to enter this war. I would like to know what your opinion is on this matter." General MacArthur, again speaking slowly and dramatically, replied, "Mr. President, they will not enter the war. This is the hour of our strength, not of our weakness. We no longer stand hat in hand. If the Chinese Communists cross the Yalu, I shall make of them the greatest slaughter in the history of mankind." He then went on to say that they would have no air support and that it was difficult for troops to fight without air support. He pointed out that even on our side only the Marine Corps had the kind of close air support for their ground troops that he felt was essential for operations. Since the Chinese could not provide this for their troops, they would be helpless before our Air Force. He concluded by saying that the war would in any case be over by Thanksgiving and that he would give Mr. Truman one or two divisions back for Christmas and one or two divisions in the new year for NATO in Europe. He spoke with great assurance and confidence on this subject and I was duly impressed.

A revealing incident occurred during the conference. General MacArthur took out his pipe, stuffed it with tobacco, put it in his mouth, took out a box of matches and paused as he was about to strike one of the matches; he then looked over his shoulder at Mr. Truman and said rather diffidently, "You don't mind if I smoke, do you?" It was not really a request. MacArthur had gone so far that for Truman to have said that he did mind if the general smoked would have made the President appear rude and arbitrary. Mr. Truman looked at him sharply and said, "Go right ahead, General. I've had more secondhand smoke blown in my face than any other man in America."

Further discussion ensued about timetables for troops leaving

Korea. General MacArthur was absolutely categorical in his belief that the war would be over by Christmas. Vernice Anderson took notes in the alcove and I took some notes, as did General Matthews, General Bradley's aide. Subsequently, all of
these were merged to form the record of this meeting, which
later leaked to the press. There were many charges and coun-
tercharges about whether General MacArthur had known that
minutes were being taken. I personally saw Vernice Anderson
introduced to General MacArthur as the person who was going
to take the minutes of the meeting. The general may not have
been untruthful; he was in his seventies, and he may simply
have forgotten that this was done right at the beginning of the
meeting. General Bradley courageously assumed full responsibility before the Congress when there was an inquiry on the
leak of the minutes that had been taken at the meeting.

At the end of the meeting, Mr. Truman indicated that he had
one or two other things he wanted to do. We went out into the
bright sunlight in the midst of a huge crowd of newspapermen
and photographers who were snapping pictures like madmen,
and Mr. Truman then proceeded to decorate General MacArthur with his third or fourth oak leaf cluster to his Distinguished
Service Medal. He also decorated U. S. Ambassador to Korea
John Muccio, who had behaved very courageously during the
fighting in and the withdrawal from Seoul. I took color movies
of this scene. Then Mr. Truman shook hands warmly with General MacArthur and the rest of us, boarded his plane and returned to Hawaii. We followed shortly thereafter, General Mac-
Arthur being particularly cordial to Mr. Harriman, to whom he
gave much of the credit for the fact that he had obtained the reinforcements for which he had asked during Mr. Harriman's
earlier visit. I must say I felt fortunate to be there. It was truly a
meeting of giants. I did not know at that time how much they
would clash later and while they were and remained in strong
disagreement, both men were truly outstanding in their own
fields.

We flew back to Honolulu and after a pause there we went
on to San Francisco, where Mr. Truman made a speech and

then returned to the White House. Two or three days later, one of the syndicated columnists in Washington published a considerable extract from the minutes of the meeting at Wake Island. There had been only five copies of these minutes made. Mr. Harriman had one. It was kept in his safe in an envelope sealed and marked "To be opened only by Mr. Harriman or Major Walters." An FBI investigation was conducted of this leakage and when the FBI came to Mr. Harriman's office, we were able to show them the envelope still sealed. It had never been opened since Mr. Harriman had received it for the first time.

During this period, Mr. Harriman also was working very hard to get me promoted. I had been six years a major at this point. He was eventually successful. He showed me a letter from General Marshall which he had just received and which said:

> Dear Harriman,
>   Frank Pace, the Secretary of the Army, has just told me of Major Walters' promotion to Lieutenant Colonel and I am delighted to pass on this information to you. As you may or may not know the old Army custom is to place the insignia in a glass of hard liquor and require the newly promoted officer to drain the glass in one swallow. Since Walters is a teetotaler, you may have to use milk or water. I am sending along the necessary insignia.
>   Faithfully,
>   George C. Marshall

At the bottom of the letter General Marshall had written in his own hand, "I am sending along the necessary insignia. I doubt if these leaves can stand hard liquor." While I was not a teetotaler, I did not drink whiskey or gin except in the service of my country! I was most grateful to Mr. Harriman, who gave me this letter. It is one of my treasured souvenirs to this day. And so I became a lieutenant colonel, a rank I was to hold for the next ten years.

I continued working with Mr. Harriman in the White House at this time and had considerable opportunity to see and observe President Truman. This opportunity confirmed my belief that this simple man had grown into one of the truly great Presidents of the United States. His simplicity, his forthrightness and his directness were most impressive. I remember hearing on one occasion that the White House was under repairs and Mr. Truman was actually living in the guesthouse at Blair House across the street, and that when he left his office in the White House at night to go home to Blair House, he left behind the following instructions: "If anything occurs that requires action by me between now and tomorrow morning, call me without hesitation, but if you call me and it doesn't, God help you." Mr. Truman had the extraordinary faculty of being able to leave his cares in the office, and God knows, no man bore a heavier burden than he did.

I heard later that at the Cabinet meeting at which it was decided to intervene, he had said after all of the members of the Cabinet had spoken in favor of some such intervention that he knew that someday he would have to stand before the throne of God and account for all the young lives that were about to be lost because of what he was about to do, but in the light of the oath he had taken as President of the United States, he could not do otherwise. He was an impressive man and to have had this contact with him was one of the great privileges of my life.

Years later, long after he had left the presidency, I was to see Mr. Truman at Independence. I worked up enough courage to ask him a question that had been bothering me for a long time. I said to him, "Mr. President, may I ask you an indiscreet question?" He replied, "Walters, there are no indiscreet questions, only indiscreet answers, and I am a specialist at them. So go right ahead and ask your question." I then said, "Mr. President, when you arrived at Wake Island and came down the steps from the plane, did you notice that—" Before I could finish the question, he broke in with "Did I notice that MacArthur did not salute the President of the United States. You are goddamned right I noticed." Then he added in a softer, more philosophical tone, "I was sorry because I knew it meant I was going to have trouble with him, and I did. I fired him and I should have done it long before I did. Right or wrong, he just did not understand how the United States is run."

This was the nub of their quarrel. President Truman was determined to keep the war localized on the Korean peninsula and to keep it a limited war. General MacArthur, on the other hand, felt that we must inflict a smashing defeat on the North Koreans or we would have other such limited wars in the future —and we did.

Each man, in a way, was right, but Truman was President and MacArthur did not fully recognize this overwhelming fact. When Truman fired MacArthur many criticized his action, but no one questioned his right as President to do it.

Both were men of iron will and determination and in the end in such a conflict one had to go, and under our system it could only be MacArthur.

The year drew on toward its end, and I did not realize that I was about to leave this job, one I enjoyed and which gave me as a young officer access to some of the highest levels in Washington. I was about to begin my next mission, my mission to NATO with General Eisenhower.

12. TO NATO WITH GENERAL
EISENHOWER

On April 4, 1948, the treaty of alliance forming the North Atlantic Treaty Organization (NATO) was signed in the auditorium on Constitution Avenue in Washington, D.C. This treaty
was the result of earlier efforts by the Western European nations to organize themselves for their common defense. Great
Britain, France, Belgium, Holland, Luxembourg and Italy set up
a Western Union headquarters, with Field Marshal Montgomery as the designated commander of their forces. It was
clear to them as it was to most thinking Americans that they
simply could not provide adequately for their own security without the participation of the United States. President Truman
had been able to achieve an extraordinary degree of bipartisan
support for his foreign policy and the United States and Canada
decided to join the Western European states in efforts for a
common defense. Negotiations with the Portuguese, Danes and
Norwegians resulted in their also joining. Sweden chose the
path of armed neutrality. Later Greece, Turkey and the German
Federal Republic were also to accede to the organization. The
Soviet takeover in Prague, military pressures on Greece by Communist guerrillas and other threatening moves by the Soviet
Union had convinced these nations that either they must stand
together or they would be devoured separately. The United
States through the Marshall Plan had promised economic help.

Now it had decided to provide political and military support for the free nations of Europe. These free nations came together in Washington to pledge themselves to consider at attack on one as an attack on all.

In early 1948 the Yugoslav quarrel with Moscow had led the Yugoslavs to withdraw the help they had been giving so generously to the Greek Communist guerrillas and the Greek government was finally able to drive the guerrillas into Albania and Bulgaria. The NATO governments in consultation worked out the broad structure of the organization of the alliance. The top body was to be a political council. Each nation would be represented on this council by an ambassador. The military structure would include an over-all command headquarters. This was to become the greatest peacetime alliance in human history. It still endures thirty years later. Some have said that it is ineffective and out of date. That may be but its dissolution remains one of the prime objectives of Soviet foreign policy. I doubt whether they would waste much effort on discrediting NATO if they did not regard it as a formidable and effective obstacle to their plans.

The Allied powers agreed that the seat of the alliance would be in Paris and that both the political council and the military headquarters would be in the vicinity of the French capital. Temporary buildings erected in 1948 for the United Nations General Assembly meeting became available for the political council. Not very much was done in the military area.

In 1950 The U. S. Chiefs of Staff went to Europe to submit to the Europeans the outline of a plan for the military organization of the alliance. These plans would replace those established earlier by the Western Union powers and would of course include the United States, Canada and the other additional signatories of the NATO treaty. The U. S. Chiefs of Staff were led by their chairman, General of the Army Omar Bradley. In World War II he was the victorious commander of a gigantic Army group that had liberated a great part of Western Europe. Next to General Eisenhower he was the most prestigious American soldier. Quiet and soft-spoken, he could be firm and steadfast.

On General Bradley's arrival in Paris he borrowed me from Mr. Harriman, on whose staff I was (serving at the Marshall plan), in order to translate the U. S. Chiefs' presentation to the European military authorities. The European Chiefs liked the concepts presented to them and the North Korean attack on South Korea gave a sense of urgency to the whole matter of organizing the defense of Europe.

From the outset in every discussion where the question of a commander arose, thought turned automatically to General Eisenhower. To most Europeans his name was inextricably bound up with liberation. His presence at the summit of the military organization would be an enormous reassurance to all. More important still, it would send a message to the Soviets that the United States was in earnest in its commitment to defend Western Europe. General Eisenhower was at that time president of Columbia University in New York City. He was not anxious to leave that post. He finally responded to President Truman's appeal and agreed to accept the post of first Supreme Allied Commander in Europe. In early January 1951 he decided to undertake a journey to the NATO capitals to meet with the political and military authorities of each country. He would discuss with them the establishment of the Supreme Headquarters of the Allied Powers in Europe.

General Eisenhower knew that I spoke a number of languages. He asked Mr. Harriman—on whose staff I was working at the White House—to make me available for this journey. Mr. Harriman readily agreed since it was understood that I would return to his staff upon the conclusion of General Eisenhower's trip. General Eisenhower took a small staff which included an experienced Foreign Service officer, Douglas MacArthur II, the general's nephew.

We left Washington on January 6, 1951, in a special military Constellation aircraft made available to General Eisenhower by President Truman. We flew all night and landed the next morning at Orly airfield near Paris. French Defense Minister Jules Moch and Chief of the French Defense Staff General Alphonse Juin met us on landing. Like most European non-Communists they were delighted and relieved to see General Eisenhower and greeted him warmly.

Despite the all-night flight General Eisenhower got right down to business. We had lunch with Moch and other officials. The French Defense Minister was a Socialist and a staunch anti-Communist. His son had been killed during the war and he was bitterly anti-German. He opposed any German participation in the defense of Western Europe. He was almost psychotic on this subject. Likewise he wanted no dealings with Franco's Spain for ideological reasons. In all other respects he was strong and helpful. General Eisenhower had many meetings with him in those early formative months of the alliance. Mr. Moch spoke passable English, but he was more comfortable in his own language so I usually accompanied General Eisenhower to these meetings.

On the day after our arrival in Paris I went with General Eisenhower to call on Prime Minister René Pleven. He also called upon Foreign Minister Robert Schuman. The latter was a most unusual man. He had been born in Luxembourg, served in the German Army in World War I and was now the French Foreign Minister. He was one of the great artisans of the movement for European unity, together with Adenauer of Germany, de Gasperi of Italy and Spaak of Belgium. Schuman was an ascetic man whose whole life was dedicated to ending the long rivalry between France and Germany. That rivalry had twice in this century led to terrible and destructive wars.

On January 9 General Eisenhower called upon President Vincent Auriol. The French President was also a Socialist and spoke with a broad accent from the South of France. During World War II he was secretly flown out of German-occupied France in a light plane and had joined General de Gaulle in London. He was a kindly fatherly sort of man but strongly opposed to communism. Later that morning I accompanied General Eisenhower to Fontainebleau to visit the Western European headquarters. That evening General Juin came by the Raphael Hotel, where we were staying, for cocktails. He and Eisenhower were on excellent terms and were good friends as well.

General Eisenhower then flew to Brussels, where he was met by the Defense Minister, Colonel de Greef, and the Chief of Defense, General Jacques Piron. The latter had led Belgian troops fighting under Eisenhower during the liberation of Europe. I accompanied General Eisenhower on all of his calls on Belgian defense officials. There were no problems. The Belgians were anxious to help and support the new NATO headquarters in any way they could.

General Eisenhower flew on the next day, January 10, to the Netherlands. Since all of the Dutch officials spoke excellent English I did not accompany him in his calls on them and in a sense had a day off. Here as in Belgium things went well. There were, however, some indications of tension between the Defense Chief, General H. J. Kruls, and the Prime Minister, who was a pacifist and a member of the Broken Rifle association. Kruls told Eisenhower that he was having great difficulty in getting the Prime Minister to agree to even the minimum requirements for the Netherlands Armed Forces.

The next few days were spent in Denmark and Norway. In Copenhagen the Danish Chief of Defense, Admiral Erhard Qvistgaard, met General Eisenhower. The admiral's son had been killed shortly before in Korea, where he was fighting as a volunteer in the U. S. Armed Forces. The admiral was anxious to be of assistance but Denmark was a country with a long history of pacifism. It had offered no organized resistance to the German invasion in 1940. Subsequently there had been some gallant resistance. Many Danes, however, were convinced that any defense effort was futile. The government was helpful and co-operative, within the limits of what was possible for them. The northern countries had traditionally been neutral, but both Denmark and Norway had been invaded during World War II. Sweden had chosen to go it alone. In Norway there were some analogies with the situation in Denmark. Norway, however, had bitterly resisted the German invasion and occupation. Norwegians knew what a harsh occupation could mean and possessed a more intense desire to defend themselves than did the Danes. Crown Prince Olav gave a dinner and General Eisen-

hower was received by King Haakon VII. I accompanied him to
both.

We left Oslo on the evening of January 12 in the midst of
falling snow. At Gardermoen Airport glycerine was being poured
on the control surfaces to prevent their freezing. We flew to
London, where the British welcomed Eishenhower as an old and
valued friend. He lunched with Prime Minister Attlee. Once the
British were assured of substantial representation in the command structure of the alliance, there were no difficulties.

An ironic incident occurred during Eisenhower's stay in London. As we walked out of Claridge's Hotel we ran into Prime
Minister Jawaharlal Nehru of India. He wore a bowler hat and
looked every inch the British gentleman. As president of Columbia University, Eisenhower had conferred an honorary degree on
Nehru. Nonetheless, the Indian Prime Minister seemed enormously embarrassed to run into Eisenhower, who was being
denounced in the Soviet press as a warmonger. As they talked
Nehru kept looking around furtively as though fearful of being
photographed with Eisenhower. To his visible relief, he was not.

From London we flew to Lisbon, where my Portuguese
proved useful. On January 17, 1951, I accompanied General Eisenhower on a call upon Prime Minister António Salazar at São
Bento Palace. I had met Salazar previously during my service
with Mr. Harriman for the Marshall Plan. Salazar recognized
me at once and as we shook hands he asked if I still had my
Brazilian accent in Portuguese. I acknowledged that I did but
promised to try to lose it while in Portugal.

Salazar spoke philosophically about the differences between
the countries of northern Europe and those of southern Europe.
Democracy might work, he said, in the United States, United
Kingdom or the Scandinavian countries, but such a system in
Portugal would degenerate into anarchy. He recalled the chaotic
situation that prevailed in Portugal before he came to power in
1926. He saw the Soviet threat clearly. He feared Soviet support
for the independence movements in the Portuguese colonies, or
overseas provinces as he called them. Soviet strategy, he pre-
dicted, would include African bases astride the West's oceanic

lines of communication—a disturbingly accurate prediction. The Portuguese leader looked nothing like a man accustomed to wielding dictatorial power for twenty-five years. He was quiet and professorial and spoke almost in a whisper. He never wore a uniform or harangued the masses from a balcony. As we departed by car General Eisenhower, musing aloud on Salazar's unusual personality, said, "He is a remarkable man. I don't agree with everything he says, but he is a mighty impressive figure." My Brazilian accent had evidently not impeded the flow of the conversation. Following the talk with the Portuguese Prime Minister, we found the Portuguese military leaders unanimously eager to help.

We flew on to Italy. The Italian Defense Minister and the Chief of Defense Staff met General Eisenhower at the Rome airport. As Eisenhower began his arrival statement, I absentmindedly translated it into Portuguese. Everyone burst into laughter. I sheepishly shifted to Italian. On January 18 I accompanied General Eisenhower to his call upon Prime Minister Alcide de Gasperi, one of the great men of postwar Europe. Alcide de Gasperi began his career before the First World War as a member of the parliament of the Austro-Hungarian Empire. He had represented the Italian minority in the Hapsburg empire. A man of great vision and historical perspective, he gave Italy leadership such as she has not enjoyed since. Later the Foreign and Defense Ministers joined the talk. De Gasperi recalled me from previous meetings when I accompanied Mr. Harriman in calls upon him. He remembered that I had worn an Italian decoration with a crown on it, which I had received from King Umberto II. General Eisenhower called upon President Luigi Einaudi at the Quirinale Palace. He then lunched with Defense Minister Randolfo Pacciardi. The Italians were pleased at being included and most anxious to help the alliance. De Gasperi was a strong proponent of European unity and common defense.

The next morning we flew to Luxembourg, the smallest member of the alliance. Because French was commonly spoken there I accompanied General Eisenhower in his calls upon Grand Duchess Charlotte, Prime Minister Pierre Dupong and

Foreign Minister Joseph Bech. The latter had been Foreign Minister longer than anyone could recall. The Luxembourg Armed Forces were tiny but there were no problems at all in this wonderful little country.

We flew to Germany. Near Darmstadt as we rode in a jeep along a country road, two little German boys pointed excitedly at the general. We stopped the jeep and I asked them in German if they knew who he was. They grinned and said that they did. Eisenhower spoke to a number of our commanders in Germany to get their views. Germany was not yet fully sovereign and was still an occupied country.

Next day we flew back to Paris, where I accompanied General Eisenhower on visits to several possible sites for the construction of the new headquarters. Finally he chose one at Rocquencourt. It belonged to the French presidency. Mr. Auriol at once made it available. General Eisenhower continued his discussions with the French and conveyed to them the fine co-operative spirit he had found everywhere. On the afternoon of January 24 he spoke to his small staff at the Astoria Hotel, the temporary headquarters until the new building could be completed.

On January 25, 1951, we flew to Reykjavik, the capital of Iceland, the only member of the alliance with no armed forces at all. We landed at Keflavík Airport in a howling snowstorm. Since my knowledge of the Icelandic language was nil, I remained aboard the aircraft during the general's brief talks with the Icelandic government. With us was an irrepressible young major, fond of wisecracks. He noted that most of the parka-clad ground personnel were Americans. As darkness fell and the wind lashed the snow across the airfield, I thought that the only thing missing to complete the eerie picture was a pack of wolves. The young major looked out through the open door of the plane and seeing a man who was servicing the aircraft, he said to him, "Hey, bud, what did you do to get sent to this hellhole?" The man looked at him solemnly and then said slowly, "I was born here. I am an Icelander and this is not a hellhole." We pulled the young major back into the plane and kept him there until General Eisenhower returned and we flew on to Ottawa. We crossed Greenland in clear weather and the sight of the gigantic ice cap was most impressive. We made our landfall in Labrador at a place with the unforgettable name of Bear's Gut. We arrived in Ottawa and were met by high Canadian officials. We stayed at the Chateau Laurier Hotel. General Eisenhower always made a point of not staying at the American Embassy to emphasize the international character of his position. Talks with the Canadians went very smoothly. They knew Eisenhower and liked and trusted him.

On January 27 General Eisenhower ended his whirlwind tour through thirteen countries at West Point, New York. Here he was to spend the weekend and to write his report for President Truman. We landed at Stewart Field in a blinding snowstorm. As the plane banked sharply to line up with the runway, I felt it sideslip and thought for a moment that it was going to crash. My brother Vincent, who was on the ground watching, told me later that he had the same feeling. Bill Draper, the pilot, straightened up the aircraft and brought it in for a smooth landing. I left General Eisenhower there and returned to Washington. While aboard the aircraft, I had after each stop dictated long memoranda of our conversations to two warrant officer stenographers we had aboard. Thus I did not have a backlog of memoranda to write at the end of the trip. Although I had not interpreted some of the conversations that General Eisenhower had had, if I was present I made a record of what was said for him.

I returned to Mr. Harriman's staff. A few days later he told me that General Eisenhower had asked President Truman to have me assigned to him at SHAPE in Paris. I had been back in Washington only six months and was not anxious to leave my job with Mr. Harriman, which I enjoyed very much. Harriman told me that President Truman had told General Eisenhower he could have anyone he wanted for this mission. I really had no choice. Either I would go quietly or they would drag me screaming. The first option made more sense. Mr. Harriman had also found out that while on the trip I had played bridge a good deal with Doug MacArthur against Generals Eisenhower and

Gruenther, both of whom were experts. MacArthur and I had not done well against them. Mr. Harriman gave me several books on bridge by Goren and expressed the hope that they would help my career. I was not asked to play bridge with the two generals again. Clearly they felt that my skill at bridge was not on a par with my proficiency at languages.

Less than half a year, therefore, after my return from the Marshall Plan I was on my way back to Europe to serve at the new NATO headquarters. As usual I left my mother behind to do all of the actual work of moving and flew to Paris.

On February 22 General and Mrs. Eisenhower arrived at Cherbourg by boat. Mrs. Eisenhower never really liked to fly. Immediately General Eisenhower went to work to set up the headquarters and organize the command structure of the alliance. Above all he was able to infuse into all who worked at SHAPE his own infectious enthusiasm and confidence. I accompanied him upon many calls on French civilian and military authorities. I went with him when he went to look at the house that the French government was offering to make available to him at Marnes la Coquette, a small village not far from the headquarters at Rocquencourt. Things moved rapidly and on April 2, 1951, General Eisenhower issued General Order № 1 establishing SHAPE.

General Eisenhower kept in almost continuous touch with the French to speed construction of the new buildings for the headquarters and the supporting service units. He was struck by the vast differences in pay between officers of the same rank but of different nationalities. This meant that these officers had very different living standards. In an integrated headquarters this was bound to cause problems. He was able to convince the French that they should build a housing complex known as SHAPE Village. Here apartments were given on a point system that involved not only rank but also the number in the family. These apartments were reasonable and went a long way toward eliminating some of the inequities of pay. They also created a situation where officers of many nationalties lived in close proximity to one another. This fostered friendship and understanding.

I was assigned to the office of the Executive for National Military Representatives. In SHAPE an officer served in a position as a staff officer and not as the representative of his country or service. This representation was handled by offices that resembled military embassies. The National Military Representatives dealt through our office with the Supreme Commander in matters that were of special national interest to their respective countries. The executive for National Military Representatives was Colonel Anthony Drexel Biddle. His experience as a former ambassador to all of the governments in exile in London during World War II was invaluable and his enormous personal charm greatly facilitated our task in dealing with the various national representatives. I worked in this section every day but needless to say when the Supreme Commander needed me for some foreign visitor this was the overriding priority.

General Eisenhower believed that all of the peoples of the alliance had to be sold on the idea of the need for collective defense and more specifically on the need for the NATO military organization. This led to an almost continuous stream of visitors from all of the participating nations. Not just political and military authorities, but civic groups, newspapermen and associations of all types came individually or in groups to the headquarters to be briefed. Not all were favorably disposed toward the alliance. One day General Eisenhower had me to a lunch he gave for the president of the Paris City Council, Mr. Pierre de Gaulle, the general's brother. The general was then heading the Rassemblement du Peuple Français and was very much opposed to the current French government.

In April 1951 I flew down to northern Italy to visit units there and to prepare for a visit by General Eisenhower. I was making the arrangements for his trip to the Udine area. Since the Italians did not judge any of the local hotels to be adequate they decided to house him in a private villa belonging to Countess Florio. Her husband had been killed in the war with Marshal Italo Balbo, the Italian governor of Libya, when his plane was shot down over Tobruk. She owned immense properties and after her husband's death she went to the University of Bologna, where she took a degree in agriculture. She managed her lands with great skill. In her living room the countess had photographs of King Umberto II (then an exile in Portugal) and of Marshal Balbo. The prefect of Udine was fearful that a photograph of the Fascist marshal might displease General Eisenhower and he did not know how the general might react to a photograph of the King, who had been dethroned in 1946. The countess was adamant. She would not move the photos and if the prefect did not like it then he could house General Eisenhower elsewhere. Since there were no other suitable accommodations in the area the countess won that battle. Soon after General Eisenhower arrived, he noticed the photographs. The prefect, who was present, grew tense. General Eisenhower recalled to the guests his good relations with King Umberto and added that when Marshal Balbo led a squadron of Italian planes across the ocean to the Chicago Century of Progress Exhibition, he had been designated as aide to Marshal Balbo and had liked him very much. The prefect relaxed and the countess smiled triumphantly. Later I went with General Eisenhower to watch a demonstration of mountain warfare put on by Italian Alpine troops. It was most impressive. The artillery fell very close to the maneuvering troops and the whole thing was extremely realistic. At the end of the demonstration the Alpini gave Eisenhower an Alpine hat complete with a long plume. The news media were delighted with the resulting photos.

Between trips to the forces under his command Eisenhower continuously received large numbers of visitors at the headquarters. He simultaneously continued the task of getting the command structure organized. He needed all of his persuasive powers to settle some of the political problems which arose. Choice commands were particularly "hot" items. The general settled every question without rancor or bitterness. He was a master of military and political diplomacy.

The neutrals watched the establishment of the NATO headquarters with great interest. They wanted to know if the United States was really committed to the defense of its allies in Europe. Yugoslavia sent General Koca Popovic to Eisenhower.

He spoke excellent French so I translated at this very secret meeting. He left reassured that the United States would live up to its commitments. A similar visitor came discreetly from Sweden. Since he spoke German, I again translated. He too went away reassured from his call on the Supreme Commander.

A French government crisis brought in Georges Bidault to replace Jules Moch as French Defense Minister. The new Minister had remained in occupied France throughout the war and had been president of the National Council of Resistance. Mr. Moch was a professed agnostic who looked with condescending amusement on General Eisenhower's efforts to emphasize the importance of spiritual values. He seemed to think that General Eisenhower was trying to organize a Children's Crusade. Bidault, on the other hand, was a devoutly religious man who understood this aspect of Eisenhower's efforts. As I accompanied the Supreme Commander to many meetings, I would often brief him about the people he was going to meet. My years with Mr. Harriman had given me the opportunity to meet with many of the same leaders that Eisenhower was meeting. His comments about them after the meeting were always of the greatest interest to me. He was a keen judge of men.

Day after day he received groups from the media, NATO members of parliament, members of the U. S. Congress, civic and patriotic groups. When these groups were large he would give a buffet and then move around the group, trying to give them all an opportunity to talk with him. I tried to stay at his side when these were non-English-speaking groups. It was not always easy to render accurately into other languages his humor, confidence and enthusiasm. Perhaps the most memorable of these visitors was Winston Churchill, who came on December 18, 1951. He spoke to us and praised NATO and General Eisenhower. His words moved us deeply. Rightly has it been said that not since Caesar has any man been so mighty with both pen and sword. On occasion Eisenhower would see people from non-NATO countries, Spanish journalists, South American ambassadors, men from all continents. On such occasions I was normally with him. Many members of the U. S. Senate and House of

Representatives came during this period. Many were trying to get Eisenhower into the presidential race in 1952. Others were trying to keep him out, telling him that he was the indispensable man in Europe. They were always treated with great respect. I could not but contrast this with the Deputy Supreme Commander's treatment of visiting members of the British Parliament. On one occasion I saw Field Marshal Montgomery lecture them like schoolchildren. When they wanted to ask questions he would instruct them to stand up, give their name and then ask the question. One did so and when he gave his name, Monty said, "Oh yes, I remember you. You are the one who said that it would be a good thing if I kept my big mouth shut, and now you want to hear my opinion."

In January 1952, the French commander in chief and high commissioner in Indochina died. General Jean de Lattre de Tassigny had commanded the First French Army, composed of eleven divisions, under Eisenhower during World War II. He had been a brilliant commander in Indochina and was struck down by cancer shortly after his only son had been killed in Indochina. De Lattre was to be given a state funeral and Eisenhower and Montgomery were invited to be among the pallbearers. This would involve walking several miles alongside the caisson carrying the casket from Notre Dame Cathedral to the military church at the Invalides, where Napoleon is buried. It was very cold and a number of Eisenhower's advisers told him that he should not do it. He listened to the discussion for a few minutes and then brought it to an end by saying, "Don't you think that this is the least thing I can do for an old comrade?" I walked in the procession some distance behind General Eisenhower. It was extremely cold and the wind was biting. Eisenhower's walking alongside the coffin made a deep impression on the millions who watched the funeral. When we reached the Invalides I was able to move briefly to his side. I asked him, "General, are you still alive?" He flashed a grin and replied, "Yes, but only just."

On one occasion I went ahead of him to the French forces in Germany to prepare for his visit. Early one morning the French told me that General MacArthur had been relieved from command by President Truman. I was not really surprised. I had a feeling that this move might come ever since I had attended the Wake Island meeting. When General Eisenhower arrived to visit the 3rd Algerian Infantry Division, he came from Frankfurt, so I thought that he had already heard the news and did not mention it to him. We were watching a French unit maneuvering to the attack and during a break the newspapermen and photographers who were accompanying him crowded around. A photographer stood in front, aimed his camera at the general and said, "I'm ready; ask him the question." A newsman then said, "General, President Truman has just fired MacArthur for insubordination. Do you have any comment?" This took Eisenhower completely by surprise. He had not heard the news and the ensuing photograph won a prize that year. As I rode back to the French headquarters with him he said to me, "You know, when you put on a uniform, you impose certain restrictions on yourself. MacArthur may have forgotten them." I knew, of course, that there was no great love lost between them since Eisenhower had worked for MacArthur in the Philippines before the Second World War. One story from that period was that MacArthur had said that Eisenhower was the best clerk he had ever had. Eisenhower noted that he had studied dramatics under MacArthur.

In early March I went with General Eisenhower to Greece and Turkey, each a recent addition to NATO. He was warmly received in Turkey. We had good discussions with the Turks and the delicate command problem arising from their unwillingness to be put under an Italian commander and suspicions of the Greeks was settled, at least for the time being. From Ankara we flew to Istanbul for a few hours of sight-seeing. As we entered the Blue Mosque, Eisenhower pointed to an inscription over the door and asked what it meant. An old Turkish general replied, "It says, 'Before you ask God for anything, first work yourself.'" General Eisenhower greatly appreciated this piece of advice.

We flew on to Salonica to inspect the Greek troops of the III

Corps. Then we went on to Athens. I accompanied General Eisenhower to lunch at the Greek Military Academy, where he talked to the cadets. That night we went to dinner with King Paul and Queen Frederika at the royal palace. Just before the dinner King Paul awarded high Greek decorations to General Eisenhower and his Chief of Staff, General Gruenther. I was sitting next to the King's ninety-year-old uncle, Prince Nicholas. He grumbled and said to me, "It's ridiculous, giving medals to those old generals who already have a lot. They should give them to young fellows like you." I found myself in sympathy with the idea.

On the way back to Paris we stopped in Italy to see Defense Minister Pacciardi. He had insisted that the Greek and Turkish forces be under an Italian commander. Both, however, had told Eisenhower that this was out of the question. During the discussion Eisenhower suddenly appeared to misunderstand something that Pacciardi had just said and I had translated. His face flushed and he pounded the table indignantly. Pacciardi, after a few feeble attempts to explain that he had been misunderstood, gave in and accepted a U. S. commander for the Greek and Turkish sector of NATO. I was greatly crestfallen as it appeared to Pacciardi that I had mistranslated what he had said and that this had provoked Eisenhower's anger. I thought that my reputation as a linguist would be shot forever in Italy. The matter of the command settled, we returned to Naples airport and took off for Paris. I was sitting in the forward cabin feeling quite glum when General Eisenhower came forward, tapped me on the shoulder and said, "Dick, if I sometimes appear to misunderstand what you say, it is just that I need a hook on which to hang my anger." He added with a grin, "It worked too." This made me feel much better but I still worried about my reputation in Italy.

Throughout this period pressure had been mounting on General Eisenhower to go back to the United States to try to win the Republican nomination for the presidency. An endless stream of politicians had been through Paris working on him. At first he remained noncommittal. On the day of the New Hamp-

To my friend Dick Walters
   With gratitude for your long
      and faithful service to
         our country, *Jerry Ford*

To my friend general "Dick" Walters
with appreciation for his magnificent
service to the nation from
Dick Nixon

For: Colonel Vernon A. Walters
 U.S. Army Attache, Brazil

a master of tongues,

Lyndon B. Johnson

"A master of tongues."

"For: Dick Walters—with deep appreciation of incalculable service—and with warm regard from his devoted friend."

"Kindest regards to a capable & efficient officer."

Vernon and Vincent Walters, 1932.

At thirteen, just before returning from Paris to school in England, May 12, 1930. My first flight.

At school: top row, third from the left.

As General Mark Clark's aide, outside my van. Italy, 1944.

Private Vernon A. Walters in blue fagues. Camp Upton, Long Island, May 4, 1941.

September 27, 1944: with the Fifth Army in Italy. Left to right: Major General Mascarenhas de Moraes; Major General Ralph H. Wooton; Major General Geoffrey Keyes; Lieutenant Antonio João Dutra, son of Brazil's War Minister; Lieutenant General Mark W. Clark; Major General Eurico Gaspar Dutra, Minister of War of Brazil; and Captain Vernon Walters.

Field Marshal Alexander visits the Brazilian Expeditionary Force in Italy, November 8, 1944.

Clare Boothe Luce visits the Brazilian Expeditionary Force, Italy, 1945.

Rio de Janeiro, 1946. With General Eisenhower and Brazilian Minister of War Goes Monteiro.

shire primary results I had flown to Germany with him. For some reason that I cannot remember there were only the two of us on the aircraft returning to Paris. All day long people had been handing me partial and later the final results of the primary. I knew that theoretically he was supposed to be uninterested in the primary. On the way home I finally said, "General, you may not be interested, but other people are. All day long people have been handing me the partial results of the New Hampshire primary. Now I have the final results and here they are." He grinned, looked at them and said to me, "Well, any American would have to be a strange kind of guy if he did not feel good that that many of his fellow countrymen feel that way about him." He had won the primary handsomely without even running. Personally, I never doubted that he would run. When a man has achieved extraordinary success in one field of human activity, he often seeks success in another.

When he finally decided to announce that he would return to the United States to run, the announcement was to be made at a press conference at SHAPE. On the appointed day a very large group of newspapermen from all over the world were gathered, waiting for Ike's chief of public relations to make an announcement that would clarify the general's intentions. General Buck Lanham did not show up at the appointed time for the announcement, which I was supposed to translate into French, the other official language of the Alliance. In fact General Lanham was sweating profusely in another nearby room. His fly would not zip shut after a trip to the bathroom. Time was running out and a desperate decision was made to sew the fly shut while General Lanham was in the pants. With several colonels acting as chaperons, a girl secretary took the necessary stitches in time and a major crisis was narrowly averted.

In the months before the announcement we had to take care of large numbers of congressmen. Sometimes they gave us serious problems by dabbling in "fringe benefits." One night I had to help carry a congressman into the Royal Monceau Hotel. He was dead drunk. Another told me that he had lost his wallet and passport in a night club and would appreciate it if I could get

them back for him. I went to the night club and they told me
that he had left with a young woman. After some difficulties I
located her. She admitted that he had visited her but denied
that he had left his passport or his wallet. I explained that I was
less interested in the money and much more so in the passport
and the papers in the wallet. I explained to her that I had good
friends in the Paris Police Department and urged her to have
another look in the bedroom. She returned a few minutes later
smiling and said, "What do you know? It was there." She
handed me the wallet and the passport. I found only ten dollars
in the wallet. An expensive evening for the congressman. He
thanked me without asking how I had located it. Another congressman bought a large crystal chandelier at the flea market
and tasked me with getting it back to the United States. Balanc-
ing it precariously from a hook attached to the roof rib of my
convertible, I drove it to Orly Airport and sneaked it aboard the
military Constellation aircraft on which the congressmen were
traveling. I hung it from a hook on the roof of the cabin and
left. The congressman later wrote from the United States to
thank me. He wrote that he felt I must have a sporting interest
in knowing whether the chandelier had made it safely back to
Washington. It had.

On many occasions during Eisenhower's tour at SHAPE
efforts had been made to get him together with General de
Gaulle, who was then in opposition to the government. De
Gaulle had been lukewarm in his support for NATO and many
thought that if he could be brought together with General Eisenhower he could be won over. Arranging such a meeting was
difficult. Eisenhower was a guest of the French government and
was even living in a house that they provided for him. General
de Gaulle was very touchy about protocol and would not go to
SHAPE. This problem was eventually solved and they lunched
together at the seat of the Order of Liberation, which de Gaulle
had founded and of which Eisenhower was the only foreign recipient. I have recounted this meeting in the chapter on de
Gaulle. At that time he foresaw that both he and General Eisenhower would be called upon to lead their peoples. Seven

years later they were to meet again, both as President of their respective countries, and once more I was to translate for them.

The news that Eisenhower was leaving was greeted with dismay, alleviated only by the thought that the alliance would have a good friend in the White House. None doubted that he would be elected. On May 21, 1952, President Vincent Auriol of France gave a formal farewell lunch for General Eisenhower. I cannot remember what each said, but I do remember that the food and wines were superb. On May 29 the officers of SHAPE gave their departing commander a farewell dinner that was very moving. On the thirtieth General Eisenhower formally turned over the command to his successor, General Matthew Ridgway, an experienced and distinguished soldier. As Ike left his villa at Marnes la Coquette a boys' choir sang "Auld Lang Syne" and there were few dry eyes among those present.

The rest is history. Eisenhower was triumphantly elected. It was in a way the end of the era of the great crusade at SHAPE. I was fortunate during this period in being closely associated with General Eisenhower. This gave me an unusual opportunity to observe him under different circumstances and to watch how he dealt with different foreign leaders. Though he often expressed appreciation for my services, I could see how much more easily he could communicate with those who spoke English. I was conscious of this and did my best to make him as little aware as possible that what he was hearing was a translation.

Eisenhower rarely used strong language. More often he would say "goldarned" than "damn." Yet on one occasion I heard him tell how in a moment of indignation he had called someone a "son of a bitch." He said that a British officer on his staff had asked whether he had given any consideration to calling this man a "spherical son of a bitch." General Eisenhower asked what that was. The British officer replied, "General, a spherical son of a bitch is one who, viewed from any angle, is still a son of a bitch."

Jovial and friendly as he was, there was a certain aura about the man and few were insensitive to it.

Often in the car returning from some meeting with a foreign

dignitary he would speak of his previous experience with this man and his reaction to what he had taken up with him. Such appraisals based on his immense experience were to be very useful to me in later years. He was a shrewd judge of character and had an uncanny ability to evaluate people. He knew this and was proud of it. I once heard him say, "If I had no other claim to fame, the fact that I had chosen Bedell Smith and Al Gruenther as my chiefs of staff would entitle me to at least a modicum of fame." Both of these men were extraordinarily able. Gruenther was later to become the third Supreme Allied Commander and an outstanding one. I had known General Gruenther since World War II. He had been General Clark's Chief of Staff during the whole of the Italian campaign. Completely American in the best sense of the word, he had won the Europeans by his brilliance and his understanding. He had a strong personality and a remarkable ability to persuade others that what he wanted was good for them. He was a man of considerable personal charm, but the life of his aides was very like mine with General Clark. He had a memory of staggering proportions. He made a point of having every officer at SHAPE to his table for lunch at least once every six months and would often take up the conversation at the point where he had left off six months earlier. He too evoked great loyalty and brought out the best in his subordinates. His wife Grace was a perfect foil for him. She had a friendly word for all and was unimpressed by his brilliance. On one occasion, against General Gruenther's advice, she drove the family car into Paris and caught the bumper on a hydrant, nearly tearing it off. She drove home not quite knowing how she was going to break the news to him. She put the car carefully in the garage. Later that evening General Gruenther decided to drive himself to the home of a friend nearby. As he backed the car cautiously out of the garage, he struck the rear bumper against the door. He got out to examine the damage and was horrified to see that the bumper was nearly torn off. He could not understand how this could have happened since he was moving very slowly when he touched the door. He came in and told his wife that he had barely touched the door and yet the bumper was almost torn off. To which she replied, "Al Gruenther, don't you give me that 'barely touched the door' stuff. You know that you crashed into the door. It serves you right for driving yourself and not using your assigned driver." This nearly drove him crazy, so she finally had to tell him the truth. By then she had him so on the defensive that he could not chide her for having done it in the first place. General Gruenther solidified the alliance and gave it intellectual conviction as well as emotional content. His unchallengeable integrity and force of personality dominated the alliance during his years as Supreme Commander. His strategic vision coupled with his ability to grasp minute details made him a formidable commander.

Twice during this period when I remained at SHAPE, President Eisenhower sent for me to go to summit meetings with him, at Bermuda and at Geneva. These are covered in another chapter.

In 1954 I had been attending an intelligence course at a U. S. Army installation at Oberammergau, in Germany. On Good Friday of that year I was skiing down from the top of the Zugspitze, the highest mountain in Germany. I was racing against the clock and as I got about halfway down the mountain to an area called Kreuzeck, I ran into some clouds hanging on the side of the mountain. I did not realize how opaque they were. When I ran into them I could no longer see the trail and traveling at high speed, struck a large rock, which shattered my right ski and broke my right leg. I fell and lay in the snow for a short period. The first person to reach me was a German one-legged skier. He looked at me, reached into his pocket, took out a pillbox and handed me a pill and said, "Take this; this is what the doctors give me to take when the stump hurts." To this day I do not know what it was, but it did make the pain somewhat bearable. He left to get the ski patrol. I had seen many skiing accidents and I knew that when the injury was severe a period of trembling set in. I was determined that this would not happen with me. They placed me on a sled and took me over to the cable car station at Kreuzeck. There they put me in the cable car, wrapped me in blankets and fed me hot chocolate. At this point when I was on the stretcher, wrapped in warm blankets and drinking hot chocolate, the trembling began. It was absolutely uncontrollable and I was embarrassed by it, but there was nothing that I could do to stop it. At the bottom an ambulance was waiting to drive me to Munich. They drove me to the American Army hospital on Koelner Platz, where I was operated on that night.

The operation was performed under a spinal anaesthetic and while I was somewhat drugged, I was conscious of what was going on. I recall asking whether they were sewing yet and they said no. The skin had not been broken, but the separation of the bones was such that they had made an incision and screwed the bones together and then put me in a cast. The pain, while intense, was not comparable to the pain I had experienced when I was burned in Italy during World War II. I remained in the hospital for a considerable period of time. The wound became infected with one of those antibiotic-resistant strains that develop in hospitals, and I was in the hospital for more than two months. This medical episode was to drag out for more than two years before I was finally released from various casts or braces. The food at the hospital was not good. I was able to drive my car with the cast on because the car had an automatic transmission, and I could place the cast on a camp stool in front of the seat on the right of the car. Moving on crutches, however, was extremely difficult and tiring. I could not go inside buildings, as the effort was too great to do any sort of indoor sightseeing. I was released from the hospital during the daytime and drove around much of south Germany.

The Germans were accustomed to large numbers of their own war wounded and were extremely helpful and sympathetic to me when they realized that I was in a cast and on crutches.

I was able to go downtown to get a good meal. I went the first time to the Vier Jahreszeiten Hotel. Here there is one of the great restaurants of Germany, the Walterspiel. It was presided over by old Mr. Walterspiel himself, who bore an extraordinary resemblance to Field Marshal von Hindenburg. After my meal there, which concluded about three o'clock, I went back to the hospital, and at four o'clock they brought my evening meal to me in my room. It was typical hospital and Army fare. I waved it away, closed my eyes and said, "Go away and leave me with my memories of the Walterspiel." During this time I kept getting short sympathetic and sometimes ironic notes from General Gruenther. The first one I received read, "After hearing what has happened to you, my first reaction was to put you before an eight-ball board, but on reflection you will be punished enough." Another of them said, "Tell those doctors to take good care of you. There are lots of doctors, but only one Dick Walters."

It was tedious for me to be confined in this way and I finally talked the doctors into letting me go back to Paris to resume my job at SHAPE despite my crutches and cast. I remained in a cast or brace for nearly two years. Six months after the accident, since the bone had not healed, I went to the Army hospital at Neubrucke near the French border and was operated on by a distinguished surgeon, Colonel Milton S. Thompson. He was successful and though the process was long my leg healed completely and has never given me any trouble since. Every year in my Christmas card to Colonel Thompson and his wife, I wish them both a merry Christmas, recalling how many merry Christmases he has made possible for me.

I resumed my normal functions at SHAPE and continued there for more than a year still on crutches and in a cast. Everyone from General Gruenther on down showed great understanding for the slowness and difficulty with which I had to move. This handicap did not, however, prevent me from doing my normal work as assistant to the Deputy Chief of Staff for Logistics and Administration. Still later after I returned to the United States I was to return to Europe for NATO Military Committee meetings on four occasions. I used to say that my cast had been across the ocean eight times. Sometimes I used to wonder about minor mishaps with the aircraft—would I be able to get out in time if anything happened? While I thought about it, I lost no sleep worrying about it. I was more concerned

whether I would ever recover the full use of my right leg. I
missed tremendously the ability to stroll or window-shop. While
I worried about my leg I made a major effort not to complain
about it to anyone, even my mother. She once said to me, "I
have never heard you complain about your leg." I shrugged and
did not tell her how much I worried whether they would eventually have to amputate it or not. The thought never left me until
I was sure that the bone had knitted.

After four years my tour at SHAPE ended. I made arrangements to return to the United States by boat, sailing from
Naples. My mother, who lived with me after the death of my father, had invited two friends to drive down to Naples with us.
Mrs. McBain lived in Paris and Mrs. Inslee came from Los Angeles for the trip. They took an immediate and violent dislike to
one another. The distance from Paris was great and I had to
drive with my leg in the cast on a camp stool. Fortunately the
car had an automatic transmission and I could accelerate and
brake with my left foot.

When the day of departure from Paris came, the moving men
were still in the apartment. My mother had gone out to have
her hair done and her room was still untouched, as though she
was going to be in it for weeks. The rest of the apartment had
been emptied, except for packing cases in the living room. The
movers were grumbling and wanted to finish, but my mother
had left strict instructions that her room was not to be touched
until she got back. The two ladies and I sat on packing cases in
what had been the living room. While we waited three women
arrived separately. They had been summoned by my mother.
One was a dressmaker, another a costume jeweler and the third
a milliner. Finally my mother arrived and I chided her for the
delay. She replied, "Don't press me or I will have a stroke, not
one of those quick ones, but a long, lingering one." Then she
did her business with the three tradeswomen and finally packed
so that the movers could clean out her room. We left with the
car heavily loaded, three women and a Siamese cat that had
never traveled by car before. Because all of these women were in
their seventies I decided to make the trip in easy stages.

My goal for the first day was the watering spa at Vichy in central France, some two hundred miles from Paris. As I drove south the bedlam of the two women arguing and the Siamese cat wailing was unnerving. My mother had developed a case of laryngitis and instead of offering me her usual advice on driving, she would tap vigorously on the dashboard. This might mean almost anything. I tried to pay as little attention to this as possible but the unending argument in the back seat was more difficult to turn off. We reached Vichy late in the afternoon. It was out of season and many of the hotels were closed. We finally found a tolerable hotel opposite the station. My mother announced that she was both tired and sick and went into the hotel followed by the two quarreling women, leaving me on crutches to try and unload the car. Finally an Algerian bellboy came out to help me. In the lobby I found my mother highly indignant. The clerk had asked her for her passport and she did not want to give it to him. I explained that he was acting in accordance with French law and most reluctantly she gave the passport to him.

Mrs. Inslee and Mrs. McBain went to their rooms still arguing. I made my way to my room with difficulty on crutches. All movement for me was slow and tiring. Next morning I got up and went down to supervise the loading of the car. My mother, the two women and the Siamese cat joined me and we continued our journey southward. Early in the afternoon, as we drove down the Rhone Valley we came to a flooded area and had to turn back. My mother tapped vigorously on the dashboard. She had driven herself to the hospital the night before I was born and felt well qualified to offer me driving advice. I examined the map and found an alternative routing that would take us around the flooded area. It was of course much longer, and we arrived at Aix en Provence about dinnertime. Here the ladies announced that they were very tired and did not want to go any farther. My program called for reaching Nice that night. This was still a hundred and fifty miles away. I decided that the best way to persuade the ladies to go on was to feed them a good meal and a bottle of wine. We stopped at a restaurant that I knew and the ladies went in to eat. As we sat down Mrs. McBain suggested that we bring in the cat so it too could eat. This is often done in French restaurants, where cats and dogs are generally welcomed. I stumbled out to the car on my crutches and brought the cat back to the restaurant. There it was admired and petted and a large bowl of tasty leftovers was prepared for it. For the first time since Vichy it stopped wailing. We had a splendid dinner and the spirits of the ladies were high. Mrs. Inslee and Mrs. McBain even stopped arguing. When I announced that we were going to drive on to Nice three hours away there was not a word of protest, only a reproachful look from my mother. We then started to look for the cat, which having eaten could not be found. Immediately Mrs. Inslee accused Mrs. McBain of being responsible for the missing cat, since she was the one who had suggested that the cat be brought in and fed. Irritated, I said that I did not give a damn whose fault it was. All I wanted was the cat, which I liked. I had bought its ticket home on the boat, as the Army would not pay for it. We searched all over the restaurant but could not find the cat. My mother announced that she was a very sick woman and had to get some rest. I knew that she was not really sick but that she must be very tired. I also realized that I was not going to get to Nice that night. I did not want to give up the search for the cat. I decided to take the ladies to the hotel and get them settled there and then continue the search for the cat. I took them to the hotel and then returned to the restaurant. I had left my mother on her way up to the room and her friends arguing in the lobby about whose fault it was. I realized that they were actually enjoying their quarrels. At the restaurant they told me that there had been no sign of the cat. I went to the local police station and was told that no one had turned in a cat since the last Roman legion had left. I then started to cruise slowly around the neighborhood in the car looking for the cat and calling it by name. It was starting to get dark. I had not realized that I was right in the area where the ladies of the evening ply their trade. Soon they spotted me cruising slowly through the area and figured that I was a bashful customer. When I paused for a stop sign, one of the girls asked me if I was looking for something and I absent-mindedly replied that I was looking for a cat. This word has the same connotation in French that it does in English and the answer doubled her up. Then she looked into the car and saw my leg on the camp stool in a cast. She asked with some concern whether I was sick and I replied, "No, only injured in a ski accident." Then she asked me rather kindly whether I was really looking for a four-footed cat and I replied that I was. I explained the circumstances of its disappearance and the fact that it was due to return to the United States with me and that I already had a ticket for it. She immediately became very sympathetic and told me that I should continue to cruise through the neighborhood. She and the other girls met on corners and she would pass the word. If any of them sighted a cat they would alert me and I could check to see if it was mine. Then she smiled and said, "After that, who knows?" Intent on getting her help, I nodded sagely and said, "Who knows," knowing perfectly well that with the cast on my leg I could not do a damned thing.

I then continued for the next half hour to cruise slowly through the neighboring streets. Occasionally one of the girls would commiserate with me and would say that the cast on my leg must prevent me from having much fun and I always agreed. Every now and then one of the girls would report that she had seen a cat under a car. I would stop mine, put a paper on the street and go through a dying swan act as I sank to the ground on crutches to look under the car. At long last I decided that the cat was really lost. I would not be using the ticket that I had bought for it. I cruised once more through the area to shake hands with the girls and to thank them for their help. They all wished me luck and hoped that I would come back when "I could do something." I assured them that I could hardly wait. As I left I decided to stop once more at the restaurant to see if they had any news. I was greeted with great excitement. They had located the cat under the wooden dais on which the lady proprietor sat so she could watch any of the guests making off with linen or silver. The space under the dais was narrow and they had not been able to cajole the cat out of it. The proprietor's dog had in fact driven the cat under the dais without any-

one noticing. I then did my dying swan act again and sank to the
floor and peered into the narrow space under the dais. I saw
Mitzi's eyes glittering and I was finally able to persuade her to
come out. I then started for the hotel, but remembering the
girls' help I figured that they must have a sporting interest in
knowing the final result of the search. I headed back into the
area and told one of the girls that I had found it. She grinned
and said, "Vive le chat," which can be translated several ways.

I returned to the hotel. My mother's two friends were still sitting the lobby trying to fix responsibility for the loss of the cat. I
told them that this was a waste of effort since I had found the
cat. Reluctantly they stopped arguing and went to bed.

The next morning I went in to see my mother and she told
me that she was going with me but that she was a very sick
woman and would probably not reach New York alive. Loading
up my passengers and the cat, I headed for Nice. This was a
relatively short drive and we got there for lunch. My mother
went to bed and announced that she was even sicker and would
probably not even reach Naples alive, much less New York. I
finally got the whole party settled in the hotel. Late that afternoon I announced that I was going over to Monte Carlo that
evening to try my luck at roulette, at least until I had lost $20.
Then I would cease and desist from further play. My mother's
two friends decided that they would go with me. This once at
least they did not argue. My mother said that she thought she
just might be able to make it too, even though she was a dying
woman. I said that it might be imprudent for her to go and she
replied that she could not think of a better place to die. We all
went off that night to Monte Carlo. The ladies broke even or
lost a few francs. I won more than a hundred dollars and my
mother announced that only a champagne cocktail would give
her the strength to drive back to Nice. I joined them in a champagne cocktail and we returned to the hotel. It is difficult to explain how tiring it was to do all of this on crutches. Only someone who has been on them can understand.

The next morning I gathered my flock for the next stage of
the journey, to Leghorn in Italy. My mother now expressed

doubt that she would reach Rome alive, much less Naples. We drove over the border into Italy and along the Italian Riviera, through Genoa to the Bracco Pass. We reached this point late in the afternoon. There were miles and miles of curving mountain roads and a high wind was blowing. My mother was getting tired and impatient and the two ladies in the back were arguing with unabated fierceness. I was intent on getting to Leghorn, where there was a large U. S. Army hospital and they could have a look at my mother to see if there was anything to her claims of imminent demise. At the top of Bracco Pass we stopped at a small restaurant and hotel for dinner. The wind was blowing so hard I could hardly stand up on my crutches when I got out of the car. The owner of the restaurant was delighted to see us and kept saying in English, "You ladies spend the night with me. I take good care of you." They looked pleased; it had been some years since anyone had made them this kind of a proposition. All the owner wanted, of course, was to rent us rooms.

After a good dinner and an even better bottle of wine, I drove on with my protesting passengers. Late that night we reached Leghorn and got settled in the hotel. Even the cat had stopped wailing. The next morning I took my mother to the Army hospital, where she was examined by a young doctor. He told her that she had a cold but would be all right in a few days. She was indignant at this, and assured him that she was a dying woman and demanded that he take a chest X ray. He looked at me and whispered that it was really not necessary. I told him to go ahead and do it, as it would make the rest of my journey a lot easier. He had the X ray taken and brought to him while it was still wet. "Ha!" said my mother. "Now what do you say?" He studied the X ray carefully and then turned to her and said, "Mrs. Walters, if I ever reach your age and my lungs look anything like this, I will be a very happy man. You will be perfectly okay in a day or two." My mother was almost speechless with indignation, but not quite. As we walked out of the hospital she said to me, "That young quack, no wonder he is only a captain. Telling me there is nothing wrong with me when I know perfectly well that I am a dying woman." By the force with which she said it I realized that she had fully recovered her voice. Back at the hotel I loaded the two quarreling ladies and the cat into the car and on we went to Rome and Naples and then to the United States. My mother was to live another fifteen years.

It had been an arduous journey from Paris. Seven days' rest on the boat would help to prepare me for my next mission.

13. THE STORY OF MOSSADEGH AND HARRIMAN

In 1951 following the assassination of Iranian Prime Minister Ali Razmara by fanatical religious Nationalists, Mohammed Mossadegh, a wealthy landowner and Iranian Nationalist, was named Prime Minister by the Shah. In his seventies, he was a consummate actor and often in the Iranian Majlis or Parliament he would weep or faint. To many Iranians this indicated the depth of his feelings and sincerity. A coalition of right and left forces gathered about the fiery, frail old man and he soon began to move boldly against the Anglo-Iranian Oil Company, which since 1911 had controlled a very large part of the Iranian oil industry with respect to drilling, production and running the huge refinery at Abadan on the Persian Gulf. Churchill, who was first sea lord, in 1911 had understood that oil would soon replace coal as a fuel for warships and wanted to secure an adequate supply for Britain. He had encouraged large British investments in Iranian oil. His chosen instrument, the Anglo-Iranian Oil Company, became a great power in the world of oil. Despite its name, it also had other sources of oil and a vast worldwide network of refinery and distributing facilities. Mossadegh, riding the crest of a wave of Iranian nationalism fueled by what Iranians believed to be an unfair purchase price and intolerable advantages for the Anglo-Iranian Oil Company, proceeded to nationalize Anglo-Iranian properties in Iran and to cancel the

Company's concession. These moves enhanced Mossadegh's popularity in Iran but seemed to the British to be a deadly threat against what they perceived to be their vital interests—access to oil and payment for it in pounds at a very advantageous price. It was also obvious that the Iranians at that time had no means of paying for the properties they were about to nationalize and furthermore had no real intentions of doing so. They felt that Anglo-Iranian had already reaped vast profits from its investment.

As Mossadegh moved against British oil interests, a wave of anti-British feeling swept Iran (still smarting from a joint Anglo-Soviet occupation of the country during World War II and the deposition of the Shah's father). Words became sharper between the British and the Iranians and when the Iranians seized the huge refinery on the Gulf at Abadan, the British began to contemplate the use of force to defend their interests. The 16th Parachute Brigade on Cyprus provided them with a force in the area that could be used. The possibility of an Anglo-Iranian conflict with all its possible consequences, including the reaction of the Soviet Union to something that might occur so close to its borders, was an unpleasant prospect. The spectacle of two friends of the United States snarling at one another was dismaying, and President Truman moved to avoid such a conflict by appointing trouble shooter Averell Harriman as a friendly mediator to see if he could not work out a compromise that would be equitable and accepted by both parties to the dispute.

Mr. Harriman, former lend-lease expediter, Ambassador to the Soviet Union and Great Britain, Secretary of Commerce and head of the Marshall Plan in Europe, was admirably equipped by his experience, diplomatic skill and personal courage to undertake this difficult task. I had worked with him at Bogotá under trying circumstances and later at the Marshall Plan and in Washington. He knew that Mossadegh had been to school in Switzerland, that he spoke admirable French and preferred to negotiate in this language. He decided to take me along on this mission. Harriman, accompanied by Mr. Truman's Air Force aide, General Robert Landry, made his first stop in

Paris on the way to Iran. I was assigned at that time to the NATO supreme headquarters in the French capital. My mission to Mossadegh was about to begin.

On the morning of July 14, 1951, I was in the grandstand of the Champs Elysées in Paris watching the Bastille Day parade. My seat was in the grandstand by virtue of my job as assistant to the Supreme Commander of NATO. I was enjoying it. This parade was memorable for several reasons, but one stands out clearly in my mind.

The closing event of the great parade was to be a helicopter bowing to the President of the Republic. First, impressive masses of infantry passed in review, followed by clanking columns of armored vehicles and then several large contingents of Republican Guards on horseback. Cavalry always leaves certain traces on the ground. A hot sun was beating down as the helicopter came down the Champs Elysées at an altitude of about one hundred feet. As it reached a point directly in front of the presidential grandstand, it began slowly to settle toward the ground, and as it did so, the rotors whipped up a small but dense brown cloud that descended upon the presidential party and the diplomatic corps. I will always retain the vision of the President of France bent almost double, clutching his grand cordon of the Legion of Honor, while simultaneously struggling to keep the brown dust out of his eyes, nose and mouth, desperately aware of the composition of this unprogrammed cloud.

Following the parade, I returned home, where my mother informed me that Mr. Harriman had phoned and wanted me to call him back at once. I had read in the papers that he was on his way to Iran on behalf of President Truman to try to mediate the British-Iranian dispute over the Iranian nationalization of the Anglo-Iranian oil properties. I called him, and after exchanging greetings, he said, "We are leaving at nine o'clock tonight." I wished him bon voyage and success, to which he replied, "I said *we* are leaving and that includes you. I have talked to General Eisenhower and he has agreed you will go with me. Dr. Mossadegh speaks French, and I want to have somebody through whom I can talk to him directly, so you are going." I pointed out that it was Saturday afternoon, July 14, in Paris, and the Iranian Embassy was probably closed. He allowed that getting the visa to enter Iran was my worry and not his. Then he said, "Didn't you get one before I came?" I replied, "No," that I thought that would have been presumptuous on my part. He then said, "Well, in any case, don't be late and don't miss the airplane. I don't like to be kept waiting."

I immediately called my old friend Agnes Schneider, who had been for many years in charge of the visa section in the American Embassy in Paris. She said she would see what she could do. Within a quarter of an hour she called back to say that she had arranged for a member of the Iranian Embassy to open their Embassy and give me the necessary visa. I got the visa and made it to the airport before nine. Mr. Harriman repeated to me that Mossadegh spoke French and that with me present he could speak to the Iranian Prime Minister very directly and very privately. He said Mossadegh was obsessed with secrecy and feared many of his own entourage.

I also met the other members of the party—General Landry, who was the Air Force aide to Mr. Truman and charged with Mr. Harriman's security; Walter Levy, a distinguished independent oil expert; and Bill Rountree, a Foreign Service officer and a Middle East expert from the State Department. He was later to become Ambassador to Parkistan and Brazil. At 9 P.M. we were airborne from Orly. We headed south along the Rhone Valley, skirting a tremendous thunderstorm which showed on our radar screen. I looked forward to seeing Iran for the first time. I went to sleep after we passed Marseilles.

I was awakened by breakfast and the news that we were almost over Baghdad. I leaped to the window but at twenty thousand feet almost nothing was visible and what was visible was shimmering in the intense summer heat. Soon we were circling Teheran, over which towered the impressive and symmetrical mass of Mount Demavand. Eighteen thousand feet high, it was eternally crowned with snow. At Mehrabad Airport we were met by the U. S. Ambassador, Dr. Grady, the British Ambassador, Sir Francis Shepherd, and high-ranking Iranians. We drove first to the Shah's palace to sign the guest book. We then walked across the palace of the Shah's mother to sign another guest book.

Then we were driven to Shimran, a suburb of Teheran with trees but about a thousand feet higher than the capital. For over a month we stayed as guests in one of the Shah's palaces. Saheb Garanieh is indeed a palace from the *Arabian Nights*. The walls of the great reception room were covered with small pieces of mirror which gave off a shimmering jewel-like effect. I later noted that this type of decoration was used in many Persian palaces. The Shah's brother, Prince Ali Reza, received us. The Prince spoke no English but excellent French.

Mr. and Mrs. Harriman were quartered in a suite beyond a great reception room and the rest of us were in quite large rooms opening directly onto the main reception area. This room was so large that our own rooms, even though they were spacious, seemed like cubbyholes in comparison and were, in fact, so described in a *Newsweek* article.

As we sat down to lunch, I recalled all the precautionary instructions I had received regarding what to eat and what not to eat in Persia. Shortly before the landing, Mr. Harriman had assembled all of us in the rear cabin of the aircraft and had mentioned how much trouble he had always had with his staff in Teheran on previous visits because they would not exercise a little self-control in what they ate and generally became ill. He portrayed himself as Florence Nightingale nursing them back to health. In any case, this first lunch was marked by extraordinarily liberal servings of caviar. As I dislike caviar, some juggling around on my plate was necessary. I was also told that vodka had excellent germ-killing qualities, so, contrary to my usual custom, I drank liberal quantities thereof. I must confess that I wondered how one could distinguish it from rubbing alcohol. The meal lasted at least three hours. The Prince then left us alone in the palace with just forty-eight servants to take care of our party.

Mr. Harriman's wife, Marie, had accompanied him on the trip. She was a remarkable woman, always full of bubbling humor and always ready with a quick and amusing anecdote. As I watched them over a period of years, it seemed to me that Averell Harriman gave purpose and dignity to her life, and she gave humor and a touch of humanity to his. They were marvelously complementary and wonderful people to be with. Only a few days later, Mr. Harriman was stricken with a minor intestinal complaint. Ironically, it was Mrs. Harriman who invited us into his room and, almost mimicking and repeating his words of a few days before on the airplane, she told us, "Now, look at who couldn't exercise any self-control in Teheran, and look who is sick now as a result of the lack of such self-control." They shared an obvious and mutual affection.

On our arrival we found an awkward situation. The Ambassador, Mr. Grady, was not particularly happy to have us there. This is often the case with special envoys. Most ambassadors feel that they are truly the President's representative and that all communications with the local government or chief of government should be through them. They often resent any attempt by the President to conduct foreign policy outside of this channel. This problem arose on a number of occasions in my career. It caused me embarrassment with some ambassadors in countries to which I had been sent by the President to deal directly with the chief of state.

Nothing prepared me for the first meeting with Dr. Mossadegh at his home in a residential part of Teheran. I had read in the papers about his fits of weeping, his dramatics and theatrics in the Iranian Parliament. Mossadegh in person was quite startling. I went with Mr. Harriman to his unpretentious home. After a brief wait, we were taken upstairs to Dr. Mossadegh's room. He was lying in bed wearing a sort of Mao jacket made of camel hair buttoned up high onto his neck. He was lying low in the bed with the palms of his hands crossed directly below his neck and he fluttered them gently up and down as we entered the room.

He greeted Mr. Harriman in French, saying how pleased he was to see him and that he just hoped that in this whole matter the United States would not prove to be a puppet of Great Brit-

THE STORY OF MOSSADEGH AND HARRIMAN

ain. Mr. Harriman assured him that this was not the case, that we were upset to see a quarrel between two of our friends and that we were anxious to do everything we could to settle the quarrel in a way satisfactory to both sides.

Dr. Mossadegh was a very small, slight man. I do not to this day know actually how old he was, but in retrospect I know he was more than seventy years old at that time. He appeared extremely frail and weak, and used this to great advantage. As a matter of fact, an Iranian doctor to whom Mr. Harriman talked, and who was a member of the Majlis, recounted his first experience with Dr. Mossadegh's dramatics in the Iranian Parliament. Mossadegh, who had become Prime Minister upon the assassination of General Razmara in a mosque, had been pleading passionately for a bill which he wanted the Parliament to pass. The doctor was a member of the opposition. Mossadegh wound up his passionate plea for the bill with a sort of slow swoon during which he moaned that he was prepared to give up his life for his beloved Iran and sank to the floor. The doctor said that his Hippocratic oath got the better of his political opposition. He leaped across a few benches, knelt beside the Prime Minister, loosened the old man's collar and picked up his wrist, expecting to feel a faint, fluttering pulse, but in fact what he felt was the healthy pounding of a strong, sound man's pulse. As a matter of fact, Dr. Mossadegh was to live into his nineties. Mr. Harriman then said to the doctor, "What did you do as a result of this?" And the doctor said, "I was so moved that I voted for his bill." This was an example of the skillful way in which Dr. Mossadegh used his apparent weakness as a powerful weapon.

Dr. Mossadegh was in an extremely anti-British mood. Everything from Iran's low standard of living to the fact that Iran no longer occupied the same prominent place in the world which it had at various times in history was in his mind due entirely to the machinations and craftiness of the British. He looked at Mr. Harriman and said, "You do not know how crafty they are. You do not know how evil they are. You do not know how they sully everything they touch." Mr. Harriman said that this was not the case, that the British were like most other people: some were good, some bad and most in between. Mossadegh repeated, "You do not know them. You do not know them." Mr. Harriman, a little irked, said, "Yes, I do know them. I was lend-lease expediter in Great Britain. I have been Ambassador to Great Britain. We have fought two wars with them, which you haven't, and I assure you they are good and bad and most of all in between." Dr. Mossadegh leaned forward, clutched Mr. Harriman's hand and smiled winsomely.

Dr. Mossadegh had a most extraordinary nose. I have often commented that his nose was so large that it made Jimmy Durante's seem like an amputee's. He was an extraordinarily friendly man but also quite deaf. Usually when he was lying in bed talking to Mr. Harriman, I sat next to Mr. Harriman on the side of his bad ear. He would pat the foot of the bed, a sign me to sit yogi style on the foot of the bed while I interpreted the conversation. Soon this became my accustomed place during the discussions. Dr. Mossadegh would sit at one end of the bed; I would sit at the other end of the bed; and Mr. Harriman would sit beside the bed between us.

Mr. Harriman attempted to explain the realities of the oil situation to Mossadegh. Mossadegh could not understand why, having nationalized the Anglo-Iranian Oil Campany in Iran, all of the profits and figures which showed in its annual statement had not become his. Two things became clear. First, Dr. Mossadegh did not understand that much of the Anglo-Iranian oil revenue derived from refining, and from retail distribution in many countries. He did not seem to understand that Iran was not the company's sole source of crude oil. To Mossadegh, the company's name meant that Iran alone was the provider for this company. Mr. Harriman had brought with him Walter Levy, an extraordinarily brilliant, perceptive and persuasive man. He had fled from Germany at the beginning of the Hitler regime. His Jewish father, who had won the "Pour le mérite," imperial Germany's highest war decoration for heroism, was protected by this decoration from harm from the Nazis. Walter had not believed that this would last and had left. In fact, his father's decoration protected Walter's mother and brothers and sisters until 1943, when his father died. Shortly after this, his mother and the rest of his family disappeared and he was never to hear of them again.

Walter Levy sat for hours at Dr. Mossadegh's bedside, trying to explain to him the complexities of the international business. He explained that Saudi Arabia, Kuwait, Venezuela and others all sold oil, and that Iran would have to create a situation in which she could be competitive. Mossadegh, however, was convinced that the oil companies had ganged up on him to make sure that the Iranian nationalization would not be successful. If it succeeded it might become contagious to other areas. There was, in fact, some validity to his suspicions. He readily conceded that he was having great difficulty in attempting to sell the nationalized oil which he had seized from Anglo-Iranian. Since Iran had no tankers of its own, he had tried to charter tankers and had found that the tanker owners were unwilling to charter their vessels to him. He felt this was a result of threats from the "seven sisters" or the other great oil companies, who, while they might wish to compete with Anglo-Iranian, had no wish to do anything to prove to countries that nationalization could be a successful solution to the problem of handling their oil.

Day after day, Mr. Harriman or Walter Levy attempted to educate Dr. Mossadegh about the realities of worldwide oil production and distribution. No one challenged his right to nationalize the oil, but he must be prepared to make some compensation. Mossadegh rejected this out of hand since he felt that over the years the profits made by the Anglo-Iranian Oil Company had more than discharged any debt Iran might have to them for the discovery and development of the oil fields.

Another complicating factor was the fact that Mossadegh had become Prime Minister as a result of the assassination of his predecessor, Ali Razmara. There was at that time in Iran a band of extreme Nationalist fanatics who had been responsible for the death of Razmara. Mossadegh constantly referred, in a most confidential manner, to the atmosphere of "terror, terror, terror," in which he must live.

Talking to Dr. Mossadegh was always amusing but enormously repetitive. It seemed to me that he reversed Lenin's adage that one must take a step backward in order to take two forward. Dr. Mossedegh had learned to take one step forward in order to take two backward. After a day's discussions, Mr. Harriman would bring Mossadegh to a certain position. The next day when we returned to renew the discussion, not only was Mossadegh not at the position where he was at the end of the previous day, he wasn't even at the position where he had been at the beginning of the day before that. He was somewhere back around the middle of the day before yesterday. I often had the impression that instead of going forward we were actually moving backward.

One day, in exasperation, Mr. Harriman said to Dr. Mossadegh (who seemed to be asking for a larger share from a barrel of oil than the total cost of the barrel), "Dr. Mossadegh, if we are going to talk intelligently about these things, we have to agree on certain basic principles." Mossadegh peered from behind his enormous nose and said rather craftily, "Such as what?" Mr. Harriman said, "Such as: nothing can be larger than the sum of its parts." (A direct reference to Mossadegh's desire for more than 100 per cent of the income per barrel of oil.) Dr. Mossadegh looked at him and said (in French), "That is false." Mr. Harriman, who does not speak much French, nevertheless understood this. He looked at me with a puzzled look on his face, and said, "Did he say it was false?" I said, "Yes, he did say it was false." Mr. Harriman turned to Dr. Mossadegh and said, "What do you mean, 'false'?" Mossadegh said, "Well, consider the fox. His tail is often much longer than he is." With that, he put the pillow over his head and rolled from side to side in the bed convulsed with laughter. Mr. Harriman was less amused.

One minute one had the impression that Mossadegh was really trying to find a solution for the oil problem, that an agreement was in sight. But the next conversation would take up on a note that made clear that any agreement was remote. He seemed to enjoy this. It was like dangling a fish on the line.

Days passed and the discussions went on and on without real

result. I was charged with writing the memoranda of the conversations and preparing the telegrams to be sent to Washington reporting "the progress" of the talks. Late one night, after a particularly unproductive day, I returned to the palace at Saheb Garanieh and wrote the following memorandum: "Today, Dr. Mossadegh and Mr. Harriman played the same record on both sides for two hours." Mossadegh would always lard these conversations with amusing anecdotes about his own past to make some sort of point. He delighted in telling us, for instance—and this was to show how shrewd and crafty he was and how he could not be outwitted—that during World War I his doctors had told him that he needed an appendicitis operation. So he decided that he would go to Russia for the appendicitis operation. He talked to an American doctor who was living in Teheran at that time and asked the doctor how much he would charge him to accompany him as far as Baku in southern Russia. The American doctor quoted him a price and that seemed excessive to Mossadegh. Mossadegh found out that the American doctor was going to Baku anyway so he arranged to leave two or three days ahead of the American doctor. At each relay station he made arrangements to make sure that the American doctor could not get horses fast enough to pass Dr. Mossadegh. Each night the American doctor would arrive at the end of the day and find Dr. Mossadegh at the inn. On the third day, he said to Dr. Mossadegh, "Dr. Mossadegh, I understand your message. Can I travel with you? It won't cost you anything." Mossadegh collapsed into a convulsion of laughter. He was proud of how shrewdly he had outwitted the American doctor and obtained free of charge the doctor's company throughout the trip without having to pay for it. This conviction that if one haggled long enough the other side would be worn down and would in the end give in was one of the difficulties in dealing with him.

Time and again, when Walter Levy or Mr. Harriman would point out how some action or failure to take action on his part would result in unfortunate consequences to Iran, Mossadegh would say simply in French, shrugging his shoulders, "*Tant pis pour nous,*" which I would translate loosely into English as,

"Well, to hell with us. Down the drain we go." Another time Mr. Harriman was attempting to explain to him that if some satisfactory solution was not found for this problem, grave consequences could ensue. Mossadegh's eyes filled with tears; the drops rolled slowly down his cheeks, and he said, "Yes, soon I will not be able to pay the Armed Forces and the police. And when that happens, they will no longer protect us." And he lowered his voice and whispered, "The party of the left [he could not bring himself to say the Tudeh or Iranian Communist party] will take over and they will liquidate all of our friendships with the West." Mr. Harriman, who had been listening to a lot of this, said to him, "But Dr. Mossadegh, you realize that one of the first people they will liquidate will be you." "Yes," said Mossadegh, roaring with laughter, "but that will fix your wagon when they take over."

He was obsessed with the idea that Iran bore no share of responsibility for her difficulties. One day he began a conversation by saying, "Iran's problems have always been caused by foreigners. The whole thing began with that Greek Alexander," referring to Alexander's burning Persepolis 2,400 years before as though the event had occurred in the recent past. He was an extraordinarily polite man, and never said anything rude. He always spoke in a most courteous, polished, almost nineteenth-century fashion, but he was strong in his feelings. When speaking of American military assistance to Iran he would whisper, "But don't make them too strong or they will overthrow me." Another day when Mr. Harriman came in, Mossadegh looked up at him brightly, flipped his hands up and down a few times and said, quite matter-of-factly, "Oh, I have had a bad day. This morning I fainted three times."

It was truly a negotiation unlike any negotiation I have ever seen in my life. Dr. Mossadegh had a violent anti-British fixation. After several weeks, in an attempt to make the conversation more personal, Mr. Harriman asked him whether he had any grandchildren. A few moments before, Mossadegh had delivered a ten-minute soliloquy on the evils and perversity of the British. Mossadegh said he had one grandson, who was the apple of his eye. Mr. Harriman said, "But I don't think I've met your grandson." "No," replied Mossadegh. "He is out of the country away at school." "Oh," said Mr. Harriman. "Where is he at school?" Mossadegh uttered a loud giggle and answered, "Why, in England, of course. Where else?" This was typical of the contradictions in the man's nature. He did, however, perceive the comic nature of his reply.

Once in an attempt to show us his craftiness, he told us how he obtained his Swiss motorcycle driving license. When he told me this story, the mere thought of Dr. Mossadegh riding a motorcycle simply boggled my mind. At the time he was a student at the University of Neuchâtel in Switzerland and he went to take his driving test. The inspector did not actually ride with him. He told Mossadegh to ride down to the lake and then come back. Mossadegh said that he rode the motorcycle down to the lake but he did not know how to stop it. When he got down to the lakeshore, the site of an open-air market, he crashed into a fruit stand run by an elderly Swiss woman, overturning the stand. She looked at him and shouted, *"Cochon, cochon!"* Mossadegh looked at us casually and said, "Can you imagine what that meant to me, a Moslem, to be called a pig?" He then picturesquely said, "I paid her money for the damages, but during this time the motorcycle was lying on its side screaming. Finally, I turned it off, righted it, got on and rode slowly back up the hill. When I saw the inspector, he said, 'Mr. Mossadegh, you have taken a long time. You must have driven very carefully. I congratulate you. Here is your driving license.'" All of these stories had helped to form Mossadegh's idea of the West and his conviction that if one held out long enough or connived carefully, one could get almost anything. This attitude led of course to unparalleled haggling over the whole issue.

While the negotiations were going on, the Minister of Railways, a close confidant of Dr. Mossadegh's, stayed at the palace with us. We often dined together and he would convey messages from Mossadegh or comment on how Mossadegh was feeling, and so forth. Mrs. Lucretia Grady, the wife of the Ambassador, a most vivacious woman, but much given to peculiar turns of expression, once said to the Prime Minister, "Dr. Mossadegh, you have a very expressive face. Every time you are thinking of nothing, I can tell by the blank stare on your face." I must confess that in translating this, I altered it to say, "Dr. Mossadegh, you have a very expressive face. Every time you are thinking deep thoughts, I can tell it by the look of concentration on your face." Fortunately, there was no one there to catch my change in the translation. On another occasion, she greeted the Minister of Railways, telling him that a large rat in the Embassy residence had almost eaten the housekeeper's baby and that they were, therefore, organizing a great rat hunt. She said to him, "Now, Dr. Bushery, if you're coming up here, you just be sure and tell us in advance so no one will shoot you." Dr. Bushery, who spoke some English, was sure he had been told he could be mistaken for a rat. Fortunately he just couldn't believe it. I forget what particular twist I gave this in translation to try and smooth out the situation.

In the midst of these talks, Mr. Harriman flew back to London in an attempt to persuade the British government to send out a negotiator with full powers to deal with Mossadegh. The British Ambassador in Iran, Sir Francis Shephard, had been in Indonesia, where he had had a very difficult time. He once related to us how he had been told of his mission to Iran by Ernie Bevin, the Labour Foreign Secretary. Bevin had told him, "Francis, you've had a rough time in Indonesia. We're going to send you to a post in a place where we never have any trouble with the natives—Iran." I do not believe that Sir Francis Shephard fully understood what was going on in Iran, but he was a man of remarkable courage. At the height of the anti-British campaign, he used to ride around Teheran in his Rolls-Royce with a huge Union Jack flying from the car. No threat of violence or anything else could dissuade him.

Mr. Harriman, keenly aware of the intense pressure which the ultra-nationalists and fanatics were bringing on Mossadegh, felt that perhaps a personal visit to the mullah, or religious leader, Ayatollah Kashani, would break the impasse. He was told that this would do no good, that Kashani was a fanatic, and that no negotiations with him could serve any useful purpose. Mr. Harriman insisted, nevertheless, that he wanted to talk to Mullah Kashani. Finally, with some difficulty, an appointment was arranged.

Mullah Kashani lived in the suburb of Gulhaq, which was halfway between downtown Teheran and our palace in Shimran. Up to this time most of the things I had seen in Iran struck me as being much more Western than I had expected, but when we reached the mullah's house, I found a place that looked satisfactorily oriental to me. The mullah himself wore a turban and a huge beard. We were taken into a heavily draperied room where it seemed to me that from time to time I could see movement behind the draperies.

Mr. Harriman attempted to discuss these matters with the mullah. The mullah again told him he knew nothing about the British, who were the most evil people in the world. Harriman replied somewhat testily that *he* did. He had been Ambassador there, he had dealt with them over a period of years and we had fought two wars with them, which was more than Iran had done. Then the mullah, looking extremely crafty and stroking his beard, asked Mr. Harriman, "Mr. Harriman, have you ever heard of Major Embry?" "No," replied Mr. Harriman, shaking his head, "I have never heard of him." "Well," said the mullah, "He was an American who came to Iran in 1911 or 1912. He dabbled in oil, which was none of his business, and aroused the hatred of the people. One day, walking in Teheran, he was shot down in the street, but he was not killed. They took him to the hospital. The enraged mob followed to the hospital, burst into the hospital and butchered him on the operating table." The mullah looked at Mr. Harriman and said, "Do you understand?" Mr. Harriman's lips tightened, and I could see that he was furious. In a very steely voice, he said, "Your Eminence, you must understand that I have been in many dangerous situations in my life and I do not frighten easily." "Well," shrugged the mullah, "there was no harm in trying." The interview was fruitless. The mullah maintained his rigid position. He accused Mossadegh of being pro-British and added ominously, "If Mossadegh yields, his blood will flow like Razmara's." And since we all felt that the mullah had something to do with Razmara's death, this was tantamount to a threat against Dr. Mossadegh's life. We were certain that if he made the threat to us, he had also conveyed it to Mossadegh and that this was one of the factors contributing to the old man's reluctance to reach some sort of agreement.

In response to Mr. Harriman's request, the British government did send out a negotiator, a Labour party millionaire by the name of Richard Stokes. He was a remarkable man who later was to acknowledge much of the validity of Mossadegh's claims. Stokes brought an interpreter with him, but Mossadegh caught Stokes' interpreter making notes on his cuff. He refused to see him again, so I was pressed into service as interpreter for both Harriman and Stokes. This revealed to me another side of Dr. Mossadegh.

At one point he said to Stokes, "The reason why we can't come to an agreement is because you are a Catholic." Stokes said, "I fail to see what connection that has with the oil business." Mossadegh said, "But you see, in your religion you don't have any divorce, whereas in ours all you have to do is say three times to your wife, 'I divorce you,' and she is divorced. What you don't understand is that we have divorced the Anglo-Iranian Oil Company." "Yes, yes," said Stokes, "but remember, Dr. Mossadegh, even if you divorce her, you still have to pay her alimony until she remarries, and the Anglo-Iranian Oil Company has not remarried." Mossadegh hugged him to his bosom and said, "If all Englishmen were like you, we wouldn't have any trouble." An interesting sidelight, the British enjoined me not to tell the Americans what was going on with the Iranians, and the Americans enjoined me not to tell Stokes what was going on between them and the Iranians.

These negotiations went on for more than two months. I went several times with Mr. Harriman to see the Shah. The Shah of 1951 was a very different man than the Shah of today. He was young, inexperienced, impressed by the popular hold Mossadegh had obtained, fearful that Mossadegh was not loyal to the throne and would seize the first opportunity to declare Iran a republic. Subsequent events proved this to be a correct assumption. I remember on the evening we arrived in Teheran, we had dinner at the American Embassy. The Minister of the Interior, General Fazollah Zahedi, was present. We ate in the garden, and during the meal the sounds of gunfire were clearly audible. We learned later there had been a riot and thirteen people were killed. Mossadegh asked for and obtained General Zahedi's resignation. This was a mistake. General Zahedi was eventually to play an important part in restoring the Shah to his throne after Mossadegh had dethroned him. And Zahedi's son, Ardeshir Zahedi, was to be on several occasions the Iranian Ambassador to the United States.

On Fridays, the Moslem Sabbath, Dr. Mossadegh would not meet with Mr. Harriman or discuss anything. On these days, Mr. Harriman generally would go out, board his Constellation, and go to one of the scenic sites in Iran such as Tabriz, Meshed, Shiraz or Isfahan. In Teheran, the temperature often hovered around 120 degrees. Our palace was not air-conditioned, nor did we even have fans. Fortunately, however, the nights were cool. On one trip out of Teheran, I remember we went up to a very high altitude and left the heating system on the airplane off. We sat with blankets around us enjoying the chill. Someone in the party said to Mr. Harriman, half jokingly, "Don't you feel slightly guilty—going for a drive on Fridays like this in an aircraft burning eight hundred gallons of gasoline an hour?" Mr. Harriman, who normally did not like any reference to his wealth, looked at him chillily and said, "If you had seen my income tax returns over a period of years, you would know that I have bought a number of these aircraft for the United States government."

One morning I was sitting in the garden with Mrs. Harriman waiting for breakfast to be served. Mr. Harriman came over, sat down and slapped his knees, saying, "I feel like a million dollars." Mrs. Harriman replied, "Gee, Ave, that's terrible. What happened to the rest?" Only Mrs. Harriman could have gotten away with that remark.

The trips were interesting and a welcome opportunity to see other parts of Iran and to get away from the political tension so apparent in Teheran.

After nearly two months had passed, we realized that Mossadegh simply did not want to arrive at any agreement because he did not feel he could sell it to his Nationalists. And so, reluctantly, Mr. Harriman informed him that we would be returning to the United States, that he hoped this would not be the end of the discussions and that we were friends of Iran. We did wish to be helpful. We did not challenge Iran's right to go through with this nationalization, but we did feel that it should make some compensation. Dr. Mossadegh spoke feelingly about the wretched conditions of the workers in the refinery at Abadan. Mrs. Harriman asked Dr. Mossadegh whether he had ever been to Abadan, and Mossadegh, laughing wildly, said, "No," but he had read about it.

Once during this trip we did go to Abadan and I was simply staggered at the heat. The temperature was close to 125 degrees at seven o'clock in the morning. We drove from Abadan to Khorramshahr, the provincial capital. The road was lined by Iranian sailors and, to my astonishment, when we drove back several hours later, the Iranian sailors were still there. How anybody could stand alongside that road for several hours in that incredible blazing heat I did not understand. The Abadan refinery was an immense installation vitally important to the world. It was lying idle at that time, since the British engineers, who were responsible for keeping it running, had left. The few Iranian engineers who were there could keep only a small part of the huge complex operating. Again, as Dr. Mossadegh had made plain, there was the problem of marketing whatever oil was refined there, since the other oil companies were reluctant to purchase from him.

Finally, we left. Mossadegh showered gifts on us. I got five pounds of caviar. I have never liked caviar but I distributed this strategically in Paris. We flew to Paris, Mr. Harriman obviously upset at not having succeeded in this mission. Once on the plane going back, he made an intriguing statement. He said, "I am simply not used to failure." Mossadegh and Iran were an extraordinary experience.

Harriman dropped me off in Paris. On his way back to Washington, he wrote a letter to General Eisenhower thanking him for my services. I was grateful, because he explained that the failure of the negotiations had in no way been due to me!

I had many talks with General Eisenhower about Dr. Mossadegh and about what went on in Iran. I think our conversations may have had some impact upon him later when he was to determine, as President, the American policy toward Iran.

The Mossadegh story does not end here. Shortly afterward, the British hauled Dr. Mossadegh before the International Court of Justice at The Hague. I received instructions to go and talk to him and ascertain how he was feeling and what his disposition was toward the possibility of reaching an agreement. I drove from Paris up to The Hague and checked into the Hotel des Indes, an old sedate hostelry, generally the place where most distinguished foreign visitors stay in The Hague. I had no difficulty in getting a room for myself despite the fact that I had not telephoned in advance for a reservation. I asked if Dr. Mossadegh was staying at the hotel. The hotel clerk looked archly at me and said, "No, we have no room for Dr. Mossadegh at this hotel." I said, "I don't understand. You have room for me but you have no room for Dr. Mossadegh." The clerk looked at me and said, "Mijnheer, Shell is not just British, it is also a Dutch corporation, and what threatens any of us threatens all of us." This, in a sense, justified part of Mossadegh's feeling that the oil companies were really intent on not letting his nationalization become a success.

A few months later, Dr. Mossadegh went to New York, where the British brought him before the United Nations. Again, since he had made clear that he liked me, trusted me and would prefer to talk through a non-Iranian interpreter, I was flown back to the United States to serve as the interpreter for Undersecretary George C. McGhee, who was dealing with Mossadegh during his stay in New York for the United Nations General Assembly session. I think at first George McGhee was a little concerned about having the rough and brutal soldiery brought into this delicate diplomatic negotiation, but since Harriman insisted on it, and said Mossadegh trusted me and I knew the old man and could contribute something to the atmosphere, he reluctantly agreed. The first time we went into Dr. Mossadegh's room and I climbed up as usual on the foot of the bed which Mossadegh had patted, McGhee looked quite startled at the spectacle of this American lieutenant colonel getting onto the foot of the Iranian Prime Minister's bed.

Mr. McGhee was an unusually compassionate and understanding human being. Mossadegh liked him immediately. I could tell that if Mossadegh had been disposed to make a deal, he would have liked to have it with George McGhee. These discussions in New York were constantly interrupted by the fact that Undersecretary McGhee's other duties in Washington necessitated his return there from time to time.

Dr. Mossadegh lived in the Waldorf Towers but slept on a camp bed so that he could be photographed in surroundings of great simplicity for the purposes of public relations in Iran. Dr. Mossadegh was convinced at this time that the United Nations was a British puppet which was going to order him to give back the Anglo-Iranian Oil Company.

During one of Mr. McGhee's absences in Washington, one of the members of the U.S. delegation to the United Nations was Ambassador Ernest Gross, who shared the opinion held by many people at that time (including, I must confess, myself) that, "If they would only leave me to handle this matter, I could soon settle it." Ernest Gross came up to me and said, "Walters, I want you to arrange a meeting with Dr. Mossadegh for me this afternoon." I knew that everybody was trying to get in on the act. But as Ernest Gross was an ambassador and I was a lieutenant colonel, I did not see how I could refuse his request. So I talked to Mossadegh, who agreed to see him that afternoon at four o'clock. At the appointed hour, I came to Dr. Mossadegh's room with Ambassador Gross, an engaging and likable man. He stepped into the room and walked over to Dr. Mossadegh's bed. As he did so, I noticed that we got from Mossadegh's hands (crossed on his chest below his neck) a very weak flutter—a very bad sign. It generally meant that one was going to have a very frustrating time.

Ambassador Gross seized Dr. Mossadegh's hand and said, "Dr. Mossadegh, I am Ambassador Ernest Gross. I am a friend. I want to help you find a solution for this problem. I want to do everything I can to help you get a just share for the Iranian people." Mossadegh peered cautiously from behind his enormous nose and inquired. "Ambassador, what are you Ambassador to?" "Oh," said Mr. Gross, "I am Ambassador to the United Nations." With that, Mossadegh let out a shriek as though he had been stabbed with a carving knife, tossed convulsively from one side of the bed to the other and sobbed wildly, huge crocodile tears pouring down his cheeks. Now this was a much more violent outburst of weeping than any I had seen previously; Ernest Gross was equally appalled by the outburst. I could not resist saying to him, "Mr. Ambassador, I don't think this is the day to continue the discussion." He said, "My God, neither do I." So he clutched Dr. Mossadegh's hand and said, "Dr. Mossadegh, we'll come back some other time when you feel better." We walked out of the room. We stopped outside the door and Ambassador Gross turned to me and asked. "Does he do this often?" I said, "Well, I've seen quiet weeping, but I have never seen this wild convulsive sobbing before." Gross said, "You haven't? Then you must never tell anybody he did it for me."

Dr. Mossadegh moved to Washington. On the occasion of his arrival, the Iranian Embassy published a small pamphlet entitled "Mohammed Mossadegh, the George Washington of Iran." In Iran there was a law at that time which said that nobody who had reached the age of seventy could (a) be Prime Minister or (b) be executed. I had talked to a number of people in Teheran who told me that they had been going for several years to Dr. Mossadegh's sixty-ninth birthday celebration. Like Jack Benny with his thirty-ninth birthday, he never aged beyond that point. At least not until he was condemned to death several years later for rebellion, at which point he claimed that he was more than seventy and therefore could not be executed.

In the best Iranian fashion, this worked. But in the pamphlet, which he showed me with evident relish, it said, "Dr. Mossadegh was born in Teheran in 1884. He was taught by private tutors in Teheran. He then went to Switzerland, where he obtained a degree in political science at the University of Neuchâtel. He then returned to Iran, where he practiced law successfully for a number of years before becoming governor of the province of Fars in 1896." He then nudged me and said, "That's not bad for a twelve-year-old boy."

Again, the discussions in Washington proved fruitless. It was clear that Dr. Mossadegh did not feel himself in a position to accept any agreement. On the last night before his scheduled departure, Mr. Harriman asked me to go up to see him alone for one last try at budging him from his inflexible position. Immediately I felt that I had been given my chance, and like almost everyone else, I was certain that I could solve the Iranian oil problem. I went up to his room at the Shoreham Hotel. When I entered, he embraced me and said, "I know what you're here for and the answer is still no." Then he invited me to have some Iranian tea. While we were talking, he said to me, "You know, I heard all that shooting outside the hotel during the night." I said, "Dr. Mossadegh, there may have been a backfire, but there was no shooting outside the hotel last night." He said, "Walters, you defend your country well, but I know shooting when I hear it and there was plenty of shooting outside the hotel last night." I could not convince him that there had been no shooting outside the hotel. We talked for a while and he reiterated that he could not change his position. I said to him, "Dr. Mossadegh, you have been here for a long time. High hopes have been raised that your visit would bring about some fruitful results and now you are returning to Iran empty-handed." He looked at me shrewdly and said, "Don't you realize that, returning to Iran empty-handed, I return in a much stronger position than if I returned with an agreement which I would have to sell to my fanatics?" I was satisfied that he simply did not want to reach an agreement at that time. I got up to leave and he said to me, "Can I ask you one more thing?"

Again, a ray of hope shone through the clouds and I said, "Go ahead, Dr. Mossadegh, ask me anything." He said, "May I kiss you goodbye?" I thought about this for a while and finally I said, "If that's all that's involved and it's only on the cheeks, go right ahead." He cackled with delight, kissed me on both cheeks and I left. That was the last time I saw Dr. Mossadegh. For years afterward, I always received a Christmas card from him portraying an elderly Persian with a long beard surrounded by a vast bevy of beautiful young half-naked dancers. I maintained erratic correspondence with him for four or five years, but I knew now that I could *not* solve the Anglo-Iranian oil problem. This whole mission was entertaining and interesting, but nevertheless fruitless. As Mr. Harriman had said so well, I too was not used to failure, and it was with genuine regret that I saw the old man leave. When the restoration of the Shah occurred, I devoutly hoped that nothing would happen to the old man. In fact, very little did. He retired to his ancestral estates, where he died many years later at an age in excess of ninety years.

It was a mission unlike any other mission. There was an *Alice in Wonderland* quality to it which led me after three days in Teheran to write back to Mr. Harriman's secretary in Washington to ask her to send me a copy of that book so I would know what was next on the program. It was in a sense a mission that failed, but it was a mission that cast a long shadow ahead of the great problems that the Western world was to have with oil two and a half decades later. These Dr. Mossadegh was not to live to see, yet in a way their true origin led back to him.

14. WITH TITO AND HARRIMAN

Josip Broz Tito was born in Croatia, part of the Austro-Hungarian Empire before World War I. He served in that war as a sergeant in the Austro-Hungarian Army and was captured on the eastern front by the Czar's troops. The Soviet revolution found him a prisoner in Russia. Attracted by the Communists' political and economic philosophy, he became a Communist and returned to Yugoslavia at the end of the First World War as an underground cadre for the Yugoslav Communist party, outlawed by the dictatorship of King Alexander. Following the King's assassination in Marseilles, his young son Peter was proclaimed King under the regency of his cousin, Prince Paul. With the swift German victories in the early days of World War II, Prince Paul led Yugoslavia away from her traditional alliance with France and closer to Germany. A sudden pro-Western coup in Belgrade in April 1941 overthrew the regent and established a pro-British-and-French regime under the young King Peter II. Days later, Germany and Italy attacked Yugoslavia after a brutal bombing of Belgrade. Within two weeks they overran the whole country. The regular Yugoslav Armed Forces collapsed before the onslaught and the country was divided into several puppet states.

At this time, the Soviet Union was still Germany's ally and

furnishing the Nazis with the raw materials for their war effort. Suddenly on June 22, Germany attacked the Soviet Union along the whole of that country's western frontier from Finland to the Black Sea. The Yugoslav Communists, quiescent until then, moved against the Germans in partisan guerrilla warfare, to which the terrain of the country lent itself perfectly. At the same time, a group loyal to King Peter, an exile in London, began to attack the German occupiers. The Yugoslav Communists were led by Josip Broz, who took the war name of Tito; the monarchist resistance group was led by General Draza Mihailovich. Both groups fought the Germans. Tito received aid from the Russians and was able to persuade the British to help him even though he was an avowed Communist. As a result, he soon became the main resistance leader inside Yugoslavia against the Germans. Mihailovich did not get such aid. He did the best he could but was less effective than Tito, who accused him of collusion with the Germans. Many Allied fliers, however, have testified that they owed their lives to Mihailovich and his Chetniks.

As the war went on, fortified by aid from both the Eastern and Western Allies, Tito grew strong enough to take Belgrade in 1944, from which the Germans had to withdraw after Romania defected from their side to the Allies. This pulled some twenty divisions out of line on the German front, which gave Tito a trump in dealing with the Soviets that no other Eastern European leader possessed. He, not the Soviets, had liberated his capital. At war's end, now a convinced Communist, he seized the Italian city of Trieste and subjected it to a savage reign of terror. Ultimately he was forced out of the city by American and British threats of military action. I recall in 1945 alerting the Brazilians in Italy of the possibility of a clash with Tito. The Yugoslav dictator captured Mihailovich and executed him after a trial that was a farce. He also imprisoned the Catholic Archbishop of Zagreb for many years, even after the Pope had made Archbishop Stepinac a cardinal. Tito loyally toed Moscow's line until February 1948, when, unable to stand Stalin's autocratic interference in Yugoslav affairs, he broke with the Soviets but maintained a Communist regime at home. In the early postwar years, he shot down several U.S. aircraft over Yugoslavia and a number of graves in Arlington Cemetery reflect his handiwork. Now in 1951 he was looking for help from America to remain outside Moscow's clutches. So he invited Mr. Truman's adviser, Averell Harriman, to visit him on his way back from Teheran. He succeeded in getting U.S. help and unlike other leaders he did not have to account for it. Tito was to maintain his position for thirty years, so-called "independent," but *never* voting against the Soviets in the UN; abstaining sometimes, but nearly always aligned with the Soviets on the really major issues—Korea, Vietnam, the Middle East, Cuba, Angola.

After two months in Teheran, Mr. Harriman realized that the mission to Mossadegh would not succeed and that we would leave the Iranian capital empty-handed. The Yugoslavs became insistent that Mr. Harriman visit Marshal Tito on his way back to the United States. After prolonged consultations with the State Department, the invitation was finally accepted. Our departure from Teheran was at hand. Final calls were paid on the Shah and Mossadegh and just before we left Saheb Garanieh Palace, minions appeared carrying gifts from the Shah. Mr. Harriman made a very liberal donation to a fund to help young Iranians studying in the United States. We left Teheran late at night in order to arrive in Europe in the early morning. Shortly after the takeoff, I went to bed in a comfortable berth and slept soundly. At this stage of my career, I did not often get a berth on a plane. These were reserved for more senior people, but since I fell into this category on this mission, I did get a berth. I slept soundly and at daybreak when I awoke, we were over Athens. The crew served an excellent breakfast as we circled over the Greek capital.

We had no clearance from the Yugoslavs to enter Yugoslavia, so we circled near Athens for a considerable time trying to obtain this clearance by radio. Athens airport reported that Belgrade airport did not come on the air until nine o'clock in the morning. We continued circling over Athens and then it became clear that if we continued to do this, we would soon have a fuel problem. Mr. Harriman made the decision to go ahead to Belgrade without the clearance. He pointed out that circumstances had changed considerably, even immeasurably, since Tito had been shooting down U. S. Air Force planes in 1946 and 1947.

We flew north and as day broke we passed over Salonika. Soon we were over Yugoslavia flying above the clouds. Despite the change in Tito's attitude, I kept an eye peeled for fighters but saw none. Belgrade radio was still not on the air. We saw an airfield that we thought was Belgrade's Zemun Airport, but it was not. We were homing with our plane radio on the Zemun Airport transmitter. At last Belgrade radio came on the air and reported the field clear. Below us we saw only a low fog through which emerged some church steeples, tall hills, and a few structures. We continued to circle, puzzled at the variance between what we could see and the conditions they were reporting on the ground. At this point, our gasoline was really running low and we had to make the decision to attempt the landing or else head for our nearest alternate field, which was Rome. We were flying along at about a thousand feet and we suddenly saw a tall radio tower sticking up through the clouds. The decision to go to Rome was almost made then, but we saw a hole through the clouds and down we went. Almost immediately we were above Zemun airfield. In a few moments we were on the ground. As we taxied up to the terminal, I could not help but feel a little peculiar as I saw the red-starred fighters on the ground. The confusion about our whereabouts had arisen from the fact that we had been homing with our radio compass on the Belgrade radio transmitter, and the Yugoslavs had moved it about thirty miles without bothering to notify the International Civil Aviation Organization.

As the aircraft came to a stop, we were met by Comrade Mates, one of the many Yugoslav vice-foreign ministers we were to meet during the thirty-six-hour stay in the country. I was later to wonder seriously whether the title of vice-foreign minister was given to everyone in the Foreign Service above the rank of vice-consul. We were then told that we had arrived an hour ahead of the time at which we were expected. Ambassador Allen had not yet returned from Bled, where he was spending the summer, and the American chargé, Mr. Beam, bade us a weary welcome. We went into the airport restaurant while trying to find out what would happen next and ordered a cup of coffee. Had my Brazilian friends tasted this coffee, they would have regarded it as an insult. After sipping at this indescribable black beverage, I became uneasy from looking at the large photographs of Lenin and Tito staring down at me and went to the airport newsstand to see what could be had in the way of souvenirs of my trip to this proletarian country. Other than the newspapers *Politika* and *Borba* the stand carried only some Yugoslav cigarettes called Drina. Although I do not smoke, I thought they would be a suitable souvenir and pulled out some Yugoslav money that I had gotten from a member of the Embassy. "How much," I asked in German, which was the language the news vendor seemed to speak. He smiled broadly and said, "Two hundred dinars." That was two dollars. I forked over the money, deciding that Drina cigarettes would be a souvenir indeed. Mr. Mates, the Vice-Foreign Minister, must have seen the expression on my face, for he rushed over as I put the cigarettes in my pocket, and said, "You paid too much. You should have used putniks." Not having the faintest idea what putniks were, I said it was all right and he returned unhappily to his "coffee." (This was the only way to approach Yugoslav "coffee.") The Ambassador arrived and took charge of the confusion. The great question of the day seemed to be whether we would go to Bled to see the Marshal or whether he would come to Belgrade. Another key question was whether Mr. Harriman would accept an invitation to a proletarian boar hunt the next day. This Mr. Harriman felt obliged to decline with regret because of prior commitments to go on to London. Mr. Mates appeared quite upset at the idea that anyone would decline an invitation from Marshal Tito. He appeared greatly relieved when Mr. Harriman offered to break the news to the Marshal himself. After two delightful hours of indecision at the airport our hosts finally decided to send us on to Bled to see the Marshal at his country retreat, or rather, one of

his country retreats. He had just gone to Bled from the former
Italian resort of Brioni, now entirely reserved for the bigwigs of
the Yugoslav Communist party.

The nearest airfield to Tito's palaces at Bled and Kranj was
at Ljubljana, Yugoslavia's third largest city, but it would rarely
take a DC-3. It was then decided that we would go in the U. S.
Air Attaché's plane. Since this would take a little time to arrange, we were whisked into Belgrade to the government guesthouse for breakfast while the plane was made ready. As we sat on
the terrace waiting for breakfast, Mrs. Harriman asked another
of the bright young vice-foreign ministers what the guesthouse
had been before the war. He replied, "Oh, it belonged to the
Karageorges, the former royal family." Mrs. Harriman nodded
and whispered to me, pointed to a dark stain on the floor, saying, "I guess that's the blood of the last owner."

Driving to' and from the guesthouse, we got a glimpse of
Belgrade. The city looked drab and run-down. We passed
through an area covered with the skeletons of huge buildings
that were unfinished but already sinking into the ground at
crazy angles. I asked the English-speaking driver of the car, a
Serb who had emigrated to the United States and returned
home, to his eternal regret, what these colossal unfinished buildings were. "New Belgrade," he replied bitterly, "a monument to
the inefficiency of the government's Russian friends. They built
it on the soft earth of the Danube's bank." I was surprised that
he had spoken so frankly. The police-state environment was
palpable.

We took off from Zemun Airport and flew in the Air Attaché's DC-3 plane to Ljubljana, passing over the superhighway
from Belgrade to Zagreb. I did not see a single automobile on it,
only oxcarts and horse-drawn vehicles. Zagreb from the air
seemed large; but again, the absence of vehicular traffic in the
streets of such a large city was striking. We landed at Ljubljana,
where we were met by another urbane young vice-foreign minister who gave his name as Vilfjan. His wife, a pretty young
woman, who spoke equally good English, took charge of Mrs.
Harriman. After our passports were stamped, we drove off along

the concrete highway through Kranj toward Tito's summer palace. It soon became obvious that we were approaching the Marshal's palace by the barbed-wire fence with the grim Tommy-gunners spaced every fifty yards or so behind it. We swept up to the entrance and stopped before the door of the palace. Thence we were ushered into the presence of the great man. As we passed through each doorway in the palace, we passed between two motionless captains of Tito's guard in smart gray uniforms. Finally, we paused before a door that was dramatically thrown open by Vilfjan, and he exclaimed, "The Marshal."

We went in and Tito shook hands with Mr. Harriman, Ambassador Allen, Bill Rountree, and Walter Levy. Then it was my turn. He held out his hand and I took it, not without an inner queasiness about shaking hands with Mihailovich's executioner and Cardinal Stepinac's jailer. The Marshal was dressed in a hand-stitched pearl gray suit and looked more like a prosperous Chicago gangster than anything else. He was beaming broadly, obviously happy to receive so distinguished and powerful a guest, Vilfjan interpreting attentively. He was completely assured and obviously a leader of men. When he smiled his whole face crinkled. He had obviously made the transition from guerrilla warfare (at which he excelled) in the mountains to life in a palace. One sensed that he understood power and enjoyed it. We were then given a few minutes to prepare for lunch, returning between the pairs of motionless captains of the guard as we proceeded to lunch on the terrace. Low-ranking though I was in this party, I had the dubious distinction of sitting at the foot of the table between Boris Kidric, Yugoslavia's chief economic planner, and the Minister of the Interior and chief of the Secret State Police, Colonel General Aleksandr Rankovich. Kidric and I spoke in German and he acted as interpreter for the conversation at our end of the table. I doubt if I have ever seen a man who looked more sinister than Colonel General Rankovich. He rarely moved his head, shifting only his eyes from one speaker to the other. The table was not too large, and it was possible to get snatches of the conversation from the other end of the table. At regular intervals we heard the shrill voice of Vilfjan's wife saying, "We Catholics" this, that or the other. Vilfjan, at the other end of the table, also used the phrase. I could only smile inwardly at the irony in the persecution that was then being inflicted on the Yugoslav Catholics by these very people who sat around the table calling themselves Catholics. It was obvious that the word had gone around to impress the Harriman party with the fact that Tito's men were not wild-eyed Macedonian comitadjis or sinister Communist killers but courageous, upstanding, independent patriots holding out bravely against the Muscovite tyranny. Only Colonel General Rankovich seemed not to have gotten the word. Or maybe he could not avoid looking sinister no matter how hard he tried. Kidric, at my side, could not have been more urbane or civilized. He told me how he had hidden Tito in his home when the latter was on the lam under King Alexander's dictatorship. Kidric allowed as how he himself had been one of the pillars of the underground Slovene Communist party at that time. I told him that I had heard numerous conflicting reports concerning Tito's participation or non-participation in the Spanish Civil War. He assured me that Tito had never been in Spain.

At one point during the lavish luncheon, Vilfjan was telling a witty story and pointing to the Minister of the Interior. He said "General Markovich." Rankovich's eyes narrowed to slits. He leaned across the table and said in a low, harsh voice, "*Vilfjan, Rankovich, ne Markovich.*" Vilfjan turned pale and gibbered almost hysterically, "*Da, da, Rankovich, Rankovich,*" as he looked into the steely eyes of the secret police chief. Tito, farther up the table, noticing that something had happened, asked what it was. When informed, he laughed uproariously and said something to Vilfjan, who was obviously in an extremely nervous state. I asked Kidric what the Marshal had said, and he replied that the Marshal had told Vilfjan, "If you want to get ahead, you must not make mistakes like that." The big brass all seemed to enjoy the slick young Vilfjan's discomfiture, all except Rankovich, who smiled only a pale, cold smile. Yet, years later Rankovich's turn was to come when he was thrown out of his job by Tito, who became suspicious that Rankovich might be plotting to replace him. He probably was.

In response to my questions Kidric explained that the palace dated from the fifteenth century and formerly belonged to the Serbian royal family. The regent, Prince Paul, was the last occupant before Marshal Tito. "Do you know what Prince Paul did?" asked Kidric in a shocked tone. "He put up a Byzantine wall around a fifteenth-century palace." I looked pretty shocked myself. Then Kidric added, "Of course, Marshal Tito had the Byzantine wall taken down at once." I was sorely tempted to remark that he had replaced it with a triple-charged barbed-wire fence with a Tommy-gunner every fifty yards as being much more in keeping with the architectural harmony and indicative of the trust, love and affection of the people.

We heard that a mysterious Madame Tito was reported to be around, but though we were introduced to Madame everyone else, no Madame Tito was produced. After lunch the conversation with Tito began privately. I was present at this. Occasionally Tito would speak to me in German and I would translate for Mr. Harriman. Tito, a remarkable linguist, spoke flawless German and Russian and has since learned a great deal of English. He emphasized the historic importance and the courage it took to break with Moscow. He understood the West. He spoke of his need for economic help. He denounced the unreasonable attitude of the Italians in wanting the Italian city of Trieste. He emphasized the importance of his help in case of a Russian attack. He spoke of his plans to industrialize Yugoslavia, and the need to develop exports. He also added, gratuitously, "Please don't mention Cardinal Stepinac. I am fed up with that subject." He had kept Cardinal Stepinac in jail for years and obviously wished to avoid discussion of the matter. Mr. Harriman listened sympathetically to Tito's problems and promised to convey them to Washington. Tito spoke forcefully, occasionally emphasizing a point with his cigarette holder. I noticed he did not smoke Drinas.

Following this conversation, the American Ambassador whisked Mr. Harriman off to his residence and, having been in

Yugoslavia long enough to have picked up proletarian protocol, he paid not the slightest attention to Bill Rountree, a class-two Foreign Service officer, nor to peasants like Walter Levy or myself. We managed to get a car and make our way to the Grand Hotel Toplice at Bled, not far from Marshal Tito's other palace on the lake. Lake Bled was beautiful, surrounded by magnificent mountains. The hotel was large and comfortable with a splendid view. Duncan Sandys and his wife (Churchill's daughter) were staying at Bled, and I saw them in the government travel agency Putnik, where I went to change some money. Now I learned the meaning of putniks. The official exchange rate for the Yugoslav dinar was completely unrealistic—fifty to the dollar, whereas in Switzerland it was six hundred to the dollar—so the government gave all those who changed their money legally in Yugoslavia coupons that entitled them to different reductions—50 per cent on the hotel bill, 60 per cent for food—but these coupons could not be used for tips, haircuts, and so forth, so that a shoeshine cost a dollar. The girl in Putnik explained all this to me in German. I said to her, "You have a very complicated financial setup." "I know," she replied. "Well, you won't get many foreign tourists with a setup like this." "I know," she replied. Then I added, "There must be some simple system." She said, "There is." And I asked, "Well, why don't you use it?" She looked carefully around the agency; we were alone. She looked at my American passport and said in a slow voice, "They have taken the red paint off the bars, but we still live in a prison." Thanking her, I departed at once.

The next morning was Sunday and I decided to go to church. I walked around Lake Bled and found the church jampacked with worshipers, young and old. Later that morning I expressed surprise to a Yugoslav who did not hide his distaste for the Tito regime. "Oh," he said, "the persecution here is very shrewd—nothing like stopping people openly from going to church. The sort of thing they do is to arrest all the young seminarians the night before they take their government-supervised examinations. They question them and threaten them all night and then release them just in time to take the exams. You can imagine what kind of marks they get, so they don't become priests. They are waging a long-term war of attrition against the church." This same man told me that he felt Tito had scored a success even greater than his victory over the Germans and his fellow resistance fighter Mihailovich. I asked him what he meant, and he replied that Tito had convinced the West that the bulk of his opposition was from Stalinist communism. "This is utterly false. Ninety per cent of the opposition to Tito is bourgeois. This," he added sadly, "the West does not want to hear about." Our visit to Yugoslavia was almost over. I had seen Tito. He had impressed me as a strong, harsh man, probably a patriot, probably quarreling to some degree with Moscow because he did not want to take orders from them, but, nonetheless, a convinced Communist.

We drove to Ljubljana in the curtained cars of the Marshal and boarded our C-47; we flew quickly across the border and soon saw our faithful Constellation on the fine Italian field at Udine. We landed and as the door of the plane opened, I took a deep breath of Italian air, the air of freedom and civilization. After greetings from the prefect of Udine, we changed planes and flew quickly to London, passing over Lake Constance. Landing there we were met by friends, and before I left the rest of the party, who were continuing on to the United States, we made up a scroll and gave it to Marie Harriman. It was signed by Mr. Harriman, General Robert Landry (Mr. Truman's Air Force aide), Bill Rountree, Walter Levy and myself and cited her for "morale building and keeping up our spirits under difficult and dangerous conditions far above and beyond that which was to be expected from the wife of an Ambassador extraordinary and plenipotentiary." She was moved and appreciated it very much. The trip to Yugoslavia did not bear much initial fruit, but it gave me the opportunity to observe Tito and briefly the operation of his so-called independent communism. Yugoslavia seemed to have the same gray drabness about it that characterized the other Eastern European countries. I did not of course have a chance to visit the beautiful Dalmatian coast.

When the Hungarian Revolution was crushed by the Soviets

in 1956, it was interesting to note that hundreds of thousands fled to Austria, but almost no one fled to Yugoslavia. Forgotten now is the fact that it was Tito's Embassy in Budapest that turned the Prime Minister of the short-lived Free Hungarian Government, Imre Nagy, over to his Soviet executioners.

15. TRAVELS WITH PRESIDENT
EISENHOWER

In late 1953 I was still serving at SHAPE. I was the Assistant to the Deputy Chief of Staff for Logistics and Administration. In November I received an advance message from Washington alerting me that I should be ready to go to the summit meeting in Bermuda, where President Eisenhower was scheduled to meet with British Prime Minister Winston Churchill and French Prime Minister Joseph Laniel, from December 4 to 8.

I flew back to the United States and was briefed at the White House and State Department on the various projects which the United States expected to present at this meeting and broadly the U.S. view of the purposes of this meeting. This was important for accurate interpretation, because it is difficult to convey correctly the meaning of words unless you know what lies behind the words.

It was winter in Washington, and I was surprised how, in a very short flight, we flew into summertime. The conference was held at a magnificent resort, the Mid Ocean Hotel, surrounded by a golf course and beaches. All three national delegations were to be billeted in this hotel. I went to Bermuda ahead of President Eisenhower's arrival to get a feel of the location and what would be expected of me. I was to see where the meetings would be held and familiarize myself with the environment of this conference. French and English were the only languages involved, so I expected no problems.

President Eisenhower arrived in his special Air Force plane, the *Columbine*. He was greeted on arrival by the governor of Bermuda in his dress uniform with a magnificent plumed hat. Churchill and the President exchanged warm greetings.

Shortly after the arrival of the three national delegations in Bermuda a press conference was held. The three principals, Eisenhower, Churchill and Laniel, were present and spoke of their hopes and expectations for a fruitful conference. The press questioned Eisenhower about a piece of plaster on his hand. He explained that he was showing Mamie how to handle a pistol and had cut himself accidentally. Churchill appeared to be in good form despite his advanced age.

The usual preliminary meetings and protocol calls began. Each chief of delegation called on the other and then the other side returned the call. I accompanied Eisenhower upon his calls on the French but not on those upon the British. Obviously he needed no interpreter for the British. I have, however, noted on numerous occasions the truth in George Bernard Shaw's remarks about two peoples separated by a common language. The British and American meanings of the expression "to table a paper" are diametrically opposite.

The staff ate in the dining room of the hotel. I was surprised to see Secretary of State John Foster Dulles come down and eat with us in the dining room. On the first day I was sitting at the table with him and he commented that ever since members of his delegation had seen Bermuda, he had received a large number of applications from people who wanted to be consul in Bermuda. No such applications had been received before they had seen it.

Because Bermuda is a British crown colony, Churchill as host presided over the conference. Considerable security was provided on the island. Part of the security was provided by a local defense force, the Bermuda Rifles, and the other part was provided by troops of the Royal Welsh Fusiliers, who were flown in from Jamaica. The Royal Welsh Fusiliers were British regular troops. One of the jokes current at the Mid Ocean Hotel referred to the bushes or trees around the hotel: "If it moves, it's a Bermuda Rifle; if it doesn't move, it's a Royal Welsh Fusiliers."

Churchill opened the conference with a passionate plea for Western unity and stressed the need to find a common path that all could follow. At one dramatic point he lowered his head as though musing to himself, and said, "I have charged on horseback at Omdurman and I have flown to Bermuda in a Stratocruiser, all in the span of one lifetime." I understood at that moment the span of history that this extraordinary man's life had covered.

The French were, at this time, heavily engaged in their Vietnam war and appealed to their allies for assistance. Shortly after the first meetings, the French chief of delegation, Prime Minister Joseph Laniel, became ill. A member of the French delegation approached me and asked if Major General Howard Snyder, who was Eisenhower's doctor, could attend the French Premier. The French had not brought a doctor with them. I asked the nature of Mr. Laniel's illness and was told that it was evidently some sort of lung problem. General Snyder indicated that this was not his bag of tricks. He was basically a cardiovascular man. He suggested that we check with Lord Moran, Churchill's physician. Lord Moran agreed to see Mr. Laniel. I accompanied him to the door of the French Prime Minister's room and started to withdraw. The French asked me to remain since Laniel did not speak English and presumably Lord Moran did not speak French. I went in with Lord Moran. He examined Mr. Laniel at considerable length. Finally he told the French Premier that he had bronchitis. Laniel said, "But I must go to the meeting or everyone will think that it is a diplomatic illness." Lord Moran assured him that he would make plain, as a doctor, to Churchill and Eisenhower that Laniel was really sick in bed. Laniel said that despite Lord Moran's recommendation he felt that he must go to the next meeting. He could not remain in bed. Lord Moran then said to him, "Prime Minister, if you go to the next meeting, I promise you that you will have pneumonia." This sobered Laniel somewhat. Finally he said,

TRAVELS WITH PRESIDENT EISENHOWER

"Well, if you promise me that I can go to the meeting tomorrow, I won't go today." Lord Moran looked at him and smiled. Then he said, "Prime Minister, prophecy is as difficult in the field of medicine as it is in the field of politics. You should stay in bed. If you get up prematurely you will get pneumonia. You must leave your delegation in the hands of Mr. Bidault, your Foreign Minister. I will explain to the British and American leaders that this is no diplomatic illness and that it is at my insistence that you are staying in bed."

Shortly before this episode, I had been talking to Prime Minister Laniel in the lobby of the hotel when Churchill came up. Knowing that he spoke some French I immediately withdrew. He spoke a few words to Laniel and then waved me back to translate for him. Speaking French had simply been too much of an effort for him. Abruptly Churchill stopped, looked at me for a minute and said, "You've translated for me before. Where was it?" I replied, "Prime Minister, it was on the twenty-fifth of August 1944 when you addressed the Brazilian troops at Vada in Italy." He said, "That's right. So it was. So you speak Portuguese too." I said, "Yes, Prime Minister, I do." He then held out a large case containing cigars. Since I did not smoke I declined the offer. I have regretted not taking one as a souvenir ever since.

As a result of Lord Moran's advice Laniel remained in bed. For the remainder of the conference Foreign Minister Georges Bidault effectively became the leader of the French delegation. Bidault was a distinguished French statesman who had been in the Cabinet ever since the liberation of Paris in 1944. For most of this time he was Foreign Minister, but he had also occupied other posts and had been Prime Minister. During the war he succeeded Jean Moulin, who committed suicide while in the hands of the Germans, as president of the National Council of Resistance within occupied France. He was the highest official of the Resistance in France. He remained there until the liberation, and stepped out of the shadows on the day on which the Allies entered Paris.

At one of the meetings Bidault made a rather passionate plea for British and American assistance for the French efforts against communism in Indochina. When he had finished speaking, Churchill replied quite harshly and said that Indochina was basically France's problem, and that France should solve it alone. I was quite surprised at the force with which he spoke, since Churchill was not exactly an anti-colonialist. As he was about to finish, he suddenly realized how sharp he had been to Bidault. In a solemn voice, he said, "If I say what I say, it is because for forty years I have stood alongside our French comrades as they sought to protect themselves from the mortal peril which threatened them. Let us never forget that Mr. Bidault, sitting here with us today, lived during the whole long night of the occupation, for every hour of every day and every night in mortal peril of his life. And when dawned the day of glory of which the 'Marseillaise' speaks, he awaited us beneath the Arch of Triumph. In so doing he has earned the undying gratitude of the entire free world." As Churchill finished speaking, his voice choked. Everyone else in the room was deeply moved. Bidault buried his face in his hands. Eisenhower was visibly moved, and I myself was deeply moved, first of all by Churchill's extraordinary eloquence and secondly by the realization that Mr. Bidault had been the most sought-after target of the German occupiers of France for four years. When Churchill finished speaking, there was a moment of silence. Then Anthony Eden, the British Foreign Minister, said in French, "Georges, after a bouquet like that you have to do something." It was an amusing statement but it spoiled the magic of the moment.

Later, Bidault, as the acting leader of the French delegation, gave a luncheon for Eisenhower. There I committed perhaps the greatest *faux pas*, or blooper, I have ever committed in my career as an interpreter. Somehow, the conversation had gotten around to literature, and Bidault was pointing out that there were some authors who were good in the original and poor in translation and vice versa. He said in French, "For instance, you have an author who is magnificent in the original, like Shakespeare, but poor in translation. To my mind you have to be an Anglo-Saxon to understand all these Henry the Fourths and

Henry the Fifths and so forth. Then," he went on, "you have a writer who is good in translation but worthless in the original, like Balzac." As I translated this into English, I translated it correctly until the end, when there came a slip of the tongue and I said in English, " . . . and worthless in the original, like Bidault." There was a gasp of laughter and horror around the table. Bidault himself laughed. I was enormously embarrassed, especially since Bidault was an author who had some pretensions at literary value. I still did not know whether he had forgiven me until I saw him a couple of weeks later in Paris with General Gruenther, who was then the NATO Supreme Commander. At the end of our meeting Bidault said to me in French. "Walters, are you still only a lieutenant colonel?" I then said to Bidault, in French, "Thank you, Mr. Foreign Minister. I see that you have really forgiven me for my slip of the tongue at Bermuda." As a matter of fact, when I returned to SHAPE from Bermuda General Gruenther had already heard the story and asked me what I was trying to do to Franco-American relations. Nevertheless, this was not lasting and on the many occasions I have seen Mr. Bidault since that time, he has been very gracious and has sometimes humorously recalled this particular anecdote.

The conference was not an intensive one. There were considerable periods of relaxation between the meetings. Then President Eisenhower would go out and putt on the green outside the hotel. I would go swimming and often Secretary of State John Foster Dulles would join some of the junior members of the U.S. delegation for swimming at the beach, not far from the hotel. Near the hotel there was a golf course and through it ran a road on which there was not much automobile traffic, since automobiles had only recently been allowed in Bermuda. There was a rather curious sign on a bridge over the road that read, "Beware of golfers and flying golf balls."

This conference, like most summit conferences, was not particularly productive, but it did give the three main leaders of the Western world an opportunity to get together and to get to know one another better. They also discussed economic and political matters as well as colonial problems and the matter of a common position with respect to the Soviet Union and its desire to dominate the world. They were able to do this quietly and privately and without the everyday pressures to which they were subjected in their respective capitals. I must say that I was greatly impressed with Mr. Bidault's dignified and effective performance, faced with these two Anglo-Saxon giants. At the end of the conference I flew back to Washington.

As always, one of my principal tasks at these conferences was not only to translate, but to produce each evening, as complete as possible, memoranda of the conversations President Eisenhower had at which I was present. This was a long and time-consuming job. Generally I took no notes at the private talks, as this inhibits the speaker and makes him less frank and forthcoming. At the conference table the secretariat, of course, produced the record. While notes of the private talks might help with the accuracy of the translation, one can lose much of the spontaneous nature of what was said and the way it was said by concentrating on the verbatim account. If one becomes so caught up in the words themselves, one can forget the meaning and the message that the speaker was attempting to convey.

I remained at SHAPE as Assistant to the Deputy Chief of Staff for Logistics and Administration. I was assigned to this job after Eisenhower left SHAPE. Previously I was the Assistant Executive for National Military Representatives and it appeared to me that that job was being phased out. I continued, of course, to translate for General Gruenther whenever he needed me. He had spoken to me and expressed a strong desire that I remain at SHAPE and had asked me in a general way where I thought I would fit in best. I regarded this as a somewhat rhetorical question and so did not give him a specific answer. One day I was driving with him to see a foreign dignitary and he said to me, "I have asked you where you should be assigned in this headquarters and you have been vague to the point of unco-operativeness." I replied, "General, I did not desire to be unco-operative. It merely seemed inappropriate for me to tell you where I should be working in your headquarters." He got the message and shortly afterward asked me whether I would like to work for the French Deputy Chief of Staff for Logistics and Administration. At that time this was Lieutenant General Olivier Poydenot, a witty, amusing and capable French officer. I worked for Poydenot, his successor General François Brissac and later for the extraordinarily able and brilliant General Jean Étienne Valluy. During World War II Valluy had been Chief of Staff to the commander of the First French Army. Later he commanded a division, had fought in Indochina and after he left SHAPE became the commander in chief of Allied Land Forces Central Europe. On one occasion it is reported that General de Gaulle told Valluy that he would soon have the Americans on their knees before him. Valluy replied, "If you really think that, then you are insane." Whereupon de Gaulle ordered him to leave his presence. Valluy was a fearless as well as a brilliant officer.

This was an interesting job and it led me to travel a great deal with General Valluy, not only in Europe but also to the United States. General Valluy had on his staff a French cavalry colonel who was also a paratrooper. He was extremely aristocratic in manner, personally very wealthy and took a rather contemptuous view of the British and Americans. On one occasion he came into my office after eating at the mess and said quite seriously, "The food in this mess is so terrible that even the British and Americans are complaining." He meant it.

General Gruenther was universally admired and respected as a man of extraordinary intelligence, understanding and wit. The Europeans regarded him with confidence and affection and the Americans knew how extraordinarily competent he was. It has always seemed unfortunate to me that General Gruenther was not used in an ambassadorial post after he left SHAPE. He was superbly qualified for such a position. I have always speculated whether if he had been Ambassador to France he could not have persuaded General de Gaulle to take another course toward NATO than he ultimately did. I have known very few men as convincing and persuasive as General Gruenther.

As my assignment to SHAPE drew to a close, I was notified that my next assignment would keep me involved with the

North Atlantic Treaty Organization. I was to go to the NATO Standing Group in Washington, where I was to serve on the U.S. delegation. The Standing Group was a sort of executive body for the NATO Military Committee made up of the chiefs of staff of the member nations. Obviously this Military Committee could meet only infrequently and the Standing Group was a sort of permanent executive body for it. The Standing Group was composed of representatives from the United States, Great Britain and France. On its staff, however, there were planners from other member nations. The chief of the U.S. delegation to the Standing Group at that time was a distinguished soldier, former Chief of Staff of the U. S. Army, General J. Lawton Collins. I served with the Standing Group as interpreter and special projects officer. In the latter capacity I helped arrange a trip for senior NATO officers to watch a series of nuclear tests at Eniwetok and Bikini in 1957. This series of tests code named "Hardtack" included both nuclear and thermonuclear tests. I saw some eight tests in all and they were an awesome sight. As someone once said of the first nuclear test, "It was something like being present at the first day of creation."

While I was serving at the Standing Group, my old chief from SHAPE, General Valluy, was assigned there as the chief of the French delegation. His wit and brilliance won him the admiration and affection of his American and British counterparts. Much of the Standing Group's time was spent in formulating military documents for the whole of the alliance, not just for SHAPE, but for the other commands as well—the Atlantic Command, largely naval, and the Channel Command.

I observed with interest and curiosity at the Standing Group that the Americans, who have a sacrosanct written constitution, wanted everything set forth in writing in the most minute detail. The British, who have no written constitution at all, always resisted putting anything in writing that they felt unnecessary. They felt that having everything in writing limited their flexibility. I was always struck by the French position, which was to go along with whatever seemed to be the consensus. I once asked General Valluy about this and he said, "The reason why we do not take a strong position on this matter is that we know that when the time comes, everyone will do what he believes to be in his national interest regardless of what has been put in writing. Therefore we do not pay that much attention to what is written."

At one time the British delegate to the Standing Group was the extraordinarily able and intelligent Admiral Sir Michael Maynard Denny. The U.S. representatives were successively Air Force General Leon Johnson, who replaced General Collins when he went to Indochina as U. S. Ambassador, and Admiral Frederick Boone. Admiral Boone and Admiral Denny clashed often, not only on substance but on punctuation. Both were greatly attached to correct punctuation and argued frequently about it. On one occasion there was a fierce discussion going on between them as to whether or not there should be a comma after the word "and." I cannot now remember who was defending the pro and who the con. I do remember the fierceness of the argument, which was getting nowhere. They finally asked General Valluy what his view on the matter was. General Valluy had long since lost interest in the discussion and was reading his overseas edition of *Le Monde* when one of them asked his opinion on this problem. General Valluy lowered his newspaper and asked innocently, "What problem?" to emphasize the lack of interest he had shown in the argument. They explained to him in general terms that it involved the matter of putting a comma after the word "and" or not. General Valluy replied with some irony, "I have two remarks to make in connection with this matter. First, in French it is compulsory but it is never done. Second, in the French Army we generally have this sort of thing done by captains, not generals or admirals." Rather sheepishly the two admirals looked at one another and one said, "Perhaps we ought to let the secretary handle this matter." General Valluy was quite adept at ending long-drawn-out discussion over trivia.

While I was serving with the Standing Group, the White House notified me that there would be a summit meeting with the Soviet Union, France and Great Britain at Geneva in late

April 1955 and that I was to accompany the President as his interpreter. Needless to say the Standing Group offered no objections and in mid-April I was a member of the White House advance party which generally precedes all of the President's visits to make all the necessary local arrangements. We went to Geneva and were most cordially and hospitably received by the Swiss. We had many meetings with them to cover all aspects of the visit. Since the conference was taking place in Geneva nearly all of the Swiss spoke French. I went out with President Eisenhower's military aide, Colonel Robert Schulz, to visit the splendid Ferminich Villa on the shores of Lake Geneva. This villa was made available to the President as his residence during the conference. Large private homes were also made available to the other delegations. The owners of these homes moved out in order to leave the homes to the chiefs of delegations. The Ferminich Villa was magnificent, with two formal gardens running down to the lake. There was a superb view. The villa also had a large guesthouse on the grounds and this is where I stayed along with other members of the President's personal staff.

On April 25, 1955, President Eisenhower with his son John and other members of the U.S. delegation arrived in Geneva for the opening session of the conference. Here the pattern of Bermuda was repeated, only this time there were four delegations, not three. There were a large number of individual conferences between the various delegations in getting ready for the actual opening of the conference. One of the chief projects that the United States was anxious to push at this meeting was the Open Skies program. This would have given reassurance to all sides that the others were not planning sudden strikes against them, by permitting controlled overflights of national territory by the other sides. None of us had any real illusions that the Russians might accept this. Their society was such a closed one that the idea of open overflights like this was bound to be abhorrent to them.

I was fascinated to see the Soviet leaders and observed them very closely. The meetings were held in the old League of Nations building in Geneva in a large room that looked out over the lake and Mont Blanc. The Soviet delegation was large. The main members were Khrushchev, Bulganin, Molotov, Gromyko, Marshal Zhukov and the able Soviet interpreter Oleg Troyanovsky. The British delegation was led by Prime Minister Harold Macmillan, with Foreign Minister Anthony Eden and Ivone Kirkpatrick from the Foreign Office. The French delegation was led by Prime Minister Edgar Faure. He had with him Foreign Minister Antoine Pinay, the French Ambassador to Moscow, Louis Joxe, and their unusually able and intelligent trilingual interpreter, Prince Constantin Andronikof. Secretary of State Dulles was with the President, as was Douglas MacArthur II, the counselor of the State Department, and Dillon Anderson.

At the first meeting the Russians sat to the right of the U.S. delegation. The British faced the U.S. delegation and the French were on the left of the U.S. delegation facing the Russians. I made some notes at that time which are reproduced below.

Khrushchev has a twitch in his left eye. He sits at Bulganin's right. Eden looks at the Russians directly when he says that in any future war there would be no victors. Bulganin, Molotov and Troyanovsky smoke, the others do not. None of the Russians wears any jewelry—no rings or cuff links. Khrushchev changed his shirt during lunch. (To later meetings they all came with Swiss shirts and cuff links, as though they had bought them on a signal.) Gromyko has a crease in his sleeve, perhaps a relic of his days in the United States. Khrushchev and Molotov both have a slightly oriental look, Molotov more so than in his pictures. I guess that their ancestors did not run fast enough from the Tartars. Bulganin and Zhukov look completely Western. Bulganin in particular looks like a kindly old country doctor and he should have a twinkle in his eye, but there is no twinkle, only a glitter. There is a considerable resemblance between Marshal Zhukov and our General Omar Bradley.

The conference began with the Russians, as usual, making a series of propaganda speeches and the Westerners trying in some way to get them to agree to some system of inspection. The Soviets made it clear that they would not go along with any system of inspection. They regarded this as a violation of their sovereignty and would have none of it.

Each day I rode with President Eisenhower in his car to the League of Nations building. As we came down close to the shore of the lake, a large number of bathers would run out to see us. Many of them were very pretty girls wearing scanty bikini bathing suits. The President called them his "Bikini Brigade."

Interestingly the Russian protocol apparently places the most senior person in a car the farthest forward. Khrushchev would often sit on the jump seat while Marshal Zhukov sat in the back of the car. We had considerable contact with the Soviet security officials who were charged with safeguarding the Soviet leaders. The newspapermen and photographers were fascinated by the whole meeting and this unusual view of the Soviet leaders. Up to that time few of them had ventured outside the borders of their own country. On one occasion while the four principals were being photographed on the lawn outside the building, I went around to join the photographers to take some movies and was roughly jostled by those photographers who were jockeying for position.

As I observed the Soviet delegation it seemed to me that while Bulganin was the titular head, there was no doubt that Khrushchev was the real boss. He seemed to know it and behaved accordingly. My impression was that Molotov and Gromyko were senior civil servants, not policy makers. Bulganin apparently was in an intermediate class, somewhere between them and Khrushchev.

I went with President Eisenhower to a number of meetings with the French to try and concert our positions. As usual I did not go to the discussions with the British. At the final meeting of the conference Eisenhower made an impassioned plea for his Open Skies proposal. He closed by saying, "I do not know how I could convince you of our sincerity in this matter and that we mean you no harm. I only wish that God would give me some means of convincing you of our sincerity and loyalty in making this proposal." As he finished, there was a tremendous flash of lightning and a clap of thunder and every light in the building went out. To this day, I am told, the Russians are still trying to figure out how we did it.

Little of substance was achieved at this conference. The leaders of the West were able to get a better feel of their Soviet counterparts and of the complex relations between the Russian leaders. This was the first good look that the Western world had of the men who ruled the Soviet Union. Later they were to travel a great deal. This conference was in a sense a premiere of their subsequent world travels.

I accompanied President Eisenhower to another summit, this one a meeting of the chiefs of government of the three countries of North America. Eisenhower met with President Adolfo Ruiz Cortines of Mexico and Prime Minister Louis St. Laurent of Canada at White Sulphur Springs in Virginia on March 26, 27 and 28, 1956.

This was largely a ceremonial meeting and a gesture to two good and close neighbors. Ruiz Cortines was an interesting man. He had the chiseled face of an Aztec emperor. At this meeting an awkward incident occurred for me. I had written up a memorandum of President Eisenhower's talk alone with Ruiz Cortines. Secretary Dulles came into my room at the Greenbriar Hotel while I was in my underwear and asked me for the memorandum. I explained to him that I had specific orders from the President himself not to show anyone any of these memoranda until he personally initialed them. Dulles turned abruptly and left the room without answering. I could not tell if he was angry at the time. Mr. Dulles was, however, very cordial to me thereafter and obviously did not hold my refusal to give him the memorandum against me. The conference was pleasant and without tension. The leaders discussed airline routes, cultural matters and other problems that were pleasantly minor after the summit with the Soviets.

The Mexican President was much taken with my Spanish and surprised that I had never been to Mexico. He invited me to go there with the President's naval aide, Captain Ned Beach. We flew to Mexico City and spent four or five days there as Ruiz Cortines' guests. He took me through his official residence, Los Pinos, and when I commented on what a magnificent residence it was he said somberly, "Yes, I live in this palace and there are hundreds of thousands who do not know where their next meal will come from." He even showed me his personal living quarters. When I saw a crucifix in the bedroom I was somewhat surprised, since Mexico is very anti-clerical and a Mexican government official cannot enter a church. He caught my look of surprise, smiled and said, "My wife, she believes."

I returned to the NATO Standing Group and resumed my duties there. As public relations officer I spoke at a number of colleges around the United States explaining what NATO was, what it meant to the United States and why it was in our interest to keep the alliance strong. I was frequently called upon to translate for the President when he received distinguished foreign guests from countries whose language I spoke—the Austrian Chancellor, President Sékou Touré of Guinea, the Prime Minister of Lebanon and many others including several NATO Prime Ministers. I was known as the President's interpreter but I was never actually assigned to the White House during this period. This service to the President was additional duty to my normal assignment in the Pentagon. I think I was used so often because the President had known me for a long time and felt comfortable with me. Sometimes on matters of less than major import that he was to discuss with foreign leaders, he would arrange to have me briefed, so that, as he told a State Department official, "Dick Walters will know when to stop me from doing something wrong on this particular issue." Obviously he did this only on lesser matters. Nevertheless, whenever possible I tried to sit in on the briefings for him. If I knew the background of a problem and the aims of all concerned, I could better represent the President's position. Similarly the more I knew about the position of foreign leaders who were to see the President, the easier it was for me accurately to comprehend what he really wanted to convey without saying certain words. Sometimes I actually knew what their real position was through intelligence sources and this made my task much easier. At other times I had to go into the conversation, so to speak, absolutely cold. I never forgot that Dwight Eisenhower was the President of the United States, but sometimes he made it difficult for me to remember this by his warmth and friendliness. Once I was in Walter Reed Army Hospital in Washington to have a metal nail removed from my right leg. It had been inserted after my 1954 skiing accident. I was sharing a room with two other lieutenant colonels. I had been operated upon for the removal of this intramedullary nail by the same doctor who inserted it four years previously in Germany, Colonel Milton S. Thompson. I shall forever be in his debt. One day a large bunch of flowers arrived in my room with a card that said, "Dick, get well soon. Affectionately, Ike and Mamie." I was surprised and grateful that in the midst of the enormous burdens he carried as President of the United States he could remember I was in the hospital and still more send flowers. I saw him after I got out of the hospital and thanked him for the flowers. He asked me whether anything special happened after the flowers came. I replied that within minutes of receiving flowers from the President I was moved into a private room. With a twinkle in his eye and a grin, he said, "I did not want to ask for any special favors for you, but I figured that if Mamie and I sent the flowers something like that might happen."

On another occasion, while General de Gaulle was in Washington, I had attended a number of functions in white tie and tails. On the last day of General de Gaulle's visit I was told that I would not be going to the French Embassy white tie dinner for President Eisenhower that night. He was taking one of the White House military aides. I informed my mother, who promptly sent my only wing collar to the laundry. At five-thirty that evening I received a phone call from the White House informing me that I would be going with the President that evening. I asked my mother for my wing collar and she told me that she had sent it to the laundry. I was much agitated and said to her, "Don't you realize that I have to wear it to a dinner with the President in two and a half hours?" To which she replied, "Did you or did you not tell me that there were to be no more such ceremonial occasions this week?" Since that was exactly what I had told her I was even more upset. I called several clothing stores and they were either closed or had no wing collars. I called John Eisenhower at the White House to see if he could help. He wore size 15 collars and his father 15½. I wore a 16½. John told me to come down to the White House and they would see what they could do. He seemed highly amused by the imbroglio. I went to the White House in full dress uniform wearing miniature medals and carrying my white tie in my hand and wearing no collar. On the third floor where John lived a search for a wing collar that would fit proved fruitless. John, who had to go out to another dinner, turned me over to the President's valet, Master Sergeant John A. Moaney. With him I took the elevator to the second floor. As the door opened the President stood there in tails wearing the sash of the Legion of Honor. He looked at me and grinned, saying, "I hear you have a problem. It sounds pretty funny to me." I replied, "Mr. President, I am sure that you will understand that I do not find it nearly as funny." He then said, "Come with me and I will show you something I learned as a young officer." We went into his bedroom and he took one of his own size 15½ wing collars. He then sat down on the foot of the bed and with a nail file carefully began to ream out the buttonhole at each end of the collar. He told me that one had to be very careful not to split the collar, but that if this was done properly it would give an extra half size at each end of the collar. He completed his task, stood up, handed me the collar and said, "There, that solves your problem for you." I tried on the collar and it fit quite comfortably. I thanked him, saying, "Yes, Mr. President, it does and I have never had my problems solved at this level before."

I marveled that this man who had ordered the invasion of Europe and launched a thousand ships and eleven thousand aircraft on D-day could find time to worry about the problems of a lieutenant colonel with a broken leg or a missing wing collar. It was a measure of the human warmth and concern of this great man for his subordinates and those he considered his friends.

During this period I was privileged not only to travel to the summits with him but also to accompany him on all of his foreign trips except the one to the Far East. These were his trip to Germany, Britain and France in August of 1959; his great sweep through Europe, the Middle East, the Indian subcontinent and Africa in December of 1959; and his trip to Brazil, Argentina, Chile and Uruguay at the end of 1960. He undertook these trips despite severe setbacks to his health. He had a deep belief that men who were personally acquainted with one another were much less likely to misjudge each other's motives. He believed that the personal contacts which he established, not only with foreign leaders, but with their people as well, made the world a safer place in which to live. Like General Marshall who had been great in war, Eisenhower yearned to be a builder of bridges between nations and a man of peace in the afternoon and evening of his life.

There are those who fault Eisenhower for one thing or another; those who believe he should have won the war more quickly and with fewer losses; those who believe that he played golf too much, or that like most generals he was not really intelligent. They mislead themselves. There was a special quality about this man that was understood almost immediately, not only by a large majority of his fellow countrymen, but by Indians, Spaniards, Brazilians and Moroccans. I do not speak of the peoples of Europe, to whom he was the Liberator. As Carl Sandburg once said of Lincoln, Dwight Eisenhower was both velvet and steel. His impact on the rest of the world has never been fully appreciated in the United States. Men tend to forget that the eight years of his presidency were years of national unity, peace, prosperity and tranquillity that we have not known since. He represented all that was best in America and he projected this image to friend and foe alike. It was impossible to ride in a car with him, as I did many times, and not see the effect he had on crowds who came to see not just the President of the United States, but "Ike." The impact was the same from Kabul in the shadow of the Hindu Kush to Bariloche in the snows of the Andes. Men recognized what many of his fellow countrymen are only now dimly perceiving, that this was one of the very great men of our time. Perception of this has been slow because he did not strut, pontificate or revel in the panoply of power.

Nearly always I went on the advance party for these presidential trips. I knew many of the security officials with whom we would deal. Sometimes when the Secret Service or the press wanted something that was particularly outrageous by local standards, we were able to arrange it. Thus in a sense I got to make these trips twice. Once with the advance party and once with the President. I found this helpful because in effect I had a sort of dress rehearsal and could tell the President what was due to happen next, or which way to go or whom he would meet at what point.

These trips also presented problems of a political nature. He could not go to India without going to Pakistan. He could not go to Greece without visiting Turkey. On the occasion of the long trip to Europe and Asia, I found that he would be going from France to Morocco. I said to Press Secretary Jim Hagerty, "You mean we are overflying Spain, which is letting us keep our bases, and going to Morocco, which is asking us to leave?" Hagerty replied, "But Spain is a dictatorship." I answered, "What do you think a lot of countries we are visiting are?" I do not know whether this had any influence on the schedule, but Spain was included in the schedule and Madrid produced a crowd second in size only to New Delhi.

These trips were exhausting for all concerned. Often they were particularly so for me. The need to concentrate continuously I found simultaneously draining and exhilarating. By a slip of the tongue in translating what the President had said, I could embarrass the United States. A mistake in the other direction could mislead the President about the intentions of some foreign leader. Most tiring of all was the need at the end of the day, while others slept, to call in two or three secretaries from the local American Embassy and start dictating the long, detailed memoranda for each of the talks the President had that day. I could take no notes and yet I had to keep clear in my mind who said what, and at which conversation. As I finished dictating one memorandum, I would start proofreading another. Often this went on until two or three in the morning. Baggage pickup as often as not was at 6 A.M. This part of my work was invisible and unknown to most people. Many did not even realize that I had to do this in addition to the actual translation. Many in the State Department resented my doing this, as it deprived them of the possibility of getting copies of these memoranda as they could easily do when State Department translators were used. I was under the strictest orders from the President to give these memoranda to no one—without exception—until he had reviewed and initialed them.

Because I was often needed as soon as the President got off the plane, I generally traveled aboard the same plane with him. Sometimes in flight after he had been briefed by the State Department, he would ask me to come up and talk to him a little about some of the people he was going to meet, or about special customs of that particular country. He did his homework and traveled with a purpose. Once he described this as follows, "To pledge again in the several capitals I shall visit America's devotion to peace with honor and justice; to support Western unity in opposing, by force if necessary, any aggression and to preserve the defensive strength required for our common security." He emphasized also the willingness of the United States to negotiate realistically with the Soviets on any reasonable and mutually enforceable plan for general or special disarmament. Many people think that these are new ideas. He expressed them fifteen or more years ago.

When President Eisenhower arrived in Paris on his state visit, he stayed at the French Foreign Office. I also stayed there with him. Later that afternoon General de Gaulle came to escort him to the Tomb of France's Unknown Soldier under the Arch of Triumph, where he was to lay a wreath. The old French general wore his uniform. Eisenhower looked at him and said, almost wistfully, "You still can?" "Yes," replied de Gaulle, "I still can." Later that day, President Eisenhower was received at the Paris city hall. De Gaulle was also there to receive him. De

Gaulle spoke at some length and I whispered a translation into
the President's ear. Then his turn came to speak. He did so for
about eight or ten minutes and then turned to me for a translation. He had ended his speech with a sentence in French, "*Je
vous aime tous.*" In translating his speech into French for the
hundred and fifty thousand people massed in front of the city
hall, I ended the French version by saying in English, "I love
you all." This brought down the house and as I walked back
from the microphone to my place behind the President, de
Gaulle nodded gravely to me and said, "*Très bien, Walters,*"
about as high an accolade as one could expect from him. It had
not been easy, as the President had spoken at some length and
never paused for translation until he was through.

On September 3 the President moved, as scheduled, to the
American Embassy and I moved to the Crillon Hotel. The President saw the Italian Prime Minister, Antonio Segni, whom I
knew well, and I translated their talk as I had translated earlier
in London for Spanish Foreign Minister Fernando Castiella y
Maiz.

One of the problems with which I had to deal was the curiosity of many people about the subjects that the President had
discussed with various foreign leaders. With senior people in
government it was relatively easy. I simply said, "The President
has instructed me not to discuss his talks with anyone." Then
they usually backed off. With the press it was more difficult and
they were a great deal more insistent. On one occasion a picture
had been taken of the President and a foreign dignitary laughing
heartily. A newspaperman said to me, "It must have been a
good joke." I replied that it had been an excellent joke. He then
asked me what it was. I replied that even though it was not a
major matter, I had made a practice of never discussing what
the President talked about with foreigners. He said to me,
"Well, the American people have the right to know." This was
my first experience with the "right" of the press to know everything. I simply replied, "Well, let them exercise that right with
the participants in the conversation, not the spectators, because
that is what I am in such matters." In no way abashed, but real-

izing that he was not going to get anything more from me, he pressed me no further.

The Italians all had a feeling of being left out of the deliberations of the major powers and not being in the "know." The President was well aware of this feeling on their part and during his talk with Prime Minister Segni, Eisenhower reassured him as he had others that the United States would not be negotiating with the Russians behind the Italians' backs, and that they would be kept fully informed. That evening we flew to Rambouillet, where the two Presidents met and discussed their experiences in World War II before the fireplace. I have described this meeting in the chapter on de Gaulle. Eisenhower slept in the Francis I Tower of the Rambouillet castle and was photographed in his underwear by an enterprising photographer outside the castle who had a good telephoto lens. The two men talked about the problems that concerned them most: for Ike, peace and relations with the Soviets; for de Gaulle, Algeria and his nuclear strike force. I think both men enjoyed their meetings far more than the wording of the communiqué would have indicated. There was a special relaxed relationship between them. De Gaulle once said, "We are two old generals who have written our memoirs and we have never said anything nasty about one another. That is almost unique." Eisenhower laughed and agreed. They were often in disagreement but there was a mutual esteem and camaraderie that I did not see de Gaulle bestow on many men.

Eisenhower felt that his trip had worked out well and I believe most unbiased observers shared that view. He had been able to quiet the fears and suspicions of the Europeans that the United States would do something behind their backs with the Russians. His own directness, warmth and personality had done much to achieve this. He radiated an honest decency that even the most jaded skeptic could not easily ignore. I think in a modest way he understood what his presence and word could do and it pushed him to undertake further travel on his journey to understanding with so many of the nations of the world. To millions of people all over the world, he typified an American President who could be trusted and relied upon. He knew the horrors of war and would certainly do his best to see that this catastrophe would not be repeated.

In late November that year, I had gone ahead with the advance party through all of the many countries he was to visit. On December 4, 1959, I was at Ciampino Airport in Rome awaiting his arrival from Washington. It was pouring rain and at the last minute the welcoming ceremony had to be moved indoors while the presidential aircraft circled overhead until arrangements to do this could be completed. Inside the airport building President Giovanni Gronchi greeted the President and I whispered a translation into his ear. Then the President replied and I had to translate that aloud into Italian. We rode into downtown Rome in a downpour. I stayed with the President at the huge Quirinale Palace. Once the residence of the Popes and the Kings of Italy, it is now the home of the Italian President. It is a gigantic building with monumental staircases up which the President slowly climbed. He had to be careful since his heart attack in 1955. Then the President met with Italian President Gronchi, Prime Minister Segni and Foreign Minister Giuseppe Pella. They spoke for about an hour. Carefully the Italians indicated their unhappiness at being excluded from many of the deliberations and decisions of the Big Four. Eisenhower was very sympathetic and said that he would pass on their views to the Big Four.

A stupendous state dinner followed. There were toasts which I had to translate as well as the conversation between the two Presidents during dinner. Then once again when all went to bed I wrote long memoranda into the small hours of the morning. The next day I accompanied the President to the Tomb of Italy's Unknown Soldier, where he laid a wreath in the still pouring rain. There were smaller crowds in Rome than in almost any other stop on this journey. Rome has seen many celebrities in its two-and-a-half-thousand-year existence and is somewhat unimpressed by them. The heavy rain also contributed to keeping the crowds smaller than elsewhere.

On the following morning, December 6, I went with the President to see Pope John XXIII. As a Catholic this was obviously a special occasion for me. I had known the Pope before his election in Paris, where as Cardinal Roncalli he served as the papal nuncio. It was a solemn occasion. Only once before had an American President met with a Pope and that was in 1919. I was to translate for the President into Italian on this occasion. The President told the Pope of his hope that his journey would help the cause of peace and understanding among nations. The Pope expressed his approval. Just before the conversation began, the members of the President's party were presented to the Pope. The President, John and Barbara Eisenhower, Secretary of State Christian Herter and others who were not Catholics shook hands with the Pope. When my turn came, I kissed the Pope's ring. He looked up with a smile and said, "Ah! Uno dei nostri." (Ah, one of ours.) He gave me a small silver commemorative medallion. Pope John was the second pontiff I had met. He radiated a warm and fatherly personality. Pius XII, on the other hand, had a spiritual, almost other-world quality. Pope John apologized to the President because he could not speak English. He said that he spoke French, Bulgarian and Turkish in addition to his native Italian. "What about English?" asked the President. "Well," said the Pope, "I am an old man, I am very busy, but I am taking one hour of English a day." The President then asked, "And how is it coming?" The Pope smiled and replied, "The more I study English, the more I understand that papal infallibility does not extend to its pronunciation." We all laughed and the photographers took a shot of the occasion that was widely published. The Pope then commented that both the President and he had some military background. He noted smiling that military life promises a good future. "You were a general and you became President. I was a sergeant and I became Pope." Again there was laughter. I felt that the Pope very much understood what the President was trying to do and approved of it. He said so publicly, invoking God's blessing on the President's efforts.

We then flew in helicopters straight to Ciampino Airport and took off for the two-and-a-half-hour flight to Ankara. Here I had no official duties to perform since I did not speak Turkish. I enjoyed the visit although feeling somewhat illiterate at my inability to talk to the Turks. The reception was warm and tumultuous as Eisenhower and the Turkish president drove through the streets in an old car that had been used by Mustafa Kemal Atatürk. That night I had a good sleep. I did not go to the state dinner and I had no memoranda of conversations to write.

The next day, we flew on to Pakistan. On these trips, the deputy chief of mission from the next stop would fly to the preceding one and ride with the President to tell him what was ahead. Thus, for instance, the DCM from Karachi boarded the President's plane in Ankara and flew with him to Karachi. This was standard procedure so that the President could be brought up-to-date on all matters of importance relating to the next stop.

Pakistan was spectacular, exotic and delightful, as here again I had no official duties. The long British presence had resulted in all of the officials speaking English with the greatest fluency. Here again the enthusiasm was enormous. Eisenhower and President Mohammed Ayub Khan rode in an open carriage drawn by six white horses for the last part of their journey into town. There were ceremonial visits and talks in which I did not participate. Again it was for me a most restful, pleasant and interesting stop. At the next stop, Afghanistan, however, I was to work even though I did not speak either Farsi or Pushtu. The King spoke French and that brought me into the picture. The flight from Karachi to Kabul was spectacular. As we flew over the deserts of Helmand I thought that this was the most desolate spot I had ever seen on earth. After a small but highly military reception at the airport, I translated French to English for the President in his talks with King Mohammed Zahir. There was not a great deal of substance in these talks. Afghanistan, directly on the southern border of the Soviet Union, had to observe strict neutrality. During the King's lunch I noticed the Soviet Ambassador watching me—probably wondering where the U. S. Army had dug up this lieutenant colonel who could speak the local language. He was far enough away that he could not hear that the King was speaking in French. When we had come to Kabul on the advance party some weeks before we had all been struck by the number of Russians on and around the airfield. As we took off on that occasion, the pilot of the President's plane, Bill Draper, put the plane into a steep climb right after takeoff and, as we zoomed into the sky, he commented on the public address system, "That was our commercial for the Russians at the airport." They were not to have jet transports for several years.

Flying to New Delhi, the next stop, took us across the fabled Khyber Pass. Delhi, capital of a country not noted for its pro-American feelings, was to provide the largest crowds anywhere on Eisenhower's many foreign trips. I was far back in the convoy of vehicles traveling from Delhi's Palam Airport. Even in the countries where my services as an interpreter were not needed with the local government, I was usually in eyesight of the President in case some diplomat should come up and speak to him. One interesting fact developed in connection with the President's speech at Delhi University. The question was asked whether any interpretation would be necessary into Hindi. The reply was that this would not be required since all of the instruction at the university was in English. Talking to a young Indian Air Force officer from southern India I asked him what happened at the Air Force Academy in the light of the many languages spoken in India. He replied that all of the instruction was given in English. I asked what happened if a cadet could not speak English. He replied simply, "If you don't speak English, you don't get into the Air Force Academy."

The motorcade from Delhi airport to the President's house, the Rashtarpati Bhavan, where DDE was to stay, was an unbelievable sight. There must have been 2 million people along the line of the cavalcade. It took more than two hours to make the ten-mile trip. Somehow, the Indians had caught the magic of the man. He spoke gravely to India's Parliament and at Delhi University, but perhaps the most moving thing he said was to a huge crowd on the Ramlilla parade ground. He quoted Gandhi, "Freedom is a gift of God and God's gift cannot be kept forever from his children." Since I was less involved in the official program, I went twice to Agra to see the Taj Mahal, perhaps the most beautiful building ever raised by the hand of man.

For the President and most of those in his party the stop in India was one of the most exhausting. For me it was one of the most restful. It was not often on presidential trips that I had relatively little to do. I was even able to do a good deal of sight-seeing. On the advance party trip, I had been able to spend a day in Agra and had seen the other sights there besides the Taj Mahal. I had lunch in the garden of an old British-style hotel. An Indian came up with a trained bird which he claimed could do tricks. I watched in amazement as the bird picked up numbered cards at my request. The bird then caught in flight tiny hoops that were thrown at him. After the incredible little show was over I asked the man how much I should give him and he said, "Four rupees" (one dollar). I replied that was a lot of money. He answered softly, "Sir, do you know how long it takes to teach the bird to do these things and do you know how long the bird lives?" I gave him five rupees.

The next stop, Iran, I knew quite well from previous visits there. It was a splendid stop for me again, as I had little to do with the official part of the program and was able to see some old friends and note the extraordinary changes in Teheran since I had last been there. Half a million people lined the streets from the airport to the palace on the President's arrival. Persian carpets lined the streets. It was a short stop and we moved on to Greece, where we arrived in rain. Three quarters of a million Greeks lined the streets to see the President and King Paul drive into town. Very enthusiastic, very Western-looking after the last few stops. The President and King Paul knew one another well from Ike's days at NATO. I had been with him at dinner in Athens in 1952 the night he was decorated by the King. I talked briefly to Crown Prince Constantine about my experiences in Greece in 1948 during the war against the Communists. After Ike had addressed the Greek Parliament, he flew out by helicopter to the cruiser *Des Moines* and I flew out to the aircraft carrier *Essex*, on which I was to travel to Tunisia and France. After a very smooth crossing of the Mediterranean with an old friend,

Admiral George Anderson, who was the commander of the Sixth Fleet, we arrived off Tunis. Here French was a much used language and my services would be required, since President Habib Bourguiba had indicated that he would be quite happy to talk to President Eisenhower in French. I flew over from the *Essex* to the *Des Moines* and went ashore by helicopter with the President. Bourguiba's welcoming address was delivered in French and I translated this for the President and in turn translated his answering speech into French. The visit was a short one lasting only a few hours. The President had a long talk with Bourguiba, who was most intrigued by my knowledge of French. I was wearing a uniform and this made the linguistic shock even greater. It was a great day for the Tunisians even though many of them did not get to see General Eisenhower. They had poor relations with the Arab League and the French were still quite irritated at them for the support they were giving to the Algerian independence movement. Ike's gesture in stopping by, even for a short time, was greatly appreciated by them. They remembered too that he had been there during World War II and had commanded the armies that had driven out the Germans and Italians. The two Presidents talked for two hours, focusing mainly on Algeria. Bourguiba was fearful that the French would take some action against him because of his support for the Algerians. Eisenhower reassured him and told him he was convinced that the French would not take action against Tunisia and that de Gaulle was actually seeking a way out of the Algerian situation. At the Tunis airport as we boarded the choppers to return to our ships, Bourguiba told the President, "Your visit here is one of the most important events of our time." Then he complimented me again on my French and we flew off.

As our ships sailed into the great French naval base at Toulon, I received a personal signal of welcome from the commander of the French forces there, Admiral Picard-Destelan, whom I had known at SHAPE. His mother was American. She had eleven children. Often people on hearing this would say to her, "You must be a devout Catholic." To which she would invariably reply, "No, I am just a sexy Protestant." After a warm welcome from the people of Toulon, the President boarded de Gaulle's private train for the nine-hour trip to Paris. I bore some responsibility for this train trip since on the advance party the French had offered their President's train for the trip. The Americans were startled at the idea of train travel. I assured them that in France it was very good, that de Gaulle's train must be terrific and that it was better not to refuse the French offer or they would think that we looked down on their trains. Jim Hagerty and Tom Stephens, Appointments Secretary to Eisenhower, agreed and that is how we happened to be riding the train instead of flying to Paris.

De Gaulle met the President at the station even though it was very late at night. Since it was not a state visit, Eisenhower went to the American Embassy. I went to the Crillon Hotel, where I was very well housed, as always, by my old friend Claude Lemercier, the general manager. In Paris, Eisenhower met with de Gaulle, Macmillan and Adenauer. The Big Four reaffirmed their strong stand on Berlin. De Gaulle was particularly tough on this. He once told the Americans and British in my presence, "I will not leave Berlin without fighting, and if I fight, you don't have any choice, do you?" It was agreed that the Western leaders would get together in Paris with Khrushchev in April of the following year. This conference was later to become the U-2 conference because the shootdown of the U.S. reconnaissance plane became the only item on the agenda. The meetings between de Gaulle and Eisenhower were as warm and friendly as ever, though there was much press speculation, later justified, of growing French disenchantment with parts of NATO.

The next stop was the Spanish capital, Madrid, an hour and a half away. Here again my services would be required. At Torrejón Air Base, Franco read a warm speech of welcome to the President as we stood on a little dais, and I whispered a running translation to the President. Then he spoke and I repeated the speech in Spanish. Ten years later I was to translate a speech by President Nixon at the same place, and the Spanish Radio gave me a cassette with my translation of President Eisenhower's speech in 1959 and President Nixon's in 1969. The crowds in Madrid were very large and their welcome extraordinarily enthusiastic. I rode in the car with the President and Franco and I can only report that there were a lot of "Viva Franco" shouts. The visible popularity of the man regarded by many as a hated dictator was not reflected in the press accounts of the visit. Eisenhower, however, was much impressed by this and the way Franco moved through large crowds.

President Eisenhower had struck just the right note at the airport with the Spaniards by asking how he could feel a stranger in Spain. He came from a country that had states called California, Colorado, Florida, Nevada, Texas and Arizona. Later the traffic circle outside the airport was renamed Glorieta Eisenhower. I could not help but contrast this with the tiny street with no buildings on it which bears his name in Paris—a city liberated by his armies. Human gratitude is fickle.

That night Franco gave a state dinner for the President at the Oriente Palace, where the Kings of Spain had lived, but which Franco preferred not to occupy himself. He lived at the spacious but much smaller palace of El Pardo a few miles out of town. When Napoleon had installed his brother, Joseph, as King of Spain in this Palacio de Oriente, he had said to him, "Now, Joseph, you will be better housed than I am." There were warm toasts at the dinner and following it there was a short concert by five violinists all playing Stradivarius violins—priceless treasures in their hands.

The next morning, December 22, I rode with the President out to El Pardo for the meetings with Franco. This started with a breakfast which was so good-humored and relaxed that Eisenhower asked me to tell General Franco a story which I had previously told Ike and which had greatly amused him. The story went like this:

In Napoleon's army there was a colonel named Dupont. He was extraordinarily brave, which is frequent among colonels, and extraordinarily stupid, which is very rare among colonels. But he was crazy to become general, which is universal among colonels. Napoleon said that he knew Dupont was brave but he simply could not have a general that stupid in the French Army. However, at the Battle of Austerlitz Napoleon saw Dupont charging at the head of the cavalry of the Guard, cutting down the Russians and the Austrians and practically winning the battle. As he watched he saw Dupont stagger and fall from his horse. He had been hit. Much moved, Napoleon dispatched his aide and his surgeon Larrey to see what Larrey could do for Dupont. Not long afterward, the young aide came riding back to Napoleon and said, "Sire, Colonel Dupont has been shot through the head. The bullet went in one ear and came out the other. Larrey says he is still conscious, but will be dead before nightfall." Napoleon thought about it a moment and then said, "Dead before nightfall. Well, go down there and tell him I have just promoted him to general." The young aide dashed off and rode back to the medical tent, where Larrey was treating the new general. Larrey had given Dupont a good slug of brandy and had then sawed off the top of his skull and placed it on the table. The brain was badly damaged and Larrey was trying to put it together again when the aide burst into the tent and announced, "The Emperor Napoleon has just promoted Colonel Dupont to the rank of general." Dupont had been powerfully slugged with Napoleon brandy, his brain was on the table, but through the brandy fumes he heard the magic word "general," staggered to his feet, put the top of his skull back in place and tottered toward the door of the tent. Larrey ran after him saying, "Mon général, you can't leave like that. Your brain is still here on the table." "To hell with that," replied Dupont groggily, "now that I am a general I don't need it anymore."

There was much laughter from all present—some of whom were generals. Franco joined in and then commented slyly to Eisenhower, "Did you notice how much harder those who are not generals laughed?" I had not suspected Franco of this kind of humor. Then he said, "The reason why generals are as bad as they are is because they are chosen from among the best colonels." At this the generals present really laughed. Later we went into Franco's study. There was a brief discussion of the U.S. bases. Franco felt that his economic situation was improving and it would not be many years before Spain became a prosperous country like the other nations of Europe and this indeed did happen. Then Eisenhower asked him for his assessment of the intentions of the Soviets. Franco, speaking calmly, gave a most detached and unemotional appraisal of what they were trying to do. Namely, stay out of a major war but press everywhere and when anything was yielded they would press on. If they encountered serious resistance, they would press somewhere else. He did predict that the Soviets would try by all means to destroy the Western nations' will to resist and conviction that they had something worth defending. In this too he proved a good prophet. I was to see him many years later in this same room to discuss what would happen to Spain following his death. He was to be just as unemotional and detached in discussing this event.

We took off from El Pardo in a helicopter and flew to the Torrejón Air Base. Franco showed no emotion as the helicopter lifted off and I was astonished a few minutes later when in reply to a question by Eisenhower as to whether he used helicopters much, the Spanish leader replied that he had never flown in a helicopter before. One would never have guessed it from his composure. He and Eisenhower embraced warmly at the airport and Ike boarded his plane. I sat in the fairly large cabin in the rear of the plane. I had a window seat and watched the Spaniards and Americans waving goodbye as the plane taxied slowly away. I said, "I can read lips and I can tell what they are all saying." Others aboard the plane nibbled at the bait and asked, "What are they saying?" I answered, "It's extraordinary— they are all saying the same thing." "What is that?" everyone wanted to know. I replied, "They are all saying, 'Thank God they're gone!'" This got a good laugh and was probably very close to the real truth. For the host country as for the U. S. Embassy in that country, a presidential visit is an exhausting and shattering experience.

We flew on to Casablanca for the visit to Morocco. Here we

were welcomed by King Mohammed V. There were the two shortest speeches I could remember at the airport and then the two chiefs of state rode into town between thousands of Moroccans on horseback. Tribesmen who had come down from the mountains rode alongside the motorcade firing their rifles into the air to the great dismay of the Secret Service, who had never before ever heard this much gunfire in the presence of a President of the United States. During lunch, Crown Prince Hassan came over and reminded me of our previous meetings in 1942. Whether he actually remembered or whether someone told him I do not know. The President told the Moroccans that we would be evacuating the air bases which the French had given us during their protectorate and the visit wound up on a very friendly note.

I also accompanied President Eisenhower to a meeting with the other Presidents of American nations in Panama from July 21 to July 23, 1956. He had barely recovered from his ileitis operation and was still convalescing but he decided to go anyway. He felt it was important to assure the Latin Americans of our interest in them. His indomitable courage and sense of duty gave him the strength to go through with it. I was with him when he received almost all of these Presidents and did not leave his side when he attended conferences or social occasions, so I know how much of an effort it was for him.

At one point in the conference, there was a ceremony in downtown Panama at which each of the Presidents would speak. It was to be a long ordeal for Eisenhower and I was sent discreetly to several of the other Presidents to ask them to be brief and to enlist their help with their colleagues for the same purpose. All of the ones to whom I talked understood and promised to do their best. The Presidents of the big countries, like Brazil, Argentina and Chile, spoke for about three minutes each. Then President-elect José Velasco Ibarra of Ecuador started his speech by saying that he would be brief. He spoke for forty-five minutes. I could not help but wonder how long his speech would have been had he not decided to make it "brief." President Eisenhower stood it well but as Velasco's long peroration drew to a close I whispered to him, "Mr. President, are you okay?" He whispered back, "Yes, but only just."

During the conference, he received each of the Presidents in turn. The Dominicans all came wearing barely concealed Colt .45s, to the great distress of the Secret Service. I translated for all of them. I also had to write the memoranda of these conversations for the record after the talks. A few of the Presidents spoke English well, like Luis Somoza Debayle of Nicaragua, but I translated for all of the others, including President Juscelino Kubitschek of Brazil in Portuguese and President Jean Magloire of Haiti in French.

This meeting, while not really productive in a visible form, did much to reassure our neighbors to the south that we had not forgotten them and that all of our attention was not concentrated on Europe and the Far East. That Eisenhower had come to the meeting so soon after his operation was not lost on them as a demonstration of the United States' interest and friendship for them and their countries.

With the Latins as with the Pakistanis and the Germans, the old Eisenhower magic worked. He has never been given full credit for what he did to project an image of the United States as a country of justice, honor and decency. In his time, we enjoyed a regard throughout the world that we have not known since. I can never forget this old soldier, tirelessly and without regard for his own health moving around the world to advance the cause of peace and to show the United States as the leader of the free world and the standard-bearer of those nations which loved liberty.

These journeys with him were extraordinary opportunities for me to learn many things and to observe a truly great American in action for his country and for peace.

Many months before the end of his term, he knew that I was anxious to escape from the interpreter's job and he decided to send me to Rome under circumstances I describe in the chapter on my services as attaché in Rome. On January 4, 1961, just before he left the White House, he wrote me in Rome a letter which I shall always cherish with pride. That he would think of

me at such a time and with so many other concerns on his mind
as he left the presidency is indicative of the extraordinary
human quality of the man. He wrote:

> Dear Dick:
>
> Before I leave the White House, I want once again to try
> and express to you my deep gratitude for giving me so
> freely of your great talents whenever I needed and re-
> quested your help. The service you rendered me over a long
> period of time was invaluable—not only because you are so
> expert in the various languages at your command, but also
> because of your intelligent grasp of the problems and back-
> ground of the various countries we together visited . . .
>
> Please give my best wishes to your mother, and to you, of
> course, my warm thanks and personal regard.
>
> As ever, your friend
> Signed Dwight D. Eisenhower

He then added at the bottom, "I am having a copy of this letter
placed in your official file."

When I saw him for the last time on February 17, 1969,
shortly before his death in Walter Reed Army Hospital, he
looked back with satisfaction over his life. He told me that he
knew he did not have long to live, but that he could not complain. Most of the dreams of his childhood had been fulfilled.

I had gone as far as one can go in the interpreting business. I
wanted to show that I could run my own organization and serve
in a capacity where I could use my languages, but that they
would not be all that I would need. He knew this and he helped
me. So I left the service of this great man with gratitude for the
opportunity of working so long and so closely with him, to go to
my next mission—to Rome as attaché.

PART II

16. TO SOUTH AMERICA WITH VICE-PRESIDENT NIXON

In 1958 the first democratically elected President in Argentina in many years was scheduled to be inaugurated. The United States, pleased with this return to popular government, and in keeping with the tradition of sending a high-level government representative to such ceremonies, decided to send Vice-President Richard Nixon as its representative to the inauguration of President Arturo Frondizi. After the announcement of his trip, a number of other South American countries extended invitations to Mr. Nixon to visit them. He had been to Brazil the previous year so that country was not on the list for a visit on this journey. The oldest university on the American continent, the University of San Marcos in Lima, had invited Mr. Nixon to speak there. This venerable institution was founded nearly a century before any similar institution in the United States. Other invitations were extended by Uruguay, Paraguay, Bolivia, Peru, Ecuador, Colombia, and Venezuela. The United States felt that such a visit would show our continuing interest in our Latin neighbors. The ambassadors in the nations involved had strongly urged that the Vice-President accept the invitations. A statement of acceptance was issued in Washington and it was received with great satisfaction by all of the governments concerned. There were, however, some negative factors which were perhaps not fully appreciated. The U.S. government had, under pressure from domestic groups, who wanted protection for their interests, taken certain measures of a protectionist nature. This had greatly irritated many people in Latin America. For instance, certain restrictions had been placed on the importation of Venezuelan petroleum. After the violence in Caracas, it was said that this had caused a number of Venezuelans to lose their jobs. The Communists knew that Mr. Nixon was a staunch anti-Communist and did not intend to lose the opportunity to try and discredit him through violence or better still to humiliate him, nor were the Communists alone in this intention. The so-called New Left, claiming to be independent of Moscow, appeared in Latin America almost before it showed up anywhere else. Then, as now, the United States was the favorite whipping boy of the New Left to explain away any problem that might arise. A foreigner once quoted me a proverb from his country which went like this: "It is raining, swinish government! It is not raining, swinish government!" He said that the proverb had now been modified. "It is raining, swinish United States! It is not raining, swinish United States!" Another negative factor was the widespread belief in the southern part of the continent that the United States gave only lip service to Pan-American ideals, but that its real interests lay in Europe and Asia. They saw themselves as some sort of stepchild that can only get attention from the United States through some sort of violence. There is, unfortunately, some basis to this belief. Many in Latin America note that the United States is rich and powerful and they are not. They believe that in some way this must be the fault of the United States. This view is held by many who are not leftists. Many on the far right, too, regard it as gospel truth. Extremists of the far left and far right are often not far apart on many issues.

The United States Government was aware of all of these facts, perhaps not in the blunt form in which I have put them. All of these factors were weighed and it was decided to go ahead with the trip as being in the best interest of the United States.

It was against this background that my mission to South America with Vice-President Nixon was to develop. My first contact with him was to occur in an unusual way. In early April 1958, I was on leave in Florida and was driving from Miami to Palm Beach when I was overhauled on the Sunshine State Parkway by a Florida State Trooper. I had been observing the speed limit and was surprised when he signaled me to stop. He then asked me if I was Lieutenant Colonel Vernon Walters and when I replied affirmatively, he told me to call the White House switchboard at once. I stopped at the next service area and made the call. The President's military aide, Colonel Robert Schulz, told me that I would be going to South America with the Vice-President at the suggestion of President Eisenhower. I was to be Mr. Nixon's aide and interpreter and we would be leaving Washington on April 26. I scarcely saw the need for the urgent message on the road, but was delighted to be going on such an interesting trip and to have a chance to meet the Vice-President —I had never met him previously.

As departure time approached, I learned that I would not be traveling to Montevideo, the first stop, on the same plane as the Vice-President. I traveled on a C-118 of the U. S. Air Force with a group that was to accompany Mr. Nixon to the Argentine inauguration. It included Senator Montoya, then a congressman. This military plane went only as far as Buenos Aires and I had to go on from there to Montevideo on a commercial flight. On landing at the Uruguayan capital, I was met by someone from the Embassy who told me to go immediately to the Uruguayan Congress Building, where the Vice-President was scheduled to make an address. I went there directly and walked into the Hall of Congress just as Mr. Nixon was to begin his speech. I had not yet been actually introduced to him. He began to speak in English and I had no advance knowledge of what he was going to say. It is always much easier to translate for someone when you have translated for them before. I had no paper with me to take notes, as I had been rushed straight to the Congress upon landing. I did the best I could using my memory when he stopped infrequently for translation. The speech was well received by the Uruguayans and afterward Mr. Nixon chatted with the members of Congress, and I translated for him.

We then called on the Council of Government which at that
time in Uruguay replaced the President in a Swiss-style organization. Thereafter, I was directed to remain at Mr. Nixon's side
at all times and rode in the same car and plane with him. I also
met Mrs. Nixon, who impressed me as a charming and gracious
woman. Still later she was to show great courage as well.

Perhaps the most interesting event of this visit to Montevideo
was a call at the university where Mr. Nixon, despite Embassy
misgivings, debated skillfully with a group of students of anti-
American convictions. I translated the rapid-fire exchange in
both languages. His willingness to engage in such an exchange,
his relaxed manner and the fact that he had obviously done his
homework won him the grudging admiration of most of the students. What had started out in a somewhat chilly atmosphere
wound up with handshakes and *abrazos*. The students, whatever
their political views toward the United States, were visibly
pleased that the Vice-President would take the time to debate
with them. So was I. He was to do it again in several other
places.

From Montevideo we flew in the Vice-President's plane to
the Argentine capital, where we were met and taken in charge
by Ambassador Willard Beaulac. I had known him in Bogotá in
1948. Mr. Nixon stayed with him at the Embassy residence and
most of the rest of the party stayed at the fine old Plaza Hotel.
The next morning was a religious holiday and I went out at 6
A.M. to a nearby church and was surprised to find there the Vice-
President's secretary, Rose Mary Woods, and his Air Force aide,
Major Don Hughes. We had all gone independently and almost
surreptitiously, but we all returned to the hotel together and had
breakfast.

In Buenos Aires I accompanied Mr. Nixon on his official calls
but did not attend the actual inauguration with him. Ambassador Beaulac, who spoke Spanish, assured me that he would take
care of everything. He got the Vice-President to the ceremony
ten minutes after it started. This was widely reported, but Ambassador Beaulac survived the embarrassment to the Vice-
President.

After the inauguration of President Frondizi, I went with Mr. Nixon, who was quite displeased with the Ambassador, to the Casa Rosada, the official home of Argentine Presidents. We watched the inaugural parade from the balcony there. During the parade a large Perónist demonstration occurred with thousands of people waving small white handkerchiefs as Eva Perón used to do. Small balloons carrying pictures of Perón and Evita were released and floated over the parade, but there was no violence.

Mr. Nixon went to the University of Buenos Aires, where the rector, a brother of President Frondizi's, was very far left in his political views. Mr. Nixon, here again, engaged in a debate with the students. It was extremely lively and I was hard pressed to keep up with the fast-moving give-and-take. Here, as in Montevideo, the net effect on the students was positive. Mr. Nixon did not talk down to them, he was obviously well informed and was quite unlike the image they had been given of him. Most of all the fact that he would take the time to talk to them during his short stay in Argentina was what impressed them.

Despite the lively Perónist demonstration and the graffiti on all the walls of Buenos Aires, one had the impression that constitutional government had really returned to Argentina and that the provisional President, General Pedro Eugenio Aramburu, had led the Army back to the barracks. Aramburu was an impressive figure of a soldier and statesman. He was quite unselfish and harbored no ambitions to perpetuate himself in office. He was later to die tragically, brutally murdered by extremists. He made a most favorable and dignified impression on all of us.

From Buenos Aires we flew to Asunción, the capital of the small, landlocked nation of Paraguay. On the way there, I briefed Mr. Nixon about President Stroessner, whom I knew well from previous visits with other distinguished visitors. The Vice-President was always most grateful for the insights and anecdotes I could give him from past experience on many of the prominent personalities he was scheduled to meet on this trip.

President Stroessner met us at the airport and after reviewing a smartly turned-out guard of honor, we drove into Asunción.

There, I stayed at the Grand Hotel, formerly the home of Eliza Lynch, who was the mistress of nineteenth-century Paraguayan dictator López. Since the hotel was overcrowded, the room I was assigned had only one bed but another officer was also assigned to it. We drew lots for the bed or the floor. I drew the floor.

A party with Guarani songs and folk dances was given for Mr. Nixon on the site where a new American Embassy chancery was to be built. One of these dances involved the dancers cavorting with a bottle (empty) on their heads. There were no real problems in Asunción and the popular welcome was warm and friendly. Stroessner and the Paraguayans were very pleased that the Vice-President had paid them a visit. We left without incident.

The next stop on our itinerary was La Paz, Bolivia. We took off from the Paraguayan capital, which is a few hundred feet above sea level, and headed for the Bolivian capital, which is the highest in the world at some 13,000 feet above sea level. On this, as on other legs of the journey, Mr. Nixon would take several newspapermen along and would talk to them for a while during the flight. After they had their talk with him, they went back to the rear of the aircraft and started drinking. At one point, one of us wondered when the pilot was going to decompress the aircraft cabin pressure to match La Paz's 13,000-foot altitude. I went forward to the cockpit and asked the pilot about it. He said that the cabin altitude was already set at 13,000 feet (he said this from behind his oxygen mask). I went back and told the newspapermen that whether they had noticed it or not, they were already at 13,000 feet. Within minutes one complained of shortness of breath and another of a headache. These symptoms had not been perceived until they knew they were at 13,000 feet. The knowledge seemed to have a great psychological impact. On landing at El Alto Airport at La Paz one is immediately confronted with a sign in English and Spanish sayng, "El Alto La Paz, 13,000 feet, the highest commercial airport in the world." One of our newspapermen read it and promptly fainted.

We drove into La Paz through thousands of cheering, flag-waving Bolivians including many Bolivian women wearing derby or bowler hats. Here again, the welcome was large, warm and friendly, but this got little attention in the American press. Only the negative aspects of the trip seemed to be featured. I am sure that it was on this trip that Mr. Nixon began to develop the feeling that the press was violently prejudiced against him. This feeling exploded in his press conference following his defeat in the contest for governor of California in 1962.

In La Paz I had a real demonstration of Mr. Nixon's vitality. He made eleven speeches in one day to different groups. I counted them because I had to repeat each one in Spanish.

One amusing instance occurred during the presentation to the Vice-President of the keys of the city of La Paz at the City Hall. The mayor made a speech welcoming Mr. Nixon in Spanish and I whispered a simultaneous translation into the Vice-President's ear. Then Mr. Nixon replied and I translated that aloud into Spanish for the mayor and the City Council. After the presentation of the key an Indian chief wearing the characteristic hat or chuno of the Aymara Indians of the Altiplano began a greeting to Mr. Nixon in the Aymara Indian language. For a second I was nonplused as I could not understand a single word of the language. Suddenly, I heard a voice whispering into my left ear a Spanish translation of what the chief was saying. A small Bolivian standing on tiptoe was giving me a translation. I turned to Mr. Nixon and said in English, "We the Indians of Bolivia are proud to extend our greetings to you in the language that our fathers spoke for a thousand years before the Spaniards came." Mr. Nixon, who knew some Spanish, realized that the Indian chief was not speaking Spanish. He looked at me with astonishment. He could not see the small Bolivian who was bailing me out and thought I was translating directly from the original Aymara. After we left the ceremony, he asked me in the car where I had ever learned the Aymara language. I broke down and confessed what had happened. He was greatly amused, even more so when we read a few days later in the American papers that "to everyone's astonishment Colonel Walters translated the Aymara just as easily as the Spanish."

The altitude of La Paz did not really bother me in spite of the running around trying to keep up with the Vice-President. In fact, most of the time I was too busy to check and see if I was out of breath. Lying in bed at night, however, I could feel my heart pounding as it sought to compensate for my being above half the earth's atmosphere. Mr. Nixon's visit to La Paz was a real success. The Bolivians had long been used to being bypassed by American and other foreign dignitaries touring South America, who were unwilling to face the rigors of the 13,000-foot altitude. From La Paz we flew on to Lima, the capital of Peru, and arrived there in the afternoon. We were met at the airport by a large and distinguished delegation. After the usual airport ceremonies, we drove into Lima. The vice-presidential party was staying at the Bolívar Hotel on San Martín Square in the heart of the Peruvian capital. The Embassy chancery was across the square, and here we met with U. S. Ambassador Ted Achilles and his staff. There was considerable concern because the Vice-President was scheduled to go to the University of San Marcos and a group of students there had already declared him persona non grata at the university. Most of the Embassy staff advised Mr. Nixon not to try and go to the university. They felt that there would be unpleasant incidents if he tried. The Ambassador said that as the Vice-President had accepted the invitation months ago, he should at least try and go. Almost every other person present was strongly opposed to his making such an attempt. Finally, Mr. Nixon turned to me and asked me what my views were inasmuch as I had lived for many years in South America and should know local conditions. I replied that in different countries different things were important. In France or Brazil, the greatest virtue was to be thought intelligent and the greatest vice was to be thought stupid, but in any country where Spanish was spoken, the greatest virtue was personal courage and the greatest vice was to be thought a coward. If Mr. Nixon felt he should not go to the university, I believed that he should cancel the rest of the trip and announce that he had been called back to the United States on some internal matter. I recommended that he should try and go to the University of San

Marcos and I added, "I give you this advice all the more freely because if you go I will be in the car with you." Mr. Nixon decided to go the following day as scheduled. The rector of the university, by this time, was having further misgivings but he still would not withdraw the invitation. Mr. Nixon said that if the invitation which he had already accepted weeks before were not withdrawn, then he must at least try and go.

I walked across San Martín Square back to the Hotel Bolívar. A large crowd had gathered outside the hotel and it was easy to sense that it was not a friendly crowd. There was a sense of hostile tension in the air. After my return to the hotel, Mr. Nixon sent for me and told me that he shared my view about going to the university and I would, as I expected, be going in the car with him. I must confess that I felt a certain anxiety at the prospect of what might happen but I would have felt far more disappointment if he had "chickened out."

The following day with a considerable police escort, we started for San Marcos. When the invitation to the Vice-President had originally been extended, the governing body had not reckoned with the leftist inroads among the student body and above all with their militance. A day or two before the Vice-President's arrival in Lima, a meeting of some of the students had declared that he would be persona non grata at the university if he were to come. It was this action that had led to our discussion at the Embassy. The rector had sent word that he was not sure what might happen. When Mr. Nixon asked whether that meant that he was withdrawing the invitation, he replied that he could not withdraw the invitation. From a distance as we approached the university, we could see that there were several thousand people massed in front of the buildings. As we got closer we noticed that a number of the students seemed well into their thirties. Our car came to a stop in front of them and there immediately arose a loud chorus of boos and catcalls. Many of the students were carrying banners or signs reading NIXON OUT in Spanish; another in English said GO HOME NIXON, still another YANKEE OUT. One of them even called him a donkey in Spanish. He noticed this and asked me whether that was what it said and

when I confirmed this he said that was the last thing in the
world he expected to be called as a Republican. The Peruvian
police were quite nervous and were holding the students back
from the car rather energetically. The hostile shouts were loud
and the Vice-President realized that he could not drown them
out. We were in a convertible and he told me to stand up and
to ask them in Spanish whether they were willing to listen to
him or not. I did so, shouting at the top of my voice in order to
make myself heard above the tumult. The answer was an even
louder chorus of boos and catcalls. Nixon then said to me,
"Ask them whether they believe in the old university tradition
of hearing both sides of a question discussed and then making
up their minds." I repeated this in Spanish at the top of my
voice. Again came the cries of derision. Mr. Nixon stood up in
the car and told me to come with him. He stepped out of the
car and walked into the middle of the jeering crowd. The students, the police and I were all taken aback by this. The police
started to push and Nixon asked me how to say "don't push" in
Spanish. I told him and he said it frequently to the police. As he
moved into the crowd of booing students, he held out his
hand. It was interesting to watch the sheepish grins of admiration for his courage that spread over the faces of many students
who stepped forward to shake his hand. More students then
crowded around to try and shake hands with him. The police
started to push them back and Nixon told them not to. Some of
the students then told Mr. Nixon that they had nothing against
him personally. It was American imperialism that they opposed.
I was astonished at the impact of his willingness to move among
them. Those farther away who could not see or hear what was
happening began to throw small stones and some fruit and eggs
toward the place where they thought he was. The students
within reach were busy shaking hands with him. As the first missiles began landing close to us, I whispered to Mr. Nixon, "Mr.
Vice-President, they are throwing some stones and fruit at us."
He replied, equally in a whisper, "I know and we will move
soon, but our exit has to be slow and dignified." From the size
and temper of most of the crowd, it was obvious that the only

During the Pan American Conference, President Truman addresses a joint session of the Brazilian Congress in Rio de Janeiro.

On the deck of the battleship *Missouri* in Rio Harbor, I translate President Truman's farewell speech. General Marshall is among those present.

Venice, 1948. With General Marshall and an unidentified Italian general.

My mother, Mrs. Frederick Walters, Field Marshal Viscount Montgomery of Alamein, and myself.

THE SECRETARY OF DEFENSE
WASHINGTON

NOV 1 ⌐ ⌐

Dear Harriman:

Pace has just told me of Walters'
promotion to the temporary grade of Lieutenant
Colonel on November 3rd.

The old army custom is to drop the new
insignia in a glass of hard liquor, drink the
liquor, and then fasten the insignia on the
tunic. As Walters is a teetotaler, it looks
like you will have to use milk or water!

I am glad to be able to pass this word
on to you.

Faithfully yours,

Honorable W. A. Harriman
Special Assistant to the President
The White House

I am sending along the necessary
insignia, I doubt if these leaves
can stand hard liquor.

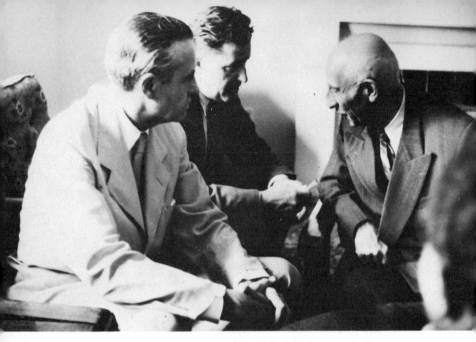

Lieutenant Colonel Walters in Teheran with W. Averell Harriman and Iranian Prime Minister Mohammed Mossadegh, 1951.

Geneva summit conference. Colonel Walters at upper right corner of the table; President Eisenhower and John Foster Dulles third and fourth to the left; and Nikita Khrushchev near the left corner of the table.

South America, May 1958. Vice-President Nixon tells reporters, "It is not easy to endure the kind of activity we had to go through." *(Paul Schutzer, Life magazine, © Time Inc.)*

Speaking to General de Gaulle at the entrance to the U.S. Embassy, Paris, 1959.

At the NATO meeting in Paris, 1959. President Eisenhower greets the Dutch Prime Minister. Also present: John Eisenhower (upper left corner), Secretary of Defense Neil McElroy (above spectacled man near Eisenhower), and John Foster Dulles. I am at right.

Sharing a laugh with U.S. and Italian Presidents Eisenhower and Gronchi upon our arrival in Rome, December 1959. *(UPI)*

Rome. From left: General Andrew Goodpaster, Ambassador Robert Murphy, President Eisenhower, myself, Ambassador James Zellerbach.

With the American and French Presidents in Paris.

The Vatican, 1960. Pope John XXIII greets President Eisenhower as Barbara and John Eisenhower and I look on.

Meeting with Generalissimo Franco in Madrid, 1960.

The most widely publicized photo of the Spanish visit: the two heads of state say farewell.

way we could have gotten into the university would have been to use force. This had been ruled out by Mr. Nixon. We then began to move slowly back toward the car. I was in uniform and to my astonishment quite a few of the students shook my hand, saying, "*El gringo tiene cojones*" ("The Yankee has balls"), about as high a tribute as can be paid in Spanish. As we moved back toward the car, Mr. Nixon cautioned the police against being rough with the students. A number of them patted him on the back as we moved slowly toward the car. We got back into the car and he stood and waved, an excellent target. Many of the students waved back.

We then began driving slowly away from the university and back toward the hotel. This was the plan that had been agreed upon beforehand in case it proved impossible to get into the university. Mr. Nixon was plainly irritated and disappointed by the intolerance he had just witnessed. He was, however, pleased with the way the students close to him had reacted. At no time did I sense any anxiety or fear on his part, but as we drove to the hotel I could tell from the grim expression on his face how disappointed he was. I said, "Sir, you tried and at least they saw that you were not scared of them." He grinned and said, "Did you see how they pressed up to shake my hand?" That thought seemed to put him in a better mood and I said, "They may not agree with your politics but at least they know that you are not afraid of them." While we were having this exchange, we passed some large buildings and he asked what they were. I replied that they were the buildings of the Catholic University, the other great university in Lima.

Suddenly Mr. Nixon said sharply, "Stop the car." The vehicle stopped and the Peruvian police and the Secret Service looked expectantly at the Vice-President. He told me to come with him and stepped out of the car and walked up the steps of what was obviously the main building. We had not been scheduled to make a stop here and there was, of course, no one to meet us. Mr. Nixon walked rapidly, almost running, up the steps and into the lobby. There was no one there except a few startled students. He climbed a flight of stairs and opened the door of a classroom. A lecture was under way and a startled professor and students looked up at us in evident surprise. The professor stopped talking as he recognized the American Vice-President. Mr. Nixon held up his hand and said, "I have just come from the University of San Marcos and I found that there they do not believe in the old university tradition of hearing all sides of a question discussed. I will only be in Lima for one more day and I just wanted to know whether this was also true at the Catholic University." I translated this at once into Spanish and almost to a man the students rushed toward him and to the dismay of the Peruvian police and Secret Service, who had caught up with us, they hoisted him onto their shoulders with shouts of "Viva Nixon," "Viva los Estados Unidos." I tried to stay as close to him as I could, interpreting the friendly exchanges between him and the students who were carrying or escorting him. The delighted professor was also moving along with us. Triumphantly, they carried him back to his car and let him down to the ground. Their action had already given him the answer to his question. He exchanged some pleasantries with them and told them that he was delighted to find at the Catholic University a tolerance he had not found at the older university. The students roared their approval as I put this into Spanish. With a final wave, Mr. Nixon re-entered his car.

I joined him and he continued to wave as we drove slowly away from the cheering students. Tad Szulc, a newspaperman with the party, who was certainly no admirer of Mr. Nixon, then and even less later on, ran alongside the car shouting, "Great show, Mr. Vice-President." I must confess that at that moment I shared Szulc's view. We have not often agreed since. As with Mr. Harriman at the other end of the political spectrum, at Bogotá and Teheran, I could not help but feel a surge of pride that a major political figure of my country would show this kind of guts. Obviously, we have it among both Democrats and Republicans.

Word of this incident spread like wildfire around Lima and wherever the Vice-President went that day he was most warmly received—by businessmen at lunch and later at a large press conference. As we moved around Lima any heckler who raised his voice was promptly shouted down. He had passed the greatest test one must pass in a Spanish-speaking country. He had shown personal courage. He spoke at the port of Callao to a group of stevedores and they applauded him with enthusiasm when he said that the incident at San Marcos clearly showed the ugly face of communism. At his press conference, he noted that the incident was an affront to Peru, to her liberator San Martín and to all who stood for freedom. The Peruvian reporters applauded him.

The following day we flew on to Quito, another high Andean capital, at eleven thousand feet altitude. Here the Vice-President was warmly greeted at the airport and all the way into town cheering crowds lined the streets. It was a warm and comforting ovation. He stopped several times and got out of the car to shake hands with the people who were cheering. After making his official calls on President Camilo Ponce Enriquez and other government officials, we went to the Embassy and were briefed there. Then to the surprise of the Secret Service and the Ecuadorians he decided to go for a walk through the central part of town. This was not on the program and I walked alongside him as people came up to greet him and shake his hand. While walking along one of the main streets, he suddenly spied a barbershop and decided to go in for a haircut. He sat down in the barber's chair and said to me, "Tell him to give me a light trim, all the way around." I did so and the barber was absolutely enchanted at this unexpected customer. A huge crowd gathered outside the store to watch the Vice-President of the United States get "clipped." Fortunately, I had some Ecuadorian money with me and was able to pay the barber and give him a handsome tip. At first he did not want to take the money, saying that the publicity was worth infinitely more to him. I finally prevailed upon him to take it and the Vice-President signed an autograph for him. Throughout the haircut, the Vice-President had been asking him how things were in Ecuador and what his problems were. The delighted barber said to me in Spanish, "This is a gold mine for me. I am going to call this place the

'Barbería Nixon' from now on." He did, for a year later when I returned to Quito the name was up on the outside of the barbershop. We then left the barbershop and proceeded on foot to a local football game. Here, too, he was recognized and got a great hand. Quito could not have been more friendly and pleasant.

Former President Galo Plaza of Ecuador, who speaks English like a native American, told Mr. Nixon that he was right in trying to go to the University of San Marcos and in debating with the students in Montevideo and Buenos Aires. He had shown both sense and courage. All too often what the students are expressing is their frustration because they are unable to get someone in a position of authority to listen to them. While we were in Ecuador we learned that a plenary of all of the students at San Marco in Lima had passed a resolution condemning what had taken place there. They too had obviously felt the weight of public disapproval. Whatever the country or the school, one can always be sure of one thing—the Marxist students are always well organized and highly militant. They know how to take advantage of the apathy of the majority and are past masters at making a minority look like an overwhelming majority.

While in Quito we received disquieting reports of planned violence for Mr. Nixon's visits to Bogotá and Caracas. I felt more concern about Bogotá in the light of my own experience there ten years previously with General Marshall. This was aggravated by the fact that for those ten years there had been a semi-civil war going on in Colombia with great violence and bloodshed. Our reception at Bogotá, however, was warm, friendly and peaceful. The members of the military junta that had recently overthrown the dictator Gustavo Rojas Pinilla had just held a free election which had chosen Alberto Lleras Camargo, a distinguished statesman, as President. Bogotá, too, was a high Andean capital, at eight thousand feet altitude, but there were no problems with this either in the official party or among the press accompanying us. I was amazed to see how Bogotá had grown, both in high buildings and in area, spreading out toward the airport. Wherever we went in the course of the official program the crowds were most friendly. The San Marcos incident had helped. True, not all of the hostile demonstrations were Communist-inspired. There was considerable resentment in many countries against various economic measures that the United States had taken either because of pressures at home or because of genuine ignorance of their impact on some of the poorer South American countries. In Colombia the Vice-President visited a remarkable Catholic priest and the radio program he was conducting in an effort to wipe out illiteracy in that country. He was a most dedicted man and the program was soundly conceived. Military rule was about to end in Colombia and the government was being returned to the civilian President who had just been elected. The Latin American military are a stabilizing force and a block to the ambitions of the Communists. The greatest skill of the latter in my opinion is their ability to seize upon a just cause and mobilize many well-meaning non-Communists to support not only that just cause, but the rest of the Communist program for that particular country as well. Outside of the military, the only other truly well-organized group in most of these countries is the Communists and their friends. They are deeply motivated. They have an ideology and a goal. They unceasingly train the cadres they need to penetrate each group, the students, the workers, the Church, the intellectuals. One cannot help but admire their organization, zeal and indeed courage. It is a tragedy for the world that all of this youthful courage and dedication are put to the service of an intrinsically evil cause. Then too, there is the frustration and envy engendered by the fact that the United States is rich, powerful and prosperous and that many of these countries which secured their independence shortly after ours are not. They seek a scapegoat to blame for this and the easiest answer is that it is in some way the United States that wants to keep them economically weak suppliers of raw materials. All of these factors make it easy to stir up anti-American feelings in many South American countries. Our own ineptness and neglect often help.

We left Bogotá on May 13, 1957, for the short flight to Caracas, where we had been told to expect problems and violence. While we were in flight we had received several warnings from the Embassy in Caracas that there would be some violent demonstrations against Vice-President Nixon on his arrival there. We were able, thanks to the single side-band radio in the aircraft, to talk to our homes in Washington, and I spoke to my mother. She asked me where I was, and I said I was flying from Bogotá to Caracas, and she said, "Oh my God, that's where the assassins are waiting!" This was not very comforting to me. One report we had received I found rather disturbing. This said that someone was going to throw a white phosphorus grenade into the Vice-President's car. White phosphorus is a particularly unpleasant substance which burns until it gets to the bone and there is no way of putting it out.

We came in for a landing at Maiquetía Airport in Caracas, and as we taxied into the terminal, I could see very large crowds on the roof of the airport building and in front of the main terminal. They appeared to be holding banners and shouting and waving. As the aircraft door opened, I walked out directly behind the Vice-President and Mrs. Nixon, and I could hear the hostile and obscene shouts and read the signs, which said, GO HOME NIXON, YANKEE IMPERIALIST, OUT WITH NIXON and other similarly hostile slogans. The Vice-President turned over his shoulder and said to me, "What are they saying?" I replied, "This crowd is entirely against us, Mr. Vice-President." We went down the stairs of the aircraft and when we reached the ground, the Venezuelan authorities were waiting for us, headed by Mr. Venturini, the Venezuelan Foreign Minister. The booing and catcalling was so loud that the Vice-President turned to me and said, sharply, "I am not going to make my usual arrival statement." These demonstrators were not only on the roof of the airport terminal building, but they were also on a balcony. The Vice-President shook hands with the American Ambassador and other assembled dignitaries present and then strolled over to a group of very solemn-looking airport mechanics who were standing there. He shook hands with each one of them; their faces brightened up a little bit when they shook hands with him, but I remember hoping that they would not be allowed to do any maintenance work on the aircraft on which we were traveling. The booing and catcalling was very loud and continued all the way through the playing of "The Star-Spangled Banner." When the band struck up the Venezuelan national anthem, I expected the booing and catcalling to die away; in all of the Latin American countries, the playing of the national anthem is a very solemn occasion and is generally respected by all, regardless of political party or belief. This, however, did not prove true in Caracas on this particular occasion. The booing and catcalling continued just as loudly through the Venezuelan national anthem as it had through "The Star-Spangled Banner." We then turned and walked directly through the airport building. Curiously, the Venezuelans did not have the car on our side of the terminal, they had it on the far side of the building, and as we walked through the terminal, the jeering mob on the balcony overhead spat down on us. It was a rain of spittle coming down. There was nothing we could do. These people were one, two or more floors above us. We walked stoically through the terminal. I could see that Vice-President Nixon was extremely irritated, and I was almost beside myself with anger and a sense of helpless frustration. The mob appeared delighted with our inability to retaliate and the obvious laxity of the police in permitting this kind of disorder. The police made no attempt to interfere with what was going on. They acted as though it was not happening at all.

The Vice-President's car was in place and a large crowd was being held about four or five feet from him by the Venezuelan police. They were being physically held away from Mr. Nixon, but they were not prevented from spitting, jeering and shouting obscenities. The rain of spit began falling again on the Vice-President, on Mrs. Nixon, on me and partly on the Venezuelan Foreign Minister, who did not seem particularly disturbed by any of this. I got into the front car with the Vice-President and the Venezuelan Foreign Minister. The Vice-President was sitting on the right rear seat, with the Venezuelan Foreign Minister sitting on the left. I was sitting on the jump seat directly in front of him, and in the jump seat in front of the Vice-President there was a Secret Service agent. Another agent was sitting in front with the Venezuelan driver. As we pulled away from the terminal through the booing, jeering, catcalling crowd, the Venezuelan Foreign Minister turned to Mr. Nixon and smiled rather wryly. He said, "You mustn't take all this too seriously. After all, it's just the excitement of young people breathing the heady air of freedom after the long night of the Pérez Jiménez dictatorship." Mr. Nixon looked at the spittle on the Foreign Minister, on himself and on me, and said to the Foreign Minister, in a level voice, "If you don't learn to control these mobs you are going to have a dictatorship that will make Pérez Jiménez seem like an afternoon tea party." The Venezuelan Foreign Minister then abruptly changed the conversation, pointing out the magnificent superhighway that leads from the coastal area around the airport up to Caracas, at three thousand feet altitude. This road climbs the coastal escarpment in spectacular sweeps, and he explained that the highway cost many million dollars a mile. He seemed quite unconcerned about the fact that the Vice-President of the United States had been subjected to unprecedented humiliation while the Venezuelan police had stood by and done almost nothing. It had struck me that there were no Army troops anywhere in evidence and that all of the security seemed to have been turned over to the police. We drove uneventfully and at a fast clip up the coastal road and soon began moving into the built-up area of Caracas. Driving in front of us were several cars. A large truck filled with the press and photographers was directly in front of us. Just as we approached the edge of Caracas, two abandoned cars were parked across the superhighway. The island in the center was so high that one could not cross to the other lane. The truck in front of us stopped and we stopped. As we did so, a large crowd came out of the bushes on both sides of the roads carrying baseball bats, lead pipes and stones. We had a motorcycle escort, but it has never been quite clear in my mind where they disappeared to but disappear they did. The mob then began beating on the car with these lead pipes and baseball bats, and sitting inside a closed car with people beating on it is like being inside a bass drum. The Vice-President remained extraordinarily calm. From the car in back of us Mrs. Nixon was watching the proceedings, several Secret Service agents moved up around our car and attempted to protect it without harming the Venezuelans, but trying to keep them away while they were jabbing at the windows attempting to smash them.

The Secret Service agent next to me on the jump seat drew his gun and said, "Let's kill some of these sons of bitches and get out of here." Mr. Nixon, very calm and very composed, said to him, "Put that away. You take it out when they open the door and grab for me, and not before. You don't shoot unless I tell you to do so." The agent complied and put away his gun.

Meanwhile, the contorted faces outside the windows of the car were really something to behold. The rage, hatred, venom and viciousness were almost terrifying. I saw a man's coat fly open and a pistol drop to the ground. I did not know whether he was one of the agitators or whether he was one of the police. Eventually, it turned out it was one of the police, but he was making no particular effort to protect us from the vicious mob at that time.

Mr. Nixon sat calmly in the back of the car. The photographers ahead of us, who were getting a grandstand view of the attack, were grinding away with their cameras. I remember wondering in considerable alarm how we were going to get out of here. While I was worried about getting a black eye or a broken nose, the absence of shooting was somewhat reassuring and I did not think anybody was going to kill me, and such a thought is generally the source of more acute fear than any other. This was probably naïve and unjustified confidence on my part.

The Venezuelan Foreign Minister seemed very upset. He was almost gibbering in the back seat and when a stone smashed through a window on his side and splattered broken glass on him, he became almost hysterical. I remember looking at a man standing outside with a large piece of metal in his hand that looked like the base of a shell and I remember hoping that he would throw it at the other window rather than mine, and this he did. As I looked out through my own window, a stone flew out of the crowd, struck the window and smashed it right in front of me. The broken glass showered all over my face.

The Vice-President asked me if I was hurt and I said that I did not think I was. I had a mouth full of glass, which I spat out on the floor of the car, and as I turned toward him to answer, he said, "Well, maybe you are not, but you are bleeding at the mouth." He then added, "Spit that glass out—you are going to have a lot more talking to do in Spanish for me today." I spat out the glass and wondered idly whether I had swallowed any or not. Meanwhile, the enraged crowd was beating at our car and it seemed quite difficult to think of some way in which we could get out of this mess we were in. However, by some miracle the two cars that had been parked across the road in front of us were moved. I do not know who moved them, whether the Secret Service or the Venezuelan police or someone else, but they finally were moved out of the center of the road, and at that point, the truck in front of us which had all the correspondents and photographers on it began moving and when it began moving, we started moving too. We gradually drew away from this crowd, they chased us a little way, but as we picked up speed, they dropped behind and the rest of the vehicles of the convoy followed us. We drove on through relatively empty streets past the main new development known as El Silencio into downtown Caracas. We turned up a small, narrow street which leads to the Pantheon in which are interred the remains of Simon Bolívar, the liberator of half of South America. The program had originally called for us to drive to this point and lay a wreath on the liberator's tomb. In fact, the Army Attaché, Lieutenant Colonel Daly, was waiting for us at the Pantheon with the wreath. As we turned into this long, narrow street, I realized that it was filled with a very large and hostile crowd. I turned around and said to the Vice-President, "Mr. Vice-President, you can't go to Bolívar's tomb." He looked at me and said, "Well, where can we go? Do you know Caracas? Have you ever been here before?" I said, "Yes, sir, if we turn off to the right here, we will quickly be in a residential area and we can go to the American Embassy residence. It is up on the top of a hill and at least they will be out of breath by the time they get there. Most of all we will be off the published route for your motorcade." Mr. Nixon said to me, "Tell the driver to make the turn." At this point, the Venezuelan Foreign Minister, who had a piece of glass in his eye and had been sitting quietly almost sobbing on the back seat, said, "But this is madness—we won't have any police escort." This was a little too much for me. I had hardly seen a policeman since we left Maiquetía Airport. I turned around to him and said in Spanish, "Mr. Minister, where *is* our police escort?" There was not a single policeman visible around our car. The Vice-President said to me rather sharply, "Tell the driver to turn right." I repeated this to the driver and he complied. We drove a couple of hundred yards down that side street. The emptiness and quiet were almost startling. We were out of the crowds in a quiet, residential neighborhood, and the Vice-President asked me to have the car stopped. I did so. He then asked me to go back and see his wife and to ask how she was and to tell her he was all right. I was to tell her that the plan was to go on to the American Embassy residence. I got out and walked back to her car and found Mrs. Nixon sitting in a very composed fashion with her hands folded on her lap and I said to her, "Mrs. Nixon, the Vice-President wants to know how you are. He says he is all right and we are going to the American Embassy residence." She looked up at me and quietly said, "Tell him I'm all right too, but it was quite a sight to watch from back here." I couldn't help admiring her courage and composure at a time like this, particularly as the car in which she had been riding had been stopped directly behind ours and she had, so to speak, "a front-row seat" in watching the attack on her husband's car. Every window in her car had been broken by the mob as well. The Vice-President's secretary, Rose Mary Woods, was riding with Mrs. Nixon and she too was quite calm.

We dropped the Venezuelan Foreign Minister off at a hospital to have his eye treated. He was not badly injured—it was just a small piece of glass that was understandably frightening him more than it was hurting him. We then drove on to the American Embassy residence. The Ambassador had been riding with us in the motorcade. His wife, Mrs. Sparks, was a Belgian woman of remarkable aplomb. Our original plans had called for us to go to the sumptuous Venezuelan Officers' Club, where we were to stay, but instead we arrived, unexpectedly, at her Embassy with a very large group of thirty to forty people. Within minutes, she had drinks and canapés being served to all of us.

A little later on, the Venezuelan President arrived. The President, Admiral Wolfgang Larrazabal, came up to express his apologies for what had happened. He, too, made light of it and blamed it on the Pérez Jiménez dictatorship and everyone else he could think of except the Communists, who were obviously mainly responsible for what had happened. His own government's neglect and weakness in entrusting the safety of the Vice-President entirely to city police rather than having some troops in the city were also to blame, all the more so in view of the warnings and threats of violence against Mr. Nixon. Certainly, the Communists were not the only participants in these violent demonstrations, but as they so often do, they provide the organization and driving force. Unquestionably, there were also many people there who were not Communists, but who felt some sort of resentment or grudge against the rich and powerful Americans.

President Larrazabal was a dapper little man who made a great issue of being a democrat and opponent of the dictatorship. Needless to say, he had served Pérez Jiménez and had actually been made Venezuela's first Admiral in modern history by the very dictatorship he now denounced.

He left and I must say that I later was delighted to learn that on the way down the hill from the American Embassy, his car was stoned and most of the windows were broken by the same mob that had demonstrated against the Vice-President. Though his car was bulletproof, he at least had some taste of what we had been through earlier in the day.

During the evening, the War Minister, General Castro Leon, over the objections of Admiral Larrazabal and the government, moved troops into the city and law and order was restored.

Then there was a press conference, for which the newspapermen came up. Mr. Nixon was rather restrained with them, saying that he was sure that the day's events did not represent the true feelings of the Venezuelan people, but rather were the result of the work of agitators and professional anti-Americans.

Then a number of Venezuelan party leaders called on him and he was a good deal more frank with them in describing his concern at the government's inability to maintain even the most fundamental type of law and order, despite numerous warnings of what was going to happen. They all insisted on blaming Pérez Jiménez' dictatorship for this, and one would have almost thought that he was still in power, rather than in exile in Miami. He would, at a later date, be turned over by the Kennedy administration to the Venezuelan government for trial. He was held for years without trial and was finally elected senator from Caracas, but in a peculiar interpretation of the democratic process he was not allowed to take his seat. His election as senator from Caracas might lead one to believe that he might not be as universally hated as we were told he was.

Seeing what an enormous crowd there was in the Embassy, I told the Ambassador's wife that I would go downtown, look around and see what I could find out, and would dine downtown. I walked downtown—it was quite a long walk—and had dinner at a restaurant. One could feel the tension in the city, but the restaurant was open, service normal, and I had an excellent dinner at the usual fabulous Venezuelan prices.

I then walked back up the hill to the Embassy and was relieved to see that by now it was guarded by Army troops, who had been brought into the city by the War Minister. Later that night, there was considerable discussion among the members of the party as to what should be done and what plans should be made for the Vice-President to leave Caracas. A number of his advisers felt he should go to the other end of town to a small airport called La Carolina and leave in a C-47-type aircraft from there rather than to attempt to go back through the city to Maiquetía Airport. I expressed my feelings very strongly that he should not sneak out the back door. He should go out the same way he came in, with his head held high, and the Venezuelan government should be made responsible for his ability to do this. This was not just idealistic talk on my part. I was going to ride in the car with him if my advice were followed.

It was also decided to try to carry out most of the previously planned programs for the following day, providing the city remained calm.

With that, we went to bed, and I must say I slept very soundly. The aircraft commander had a single side-band radio he carried up with him from the plane, and with it we were able to communicate with Washington, which had become extremely alarmed and had ordered two companies of Marines to stand by to rescue us. What two companies of Marines could have done in a city of a million people I am not sure, but anyway, that was the order that was given. Mr. Nixon was annoyed by this and felt it was unnecessary and sensationalistic.

The next day we got reports that the city was quiet, and the Vice-President went through with his schedule accompanied by Mrs. Nixon. He visited a medical laboratory and various other installations. As we went by the university, the authorities were obviously nervous. The University of Caracas enjoyed the medieval right of asylum and the police were not allowed to enter it, so that any criminal could take refuge in the university without being chased by the police. It was and is a hotbed of Communist-sponsored violence. Years later the police entered the university and a number of graves were found.

It was hard to believe that this kind of archaic privilege still existed in the twentieth century, and it was a source of a great deal of trouble in Venezuela.

We visited the various places we were supposed to visit, and finally on the morning of the third day, we drove out of the city through the rather empty streets with a whiff of tear gas here and there, which had been used to disperse gathering mobs. We drove down to Maiquetía Airport without trouble and departed. As we took off from the airport, a loud cheer arose from all in the aircraft. I think every one of us felt a certain amount of relief at leaving a country run by a government as incompetent as that which had succeeded Pérez Jiménez and which under the guise of restoring democratic liberties was actually granting every kind of license to the parties of the extreme left to carry out this type of violence and intimidation. If they were allowed so to frighten the United States that our statesmen could no longer venture abroad, then truly we would find ourselves in a defensive if not helpless position to counter their efforts to create trouble between us and our brothers in other Americas.

We had a smooth and pleasant flight to San Juan in Puerto Rico. There we were received by Governor Luis Muñoz Marín. He was far from Mr. Nixon politically, but he greeted him with warmth and admiration. We spent the night in San Juan and then flew on to Washington, where President Eisenhower led a large and enthusiastic welcome for Mr. Nixon. The next day a high government official took me aside in the White House and said, "I think the world and all of Dick Nixon, but tell me, how did he really behave when they were trying to get at him in the car?" This man was close to the upper level of government officials, and I was irked that he would ask me such a question. I replied stiffly, "All I can tell you is that as an American, I was proud of the Vice-President of the United States." He said somewhat sheepishly, "I guess it was not fair to ask you that question." I made no reply. This picture of Mr. Nixon may not jibe with much that has been reported. I can only say that I have recorded faithfully here what I saw and observed on this trip. Mr. Nixon showed intelligence, courage and judgment. I was to testify before the Ervin Committee in 1973 of my admiration for those qualities.

17. THE U-2 CONFERENCE

In the years following World War II the Soviet Union had remained to U. S. Intelligence what Churchill once called "a puzzle inside, a riddle wrapped in an enigma." The Soviet Union had not, like Britain and the United States, in great part demobilized its Armed Forces following victory over Germany and Japan.

This vast totalitarian society covering a sixth of the earth was working feverishly to catch up with U.S. technology. The Soviets had developed both the atomic and the hydrogen bomb and in the late fifties were striving to create the means to launch and deliver them if need be against the U.S. heartland. The United States, deeply scarred by the costly and tragic memory of our unpreparedness at Pearl Harbor, was determined not to be surprised again. But if the United States was to be kept informed of what was going on inside the Soviet Union and was not to be surprised, something imaginative would have to be done. Only by some new means could the United States keep abreast of technological developments inside the closely guarded borders of the Soviet Union, a nation obsessed with security. American ingenuity and American imagination and technology had to find an answer to the difficult problem of obtaining intelligence on the Soviet Union.

The need for such intelligence led to the conception and construction of an aircraft that could fly so high and so far that it would be beyond the reach of Soviet surface weapons or aircraft. Such a plane must necessarily have a range sufficient to take it across the vast land mass of the U.S.S.R.

This plane, the U-2, was built in great secrecy (at a time when secrecy was still not regarded as a crime). For nearly four years prior to 1960 these planes had overflown the Soviet Union and their highly perfected cameras had produced vast quantities of intelligence on what was going on inside the U.S.S.R. in the area of weapons development. The Soviets knew from their radars and from visual observations that they were being overflown, but to protest or admit this publicly would have been an intolerable humiliation by their standards. They started instead to work on the development of a surface-to-air missile to shoot down the U-2. During these nearly four years, none of the many U-2 flights had been seriously threatened and the flights had become almost routine. The President of the United States, of course, had approved the entire program, and senior officers in the U.S. government were aware of it since they received the superb intelligence which these flights provided. This photography gave America its first real look at what was going on in the great factories and military bases behind the Iron Curtain.

Suddenly, on May 1, 1960, a U-2 plane flying from Pakistan to Norway was shot down by a surface-to-air missile near Svordlovsk deep inside the Soviet Union. The pilot, Gary Powers, parachuted out of the falling plane and was captured alive by the Soviets. The Soviets reacted with a frenzy of outrage. They exhibited Powers and the wreckage of the plane to the world press and lashed themselves into a storm of indignation.

Well before Powers was shot down and quite independently of these flights, the four powers (Britain, France, the U.S.S.R. and the United States) had scheduled a meeting of the respective chiefs of government for the month of May 1960. My next mission as aide and interpreter to President Eisenhower took me to the four-power conference in Paris. Khrushchev was to demand an abject apology from the United States and when it was not forthcoming, the Soviet leader stalked out of the conference threatening dire reprisals. The allies of the United States stood firmly with us.

On May 14, 1960, I left the United States with President Eisenhower to attend the four-power meeting in Paris. The actual meeting had been in doubt following the shooting down of the U-2 aircraft in the Soviet Union, the capture of Powers and the United States' admission, much to the chagrin of the Soviets, that it was ours. After a period of doubt and consultation, General de Gaulle, the conference host since the meeting was to be held in Paris, had announced that the conference would be held as scheduled and the other chiefs of government had successively announced that they would attend. When Khrushchev announced that he would be present, a worldwide sigh of relief went up. Things could not be so bad after all, if he was willing to attend.

We arrived in Paris on May 15. I accompanied President Eisenhower on his call to General de Gaulle. As always, the meeting between the two men was friendly, cordial and almost affectionate. I have accompanied a number of American dignitaries to see General de Gaulle over some thirty years, and the only ones to whom he did not talk down were Presidents Eisenhower and Nixon and Governor Harriman. To them he showed not just respect but real warmth and, to Eisenhower, affection. The two men had, after all both been called upon by the free choice of their fellow citizens to lead their respective nations in peacetime as well as war. It was more than just a meeting of two chiefs of state. They met as two old comrades as well.

De Gaulle told Eisenhower that Khrushchev had been to see him and was highly agitated about the U-2 overflights. He simply could not understand why Eisenhower had to admit publicly that he knew about the flights. By Khrushchev's standards this indicated not American truthfulness, but rather contempt for the Soviets. Khrushchev simply did not understand the deep American compulsion to confess, and neither did de Gaulle. Khrushchev had read to de Gaulle a long statement denouncing the overflights and demanding an apology from President Eisenhower. De Gaulle, who had with him only his superb English and Russian interpreter Constantin Andronikof, added, "Obviously you cannot apologize, but you must decide how you wish to handle this. I will do everything I can to be helpful without being openly partisan." He said he had asked Khrushchev whether under these circumstances they should go ahead with the conference. His Ambassador in Moscow had put this question to Khrushchev before the Soviet leader had left Moscow, and Khrushchev had said that they should meet. He had repeated the question to Khrushchev after his arrival in Paris and again he had said that they should go ahead. De Gaulle had indicated to Khrushchev that he could not seriously expect that the U. S. President would apologize to him. That sort of thing was not done among responsible chiefs of government. Khrushchev had been adamant that Eisenhower must apologize for the U-2 flight. De Gaulle felt that Khrushchev's readiness to go ahead with the conference after he had told him that Eisenhower could not be expected to apologize was a hopeful sign, but he added, "We shall see." De Gaulle discussed this matter with a sort of Olympian detachment. He told Eisenhower that he did not think that the peccadilloes of intelligence services were appropriate matters to be discussed at meetings of chiefs of government.

De Gaulle maintained great composure throughout this whole episode. He seemed to me to be the allied leader who was the least dismayed by the whole thing. At no time did he show the consternation of Macmillan or the irritated embarrassment of President Eisenhower. De Gaulle's attitude seemed to be one of irritation that his misfortune along the intelligence road (*accident de parcours*) had been elevated to the level of the chiefs of government. He said to Eisenhower comfortingly that this is the sort of thing that all intelligence services do but usually they are discreet about it, and it is not dragged out for all of the public to see. It does not involve their leaders. To my surprise at no time did he chide Eisenhower for the overflights of the Soviet Union. He even recalled that I had shown him the photograph of Vinnitsa and he had not asked how it had been taken.

One other curious episode occurred during this conference. A very senior U.S. official asked me whether I would take into the conference (where I would sit as one of the interpreters) a suitcase containing a recording device. Despite his rank, I told him that I would not do this unless I was personally ordered to do so by the President. This would involve eavesdropping on him and I would do it only if he himself wished it done. I cautioned this official that the French were sophisticated in this area and might well have equipment in the Elysée which could detect the presence and operation of such machinery, and I was sure that General de Gaulle, who had after all been very helpful, would be furious if this were to be done without his knowledge. For all of these reasons, I would take this equipment into the conference only if President Eisenhower told me to do it. The official was obviously irked but he pressed me no further and that was the last I heard of the matter. When the conference convened, I looked around the U.S. delegation and did not see anything that looked like a recording briefcase.

The U.S. delegation was clearly embarrassed by the shoot down and Powers' confession, but it was determined that Khrushchev would not be allowed to use this publicly to humiliate the United States. President Eisenhower clearly felt that in the discharge of his responsibilities to the United States he must ascertain the measure of the threat against it, and with a closed society such as the Soviets which we faced, there was no other way than by such imaginative methods as the U-2. After all, Soviet satellites had already overflown the United States and the Soviets had published pictures taken by cameras aboard such satellites.

The conference was held in the Elysée Palace, the traditional residence of the President of France. The meeting convened in a large high-ceilinged room on the second floor of the Elysée, only a few rooms removed from General de Gaulle's own office. The windows looked out to the south and west over the gardens of the palace. In the center of the room there were large tables arranged in the form of a square. General de Gaulle and the French delegation sat on the east side nearest to de Gaulle's office. Opposite him sat the U.S. delegation (I was seated at the far right of the U.S. delegation, closest to the Soviets). On the right of the U.S. were the Soviets and facing them were the British. I entered the room with President Eisenhower and General de Gaulle, who had met him at the top of the stairs. De Gaulle was very conscious of the fact that only he and Eisenhower were chiefs of state, while the two other delegations were led by chiefs of government. The Russians were already in the conference room standing around talking together. Eisenhower greeted the other French delegates and the British, but the Russians kept talking among themselves and so Eisenhower walked around to his own side of the table and sat down with the Secretary of State alongside him. After a few minutes, General de Gaulle called the meeting to order and all who were still standing sat down. General de Gaulle then greeted the chiefs of delegation, thanked them for coming and expressed the hope that the meeting which was about to begin would be fruitful and contribute to world peace. He noted that the eyes of the entire world were on them. He then said that inasmuch as President Eisenhower was the only other chief of delegation who was also a chief of state, he would give him the floor first. Khrushchev, obviously agitated, stood up and said angrily that he had asked to speak first and that as chiefs of delegation they were all equal. He demanded the right to read a prepared statement first. De Gaulle, when this outburst was translated, raised his eyebrows and looked questionably at General Eisenhower, who nodded. De Gaulle then gave the floor to Khrushchev. Khrushchev stood up and began to read in a very loud voice. This was clearly the same statement he had read to de Gaulle previously. De Gaulle assumed a pained but patient expression as Khrushchev rambled on. From time to time he would pause for translation and take a drink of water.

I had been strongly enjoined by the State Department not to wear my uniform, as this was a "peace conference." Notwithstanding this, Soviet Defense Minister Marshal Rodion Malinovsky was there at the left side of the Soviet delegation sitting right next to me, glowering in full uniform. As Khrushchev thundered on, I fell to counting the ribbons on Malinovsky's chest. There were fifty-four, including, as I noted with some interest, the U. S. Legion of Merit. At one point as Khrushchev read (and I noticed that his hands trembled as he held the piece of paper he was reading—whether from agitation, anxiety or anger, I do not know), he raised his voice even louder. De Gaulle interrupted, turned to the Soviet interpreter, rather than his own, and said, "The acoustics in this room are excellent. We can all hear the chairman. There is no need for him to raise his voice." The Russian interpreter blanched, turned to Khrushchev and started to translate. De Gaulle then motioned to his own interpreter, who unfalteringly translated what the French leader had said. Khrushchev paused, looked over the top of his glasses and cast a furious glance at General de Gaulle and then continued reading in a somewhat lower voice. As Khrushchev read, he was clearly lashing himself into an even greater frenzy and as he denounced the U.S. overflights, he pointed at the ceiling as though a U-2 were overhead at that moment, saying, "I have been overflown!" De Gaulle interrupted to say that he too had been overflown. "By your American allies?" asked Khrushchev. "No," said General de Gaulle, "by you. Yesterday that satellite you launched just before you left Moscow to impress us overflew the sky of France eighteen times without my permission. How do I know you do not have cameras aboard which are taking pictures of my country?" De Gaulle crossed his arms and looked at Khrushchev questioningly. Khrushchev's jaw dropped. Then an almost beatific expression came over his face. He raised both hands above his head and said clearly, "*Bog minya vidit. Moi rukhi chesti.* (God sees me. My hands are clean.) You don't think I would do a thing like that?" "Well," said General de Gaulle, "how did you take those pictures of the far side of the moon which you showed us with such justifiable pride!" "Ah," said Khrushchev, "in that one I had cameras." "Ah," said General de Gaulle, "in that one you had cameras. Pray, continue."

This exchange had upset Khrushchev and his hands trembled even more as he continued reading his long statement. While he was talking, State Department Counselor and former Ambassador to Moscow Chip Bohlen kept grumbling, "We can't sit still for this. We've got to answer." Eisenhower sat silently listening to the original and its translation. He doodled impatiently with a pencil. (I still have the doodle, as I picked it up when he left the table.) However, his face and neck were flushed and I could tell from experience that he was extremely angry. I worked very closely with General Eisenhower for a number of years, yet I had never seen an outburst of temper from him. However, long experience had taught me the signs of anger on his part and they were all present here. Once or twice he looked at de Gaulle, who was sitting there with a slightly bored expression that plainly said, "Why do I have to sit through this again?" He had already heard all of this from Khrushchev once before. The British Prime Minister was uneasy as he looked at the angry Khrushchev, the flushed Eisenhower and the bored de Gaulle.

At one point Khrushchev exclaimed, "What devil made the Americans do this?" De Gaulle observed that there were devils everywhere, on both sides, that this was a matter of espionage such as went on all the time and was really not worthy of the consideration of chiefs of government to whom the peoples of the world were looking for hopes of peace. Khrushchev shook his head like a bull and went on reading. He finally ended his long diatribe by announcing that unless President Eisenhower apologized he would not attend further meetings of the conference.

President Eisenhower then made a mollifying statement containing many of the justifications used publicly for the U-2 flights, and promised that U.S. aircraft would not overfly the U.S.S.R. again. Khrushchev angrily repeated that he would not attend any further meetings of the conference if Eisenhower did not apologize. There was a long, awkward pause after this was translated. Then General de Gaulle said, "Chairman Khrushchev, you have imposed conditions that are obviously impossible for General Eisenhower to accept. Before you left Moscow and after the U-2 was shot down, I sent my Ambassador to see you to ask whether this meeting should be held or should be postponed. You knew everything then that you know now. You told my Ambassador that this conference should be held and that it would be fruitful. I repeated this question to you when I saw you long before this meeting and once again you said it should be held. Now, by imposing conditions that obviously cannot be met by the American President, you make it impossible for us to go further. You have brought Mr. Macmillan here from London, General Eisenhower from the United States and have put me to serious inconvenience to organize and attend a meeting which your intransigence will make impossible. We should all reflect on this and on the hopes that the people of the world have placed in this meeting and meet again here tomorrow at the same time. The meeting stands adjourned."

Khrushchev jumped to his feet and said once again that unless Eisenhower apologized he would not come. De Gaulle looked at him as one would look at a naughty child and announced that the conference would meet on the following day. Khrushchev, accompanied by his whole delegation, strode out of the room and down the stairs. The other delegations looked at one another. De Gaulle said that he would stay in touch with the Russians. All then rose and started out of the room. De Gaulle came over to Eisenhower and took him by the arm. He took me also by the elbow and, taking us a little apart, he said to Eisenhower, "I do not know what Khrushchev is going to do, nor what is going to happen, but whatever he does, or whatever happens, I want you to know that I am with you to the end." I was astounded at this statement and Eisenhower was clearly deeply moved by this unexpected expression of unconditional support. Only the three of us heard it, but it remains as vivid in my mind to this day as it was when I heard it. Eisenhower thanked de Gaulle, who walked down the stairs with him to his car. As we entered the car, Eisenhower, still upset by the whole episode, looked at me and said, "That de Gaulle is really quite a guy." I nodded my wholehearted agreement. We drove the short distance to the U. S. Embassy residence, then on Avenue d'Iéna, where the U.S. delegation went into a meeting to decide what to do next.

I was not privy to this discussion and do not know what was

decided, since President Eisenhower's mollifying statement and promise that the U-2s would not overfly the Soviet Union had evidently not done the job of bringing Khrushchev back to the conference table and Eisenhower's pending invitation to visit the U.S.S.R. was obviously withdrawn.

In the meantime, Khrushchev had been holding a stormy and furious press conference, making veiled threats and inveighing against the treacherous nature of the United States. Next day at the time appointed by de Gaulle, he, Macmillan and Eisenhower met in the same room in the Elysée where the meeting had taken place on the previous day. The three delegations sat looking slightly sheepishly at one another. General de Gaulle said that he had no word from Khrushchev, but he was out "kissing babies on the street and generally electioneering for the French Communist party" while Marshal Malinovsky was out near Verdun, where he had fought in World War II and "where he had attempted to subvert the Russian troops from fighting with the Allies." After some waiting, de Gaulle gave an order to contact Khrushchev and ask him whether or not he would attend the meeting. After a further delay, an assistant came into the room to say that Khrushchev had sent word he would not attend the meeting unless President Eisenhower apologized. De Gaulle looked furious, Macmillan seemed crushed by the news and Eisenhower was torn between embarrassment and anger. De Gaulle turned to the assistant and said that Khrushchev had been invited in writing; therefore, he should reply in writing. A few minutes later the aide came back in to say that Khrushchev had answered that he would not answer in writing. De Gaulle said to the aide, "Tell him it is the usage between civilized nations to reply to written communications by written communications." The aide departed, to return a few minutes later to announce that Khrushchev would answer in writing but would not come.

De Gaulle, who appeared pleased to have won this minor point, adjourned the conference. To my surprise neither de Gaulle, who did not seem unduly shaken, nor Macmillan, who was clearly staggered by the whole business, ever suggested, even indirectly, that Eisenhower should apologize.

Adenauer, who was still in Paris, appeared relieved that at least Germany would not in some way pay the cost of a four-power agreement. President Eisenhower then departed for Portugal, where he was given a most warm welcome by President Tómas and Prime Minister Salazar.

It seemed to me that the Soviets had gambled on a capitulation by Eisenhower and were disoriented when it was not forthcoming. They had counted on both de Gaulle and Macmillan to pressure Eisenhower for some form of apology and this had not happened.

Historically, de Gaulle dominated the whole conference. Neither enraged like Khrushchev, nor embarrassed like Eisenhower, nor appalled like Macmillan, he used his position as host for all it was worth. While not openly partisan, he made clear to Khrushchev that he thought the whole matter was a tempest in a teapot. Through technological advances overhead, photography was here to stay and since the Russian satellites were the first to overfly other countries, they were scarcely in a position to pose as innocent victims. De Gaulle in a real crunch showed himself a stalwart, unshaken ally and friend.

18. IN ROME AS ATTACHÉ

During President Eisenhower's visit to Rome in 1959, he had noted that I had many friends there and at one point in the visit he said to me, "You would make a great attaché to Rome, as you know everybody here." I was pleased but thought no more about the remark until early 1960. General Andrew J. Goodpaster, Chief of Staff to the President, called me one day and informed me that I would be going to Rome as the Army Attaché. In the light of this, I reported to General John Willems, then the Assistant Chief of Staff for Intelligence to the Army. He was very cold and I could tell that he was displeased by this nomination. He had not been consulted on it and he had already selected someone else for the job. I spoke Italian and this officer did not, but that did not carry much weight with him. As I went around Army Intelligence seeing the people necessary in relation to my going to Rome, I could sense a certain chill. It was clear they all thought that I had used the fact that I had been Eisenhower's aide to arrange this job for myself. The person who was the least upset was the officer who had been first selected to go to Rome. He did not speak Italian. He understood that I had simply been told that I was going, and he himself was assigned to another billet in Italy at the NATO headquarters in Naples. Gradually, however, as I talked to the people, they became aware of the fact that I knew a great deal about Italy, that I spoke the language fluently and that perhaps my going there would not be a totally negative factor.

I was called upon to attend the Attaché School in Washington even though I had been an assistant attaché to Brazil previously. A great deal of the schooling was devoted to the administration and the procedure of running an attaché office. I also, during this time, received briefings both in the Pentagon and at the CIA, and I must say these briefings gave me the impression that the Italians had a fairly effective intelligence service, but that they were not up among the great intelligence services of the world because they simply did not have that kind of money. I was not told some of the things that I was to learn later, namely that the Italian Intelligence Service had succeeded in planting a man at Los Alamos during World War II. Even though they did not know what was going on there, they knew it was an interesting project; after Italy signed the armistice, this man gave himself up. Nor was I told at that time that the Italians had broken a number of U.S. naval codes during World War II, as well as some of the British diplomatic codes. I was inclined to believe what they had told me. The intelligence organization in Italy was highly centralized. The same service ran what in the United States would be the CIA, the service intelligence agencies, the National Security Agency and the FBI.

I had a most pleasant trip over to Italy on the U.S.S. *Constitution* and arrived in Naples, where I was met. After spending the night in Naples, I went on to Rome, where I arrived almost on the eve of the Olympic games. The city was in a great state of agitation and it was very difficult to get the necessary hotel rooms for my mother and myself. We were able to do so through my predecessor. Shortly after I arrived, he took me down to meet the chief of the Italian Intelligence Service. I noted the uncertainty with which he entered the building. He was not sure on which floor the chief's office was. I understood that he did not have close contact with the chief of service. I knew that the chief was a General Giovanni de Lorenzo. I had known General de Lorenzo briefly during World War II when he was a lieutenant colonel and the Italian liaison officer to the

U.S. 92nd Division, which was fighting on the left of the Brazilians, with whom I was as liaison officer. Once in a while we would get together in good humor and complain about the people whom we were serving as liaison officers. I later saw General de Lorenzo when he was a brigadier general and Chief of Staff of the V Corps at Padua, when I went there with General Eisenhower on a trip. At this time an incident that was to be helpful to me occurred. General de Lorenzo had a photograph taken with General Eisenhower and mailed it to me in Paris and asked me to get General Eisenhower to sign it. I did so and sent it back to General de Lorenzo with a little note, not knowing that I was later to meet him as chief of the Italian Intelligence Service. Then I realized that my bread had not been cast upon the waters.

General de Lorenzo was a remarkable man. He wore a monocle, which gave him a very aristocratic appearance. He had been running an anti-German intelligence setup in German-occupied Rome during the war, while his wife ran a clandestine radio station in northern Italy. On one occasion the building in which he was meeting was surrounded and he was one of the very few who escaped capture by the Germans. This he did by jumping out of the second-story window. I was told by a number of people later on that he landed with the monocle still in his eye.

When my predecessor took me in to see him, he greeted me very warmly and we spoke, of course, in Italian and recalled our previous meetings. He expressed Italy's strong support for NATO and his desire to do everything he could to be helpful to me in my new job as an attaché. I was very grateful for this because for many years I had been caught in the process of being an interpreter to Presidents and Cabinet officers, and this was the first chance I had had in a very long time to prove that I could operate on my own and run an office to the satisfaction of my superiors.

Shortly after I arrived in Italy, I arranged with General de Lorenzo to make my first official call on an Italian Army unit. This was to be the III Corps in Milan. I decided to drive to Milan myself and save the per diem for my driver, which I could use for further travel. I knew that on arrival in Milan the Italians would give me an escort officer and a car. So I set out on my first trip. I drove myself to the U.S. base at Livorno and spent the night there. The next day, instead of going straight on to Milan, I recalled that I had been several times before to an excellent restaurant in Florence called Otello's and remembered that they had terrific green lasagne. I estimated that by going to Florence rather than directly to Milan, I would lose a few hours' time, but it made no difference since my official program in Milan did not begin until the following day. I drove up the autostrada from Livorno to Florence. As always when driving in a foreign country on an intelligence mission, my eyes drifted frequently to the rear-vision mirror to see whether I recognized the car or any face behind the wheels behind me. I saw none. I drove into Florence, a large city, parked in the square in the front of the station—it was still possible at that time—and then walked the two blocks to Otello's, where I sat down in a very pleasant environment surrounded by greenery and ordered my lunch. While I was eating the lunch, which was fully up to my expectations, a man approached my table, clicked his heels and introduced himself as Maresciallo (Warrant Officer) So-and-So of the carabinieri. He said to me, "Colonel, there have been several changes in your program and the chief of service wished them to be given to you before you arrived in Milan." He then handed me a piece of paper covering the changes and added, almost as an afterthought, "By the way, you are the guest of the chief of service for lunch." I thanked him and he then disappeared. I did not fully comprehend what was involved until I asked for the bill and was told that there was no bill, that I was indeed the guest of the chief of service. I understood that what General de Lorenzo was doing was giving me a demonstration that he knew where I was at any given time and what I was doing. I bore this in mind many times in the future. Americans frequently have a tendency to underestimate the local service. This is a mistake. The local service may not have the budget that we have, but it is usually very good in its own country.

I proceeded on to my visit to the III Corps in Milan and it

went off very well. On my return to Rome, I had lunch with de Lorenzo. I did not immediately bring up the Otello incident, but we were discussing the activities of the various Soviet bloc attachés in Rome and I asked him whether he was fully up on what they were doing. De Lorenzo adjusted his monocle, looked at me with a smile and said, "Walters, do you remember Otello's? Well, if we do that for our friends, you can imagine what we do for our enemies." This event, small as it was, gave me new respect for the Italian service and for General de Lorenzo. I was to have close and friendly relations with him throughout my tour as attaché.

General de Lorenzo could be very tough on occasion, as he once was with the Mexican attaché. Our Spanish colleague had died suddenly and the habitual thing at that time was to hold a religious service which the other attachés would attend. The Mexican admiral, who was the dean of the attachés, refused to hold such a religious service, claiming that he was not allowed inside a church in uniform by virtue of Mexican law. The Swiss attaché, Colonel Luciano Respini, was indignant at this breach of attaché etiquette and asked me about it. I said that I was perfectly prepared to support him in going to de Lorenzo and asking that Respini, as vice-dean, might be allowed to organize the mass. The Mexican admiral got wind of this and forbade it. De Lorenzo then sent for the Mexican admiral. The Mexican admiral did not go. De Lorenzo then sent his own car with two carabinieri to escort the Mexican attaché to his office. When the Mexican admiral came in, he proceeded to explain to de Lorenzo that Mexico had no diplomatic relations with Spain and besides, as a Mexican officer, he could not go into church in uniform. De Lorenzo coldly told him that he had evidently not read the small print on the attaché regulations, which indicated that the dean of the attachés is dean only by virtue of the consent of the chief of the Italian service. Since the Mexican admiral had failed in his duties to his colleagues, he, de Lorenzo, was withdrawing that consent, and the dean would then be the Soviet attaché, General Trousov, who had assured General de Lorenzo that he had no restrictions about going to religious services or wearing his uniform inside a church. Shortly thereafter, the Mexican admiral left.

There was at this time in northern Italy a U. S. Army detachment to provide missile support to the Italian forces. This was known as the Southern European Task Force or SETAF. When I arrived in Rome, relations between the attaché office and this force were extremely bad. I proceeded to call on General Eugene Cardwell, the commander of the detachment, and established very cordial relations with him, which were of great help to me as he frequently furnished me with an aircraft for travel that I could not effectively perform by car. It seemed to me that all of the Americans serving in the same country should be co-operating closely.

As I moved about the Italian Army, I must say I was amazed at the military miracle that had taken place as well as the economic miracle. The Italian forces had been badly battered during World War II and had had vastly inferior equipment to the other combatants—for instance, the Italian Navy did not have radar at a time when it was fighting a British Navy equipped with radar; nevertheless, that Italian Navy sank more Allied shipping tonnage in the Mediterranean than the Allies sank of Italian shipping. The rebuilding, discipline and effectiveness of the Italian Army was, to me, extremely impressive. During my period as attaché, I went off on two extraneous missions. One was a second visit to Iran with Mr. Harriman, which lasted only a few days, and the other was a visit to Paris to make the arrangements for President Kennedy's visit there. This is described in another chapter, as the mission which was aborted and never took place.

One of the rather pleasant things that occurred during this period was that I started to ski again. I had not skied for seven years, since my serious accident in 1954. On one occasion, I was visiting an Italian Alpine brigade at Mondovi and was taken up in a cable car to the top of the mountain where the maneuver was going on. When we got to the top, the young battalion commander told me that I would have to put on skis or I would sink in the snow up to my waist. I did so and felt quite comfortable on them. At the end of the day, the battalion commander said to me that I could ride down in the cable car, but that he would ski down. I told him that I felt the honor of the U. S. Army was at stake, that he should lead off and I would follow him down. I followed him down without any difficulty and was very happy to take up skiing once again. I have always found it to be a most extraordinarily exhilarating and satisfying sport. Since the Italian Army had five Alpine brigades and an Alpine Mountain Warfare School, I was able during the two years I was in Italy to mix business and pleasure by visiting these Alpine brigades and at the same time enjoying a good deal of skiing myself with them on maneuvers or alone.

During this time I had quite friendly relations with the Soviet attaché, General Trousov. General Trousov was a slight, rather timid man with a slight impediment in his speech. I recall that on the day Gagarin went into orbit there was a lunch for the foreign attachés in Italy, and as I arrived at the lunch, I found Trousov already there. I could see that all of the attachés were watching me to see what I would do. I immediately went up to Trousov and told him in Russian, "I congratulate you on the first human flight in space. It is a very great achievement." He was very moved by what I said and replied graciously, "Today, us; tomorrow, you." As a matter of fact, when Trousov was leaving Rome, he insisted on calling upon me. I said no, that he was a general, and I was a colonel, I should call on him. He refused, saying he wished to call on me. I received him in my office and he made a little speech, saying that he had served as an attaché in a country which was an ally of my country and that I was therefore in a favored position and I could on many occasions have embarrassed him or put him in an awkward position, but I had never done so and he was very grateful for that. I told him that I did not have any thought of embarrassing him or any of my Soviet colleagues. We had differences but each of us was serving his own country in his own way. He shook hands, visibly moved by what I had told him.

I recall that on one occasion I was talking to the Russian Air Attaché on a particularly hot day. He was wearing a heavy blouse. I asked him whether in the Red Air Force they did not have a summer uniform and he said they did not. One year later when I saw him resplendent in a lightweight white blouse, I asked him about it. And he said, "Now thanks to Gagarin, *slava Gagarinu*, we do have one." They designed one for him when he went to the tropics.

Curiously, my relations with the Russians were better than those with the Yugoslavs. The Yugoslav attaché, Colonel Ugritza, was a particularly aggressive Communist and was always making snide remarks. I simply would not sit still for these and took him to task for them. The Italians used to be greatly amused by some of the very long arguments and discussions that Ugritza and I would have on some of the attaché trips. His wife was a beautiful, charming ballerina who had never suspected that the West was anything like she found it.

I had very good relations with all of my colleagues, and I formed a particularly close friendship with the Argentine attaché, Colonel Juan Carlos Sánchez, who many years later was tragically to be assassinated by leftists in Rosario. I cannot forget that one night sitting on the floor at his apartment in Rome with his wife and son, who were playing the guitar and singing Argentine songs, his wife said to me quite seriously, "I would rather be dead than red." That sacrifice was not to be made by her, but by her husband.

I had quite cordial relations with the CIA representative there with one exception. I once discussed with him a talk I had had with General de Lorenzo. I could tell from his manner that he was displeased that I knew the general this well, and finally, he said to me, "Well, if you tell me everything that he tells you, you have my permission to see him." I replied, "As an American, I will always tell you what he tells me. However, let me make one thing clear right now. He is a lieutenant general on active duty in the Italian Army and I do not need your permission to talk to him." After that, our relations were cordial and good and he made no further attempts to exercise any control over me. We did disagree somewhat about political developments in Italy at this time. There was much agitation for the opening to the left; that is, the inclusion of the Socialists in the government. This was going on inside the U.S. government as well as in Italy. The Christian Democrats and some minor parties had been running Italy since the end of World War II, and had brought about a quite extraordinary recovery in an atmosphere of freedom, and I personally did not see the need to unbalance what I thought was a rather delicate political situation. Nevertheless, this whole question had become a domestic issue in the United States. Various envoys had come from President Kennedy to push the Italians toward the inclusion of the Socialists in the government coalition. A large part of the political section in the Embassy thought it would be a good thing. I was convinced that it would cause instability and upset a delicate political balance. Subsequent events have not proved me wrong in this respect. We had a number of meetings in the Embassy and I spoke out rather strongly on my feelings on this subject. The fact that I was opposed to the opening to the left became known, and in later years a series of phony stories in the leftist press—in both Italy and the United States—stated that I had wanted to bring in U.S. troops from Germany to stop the opening to the left. This, of course, is absolute nonsense. No thought was ever given to any such idea by me or by anybody else at any time. I knew Italy and the Italians well enough to know that one of the great war songs of World War I had been "Go Out of Italy, You Foreigner." I knew that any foreign intrusion into Italian internal political affairs would be counterproductive, and furthermore, there was no way one could bring troops from Germany into Italy across neutral Austria or Switzerland. This phony story has followed me around for a number of years. The idea of the opening to the left was pushed and eventually was adopted and led to the situation in which we find Italy today— giving new respectability first to the Socialists and then carrying the idea further to give ever greater respectability to the Communists.

One of the more interesting events that occurred during my service as attaché in Rome was the visit of Lyndon B. Johnson, then Vice-President of the United States. Once again, even though his trip did not have any military implications, I was assigned by the Ambassador because of my fluency in Italian to serve as his interpreter during his calls on members of the Italian government. I had met Mr. Johnson when he was the Senate Majority Leader during General de Gaulle's visit to Washington in 1960. When he arrived in Rome he was returning from a visit to Iran, Greece and Turkey. In all of those places, the Vice-President had been greeted by large and enthusiastic crowds. Sophisticated and blasé Rome was different. Outside of Italian and U. S. Embassy officials, there were no crowds at the Rome airport for his arrival. He noted this and was not happy. I was amazed at the sheer size and vigor of the man. I had always thought of him basically as a run-of-the-mill politician, but as I accompanied him on his calls on the Italians, I grew aware of the fact that this was indeed a shrewd, tough, aggressive and dynamic man. At that time, he was pushing hard to get Italian budgetary support for Greece, which had to maintain unusually large military forces that were almost beyond her capacity to support. He did not give the Italians the impression that he favored the opening to the left, but regarded it as a pet project of some of President Kennedy's more progressive advisers. Lyndon Johnson was still somewhat irked over the low-level public reception he had had in Italy. Some bright man in the Embassy dreamed up a visit to Naples, where I think a rumor was circulated that anyone who cheered the U. S. Vice-President loudly enough would get a visa to go to the United States. True or not, when we flew to Naples there were large and enthusiastic crowds everywhere. Friendly people surged around his open car and he delightedly shook hands with them. As they pressed in toward his car, the carabinieri tried to hold them back. The Vice-President said, "Let those people come in. I came four thousand miles to see them." The carabinieri looked helplessly at me as he got out of the car and plunged into the crowd shaking hands and admiring babies that were held up for his admiration. We were pushed and shoved from all directions and finally found ourselves in the door to a shop with delighted Neapolitans crowding around and shaking hands. It made quite a picture

and the U.S. and Italian news photographers got themselves
into position to take pictures of what was going on. As he shook
hands, Mr. Johnson said to me out of the corner of his mouth,
"What kind of a shop is this anyway?" I replied that it was a
wine shop. At that he plunged out of the doorway and back into
the crowd. I understood that he did not want to be photographed in the entrance to a wine shop. Finally, we got back
into the car and continued the visit to Naples. This had a very
good effect on the Vice-President and he was positively benign
as we flew back to Rome for dinner with the Italian government
that night.

This dinner was held in a most elaborate guesthouse of the
Italian government for distinguished foreign visitors. It was
called Villa Madama. The dinner was given by the Italian government and I attended as the Vice-President's interpreter. During the course of the dinner, Mr. Johnson began talking about
the severe earthquake that had occurred in Iran about two
weeks before. He paused as though meditating and then said
that he thought he ought to take some doctors from the U. S.
Sixth Fleet in the Mediterranean and go back and help the
Iranians. Lady Bird Johnson, who was with him, had her Red
Cross uniform and she could help too. Then he turned to Italian Defense Minister Giulio Andreotti and said that he was sure
that the minister could give him twenty or so Italian military
doctors to go along and help the Iranians. Andreotti said that he
could. Then Foreign Minister Amintore Fanfani's wife said that
she too had a Red Cross uniform and could go along. The pretty
blond wife of Rome's elderly mayor said that she too had a Red
Cross uniform and could go along and help. At each new offer,
Johnson said, "Great, great." I could see that the plan was creating some consternation among the Italian ministers. One of the
U.S. officials present said, "But Mr. Vice-President, you have an
appointment tomorrow with the Pope." "That's okay," replied
the Vice-President, "he's a great humanitarian and he'll understand." Consternation grew among both Italians and Americans
at this enormous change in the Vice-President's plans. Johnson
then turned to Andreotti and said, "Can you have those Italian

military doctors at the airport tomorrow morning?" Andreotti replied that he could and told the chairman of the Italian Chiefs of Staff, General Aldo Rossi, to keep in touch with me as to the location and transportation for the military doctors. We then adjourned to the garden for coffee. Foreign Minister Fanfani came up to me and said in Italian, "Walters, this is madness. I have seven children; if my wife goes off to Iran on this wild goose errand, who will take care of them?" The elderly mayor of Rome was also clearly disquieted at the idea of his pretty blond wife going off with all these young military doctors.

Upon this note, the party broke up and I returned with the Vice-President and Ambassador G. Frederick Reinhardt to the Excelsior Hotel, where Lyndon Johnson was staying. It was very late at night and the Ambassador commented that he would have to notify Washington and Teheran of the changes in the Vice-President's plans. Lyndon grinned and said, "You don't really think I am crazy enough to go back to Iran, now do you?" He added that he was just trying to shake up the State Department escort officer who was traveling with him and who had done something to irritate him. I excused myself, went into the next room and telephoned General Rossi at his home to tell him that the Italian military doctors would not be required after all. He was astounded and said, "But Walters, they are all at Ciampino Airport being vaccinated against cholera, bubonic plague and other things." I assured him that the project was off. Next morning, Mr. Johnson saw the Pope and held a press conference at which I translated for him. He handled it with great skill and aplomb. Despite the Iranian nonsense, I developed a new respect for the ability and force of Lyndon Johnson. His wife Lady Bird was with him, and I can only say that she impressed me as one of the most charming and gracious ladies that I have met. In later years when I read her book, I noted with interest that she did not have an unkind word to say about anyone, even those who had stabbed her husband in the back politically. It was a fascinating and exhausting experience to serve Lyndon Johnson, even for only a few days. When he left Rome, a collective sigh of relief went up from both Italians and Americans.

The physical vigor and vitality of the man was almost unbelievable. He even found time to have me take him to a shirt-maker to have some custom shirts made.

Another visitor during this period was Secretary of State Dean Rusk. Once again, the Embassy assigned me to accompany him on his calls on Italian officials and to interpret for him. The State Department did not particularly like asking an Army officer to do this, but the simple fact was that my Italian was more fluent than that of most of the Foreign Service officers in Rome. Dean Rusk also made a deep impression on me. I had first met him in the weather shack at Wake Island many years before when Truman and MacArthur had met. When he called on Italian Foreign Minister Fanfani, the latter had just returned from a visit with Khurshchev in Moscow. The Soviet leader had been very tough and threatening with Fanfani. He had noted that the United States had missiles in southern Italy and had told Fanfani that he could blast them out of the orange groves. Fanfani had somewhat worriedly replied they were in the olive groves. Khrushchev said that he did not care what kind of groves they were in, he could blast them. Fanfani also said to Rusk, "Mr. Secretary, you must understand that Khrushchev is not prepared to tolerate the presence of the Western garrisons in Berlin any more." Rusk looked at him impassively and replied, "Mr. Minister, neither is he prepared to face the alternative." Fanfani had gotten the answer that he had been seeking. The United States was not prepared to have the Russians bully us out of Berlin. I think Americans sometimes forget how Europeans and others watch us to detect any lessening in our leadership and willingness to defend the free world. I was greatly impressed by the strength, dignity and brilliance of Dean Rusk. He has been one of America's great servants.

Bobby Kennedy, then Attorney General, was another visitor who came during this period. Once again with some gnashing of teeth in the State Department, I was assigned to accompany him on his calls on the Italian Minister of Justice and others. Bobby Kennedy gave an extraordinary impression of youth and force. During his first visit he and his wife Ethel became greatly

taken with the motor scooters that then abounded in Italy.
They borrowed one and Ethel ran it into the car of an indignant
Italian. It took some diplomacy, money and negotiations in
which I participated to settle the matter; but we were able to do
so successfully before the Kennedys left Rome. At the end of his
visit Bobby Kennedy said to me, "I have heard of your ability
before, and after this trip I can only say that it is all true." I was
to see him again twice in Brazil.

One of the political visitors who came to Rome to look into
the political situation and the problem of the opening to the left
was historian and writer Arthur Schlesinger, Jr. I had known
him during my service with Mr. Harriman at the Marshall Plan.

When Schlesinger arrived Ambassador Reinhardt, feeling
that my Italian was equal to the task, assigned me to accompany
Schlesinger on his visit to various Italian political leaders. The
Deputy Chief of Mission, Outerbridge Horsey, shared my misgivings regarding the inclusion of the Socialists in the government. Many of his subordinates went behind his back to
Schlesinger and other visitors from Washington to advocate the
opening to the left. Schlesinger in his talks with Italian political
leaders made plain that he was in favor of the opening.

I accompanied Arthur Schlesinger on his call on the President
of Italy, Antonio Segni. Some years before I had accompanied
Segni, then Prime Minister of Italy, on a long trip around the
United States, and so I knew him well. In answer to Schlesinger's questions, he guardedly made plain that he had some
reservations about the inclusion of the Socialists in the Italian
government, at least until they had clearly detached themselves
from the Communists.

At one point in the talk, Schlesinger told Segni that he would
like to know, for President Kennedy's ears alone, what President
Segni thought personally of the major Italian political leaders.
This was an awkward question. Segni, as President of Italy, was
supposed to be above the fray. Segni hesitated, and Schlesinger
repeated that the information he sought was for President Kennedy alone. It would not be reported to the State Department
or the Embassy in Rome. Schlesinger told me to make no writ-

ten record of Segni's reply. Segni, a frail, old man, was reassured and proceeded to give his frank views of the Italian political leaders.

It is interesting to note that Schlesinger subsequently made public in a book much of what Segni told him about these leaders. When Schlesinger's book was published, these revelations caused a great furor in Italy, and there were widespread demands for Segni's resignation. In the midst of this turmoil Segni had a stroke and had to resign as President and retire as an invalid to his home in Sardinia. There he died not too long afterward.

During all these calls, and indeed throughout my career, I have almost never made notes while translating, but after the conversations I have nearly always prepared for the American participant an extensive memorandum of the conversation so that he would know, basically, what he had said and what the other side had said. It has been my experience over many years that most U.S. public figures like memoranda that say a great deal about what the other man said and relatively little about what they had said, unless they got off a particularly humorous or telling point.

During this time, I called with my mother on Pope John and was very impressed by his kindness and wit. While I was on a trip to Sicily around this time, I received a phone call from my assistant, Colonel Jim Strauss, telling me that my mother was sick and required an operation, and because of her age—she was then seventy-eight—he did not wish to authorize it. I left the car in Sicily, flew back to Rome, discussed the matter with the doctors, who told me my mother had a hernia and if it was not operated upon, she would die. If she were operated on, because of her age they could not guarantee how well she would stand the operation. I then said to them, "Really, what you're telling me is that she has to be operated on or she will die." They said, "Yes, that is correct." I therefore authorized the operation. My mother stood it very well. The operation was performed in the Salvator Mundi Hospital, one of the most pleasant hospitals I have ever seen. It had neither the odor nor the appearance of a

364 · SILENT MISSIONS

hospital and looked more like a hotel. When my mother came out of the operating room into the recovery room, I went in to see her as she recovered consciousness. She looked at me for a little while and then she said, "Tell me, was it a boy or girl?" I said, "Mother, that's ridiculous. You're seventy-eight years old. You were not here to have a baby. You were here for a hernia operation." She looked at me, still drowsy from the anesthetic, and said "Don't give me any of that hernia business. The only times I have ever been in a hospital were to have a baby. Now tell me, was it a boy or girl?" I talked to her for a while and finally thought I had convinced her that she had not been in the hospital to have a baby. Shortly thereafter, our cook, Silvana, went in to see my mother and emerged from the room chuckling. I asked her what she was laughing at and Silvana grinned and said, "The signora asked me, 'What did the colonel say when he saw the baby?'" Needless to say, the next day my mother returned to normal and was able to continue to play her part as my hostess.

Around June 1962 I began to hear rumors that I was going to be transferred to another post. I tried all of my usual best sources in Washington and was unable to obtain any hard information other than that there were discussions going on about transferring me to another job. I finally appealed to one of my best sources, a warrant officer whom I had known for many years, and he replied with one sentence, "You are going to Brazil." A few days later I discovered that I *was* going to Brazil. Ambassador Lincoln Gordon, whom I had known during my assignment to the Marshall Plan and who was now President Kennedy's Ambassador to Brazil, had asked that I be transferred there since a dangerous situation was developing in which the military would obviously play a key role of some sort. And he wished to be informed of what the military were thinking and what was going on. The Army had refused to consider this lateral transfer and Gordon carried this matter all the way to President Kennedy and obtained the decision that I would be transferred. I was subsequently notified that I was to be transferred to Rio as Army Attaché, but before I went to Brazil I was to accompany Italian Defense Minister Giulio Andreotti (who was later, on several occasions, to become Prime Minister) to the United States. He was to make an extensive visit and we were very anxious to sell military equipment to Italy to make up deficiencies in its forces, particularly heavy equipment which Italy did not manufacture at that time such as armored personnel carriers. It was understood that if Italy purchased such armored personnel carriers, she would also acquire the right to build them in Italy under license, thus creating many jobs in that country.

I flew to the United States and met Mr. Andreotti in Washington and we then set forth on a trip around the United States. Prior to our departure from Washington, I discovered that they were going to fly him around the United States in a propeller-driven Convair, which was very slow in comparison to the jets. I suggested that he be flown in a Lockheed Jet Star, a C-140, but was told that these were all unavailable. They were all at the Air Force Association meeting in Las Vegas. By harping on this matter, I was finally able to get one and we set forth on our trip. One of the first stops was at Fort Knox, Kentucky, at the Armored School, where Mr. Andreotti had an opportunity to see the latest models in U.S. armored vehicles and tracked vehicles of all sorts including the armored personnel carriers.

We then flew on to San Antonio, Texas, and were cordially received there by the Air Force general in command. As we took off from San Antonio, there were some very strange noises and the aircraft bounced around considerably. I was sitting on the other side of the aircraft from Mr. Andreotti, who was reading his newspaper. He lowered the newspaper and in a very calm and casual voice asked me in Italian, "Is this aircraft going to crash or not?" I was not too sure, but I said, "Oh no, Mr. Minister, its nothing at all. Pay no attention to it." He nodded and went on reading his newspaper. In a few moments the pilot asked me to come up to the front of the aircraft, where he explained to me that he was unable to get the doors of the landing gear compartment closed, as a result of which the aircraft could not fly above twenty thousand feet and certainly could not fly to

San Francisco, which was our destination for that day. I asked him what he could do under the circumstances, and he said he could only fly as far as El Paso. I then asked him what the situation would be when he got to El Paso. He replied that he would simply be one thousand miles farther from the spare parts at Andrews Air Force Base in Washington, D.C. He asked me to ask the Italian Defense Minister what he would like to do under the circumstances. I went back to Mr. Andreotti, who was still calmly reading his newspaper. He looked up at me and grinned and said, "Well, are we going to crash or not?" I assured him that we were not. I explained the situation to him and told him that the pilot had asked me what his desires were. Andreotti looked at me and said, "Walters, you tell that pilot to do exactly what he would have done if I had not been aboard the aircraft," and then he went back to reading his newspaper. I told this to the pilot and he decided to return to San Antonio. Shortly thereafter we landed and were met once again by the general who had seen us off. He laughed and said, "When you left, I told you to come back, but I did not mean this quickly." He was resourceful and was able to get us two small jet aircraft. We divided the party into two groups and flew to San Francisco.

In San Francisco Mr. Andreotti visited the factory which made the armored personnel carrier in which the Italian Army was interested, and eventually the Italians did buy a certain number of these carriers, as well as the right to build them under license in Italy, which they have done since then. We were received by the Italian consul general in San Francisco. The San Francisco stop outside of the visit to the armored personnel carrier factory was really in the nature of a weekend rest stop. The Italian consul general, however, had filled it with a series of engagements on Saturday and Sunday, visits to Italian fraternal organizations and, finally, a visit to a California vineyard run by Italians. Mr. Andreotti was quite irritated at this. He had hoped to have a free weekend in San Francisco, instead of which both Saturday and Sunday were fully organized by the consul. Andreotti grinned at one point and said, "That consul thinks I may be Foreign Minister some day and he is trying to get a good job. If I ever become Foreign Minister, he's going to some obscure and distant post." Needless to say, this did not happen.

After that we flew back to New York and I recall a rather warm and human incident there. Mr. Andreotti confided to me that he had saved up $400 and would like to buy a gift at Tiffany's for his wife. He wondered whether they had anything for $400. We went over to Tiffany's and he was able to get a very attractive silver gift for his wife and thus bring her "a gift from Tiffany's."

I was struck by his courage under awkward circumstances, by the calm he always manifested and by the dignity with which he bore himself. Yet it was utterly without pompousness. I have always regarded him as a man of independence and courage, a true democrat, an Italian patriot and a good European and loyal supporter of NATO.

Upon my return to Rome, Mr. Andreotti gave me a farewell dinner and I received a high Italian decoration. On the day before I left I gave a farewell reception to say goodbye and to present my successor who was already well known to the Italians. He was the Assistant Army Attaché, Colonel James P. Strauss, a distinguished officer and a great friend and helper. At the party one of the Soviet naval attachés, a Commander Bykov, whom I had seen once before at the Pierra Marquez Hotel in Acapulco during Eisenhower's visit, asked me what I thought of the Cuban situation. At this point, I knew nothing whatever about the developing Cuban missile crisis, but I knew that the Russians were tampering with Castro and I knew that a provocative situation could develop. So in reply to his question I replied in Russian with an old Russian proverb, "Do not throw oil on the fire." I am sure that to this day Captain Bykov feels that I knew something about the Cuban crisis at that time, whereas I actually knew nothing and discovered what was going on only after my arrival in Rio de Janeiro.

I left Rome with great regrets. These had been two extremely happy years. There had been no crisis, no great difficulties. The environment was friendly. I got along well with the Italian

Armed Forces, and I had had the opportunity to prove to my superiors in Washington that I could successfully run an attaché office. The inspectors had given me high marks. I had traveled all over the country visiting most of the units of the Italian Army. I had to keep my government well informed and tried to project to the Italian Army the image of a U. S. Army officer who was friendly, interested and sympathetic. This was easy to do because I felt that way toward them. It was with great reluctance that I left Italy at this time. I decided that I would stop over for a day in Dakar, which I had not seen since World War II, and I left Rome on October 10, 1962, on my way to my next mission, my second mission to Brazil.

19. IN PARIS WITH KENNEDY

In the summer of 1960 after I had been a few months at my post as Army Attaché in Rome, I received a telegram from Major General Ted Clifton, an old friend who was the Army Aide to President Kennedy, alerting me to prepare myself to go to Paris to meet the advanced detachment from the White House that would be going there shortly to discuss the arrangements for President Kennedy's impending visit to General de Gaulle in the French capital. I was quite pleased to receive this instruction as it indicated to me that the new Administration had understood that I was simply an Army officer who served whatever commander in chief was in the White House at the time. I had previously served both President Truman, a Democrat, and President Eisenhower, a Republican. I had heard rumors that there was more partisanship in the new Administration, but this telegram from Clifton served to reassure me that this was not the case.

I informed Ambassador Reinhardt and he was very pleased and felt that I might be able to make a useful contribution inasmuch as I already knew General de Gaulle quite well and could help bring the two Presidents closer together at a time when France and the United States seemed to be drifting apart. A few days later I received a telegram ordering me to go to Paris to meet with Pierre Salinger, the press secretary to President Kennedy, and Kenneth O'Donnell and other members of the advance party. I notified the Army of this and received their authorization to go to Paris. I proceeded to Paris, and on arrival there I reported to Pierre Salinger. Salinger was the son of an Alsatian who had settled in the United States, and he spoke quite good French at that time. Since then he has become much more fluent, lives in France permanently and often speaks on French television. He gives public lectures before various societies and organizations in France.

They received me cordially enough and I met other members of the party and we then proceeded to contact the French presidential and Foreign Office staff. Many members of de Gaulle's personal and security staff were well known to me from previous visits by General Eisenhower and they greeted me very warmly. I sensed that this was not entirely welcome to Salinger and O'Donnell. I was on close, friendly terms with General de Gaulle's aide and some of his chief assistants. In the discussions we had relating to the President's visit, they were extremely forthcoming and co-operative. There was just something about the attitude of Salinger and O'Donnell that made me feel faintly uneasy throughout all the discussions, but nevertheless, we proceeded to make the various arrangements for President Kennedy's schedule. I knew that the one thing I must never say was, "This is the way we did it before." This always has an agitating effect on new administrations, so I let the French do most of the talking in this respect. Once in a while they asked me how it was done before, and only in answer to such a question would I reply and describe the particular form of the arrangements for General Eisenhower's visit.

This discussion with the French involved many things—the program for President Kennedy's visit, the people he would see, the official entertainment that would take place by General de Gaulle, the return entertainment by President Kennedy at the U. S. Embassy, as well as the rather complex arrangements for the press and television people. In this, as in all presidential advance parties in which I have participated, almost as much attention was paid to taking care of the press and the media and keeping them happy as to the arrangements for the President himself. Since Salinger was the press secretary, these matters were given particular attention. It was always a matter that slightly irritated the French since they did not pay the same attention, at that time at least, to their press as we did to ours. They once said to me, "You Americans worry more about keeping your press happy than your President. We do it the other way around."

In addition there were the complex arrangements relating to the security of the President. These involved lengthy discussions between the U. S. Secret Service and various security authorities in France, all of whom, again, were well known to me—the Internal Security Service, the D.S.T., the Presidential Security Staff and the Paris Police. In addition to this, we discussed the arrangements for the actual arrival and departure at Orly Airport and, since I had been through this drill on a number of occasions with General Eisenhower, I was familiar with the way the French wanted to do it. However, I kept my knowledge to myself unless asked and attempted to be as unobtrusive as possible, yet I could feel the growing chill from this advance party as they realized that I knew all of the French authorities with whom they were dealing.

However, nothing was said and right up to the time when they returned to the United States and I returned to Italy, the understanding was that I would return for the presidential visit and serve as President Kennedy's interpreter. I knew this always put the State Department's nose slightly out of joint since when their interpreter was present, they always got the memoranda of conversations of the President's talks with foreign leaders. In my case, I had always been strictly instructed by President Eisenhower never to give anybody a copy of his memoranda of conversations until he had initialed them. On one occasion I was obliged to refuse such a memorandum to the Secretary of State, John Foster Dulles. Dulles, however, while initially irritated by my refusal, did not hold it against me and was very cordial to me the next time he saw me. Salinger, O'Donnell and their party returned to the United States and I returned to my post as

Military Attaché to Italy with the understanding that I would be returning to Paris one or two days before President Kennedy's arrival.

As I returned to Italy, I began thinking about the atmosphere in which I had found myself, and it was clear that at least Salinger and O'Donnell viewed me as an Eisenhower political appointee of some sort. Neither of them fully comprehended that I was simply an Army officer who did what I was told and served whatever President happened to be in office. As I thought about this, it seemed to me that the best thing to do would be for me to send a telegram to General Clifton and indicate to him that as a result of my contact with the party, I had a feeling that I should not return to Paris for the visit unless I received confirmation from him that my presence in Paris was desired. This would get him off the hook gracefully if my presence was, in fact, not wanted. I sent such a telegram to Clifton and shortly afterward received a reply from him to the effect that my impression was correct and that I should not return to Paris for the visit. This did not surprise me.

President Kennedy's visit to Paris went off very well. Mrs. Kennedy was a great success, and at the end of the visit she flew to Greece. She was making a short stop in Rome to change planes and I received a message from the Secret Service asking me to meet her and make arrangements for a waiting room where she could stay for a short period while waiting to continue her journey on to Athens. I was delighted to do this and on the appointed day I made the necessary arrangements at the airport with the commander of the airport, a Colonel Salaris, who was an old friend of mine. When Mrs. Kennedy's plane arrived, I made arrangements to go on board while the passengers were still aboard. I walked up to Mrs. Kennedy and introduced myself as the American Military Attaché in Italy and told her that I was to take her to a waiting room where she could wait until the onward flight to Athens was ready. She looked up at me and, in her rather deep and very attractive voice, said, "Colonel Walters, you were the most missed man in Paris." I have often said that anyone who says flattery will get you nowhere has never had any. This made a most favorable impression on me and I must say that I became a devoted admirer of Jacqueline Kennedy.

20. BRAZIL AGAIN

After accompanying the Italian Defense Minister to the United States, as described in a previous chapter, I flew to Rio, leaving my mother to close the Rome apartment and follow later, repeating a pattern of many previous transfers. On my arrival in Rio, I was met, to my surprise, by some thirteen general officers of the Brazilian Army who had served in Italy with me. They had of course been much junior officers during our service in Italy. Their meeting me at the airport was a typically warm Brazilian gesture of friendship. They ranged across the political spectrum from José Ulhoa Cintra on the right to Luiz Cunha Mello on the left. I was, of course, most grateful to them for the gesture and it stirred anew the affection and esteem I have always had and will always have for Brazilians.

The next morning I reported to the Ambassador in his office. I said, "Mr. Ambassador, here I am. What is it you want of me?" He walked me to a chair, told me how glad he was to see me again after so many years. He then described the deteriorating political atmosphere in Brazil from both the point of view of Communist progress and the steady cooling of relations with the United States. He then said, "From you I want three things: First, I want to know what is going on in the Armed Forces; second, I want to be able in some measure to influence it through you; and third, most of all, I never want to be surprised." In the years since this talk I have often thought of that charge and admired it. It seemed to me complete. I must confess, I have on occasion used it on my own subordinates.

The Ambassador then told me about the Cuban missile crisis and showed me the photographs of the missiles which he had been instructed to show to Brazilian President João Goulart. He told me that he wanted me to go with him in case Goulart wanted any technical explanations. Ambassador Gordon had no need of my services as an interpreter since he spoke superb Portuguese.

At the appointed time the following day, I went with Ambassador Gordon to Laranjeiras Palace in Rio. We were met by a young military aide to Goulart whom I had known in Italy when he served with the Brazilian Expeditionary Force. This young officer and I had had many talks and I knew that his political convictions were very far to the left. His wife was even more so. His father, a distinguished Brazilian general, had once told me, "I will die sad because my son is a Communist." The young officer seemed most surprised to see me. After a short wait, the Ambassador and I were ushered into the presence of President Goulart. He received us most cordially and the Ambassador introduced me to President Goulart, whom I had never met before. The Ambassador then described the development of the Cuban situation and showed the President the photos of the Soviet missiles in Cuba. Goulart examined the photos closely. I noted the proximity of the two missile fuels which are only brought together shortly before use. He looked up at the Ambassador and asked, "Why don't you blow the whole island out of the water?" The Ambassador replied that this would cause the death of millions of innocent people and we did not do that sort of thing. Goulart replied, "But what would that be alongside a single American life?" The Ambassador then asked for the President to order the Brazilian delegation to support U.S. initiatives at the UN and in the Organization of American States and Goulart promised to do so. After partaking of the usual cups of coffee the Ambassador and I left. My young leftist friend walked us out to our car musing almost to himself, "So you're back in Brazil."

Two days later the Communist daily *Novos Rumos* came out with a long story to the effect that Colonel Walters, "the Pentagon's chief specialist in military coups, has just been sent to Brazil for the sole purpose of overthrowing President Goulart and establishing a regime that would be a puppet of the U.S." The article went on to say that I had been the artisan of the overthrow of King Farouk in Egypt, President Frondizi in Argentina, President Prado in Peru, and that I had threatened the Arab oil sheiks with coups to make them sign oil agreements beneficial to the U.S. oil companies specifically and imperialism in general. I forwarded this article to Washington. Since we were generally asked to comment on such things, I added the following comment: "And on the seventh day I rested." It was not an original phrase. It had once been used about Colonel McCormick of the Chicago *Tribune*. This was but the first shot in a campaign against me that has continued sporadically until this day. Its purpose then was to intimidate me and to make Brazilians unwilling to talk to me. Years later in a slightly different version, it was to be naïvely reported by Jack Anderson in his column. This campaign made it necessary for me to be very careful not to damage my friends by seeing them too often. The campaign was not to let up until the 1964 revolution, eighteen months later. On one occasion Roberto Campos, a brilliant economic miracle, who was then Goulart's Ambassador to the United States, took me aside and said, "Walters, what truth is there in these stories that you are plotting? President Goulart himself has asked me whether you should be expelled." I replied, "Mr. Ambassador, I give you my word of honor as a U. S. Army officer that there is not a word of truth in it. I know Brazilians too well not to know how they would resent a foreigner interfering in their internal affairs. To do so would be contrary to my instructions. I do work hard, however, to find out what is going on and what may happen, just as you or any other Brazilian official does in any country to which he is accredited." He thanked me and said that he believed me and would pass this on to President Goulart. Whenever I saw Goulart at any official function he was always most courteous to me and complimentary about my Portuguese. Nevertheless, it was clear that, if not Goulart, at least some of the far leftists in his immediate entourage were working hard to divide the Brazilian Armed Forces by encouraging the non-commissioned officers of all three forces to take a strong political stand against their officers. It was to be these efforts to divide the Armed Forces and destroy their cohesion and discipline that would in the end bring about the revolution and Goulart's downfall. There were sinister precedents. During the 1935 Communist revolution in Brazil a number of officers were killed in their sleep by Communist NCOs setting the enlisted men against their officers, which is an old tactic of the Communists—until, of course, they take power. We ourselves were to see it years later in Vietnam with the "Fragging" incidents by enlisted men against their officers. Many of those who took part in such incidents did not, of course, realize that they were being exploited in this way in accord with Communist principles of subversion.

I was able to visit many Brazilian units because the Brazilian Military Attaché in the United States had similar freedom to visit U.S. units. I was nearly always received most cordially, only rarely, coolly. Still, it was very formal, except when I was alone with old friends who would pour out their worry at seeing their country drifting toward becoming what so many called "another Cuba." They spoke of the growing use by Goulart of the power to promote far leftist officers to key positions. I found very few officers who actually believed that Goulart himself was a Communist or a subversive. Most worried at his apparent belief that he could use the Communists and yet escape from their control. Many times I heard the Chinese proverb quoted, "He who rides the tiger dare not dismount." The real far leftists around Goulart were using power skillfully to remove officers they suspected and replaced them with officers who were either convinced and sincere Marxists or else opportunists. A number of my friends expressed their frustrations and some even despair.

The best among them, however, never ceased to hope that somehow, some way, the trend would be reversed.

After a few months it became apparent to me that in their frustration and fear for their country, a number of officers were beginning to think about some sort of military action to prevent Brazil from becoming another Cuba. This was done with extreme reluctance. Most Brazilian officers were anxious that their country not give the impression to the world that it was just another "banana republic." Successful revolutions have been extremely rare in Brazilian history. Even independence from Portugal was obtained without a revolution. Successful revolutions were the ones that overthrew the empire in 1889, the one that brought Vargas to power in 1930, the one that overthrew him in 1945 and the one that overthrew him again in 1954. It was also clear to me that most of this thinking was isolated and that the many small plotting groups were not yet in communication with one another. There did not appear to be any sort of co-ordination at all. One very senior officer once threatened in despair to commit suicide. Frustration bordering on hopelessness was widespread as many of the military felt themselves isolated and being enveloped by the wave of what many called "supraversion" or revolution from the top rather than the bottom.

On one occasion I was at the home of a Brazilian officer who was known as an activist and a violent man. While we were talking, he was called from the room. Shortly afterward, he returned and said to me, "Walters, out there I have a guy who for five thousand dollars guarantees he can knock off Goulart. What do you think?" I replied, fundamentally, this is none of my business as a foreigner, but I will tell you this. I don't believe in assassination for three reasons. First, it is against the law of God. Second, it is against the law of man. And third, it does not work. Whoever is assassinated is generally replaced by someone even more fanatical. He nodded regretfully and abandoned the idea. It was totally un-Brazilian. No Brazilian President has ever been assassinated. As a people, whatever their political differences, they rarely forget that their opponents are also Brazilians. There has been no death penalty in Brazil for over a hundred years.

The victors have rarely physically mistreated the vanquished. Such an assassination would have outraged all Brazilians and this officer knew it.

Inexorably the leftward drift continued in all areas. After Goulart's promise of support in the United Nations and the Organization of American States, the Brazilian delegation voted against the U.S. motions or abstained. When Ambassador Gordon called the President on this, Goulart said that they had not followed their instructions but took no punitive sanctions against them. The Brazilian Ambassador to the United Nations at that time was to become Goulart's Foreign Minister at the time of the revolution, and, Brazil being Brazil, this same man served for many years as the revolution's Ambassador to the United States.

A radical land reform bill was announced by Goulart that would seize and divide large properties. This was ironic since Goulart himself was probably the largest landowner in Brazil. It gave rise not merely to concern but, as everything eventually does in Brazil, to jokes, one of which went as follows:

> Goulart flew over to see a neighboring rancher in Mato Grosso. It took him an hour to get there and he flew only over his own land. As they were talking, his neighbor asked whether the agrarian reform was truly inevitable. Goulart said that the masses demanded it and it really could not be avoided. The rancher then shook his head in resignation and said, "Well, I suppose the only thing I can do is put my land up for sale." Instantly, Goulart said, "How much do you want for it?"

Tension continued to grow and the Armed Forces appeared divided. There is a popular delusion in the United States and Europe that officers in Brazil come from the wealthy landowning class. This is quite false. Most of them come from the middle class. Few rich young men in any country voluntarily accept the limitations and continuous transfers of military life. A Brazilian officer can expect long years of service in remote areas and a life of many hardships and sacrifices. The Brazilian military view themselves not merely as the defenders of the fatherland but also as guardians of the values of the nation and the ultimate arbiters of the national scene. This is true in many less developed countries, though not in the English-speaking countries or those of most of Western Europe. Yet despite the mistrust many officers felt toward Goulart, there was a deep reluctance to move against him unless the fundamental values of the nation were threatened. Yet during this period of 1962 to 1963, there was a clear sense of leftward drift and growing strength of the Communists and other assorted far leftists. Goulart's own brother-in-law Leonel Brizola was the standard-bearer of these forces.

Because my job was to keep my Ambassador and my country informed, I tried to maintain contact with military men of all views, leftists as well as rightists and centrists. Curiously, despite the fact that I was an Army officer, I believe that I had more contacts and discussions with far leftists than almost any other member of the Embassy. My knowledge of Portuguese greatly facilitated these contacts. I was helped in this by the fact that I had known many of the far leftists for many years and had always remained on friendly terms with them. In many cases I was to continue these friendly personal relations even after the victorious revolution in 1964. On one occasion, General Argemiro de Assis Brasil, a far leftist, but a courageous and forthright officer, invited me to a party at the Copacabana Hotel. When I came into the room, where he was surrounded by many of his friends and co-believers, he called out to me in a loud voice, "Hello, Walters. You Americans think I am a Communist, Castroite or Maoist. I am none of those things. I am a Brazilianist." I replied, "Assis, I know how you feel. Many of your friends think I am a capitalist and the long arm of American imperialism, and I am none of those things." He came over, gave me a bear hug and said, "Walters, if all Americans were like you, we would not have any trouble." I was to visit him several times after the revolution and his expulsion from the Army. I disagreed, and still do, with his political philosophy, but we were and are, I hope, friends. I had good relations on a personal basis with many other members of Goulart's *dispositivo* (or unofficial organization of military support), including Generals Benjamin Galhardo Napoleão Nobre and Euclydes Zerbini and my old comrade from Italy General Luiz Cunha Mello, who has remained a close friend and whose courage I have always admired. Despite this, the whispering and press campaign against me continued. My old commander in Italy, Marshal Mascarenhas de Moraes, who had led the Brazilian Expeditionary Force, worried by this, gave a large public luncheon for me at which he made a speech emphasizing the services I had rendered to Brazil. He wound it up by saying, "There are those who would like to drive you out of this country, but the Army of Monte Castello and Montese will not stand for it." Those words by Brazil's most respected hero had a calming effect on the campaign. I have also been told that some of my friends on the left also passed the word to stop the campaign against me. Be that as it may, as 1964 began, things were easier for me. Early in 1964 from many friends I finally got the impression that some of the plotters were beginning to get in touch with one another on a co-ordinated national scale. Couriers began to travel. Contingency plans began to become more specific. Directives and think papers began to circulate. Through friends I was aware of this. I saw very little during this period of the officer to whom I had been closest in Italy. General Castelo Branco was commanding the Fourth Army in Recife in northern Brazil. Once or twice he came to Rio and I had lunch or dinner with his wife and him. She was a very close friend of my mother's and they enjoyed speaking French together. Castelo Branco had always spoken with pride of the professionalism of the Brazilian Armed Forces and of his unwillingness to take part in any revolutions. When we would meet, we would speak of the world, the United States, Vietnam, Europe, the Soviet Union or China. Rarely did we speak of internal Brazilian affairs and he spoke of them only with great circumspection. There have been many reports, all false, to the effect that I in some way pushed him to take the leadership of the plotters and overthrow Goulart. Castelo Branco was a proud Brazilian and had I or any other foreigner ever made any such suggestion to him, he would have indignantly rejected it and it might well have terminated our friendship. I knew this and therefore was never tempted to try to influence him or to seek information from him. I valued his friendship too highly.

Eventually, Castelo Branco was named Chief of Staff of the Army and returned to Rio. I saw him frequently but almost never did our talks touch on current Brazilian affairs. He had always expressed the belief that Brazilians could and would solve their own problems. He was no reactionary but a thoughtful patriot with a real social conscience, outraged by many of the injustices he had seen in the northeast, convinced that all, especially the rich, must make sacrifices if the nation was to live. He was a man of brilliant intellect, extraordinarily well informed on social, political and economic matters; a man to whom God was real, a man of extraordinary rectitude of character, as unselfish and dedicated as any man I have ever known.

His example and nobility have served as an inspiration to me. I had seen him in the storm of war, in stress and in peace, and later as President, and I have never known him to do a mean or base thing. His wit was biting. He was intolerant of incompetence. He held high ideals and lived much closer to them than most men I have known. He never spoke disparagingly of President Goulart nor did he ever discuss with me any action he might contemplate taking. My information on the situation came from other old friends.

One day one of my closest friends was to tell me, "Castelo Branco has finally agreed to lead us and this has given us all hope that Brazil is not yet lost." Castelo Branco was never to mention this to me until after the revolution. Another brigadier general I had known in Italy was extremely forthcoming with me because he truly feared that his country would become Communist and another Cuba. One night at his house I spent my "longest night." He had sent me word that he wanted to see me. I went to his house, leaving my car several blocks away. I was received by his wife, who told me he would be back shortly. Several hours passed and still he did not return. I finally said I would go, but she insisted that he was most anxious to see me, so I waited.

Finally he arrived with his aide and said, "This is it. We have decided to go right at the beginning of next week." At this moment, his phone rang and a friend told him that there would probably be a police raid on his house at any minute. The house was a veritable arsenal. He had submachine guns, rifles, hand grenades and ammunition. I could see the headlines already. I had come there to be able to inform my government, not to participate in any plot, but if I were arrested in the apartment, who would believe it? Yet I could not flee at once or he would have thought me a coward. I said to him, "I will do whatever you want. I will stay if you want me or leave if you prefer." Somewhat to my dismay, he said, "I want you to stay." I stayed and was rehearsing what I would say if arrested. The minutes and hours dragged by and nothing happened, and it became clear that there was not going to be a raid. He said I could go and finally at 3 A.M. I left, after what had seemed to me an eternity. This officer was a close friend. He died not long after the revolution, and in his will he left me his ivory and gold swagger stick. I knew then that he had appreciated my not running out on him on that longest night.

During this period, from time to time, I would visit Castelo Branco at his home and we would talk of China, the U.S.S.R. or the United States and Europe, almost never of Brazilian politics. On the evening of March 13, 1964, I was at his home watching on television the mass meeting Goulart had called in front of the War Ministry. Hammer and sickle emblems were everywhere. The oratory was inflammatory. Castelo Branco switched off the set and said quietly, "That man is not going to leave when his term is up." That was as close as he ever came to discussing the internal situation with me. Sometimes I would drop by and, seeing that he had visitors, I would not go in. Though he was extraordinarily discreet, I knew from others that things were heading for the long-postponed showdown. The leftists' efforts to set the non-commissioned officers against their officers became more open and restlessness increased in all of the armed services. Still, there was a continuing reluctance to do anything outside of the constitution without extraordinary provocation.

It was Goulart himself who finally provided this provocation by a series of unwise actions that could only have been recommended to him by overconfident far leftists in his entourage who felt strong enough to face a showdown. Many of them, I knew from discussions with them, felt that they had the situation in hand. This confidence was shared by Soviet Ambassador Andrei Fomin, with whom I talked often at receptions. On one occasion while speaking to me, and he spoke good English, he said, "The trouble with you Americans is that you never want to learn anyone else's language. You always demand that people speak English with you." My first thought was that he had not read my biography as I had read his, because I do speak some Russian. I said to him in English, "Mr. Ambassador, that may have been true fifteen years ago, but it is no longer true. All of my assistants speak Portuguese, much better than yours." "Yes, it is true," he insisted, "and besides, you do not have a gift for languages like us Slavs." I said to him sharply in Russian, "Mr. Ambassador, that is bullshit and I am amazed that an intelligent man like you who has lived outside the Soviet Union still believes *eti Kommunichestiki basni Krylova*, these Communist fairy tales." He was visibly shaken and I hastened to press my advantage. I asked him in Russian if he would like to try Portuguese, knowing that mine was far better than his. Then disaster struck. He looked at me and grinned and said in English, "Walters, you may be good soldier, but diplomat you are not." That was his round!

I had calculated for some time that the anti-leftists were running out of time. The revolution could not occur during the carnival or Lent, especially not during Holy Week, and it would fail if they tried it on April Fools' Day. Easter fell that year on March 30. It could only be on the thirty-first. I had so informed my superiors. I had been aware of some U.S. contingency planning for an upheaval in Brazil. After all, the world was in great measure polarized into two camps and any government would fail in its duty if it did not plan for all eventualities. Apparently, in the United States this planning received the code name "Brother Sam." The first time I ever heard this expression was in January 1977 when some of the papers were made public. Perhaps this was because on one occasion I was asked by a four-star U.S. general what I thought of contingency planning in case of a prolonged civil war in Brazil. I replied that that was nonsense. There would be no prolonged civil war. At most, it would last a few days and I was quite confident the Brazilian Army could do all of their own planning. This U.S. officer was highly displeased with me and I was not taken further into his confidence. Much has been made of this contingency planning. All nations do it under almost all circumstances so that sudden changes will not catch them by surprise. Rarely does it indicate intention. Rather, it is a precaution. The Communists had recently taken over Cuba and this planning was predicated on a civil war in which the Soviets would try and help their Brazilian friends. The publication of such contingency plans has been used to try to show that the United States was in some way connected with the Brazilian revolution of 1964. It was not in any way. Ambassador Gordon once said under oath when testifying before Congress, "The Brazilian revolution was not 99 per cent Brazilian. It was 100 per cent Brazilian." I would be happy to make the same statement under oath at any time. The Communists and their friends see the need to denigrate those who have defeated them. So they spread the word that the Americans were really behind the Brazilian, Chilean or any other revolution they don't like. Unfortunately many guilt-ridden Americans naïvely believe them. The United States' uncontrollable urge to tell everyone about everything reveals contingency planning for this or that eventuality and that is then used to document U.S. complicity. The U.S. media, which enjoy the sensationalist character of the story, help unintentionally in spreading the far-left version of the event, because it is always sensational.

In March 1964 events began to take an ominous turn. On the thirteenth Goulart's brother-in-law, Leonel Brizola, in the President's presence, made a highly provocative speech. President

Goulart appointed a scoundrel who had been cashiered out of the service as commandant of the Brazilian Marine Corps and the President himself made an extremely provocative speech to the Sergeants' Club. Navy mutineers carried the Marine admiral in the streets in triumph. I told the Ambassador on Sunday, March 30, that all of my information pointed to imminent action by those Brazilian officers who feared that further delay would create an irreversible situation. I told the Ambassador that I felt the provocation the plotters had been awaiting had just been given by the President in seeking to disrupt the discipline, unity and hierarchy of the armed services. The Ambassador had planned to fly up to the northeast to inaugurate a housing project in Maceió built with Alliance for Progress funds. Despite advice by many that the showdown would be postponed again, he decided to cancel his trip to the northeast. The revolution was not planned to go quite as early as March 31, but the provocation given was intolerable to peppery little General Mourão Filho, who had been sent to the small town of Juiz de Fôra in Minas Gerais to get him out of his command in the crucial center of São Paulo. He had once told me in front of his whole staff that he would revolt—"overturn the table"—rather than see his country turned into another Cuba. That was a phrase many of my friends in Brazil used. I myself feared that Brazil would not be another Cuba, but another China. The hour of decision was almost at hand on the morning of March 31. General Mourão announced that he was marching on Rio. General Cunha Mello was appointed to repel Mourão. He attempted to form a task force of the 1st, 2nd and 3rd Infantry regiments together with armored and engineer units which were all part of the Rio garrison. Almost immediately several of these units, as they made contact with the forces of the rebellion, joined it. Cunha Mello tried to do what he could, but ascertained that Goulart had already fled from Rio. First Army Commander General Armando Ancora had gone to the military academy at Resende on the road to São Paulo to negotiate a settlement. Cunha Mello asked Assis Brasil, Goulart's military aide, what he should do and was told to do whatever he wanted, as the whole matter was beyond salvation. Cunha Mello ordered his troops to return to their barracks and the next day courageously presented himself at the War Ministry. There I saw him when I was calling and shook hands with him.

Guanabara State Police occupied key posts including the headquarters of far-left unions and the national student federation. As I moved around the city, I realized that Fort Copacabana and the various military schools in the Praia Vermelha area had gone over to the rebellion. In the late afternoon, I went to the Embassy to report to Washington on what was occurring. Darkness found me still there. As I attempted to return home and left the Embassy driving my own car, several shots were fired. The Marine guard at the Embassy ran out into the street and waved me back into the garage. I spent the night in the Embassy, and during the night I received information that Goulart was preparing to leave the city and fly to Brasília. It was also apparent that the Fourth Army in northeastern Brazil had also joined the rebels. All that remained was for General Amaury Kruel and the Second Army to join forces with the rebellion. This occurred in the early hours of the morning of April 1, and from then on the outcome was never in doubt. Late in the morning of April 1, Goulart left Rio and his supporters simply fell apart. Goulart, who would not believe that his support had evaporated, blamed the CIA for the situation. This was absolute nonsense. The CIA was following developments, not leading them. This was also true of my office, which was not part of the CIA. We, too, were trying to follow events and, if possible, trying to alert our government as to what was to come. Any American attempt to interfere in developments would have been bitterly resented by the Brazilian military, who felt and proved that they were quite competent at handling their own affairs. They did so, taking over the whole huge country almost without bloodshed. Only a few instances such as the bold capture of Fort Copacabana by Colonel César Montagna gave rise to any fighting and it was brief. The Brazilian Armed Forces knew their country well, far better than any foreigners possibly could. The United States, fearing a prolonged civil war and possible

Soviet intervention in it, had done extensive contingency planning that foresaw a much longer duration of a conflict. I had shared the Brazilians' belief that either the movement would succeed almost immediately or it would fail. I had told this to the senior U.S. commander responsible for the planning and he had not been pleased. I told him that the only U.S. troops that I felt might be needed would be those necessary if he were invited to put a symbolic platoon in the victory parade at the end of the rebellion, just as in the victory parade at the end of World War II there had been a composite platoon of American troops from the 10th Mountain Division invited by the Brazilians. In consequence, I was kept outside most of the contingency planning.

Brazilians, essentially, have a strong sense of belonging to the same community. They do not kill one another for political reasons, as occurs in many other South American countries. Not too long after the revolution one could see the victors and the vanquished sitting at the cafes in Copacabana arguing the merits of their case. On April 2 the Brazilian Congress declared the presidency vacant and the constitutional successor to Goulart, the president of the Senate, Ranieri Mazili, took office. It was his government that the United States recognized that day. Much has been made of the speedy U.S. recognition for the new Brazilian government. The United States was well informed of the likelihood of a change in the government. The United States did not participate in any way in this change. It clearly welcomed it after the fact, since it had been obvious that Goulart's belief that he could use the Communists was naïve and unrealistic. Anyone who saw the March 13 demonstration in front of the War Ministry at which the President spoke could not have had any illusions about how the Communists felt concerning their influence in the Goulart regime. Goulart was basically a good man with a guilty conscience for being rich. As someone once said, inside João Goulart the friend of labor was constantly clashing with the largest landowner in Brazil. He was not a Communist but he entertained an almost childlike belief that he could use them without coming under their control. No one uses the Communists.

A regime basically unfriendly to the United States had been replaced by another one much more friendly. Some may regard this as bad. I do not. I am convinced that if the revolution had not occurred, Brazil would have gone the way of Cuba. Perhaps there have been some excessive shows of zeal under the present regime. They are very small alongside of what would have happened if Brazil had gone Communist. We would not have isolated cases of police brutality such as occur in many countries. We would have had another Gulag archipelago. Authoritarian rightist regimes always disappear eventually. They have never been able to perpetuate themselves. Communist regimes, once they seize power, never let go. For unlike the rightists, they do know how to perpetuate themselves in power. They retain absolute control of the school system. They do not tolerate any opposition such as we see in Brazil today. Despite allegations that there is no opposition in Brazil, at the last election the opposition party won control of 59 per cent of the hundred largest cities in Brazil. Both senators elected from the city of Rio de Janeiro belong to the opposition. It is not a society that enjoys exactly the same freedoms as ours, nor is it as free as the democracies of Western Europe, but it is infinitely more free and tolerant than the societies of the Communist world. We cannot expect everyone to govern their country the way we do ours. The revolution of 1964 gave Brazil stability that brought about the economic miracle that has moved Brazil far up the ladder of world powers. A million cars a year are sold within the country. Someone must have purchasing power to buy them. Thanks to the confidence inspired by the stability, enormous foreign investments have brought vast quantities of industrial and scientific know-how into the country and have built plants that have given jobs to many Brazilians. The whole country has been thrust forward along the road to the great destiny that undoubtedly awaits Brazil.

Shortly after the revolution the governors of Brazil met and indicated that their choice for the presidency of Brazil was General Castelo Branco. He was duly elected by the Congress. Two days after the revolution, I went with Ambassador Gordon on instructions from the U.S. government to see War Minister Arthur da Costa e Silva to express the U.S. government's hope that human rights and freedom of the press would be observed. Costa e Silva was, to put it mildly, shocked and surprised by this *démarche*. He said that the United States should be happy to see this vast country saved from communism and economic ruin. Obviously they could not and would not conduct their society like the rich, unthreatened United States, but neither would they run a brutal totalitarian dictatorship. He noted the *démarche* and gently reminded the Ambassador and me that these were matters involving exclusively Brazilian sovereignty, but he nevertheless noted our interest.

I went to Brasília for the inauguration of the new President. He called me at the Embassy to invite me to lunch on the following day. This is the meal that gave rise to reports that I had met with him the day before the revolution. I did not meet with him the day before the revolution. I had met with him long before the revolution but I at no time urged him to assume the leadership of the plot or overthrow Goulart. He would have thrown me out of his house and it would have ended our friendship. We lunched alone. He spoke of his reluctance to use force to overthrow the regime and his acceptance of its necessity only after he became convinced that Goulart would not voluntarily leave the presidency of Brazil and was clearly contributing to the breakdown of discipline in the Armed Forces. He told me that he had never aspired to political power, but a combination of circumstances had thrust it upon him. He said, "When I married Argentina [his wife], she was rich and beautiful. She had humor, grace and wit. I was a poor young lieutenant and all I could bring to our marriage was whatever I could achieve in my career. Isn't it ironic that now that I have achieved everything a man can hope for, short of the salvation of his immortal soul, she is no longer at my side to help me bear this crushing burden." She had died very shortly before the revolution. The fact that I had lunch with him became public and was twisted to show that he was taking orders from the Americans or that there was some other sinister purpose inimical to Brazil. I think he invited me that day because he wanted to talk to an old friend who would not ask him, as many people had, for a job. We did not discuss Brazilian policy, nor did he solicit any advice from me. I offered none. He told me that he had high regard for the economist Roberto Campos, who had been Goulart's Minister and Ambassador to the United States. I told him that I shared that regard. Campos, a brilliant man, was truly devoted to giving Brazilians a better life.

After the revolution I saw President Castelo Branco from time to time. We spoke of the world, of NATO, of Europe and Asia. We did not discuss Brazilian politics. Had I attempted to do this, he would have told me that it was none of my business. I knew how jealous he was of Brazilian sovereignty. This knowledge kept me from any temptation of getting into such matters. Only once did I venture to do so and that was on specific orders from Washington. About this time I was selected for promotion to brigadier general. This was a proud moment for me. My mother shared in this. She died a month later. General Patton's daughter, Mrs. Ruth Ellen Totten, gave me one of her father's stars to wear. I kept it carefully and a year or two later I saw her again. She asked me whether I was wearing her father's star. I replied that it was in a glass case in my home. She told me to wear it, as it had the faculty of reproducing quickly. It did in less than three years as I became a major general.

Sometime after the revolution, three Americans were arrested while smuggling television sets and other valuable appliances into Brazil by air. They commanded astronomical prices. These men would fly planeloads of this merchandise into deserted airfields, where two or three Brazilian airmen kept a guesthouse in case crews were weathered in. In this particular case, they had bribed the corporal in charge but were caught in the act and were taken to Brasília, where they were held in the house of the commander of the Brasília garrison. By U.S. standards this was probably a $250,000 house. Immediately part of the U.S. press set up a great hue and cry about these poor innocent Americans who were being held by the Brazilian military and pressure began to be felt from Washington to get these men freed. They confessed to the Brazilians and the Embassy that they were guilty. They were caught in the act, and it was difficult to see what reasons could be advanced to persuade the Brazilians to set them free. The Brazilian press, in addition, had floated a phony story that they were stealing nuclear materials. Their "imprisonment" was a farce. They would come to the Embassy in the morning with their guards and swim in the pool. Then they would have cheeseburgers by the pool. Then they would nap until around 5 P.M., when, accompanied by their guards, they would go to the National Hotel for drinks and dinner. This would be followed by a visit to a nightclub or a brothel, and they would return to their "prison" about 2 A.M. or later. One day a telegram came from Washington on this matter, asking whether the Military Attaché, Colonel Walters, was not a close World War II friend of President Castelo Branco's, and whether this channel could not be used to secure their release, since the senator from their state was bringing great pressure on the State Department to get them out. This senator was a great liberal in Washington and a considerable racist in his home state. The Ambassador replied that I was in fact a friend of the President's but strongly recommended that this channel not be used for this purpose. Shortly after that I received a personal telegram from Secretary of Defense Robert McNamara which said that this senator had told him that unless these men were released, this senator would use his position on the Senate Foreign Relations Committee, and it was an important one, to defeat not only all further military assistance programs for Brazil, but also all other military assistance programs. I was therefore to go to the President of Brazil, "using my World War II friendship or anything else susceptible of gaining the desired result and secure the release of these men." I was appalled that a United States senator would cast his vote capriciously rather than according to what was in the interest of the United States.

I discussed this matter with the Ambassador and explained that I had never asked Castelo Branco for anything before and I

was almost reluctant to do so in a matter where there was no ju-
risdiction at all except for the crusty demands of a U.S. senator.
Finally, the Ambassador told me that I could do as I wished
but, in fact, McNamara's telegram was really an order from the
Secretary of Defense. With reluctance bordering on embarrassment, I talked to the President about it. His son, who was
present, exploded with indignation at this interference with the
Brazilian judicial process. Castelo Branco looked at me for a
minute and then he said, "Walters, you are much too intelligent
to ask me to do such an outrageous thing by yourself. You have
obviously been ordered to do it and if you have agreed to talk to
me, it must be because this matter has some special importance
in the United States which escapes me. If I were to reach into
this case in this manner, I would really be the kind of dictator
some of those people in Washington think I am. I simply cannot interfere with the procedure of our courts. But let me think
about it." I have rarely been as embarrassed in my life as I was
on this occasion, first at having to ask President Castelo Branco
for something and secondly to think that one of our senators
would condition his vote on getting what he wanted. This was
truly a demonstration of the power of arrogance.

Shortly after this episode the imprisoned men "escaped" to a
deserted airfield where a plane happened to be waiting, and they
were flown out of Brazil. Whether this escape was connected
with my request or not, I never found out. This was a time
when a great deal of U.S. assistance was needed for Brazil to get
back on its feet after the chaos of the Goulart era. Perhaps it
was the fact that this aid might have been endangered that
made me overcome my reluctance to speak to Castelo Branco
about it. It is not an episode of which I am proud. I yielded to
the power of arrogance. I was not to do it again.

After the initial euphoria following the revolution had worn
off, the new government had a very difficult time. Brazilian
finances were in chaos. The Bank of Brazil's checks were bounc-
ing on the day of the revolution. There was less than $90 mil-
lion in the treasury and a stern program of austerity was necessary. Finance Minister Roberto Campos, Castelo Branco's

appointee, elaborated such a program, but it stepped on many toes and there was a great hue and cry against him and against his policies. There were accusations that he was being subservient to the United States and his name was literally translated into English, Bob Fields, by the opposition, a real and vocal political entity which was very much alive in spite of the allegations to the contrary. This campaign became so harsh, both on the far right and on the far left, that several times Castelo Branco was forced to interpose his person into the struggle and to make plain that these were his policies and that he bore the ultimate responsibility for them. After a long, arduous and difficult time, Brazil began to show signs of recovering and the foundations were laid for the great progress that was to come in the years ahead, which Castelo Branco was not to see.

Castelo Branco had made plain that he had no political ambition, and he told me on one occasion that the trouble with Brazil was that there were Presidents who did not know when the time came to leave. He was not going to do this and despite all the pressures brought on him, he would not serve more than the three years for which he had been elected. There were great pressures brought to bear on him. On one occasion he told me that some visitors had told him that he was absolutely indispensable to ensure Brazil's progress and stability. He took them out on the balcony of Laranjeiras Palace, pointed to a cemetery and said, "Everybody in that cemetery was indispensable at one time or another. No one is indispensable, not I more than anyone else." He said, "In addition, no man knows when senility overtakes him, and it is not going to overtake me in the presidency of Brazil." On another occasion he mentioned casually that he would leave at his appointed time and that he would make all of his successors the prisoners of his example and thus remove the possibility that any one of them would seek to perpetuate himself in office in the years ahead.

It was clearly Castelo Branco's design as soon as possible to return the government to normal control. However, the most obvious candidate, Governor Carlos Lacerda, by his verbal excesses and impatience, removed himself from the position of heir apparent. When it became clear that Castelo Branco was not going to run for re-election, the number of candidates that appeared was small.

After Castelo Branco had announced that he was not running for re-election, I met my old friend Soviet Ambassador Fomin. He told me that he would be returning to Moscow shortly, where he would be in charge of Latin American affairs. He said that President Castelo Branco had announced that he would not run for re-election but he, Fomin, had to know who the next President would be, and since the Americans pulled the strings on these puppets, and I had selected my former tentmate for the job of president, would I please tell him who was going to be the next president. I replied somewhat sharply that what he had just said proved to me that he was far less well informed than I thought he was if he thought I had any influence whatsoever on the selection of Brazil's President. I said he was confusing one B with another. He asked me what I meant, and I said that Brazil and Budapest began with the same letter, but the method of selecting the two governments was entirely different in the two places. He laughed and said, "Yes, yes, but tell me who is to be the next President of Brazil." I replied, "Mr. Ambassador, only God knows, but since you don't believe in him, I don't know what advice to give you to find out." I told him this in Russian. He grinned sheepishly and said, "Well, anyway, I'm going to invite you to my farewell cocktail party." Thus, I had a minor revenge for my previous discomfiture at his hands some years before. In later years I was to ask while at the CIA where Fomin was and I was asked *who* he was. I said that I didn't know who he was at the time that I asked, but in 1964 he had been the Soviet Ambassador to Brazil. My Soviet experts checked and came back a few minutes later to tell me that he was now the Soviet Ambassador to Bangladesh. My only thought at that time was, "Twelve years after Brazil he is in Bangladesh. Diplomat he is not."

President Castelo Branco would come to my house fairly frequently for a cup of coffee, or ice cream, to talk about our experiences during the war, or about many other subjects. I recall that close to the end of his term when War Minister Costa e Silva announced his candidacy and, therefore, under Castelo's regulations had to resign his office well in advance, he asked me whom I thought he would appoint as War Minister. I named three or four possible candidates and gave the reasons why I believed that he would not appoint them. He broke in at this point to tell me, "Even if you guess right, I'm not going to tell you the answer." I asked him how I could win the game if there was no way I could tell whether I was going to win. He said, "Go ahead and guess anyway." I then said, "In this difficult period you will want a man who has your absolute confidence. You will therefore appoint the present president of Petrobras, Marshal Adémar de Queiroz, as the next War Minister." I have been a prisoner-of-war interrogator and I have found that when you put your finger on the thing a man is trying to hide, something usually shows in his face. As I said this, not a muscle in Castelo Branco's face moved and he commented, "Well, we'll see in a day or two." The very next day at six-thirty in the evening he called me on the telephone and asked me whether I had been listening to "The Hour of Brazil," which is a period of government announcements that occurs at six o'clock every evening. I replied that I had not and he then said, "Well, then you don't know whom I appointed as War Minister." I said, "No, I do not." He then said, "I appointed as War Minister the president of Petrobras, Marshal Adémar de Queiroz, and do you have any other good tips for the races on Sunday?" This was about as close as we ever came to discussing internal matters.

On another occasion I had some American visitors who were very interested in population control. They were having dinner with me when Castelo Branco came over. I introduced him and he had a cup of coffee with them, and when he left, one American asked me to give the President some material on population control. I refused absolutely, saying that I could not do this on a number of grounds. First of all, I was a Catholic. Secondly, the President would regard this as intolerable interference with his internal affairs, and third, I thought population control in a country the size of Brazil, with a hundred million inhabitants, was preposterous. And so I did not do it.

Many times I had people, both Brazilians and Americans, hint to me that I should use Castelo Branco's friendship to obtain some sort of information. I indignantly rejected this. It seemed more important to me that he have a good opinion of the United States and of the Army and of me than that I obtain any particular piece of information. And I knew that by asking him for information, by attempting to find out something or to influence him in any way, I would lose his friendship and esteem, and I was determined not to do it. At no time did my Ambassador or any of my superiors ever ask me to do any such thing, other than the single incident of the senator which I have already mentioned.

President Castelo Branco was one of the most extraordinary men I have met in the course of a long career dealing with chiefs of state and other important personalities. His quick mind and his broad grasp of major problems struck me at once. His sardonic sense of humor and his ability to laugh at himself singled him out. As I got to know him better, what struck me perhaps most forcibly about him was his intellectual brilliance, his interest in everything and, above all, his enormous personal integrity. During the war I had occasion to see the combination of strength, firmness and tact he exercised during the period in which the Brazilian Expeditionary Force was completing its training and receiving new equipment with which to fight. In his dealings with the U. S. Army he was firm in demanding that to which he felt the Brazilians were entitled, but always reasonable and never subservient. His ability to introduce a humorous note into a discussion which appeared to be sliding into acrimony together with his complete grasp of what he was handling won him the respect of all the Americans who had dealings with him. They recognized him as a man who would not demand more than his share, but who would never settle for less unless some reasonable explanation could be provided him along with the promise that the Brazilians would subsequently receive that to which they were entitled. In his many contacts with senior

U.S. officers he made a profound impression on them for his brilliance, courage and judgment.

Following the war when the Brazilian Expeditionary Force returned from Italy, I saw a good deal of Colonel Castelo Branco and his family while I was Assistant Military Attaché in Rio. His wife Argentina and my mother became close friends. Both spoke French and retained happy memories of Paris. Dona Argentina Castelo Branco was a beautiful, cultured woman. She and her husband were very close and shared one another's life to an unusual degree. Where Castello was sometimes formal, she was warm and friendly. Between them there was not just love and affection, but also a real camaraderie. During my first lunch with Castelo Branco after he became President, he said to me, "Here I am where I never expected to be and sitting in a seat I have not sought." I quoted Mr. Truman to him: When you are President, the only future you have is in the memory of the people. He agreed thoughtfully and said that this was indeed so. Then I told him about the card on Mr. Truman's desk which said, "The buck stops here." In Portuguese the sense of the word "buck" is conveyed by the word "pineapple" because it is prickly wherever you try to get hold of it. I then gave him a life-sized wooden pineapple appropriately and realistically painted. He smiled and asked why I gave it to him and I said that I felt it would symbolize that he now had to handle the largest and prickliest pineapple in Brazil. He laughed and acknowledged the truth of this observation.

The years of the presidency did not greatly change Castelo Branco. Perhaps the loss of his wife and his election to the presidency made him more lonely, although he always enjoyed his children and their children. His dry sense of humor never left him. He was ironic and self-deprecating. I never addressed him other than as "Mr. President." I never gave him a public *abraço* again after he became President. I held my distance and behaved as the U. S. Military Attaché should behave in the presence of the President of Brazil. When on his last day as President he invited me to dine with him, I said that this might be used against him. He replied with a smile, "They have accused you of having the first lunch with me. Now all they can say is that you also had the last supper with me." I went. I saw him even more often after he left the presidency. He was organizing his papers. The one theme of which he often spoke was that he had not shrunk from doing many unpopular things, particularly in the economic field, in order to ensure the stability and prosperity of Brazil in the years ahead. He joked about the attacks on him as he did about his own physical appearance. He was notoriously ugly. He felt quite capable of living with both burdens and did so serenely. On the night I left Brazil several months after he had left the presidency, he came to the dock with his son to see me off and promised to visit me in Paris. This was the last time I was to see him. Several months later in Vietnam, I learned of his tragic death in a plane accident. I had a mass said for him by the chaplain, knowing that he would like to be remembered on the battlefield as a soldier. I sent a message to his children, saying the world had lost a great statesman, Brazil a great leader and I a dear friend. I felt a better man because Humberto de Alencar Castelo Branco, despite the differences of our ages and origins, honored me with his friendship. I valued it all the more because he did not give it lightly.

A revolution broke out in the Dominican Republic. It was headed by a Colonel Francisco Caamano Deno, a far leftist, masquerading as a moderate progressive. He was to show his true colors later when he fled to Castro's Cuba. The junta then governing the Dominican Republic asked for American help and in the light of the Communist takeover a few years earlier in Cuba, President Johnson ordered the U. S. Armed Forces into the Dominican Republic. This temporarily prevented a Communist takeover. However, in a way that forecast the tactics to be used later to paralyze the United States in Vietnam, a great outcry arose in the United States to the effect that Caamano was not a Communist, but a fine progressive. Years later, his wife, whom he abandoned in Madrid while on a trip there from his job as Dominican Military Attaché in London, was to ask me in Paris to get in touch with Caamano's father to ask him for help as the colonel had left her stranded and penniless with children in Spain. Caamano's father did help her. Caamano himself was later to be killed leading a Cuban-based invasion of the Dominican Republic. However, in 1965 there was much agitation in the United States against President Lyndon Johnson's decision to help the Dominican non-Communists. Because of these developments within the United States, the President did not wish to have the United States carry the whole onus for the intervention. The Organization of American States supported the U.S. decision and feelers were put out by the United States to see if the whole matter could not be handled by a peace-keeping force made up of contingents from several of the countries of the hemisphere. Governor Averell Harriman was sent on a trip through the Americas to try and get contributions of contingents for this peace-keeping force. Outside of a few of the smaller Central American republics none of the larger nations responded to the appeal. I was instructed to go to President Castelo Branco of Brazil and tell him in advance the purpose of Mr. Harriman's visit and to try and prepare a favorable atmosphere for that visit. I flew to Brasília to see President Castelo Branco. He listened carefully and indicated sympathy with the idea. He then asked me how many troops would be needed from Brazil. I had no instructions on this and told him so. He asked me to hazard a guess and I said I thought we might ask for several thousand soldiers from Brazil. He then said that he would have to send a message to the Brazilian Congress requesting authorization for such a move. He then looked me right in the eye and said, "Walters, let me make one thing clear. If I do this, it is not to please the United States. It is because another sister American republic is threatened with losing its freedom as we were threatened with losing ours a short time ago. It is for this reason alone that I will ask the Congress to authorize the sending of this force to the Dominican Republic."

Later that day, I met Governor Harriman at the Brasília airport and as he was walking from the plane that had brought him from Rio to the helicopter that the President had sent to take him to the presidential palace, I handed the governor a note on which I had written. "Don't push too hard. The door is open."

The Brazilian Congress authorized the dispatch of the troops and Brazil sent a force of some fifteen hundred men to the Dominican Republic and kept them there for months. They rotated the garrison several times, using their own Brazilian Air Force planes. This was the year when the U. S. Congress decided to reduce military assistance to Brazil by almost exactly the same amount as the Brazilians were spending to maintain this force in the Dominican Republic at our request.

In response to a request from the Organization of American States, President Castelo Branco appointed as the commander of the peace-keeping force a distinguished Brazilian general who had served in Italy during World War II, General Hugo Panasco Alvim. He had commanded a battalion of 155-mm. guns. As commander of the Brazilian contingent, President Castelo Branco named Colonel Carlos de Meira Mattos, a brilliant geopolitician and a gallant company commander in Italy in the Brazilian Expeditionary Force. He had won the Combat Cross, Brazil's highest award for heroism.

The Brazilian President was anxious that all go well on the arrival of the Brazilian contingent, and remembering my service with the Expeditionary Force in Italy, he asked that I go to the Dominican Republic with Colonel Meira Mattos to make the necessary arrangements for the reception of the Brazilian contingent. The Ambassador communicated this request to Washington, where it was approved at the White House and State Department. I boarded a plane in Rio with Meira Mattos and after a bomb scare aboard, we made it safely to Panama, where we were to be briefed at the headquarters of the U. S. Southern Command. We were received most cordially by Commander General Robert Porter, a great soldier and a great human being. He had said two things to me on previous occasions that profoundly affected my life. He had said, "When you run yourself or anyone else at top pressure, you get the most but hardly ever the best." Another statement of his that had left its mark on me was "When you run your subordinates scared, you gener-

ally get back the echo of what they think you want to hear and
only rarely a creative idea." After our talks with him, he gave us
a military aircraft to fly Meira Mattos and me to the Dominican
Republic. We boarded the aircraft and as we taxied out to the
runway, the pilot received a message from the tower and
stopped. A jeep drove out to us and when we opened the door to
find out what the message was, a major in the jeep said to me,
"General Walters, you are to remain in Panama and Colonel
Meira Mattos will go on to Santo Domingo. It is an order from
Washington." Meira Mattos expressed surprise when I told him
of this order, then he grinned and said, "You are going to send
me there to face all those gringos by myself." I nodded and said,
"Carlos, orders are orders." I shook hands with him and wished
him luck. I climbed out of the plane and drove back with the
major to the headquarters of the Southern Command. Meira
Mattos then took off for the Dominican Republic, where he
served with great distinction, winning the high regard of all his
American colleagues. I then tried to find out the source and
reason for the order for me not to go to the Dominican
Republic. All I could ascertain was that the order had emanated
from the small high-level group that President Johnson had sent
to the Dominican Republic to oversee the situation there. This
small group was composed of Secretary of the Army Cyrus
Vance and Ambassadors Ellsworth Bunker and Tapley Bennett.
I was baffled by the order because only a few days previously the
White House itself had authorized me to accompany Colonel
Meira Mattos to that unhappy country. To this day I have never
been able to find out who was responsible for the order that
took me off the plane. It posed a difficult problem of "face" for
me in trying to explain to President Castelo Branco why his
wish was not fulfilled. General Porter helped me greatly by sending me to Norfolk to see the admiral there who was the theater
commander. I could then say that he wanted to know what the
Brazilian troops would be like, what would be the state of their
training and equipment. The Brazilians behaved very well in the
Dominican Republic and their presence there helped, as Castelo
Branco hoped it would, a sister nation to resist a brutal Commu-

nist takeover and to find its way to stable, orderly democratic government again. Brazil, too, had taken another step onto the world stage beyond that of pure power. Castelo Branco had said that as Brazil grew in power it would also have to shoulder its share of responsibility. Brazil could not stand idly by and watch a sister nation lose her freedom.

During the remainder of my tour in Brazil, I traveled extensively around the country by road and by river boat. In 1965 I drove the new road from Rio de Janeiro to Belém at the mouth of the Amazon. This was a fascinating trip through a hinterland that had only just been opened by the road and the vision of Juscelino Kubitschek, the great Brazilian President, who dreamed of the greater Brazil of tomorrow. He built Brasília and helped make it a reality. The road was almost as deep in places as it was wide. It was rutted, unpaved, primitive, with precarious and rickety bridges and unbelievably modest accommodations along the whole two thousand miles. I loved every mile of it.

I drove extensively into western Mato Grosso and the area along the Bolivian border. All of these journeys were made in a truck with a low gear ratio, four-wheel drive and a winch and cable on the front. When stuck, I could pay out this cable, wrap it around a tree and then winch the truck out of whatever swamp or morass in which I found myself. Without that winch I could not have made it. On one occasion I flew to Asunción in Paraguay and took a tiny river boat for three days upstream to Corumbá in western Mato Grosso, returning from there to Rio in a three-day train journey. I drove to the far south, the state of Rio Grande do Sul, and drove along the Argentine and Uruguayan borders, occasionally watching small ostriches racing me along the side of the road. I crisscrossed the impoverished and drought-stricken northeast and drove all along the long coast. Finally, I made the longest trip of all. I drove from Rio, through Brasília, to Cuiabá. Here there is a marker that indicates that this is the geographic center of the South American continent. On I drove through Mato Grosso to Rio Branco, the capital of Brazil's westernmost state of Acre. This covered some 3,500 miles on incredibly primitive track. I made this trip with two lieutenant colonels. One was Rubens Negreiros, a Brazilian and a great traveling companion, never fazed, always ready with a funny story to lighten the more difficult moments. Tom Lynch of the U. S. Army was my other companion. Steady, unflappable and resourceful, he was never at a loss or dismayed. All along this immense distance we stayed with or were supplied by small detachments of the Brazilian Army's 5th Engineer Battalion. These men won my undying admiration. Living under the most primitive and lonely conditions which they gladly shared with us, they showed pride in what they were doing and in the fact that they were engaged in nation-building in the very best sense of the word. They were always invariably hospitable and friendly. The devotion of these young soldiers and officers was really inspiring. They were always glad to see us. Not many generals of any army came that way. Before I left Rio, a friend asked me how far I was going toward the Peruvian border. I replied that I was going until the Amazon forest grew across the road. Forty-three kilometers west of Rio Branco, near the Miguel Couto School, the trees grew across the road and I had reached the end of this longest road and reluctantly had to turn back.

I sailed for four days down the mighty "River Sea," as the Indians call the Amazon. I sailed from Manaus, a thousand miles inland, to Belém at the mouth of the river. This mighty river dwarfs all others. Almost half of the fresh water flowing to the sea in the world is flowing in this mighty system. There is an island in the river—Marajó—which is larger than Belgium or Switzerland. A thousand miles from its mouth the river is twenty miles wide. Along the whole four thousand miles of its course from its source in Peru to the sea, a man has thrown neither bridge nor dam across it. We will feel the sands of Mars crunch beneath our boots before we tame this greatest of all rivers.

Finally, on a paddle-wheel steamer built in Pittsburgh in 1865, disassembled, carried into the interior of Brazil in pieces and then reassembled, there I sailed down the São Francisco River for nine days. Here again, we moved centuries into the past. I was trying to see something of Brazil other than its mighty urban centers. I sought to learn something of its rural and primitive interior. It was truly a fascinating experience that cannot be repeated because paved roads and mighty power stations have changed many of these areas. But I saw these things at a time when it was an adventure to get there.

President Castelo Branco felt that he should not get himself involved in the process of the selection of his successor. He was outflanked by his War Minister, General Costa e Silva, who was very popular in the Army. He declared his candidacy and won the support of the majority party, the ARENA. Castelo Branco was thus forced to accept Costa e Silva as his successor even though this was probably not the man he would have chosen to succeed himself if he had been entirely free. Castelo Branco withstood all pressures to remain in office himself. He felt that no man was indispensable and that change was healthy.

Following Costa e Silva's election to the presidency, I accompanied the President-elect on a trip from Honolulu around the United States. We stopped at Los Angeles and since Costa e Silva and his wife Dona Yolanda were very fond of horse racing, we went to Santa Anita race track. During a lunch there he noticed that one of the horses on the board had particularly strong odds against him. He told me to go place a bet for him on this horse. Our host in Los Angeles pointed out that this horse had never won a race. Costa e Silva replied, "Yes, but the Bible says that the last shall be first. Walters, go put twenty dollars on that horse for me." The horse won and the President-elect was delighted. The next day was Sunday and the President-elect wanted to go to church. We went to the Church of the Good Shepherd in Beverly Hills. The priest went up into the pulpit to deliver his sermon. His theme was "And the last shall be first." Costa e Silva leaned forward in his pew and gave me a long look. As we left the church, he said to me, "Walters, I have seen organization before but never anything like that." I protested that I had nothing whatever to do with the sermon but I do not believe that I ever succeeded in convincing him. Costa e Silva was a good soldier, a kindly, thoughtful man. He had a way with people though he was not an intellectual in the usual sense of the word. I liked him very much.

While we were in Washington and just before he was to see President Johnson, the President-elect asked me whether I wanted to remain in Brazil. If so he would talk to President Johnson about it. I thanked him and told him that I had been in Brazil for four and a half years on this tour, and that I had made a commitment to myself and to the U. S. Army that I would go to Vietnam before my next assignment in Paris. I therefore asked him not to speak to President Johnson about it. As a soldier he understood. While in Washington he went to Arlington Cemetery to lay a wreath on the Tomb of the Unknown Soldier. He visited the museum there and noted that Britain had bestowed the Victoria Cross, its highest decoration, on the Unknown Soldier, France had given him her Legion of Honor, and many other countries had done likewise. Shortly after his return to Brazil, he told me one day that he was going to "break my monopoly." I asked, "What monopoly, Mr. President?" He answered that I was the only non-Brazilian who had been awarded Brazil's Combat Cross. I was a little annoyed that he should be thinking of giving this medal to someone twenty years after the end of the war. He grinned and said, "You won't really mind. I am giving it to the Unknown Soldier in Arlington Cemetery." Relieved and pleased, I replied that I would be honored to share my monopoly with him.

So it was that I concluded my second mission to Brazil, a country that had exercised such extraordinary influence on my whole life and career. I left that great country with regret, but I have always felt that one should not outstay one's welcome. I had been there nearly five years and felt that it was time to go on to my next mission. I left Brazil confident that that country was moving toward its great destiny that will one day make it one of the superpowers of the world. It has all of the requisites for achieving such status.

21. TO VIETNAM

In the course of my career I have served five times as a Military or Army Attaché. In addition to other qualities it has always seemed to me that an attaché, to be successful, must have some sort of special quality or gimmick. Speaking the local language very well is one such gimmick, but if the attaché remains a long time in the country, he has to develop something new after a while, as his knowledge of the language comes to be taken for granted. For instance, in Brazil I began to travel extensively in the hinterland and distant parts of the country. I used a three-quarter-ton truck since no other vehicle could get where I wanted to go without four-wheel drive, low gear and a winch on the front that could be used to winch oneself out of the mud or the sand. When I heard that I was to go to France as attaché, I felt that in the difficult circumstances I would encounter there I would need something more than a thorough knowledge of the language, which I already had from childhood. I have always believed that an attaché, to be professionally credible, must also be able to talk intelligently about his profession, that is, the profession of arms. If he is an infantry officer, he must be able to talk intelligently about infantry tactics and weapons. If he is an armored officer, he must be able to discuss the characteristics of tanks, muzzle velocity, guns and all of the various aspects of armored warfare. If he does not have the ability to do this, he will be regarded with scorn or suspicion. I had been almost constantly in intelligence assignments and it had required a great deal of homework for me to remain credible in these respects.

Now I was told that I was going to France shortly after the French had withdrawn their forces from the NATO integrated command structure and had requested us to evacuate the bases we had been using in France, for their defense as well as ours. In addition to this, there appeared to have grown up in France a strong conviction that the Americans might not fight for anything other than a direct attack upon themselves. The year 1967 was a time when the U. S. Army was heavily engaged in Vietnam. Almost everyone in the French armed services above the rank of major or lieutenant commander had served at least once and more often than not several times in Vietnam during the French war there that lasted from 1945 to 1954. They would be talking to me about something of which they would have considerable knowledge and about which I would have none. Further, it would seem strange to them that I had moved from attaché to Rome, to Rio de Janeiro and then to Paris without ever going near the war in which almost all of my contemporaries had taken some part. I felt very strongly that for me to go straight from the cocktail circuit in Rio de Janeiro to the cocktail circuit in Paris would put me in an almost intolerable situation as the representative of the U. S. Army, intolerable in my relationship both with the French and with my own American contemporaries, who would share the doubts of the French. To many it might seem that I had somehow arranged to stay out of the Vietnamese war and I was simply not prepared to accept this kind of onus. I sincerely believed that I could not do my best for the United States at a difficult time in Franco-American military relations unless I, too, had shared even briefly the hardships that were being endured by so many Americans. In all, some 2,500,000 Americans were to serve in Vietnam during that long war.

I was being asked in a sense to pick up the fragments of the Franco-American military relationship and do my best to put them together. I would need everything I could muster for this difficult task. I felt it was important for me not to arrive in Paris coming from Rio or even from Washington. It seemed to me that if I were to arrive in Paris coming from Saigon, I would have far more credibility and ability to influence the French military than if I came from either of the two other places. As soon as my assignment to Paris was firm, I discussed this problem with the director of the Defense Intelligence Agency, Lieutenant General Joseph Carroll, who was my immediate superior. I think I failed to convince him of the necessity of my going to Vietnam. He seemed to regard it as an interesting boondoggle, but finally he said that DIA would not pay for my travel there, but if the Army would, then he would let me go. I then discussed this matter with the Chief of Staff of the U. S. Army, General Harold Johnson, and he understood at once and said that the Army would take care of the matter. He would tell General William Westmoreland, the commander in chief in Vietnam, to give me every opportunity to visit various areas and to see different types of operations. General Johnson, who had been captured in the Philippines in 1941 and had survived four years of Japanese captivity, was a figure of great prestige and integrity. I was most grateful to him for his understanding. He also suggested that on my way out I stop off briefly in Korea and see the commander in chief there, General Tick Bonesteel, for whom I had worked in Paris in 1948 at the Marshall Plan. While there was no specific time set, it was understood that I would remain a few months in Vietnam and report to the Paris assignment in the autumn. While I would have preferred to remain longer in Vietnam, this seemed to fulfill my purpose of acquiring some credibility for the job that lay ahead in France.

I felt strongly about participating in the Vietnam War. It seemed to me—and this may shock some of my readers—and it still does, to have been one of the noblest and most unselfish wars in which the United States had ever participated. We had not been attacked as a nation. We stood to gain very little by our participation in that war. All we were trying to do there was to help a small people retain whatever measure of freedom they enjoyed, not perhaps as much as we had, but infinitely more than they were to have when the North Vietnamese finally reached Saigon. I harbored a secret hope that once I got to Vietnam, I could somehow work myself into an assignment there. I think that General Carroll may have sensed this and he wanted me in Paris. This may have been one of the reasons for his lack of enthusiasm for my trip to Vietnam. Later, in awarding me an Air Medal for Vietnam, he was to point out that I had gone there as a volunteer at my own request and over some opposition. I thought this was a rather handsome gesture on his part.

On June 30, 1967, I flew from Seattle to Tokyo on my way to my mission to Vietnam. I spent a few days in Tokyo and then went to Seoul, where I visited General Bonesteel and was briefed on the situation in Korea. I also went up in a helicopter to the demilitarized zone where the North Koreans faced the South Koreans and the Americans. I then flew on to Hong Kong, where I spent two days sight-seeing and shopping. It was the first time I had ever been there. Then, finding that the best way to get into Saigon from Hong Kong was by a commercial flight, I took off from Hong Kong on an Air France plane around noon on July 6. It was a commercial flight directly to Saigon. Someone had told me that the Air France alternative to Saigon was Hanoi. I replied that that would be the case for me. I had a gun with me and I would use it to prevent the aircraft from going to Hanoi. I was traveling in civilian clothes, before the days when passengers were searched. I had my uniform cotton khaki pants, shirt and cap in the clothes bag in the cabin with me and intended to change in flight. We had a very smooth flight over the South China Sea and saw some of the reefs of the Paracel Islands. We came in over land near Danang. At this point, I went to the lavatory on the aircraft and changed into my uniform and came back. The stewardesses were quite startled, as I had been speaking French to them and I do not think it occurred to them that I was an American, much less a U. S. Army general.

I looked down at Vietnam for signs of war and from 35,000 feet I saw none. This was the third time in my life—the fourth if one counts the Greek civil war—in which I was going to a war.

It was a fine trip in bright blue skies over a turquoise sea, the mountainous shore of Vietnam stretched away to the south. Straight inland we flew into the cloud build-up over the disputed land into the thunderstorms that duplicate aloft the thunder that man unleashes below. We dropped down and at 1,500 feet we broke out of the storm clouds and saw the waterlogged plain below us. Parts of it were ours and parts of it were theirs. We circled, obviously in a holding pattern. Saigon's Tan Son Nhut Airport was the busiest in the world. I wondered about ground fire as we came in, but I could see none. We circled over gigantic military installations reminiscent of World War II. Finally, we descended steeply and landed on the runway.

We could see at once that this was not just another commercial airport. Military aircraft sheltered in high concrete revetments were everywhere. I was met at the terminal by friends and a Colonel Jack Morgan, who was to be my shepherd while I was in Vietnam. We drove through the teeming streets into the heart of Saigon. As darkness fell and I got settled, the distant thunder of guns was unmistakably clear, and bright flares illuminated the sky as our troops searched for the Viet Cong around the edges of the city. The sky was never empty of the roar of jets overhead.

The first week I was in Vietnam I spent getting oriented in visiting the units and headquarters in the immediate vicinity of Saigon, calling on senior U.S. and Vietnamese commanders. On the day after my arrival I had gone to the finance office in Cholon, a suburb of Saigon, and had taken my place in line to submit my travel voucher, when a master sergeant came up and took me to a special desk for general officers. I was not used to this kind of treatment and even more surprised when he told me I could come back and get the voucher paid that afternoon. In Saigon, Armed Forces installations ran around the clock. There were no weekends and very little free time. There was no clock-watching, and if there was any grumbling, it escaped me at that time. All of the people to whom I talked seemed to realize the seriousness of our commitment there. Most felt, as I did, that this was perhaps the wrong place to commit the credibility of

the United States, but, for better or for worse, that is where our
political masters had committed it. We were not there to defend the selfish interests of the United States but to uphold the
principles which are an essential part of our heritage. If we were
to abandon them, history would charge us a high price. Several
American Presidents of both parties had sustained the importance of this commitment. On the first day when I was about to
go back to the finance office to get my voucher paid, I received a
phone call in which the caller asked me if I would mind coming
back the next day instead of that afternoon. I said that would be
fine but wondered why. I was told that a Claymore mine had
been detonated in front of the finance office and that had
shaken things up a bit.

Saigon was a city of contrasts. On one day when I had no particular item on my program, I played tennis at the Cercle Spor-
tif, a fine country club left over from the French. That same
night planes dropped flares over the city and the distant
thunder, man-made, rolled across the night. I noticed that out-
door cafes and restaurants were covered with chicken wire
screens to ward off hand grenades casually tossed by Viet Cong
(VC) terrorists. Vast hordes of people on bicycles, scooters and
motorcycles swarmed through the streets. I was told to keep the
windows of my car rolled up lest a passer-by or a motorcyclist
deposit a hand grenade in my lap. Yet my car carried the flag
and single star of a brigadier general. At night what General
MacArthur called the mournful mutter of the battlefield was audible in my room. For twenty years war had been the lot of this
unhappy country and I could not help but ponder the words of
the man who said, "Peace is the dream of the wise, but the history of mankind is war." Alas, how true.

During my week in Saigon I visited the U. S. Army in Vietnam headquarters. I had lunch with an old friend, General
Bruce Palmer. He briefed me on the problems of preparing the
troops that were to be used in the tactical situation. I visited the
Vietnamese Air Force. I visited the Vietnamese Capital Military
District Headquarters. I visited the U. S. Seventh Air Force and
had lunch with its commander, as well as the various foreign mil-

itary attachés accredited to Vietnam. I also visited the naval headquarters in Saigon and talked to the U. S. Embassy people who worked in the socio-political area. I had dinner at the Italian Military Attaché's, whom I had known from my days in Italy, with the sister of Gianni Agnelli, the Fiat automobile magnate. The Countess Ratazzi was very opposed to the U.S. presence in Vietnam with a sense of political commitment and leftist views that the super-rich often feel.

On Sunday, July 16, I flew to Danang to visit the 3rd Marine Amphibious Force commanded by Lieutenant General Robert Cushman, whom I had known when he was Mr. Nixon's military aide on the trip to South America in 1958. A swift two-hour-and-ten-minute flight over the central highlands in a twin-engine U. S. Army U-8 brought me to the northern city before noon. A quick visit to the headquarters of the 3rd Marine Amphibious Force and then out by helicopter to the headquarters of the 1st Marine Division north of the city. Here there were more briefings.

The watchful seriousness of the two young Marine machine gunners on our helicopter told me that "Charlie" was below. As we flew from the 1st Marine Division to the 1st Marine Regiment, we hurtled along less than one hundred feet above the plain below. Moving at this altitude was the best tactic. It is hard for anyone on the ground to have time to take an aimed shot. Both gunners sat watchfully, one at the door in front of me and one at the window alongside me. Their cartridge belts were inserted and their fingers were on the trigger. Both of them were wearing the armored flak jackets that are regularly worn by personnel in this kind of job. Behind us with equal watchfulness flew another helicopter, the gunship that must accompany all general officers. Among the general officers there was a story that if you were forced down the real purpose of this helicopter was to shoot you so that you would not fall alive into the Viet Cong's hands. We were told, however, that the official purpose was to pick you up in case your helicopter was forced down.

We landed at the fortified command post of the 1st Marine Regiment and the commander told us that he did not think I was aboard because he did not think the helicopter pilot would fly like a fighter pilot with a general aboard. He then described the situation of his regiment and each of his young staff officers told me what they did. A spirited young major from the Reconnaissance Battalion told me how his outfit sent out patrols far behind the enemy lines. He described in detail how they went in or were "inserted," what they did and how they came out. He told me that a patrol was going out the next day. This patrol came in, commanded by a young Naval Academy graduate. In camouflaged uniforms and with darkened faces, the young Marines filed in. Each presented his weapon and told me what he did. They had been out on such patrols before. On the following day they were going out again. I thought, "What shall I say to these young men who, more than most, fight our country's battles?" I congratulated them on past successes, told them a joke and wished them well. They saluted and marched off. And as they went I could not help but feel a tightening in my throat.

Back to our helicopter, we lifted off the pad, up several thousand feet, and spiraled around and around over the regimental command post. There are mountains and in this area the safest tactic is for the helicopter pilots to fly so high that aiming was difficult for the Viet Cong below. Soon we were at a battalion command post. Down the valley we saw the artillery bursting on the VC positions. Lieutenant Colonel John D. Conzelman greeted us and led us to his battalion command post installed in an old French fort high on a hill at the curve of a river. Dai Loc was its name. It had never been taken by assault. We watched his operation unfolding before us. He spoke of his problems. He, too, showed the same confident spirit and pride that we have come to expect from the Marines. His operation, combined with that of two Vietnamese battalions, was going well. We left him, lifted off the helicopter pad and climbed high, heading back to Danang. As we came into Danang the results of the rocket attack staged the day before on the airfield showed clearly. The destruction was quite apparent but already replacements for the aircraft were there. Unfortunately, however, a number of young airmen died while fighting the fires set by Charlie's sneak attack. Back to the 3rd Marine Amphibious Force, where we had dinner and went to bed early, for the next day was a full one. I reflected just before I fell asleep that a good part of my day had been spent flying over areas held by the Viet Cong and yet I felt more pride than fear.

On the following day I attended a briefing at the 3rd Marine Amphibious Force, which is really a corps. Following that I was briefed on the revolutionary development program and taken out to see an operation in a small hamlet ten miles south of Danang. Here, the team leader described it to me in Vietnamese through an interpreter. He told me that what he was trying to do was to offer a new life to the villages and thereby commit them to the Vietnamese government. Then I saw a combined action platoon in which twelve American Marines and twelve Vietnamese soldiers lived, worked and fought together. This was a program devised by the Marines to motivate the Vietnamese. It had shown terrific results when proper support had been forthcoming through the Vietnamese channels. No Vietnamese had ever deserted one of these units. Sixty per cent of the Marines serving in such units had voluntarily extended their thirteen-month tour in Vietnam. When one knew how much that thirteen-month tour meant to them (twelve months for the Army and Air Force), one realizes the full impact of such a figure.

I went to lunch at the home of Ambassador Bill Koren, who headed the program in this area. That afternoon I visited the offices of the senior U. S. military adviser with the Vietnamese I Corps. We boarded his helicopter and flew north over the Hai Van Pass, north of Danang, where a convoy had been ambushed the day before; on over Hué, the imperial capital; and over much territory held by the North Vietnamese—but they gave no indication of their presence. On north to the provincial capital of Quang Tri, later to be the scene of very bloody fighting. Still farther north we flew, past the much-shelled town of Dong Ha. On still closer to the demilitarized zone which divided the two Vietnams. Suddenly below us was the utterly destroyed village of Gio Linh and there, gleaming in the glorious afternoon sunshine, was the silver ribbon of the Ben Hai River, which was the boundary between the two contending parts of Vietnam. Directly ahead lay the bridge over the river. At its north end, a gigantic red flag abutted from a flagpole and defiantly at the southern end of the bridge was an equally huge gold and red Republic of Vietnam flag flying from an equally tall flagpole. By some unwritten mutual consent neither side shot down the other's flag, yet a thousand yards to the east or west there was mortal combat. The pilot evidently sensed my concern at being so close to North Vietnam and assured me that we were at "optimum altitude"—too high for effective small arms fire and too low to enter the danger area of the surface-to-air missile envelope.

We turned west and flew along a no man's land where the North Vietnamese and the Marines clashed by day and by night, over the bloodied town of Con Thien which was finally in the Marines' hands. South we flew to the resettlement village of Cam Lo. Here we landed our helicopter and walked into the village to visit an extraordinary Vietnamese Catholic priest, Father Ko. He had led his flock south from North Vietnam in 1954 when the Communists took over. Here he had resettled thirteen hundred villagers, built a chapel, a dispensary, a school. On the steps of the rickety chapel I found a hundred refugees—women, children and old men—who had just arrived from the ruined town of Gio Linh over which I had flown earlier in the day. I asked Father Ko in French, which he spoke fluently, what he was going to do with them. He said that on the following day he would try and lodge them but that night since they were God's children they would sleep in God's house, the chapel. The man's dedication and courage were moving. I left him all the Vietnamese piasters I had with me. He said that a majority of the villages around, outside of his flock of course, were VC sympathizers. We left him and flew back to Dong Ha, which had been under almost constant shellfire; we dropped down on the pad where, because of the intermittent shellfire, one had to refuel one's own aircraft. It was the first self-service gas pump I had seen in Vietnam. After refueling, we flew south back to

Danang and had dinner that night with Admiral Paul Lacy, Jr., who commanded the Naval Support Agency in Danang.

Then I went back to my quarters and reflected. The strange nature of this war, the constant flying over enemy-held territory led me to the conclusion that in the two days I had been with the III Marine Corps, I spent more time flying over enemy territory than in the whole of World War II. I felt better; perhaps I was earning my hostile-fire pay of $65 a month.

The following day I boarded a helicopter and flew across to Danang Air Base. There I boarded a C-130 Transport and flew north. The plane was filled with Marines, eager, worried replacements and veterans returning from leave. We touched down briefly at Phu Bai, a base near Hué, and flew on north to the much-shelled town of Dong Ha. Here I was met by Brigadier General John Metzger, the assistant division commander of the 3rd Marine Division. A dynamic figure, he asked me what I wanted to see and I told him that I wanted to see anything he could show me. We then boarded a UH-1E helicopter and flew east to the coast, flying low over the Marine Amphibious Vehicles Battalion. This unit patrolled north to the demilitarized zone and kept traffic moving from the mouth of the river to the port of Dong Ha. Then we flew north again to the bridge over the Ben Hai. That day the ground below was quieter and the puff of shells bursting below was not to be seen as it had been on the previous day.

Once again we flew along the front to Con Thien, the troops there deeply dug in to defend their position on a 360° perimeter. The Viet Cong were all around, but the trucks, escorted by tanks, roared up the dusty supply road leading north into the village. Then we turned south and landed at the command post of the 9th Marine Regiment. Here another fortified perimeter with tanks dug in. One tank crew was using the depressed barrel of the tank to support the shelter-half under which the crew slept. Another had his washing hung to dry from his gun barrel. The young Marines were mostly under twenty. They seemed cheerful and unconcerned. The general joked with them and they replied in kind. Colonel John Jarue told us of his regiment's situation.

Nearby new replacements were firing their pistols and the M-16 rifle. Newspaper reports notwithstanding, the Marines seemed to like this rifle. They said all you had to do was keep it clean. Then we lifted off the pad and flew southwest to Camp Carroll, where huge Army 175-mm. guns, dug in with a company of Marines in close support, were firing across the Ben Hai. This position had been attacked repeatedly by the North Vietnamese, yet once again we found the same spirit of easy banter and good humor that is the earmark of high morale. The Army gunners and the Marine infantrymen may have heard stories of interservice rivalry but it played little part there.

We lifted off that pad and flew west toward the bloody position of Khe Sanh, up the valley into the jungle-covered hills. In the middle of the valley a weird rocky mountain jutted suddenly skyward, on its jagged peak my unbelieving eyes saw a tiny helicopter pad built of wood. We dropped unerringly onto it. Here again, a young Marine lieutenant with twenty-five Marines commanded superb observation all up and down the valley. Alongside the platform were the bunks of the Marines and I gazed at these with astonishment, for it seemed to me that if anyone rolled out of bed on the wrong side, he could roll down to the foot of the mountain. The young Marines were astonished to see not one but two generals get out of the helicopter. One of them surreptitiously tried to take our picture with a miniature camera. General Metzger told him to get up on the platform. Sheepishly, he got up, expecting to be reprimanded. Instead, General Metzger stood him between us and told another Marine to take our picture. Then he had his picture taken between a Marine general and an Army general. The lieutenant told us that if only he had better field glasses he could observe much more accurately what was going on in the valley. General Metzger promised him a pair before sundown. We climbed perilously onto the platform and lifted off. We flew farther west toward Khe Sanh and beyond it we could see our artillery falling on a hilltop. Khe Sanh was a very isolated position, an island of Marines in the middle of territory held by the North Vietnamese. In fact, it was to sustain successfully an epic siege a

As attaché, with Jacqueline Kennedy during her stopover at Rome airport, 1961.

Averell Harriman arrives in Rio de Janeiro in November 1965, following our intervention in the Dominican Republic. With me to greet him was Sylvan Loupe, Administrative Counselor of the U. S. Embassy, Paris.

Mekong, July 1967

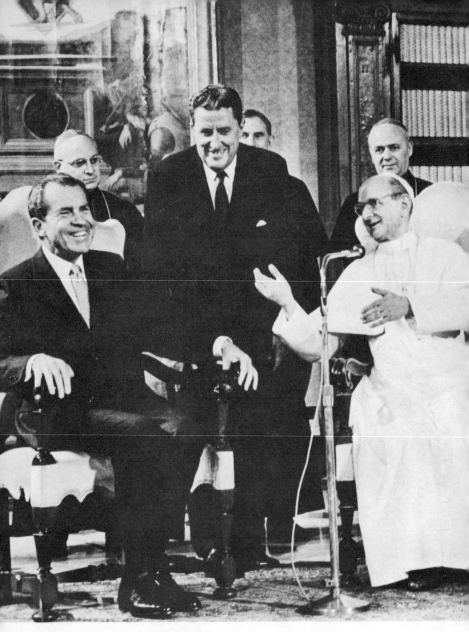

The Vatican, February 1968. *(Wide World)*

Maurice Chevalier and I escort Mme. Giscard d'Estaing and Eunice Kennedy
Shriver to the Paris Opéra.

French President Pompidou visits President Nixon in the Oval Office, 1970. At left, Pompidou's interpreter, Prince Andronikof.

Paris, 1971. A lighter moment with Soviet Military Attaché Colonel Stepan Sinitsine.

Arriving in the Azores with President Nixon, December 1971. Portuguese Prime Minister Caetano is with us.

Deputy director of Central Intelligence, May 2, 1972. My sister Mrs. Laureen
Masini holds the Bible.

The Oval Office. Presentation of
the National Security Medal.

year later. We dipped down for a landing and walked around the camp. It, too, had a mined barbed-wire perimeter, but in the PX I found color film. After a brief talk with the battalion commander there we lifted off again and flew a short distance farther up the valley to bloodily contested Hill 881. Here a company of Marines held the farthest west position of the division. We landed on their position. A young captain, the company commander, greeted us and through his glasses showed us his patrol outside his position to the west. This was the first time I had been in a company position in a combat situation in some years. Despite their isolation and the danger, for the wooded hills around were infested with North Vietnamese, I found the same morale and the same spirit. We talked to these young Marines for a while and they were obviously pleased to have visitors.

The captain said he must patrol vigorously, it was his only protection against the surprise mass attack that could overrun his position. To see these young American fighting men in this lonely, exposed and dangerous position and to see how they reacted to their circumstances filled me with pride. We lifted off and flew back to Dong Ha. General Metzger showed me where shell fragments ripped through his shower and across the top of his bed. Fifty feet away two Army officers were killed by a direct hit from a shell fired from across the Ben Hai River.

We had dinner that night with General Bruno Hochmuth, a tall, distinguished officer who commanded the division. He was wounded in the shelling just described. We visited the hospital and the surprise and pleasure of the wounded Marines at being visited by their division commander were evident. Then we went out to our own chopper, and as we did, we passed the morgue of the Graves Registration Company—a grim reminder of the cost of war. We lifted off the field at shell-torn Dong Ha and headed south. We flew past the old imperial capital of Hué with General Hochmuth. I was surprised we were flying at about 150 or 200 feet, which seemed to me to be a not favorable altitude. Generally one flies at several thousand feet or on the deck, as the expression goes, a few feet above the treetops or the ground.

I was told that this was General Hochmuth's normal practice; shortly after my trip with him, he was killed when his helicopter crashed, possibly after being hit by ground fire. We flew past Hué, the old capital, and saw the imperial tombs of the emperors of Annam. A glance backward showed that our "playmate," the accompanying gunship, was with us, its machine guns at the ready.

We landed at Phu Bai and I went over to my scheduled plane, an old C-47, and found it filled with combat-weary Marines on their way to leave. The sergeant told me that he had no more room but if I wanted, he would pull two of the Marines off. I shook my head and told him that I would find another ride. A little while later, I did hop a ride in an Air Force C-123. A troop of Vietnamese girl entertainers got aboard and the tired Marines clutching their rifles grinned at them and settled back as we took off for the short flight to Danang. I went to the Marine Air Group, where they showed me the grim damage of a deadly rocket attack on July 14. I watched with mixed curiosity and apprehension as a five-hundred-pound bomb was attached to the wing of an F-4. I photographed a Cougar for my sixteen-year-old nephew, whose favorite plane this was. Then we flew to Marble Mountain just south of Danang to visit the helicopter wing. This strange outcropping of rock rose from a flat beach near the ocean. All around it were helicopter pads. It, too, was to have its time of shelling and rocketing. Then we went back to the 3rd Marine Air Base and over to dinner with General Charles S. Robertson of the 1st Marine Division. We spoke of the morale of his men. He told me that 21 per cent of his Marines volunteered to extend their tour in Vietnam. We believed that these were some of the finest soldiers that America ever fielded. I felt that those who worried about the next generation should see their sons here, their weary, cheerful, gallant sons. A quick chopper ride back to the 3rd Marine Amphibious Force. This was my first nighttime helicopter ride in a combat area. Danang with its huge military complexes glittered below. The moon was so bright that we cast a shadow on the ground and only the flickering man-made lightning to the west and north spoke of the mortal struggle so close at hand.

Then I flew in a Marine Grumman to Chu Lai, twenty minutes south of Danang. The air traffic around Danang Base was so heavy that coming in and out was always a matter of some concern to me. The first plane we tried wouldn't start so we got another one. We flew down over the North Vietnamese-held coast at about 2,500 feet and landed at the big base at Chu Lai. It, too, bore the marks of war, everything dug in and sandbagged. It had been mortared but without the spectacular results that they were able to achieve at Danang. We took off in a helicopter and flew to the headquarters of Task Force Argone, a composite unit that was really an Army division and later was organized as such. We had lunch and a briefing there with General Richard Knowles, whom I had known previously. He was six feet four and a half inches tall and looked very much the way a division commander should look. After a lunch consisting of a bowl of soup and a grilled cheese sandwich with Jell-O for dessert, we flew in his chopper to the headquarters of Company B of the 31st Infantry. Dug in on a hillock, the company position looked like a pueblo in Arizona or New Mexico, but instead of adobe the houses were made of sandbags. I was met by Brigadier Commander General Frank Norrell, whom I had also known before. He introduced his intelligence officer, a major who particularly wanted to meet me. The company commander then briefed us on his situation while watchful sentries with their rifles at the ready scanned the surrounding countryside for "Charlie," unseen but there. It was a quiet day and many of the soldiers were enjoying the warm sun, but the sandbags and slit trenches were sharp reminders that this was no holiday. The brigade was building a road to enable the fishermen to get their produce back to the consuming centers but they were constantly harassed by the rifle fire of snipers and by mines planted in the road. I went down to the little hamlet to see the combined action platoon, in which the Marines and the local popular forces defended the village. A young sergeant by the name of Sennef led the platoon. The Army men finally convinced him that he should go to Army Officers Candidate School. He was not yet twenty. The platoon built two bunkers of sandbags at the edge of the hamlet and the villagers built two more. Sergeant Sennef almost completed the dispensary he planned to treat the villagers to. His current dispensary was a miserable room in a shack. He told us that there was a plague scare in the hamlet and he had immunized all of the villagers. Then I walked through the village. Nearby a VC suddenly jumped out and shot an Army sergeant, but I walked through the village and all I saw was a little girl, age five or six, playing with another little girl of the same age a game with small round stones. I picked them up and showed her several tricks with them. Sergeant Sennef asked me where I learned the Vietnamese game. I didn't. They were just tricks I sometimes did with coins. The little girl was shy, she hid her face behind her hands and peered at me through her fingers. As I walked through the village, it seemed that a sewing machine was some kind of a status symbol. Almost every hut had someone seated in front with a sewing machine. There were five kerosene refrigerators in this tiny hamlet. I looked over my shoulder and observed that we were being followed by a jeep with a 106-mm. recoilless rifle. The Viet Cong were only just beyond the edge of the barbed-wire enclosure surrounding the hamlet. These were islands in the countryside around which security grew for the people.

We toured General Knowles' area and then flew back to Chu Lai, boarded our Grumman, and as we neared Danang I could hear in my headset that one of the C-130s I could see in the landing pattern had an emergency. He peeled off and headed for the runway; his hydraulic system had failed and he might need arresting gear to stop him at the end of the runway. I watched anxiously but his landing was smooth and he taxied over to the operations tower. We came into the crowded traffic pattern and landed.

Over to the 3rd Marine Amphibious Force, back to Danang to see a trawler sent down from North Vietnam which had been captured—brand-new Chinese machine guns, three thousand Soviet rifles and masses of other equipment, the sort of booty that one would pick up at a major victory. Back again to the 3rd Marine Amphibious Force. Once again to the 31st Regiment's company headquarters. I saw the same kind of young men I had seen on the previous day with the Marines, American soldiers and proud of it. They, at least, knew why they were here. America meant something to them beyond the geographic expression. Its values were their values. It was so real and so precious to them that every day and every night they were prepared to lay down their young lives for it. Too little credit has been given to them for this. Too much attention has been paid to the oddballs who have made trouble. The sad thing is that in Vietnam most of those killed were twenty; the next most numerous group was nineteen. Most of these kids were not rich, they came from the average American home. As we flew to Danang the young airman aboard confided that he had just voluntarily extended his tour in Vietnam for another thirty days. These men knew the reality of war, they were not children blinded by glamour. They had watched the dead piled on the Army personnel carriers. They had seen the maimed and the blind. But instinctively they knew what they must do if America was to remain what they wanted it to be.

After this tour in the north, I went down to the area of the delta of the Mekong River. Early on the morning of July 21, I boarded a U-8 twin-engined aircraft at Tan Son Nhut Airport and flew to Can Tho in the delta. Most of the flight as usual was over VC- or North Vietnamese-controlled territory. We landed at Can Tho, a surprisingly big town, and went to see the senior U.S. adviser with the Vietnamese IV Corps which had its headquarters there, a General Desobry. Then I called on General Minh, the Vietnamese corps commander, who spoke excellent French, and we had a good talk. I visited the 13th Aviation Battalion, which provided helicopters and light aviation support throughout the delta. Later I visited an air base and went out on the river with the Navy in one of their fast Patrol-Boat River Craft. This was a really interesting experience. The boats were lightly armored but heavily armed and they were most effective against the Viet Cong. It was an interesting trip out, firing at targets ashore, and then back to Can Tho for dinner that night. The night was quiet and only occasionally could we hear the distant grumble of artillery.

The next morning we flew after some delay across the water-logged delta—this was the rainy season—to the little town of My Tho, where we visited the senior U.S. adviser to the 7th Vietnamese Infantry Division. This division commander, like so many others, spoke good French, and after lunch at the little American compound, we flew by helicopter to the little provincial capital of Go Cong. I asked jokingly whether this was a name or a slogan. We were taken around by the Nisei U.S. security adviser and also saw the Spanish medical Army team there. I spoke to them and thanked them for making Spain present on this battlefield of freedom. They were delighted to have an American visitor who could speak Spanish. I had some sherry with them and then flew by chopper to the little village of Hoa Binh, where we visited a village in which a revolutionary development team was at work. They were called New Life Villages and it was the purpose of these teams to lead these villages to a new life and thus win them from the Viet Cong or the North Vietnamese. The young Americans, civilians and military, with them were terrific. The local Vietnamese "Dai Uy," or captain, was a dedicated officer. From there we flew into the strongly Viet Cong province of Kien Hoa to the little town of Ba Tri, where we visited the headquarters of the Vietnamese battalion. The commander, Major Ninh, also spoke excellent French and appeared to be an energetic and dedicated officer. From there I flew on to the village of Giong Trong and visited the young American adviser there, Major Bolton. We also met a young Vietnamese lieutenant who commanded the artillery section of 105-mm. guns. A fine young State Department section chief named Burnham flew with us and we dropped him off at Ben Tre and flew back to My Tho.

After dinner we went up to the third story of the building to watch the artillery and small arms fire not far off. Puff, the Magic Dragon—a C-47 plane with three Gatling guns that fired eighteen thousand rounds a minute—breathed his fiery breath on the enemy in the distance. It looked almost like a bolt of lightning coming down in slow motion. The war in the delta was much more elusive and invisible than up north, but it was present everywhere. After dinner, firing was almost continuous and the crackle of small arms was audible.

One thing was the same in the delta as up north with the Marines, and that was the morale and spirit of the American soldiers. They had left the most comfortable and affluent life of which history has record, and were a real credit to the nation. They had come halfway across the world to this alien struggle, and in a war-torn land unsupported by their own press, attacked as criminals by many in the media and by protesters at home, they were doing their duty with lighthearted banter and it was a moving sight to me. I went to bed that night at My Tho only to be awakened about 1 A.M. by the thunder of artillery and the crackle of small arms. I got up and went out to see what was happening. On the command radio net we learned that the VC were attacking the U.S. camp under construction nearby. They then attacked a Vietnamese battalion nearby. Flares began to light the night sky and at one time I counted fifteen of them in the sky at once. We could hear the Dragon Ship pilots asking the ground controllers for the co-ordinates of targets and we could see the navigation lights on the tails of the aircraft as they dived down on the target. Suddenly that awesome tongue of fire would lash down from the sky. These Dragon Ships, called Spookies by some, saved many a beleaguered outpost. It was a tremendous spectacle and it went on right in front of us until three in the morning; then the fight petered out.

Next day I flew in a Huey helicopter which I had used continuously around the delta to see several companies and villages. It was a great way to get around. I usually rode in the right-hand seat next to the door, which was generally open. It was quite a thrill to look down a couple of thousand feet at the ground below, but instinctively one checked to make sure that one's seat belt was tightened and somehow the left buttock seemed to be carrying a lot more weight than the right cheek, which was on the outside. This chopper could carry nine men, including the pilot, co-pilot and two machine gunners. In the many isolated positions and villages I visited, I saw these terrific U. S. Army officers and soldiers briefing and advising the locals as well as defending them. After about ten stops I flew to Sadec. All of the flying was over territory that was mostly held by the Viet Cong. I had dinner with the Americans at Sadec and after dinner I watched a movie, a crazy Italian-made Western called *A Gun for Ringo* which was lots of fun. The soldiers who were off duty changed into civilian clothes to watch it. Here were these men who only a short time before had been out in the countryside fighting Charlie getting a great kick out of watching people shooting one another on the screen.

Meanwhile back at Sadec in the Mekong Delta, things were quiet. The night I spent there was, I think, one of the few nights in Vietnam when I did not hear artillery or any other sound of the war. The next day I flew by chopper to Soc Trang in the southeast delta. Here we landed at a Vietnamese division headquarters just as two battalions of Vietnamese troops were about to be lifted in U.S. helicopters into an area infested with the Viet Cong. Here I took part in my first combat mission in Vietnam. From the ground I watched forty U.S. helicopters lift the first wave. Then we took off and passed them on the way to the landing zone, which had been marked by liaison planes with smoke. We circled a few hundred feet above the ground and watched the Vietnamese Air Force strike the targets around the landing zone. Then we saw the first wave of helicopters go in and land the tough little Vietnamese soldiers into the rice paddies, where they jumped out of the choppers. They were immediately waist-high in the water, as most of them were only about five feet tall. Then as the helicopters brought in the second wave, we went down and landed with them. It was spectacular. The little Vietnamese soldiers jumped out of the choppers and moved out toward their objectives. Anybody who believed they would not fight had simply never seen them. Shortly after we landed the Viet Cong mortared the immediate area, and since I had my camera with me, I was able to get some good moving pictures of this incoming mortar fire. As the attack continued, we took off again and circled the landing zone. There was not much enemy fire in the area around the landing zone. The VC were somewhat appalled at having two battalions dropped on them out of the sky.

That morning I went to mass in Sadec and for the first time since World War II heard the priest give the congregation conditional absolution, which is done only under war circumstances. Later in the day we went to places like Vi Thanh, a provincial town where a small group of Americans advised the local Vietnamese garrison. We controlled nearly all the towns and villages in the delta to a degree I had not imagined before I came there. In these towns, three, four, five Americans lived among the Vietnamese and the VC were unable to do anything against them.

On July 27 I flew to Phu Loi north of Saigon, where I visited an Army aviation battalion and was enormously impressed by the large numbers of aircraft they had. I visited other units at length. The aircraft were all in revetments, as were the artillery pieces. There was no way I could know that very night they were to be mortared and men killed and wounded. They also lost some aircraft. Both these units gave an impression of efficiency and businesslike thoroughness. I flew west in my helicopter to the huge base camp of the U.S. 25th Division at Cuchi. As we came in I was struck by the size of the camp; it looked almost as large as one of the major installations in the United States.

We landed and drove to the division headquarters for the afternoon briefing. I met General John C. Tillson, the quiet, effective division commander. Following the briefing, I was told that I would go to a town that had just been freed from Viet Cong control after three years of occupation. A day earlier it would have been unsafe. Now we could see the town being reorganized for defense and a large number of houses were being razed and the inhabitants resettled in the southern part of town where they could be kept under observation. As we approached Phu Hoa Ben in our helicopter, it had a grim look, and as we landed on the small helipad at the edge of town, it was soon apparent that everything was not normal. My jeep was followed by two jeeps loaded with soldiers, and one with a crew-served machine gun. We drove slowly through the town and the faces of the villagers were masks that showed neither friendliness nor hostility, simply inscrutability. At the edge of town an infantry company was constructing a position for itself and one two-gun section of 105-mm. guns was digging a position for itself surrounded by earth and barbed wire. In answer to my inquiry the company commander said that sometimes the VC came out of the woods to the south of his position and took pot shots at either his men or the engineers who were helping them. We came back through Phu Hoa Ben, past the stolid, staring inhabitants, and the tension was thick. As we entered the square, there on the ground lay the body of a Viet Cong shot a few minutes before as he tried to sneak into town carrying three hand grenades hidden in his black pajamas. He had been shot by Vietnamese troops and they had left his body there as a lesson to those who might be tempted to follow his example.

We then took off in our helicopter and flew northwest to Trung Lop. We circled and watched our artillery striking the zone in which our forces were shortly to land. Suddenly in the sky I saw the mass of helicopters coming carrying the first assault wave. Straight down into the field, struck only minutes before, they settled like migratory birds. Through the open door of our helicopter it was an impressive sight, and down into the landing zone we went also. This was my second combat assault in Vietnam. We landed close to the other helicopters as the troops they had disgorged moved out toward some houses at the edge of the zone. Some small arms firing was audible but it did not appear to be in our immediate vicinity. We waited until the troops had occupied the houses on the edge of the landing zone and then once again moved on.

Boarding the helicopter, we lifted off into the sky and headed back to the division camp at Cuchi. Here I had dinner with General Tillson and his staff and we discussed various phases of the division's activity. After dinner there was a movie called *The Sandpiper* with Elizabeth Taylor and Richard Burton, a useless picture without a point except perhaps to prove that everyone was no good, typical of the "debunk everybody and everything" school so prevalent in many circles in our country at that time. After that I went to bed in a comfortable trailer and slept quite a lot despite the intermittent rumble of artillery firing and harassing and interdiction fire all night. The next morning after a good breakfast, I boarded the helicopter and flew south to Bao Trai, a subsector headquarters, and visited briefly with the Vietnamese subsector chief and the U.S. advisers. I felt a special sympathy with these advisers whom I had seen all over Vietnam, as I had had a very similar job in World War II when I was the liaison officer with the Brazilian division in Italy. This was a complex war where the enemy was everywhere and nowhere. Most admirable, I think, were the battalion advisers, generally lieutenants or brand-new captains. They were literally living in the mud and rice paddies in pup tents, sharing the hardships, dangers and food of the Vietnamese units with which they worked. They were a cheerful and dedicated group living under dangerous and difficult conditions. At most, they had three or four enlisted men with them. They knew that they were the number-one target for the VC. Next to them were the revolutionary development advisers and subsectors. Normally there were jobs also for civilians, but because of the dangers involved and the isolated nature of their work, there were relatively few civilians in these jobs. Instead, young Army officers, earning a small fraction of what they might be earning at home, handled these risky jobs. They handled them without complaint and their dedication to their work in the subsector did my heart good. The young civilians I saw there were just as highly motivated and did a magnificent job. They had earned the respect of the United States and the Vietnamese military.

From Bao Trai we flew to various small units of the 25th Division. Everywhere the same tired, cheerful young faces, the same feeling that they knew what they were doing. One of the more interesting units I visited was the 2nd Battalion of the 27th Field Artillery. This unit had its guns deeply dug in, and contrary to the usual practice, it did not have infantry to protect the guns. The artillerymen had dug bunkers and positions and with a few M-41 tanks had built a fortified perimeter inside of which they had dug and revetted their guns and living quarters. They were hell-bent on proving that an artillery unit could live by itself, fight by itself and defend itself without infantry.

Later in the morning I also visited a Vietnamese battalion building its own defensive position at Thom Mo. A very young-looking Vietnamese major explained the position of his outfit and what they were attempting to do. It seemed to me that many of the criticisms I had heard addressed to the Vietnamese Army were the same as those I had heard sixteen years before regarding the Korean Army. In Vietnam the Korean Army fielded an expeditionary force of fifty thousand men. There, Korea paid part of her debt to freedom and to the United States. If anyone had told me in Taegu, Korea, in August 1950 that this could happen sixteen years later, I would have laughed. My own experience had taken me to World War II, the Greek civil war, Korea and now Vietnam. I had also been involved in the 1948 Communist riots in Bogotá. It seemed to me that a large part of my adult life had been spent during such conflicts.

I then flew to Long Hun Island in the Saigon River below the capital. This area had recently been taken by the 25th Division and was quite pacified. On the hill overlooking the river, there was a massive old French fort that commanded the river access to Saigon. Though it had long since been deactivated, we could nonetheless see the U.S. guns emplaced in it for use in another day in another conflict. Back to Doc Hoa, where I took leave of the 25th Division, and then off to the base camp of the 1st Division, the Big Red One, at Di An. Here again as we flew in aboard the helicopter, I could not but marvel at the size of the base camp. At this camp, as at all others, everything was dug in and the tents and such temporary buildings as there were for troop quarters were sandbagged to a height of three or four feet. Between the sandbag bunkers there were shelters with overhead covers in case of mortar attack or recoilless rifle attack. In a war without fronts, these things could happen at any time. Upon arrival at Di An, I was met by Assistant Division Commander

General William S. Coleman, recently promoted to brigadier general and a member of a class I had addressed a year earlier at the Army War College. General Coleman was very cordial and promised me an interesting visit. He was to keep his word.

I went to the division headquarters and met General John H. Hay, the division commander, and Brigadier General Bernie Rogers, his assistant division commander, whom I had known previously when he was executive to General Maxwell Taylor. Bernie Rogers was subsequently to become Chief of Staff of the United States Army. After dinner I saw another Italian-made Western movie which was silly but entertaining. All night I could hear artillery fire. Earlier a truck with two soldiers taking laundry to a nearby village had been Claymored only a few hundred yards from the camp. Fortunately, neither of the soldiers was hurt. This was lucky, as the Claymore is a particularly vicious mine that is stuck in the ground and when it explodes it discharges thousands of steel pellets in one direction. It seems that every day these soldiers used to take the laundry at the same time on the same route. Undoubtedly, the VC watched the routine trip every day and on this particular day set up the Claymore and waited for the truck to appear at its usual time. At the evening briefing I was told that the division had fired an incredibly large number of rounds in H&I (harassing and interdiction fire) at areas where the enemy might be. When I asked how much was fired at targets which intelligence had indicated, it was claimed that there were not many, and that most of the firing was simply into the landscape covered with a triple canopy of trees.

After a good night's sleep and a good breakfast, we heard on the morning news that Phu Loi—which I had visited two days before—had been heavily mortared with considerable loss of aircraft and lives. So had Lai Khe. We took off in the helicopter and flew at once to the place from where Phu Loi had been mortared. We found it by the huge burn marks on the ground where the back flame of the rockets as they were launched burned the ground. We came down low and saw that there were two bodies of VC lying close to the burn marks. They had been killed by the counterbattery fire, which went into action almost as soon as the rockets hit Phu Loi. Knowing the fanaticism of the VC about not leaving their bodies, it was clear that they must have left in a real hurry and abandoned the bodies contrary to their custom. Most VC soldiers carried a little hook attached to a strap. This hook is locked onto a dead VC's belt and he is dragged away so that we will not find the bodies and know how many of them we have killed.

From there we flew on to an isolated infantry battalion that was holding a position in a clearing largely of their own making. We landed in the highly defended position built in a circle, with tanks and armored personnel carriers dug in around it. This was the position of the 1st Battalion of the 18th Infantry. We were met by the battalion commander, a tough Mexican from Texas named Richard Cavazos, who was later to become a major general in the Army. He took us around his battalion position to see his men, who were surprised at being visited in this location not by one but two generals. We met a baby-faced lieutenant, nineteen years old, commissioned on the battlefield. A child in years but a man in experience. I noted the cheerful respect with which Cavazos' men treated him. It was easy to see that this was a born leader. One of the soldiers was grumbling because they had taken away the wire in front of his foxhole. The battalion was scheduled to move the next day and in order not to waste wire, it had been rolled up. Cavazos told us that earlier that day the VC had come out of the woods and wounded one of his men. He had also lost a jeep to a mine but no one was hurt. I wandered around talking to the men and once again I could only marvel at their cheerfulness and wry good humor about their own plight. While we were there a few rounds of mortars came in and I was able to catch a picture of them on my movie camera. As I watched these young Americans who lived with danger and death and hardships for every hour of every day and night, I wondered if it was not true that perhaps the Army is one of the greatest universities when it comes to molding a man's character. These young Americans understood that they were their brothers' keepers and if they did not like it, at least they understood it. They were not yet ready to give Cain's answer, "Am I my brother's keeper?"

The helicopter lifted off the mud and we flew out to see a bomb strike. We circled the area that was to be struck after a VC unit had fired on some of our men from it. We saw the gallant little O-1 forward air control plane circling over the area until he sighted the VC. Then we saw his smoke marker drop into the area, and circling in our chopper about five hundred yards away, we watched the fighter bombers roar down and had a first-class view of the bombs striking the target. In Vietnam every bomb strike had to be checked out with the province or sector chief for approval. Great care was taken to avoid hitting targets other than the VC. From there we flew to Phu Von to visit an engineer group that was taking down a swath of trees through a forest so that we could control the movements of the VC through the area. This, like bombing and defoliation, had to be cleared with the local authorities. The harassed engineer group commander told us that one of his bulldozers had hit a mine a little earlier and had lost a blade. Fortunately, no one had been hurt. The engineer group, too, was providing its own defense, as would so many units in this area, where the enemy might be anywhere.

From here we flew to a mechanized outfit and they, too, were providing their own security. We saw a road patrol come back from opening a road, a dangerous and thankless task, for the VC mined the roads indiscriminately, caring little for their peaceful compatriots who might be riding a bus, for, strange to say, the civilian buses ran everywhere in Vietnam. Sometimes they were blown up, sometimes they were fired upon and other times they were stopped and some passengers were taken off by the VC. The VC often levied a tax on the bus. In spite of all this, the buses still ran. One could take a bus from Saigon to Danang in the far north and Rach Gia in the far south. We flew back to the 1st Division camp, where we had dinner and spent a quiet night.

In the morning we were scheduled to fly north to Loc Ninh near the Cambodian border. The weather looked grim, the ceiling was low and a heavy drizzle was falling. The weather forecast was not good but this was a combat situation and I suggested that we try and see how far we could go. We boarded the chopper, lifted off the pad and headed north at one hundred knots, inches above the treetops under the lowering ceiling. Northward we flew through the gusts of rain and many times it seemed to me that we must be touching the tops of the trees. Once I saw the machine gunner behind me wince back as a tree went by the open door of the helicopter, barely inches away. Finally, the helicopter pilot turned, shook his head and said to me through the intercom that it would be foolish to go on. Our destination reported ceiling and visibility zero. Reluctantly we turned and headed back to Lai Khe, which had been mortared during the night. We flew in and saw the runway and the men working to repair the crater on it caused by a rocket which had landed during the night. We landed and were met by the base commander, who was busy getting barracks ready for infantry replacements who would be in from Vung Tau later in the day. We visited the barracks, where the men were working furiously to get them ready. All of the barracks were already sandbagged to prevent a repetition of the night's event when a young lieutenant was killed in his bed by the fragments of a mortar shell which burst in the trees and entered the barracks above the line of sandbags. A truck, too, had been hit and a ten-foot hole between two barracks told of still another hit. If anyone was really perturbed by all this at Lai Khe, it did not show.

Here I left General Coleman and went over to Xuan Loc to visit a U.S. unit serving with the 18th ARVN Division. We found the artillery unit at its small camp defended by an all-around perimeter at the eastern edge of town. They were pleased and enthusiastic about the ARVN division with which they served. They were well dug in, and sandbags were piled about three feet high around their tents. The soldiers themselves with a little help from the engineer had built a beautiful modern wood chapel. They had done it voluntarily in whatever spare time they had in a war which kept no hours and where overtime was not only *not* paid, but often brought wounds and death. To the soldiers who built it with their own hands in a distant war-torn land far from their own homes, God was very definitely not dead.

From the artillery unit we went to the headquarters of the Vietnamese division. The commander received me warmly and briefed me on what his division's mission was and spoke of some of the bitter fighting that had taken place in his tactical area of responsibility. At his headquarters, I met Major Bruce Simnacher, whom I had known in Brazil, where he had attended the Brazilian Army Command and General Staff School. Simnacher, who was a Medical Service officer, had also served with the division, not only as a Medical Service adviser but also as an infantry adviser, and had won the Combat Infantry Badge for his participation in combat operations. He looked great and spoke enthusiastically about his Vietnamese counterparts. He accompanied us as the Vietnamese commander took me out to the edge of town in his jeep to show me the village he was building for his dependent personnel. Only a short time ago traveling over this road we would have come under sniper fire. The small houses he was building were unpretentious but they meant hope of a better life to his soldiers' families, who had been living in tents or broken-down wooden shacks. Then we rode back to our helicopter and took off to fly to the 9th Division somewhere east of Saigon at a place known to the Americans as Bear Cat.

We flew westward from Xuan Loc over miles of still operating French rubber plantations and then through a darkening sky I looked ahead and saw the huge base camp that housed the largest part of the 9th Division, a camp as big as many of the military installations in the United States. As our chopper sank down onto the helicopter pad just in front of the 9th Division headquarters, my memory ran back twenty-six years to that rainy dark night on November 8, 1942, when I had gone ashore on the coast of North Africa at Safi, Morocco, with the 3rd Battalion of the 47th Infantry of the 9th Division.

We were met by General Morgan Roseborough, the assistant division commander. Major General George G. O'Connor, the division commander, returned later. We had dinner with him

and went to the movies, another silly film, and then to sleep in
the comfortable trailer which seems to be the lot of many general officers in Vietnam. Before retiring, I was shown where the
sandbagged bunker was to which I should repair should there be
a shelling during the night. This is a courtesy extended to visitors almost everywhere in Vietnam. Sometimes the place where
the visitor is to sleep is sandbagged higher than the level of his
bed and then he is told that he is safe from everything but a direct hit. Outside of sleeping in a deep shelter, there is very little
that will protect you from a direct hit. Next morning, July 30, I
woke up and had a good breakfast with hotcakes and maple
syrup, and right after that I attended the division's morning
briefing for General O'Connor. Then I boarded a helicopter and
took off for a brigade of the Riverine Force, 9th Division, which
was embarked on river craft operating on the Mekong south of
Saigon. These were the only U.S. forces operating south of
Saigon.

Normally the delta is an all-Vietnamese area held by several
ARVN divisions with U.S. advisers but no ground unit. It was a
considerable distance and took us the better part of an hour to
get to our destination, Operation Coronado II, a river landing
on the north shore of the Mekong, west of My Tho. During the
night I listened on the radio to reports of the first landing. I
heard how a medical helicopter had gone in to pick up some
wounded men and had been shot down and attacked by the
VC, who were only a short distance away. The crew, who were
unhurt in the landing, fought back with their machine guns and
hand weapons. The attack grew in intensity during the night
and at midnight a lieutenant and ten men were "inserted" by
helicopter to reinforce them and help repel the VC attackers. At
dawn we heard that help had reached them and that they had
been extracted after our ground forces had driven off the VC.
The pilot of the helicopter that went in during the night was
wounded and the lieutenant who came in was killed. A few
others were wounded when two rifle grenades fired by the Viet
Cong struck the downed helicopter. Now as I landed on the
riverbank where the assault craft were waiting, I saw a young

sailor wounded in the neck by a fragment from a 57-mm. VC recoilless rifle. He was lying on the shore and I was told that a dust-off helicopter had been called to take him to the hospital. The sailor had a jagged hole in his neck. He was painfully wounded but his life did not appear to be in danger. After a few minutes waiting for the medical helicopter which did not come, I asked the colonel who was there what he planned to do and he said he planned to wait until the medical evacuation helicopter came. I could see that the young sailor was in pain. I turned to the colonel and said, "Colonel, put that sailor in my chopper and take him to the hospital in My Tho right now." This was done and less than thirty minutes after he was wounded the young sailor was on the Army operating table in My Tho.

We then flew to the area where the helicopter had been shot down during the night and saw the M1-13s or armored personnel carriers that had effected the rescue alongside the helicopter. As we watched, a huge crane helicopter moved into position to lift the damaged craft and fly it back to its base for repairs. It was an impressive sight as the huge helicopter lifted the downed craft and flew off with it. We then flew to an area where 9th Division troopers had pushed the VC up against two battalions of Vietnamese marines. Occasional puffs of smoke and moving men were all that could be seen. As we flew we heard the two helicopters had "fluttered together" at the U.S. camp at Dong Tam. For a moment we were concerned, but later we found that no one had been injured as the two helicopters collided. Why this did not happen more often I did not know, as there were helicopters everywhere. We then landed on the deck of a ship, the U.S.S. *Bien Hoa*, a large tank landing ship with a helipad built into her superstructure.

We visited briefly with Captain Smith of the Navy, who commanded the river flotilla engaged in these riverine operations, and a Colonel Fulton, who commanded the brigade. The latter had just received word of his selection for brigadier general. We congratulated him and took off from the U.S.S. *Bien Hoa* and flew to a strike against a reported VC position and ammunition dump in a village. Here again, I was able to get some good pic-

tures as the rockets struck the target and it exploded with fragments flying past our chopper. We flew back to the *Bien Hoa*
and then to the division headquarters. It was Sunday and I
wanted to go to church, so we went to an engineer outfit at the
nearby village, Company C of the 93rd Engineers, and went to
mass there. Again, I had the feeling that God may be dead to
some of the weekly magazines, but he certainly wasn't to the soldiers here. After mass we boarded the helicopter and flew over
the bloody mangrove swamps of the Rung Sat, the vast marshy
archipelago in the mouth of the Saigon River, to the coastal
resort of Vung Tau, which the French called Cap St. Jacques. It
is on the end of a long spit of land. It was the site of a very large
air base and a rest and recuperation center for the Armed Forces
and the training camp for the revolutionary development teams,
as well as a vacation colony for many people from Saigon. As we
flew in I was once again amazed at the size of the huge air base
and the number of aircraft on it. We circled the peninsula and
got a fine look at the small town and the many ships standing in
to the shore to unload. We landed at the airport and found that
we were at the wrong place.

We were expected at the Revolutionary Development Training Center so we flew over there by helicopter and were received
by the commander, a remarkable young Vietnamese major wearing the traditional black pajamas of the RD teams, Major
Nguyen Be, a dedicated officer who had written a book about
civic action. He spoke good English and French and we drove
through his vast training camp, which trained almost all the
hundreds of fifty-nine-man RD teams that were scattered all
over South Vietnam. They worked in the hamlets to teach the
people the essentials of sanitation, hygiene, agriculture and ani-
mal husbandry. They dug wells, built markets, and pig sties
and generally tried to give the people of the hamlet a stake in
their country's tomorrow. Success could best be judged by the
intensity with which the Viet Cong and North Vietnamese attacked them. The Viet Cong knew that the RD constituted a
real long-term threat to them. These teams had their own security teams, who not only defended them, but worked closely

with the hamlet's local popular forces. Major Be's contribution to his country was a significant one and his teams were all over the country, surviving and working with success. After visiting the RD center, I made a quick trip to Vung Tau.

Back to the helicopter, where the pilot said that there were four girl secretaries from Saigon who worked for the Navy. They had gone down for the weekend and were looking for a ride back and would I let them ride back in my helicopter. I said that I would be delighted to return to Saigon in such company and the girls all climbed aboard for the one-hour flight back to Tan Son Nhut. We arrived there in a driving rainstorm, and as we ran for the airport terminal, I could see the envious looks on the faces of the young airmen standing around as they watched the four girls dash from the helicopter to the terminal. It would be difficult to convince them that generals don't travel around with bevies of beautiful girls in tow.

I drove into Saigon through the tremendous traffic jams that characterized that city and back to my quarters at the Rex Bachelor Officers Quarters after dropping the girls off at their quarters. Spent a quiet night at the Rex BOQ and went up on the roof at night for a few minutes and watched the flares dropping and listened to the rumble of distant artillery and then went to bed.

The 199th Brigade was the next unit I visited. I flew from Saigon on the morning of July 31 to the headquarters of this brigade, which was part of the forces defending the Vietnamese capital. As I came into the helicopter pad I was received by the brigade commander, Brigadier General Fritz Freund, an unusual and effective officer. A graduate of the Naval Academy, he had gone into the Army when his eyes were judged not good enough for the Navy. The son of a German father and a French mother, he was extraordinarily fluent in both languages, and had learned a good deal of Vietnamese. Prior to taking command of the brigade, he had, in a sense, been General Westmoreland's special liaison officer to the Vietnamese High Command. He had developed a very close and personal relationship with many of the senior Vietnamese officers and their families. This was an area that had struck me as being somewhat neglected. What we needed were a dozen Fritz Freunds. He briefed us on the mission of his brigade and then took me by chopper and jeep to visit various units of his command.

At one point, on the periphery of Saigon, we visited a unit of the 3rd Infantry, which normally does garrison duty in Fort Meyer across the river from Washington and provides the Honor Guard for the Unknown Soldier's tomb in Arlington Cemetery. Here, on one of the shacks someone had painted a large sign saying "Fort Myer" as a reminder of calmer and happier days. All morning we moved around the periphery of Saigon visiting these small units, who together with their South Vietnamese colleagues kept Charlies out of town. Just before lunch we returned to Fritz Freund's trailer for a drink. He took out his accordion and sang a number of songs, both popular and traditional. He handled the accordion and sang like a professional. He could have earned his living that way if he had not been an Army officer. He had chosen the harder, thornier path, which had led him to this distant place at a difficult time. His enthusiasm and dedication impressed me greatly. He spoke with great feeling of the need for a more personal relationship with the South Vietnamese Army. He had certainly done his best. Americans who do most things because of "policy" think that foreigners operate the same way. They do not. Often the decisions are made on the basis of human feeling or personal relationship. It is a lesson that we as a people have difficulty in learning.

Then we had a simple lunch with Fritz and his Chief of Staff, Colonel Brandenburg. During lunch he urged me to accompany him on an operation he was conducting that afternoon. It sounded tempting but I had a very firm schedule and did not feel that I could put it off since it involved going to Tay Ninh to see the Philippine forces there. That afternoon while at the Philippines' headquarters, I heard that Fritz Freund had been seriously wounded while landing his chopper to pick up one of his men who had been shot. He was wounded in the leg and his aide, who had been with us all morning, had been shot through both legs. Upon inquiring, I found that he had been taken to the 3rd Field Hospital just outside Tan Son Nhut Airport, and I flew there immediately to see him. I found him drowsy from the anesthetic that had been used in the operation on his leg. He was sitting up in bed getting a back rub from the wife of the chairman of the Vietnamese Chiefs of Staff, General Cao Van Vien, who immediately on hearing that he had been wounded had gone to the hospital to see him. This told me worlds about the kind of relationship he had developed with his Vietnamese counterparts. Shortly after I got there the commanding general of the 1st Field Force, Lieutenant General Fred Weyand, came in to see Fritz. Weyand and I were to meet later in Paris when he came there as adviser to the U.S. delegation in the talks with the North Vietnamese. Still later he was to become the deputy commander in South Vietnam and subsequently Chief of Staff of the United States Army. In that capacity, he presided over my retirement ceremony in July 1976 and presented me with my third Distinguished Service Medal. This, however, was still nearly ten years in the future. Reassured that Fritz was not in danger of his life, although painfully wounded, I returned for my visit to Tay Ninh. Fritz was eventually to recover fully, and after his retirement as a major general, he became the adjutant general of the Connecticut National Guard. He would have gone much further had his personal friendship with President Marcos of the Philippines not aroused jealousy among some narrow-minded Foreign Service officers, who demanded, and perhaps got, his head.

Upon my arrival in Vietnam I determined that I wanted to visit all of our allies who had joined us in this difficult and unpopular war, not that there are any really popular wars. This one, however, aroused more hostility and defeatism than any other in my lifetime, hostility and defeatism on the home front. To most soldiers, the idea of a limited war in which one did not use all of one's strength to win as quickly as possible seemed both immoral and impractical. Limited war is like partial pregnancy or slight virginity. Despite the wishful thinking of many in our country, basically only a harsh totalitarian dictatorship like Nazi Germany or North Vietnam is equipped to fight a prolonged war. The Communists know this and use it to the hilt in their struggle with democracies. The Duke of Wellington once said, "A great nation cannot fight a little war."

I flew to Tay Ninh, near the Cambodian border, through violent thunderstorms and rain squalls. Tay Ninh, the holy city of the Cao Dai religious sect, was a large town and the headquarters of the Philippine Civic Action Group, where a dedicated group of Filipinos tried to assist the Vietnamese villagers to increase their agricultural and livestock production and at the same time defend them. After landing at Tay Ninh we went over to the Philippine headquarters for a briefing and to visit one of the Civic Action units just south of Tay Ninh. After lunch with them I drove into town, as I wanted to see the Cao Dai Temple, a truly extraordinary building, the headquarters of an equally exotic cult—a combination of Christianity, Buddhism and Confucianism with overtones of modern nationalism, with a Holy See, currently vacant, and a College of Cardinals, a cult whose saints included Victor Hugo, Joan of Arc and Winston Churchill. The temple itself was a fantastic building. Entering the compound in the rain, we were met by a French-speaking monk who acted as my guide. Entering the temple decorated with the sect emblem, the all-seeing eye, we found a vast building whose roof was supported by two great rows of columns around which plaster dragons curled. We visited the sanctuary, as no services were going on. At the monk's request I signed the guest book.

My chopper pilot was anxious to return, as the weather was bad and getting worse. I boarded the chopper and he said to me that in view of the lowering ceiling there were two ways we could go back to Saigon; either in the overcast or on the deck, a few feet above the ground. Knowing from experience how many other aircraft and helicopters would be in the overcast with us, I opted to go back on the deck. I had not realized what a hair-raising experience this would be. Just a few feet above the road, under a lowering thunder-filled sky, we flew back passing armored personnel carriers, civilian buses and often a lonely and isolated U.S. or Vietnamese position. We had no way of knowing where Charlie might be. At this point, I was more worried about our chopper engine than anything else. Had it faltered even for a second we would have dug a long trench in the ground. Soon through the rain squalls I saw with relief the built-up area of Saigon and we touched down at Tan Son Nhut in the midst of a blinding rainstorm. Nevertheless, air operations were continuing; every few seconds military aircraft were taking off and landing. Weather that would have grounded all aircraft under normal conditions was just a nuisance to these American airmen.

On August 1 I flew to Nha Trang to visit the 2nd Field Force commanded by General Bill Rosson, who had been at SHAPE with me in early 1951. He received me warmly and I was briefed on the mission of his command. Then I visited the Green Berets Special Forces headquarters, where I ran into the Chief of Staff of the Army, General Harold Johnson. He asked me how my trip to Vietnam was working out and I told him that it was going very well, I had had a most interesting visit. I later called on Colonel Gene Kelly of the Special Forces and told him I intended to visit a number of his camps to the west. A house was pointed out to me in Nha Trang as having belonged to Madame Nhu Diem's sister-in-law. I asked a local French-speaking Vietnamese whether it was really true and he answered, "Of course not." Later in the afternoon I flew to the headquarters of the 4th Division inland at Dragon Mountain, where I was received by the division commander, Major General Ray Peers. He had me to dinner that night with a French tea planter who managed the Catecka Plantations. He told me feelingly in French that his life was difficult, squeezed as he was between the Viet Cong and the North Vietnamese, who demanded that he pay taxes, and the South Vietnamese government, which forbade him to pay taxes to them. I asked him what he actually did and he replied that he paid enough taxes so the Communists left him alone and not so much as to get him in trouble with the Saigon government.

The following day I flew to Pleiku at treetop altitude by helicopter and visited the Vietnamese headquarters there. Then I flew west to Dak To to visit the 173rd Infantry Brigade commanded by Brigadier General John R. Deane, the son of my old chief when I worked for Averell Harriman in the White House. He explained the function of his outfit and then flew me in his chopper over some of his more recent battle areas. He had been shot down several times before but had always made it back. We had several close looks at some of his positions and some of the enemy's. Once or twice we drew fire and could see the tracers.

Then we flew back to Dak To and I took our chopper and flew west to a Special Forces camp at Dak Seang. This camp was completely isolated behind the Communist lines. It was fortified and heavily dug in. I visited there with a small garrison, who were delighted to see me and to realize that they were not forgotten. Usually visitors are a nuisance but their delight was so obvious it was clear they did not have many visitors at that particular camp. Some mortar rounds fell on the camp while I was there and when we left our chopper climbed straight up in a sort of corkscrew climb as we flew north to another Special Forces camp at Dak Pek. This was a larger camp but it, too, was completely isolated and supplied by air. Here I found a young lieutenant who had been brought up in Argentina and spoke absolutely perfect Argentine Spanish without any trace of accent. He told me that he was making good progress in Vietnamese. At this camp they had captured a North Vietnamese prisoner and asked me if I would take him back to Dak To for them. I said that of course I would. After having coffee with the Green Berets at Dak Pek, I flew out to that point where the Cambodian and Lao borders meet the Vietnamese border, then back to Dak Pek, where I picked up the prisoner. I had been greatly impressed by the spirit of the Green Berets at both Dak Seang and Dak Pek, young officers and men totally isolated, far behind the enemy's lines and in a sense under siege twenty-four hours a day, seven days a week.

We lifted off Dak Pek for the second time, heading for Dak To. As always, I flew with both doors of the helicopter open with the prisoner sitting next to me and beyond him, a tall young lieutenant who was Jack Deane's aide. As the chopper lifted the prisoner began to tremble and mutter something I did not understand. Then I realized that to prevent their men from surrendering, North Vietnamese told them that if they were captured the Americans would throw them out of the helicopters. Seeing that we were flying with the open doors, he thought his hour had come. I patted him on the back, pointed out of the chopper and shook my head, saying, "No, no." After a while he seemed more reassured and stopped trembling. He could not have been more than sixteen years old. We flew past Dak Seang, where we had been earlier in the morning; they were being mortared again as we passed overhead, and we could see the explosions inside the perimeter. At this the pilot dropped down to a few feet above the ground and we flew, as they called it, "the nap of the earth." We returned to Dak To and turned our startled prisoner over to the 173rd Brigade.

Then, still flying very low, we flew to Kontum and visited the Vietnamese headquarters there. I also met Catholic Bishop Monsignor Seitz, the last French bishop in Vietnam. He had been there more than forty years and I was to see him later in Paris. From Kontum we flew to Pleiku again, just a few feet over the vehicles moving on the road. At Pleiku there was a large U.S. base and it was here that I spent the night. I met a young Signal Corps lieutenant, Bill Marsh, who was the nephew of my brother's wife, and arranged for him to accompany me as my aide and escort officer for the rest of the trip. He was absolutely delighted. He was later to say that in a few days with me he saw more of Vietnam and the war than he had seen in the preceding eight months. Next day I went to visit a camp for North Vietnamese and Viet Cong prisoners at Pleiku. As I was entering the area, I was asked to leave my .45 pistol behind so it could not be stolen by a prisoner and I was also asked to give up my camera by the young captain in charge. He explained that it was against the Geneva Convention to photograph the prisoners in a humiliating way. I turned over the camera and could not help but contrast this with the performance of the North Vietnamese, who never failed to photograph their American prisoners in as humiliating and penitential a pose as they could any time a Jane Fonda or a Ramsey Clark showed up. It indicated to me the difference between our sides. I did not like the fact that prisoners in this camp were not required to work and, in fact, did absolutely nothing. There was no attempt by the Americans to re-educate them away from communism.

Later that morning I flew back to the 4th Division headquarters at Dragon Mountain and then visited two of their brigades to the west. At the first brigade, a sharp young black major who was the intelligence officer explained to me the brigade situation. It was quiet at the time and we then flew to the other brigade, where they also told us their mission and problems. All of this flying was done literally a few feet above the ground, dodging trees or church steeples. I recorded it on film and to this day it chills me when I watch it. In the late afternoon, we took off by chopper for Bongsan, the headquarters of the 1st Air Mobile Division. Weather predictions were bad and the pilot said he did not think that we could get over the coastal range. I suggested that we try and we did. The clouds seemed to come down to the mountaintops as we approached the pass on the road between Pleiku and Qui Nhon, but as we were about to turn back a small hole in the clouds appeared and we could see the blue sky beyond. So we plunged through it into much better weather and flew on down to the 1st Air Mobile headquarters at Bongsan.

Here I was met by the division commander, General John Tolson. He too was an inspiring officer and a first-class commander. With him was an old friend of mine, Warrant Officer Jack Good, who had been with me on many trips with General Eisenhower. We had dinner that night and General Tolson spoke enthusiastically of his command and its extraordinary mobility. He promised me that on the following day I could go in with an air assault on a Viet Cong-held town on the coast. As I retired, I noticed some 155-mm. guns firing not far from my tent; they fired all night. I slept anyway, as it had been a long, tiring and exciting day. On the next morning I flew down to the coast to an English air base, where I saw several units of the division and had explained and demonstrated to me their great mobility. Then we went off for the promised air assault on a village called Kim Gia on the coast. From my chopper at two hundred feet I watched the first wave of choppers set down on the beach. There was a standard practice that they would not let me as a general go in with the first wave. I followed them in immediately and jumped out onto the sand and began moving toward the village. Almost immediately we came under small arms fire and hit the ground. As I glanced around at the others, who were also pinned down, I recognized, to my surprise, very close to me young Major Hal Dyson, who had been a student in the Brazilian Staff College and attached to my office in Rio in 1965 and 1966. I said to him, "Hal, what are you doing here?" He replied, "General, I have a reason to be here. I am the S-2 of the battalion which is carrying out this operation. What the hell are you doing here?" I explained to him that I was acquiring credibility for my next job. He seemed to think that was a huge joke.

Our troopers dislodged the snipers and we moved into Kim Gia without further resistance. We immediately began to search for arms caches which had been reported in the village. While the search was going on, I noticed some large billboards in the middle of the village with violent anti-American signs on them in English and alongside what I presumed to be the Vietnamese translation. The billboards attacked President Johnson and the American imperialist warmongers. I beckoned to the young major who was in charge of the operation. He was nervous in the first place at having me along and said he did not want to get a general killed, it would be awful. I agreed heartily and told him I would do my best not to get killed. I pointed to the billboards and asked him what he intended to do about them. "Nothing, I guess," he replied. "Hell," I said, "the minute we leave the VC will emerge and point to them and tell the villagers that we were afraid to remove them." He then asked what he should do. I told him to get the village head man, which he did. I asked the head man if he spoke French and he grinned and said that he did. Incidentally, the one phrase of Vietnamese

I learned during my stay there was to ask whether one spoke French. I pointed to the signs and told him to take them down. He asked how he was to do this and I replied that that was his business, not mine. He had put them up, now he must remove the signs. We would not leave until he had done so. He shrugged, got some of his men and they removed the signs.

The search having been completed and a few weapons found, much less than we had been led to expect, we headed back toward the beach and our choppers. Once again, on the beach we came under sniper fire and were briefly pinned to the ground. I heard the young major in command say, "Get the goddamned general in his chopper and out of here!" After a few minutes the snipers stopped firing and I boarded my chopper and lifted out of Kim Gia. As we took off, I saw a sniper on the other side of the village raise a rifle and take a shot at us. He missed. One of our attack helicopters, however, did not miss him.

The whole operation left me with an unpleasant feeling that there was not much sense in occupying a place for a few hours and then turning it back to the enemy. Yet this tactic seemed to be widely used in Vietnam. I felt nothing could be more disconcerting for non-Communist villagers than to be briefly liberated and, after showing their joy, then a few hours later to have the liberators depart, leaving them to the not so tender mercies of the North Vietnamese Communists. It was my third air assault landing at Vietnam. None of them had been really hot but they were exciting and interesting.

I spent the night with General Tolson and talked until late with Jack Good, who probably had spent as much time in Vietnam as any other man in the U. S. Army. This was his fourth or fifth tour there. Early the next day I flew to the great port of Qui Nhon. We had built an entirely new military port so as not to hamper the operation of the regular commercial and fishing port. Qui Nhon was a large town and had formerly been a resort in the time of the French, with beautiful villas along the beach facing an incredibly blue sea. I then flew to Nha Trang and refueled the chopper. Two young soldiers asked if I would give them a ride in my plane to Cam Ranh Bay and I told them to hop aboard. We took off and flew in very rough air and had an extraordinarily turbulent trip. One of the young soldiers, who was black, suddenly became airsick all over the plane. He was enormously embarrassed; I told him not to be, it was all part of the war.

I was taken for a tour of the huge logistical base at Cam Ranh and beyond that I flew to the old resort of Dalat in the mountains. No American personnel were supposed to go here. It was a peaceful mountain resort at six thousand feet where a sweater was welcome. I had lunch at the hotel with a young French doctor and his wife who were providing voluntary medical services to the Vietnamese. The town was beautiful, with French-style villas in the pine forest and around the lake. It was also the seat of the Vietnamese Military Academy and the country's only nuclear reactor. It had been spared from the war but the following year the Tet offensive brought the war to this beautiful little town.

In the afternoon, I flew back to Saigon, arriving in the midst of the usual afternoon thunderstorms. I was glad to be on the ground.

I had asked to see one of the carriers operating against North Vietnam in the Gulf of Tonkin and the following day I flew north to Danang in an Army U-8. Then I changed to a Navy Grumman Cod and flew out aboard the U.S.S. *Oriskany*. In the course of my career, I have landed and taken off carriers about fifteen times. That is a large number for any Army officer. Every time I have done it it was because I could not get out of it without intolerable loss of face. This time was the exception. I had asked to do it. As always, I was uptight for the landing on the deck and it was as always, to me, a noisy and frightening experience. It was a Sunday and I attended mass on the carrier and offered up a prayer of thanks for the safe landing and hopefully included another one for a safe takeoff. I spent the afternoon watching flight operations on the deck. This is one of the most exciting and complex things that can be imagined.

Just as darkness fell, a stick of planes was to be recovered aboard the carrier and my naval escort officer, who had taken me in charge after my lunch with the admiral, asked me whether I would like to see this recovery from the landing safety officer's platform. I readily agreed, not knowing where the landing safety officer's platform was. Had I known what was involved, I would have been less enthusiastic. I was led to a small platform on the aft part of the flight deck and here I saw a net suspended over the side. I was told to dive into the net if one of the planes appeared to be about to run directly into me, but not to stay there, and to squeeze through a sort of porthole, as otherwise burning fuel might get me. The first planes began to approach the carrier. It looked to me as though the first plane was aimed directly between my eyes, but I was determined that I would not move before the Navy man did. The plane landed on the deck but the wing tip was not far away. In this fashion, I watched some sixteen planes recovered, one of them with a "hung bomb"—that is, a bomb that had not dropped off when released. The landing of this plane made me particularly nervous. I did not realize the bomb was not armed until it had dropped clear of the aircraft. After watching the stick, we had, as always aboard ship, an excellent dinner. Then my Navy escort asked me whether I would like to watch the recovery of another stick. Frankly, I did not particularly want to do so. One such experience had been quite enough for me from the little platform so close to the landing aircraft. Again the question of loss of face arose and I found myself saying that I would like to, whereupon after a brief respite listening to the planes over their targets—it was dark by now—I heard one of the pilots over the coast explain, "Jesus Christ, their trucks are running with their lights on and it looks like the Shirley Highway." Like a condemned prisoner, I went back to the LSO platform and went through the whole ordeal again. When it was over I returned to the ship's island bridge, where I met the admiral, who asked me what I had been doing. I told him what I had done twice. He looked reprovingly but understandingly at my lieutenant commander, who had clearly had a lot of visitors, and the thought occurred to me that this might be his way of making sure that they did not come back too often.

The next morning at eight, with my heart in my mouth, I was catapulted off the deck. As always when the thrust of the catapult let go I had the feeling that the engine had stopped and that we were falling into the water. Then I heard the blessed sound of the engine and thought, as I had on all such previous occasions, "My God, I've survived." As we gained altitude for the flight back to Danang, I could see the Chinese Communist island of Hainan on the horizon. I asked one of the plane crew what would happen if the strap harness broke as we were catapulted off. He told me that this had happened to a previous commander of the Seventh Fleet. He had smashed against a partition in the plane and had broken nearly every bone in his body and been retired from the Navy. This confirmed my unbounded admiration for the men of the Navy who did this day after day. I was happy that I was not required to do it often. My nephew, at that time eighteen years old, also wanted very much to be a Navy flier. I told him we would talk about it after he was launched from a carrier. As an ROTC student, he was launched and to my amazement he still wanted to be a Navy flier.

We flew back to Danang, changed planes and then went on to Saigon in time for a good lunch at an excellent French restaurant. That night I had dinner with an old friend, Bill Knowlton. The next day I flew out to Phu Quoc Island in the Gulf of Cambodia. I visited a large prisoner-of-war camp there and the Green Berets Training Center. Some Vietnamese friends in Saigon had asked me to bring them back some nuoc mam, a fish sauce much used in Vietnamese cooking; some of the best came from Phu Quoc. As we prepared to fly back to Saigon and I put the bottles of the powerful-smelling substances aboard, the young pilot said to me, "General, please be careful with that stuff. If a bottle of it breaks, my plane will never be the same again." I was very careful and none broke.

My last night in Vietnam I had dinner with General Westmoreland at his quarters and told him my impressions of my visit and thanked him for the many courtesies I had received and the many opportunities I had had in such a short time to see many units and many different kinds of operations. I asked him also to express my thanks to the Seventh Air Force commander for all his help and support. The next day I departed on my new mission to Paris as attaché, not with all the credibility a longer stay would have given me, but at least with some knowledge of this war. I had flown 145 times around this war-torn land, moving most of the time over enemy territory. It had been an interesting, sometimes frightening, but always exciting experience and would, I felt, help me in my next mission. It was in a sense the Tenth Crusade; unfortunately our resolution flagged and 20 million Vietnamese passed into the tyranny of communism. Certainly, South Vietnam was not a model democracy but now it is a slave state.

22. TO PARIS AS ATTACHÉ

While still in Vietnam, I was conniving to get myself assigned there permanently. I felt that there was not nearly enough human contact between Vietnamese leaders and the U.S. senior staff there. It is difficult for me to describe why I wanted to stay, but I guess there was some sense of guilt at the fact that I had not been with military units for a long time, that there was a war going on and I felt I should participate in it because I believed in that war. I believed, and still do, that we were trying to help a small nation preserve the measure of freedom which it had. One day during my stay there, I was called in by General Abrams, who was the deputy to General Westmoreland, the commander in chief, and he congratulated me. I asked him whether I had been successful in my attempt to get assigned to Vietnam. He said, "No." I then asked him whether I had received some medal, and he said, "No." And he then proceeded to tell me that I had been selected for promotion to major general. I told him that I believed there was some mistake and it was some other General Walters. He then quoted my serial number to me and asked whether I was the attaché-designate to France and I replied that I was, and at this point I became convinced that I had been selected for promotion.

This was truly a very great surprise to me because I did not think that my career had followed the kind of a pattern that would get me selected for major general. I thought I had been lucky to make brigadier general, but I did not believe that lightning would strike twice in this particular way. Then the question arose as to whether I would still go to Paris as Military Attaché inasmuch as the post was normally occupied by a brigadier general. I soon received confirmation from Washington to the effect that I should go to Paris and that I would still be assigned there as a major general. At this point I realized that I was actually going to Paris and was not going to stay in Vietnam. I therefore wrote a letter to Ambassador Bohlen, who was our Ambassador to France and whom I had known for at least twenty years, and told him that I looked forward to working for him. He replied with a somewhat stiff note indicating that he would be happy to co-operate with me. I was a little surprised at this, since, usually, I do not co-operate with my superiors—I work for them. I then received a telegram from the director of the Defense Intelligence Agency, under whose authority I came as an attaché, telling me that events in Paris had changed and that I was to report there without fail on August 15, thereby cutting my stay in Vietnam short by a considerable period of time. I was all the more startled since the month of August in France is the month when everybody goes on vacation and I knew perfectly well that there would be no senior French authorities around to whom I could present myself when I got there. The telegram not only directed me to report there on August 15, it also instructed me to report back by telegram that I would carry out this order. I found this somewhat irritating and replied tersely with a two-word telegram, "Will comply." I think this conveyed my displeasure at having my stay in Vietnam cut short and at the fact that I was directed to say that I would comply with the order by telegram, since I had always complied with orders throughout my service in the Army.

I flew via Bangkok, New Delhi and Rome to Paris, where I was met by my staff, and assumed command of my office on August 15. No Frenchman works on the Feast of the Assumption. I was tempted to send a telegram to the director of the Defense Intelligence Agency, who is a Catholic like myself, and say, "On this Assumption Day I have assumed command of this office but there was no one around to witness my assumption." Then I thought this would rightly be regarded as impertinent and decided against it.

I was not presented to the French Army authorities until September, when they all returned from their vacations. I was introduced to the Chief of Staff of Defense, the Chief of Staff of the Army, the intelligence officer of the Defense staff and the intelligence officer of the Army staff. The intelligence officer of the Army, Colonel Guy Tartinville, was a rather crusty officer. Nevertheless, before I left France we became good personal friends. I found the best way to deal with him was to be just as crusty as he was. I sensed somewhat of an atmosphere of suspicion when I arrived. This was explained to me four years later when one of the intelligence officers of the Defense staff retired. After his retirement I had lunch with him and he told me that when I was assigned to France shortly after the French had asked the Americans to leave their bases in France, the French had felt sure that I was being sent there to stir up the Army on behalf of NATO and against General de Gaulle. They therefore watched me quite closely. And the fact that I was a bachelor had provided them, as they thought, with two opportunities or two handles that they might get on me, namely, girls or boys. "When neither of these worked out," said my friend, "we decided that you were like the traditional bishop—never in your own diocese."

After I had visited the first French units, the crusty G-2 said to me, "We notice that you never ask awkward questions when you visit a unit." I said, "I presume France is a sophisticated country, that when I visit a unit the commander is told what he can tell me, and I see no point in asking a question which will embarrass him when he tells me that he can't answer and embarrass me when he does so. I am really not interested in knowing the strength of a battalion. It may change tomorrow. I am more interested in projecting a favorable image of my country in the service which I represent." He grinned wryly and said, "Well, you are doing that."

Early in my stay in France the French, to show me that they really knew what was going on, recalled to me an incident that occurred when I was living in France at the age of eight. I had been arrested for riding a bicycle without a license plate and was released after payment of a hundred-franc fine by my mother. I was impressed that this information was still in the files, and they told me that the file of any foreigner who had any difficulty with the police remained alive as long as he did. France is a democracy but they do keep track of foreigners.

Early in my tenure in Paris I was told by the French that I should call on the dean of the corps of military attachés there, a Soviet general by the name of Sergei Sokolov. I called him for an appointment, which he gave me. In the course of the conversation I mentioned my intention to come in civilian clothes. He replied rather archly that he would be in uniform, whereupon I said, "Then I will be in uniform also." He received me in a small reception room in a building on Rue de Longchamp, with his assistant, Colonel Yaroshenko, who later succeeded him. We talked platitudes for some time and, finally, he said to me, "What do you think of the situation in Vietnam?" I replied, "General, I presume you know my government's view on Vietnam and want to know my personal view." He said, "Yes, that is correct." I said to him, "Well, first, you must know that I believe in the war in Vietnam and I went there as a volunteer when I had no need to go. Secondly, I think you should know that I believe we are rendering you Soviets great services by being in Vietnam for which you are showing the most unbelievable ingratitude." This staggered him and he said, "I don't understand what you mean." I told him, "As long as we are in Vietnam, the Chinese are going to be concerned about their southern border. When they cease worrying about their southern border, they are going to become concerned about their northern border. Now, we Americans have difficulties with the Chinese, but thank God we do not have six thousand kilometers of common borders, nor do we have any territory they believe to be theirs, and there are eight hundred million of them." I added, "Frankly, General, for nothing in the world would I want to be in your shoes." He was so staggered by this that I took advantage of it to take my leave of him. Two years later Colonel Yaroshenko, who had become a general, said to me, "You know, those Chinese are crazy. They believe war is a good thing." I said, "Yaroshenko, do you remember what I told you the first time we met?" He said ruefully, "Yes, indeed, I do."

I had not been in France long before I realized how wise had been my decision to go to Vietnam. Nearly every officer in the French Armed Forces above the grade of major had served there. The fact that I had been there had increased their respect for me. Had I not gone to Vietnam, I would have simply been a cocktail general going from one attaché post to another. I had taken many moving pictures in Vietnam, some of them showing considerable action taking place, and I would often show these to French officers I would invite to my home. Once I showed a film of a small Vietnamese town and a French officer present told me he had married in the church in that town. When I visited French units, almost as soon as I found myself alone with the commander, he would say to me, "Our government is not enthusiastic about what you are doing in Vietnam, but I want you to know that the people you are fighting killed our people, murdered our wounded and whenever you have a success against them, we feel warmth in our heart for you." This feeling was widespread throughout the French Army. They understood what we were doing there. One of them said to me, "You have picked up the pieces of our broken sword." Alas, we were to drop them even as the French had.

Early in my stay in Paris I was invited to lunch by an old friend, Major General André Lalande. We had served together at the NATO Standing Group in Washington. Lalande, one of the most distinguished and gallant officers in the French Army, had behaved with great heroism at Dien Bien Phu. He was, at the time that I was assigned to France, military aide to the President of the Republic, General de Gaulle, and he lived in the Elysée Palace, which was also the President's residence. I went to lunch with him at his handsome apartment on the third floor of the palace overlooking the gardens. He had several other guests present, and after a few drinks, we went into lunch. The main course of the lunch was chicken. While I was eating the chicken, I suddenly realized that a chicken bone had become lodged in my throat. I tried by moving my tongue to dislodge the bone. Then I realized that I could not and began to worry about choking. I excused myself, stood up, turned around, opened the nearest door and went through the door. I had hoped to find myself in another room where I could reach down with my finger and dislodge the bone. Instead, I found myself inside a pitch-black closet. Nevertheless, since the situation was urgent, I reached down with my finger and was able to dislodge the bone. With some relief I came back and resumed my place at the table. No one said anything during the meal, but after the other guests had left, Lalande said to me, "Dick, why the hell did you suddenly plunge into that closet and out again?" I said to him, "André, I had a bone stuck in my throat. I did not want to stick my finger in my mouth at the table lest everyone regard me as a coarse American peasant. I thought I was going into another room. I was amazed to find myself in a dark closet, but it served my purpose since I was able to put my finger down my throat and dislodged the bone." He said, "My God, I am glad you were able to do it. Imagine, if you had died of suffocation in the Elysée, everyone in America would have said, 'Aha! Another low blow by General de Gaulle.'"

Again, early in my tenure, Ambassador Bohlen left France and General de Gaulle gave him a lunch. I was invited to this lunch and as I was presented to General de Gaulle, he recalled our previous meetings on various occasions. I did not prolong the conversation but went on through the receiving line, and at the luncheon I was seated quite far down the table and did not have occasion to talk directly to him. Following the lunch, coffee and liqueurs were served, and at this point the general's aide, Captain François Flohic, came over to me and said, "The general would like to talk to you." I immediately went over and presented myself to him, and he recalled the name of the village where we had met in Italy, justifiably pleased as always to show his prodigious memory. He asked me how long I had been back in Paris. I was tempted to tell him that it was probably on that card that the DST, the French Internal Intelligence Service, gave him before the lunch concerning the guests, but thought better of it. He was very cordial to me even though he thought I worked for the CIA, which I did not until several years later.

In May 1968 the new American Ambassador to France arrived, Sargeant Shriver. He was President Kennedy's brother-in-law, married to Eunice Kennedy. Again, at his presentation of credentials to General de Gaulle, I saw the general and had some small conversation with him. The rioting that was to shake France had already started and General de Gaulle said that he would do what he could but that the future was in God's hands. This had a rather ominous sound to me and concerned me quite a lot. The rioting started in early May with the occupation of various buildings by rioting students. They took over the Boulevard St. Germain and renamed it the Avenue of Heroic Vietnam. The rioting spread rapidly throughout the city. The President and the Prime Minister were both out of the country. By the time they returned, a large part of the Left Bank was occupied by rioters and they were drawing great support from the Communists and from other far-leftist elements in France. Red flags and even the black flags of anarchy were flying over many factories that were occupied. The events degenerated into a general strike which almost paralyzed the country. For the first time in my life the gates of the Gare St. Lazare, the largest railroad station in Paris, were closed. The rioting spread around France. Political leaders opposed to General de Gaulle began to talk about forming a provisional government. Many Americans in the Embassy were strongly against General de Gaulle; some of them almost seemed to welcome these events as promising his overthrow. It reminded me of the situation in Cuba. We did not like Batista, yet he was replaced by Castro, who ran a far more repressive society and allied himself with the Soviets. I feared that in this case, General de Gaulle would be replaced by the Communists or someone very close to them and I did not view that prospect with the same equanimity as some of my American colleagues. When I expressed my misgivings to them, they explained tolerantly that I must understand that France was very different from Brazil. In France the Armed Forces played no part in the political life of the nation. One of my colleagues bet me thirty dollars that General de Gaulle would be out of office in thirty days. I took that bet—and won. (I have yet to see the thirty dollars. I doubt if he even remembers the bet.)

In talking to the French military, it was clear that whatever hostility they might have felt toward General de Gaulle for abandoning Algeria and for whatever measures he took against the military after the generals' revolt in Algiers, the prospect of rule by the Communists seemed far worse to them and they would certainly defend him and the legitimate government of France. The Embassy reporting during this period was quite panicky and I was forced simply to append to the Embassy telegrams a statement to the effect that the service attachés did not agree with this assessment. In fact, my Navy and Air Force colleagues, who were also experienced and knew France, agreed with my assessment that this rioting was not going to overthrow General de Gaulle. Again, I was told that I simply did not understand the problem. I was so disturbed by the Embassy reporting that I started a series of telegrams from the Defense Attaché to the Defense Department entitled, "Impact of Current Events on the Armed Forces." I had a few lines about the Armed Forces and then I gave my assessment of what was happening in a political sense. I did not like to do this, but I felt that it was my duty to make sure that the U.S. government was receiving what I believed was the correct view about the events that were taking place in France, and this was the only way I could do it. I did give copies of my telegrams to the Ambassador, the political section and others in the Embassy.

Several times in my messages I referred to the fact that General de Gaulle held the "trump cards," which were the loyalty of the Armed Forces and, above all, the loyalty of the gendarmerie. The gendarmerie is a highly militarized police force organized both in local units and in military-type units in barracks. It has some 65,000 men spread all over France, generally in the upper twenties age bracket or older, highly disciplined men with a great tradition of loyalty to the national government. By this time they had called up their reserves and were some 100,000 strong. The political side of the Embassy kept pressing me for information as to what I believed the Armed Forces and the draftees in the Army would do. They were being called upon to revolt by the various left-wing organizations. I replied that the situation was quite different to what it had been in Algiers when the French Army was being asked to revolt against the legally constituted government of the republic. In this case even General de Gaulle's worst enemies did not challenge the legality of his presidency, and I also felt that there was no parallel between these events and the situation in Algiers when the draftees had refused to obey their officers' call to revolt against General de Gaulle. About this time certain Army units began moving into the area around Paris. Some French units had no draftees in them at all. These were the marine infantry units and these seemed to be the ones that were moving into the Paris area. Several armored units were out on maneuvers when the riots began and after the general strike they could not return their tanks to their home garrisons by rail—the normal procedure. They returned by road on the tracks of their tanks. Many of them moved close to the Paris area and at nighttime would move into the area of the "Red Belt" around Paris, where the clanking of the tanks could be heard in the middle of the night. There were reports that the Foreign Legion might be used, but I doubted this because a considerable percentage—though less than half— of the Foreign Legion was foreign. It would be unwise to use them to restore order within France.

I referred in my telegrams again and again to the fact that the Armed Forces and police would remain loyal to General de Gaulle and would defend the constituted government of the French Republic. This was essentially the fundamental trump in General de Gaulle's hands. During this period I had my young nephew Jimmy Walters and his friend Jay Smither staying with me. Both boys had come to visit me two years before in Brazil. Naturally they were very anxious to get a view of the riots. I normally went out every night and moved around the rioting area in French clothes and wearing my Legion of Honor boutonniere so that I would not stand out as a foreigner. Later, the author of a somewhat silly book on intelligence wrote of this period and described how he had watched the "fat military attaché look out of the window of his office counting trucks." At this time, I did not have an office that looked out on the street, and I was not counting trucks. One evening I went out and found things relatively quiet so I decided to take the boys out with me since they were becoming most pressing in their demands to see some of the riots. We drove down across the Concorde bridge toward the War Ministry on Boulevard St. Germain. I left the car behind since it had a diplomatic license plate, and we walked down the boulevard toward a barricade. As we were walking toward the barricade, we were caught by tear gas and stumbled weeping back to the car. I decided to take them elsewhere. I then drove back across the Concorde bridge and along the banks of the Seine. Jay said to me, "General, there are people around us picking up stones." I had seen them myself and was concerned but in an effort not to alarm the boys I said, "Oh, they do that all the time. Don't pay any attention to it. If they stop the car shout, 'À bas les États-Unis' and help them turn it over. You will be protected by your age. I will flee." Suddenly we drove into a square and found ourselves facing a massed group of police on one side and rioters on the other. As we arrived, the rioters threw a Molotov cocktail, a flaming bottle, across the top of our car at the police. The police replied by firing sonic grenades, sound grenades, into the rioters. I immediately took off at full speed down the quai but was stopped by a policeman. I backed up and tried to drive down a side street, where I was stopped by rioters. I backed up again and tried another side street, where I was again stopped by rioters. I then determined that I would continue down the quai despite the policeman. I drove by him at high speed and he made no further attempt to stop me. As we drove out of the area of the riot, my nephew Jimmy laughed and I asked him what he was laughing about. He replied that just before they left Atlanta, my brother Fred had said, "There is rioting going on in Paris, but don't worry, Uncle Dick will keep you out of it." If I had they would never have forgiven me. I understood how they felt.

I think I saw the night that popular sentiment turned against the rioters. I was down in the eastern working-class end of Paris at the Place de la République. Student rioters were sawing down the hundred-year-old trees with a power saw to create barricades. I saw the indignation of the working people. A woman said to me, "The little bastards, it will take fifty years for those trees to grow back." That night the rioters set many cars afire. As I watched these riots, I realized that most of the participants did not belong to the working classes. Most of them were rich leftist kids from the 8th and the 16th districts of Paris where the wealthy people lived. They had been caught up by a combination of Marxist dialectics, chic leftism and guilt for their inherited wealth. One of the better stories told about this time was that one of these rich kids came home and told his father that he had set fire to seven cars that night. His father said, "Seven? Well, you've got me beaten. I only set fire to one." The boy, surprised, said, "Which one did you set fire to, Dad?" And the father said, "Son, I set fire to your sports convertible." This was one of the reasons why I felt this rioting would not be successful in overthrowing General de Gaulle. If I had seen the working-class youth of Paris at the riots, I would have been concerned because there were enough of them to overthrow the French government. The rich kids were too few in number to overthrow the French government.

Each night as I went out I would first pass the barracks of the only gendarmerie tank battalion. If the tanks were still in the courtyard of the barracks, the situation was not really grave. From there I would go on to other sensitive points where there was rioting so that I could measure what was happening. I was deeply impressed with the discipline and restraint of the gendarmerie. In spite of the most irritating provocation, of the most obscene statements to them by the rioters, there were no deaths in Paris. There were only two deaths in the whole of France during this month-long rioting. I truly envied France a disciplined police of this kind. They were never provoked into firing, but

God knows they were provoked. Many of them were injured by stone paving blocks hurled by rioters which broke their legs. Chemistry students from the University of Paris would dissolve the tar holding the paving blocks in place and they would then be used as missiles against the police.

The thing that puzzled me was the indecision of the government. I felt that they had all the means to put an end to this rioting and could not understand why they didn't use them. It was only later that I understood that General de Gaulle's tactics were to let the population become totally exasperated by the inconveniences of the general strike. I did put this thought in a telegram to Washington—I said that he was waiting for this to occur and that he would then strike and restore the situation. Then to general surprise and dismay, General de Gaulle disappeared. Ambassador Shriver called me in and said, "Where is he? Where can he have gone?" I said, "Mr. Ambassador, I don't know where he has gone, but I can tell you what he is doing. He is talking to his generals and he is going to ask them whether they are going to support him. And they are going to tell him they will support him. He is going to come back to Paris and put an end to all of this nonsense." Looking at the political officer, who had bet me thirty dollars that de Gaulle would be out of office in thirty days, I said, "You know, Brazil and France may be very different, but the President is talking to his generals to see whether he can stay in office or not, and the resemblance is greater than you seem to think it is." General de Gaulle returned from Germany, where he had gone to see General Massu, the commander of French forces there, who had assured him of his support. De Gaulle then spoke to the nation on the radio. I was returning from a ceremony for Decoration Day at the American Cemetery in Suresnes, near Paris, when the radio program was interrupted to say that General de Gaulle was coming on the air. I ordered the driver to stop, as I wanted to be sure I heard what he had to say. As I looked around, I noticed that all the other cars had stopped too. His speech was short. He announced that he was reopening the gasoline stations, that the general strike would now come to an end and that everyone would go back to work. I drove to the Embassy and sent a telegram to Washington. I knew that the political section had undoubtedly given the text of what General de Gaulle had said. My telegram, one of the shortest I have ever sent as a Military Attaché, simply said, "This afternoon at four o'clock General de Gaulle played the trumps referred to in my previous messages and the game is over." I had reported that for two days the Gaullists were going around Paris organizing a demonstration of support for General de Gaulle, and I added that when the Gaullists' counterstroke came, it would be a massive one. Late that afternoon huge flag-waving crowds of Gaullists and people opposed to leftist takeover began to assemble in the Place de la Concorde. I had commented previously to my political colleagues that many people in France were disturbed by the red and black flags flying over the occupied factories without a French flag alongside them. The Communist red flag had become somewhat respectable during the resistance to the Germans, but it was always accompanied by a French flag. One of the political officers said to me, "Walters, you really are old-fashioned. You still think that flags mean something." As the afternoon of May 31 wore on, the crowds in the Place de la Concorde in front of the Embassy grew larger and larger. We had an excellent view of this from the Ambassador's office, and as darkness fell, I looked out and saw what must have been half a million people in the square. They were all waving flags. Standing on top of the statues, symbolizing the French cities, around the square were young men waving large French flags. I then went over to the Crillon Hotel next door for dinner, and as I came out, a crowd of young people came up to the door and asked to see the manager. I waited to see what would happen. They said to him, "Monsieur, you do not have a French flag flying from the hotel. Hoist one." He seemed rather startled and said, "Well, I'll have to check with the owner of the hotel," to which they replied, "Monsieur, this is a French hotel in the heart of Paris. You have five minutes to put up that flag." He hastened upstairs and hoisted the flag. As the flag went up, the crowd in front sang the "Marseillaise." A stirring "Marseillaise," not unlike the one I heard in the Place de France in Casablanca on November 11, 1942.

These people seemed to sense that they had come close to the fate of Czechoslovakia, where the population had gone to sleep in a democracy and had awakened in a Communist state. Many of the people in that square were not Gaullists. As a matter of fact, it was curious to see that in addition to the French flags, there were many British, Belgian and American flags in the crowd. The huge mass of people started to surge up the Champs Elysées toward the Arch of Triumph. With great effort I worked myself out to the corner of the Champs Elysées and looked up and saw the avenue solidly filled with people from the Arch to the Place de la Concorde. I imagine it is one of the few times in my life that I have ever seen a million people. The automobile owners were driving around honking their horns with a coded blast that meant "De Gaulle will remain." Remain he did.

That night I went to dinner at a restaurant owned by a man I knew to be very much against General de Gaulle. He was not there when I began to eat. A little later he came in surreptitiously carrying a French flag. I could not help but needle him and said, "Where have you been?" He said, "I was down on the Champs Elysées." And I said to him, "But I thought you didn't like General de Gaulle." He said, "I don't, but when I considered the alternative, I thought the best thing I could do for France was to go down and join that demonstration and show the other side that France is not Czechoslovakia." If that was his purpose, he was successful.

After the riots ceased, my normal duties as attaché resumed and I continued to visit many of the units of the French Army. Among the things I had to do that summer was to take Ambassador Shriver and his family to the Normandy beachhead, and here an amusing episode occurred. Ambassador Shriver had told me that this was to be an incognito visit, but he was going to give an interview to the French television. I wondered how incognito that would make the visit. He asked me where would be the best place to do this. The weather was not good so I suggested that he do it indoors at Ste. Mère Église in the Airborne Museum, which would provide shelter and light for the interview. When we got to the town, he began to give the interview in the Airborne Museum. Mrs. Shriver and the children soon lost interest in the proceedings and wandered over to the church made famous by the film *The Longest Day*. (A paratrooper's chute became entangled on the steeple and he was deafened by the ringing of the church bells.) We went into this old church. It was Saturday afternoon and the priest was in the confessional hearing confessions. Since I had not been for some time myself, I went in to confession. When I came out, Shriver's young son, Bobby, aged about fifteen, said to me, "How do you go to confession in French?" He spoke very good French and I told him what the formula was at the beginning. And he said, "Yeah, but tell me how you confess your sins." To which I replied, "Bobby, I confess my sins to the priest, not to you. You go in and tell him your sins as best you can." Bobby shrugged and went in. While he was in there, Shriver arrived and said, "Oh, confession! How do you go to confession in French?" I told him the formula and when Bobby came out, Shriver went in. While he was in the confessional, the representative of the French television who had interviewed Shriver arrived with the prefect, a position similar to that of a state governor in the United States. The TV man asked me, "Where is the Ambassador? I want to say goodbye to him." I replied, "The Ambassador is going to confession." "*Merde*," said the French television representative, "I knew he told me a bunch of lies, but he sure didn't lose any time in getting forgiveness for them!"

Later we went on to Mont St. Michel, where the prefect put his helicopter at the Shrivers' disposal. The Ambassador, his wife and Bobby flew around the mountain several times in the helicopter. The view was truly spectacular from the seaward side. Then I flew around it with their daughter Maria and their younger son Timothy. We only flew around once and started back. Timothy protested that the others had flown around three times, so I explained to him that as a major general I was only entitled to one circle. You had to be an Ambassador to be entitled to three. That seemed to satisfy him.

During this period, Mrs. de Gaulle returned Mrs. Shriver's call. Mrs. Shriver was intensely interested in retarded children and as the de Gaulles had had a retarded child, Ann, who had died at twenty, I knew that Mrs. de Gaulle was very sensitive about this subject. Mrs. Shriver spoke a great deal about it and I was translating for her. Madame de Gaulle seemed very taken with Mrs. Shriver's interest and at one point Mrs. Shriver said, "I note that in the future retarded adults will be covered under French social security. I suppose it's because you spoke to the general about it." There was a pause and then Madame de Gaulle said, "Yes, because I spoke to the general about it." It was the only time I can recall that she ever acknowledged any influence over the general.

Not long after I got to France, and on my recommendation, the United States Defense Department invited the Chief of Staff of French Defense, General Michel Fourquet, an Air Force general, and his wife to go to the United States. They accepted and I was designated to go with them. It was the first time in six or seven years that a senior French Defense official had been to the United States. In the course of preparing General Fourquet's itinerary, the Pentagon asked me what he would like to see, and I replied without consulting him that I thought he would like to see missile silos. This evoked a great fuss and much discussion, but finally the Pentagon gave in and it was agreed that he would see missile silos. In the course of his trip around the United States, we were taken to Vandenberg Air Force Base on the Pacific coast and into missile silos there which he inspected with great interest. Photographs were taken of him visiting these missile silos. These were extremely useful to me several years later. This did a lot to warm up Franco-American military relations from the extremely cool situation in which I found them on arriving in France. Subsequently there were further interchanges of visits at fairly senior levels that did a lot more to rekindle friendly relations between the two armed services. During the early part of my stay in France, I attempted not to get involved in anything political concerning NATO or General de Gaulle. I made a practice to try to attend all the commemorations of World War I and II feats of arms carried out together by French and Americans, and this very often evoked emotional outbursts from the people of these towns, who would come up to me and say, "General de Gaulle may have forgotten what you Americans did, but we haven't." Sometimes they would say this to me in front of the French authorities and this was somewhat embarrassing.

I had good relations with my attaché colleagues, one of whom later became President of Peru, General Juan Velasco Alvarado, and I was able to use this friendly relationship in the interest of the United States during a later difficult period of Peruvian-American relations.

On one occasion I was visiting the French Mountain Brigade and I had gone skiing with them, and I had invited the commander of the Brigade, General Etcheverry, and his staff to dinner with me on the last day of my stay. At four o'clock that afternoon I had a skiing accident and broke my leg. I was taken to the hospital and my leg was put in a cast. I received a phone call suggesting that I cancel the dinner. I decided to go ahead with the dinner. I was in great pain and had a wet cast on my leg, but I hosted the dinner for the Alpine Brigade staff that night. The story circulated through the French Army that not only did I speak good French, but that I did not let a broken leg interfere with my planned dinner for my French colleagues.

The French also allowed me for the first time to visit the Foreign Legion in Corsica. They had been reluctant to do so previously inasmuch as there were a few Americans serving in the Legion and they did not want me to have any contact with them. I said I couldn't care less whether there were Americans serving in the Legion. That was their business, not mine. I had an extremely interesting visit with various units of the Foreign Legion in Corsica. The Legion had borne the brunt of the French war in Vietnam, and their feelings were particularly warm toward me when I visited them. As a matter of fact, when I paid a visit to the first Legion installation, I was greeted with an old Legion song called "Against the Viets." Despite the name, a vast Foreign Legion majority of the men are French, with the Germans, Yugoslavs and Spaniards following, probably in that order. Much of the Legion is now stationed in Corsica. The reception center is in France, and they still have units in Djibouti and in the French territories in the Pacific.

I had many U.S. visitors, often very senior people, who would come to attend exercises at NATO or at SHAPE. They would invariably find an excuse to go to Paris, where they would expect to be entertained by me. Unfortunately, such entertainment funds as I had at my disposal were to be used only for entertaining foreigners, and this was a considerable burden on me. Some of these visitors were very welcome. I recall on one occasion Cardinal Cooke, the Archbishop of New York, came and, as he was the vicar-general of the Catholic chaplains, I was asked to take care of him. I invited him to dinner at my club in Paris, and since it was a very nice day, we were dining out in the garden. A sudden rainstorm came up and each diner promptly seized his own table and carried it back into the building. I did not know what one did under such circumstances with a cardinal archbishop, but when I looked at him, he was standing up holding his side of the table, so I took the other side and together we carried it into the building. On our way in, the young manager of the club ran up to me, shocked that I was carrying the table, and he said, "*Mon général*, I cannot have a general carrying a table." I looked at him and smiled and said, "You only know half the story. Do you know who is carrying the other half of this table? It is the Cardinal Archbishop of New York." He was even more shocked, but by the time he recovered, we had the table indoors and resumed our dinner.

The improving Franco-American relations were greatly facilitated by the visit President Nixon paid to France very shortly after he became President. I was, as usual, commandeered to translate for him on arrival. A statement had been prepared for him to deliver at the airport. However, when he arrived, General de Gaulle made such a warm speech to welcome him that the President departed entirely from his prepared text and proceeded to make a very much warmer and more complimentary reply to General de Gaulle. Some of the news correspondents who had some knowledge of the two languages, but not a complete one, accused me of changing what the President had said. I said to them, "You may have a prepared statement that was given to you, but I translated what the President said at the airport."

General de Gaulle always had a particularly warm spot in his heart for Mr. Nixon and viewed his career as somewhat paralleling his own. On one occasion he had told me in no uncertain terms that Mr. Nixon would yet be President of the United States. Following President Nixon's arrival, various meetings were held, including one at Versailles, where General de Gaulle had restored the Trianon Palace. General de Gaulle recalled at the lunch that he had known me longer than any of his ministers who were sitting at the table with him, since we had met in London in 1942 and he had met his ministers either later in London, in Algiers or after he returned to metropolitan France. This produced a considerable thaw.

Somewhere along the line General de Gaulle had gotten the idea that I worked for the CIA. I talked to one of his aides and told him in no uncertain terms that I could give him my word that I did not work for the CIA. In fact, I did not work for the CIA for several years after this, and the first time in my life that I ever worked for them was when I became deputy director in May 1972. General de Gaulle was always extremely cordial with me, and the French really allowed me as much freedom of action or more than most other attachés in visiting units of the French Army, not only those in France, but also the French forces in Germany.

It also fell to me to accompany Mr. Nixon on his visit to France the second time he came, and once again, the relationship with General de Gaulle was extremely close and cordial. Later, after General de Gaulle had resigned, Mr. Nixon asked me to deliver a handwritten letter to him at his home in Colombey-les-Deux-Églises.

In August 1969 I became involved with Henry Kissinger in

the secret negotiations with the North Vietnamese that are
covered in a later chapter. Somewhat later in 1970 I became involved in the secret negotiations with the Chinese Communists
that led to Mr. Nixon's visit to China and a new relationship
with them. However, these negotiations and the constant smuggling into France of Henry Kissinger to meet with them made
my life as attaché very difficult. I could not take most of the
trips that attachés normally take. I could not tell the Ambassador about the negotiations when he wanted me to go to some
particular celebration with him. I had great difficulty in continuing to perform my duties as attaché to France. I do not believe
that President Nixon or Henry Kissinger ever realized how complex my situation was. They had instructed me to tell no one
what I was doing—neither the Ambassador for whom I worked
nor my superiors in the Defense Department. In fact, shortly before I returned to the United States, I was paying farewell calls
on the French forces in Germany and on two of the four days I
was there, I received phone calls from Dr. Kissinger ordering me
back to Paris to see either the Chinese or the Vietnamese. The
first time I went back by commercial plane. The second time I
insisted that he get me a military aircraft to take me there and
back. He did so very promptly. The French, of course, were obviously puzzled by my actions and these sudden trips to Paris
only increased their curiosity.

General Earle Wheeler, the chairman of the U. S. Joint
Chiefs of Staff, came to France close to the end of my tour. The
French asked me what General Wheeler wanted to see, and
without consulting him I said he wanted to see missile silos.
They protested that no foreigners had ever been in their missile
silos and besides, we had never shown them our missile silos. At
this point, I triumphantly produced the photograph taken three
years earlier of General Fourquet in the missile silos at Vandenberg Air Force Base. This made the necessary impression, and
the French included a visit to their missile silos on the Albion
Plateau for General Wheeler. He was, I believe, the first foreigner to visit them, and, needless to say, I went along with him
as his interpreter. This was a symbol of the improvement in

Franco-American military relationships. They also decorated General Wheeler with the Grand Officer of the Legion of Honor.

Toward the end of my tour in Paris the North Vietnamese and Chinese negotiations took up nearly all my time. Yet when the time came for me to leave, the French were extremely cordial and subsequently elevated me for the third time in the Legion of Honor to the grade of Commander. The decoration was actually presented to me after my return to the United States by the French Ambassador to Washington, Mr. Jacques Kosciuszko-Morizet. After President Pompidou succeeded General de Gaulle I accompanied him on a trip to the United States, which was a sort of bittersweet trip. We visited various places in the United States, including Cape Kennedy, Los Angeles and San Francisco. This was an awkward time for his visit as there were many demonstrations against Pompidou because of the French sale of aircraft to the Arabs and the embargo on sales to the Israelis. All of this made the situation difficult. France is a democracy but such demonstrations would never be permitted around a visiting foreign chief of state. I tried at some length to explain the federal system and the municipal system of the United States, but it made very little impact on President Pompidou. In France the federal government can remove any mayor who embarrasses the national government in any way. From San Francisco, which Pompidou liked very much, we went out to Stanford University by helicopter. Long lines of students picketed Pompidou, both on account of the Arab-Israeli matter and also because as Prime Minister in 1968 he "repressed" the student riots. At the end of the visit Pompidou met with the faculty and a representative of the students. He had a short discussion with each member of the faculty. Frequently something was said to which the representative of the students would comment, "The students don't agree with that." Finally, Pompidou got to him and asked him how he became the representative of the students. He said that he had been elected to this office. Pompidou, with a twinkle in his eye, said, "And how many of the thirteen thousand students at the university voted in this election?" The boy said, "Five thousand." Pompidou said, "What percentage of the five thousand votes did you get?" The boy said, "Well, there were a lot of candidates. I got 32 per cent." Pompidou, with an even brighter twinkle in his eye, leaned over and said, "Son, I got more than that." Even the youngster himself grinned sheepishly.

As we were leaving the hotel for the helicopter pad, Pompidou asked me what we were waiting for. I passed the question to Protocol Chief Bus Mosbacher. He replied that Foreign Minister Schumann had not yet arrived. When I translated this to Pompidou he said, "They are lined up six deep in Paris waiting for his job." I told this to Mosbacher and he asked me what he meant. I replied that to me it meant that in the future we would wait only for Madame Pompidou.

Next we flew to Chicago, where the most awkward and difficult incident of the whole trip occurred. As we walked into the lobby of the hotel, the shouting demonstrators were allowed very close to Pompidou and his wife. What they were saying was actually "Shalom," which means "greetings" or "peace" in Hebrew. The Pompidous thought they were saying, "Saluad," which is an insult in French. Mrs. Pompidou was greatly upset by this and that evening when he got back to the hotel, Pompidou had decided to go home. U. S. Chief of Protocol Bus Mosbacher, who was running the trip, was appalled. Pompidou had told me that he simply would not subject his wife to this kind of insult. The United States might be prepared to put up with this sort of thing, but he was not, especially when his wife was involved. The Pompidous were an extraordinarily devoted couple. They often unobtrusively held hands while riding in cars. Pompidou keenly felt his inability to speak English. Madame Pompidou, a charming and gracious woman, spoke fluent English. Pompidou decided to stay and continue the trip but he was sending his wife home the next day. Mosbacher asked me what I thought we ought to do. I said I was convinced that the only thing that would mollify Pompidou and might prevent his sending his wife home the next day would be a personal phone call from President Nixon. Mosbacher then telephoned the President and told him what the situation was. The President then phoned Pompidou and told him that he himself would replace Vice-President Agnew at the dinner for Pompidou in New York. This pleased Pompidou and he canceled the plans for Madame Pompidou to leave the next day. We then flew to New York and stayed at Mosbacher's home in White Plains. A priest came out to say mass for the Pompidous in Mosbacher's home. I served the mass and read the Epistle in French. There was a large reception for Pompidou at the Waldorf-Astoria, but here again the demonstrators were allowed quite close to him and this seemed to offend Pompidou. His attitude toward the United States remained scarred by this visit until his death. I have been told by friends that he had made a vow never to return to the United States. The incidents occurred at the height of the anti-Vietnam demonstrations, when large groups of agitators were doing everything they could to embarrass the Nixon administration, domestically and internationally. Foreign guests had no immunity from this venom.

A European has difficulty in understanding why the American federal government has problems in preventing crowds from insulting foreign visitors. In Europe such things simply do not happen, even in democracies like France or Great Britain. This trip to the United States with the Pompidous was to prove extremely useful when I needed Pompidou's help not long afterward to extract Henry Kissinger from an awkward situation that might have compromised his ongoing negotiations with the Chinese and the North Vietnamese. President Pompidou gave that help without hesitation. Yet, he was to retain to the end of his life a cooler feeling about the United States because of the hostile demonstrations against him during his visit.

In 1971 when the United States forces moved into Cambodia to attack the long-established North Vietnamese sanctuaries a great hue and cry went up in the United States and throughout the world, orchestrated by the New Left rather than the Communists. Disorders occurred on American campuses, in the streets of American cities, in front of American embassies all over the world. Perhaps orchestration is not the right word, but the synchronization was superb. In Paris an American college is located on the Quai d'Orsay close to the French Foreign Office. The building is of Gothic stone and has a very Ivy League, wood-paneled look. The students at this college seized the building and demanded that the United States Embassy send someone over to explain to them why the United States had invaded Cambodia. They never to my knowledge wondered why the North Vietnamese had invaded Cambodia many years earlier and had been occupying large parts of the country. The atmosphere was heated and there was great reluctance in the Embassy to go and face the students. Irked by this I said that I would go in civilian clothes, so that if there was any indignity (and I confidently expected some) it would be personal and not directed at the Army. I sent word to the students that I would be there at 2:30 P.M. on May 12, 1970. As I got out of my car in front of the building, I saw the daughter of a Sixth Fleet Navy captain who was attending the college. She recognized me and said, "Don't go in, General, there is going to be some unpleasantness." I replied, "My dear, most of my adult life in the Army has been spent facing some sort of unpleasantness, most of it practiced with more expertise than I expect to find inside." I went into the building and was met and taken to the auditorium. I passed groups of students standing around and many of them cast hostile looks in my direction. The auditorium was filled with about 250 or more students sitting facing me. When I realized that they were all sitting between me and the only exit I felt less confident than I had when speaking to the girl outside the building. The meeting began with one of the professors of the school uttering a passionate denunciation of the U.S. action in Vietnam. Professor Pike made clear, however, that he was not opposed to all wars, just this one in Vietnam. When he finished speaking he received tumultuous applause. My turn to speak had come. I stood up at the small table on which the microphone was placed. As I began to speak, a group of about ten students moved down the central aisle toward me led by a young American who was carrying a package wrapped in a newspaper. They approached me silently and laid the package on the table.

It fell open revealing a fetus. A girl laid three flowers on it saying, "For the dead in Vietnam." I said softly, "for those in South Vietnam too, I hope." She looked startled but said nothing. This group then went to the rear of the room and began shouting, "Don't listen to the fascist pig; he has nothing to say to you. People are dying in Vietnam and he is talking to you." This was soon followed by incoherent words. The great majority of the students looked startled at this interruption and some shouted, "Shut up, we want to hear what he has to say." The noisy group shouted the same slogan louder. The main body of students began to get angry, shouting, "Maybe we don't agree but we want to hear what he has to say." One boy shouted at the demonstrators, "You don't belong to this school. We invited you over here to hear this debate. Now shut up or get out." The boy who had laid the fetus in front of me and who seemed to be making the most noise replied, "I'm too poor to pay the tuition at this rich kids' school." While this was going on, I had the microphone and decided to use it, as the public address system was loud enough to drown out the cries. I said, "If I had staged this whole incident to prove my point, I could not have done a better job. This is what it is all about. Will you be allowed in the old academic tradition to hear all sides of a question and then make up your minds, or will a small, noisy group like this one in the back of the room decide what you are old enough, safe enough and mature enough to hear? I did not ask to come here. You invited me to come and if you don't want to hear me, I will leave. But if you want to hear me, you will have to do something to defend your right to hear." Many applauded this statement, including Professor Pike.

One boy with very long hair stood up and shouted at the noisemakers, "If you don't like it, get out. We want to hear." The noisy group shouted back, "The fascist pig has nothing to tell you." The long-haired boy then said, "Who wants to hear?" An overwhelming majority held up their hands. The long-haired boy, shouting at the top of his lungs, then said, "Get out or we are going to throw you out." The temper of the majority was such that the interlopers decided to go, and shouting, "Okay, then, listen to the fascist pig if you want to," they left. I pointed out to the students that World War II had broken out after Britain and France had lost their credibility. They had let Hitler reoccupy the Rhineland, take the Saar, then Austria, Sudetenland, then the whole of Czechoslovakia and Memel. Finally they had to stand at Poland and a great world war had ensued. Had they faced up to aggression earlier, when it was easier, this holocaust might have been avoided. We faced the same problem in Asia. Vietnam was probably not the best place to commit American credibility, but for better or for worse, four American Presidents had supported that commitment. If we were now to abandon our credibility, who would trust us in the future? How many real friends would we have? Perhaps South Vietnam was not the ideal democracy, but some opposition was tolerated. If the North Vietnamese ever got to Saigon, no opposition at all would be tolerated, just as none was tolerated in North Vietnam. The North Vietnamese had invaded Cambodia years ago and had been using it as a privileged sanctuary to attack South Vietnamese and U.S. forces. Was it wrong for us to enter Cambodia, but right for them? Occasionally, there was a boo or a catcall but basically the students listened attentively. When I had finished I said that I was prepared to answer questions.

One young man got up and told me that I had to understand that this political commitment of youth was something new and it had never happened before. I replied that I did not agree. Youth has always been highly motivated politically. I said, "Let me tell you what was the great protest song of my time. It went like this. 'A young generation is rising ready for the storm. Before our fists all walls will fall. Nothing can stand against us, for we are a young generation rising ready for the storm and we carry the flag of a new time.'" I went on to say that none of them were old enough to remember what it was. It was the first verse of "Unsere Fahne Flattert Uns Voran," the song of the Hitler Youth. One of the boys stood up and said, "But we are sincere." I replied that three million young Germans had died on every battlefield around the world—did he think by any chance that they were not sincere? The greatest tragedy I knew was the sincerity of youth twisted to the service of an evil cause. One or two brave young people applauded this. I went on to say, "In our system there are all the mechanisms for change. If enough people agree, you can change anything in our system. No other alternative system provides for this. There are many inequities and shortcomings in our present system but it has provided more of the good things of life to a greater percentage of its members than any other system man has invented. When Marxism can match the freedom and achievements of our system, I will give it a more attentive ear." (This produced considerable applause.)

Another question was, "Why don't people listen to us?" I replied that, "They do, but what you really mean is why doesn't the government do what you want it to. You must realize that while intelligence and education are important, so is experience. Would you rather fly with a pilot with little experience and lots of correspondence course diplomas or with a pilot with little in the way of diplomas but a lot of flying hours? You simply cannot expect those who bear the responsibilities, have most facts and the most to lose to steer whatever course you shout for."

I wound up by reading three quotations, one each from President Kennedy, Senator Robert Kennedy and Adlai Stevenson, on why we are in Vietnam and what we seek to defend there. At the end there was applause by about one third of the audience and many of the others came over to say that while they were still opposed to the Vietnam War they wanted to thank me for coming over to talk to them. I left walking through the students with no manifestations of hostility. All the students made a point of telling me that those who tried to break up the meeting did not go to the American college.

I was later to receive sixteen letters from the students thanking me for coming. Some agreed with me, some did not, but all thanked me for coming. Later that evening, the Albanian Radio reported that the "democratic students at the American college in Paris had prevented the fascist Military Attaché from defending the shameless American war in Vietnam." Later the French gave me an eyewitness account. They too had evidently been present. The great lesson I learned from this is that much of the rage and frustration which young people showed during this time was because they did not feel they could get a hearing. I did not greatly change the views of most of the students who heard me, but the difference in atmosphere when I entered the building and left it was striking.

Two other major events occurred during my tour in Paris before I was to leave for my next assignment. I was ordered to accompany Mrs. Nixon on a trip to the earthquake-stricken areas of Peru. On July 26, 1970, I flew to Los Angeles and went from there to San Clemente. On Sunday the twenty-eighth I flew in the presidential aircraft with Mrs. Nixon straight from El Toro Marine base to Lima. Before I left, the President took me aside and asked me to keep an eye on Mrs. Nixon and be as helpful to her as I could. We arrived in Lima carrying medical supplies and food. We were met on arrival by President Velasco Alvarado's wife Consuelo, and I stayed at the Embassy residence. The Peruvian government of Juan Velasco Alvarado had not been friendly to the United States. I had known Velasco Alvarado some years earlier when he was the Peruvian Attaché to Paris. He was greatly moved by the fact that Mrs. Nixon had come. He took me aside and said, "You know, it is only when one goes to bed sick that one finds out who one's friends really are." On Sunday we flew in a C-130 up into the Callejón de Huaylas, where the major earthquake damage was. Mrs. Velasco Alvarado flew with us. She was a handsome, attractive woman. When I saw the dirt airstrip on which we were to land at the bottom of a deep valley at Anta, I could not believe that they would bring the first ladies of the United States and Peru into such a hazardous strip. It was short, unsurfaced and located at about nine thousand feet altitude with gigantic mountains towering many thousands of feet higher on both sides of the narrow valley. Neither Mrs. Nixon nor Mrs. Velasco Alvarado seemed concerned. I was. On landing, we were taken by helicopter to various camps and destroyed villages in the area. Many of the victims had been killed in a town called Yungay that had been buried by a landslide of mud. Some twenty thousand people had been killed. The only trace of the town was the upper tip of a few very tall palm trees that had stood in front of the church. Everything else was buried under thirty feet of mud. Everywhere we went in the valley people wanted to talk to Pat and Consuelo. Over and over they asked that the town be rebuilt at the same location despite the fact that this was not the first time their homes had been destroyed by earthquakes. I could only marvel at the attachment of people to their soil. Mrs. Nixon was greatly moved by the distress of the people. At one point a little boy with tears rolling down his cheeks ran toward her. She swept him up in her arms and hugged him till he stopped crying. The fact that the wife of the President of the United States had come this far to be with them at a time of sorrow and suffering was not lost on the Peruvians. Later that afternoon, we took off from the precarious dirt strip, climbed between the walls of the towering mountains on both sides of the valley and then flew back to Lima. Next morning I went with Mrs. Nixon to visit the Children's Hospital. We were struck by the very large number of cases of skull fracture. The adobe houses generally had heavy roofs and when the walls collapsed the beams fell in, causing the head injuries. It was truly a pathetic sight. On June 30 we flew back to El Toro and were taken by chopper to San Clemente. Next day I left to return to Paris. I was later to get a most gracious letter from Mrs. Nixon thanking me for helping her in talking to the Peruvians during her visit.

23. DE GAULLE 1942–69

My relationship with General Charles de Gaulle extended over more than a quarter of a century—from my first meeting with him in mid-December 1942 at his office in London in Carlton House Terrace, when he was head of the Free French, until I went, after his resignation, to Colombey-les-Deux-Églises to deliver a hand-written letter from President Nixon, reiterating to General de Gaulle the invitation that the American President had previously extended to the President of France. The mission was not continuous, but did involve many meetings during the intervening years. First, in London; then in Italy—twice when he came to visit the Fifth Army; again, when he saw General Eisenhower during Eisenhower's tour at SHAPE; in 1958 when he gave me a silver cigarette case with his signature engraved on it; in 1959 when I went with NATO commander General Lauris Norstad to show him U-2 photographs; in 1960 when he helped pin on my eagles the day I was promoted to full colonel—he gave me a cigarette lighter to complement the cigarette case. I saw him in Brasília and Rio in 1966 when he visited Brazil. We met again when I arrived in France in 1967, and on a number of occasions during my tour of duty there. Finally, in the end after he had left power, I brought him the American President's invitation.

General de Gaulle was a most unusual man. He maintained

about himself an aura of aloofness and mystery that he felt was absolutely necessary for greatness. Perhaps only once or twice did I see him unbend—at a dinner with Eisenhower in 1952 and again when he went to General Eisenhower's farm and played with his grandchildren in 1960. He was an austere man, but he always bore himself with great composure. He gave an impression of having thought out carefully what he was going to say and he articulated it in absolutely beautiful French. I am personally convinced that the superb language of his memoirs, published prior to his return to power in 1958, contributed substantially to that return. The French were inclined to refer to him as being stupid. It is intellectually "in" throughout the Western world to say that generals are stupid. The grace and the language of General de Gaulle's memoirs showed that he was truly a master of the language, and this gave him a popular psychological advantage that was to help him return to power, first as Prime Minister and subsequently as President.

I really cannot say that I saw a substantial change in the man between 1942 and 1969. He was more impetuous and he had more of a sense of hurt in London in 1942. He was more philosophical toward the end of his life when he had achieved his ambition to be the leader of the French people. There was a fire burning inside him in London. Later there was simply a steady glow that gave off warmth and power. In London, he was quick to see or perceive real or imagined hurts. He mentioned that the British had deliberately given him space in Carlton House Terrace because it was a dead end, with the only way in or out through Waterloo Place. I doubt very much that the British gave any thought to the matter. By a curious coincidence, General de Gaulle's appeal to the French people—stating that France had lost a battle but not the war—was issued on the 125th anniversary of the Battle of Waterloo, June 18, 1940.

In his London Headquarters he questioned me about the situation in North Africa. I told him my opinion that a large majority of the population looked to him for leadership rather than to General Giraud or Admiral Darlan. He said this confirmed what he himself knew of conditions there. He said it was difficult to convince Mr. Roosevelt and Mr. Churchill of this fact. He said that time and again they had gone out of their way to make him feel like a second-class ally.

General de Gaulle thanked me for bringing the letter. He was curious about how I had learned French. He asked me how long I was staying in London. I said not very long, that I was going on. He said that was a pity, ". . . you have qualities that could be used on this side of the ocean." I told him that I hoped to return to the European Theater as soon as I could. I had no ambition to live out the war in the United States. "That is good," he said, "good. You must return." We shook hands. I was not to see him again for nearly two years.

The next time I saw him I was General Clark's aide at Roccastrada in Italy. Upon his arrival, General de Gaulle was received by General Clark with a smart guard of honor, and was then ushered into General Clark's van. I went into the van with the two generals. No one else was present. A discussion began concerning withdrawal of the French Expeditionary Corps in Italy for the landings soon to take place in the South of France. General de Gaulle emphasized how important it was for the French to take an active part in the liberation of France if the Communists were not to take over the government at the end of the war. He felt that the French divisions fighting in Italy had redeemed in some measure the fighting honor of France. He spoke highly of General Juin but said that he had another full general on his hands, General de Lattre de Tassigny, and he had to give him his chance. He would be in command of the French Army Detachment B which would land in southern France. General Clark urged him again to name Juin as the commander of the French forces to be landed in southern France. General de Gaulle smiled a wintry smile and said to General Clark, "Isn't it a little odd for you, an American general, to tell me, the head of the provisional government of France, who should command my troops?" General Clark pushed the matter no further. General de Gaulle listened with interest to General Clark's description of the fighting prowess of the French corps and his praise for their behavior in combat in very rough terrain against

a very tough enemy. They discussed the timing of the detachment of the French divisions from the Fifth Army and their
movement into the staging area in Naples, from which they
would then go forward into the South of France. In the meantime, an operation was planned to take the island of Elba, but
this would be done with other French troops from North Africa.

Subsequently, I was to see de Gaulle still later in Italy when
he came to decorate General Clark with the insignia of Grand
Officer of the Legion of Honor. Again, there was a warm and
friendly discussion between the two. I got the impression that
General de Gaulle by and large felt that his troops in Italy had
been fairly treated. They had been given an appropriate chance
to distinguish themselves under General Clark's command and
had done so, and for all of this he was grateful.

After Italy I was not to see General de Gaulle for eight years.
I saw him shortly before General Eisenhower returned to the
United States to run for the Republican presidential nomination.
There had been attempts over a period of time during General
Eisenhower's stay in Paris as NATO commander to get him and
General de Gaulle together. This, however, involved a rather
awkward situation, since General Eisenhower was theoretically
working for all the NATO governments and that included
France. He was living in a house provided by the French government, and General de Gaulle was the leader of the opposition to
that government. A number of people were anxious to bring the
two generals together and a means was finally found at which no
offense could be taken by the French government. General de
Gaulle during the war had created a very select order called the
Order of Liberation for one thousand people who contributed
greatly to the liberation of France. Five hundred recipients were
named posthumously. The only ones awarded to foreigners were
to the Sultan of Morocco and General Eisenhower. The grand
chancellor of the order was a priest, a monk, who was also a
reserve naval officer in the French Navy and had risen to the
rank of full admiral. At the end of the war after being governor
of French Indochina, he returned to his monastery and would
emerge occasionally to act as chancellor of the order. In April

1952 he arranged a dinner for General Eisenhower with the other high dignitaries of the order; namely, the admiral himself, General Juin, General de Lattre de Tassigny and Prince Ponia-towski—a close friend of General de Gaulle's and later to be Minister of the Interior in France.

The meeting was held at the building then housing the Order of Liberation in Rue François Premier in Paris. As General Eisenhower walked up the steps of the building, General de Gaulle awaited him. They shook hands with the warmth and delight of old friends. General Eisenhower then said, "I would like to introduce my aide, Lieutenant Colonel Walters." General de Gaulle looked at me, smiled, held out his hand and said, "Walters and I know one another. The last time I saw him was at Roccastrada in Italy, where we discussed the withdrawal of the French corps in Italy with General Clark, and he was present and served as our interpreter." I was astonished as his exact recollection, even naming the place where we had met. Later I learned that General de Gaulle's memory for detail was absolutely legendary. It was to serve him well as his eyesight began to fail. When he came to the United States many years later, he addressed a joint session of the United States Congress. Advanced texts of what he was going to say were distributed to the Congress. General de Gaulle went to the rostrum without a single note and proceeded to deliver a speech almost verbatim to the advance text. This prodigious memory made a profound impression on all those who knew him.

The meal that followed at the Order of Liberation was one of the times I have seen General de Gaulle most relaxed. What was particularly surprising to me was to hear General Juin refer to him in the familiar "tu" form of speech, which is traditional in France between classmates. The idea of anyone using this form of address to General de Gaulle was almost mind-boggling, and yet he did. General de Gaulle was relaxed and happy that evening, and after the dinner he and Eisenhower went out onto the porch overlooking the garden and sat there together. I sat between them and translated what they had to say. De Gaulle said, "We both will be called upon to lead our nations. You will be called before me, but I will be inevitably called upon to lead France, as there is no alternative to me, and while we are together, I think it would be well for us to understand some of the things that cause friction and trouble between us." He said, "For instance, one of the things that irritates the French is the American consulates in our colonies and the U. S. Embassy's willingness in France to listen to and receive people who are anxious to rebel against French rule. This the French do not like." Eisenhower said he could understand that but the United States had a long tradition of being sympathetic to independence movements, and while we would not in any way support those revolting against the French, we could not refuse in the light of our tradition to hear them. General de Gaulle said another problem that concerned the French were small American actions disregarding French law. He pointed out that in France the law required all automobile headlights to be yellow, whereas nearly all of the American officers and enlisted personnel attached to SHAPE still were driving around France with white headlights. General Eisenhower looked sharply at me and said, "Walters, what color are the headlights on your car?" Somewhat embarrassed, I said, "White, General." He said, "See that they are yellow by tomorrow." Turning back to General de Gaulle, he said, "I can understand the irritation value of some of these pinpricks and you can be sure that I will give orders that French law is complied with in this area." De Gaulle then said that as NATO was now constituted it was unwieldly. In his opinion it could work effectively only if there were a small group composed of the United States, Great Britain and France working in close harmony as an executive agent for the rest of the alliance. He believed that twelve, thirteen or fourteen were just simply too many people for useful discussion. He also expressed some reservation about the unanimity required to do anything in NATO and expressed grave concern if a serious crisis came whether such unanimity could be achieved in time to permit the alliance to take effective action. General Eisenhower took an optimistic view on this subject and General de Gaulle expressed satisfaction at the fact that he knew General Eisenhower would get the Republican nomination and would be elected President of the United States. He repeated his confidence that within a few years he himself would be called to lead the French nation. It would be more complicated for him since he would have to change the constitution and the institutions, which were those of the Fourth Republic and not really adequate for the situation in which France found herself. He then said to General Eisenhower, "Sometimes some of the things that I say may irritate you, but you must remember that I am trying to take a nation which was once great and has fallen into the gutter and lift it out of the gutter. And sometimes I must sting them with words, and sometimes those words are not friendly or acceptable to foreigners. But when someone tells you that I have said something like this, try to remember the larger purpose I am trying to serve of restoring French self-respect, of restoring the French people's feeling that the security of France will depend in large measure on the efforts that they themselves are prepared to make."

General de Gaulle said that he looked forward with confidence to the period in which General Eisenhower would lead the United States and he was sure that when his turn came they could do great work together to serve the cause of human freedom and the cause of their countries. They promised to see one another again and keep in touch. General de Gaulle walked Eisenhower out of the building, down the steps and to his car. He shook hands with me and said, "Walters, I know we will see one another soon." I then drove off with General Eisenhower, on whom once again General de Gaulle had made a strong impression. He said to me in the car, "Roosevelt didn't like him. A lot of people don't like him, but I can't help but feel that he is truly and sincerely devoted to his country and to restoring its self-respect and its sense of responsibility for its own future, and you can't really fault him for that."

Seven years were to pass before I saw General de Gaulle again. When I returned to France with President Eisenhower, General de Gaulle was the President of the French Republic and his prophecy had been fulfilled in both cases. Their greeting once again was extraordinarily warm and cordial. There were already shadows on the NATO alliance and France's attitude toward it, but none of this showed as President Eisenhower stepped from the airplane and General de Gaulle, looking at him, said, "Whatever may come in the future, whatever may happen in the years ahead, you will for us forever be the generalissimo of the armies of freedom." A compliment like this was not given loosely by General de Gaulle. Before I translated I knew it was going to move Eisenhower very much. Indeed, when I translated it, I saw his eyes fill with tears and he warmly shook General de Gaulle's hand in both of his.

During the discussions which they had, all sorts of questions were touched upon—nuclear questions, the German question, the Soviet leaders, the colonial questions confronting France at that time and particularly the Algerian War, and a number of other, lesser matters. The two men spoke with great frankness. There was a series of meetings with their ministers and with their advisers and there were several meetings of the two men alone, General de Gaulle with his interpreter and General Eisenhower and myself on the American side. For me one of the truly dramatic moments of this visit and indeed of my whole life was the evening of September 3, 1959, when the two Chiefs of State met at Rambouillet Castle some thirty-five miles from Paris. After all the formal program was over, the two generals came together in front of the fireplace in their bathrobes and began to talk about World War II and their relationship at that time. De Gaulle spoke feelingly of the difficulties he had with both Churchill and Roosevelt. De Gaulle started out by saying, "Isn't it curious that we are two old generals who have written our memoirs and we have never carped or recriminated at the other." He then went on to say, "Roosevelt thought that I took myself for Joan of Arc. He was wrong. I simply took myself for General de Gaulle." His tone indicated that he did not think that this was anything less. He also spoke of his difficulties with Churchill. He said that he knew Churchill had said during the war that the heaviest cross he had to bear was the cross of Lorraine (de Gaulle's symbol), but in spite of this, he knew how much not only he and France but the whole free world owed

Churchill. And he added with some irony, "I also knew how he loved medals. When I returned to power, I conferred upon him the Order of Liberation and I gave it to him under the watchful eye of Napoleon. As I gave it to him, I said, 'Sir Winston, France gives you this in order that you may know that she knows how much she owes you.' How he wept! But what an actor."

Then the conversation drifted to the efforts France was making in the nuclear field. General de Gaulle pointed out that he had not started the French nuclear program. It had been, in fact, started by a Socialist Prime Minister and continued under a number of other Prime Ministers and when he became chief of government, he found the project well along already. He said that he was spending millions of dollars to find out things that the Americans had already discovered, but he said, "I am not asking for anything (*Je ne suis pas demandeur*). He said that it was ridiculous for France to have to spend this amount of money to find out some things her allies already knew, as well as her potential enemies. General de Gaulle said he was determined to go through with the effort to develop a nuclear capability for France as he felt it was essential to the defense of her interests and to her survival. The incident at Suez had shown that the United States did not always regard as its vital interests what some of its allies regarded as their vital interests. It was too bad that he had to spend these vast sums, but he had no choice. Eisenhower pointed out the dangers of nuclear proliferations and the restrictions placed on the exchange of nuclear information by the McMahon Act. De Gaulle snorted, "McMahon Act indeed! I changed the constitution of France when I found it was not practical." He then went on, "You tell me it is dangerous for me to know something that a thousand Soviet corporals already know. This I cannot accept. France retains the desire to be great. A weapons program gives you a technical ruboff that makes you competitive on world markets in a thousand other ways." He added, "Unlike the British, we have not lost our taste for excellence." He then told President Eisenhower that he would detonate his first nuclear weapon on February 13 of the following year and that it would have a yield of sixty kilotons. Eisenhower enjoined me sharply to secrecy, but told me I could tell the G-2 of the Army, General Willems, and tell verbally, and to put nothing in writing. On that day, indeed, General de Gaulle did detonate his weapon and it did have a yield of that order.

General de Gaulle also expressed concern about the future, saying that "You, Eisenhower, would go to nuclear war for Europe because you know what is involved and what is at stake. But as the Soviet Union develops the capability to strike the cities of North America, one of your successors," he said, "will be unwilling to go to nuclear war for anything short of a nuclear strike against North America. When that comes, I or my successor must have in hand the nuclear means to turn what the Soviets may want to be a conventional war into a nuclear war. I do not seek to compete with the Strategic Air Command or the Long Range Air Army, but I wish France to have some means of tactical and strategic strike against the Soviet Union. You see, the addition of another center of nuclear decision will multiply geometrically the uncertainties for the Soviet planners of what will happen if they invade Western Europe." He then said, "You Americans could survive for a short time the loss of Western Europe. We Europeans could not. The Soviets know me and they knew that if I have this capability and they invade Western Europe, I will use it, and this will be one more deterrent as far as they are concerned. I must have the ability to be unbearable by myself."

General de Gaulle went on to say that the United States was making a great fetish out of the United Nations because we controlled a majority in that body. But he said that with the "flowering of independence," which the United States was sponsoring, we would gradually lose control of the United Nations to the third-world nations, which included and would include in the future many small states or city-states of a few hundred thousand population. The day would come when these third-world nations in control of the United Nations would order the United States to do something contrary to its fundamental interests, and the United States would have made such a golden calf of the United Nations that they would have no alternative but to obey what the United Nations told them. General de Gaulle assured him that it would, and he was right.

I have translated a number of conversations between the two men, but almost none reached such a degree of frankness as this one by the fire in the old French castle. They spoke of the past, of what each had known and had not told the other and why. For a few moments it was not a conversation between chiefs of state, but two old generals telling war stories. I felt lucky indeed to be there.

That afternoon as we flew out to Rambouillet, the Prime Minister, Mr. Michel Debre, was with us in the helicopter and President Eisenhower, looking over the suburbs of Paris, noted the extraordinary amount of construction that had taken place recently. This was in marked contrast with the period he had spent at SHAPE, when there had been building all over Europe, but not in France. He asked Debre why this sudden change had come about. Debre answered very simply and frankly, "Since General de Gaulle has returned, we now know that there will be a future for France." This statement made a deep impression on President Eisenhower and he was to mention it several times to me later. He also said ruefully, "You know, de Gaulle has a point with his desire for a nuclear program. I wish there were some way I could help him, but I simply cannot. He is going to go ahead with it anyway." I expressed agreement and said that there was no question in my mind that he would. The French, while still militarily weak, nonetheless yearned to do sophisticated things in a scientific way.

On this visit Eisenhower received an extraordinarily warm welcome from the people of Paris, despite a strong Communist campaign against him. I had seen, on many occasions, the affection of the French for him while traveling around France, both when he was at NATO and when he was President. One had only to look at the faces of the crowd to see that there was something very special and that he was truly in the eyes of many Frenchmen the generalissimo of the armies of freedom. It was interesting, though, that two of the most powerful men in the world rode in from the airport in a convertible, and were unable to exercise their power. It had been agreed between the U. S. Secret Service and the French Service that for the protection of the Presidents the top of their car would not be put down until the car was well into the central area of Paris where the streets were very wide. The car coming from Le Bourget Airport had to pass down a long, narrow street called the Rue de Flandre, where there were tall buildings from which it would be easy to toss a hand grenade into the car or to take aim at them. It was curious, in the light of what was to happen to another American President, that the police and the Secret Service both feared sharpshooters with a rifle in a building as well as the throwing of a hand grenade. The convertible top would make it more difficult for anyone to aim at the two men in the car from one of the buildings overlooking the road, and there was a fair chance that a hand grenade thrown from above might bounce off the convertible top. As the two presidents rode down the Rue de Flandre and there was great popular enthusiasm and cheering, they began to wonder why the top could not be put down. General de Gaulle's aide, Commander Flohic, and I knew that the top was going to be put down much farther into Paris and not before. Both Presidents began asking rather querulously, Eisenhower of me and de Gaulle of Flohic, why the top was not put down. We were mumbling some sort of excuse that it required specialists and technicians when finally Eisenhower, half angry and half laughing, said, "Here we are the Presidents of our countries and we can't get a simple thing done like putting down the top of this car." The two Presidents continued to discuss this until we finally reached the place where it had been agreed the top could be taken down. The top was then taken down and the enthusiasm of the crowd was truly enormous. We drove into the center of Paris and up the Champs Elysées, where I had often walked as a child and never dreamed that someday I would ride up in a triumphal procession like the one in which I now found myself.

The adulation and enthusiasm were directed at the two men

in the back of the car, and yet in some way I was caught and gripped, and I could see how intoxicating it could be if you were the recipient of this kind of affection and enthusiasm. Looking at the two leaders, I saw that this trust and this confidence of the people had moved them very deeply. General de Gaulle accompanied President Eisenhower to the Foreign Ministry, where he was staying the first night of his visit. The second night was spent at Rambouillet, which I have already described.

During the visit, President Eisenhower extended a very cordial invitation to General de Gaulle to come to the United States and return the visit. General de Gaulle commented that it had been many years since he had been there. In fact, he had not been there since World War II, and he was very anxious to come. President Eisenhower expressed the hope of receiving him not merely in Washington, but at his farm in Gettysburg, where he could go over the battlefield with him. Once again, General de Gaulle demonstrated his prodigious memory by describing events of the Battle of Gettysburg, the actions of various commanders on both sides during that historic battle.

During this visit General de Gaulle was to give me a silver cigarette case with his signature engraved in it. In a curious way, he recalled this the following year when he came to the United States to visit President Eisenhower. At that time, he gave me a gold cigarette lighter and added lightly, "Now, Walters, you who do not smoke have everything you need." Once again, he demonstrated his prodigious memory and ability to notice trivia such as the fact I did not smoke.

I had always thought of General de Gaulle as a rather lofty individual, not much concerned with those who worked for him, and yet once I had a striking demonstration to the contrary. At a lunch at the Elysée he walked out into the garden with General Eisenhower after the lunch where the coffee and liqueurs were served. His French interpreter Prince Andronikof, a truly extraordinary individual, a gifted linguist who was trilingual in English, Russian and French, declined the tray of liqueurs. General de Gaulle looked and said, "If there is something else that you would like which is not on the tray, we'll be glad to send

and get it for you." It was a curious gesture of consideration that
I had not expected of him and it made a very considerable impression on me. That night at dinner, General de Gaulle said to
President Eisenhower as they walked into the dining room, "At
this table you will find all the Prime Ministers of France. There
are a great many of them. I hope that in a few years there will
be fewer." During this dinner, an interesting and somewhat embarrassing incident occurred for me. President Eisenhower was
making a speech or a toast to General de Gaulle and he was
pausing from time to time for translation. In this speech, he
came to a phrase that said, "There are those who say that General de Gaulle is a very stubborn man." At this point he paused
for translation. This was awkward for me because the French
word for "stubborn," *entêté* or *têtu,* is not a kindly word and is
more pejorative than the word "stubborn" in English. Since I
did not know what the next sentence would say, I was caught on
the horns of a considerable dilemma. So, in translating it, I said
in French, "There are those who say that General de Gaulle is a
very tenacious man." General de Gaulle roared with laughter, as
did most of the other people in the room who understood what
had happened. President Eisenhower then went on, "But when
that stubbornness is in the service of his country and the cause
of human freedom, then it is a quality to be admired rather than
reproved." A French newspaper, describing what had occurred,
said, "The colonel diplomat drew a delicate veil across the sensitive word." Here, once again, I had demonstrated to myself the
danger of attempting to tamper with what is being said by one
of the principals for whom one is translating.

The visit was a diplomatic triumph for both General de
Gaulle and President Eisenhower, and I think it did a lot to
warm feelings between France and the United States. The following year, 1960, General de Gaulle did come to the United
States, did return President Eisenhower's visit. I was present at
nearly all of the major occasions of this visit. I was with General
de Gaulle when he laid the wreath on Lafayette's statue in front
of the White House and when he went to the Tomb of the Unknown Soldier in Arlington Cemetery. Here, because we had

been warned of General de Gaulle's nearsightedness, bands of orange tape had been put on the white marble steps so that they would make the steps more clear, and I was told to walk alongside him and be ready to grab him if he should stumble at any time. This visit went off very well and the ceremony unfolded in a very dignified and moving fashion.

During this episode I attended a reception at the French Embassy, and as David Rockefeller came in, he said to me that he was sure that General de Gaulle would not recall him from his brief service in Paris at the end of the war. I said to him, "Mr. Rockefeller, I wouldn't bet on it. You might lose." As I introduced him to the general, de Gaulle looked at him and said, "Mr. Rockefeller, if I remember correctly, you were an Assistant Military Attaché in Paris at the end of the war, and unless I am mistaken, you were in charge of handling scientific questions." David Rockefeller and I exchanged a glance, he more surprised than I, since I had had considerable demonstrations of the general's prodigious memory for this sort of detail.

Then General de Gaulle went up to Gettysburg with President Eisenhower and visited him on the farm. I accompanied the two generals as they wandered around the battlefield, discussing various episodes of the battle, which General de Gaulle clearly knew at least as well as President Eisenhower. Then we returned to the Eisenhower farm, and President Eisenhower's grandchildren came in to talk to General de Gaulle. One of the little girls was intrigued by General de Gaulle's heavy glasses with thick lenses and took them and fondled them. General de Gaulle, noting that she was intrigued by the thickness of the lenses, said, "Yes, you see, I am an old man with whom many people are angry, and I am almost blind, but I must go on anyway." It was a wistful moment. Usually he was quite sure of himself, convinced of his authority and his place in history. This is one of the few times where I heard him, in a sense, feel sorry for himself. He did not feel this way often, or at least he did not express it in public often. This day spent together on the battlefield of Gettysburg and at President Eisenhower's home seemed to me to bring the two men even closer together.

President Eisenhower had been irritated by the French refusal to accept the European Defense Community, by General de Gaulle's insistence on a three-nation directorate for NATO and by a number of other things. Yet when the two men got together, the political and national differences between them seemed to fade away and give place to the warm comradeship of two old soldiers who had lived through the bitter and glorious hours of World War II in the service of their countries and human freedom.

In discussing once more at Gettysburg his need for nuclear weapons, General de Gaulle said that he was going to withdraw the French Army from Algeria as it had been withdrawn from Indochina, and unless he could give that Army a sense of having a modern capability to perform its mission in the last quarter of the twentieth century, he would not have an organized army on his hands—he would have 600,000 armed malcontents and French democracy would not survive. A year later I was to see him again with Governor Averell Harriman, who had come to Europe and the Middle East on a mission for President Kennedy. Governor Harriman was one of the very few Americans to whom General de Gaulle spoke as an equal. He reaffirmed to Mr. Harriman his determination to end the Algerian War by negotiations, and he commented that his Prime Minister, Mr. Debre, was going along only halfheartedly. He said that he was not ready to turn over the Sahara's oil and was thinking in terms of some sort of a consortium of various nations to develop the oil fields. He was also considering the retention of some military bases in Algeria. De Gaulle said that the situation had not changed greatly in Europe. The French were not terribly in favor of German reunification. Yet he took an extremely tough stand on Berlin and said that if the Russians wanted him out of Berlin they would have to drive him out with force and if he resisted with force, it would be difficult for the British and Americans not to resist also. He said that the withdrawal from Algeria would be very distasteful to the Army and there might be some trouble. He was confident that he could deal with it. He again repeated to Governor Harriman what he had said previously to General Eisenhower, that he was trying to lift France out of the pit into which it had fallen and this made him say things to the French public which were distasteful to some of France's allies and if they seemed harsh, he hoped that the allies would remember the context in which he was saying them. He did appear in better health than the previous time I had seen him and he appeared optimistic about the negotiations which he hoped to conduct with the Algerians.

Five years were to pass before I saw General de Gaulle again—in Brazil, where he was on a state visit. He was not surprised to see me there, and I recall at the end of a state dinner at Brasília in the Presidential Palace there was a reception for members of the diplomatic corps and he had one of his aides come and get me and bring me to him. He asked me about President Castelo Branco, saying that he knew I had known the President well during the war, and he added, "Nothing and no one prepared me for the stature of President Castelo Branco." He clearly had been deeply impressed by the President of Brazil and not the least by the fact that Castelo Branco spoke very fluent French and was a graduate of the French General Staff School. Castelo Branco was later to tell me a somewhat amusing story. General de Gaulle had asked him what was the typical Latin American dictator. Castelo Branco, never one to miss a malicious dig and having already announced that he would not serve beyond his own three-year term, said, "Mon général, it is a military man who comes to power and then feels great difficulty in giving up that power." He commented that he thought General de Gaulle had taken that particular dig quite well.

General de Gaulle asked me what I was doing in Brazil and I explained that I was the Military Attaché there, and he then commented that it seemed to him that wherever he went, he found me. He asked me if he had not seen me on a previous stop on his South American tour and I assured him that he had not, that I had not left my post in Brazil in the preceding weeks. He had visited a number of other Latin American countries, but he clearly was very deeply impressed by Brazil and most of all by the remarkable personality of its President, Castelo Branco. He was to receive President Castelo Branco to lunch in Paris after Castelo Branco had left the presidency of Brazil, a clear mark of General de Gaulle's high esteem, as he neither received all visitors nor particularly had to lunch many of those he received, especially after they had left office.

One more year was to pass before I was to see General de Gaulle again. In the meantime, I had been to Vietnam and was assigned to Paris as Military Attaché. Not long after I arrived, Ambassador Bohlen, who had been Ambassador for six or seven years, was leaving and General de Gaulle gave a state luncheon for him. I had made it my practice never to come up to General de Gaulle, or any other President that I knew, and present myself presuming upon previous acquaintance. Rather I let them have the freedom of sending for me if they wanted me, and not bothering them if they did not. On this occasion after lunch while coffee was being served, General de Gaulle's aide came over and said to me, "The general would like to speak to you." I walked over and he said, "Well, Walters, you are a Parisian again. How long have you been here?" I was tempted to tell him, "It's probably on that card that the French Internal Intelligence Service gave you about the guests at the luncheon today," but I decided that this would be neither tactful nor diplomatic and did not say it, but told him that I had arrived on August 15. He then paused for a minute and said, "Let me see, I have seen you at many places. I recall seeing you in Italy during the war as well as in London." And I said, "General, once again you are showing the tremendous memory that enabled you in 1952 to tell me the name of the village where you had seen me in Italy." He said, "I can't remember the name of the village right now, but we were there to discuss the disposition of the four French divisions in Italy which would be going into the South of France." I said, "That is absolutely correct, General." He paused, smiled and then said, "Tell me, wasn't the name of the village Roccastrada?" And indeed it was. This was twenty-three years after the event, and he was able to name with accuracy the town where this had occurred.

I was to see him shortly afterward at the time of the presentation of Ambassador Sargent Shriver's credentials. I recall the rioting that was going on in Paris and a difficult situation had developed. This was in May 1968. General de Gaulle expressed his determination to defend the legitimate governments of France, and he said, "As for the future, that is in God's hands." This struck me as being somewhat fatalistic and somewhat pessimistic and not really in keeping with his continuous faith in the future.

After General de Gaulle retired from public life to his home at Colombey-les-Deux-Églises, I was ordered by President Nixon, on a very personal basis, to deliver to General de Gaulle a handwritten letter reiterating to him personally the invitation Nixon had previously extended to him as President of France to visit the United States again. I recall the letter was open and I made a French translation of it, even though I knew General de Gaulle could read English. But as a courtesy, I enclosed the translation. President Nixon said, "In a world where there is so much mediocrity we all need greatness like yours."

Delivering this letter was a very difficult task. I had had a skiing accident and one of my legs was in a cast. Since I was enjoined to let no one know, I could not take my driver and I had to drive my own car, which, fortunately, had an automatic transmission. Since I had been strictly told that no one in the Embassy should know that I had delivered the letter, there was the additional problem of the newsmen who were mounting guard outside General de Gaulle's home. I went to the apartment of General de Gaulle's long-time aide, Captain Flohic, who was a friend of mine. Neither Flohic nor his wife was there, but the Spanish maid was. I told her it was essential that I see Flohic at once. She looked dubious and said she had been told not to say where he was. When I reminded her in Spanish that I had been there only recently as Flohic's guest, she finally told me that Flohic was at the Hôtel du Commerce at Bar-sur-Aube near the general's home.

It was difficult for me to explain my absence and my failure to take my driver along. My leg propped on a camp stool, I drove my personal car, a 1966 Chevelle, to Bar-sur-Aube, a two-and-a-half-hour drive from Paris. When I got to the hotel, Flohic was not there, but he later returned and I was able to make arrangements to deliver the letter at General de Gaulle's home at Colombey known as La Boisserie. General de Gaulle was deeply touched. As he put on his glasses, he said, "He is a true comrade." After he read the letter, he sat down and wrote a letter in his own hand to President Nixon in which he said, "Your noble official message and your surprising personal letter have deeply touched me, not merely because they come from the President of the United States, but from Richard Nixon. I have for you, and I speak from knowledge, esteem, affection and friendship as great and sincere as it is possible to have. Believe me, my dear Mr. President, my warmest regards and highest esteem." In the letter he thanked President Nixon for the invitation and he left open the possibility that he might come to the United States at some later time, but for the time being, he intended to stay quietly at Colombey and take no further part in French political affairs. I promised to deliver the letter to President Nixon and returned to Paris. The letter and its delivery have never before been made public.

I was not to see General de Gaulle again. On the day he died, November 9, 1970, I was in Florida with President Nixon. The President immediately made the decision that he would go to Paris and attend the funeral. He was told that General de Gaulle had expressed the desire for no great official funeral and for burial in his small home town. President Nixon said, "Nonetheless, we'll go to Paris and we'll see when we get there." He took off that afternoon and flew to Paris to attend the funeral. Each country was allotted four spaces for the chief of delegation and three others. When the French learned that I was with President Nixon, they made an additional space available for me, in addition to the President, Dr. Kissinger, General Haig and Brent Scowcroft, who was Kissinger's deputy.

After attending General de Gaulle's funeral with President Nixon the latter gave me a handwritten letter for Madame de Gaulle, which I delivered in Paris to Colonel des Grées du Loup, who had been General de Gaulle's aide.

I cannot help but remember a somewhat sardonic moment during President Nixon's call on President Pompidou following General de Gaulle's funeral. As we were ushered into President Pompidou's office, he looked at Nixon and opened the conversation by saying, "*En fin, seuls*," which translates, "Alone, at last." While he did not explain what he meant, I understood it to mean that he no longer had General de Gaulle looking over his shoulder and felt Mr. Nixon no longer had General Eisenhower looking over his shoulder.

I have often been irritated and antagonized by some of the things General de Gaulle said publicly, when he appeared to equate the U.S.S.R. and the United States as threats to the grandeur and independence of France. But I have not forgotten the statement he made at the crucial time of the U-2 conference to Eisenhower: "Whatever happens or whatever he does, we will be with you to the end." Seven years later, I returned to Paris as Military Attaché shortly after General de Gaulle had taken France out of the military structure of NATO and had requested the United States to remove its military presence from France. I could not help but wonder what had led us from the first statement of unconditional support to the second situation.

During the years between 1967 and my departure from France in 1972, I tried as a matter of personal curiosity as well as of national interest to ascertain what had led General de Gaulle to undergo such a change. I never asked him point-blank, but I did talk to him on a number of occasions about his philosophy of the defense of France. I have talked to many of his closest military and naval aides, some of whom I had known for more than twenty-five years, and I came to the following conclusion, based not just on what they told me but also on what I remembered on the discussions on nuclear weapons and their use between General de Gaulle and General Eisenhower. I remembered that in 1959 I had gone with General Lauris Norstad, the NATO Supreme Commander, who was trying to get General de Gaulle to put the French fighter defense under the Supreme Allied Commander, Europe. General Norstad explained that the real air defense of Western Europe would not so much be in the air battles over Western Europe but what we did to the Soviet Air Force on its bases. General de Gaulle then asked, "How would you find them?" And General Norstad indicated to me that I should show General de Gaulle the U-2 photograph of a Soviet Air Force base deep inside the Soviet Union. De Gaulle, who could not see very well, examined the large photograph very carefully and then said, "*C'est bien, c'est tres bien*" (It is good, it is very good). I expected him to ask how we took the picture, but he did not. He asked General Norstad with what kind of weapon and with what yield one should attack a target like this. General Norstad told him specifically. He thanked us both courteously, but he did not put French Air Defense under NATO.

When in 1962 President Kennedy had sent Dean Acheson and Sherman Kent to see General de Gaulle to show him the photographs of the Soviet nuclear-tipped missiles in Cuba, General de Gaulle, unlike many of the European leaders, had accepted that it might be necessary for the United States to take pre-emptive military action against Cuba. He was a man who understood the uses of power and he watched carefully to see what we would do. When he saw that instead of taking such action we appeared to have made an agreement with Khrushchev by which we took our missiles out of Greece and Turkey and guaranteed no further action against Castro in return for removal of Soviet missiles from Cuba, he felt that we had not really won the Cuban missile confrontation. He quoted Khrushchev, who had said, "I put the missiles into Cuba to keep Castro in power, and if Castro is still in power, who then really won the Cuban missile crisis?" One of his closest aides said to me that General de Gaulle once told his entourage, "If the Americans will not fight for Cuba ninety miles from the United States, they will not fight for Europe three thousand, five hundred miles away. I must draw the conclusions from this that affect France's independence and defense." I cannot prove this, but nearly all of my contacts close to de Gaulle reflected something very like this. I recall the conversation with Eisenhower concerning the French nuclear capability and de Gaulle's desire to have some means of nuclear deterrence of his own. I recall well his feeling that the United Nations would eventually be controlled by the third world, when he said to Eisenhower, "You are pushing these independence movements because you live forever under the illusion that George Washington was an Indian chief who drove out the British landlords, and therefore you feel you have to support all those who demand independence. The Soviets are pushing their support to independence movements because by evicting the colonial or metropolitan power, they hope to create a vacuum into which they intend to move. Because the two most powerful nations in the world are supporting this for entirely different reasons, it will be successful. Thus you will lose control of the United Nations to the third-world countries, who will inevitably be easily manipulated directly or indirectly by the Soviet Union." General de Gaulle has not always been proved right, but he has on a number of such occasions shown remarkable foresight. He was a complex and difficult figure. He was torn many ways by different emotions, but I think that he lived more for France than for anything else. Sometimes he loved France so jealously that it made him a difficult ally. But he was a giant in every sense of the word. By the force of his personality, he again gave France a position in the world that its material strength alone would not have justified when he became its leader. I think probably a description of what he meant to France was best given by President René Coty, his predecessor, on the day General de Gaulle became President of France. Coty said, "Now the first among Frenchmen is the first of Frenchmen." He was a towering figure and left on me a lasting impression.

For more than a quarter of a century, I had seen him under rather privileged circumstances, either alone or talking to very prominent world figures. On the day in 1960 when I became a full colonel, he was in General Eisenhower's office in the White House, and General Eisenhower at the end of the conversation said, "General de Gaulle, today Lieutenant Colonel Walters has become a full colonel. He has worked hard for both of us today. I am going to pin on one of his eagles and I am going to ask you to pin on the other one," which General de Gaulle did, adding,

"Only Churchill is missing from this celebration." And so this very great man, whom I had known over a long period of time, touched my career and my life very closely and in a most memorable way. With the delivery of President Nixon's letter and de Gaulle's death shortly thereafter, the chapter of my several missions to General de Gaulle across twenty-seven years was closed.

24. THE NORTH VIETNAMESE

When I arrived in Paris in the late summer of 1967 to take up my duties as Army and Defense Attaché to France, I had just come from a brief period in Vietnam. I had traveled all over the battle area and had taken part in a number of operations. The United States Army was heavily engaged there. The requirements for intelligence on the country were many. I do not think that there was a full realization of the fact that Vietnam had been under the French for almost a century and that there were vast masses of information about the country in the French archives and files. I made it my business to find out as much as I could about installations, communications and transportation in North Vietnam. Nearly all of these installations and facilities had been built by the French and if one looked carefully all of the information was available in Paris. Furthermore from their own long-drawn-out war in Indochina the French had gathered vast stores of information on many of the leaders who were now fighting us. This information was not easy to come by but I was gradually able to develop a capability to dip into these stores of intelligence.

There were many Frenchmen with a lifetime of knowledge concerning this area. Americans had tended to dismiss them as being out-of-date. When we were contemplating the rescue of the prisoners in the Hanoi Hilton I was able to locate two former warders of that prison with an intimate knowledge of the building, its weaknesses and strengths. We were not, however, to use their services.

I was able to locate Frenchmen who had gone to school or worked with some of the leaders in Hanoi. During my first year in Paris a large percentage of my reports to the Defense Department related to Vietnam. On several occasions I was to receive the thanks of commanders in that embattled country. On one occasion I was able to get information on a plot by the North Vietnamese to assassinate General Abrams.

Elsewhere I have articulated my feelings about the war in Vietnam. I will not repeat them here other than to say that I felt strongly we were doing the right thing in trying to help the South Vietnamese retain that measure of freedom which they had—far more than they have today. To me the North Vietnamese were the enemy. They stood for everything in life that is abhorrent to me. Little did I know that I was to be called upon to deal extensively with them, even while we were locked in battle in South Vietnam. I did not volunteer for this task. I was ordered to do it and I complied. I had seen the North Vietnamese representatives in Paris often at receptions by the Soviet bloc, but as with the Chinese we never spoke or acknowledged the presence of the other. Since the North Vietnamese had no Military Attaché to France as the Chinese did I had fewer occasions to see them than I did the Chinese. Perhaps the only one I knew by sight was Mai Van Bo, the North Vietnamese High Commissioner to France. Like many of them he had been educated in France and spoke native French.

When President Johnson announced the opening of peace talks with the North Vietnamese and sent Averell Harriman to head the U.S. delegation to these talks I met Mr. Harriman at Orly Airport on his arrival. He had commented that it was twenty years to the day since he had arrived to head up the Marshall Plan.

I was not directly involved in those talks at the initial stage. I did as Defense Attaché provide some logistical support to the U.S. delegation until it was organized enough to provide its own. I knew Mr. Harriman, Mr. Cyrus Vance, Mr. Philip Habib and other members of the delegation from previous experience. I was in a general way aware of the fact that the discussions were getting nowhere. I knew of the interminable discussions over the shape and position of the table at the conference and who would sit where. I knew also from French contacts that there were meetings between the two delegations other than those going on publicly at the Hotel Majestic. I knew, for instance, that Mr. Harriman had secret meetings with the chiefs of the North Vietnamese delegation. Their leader, Xuan Thuy, was well known to me from information I had obtained from the French about him. He had once been sent to jail for swindling his French employer. That employer was still alive and living in Paris. I had passed all of this biographical information to the U.S. delegation but they did not seem to know how to use it, or perhaps they suspected it to be biased. From May 1968 these talks dragged on without any result at all through the U.S election and the inauguration of the new President. Mr. Harriman resigned as the chief of the U.S. delegation and was replaced by Henry Cabot Lodge, a former United States senator and Ambassador to South Vietnam. This did not bring about any change in the interminable discussions at the Hotel Majestic. It was clear that the North Vietnamese saw in the public discussions a propaganda forum to use against the United States in Europe as well as within the United States itself. Their principal target was American public opinion.

At some point a decision was made in Washington to attempt to conduct private discussions with them. The public discussions would continue so that they would not feel deprived of their propaganda forum but there was hope that at the private discussions some progress might be made to find a way to end the war honorably.

Dr. Kissinger came to Paris and while he was in the Embassy he sent for me. He told me in great confidence that he was going to meet the North Vietnamese delegates and he wanted me to go with him, both to translate and to serve as a channel for any subsequent exchanges that might follow. He had made arrangements to meet with them through Jean Sainteny, who had been the French High Commissioner to North Vietnam. Mrs. Sainteny had been one of Dr. Kissinger's students at Harvard. The first meeting took place in August 1969. We met at Sainteny's apartment on the Rue de Rivoli in downtown Paris. We arrived before the North Vietnamese did and Sainteny offered us a drink while we waited. As we waited I wondered how one talked with the enemy. Did one shake hands with them? How did one behave? I had no idea. The doorbell of the luxurious apartment rang and we walked to the entrance hall. There stood Xuan Thuy, whom I recognized at once from photographs, and two other Vietnamese. Kissinger held out his hand to Xuan Thuy, who shook it with an embarrassed smile. Kissinger then shook hands with the other two Vietnamese as Sainteny introduced us. One of the Vietnamese was a superb interpreter with great command of both French and English in addition to his native tongue. He was not, however, a pleasant person and always translated unpleasant statements with an expression that made it clear he was enjoying what he was saying.

Sainteny then ushered us all into his living room and after arranging for drinks he left the apartment to Dr. Kissinger, myself and the North Vietnamese. Dr. Kissinger said that the United States government was willing to engage in private talks with the North Vietnamese in an effort to see if some way could not be found to bring this long and devastating war to an end. This could be done only if the talks were private and neither side used them for propaganda purposes. The North Vietnamese immediately observed that they never did this. There was a long discussion not without some acrimony from the North Vietnamese and some sharp replies by Dr. Kissinger. We drank tea and gradually it became clear that the North Vietnamese were feeling the pressure of the war and would be glad to have such private discussions. They did not say this directly nor did they agree then that there would be further talks. They promised to convey this message to Hanoi and they would be in contact with me to give our side the reply. I gave them my phone number and it was agreed that we would each use the code name André in calling the other. They were emphatic in citing the need for absolute secrecy. They made it plain that if this secrecy was not observed they would break off the channel if it were established. I was to call the Vietnamese High Commission in Paris if I had a message and was to talk only to Mai Van Bo, the High Commissioner, identifying myself as André. If he had a message for me he would call me and say that André had called and wanted to see me. They emphasized again that the whole matter would have to be decided in Hanoi, and that a reply would come later. They left the apartment. Dr. Kissinger and I remained there for a few minutes drinking tea and then walked back to the Embassy. That afternoon I flew on to Brussels with Dr. Kissinger. He gave me strict instructions as to how I was to handle dealings with the North Vietnamese. I would also be provided with special code to communicate directly with him at the White House. I would have to do the encoding and decoding myself. He enjoined me that I should tell absolutely no one in the Embassy of these talks, nor should I notify my superiors in the Defense Department. When I expressed some misgivings about this he said that this was very important and that shortly I would come back to Washington and the President as commander in chief would confirm these instructions. I should remember that the President was charged with the conduct of foreign policy and within the law could conduct it any way he wanted. I said that it might be wise to tell the French at a very high level. He asked why this was necessary and I said that France had highly sophisticated intelligence services and they would certainly pick up the contacts and if they were not told it might cause hard feelings with them. He then asked how this could be kept from splattering all over the French intelligence community. I suggested that he talk to President Pompidou personally and ask him to handle it very discreetly and to keep knowledge confined to the uppermost levels of French Intelligence. He thought that this was a good idea. I told him that I would also have to tell my secretary. She was the soul of discretion. He asked why this was necessary and I said that someday if I went to meet the North Vietnamese and did not come back, it was essential that someone know where I was. He reluctantly agreed to let me tell her. I left him in Brussels and returned to Paris, where I awaited the first message from the North Vietnamese. In the meantime someone came from Washington bringing me the special codes that I was to use for communicating with Dr. Kissinger. I was also instructed in how to use this equipment.

I could not but reflect upon the irony of the situation. There were few people who felt as strongly against the North Vietnamese as I did and yet I had been chosen to deal with them. As a soldier I took my orders and prepared for this task which I had not sought.

I tried to find out as much as I could about Mai Van Bo and Xuan Thuy to make it easier to deal with them.

Soon after Kissinger left I went to Washington, where the President confirmed Dr. Kissinger's instructions to me and reiterated that I was not to discuss this channel of contact with the North Vietnamese with anyone.

Not long after this I received the expected phone call from Mai Van Bo and was told that the North Vietnamese would see me at a private villa in a working-class suburb of Paris. This presented a minor problem for me. My car had diplomatic license plates clearly indicating that it belonged to the U. S. Embassy. Its presence in a largely Communist suburb like Vitry s/ Seine could not fail to attract attention. I therefore had to leave the car at a great distance and take the bus to the neighborhood of the North Vietnamese villa. Most of the top-ranking North Vietnamese lived in the elegant 16th District of Paris. They even had a brothel there for their personnel, staffed entirely with women from North Vietnam. They always met, however, in a working-class district. At the appointed time I went to their villa at 73 Rue Jules Lagaisse in Vitry. Ironically it was almost directly across the street from a Catholic church. For the first meeting I took the bus and then walked to the villa. If I was followed I did not detect it. I was received by Mai Van Bo and another Vietnamese. We sat down in their living room and had Vietnamese tea. They told me that they were agreeable to the private discussions that had been proposed and suggested that

Dr. Kissinger select or propose a date for a meeting with them. I made clear to them that Dr. Kissinger would expect to find someone from Hanoi on a corresponding level with his own position in the U.S. government. They said Le Duc Tho, who was a member of their politbureau, would come. They then asked me some questions about myself. Had I served in Vietnam and where. They did not get into polemic matters and the fact that I had served in Vietnam did not seem to bother them at all. They were very curious as to how I had learned French. We always spoke in French. Most of them had been in French schools and were completely at home in the language. Mai Van Bo himself spoke French without any accent at all. They asked me many other questions and it became clear that they were making up some sort of biographic sheet. We talked under a picture of Ho Chi Minh smiling inscrutably down on us. They then gave me a letter from Ho Chi Minh to President Nixon. I told them that I would pass this letter to the President and that they could expect a reply shortly. I then left and went to the Embassy to undertake the laborious task of encoding the message for transmission.

Thus began a series of meetings that were to go on for several years. It also led to my having to make arrangements to smuggle Henry Kissinger into France without anyone in the Embassy finding out. Above all, I was told, the press must not find out, as this would lead to publicity. The North Vietnamese had said that if there was any such publicity they would break off the talks.

Dr. Kissinger would generally fly to Europe aboard *Air Force One*. This had the advantage of discretion since the passenger list was not given out. The plane frequently flew for training purposes for the crew and that fact alone would not excite undue attention. Dr. Kissinger would arrange to be seen publicly somewhere in Washington on Friday night and would then fly to Paris. Immediately after his return he would again arrange to be seen publicly and it would never occur to anyone that he had had the time to go to Paris and back. He would make the arrangements for his air travel but I had to make arrangements to get him into France without going through either the customs or the immigration formalities. Sometimes he would come into Europe through England, sometimes through Germany and sometimes directly into France. I had talked to Pompidou's adviser Michel Jobert, and he was on many occasions extremely helpful. I was instructed by Dr. Kissinger to brief him from time to time on how things were going. All in all I was to bring Dr. Kissinger into France discreetly more than fifteen times. Not once did he ever see a French customs inspector or an immigration official. I made arrangements with friends at Orly Airport to have a spot for military aircraft and there we were not troubled. Sometimes he would come into another French airport where thanks to Jobert all facilities were made available and no questions were asked. Several times U. S. *Air Force One* was filled with fuel by the French and I do not believe to this day they have ever been reimbursed. I used the French airport at Avord several times, as this is where the French kept their tanker aircraft for their nuclear strike force and these aircraft from the outside look very much like *Air Force One*. From there I would fly him either in my own attaché plane or in a French plane. About this time I lost my attaché plane through economy measures and was not able to justify retaining it since I could not tell the Defense Department I was using it to smuggle into France the Special Assistant to the President for National Security Affairs. I talked once to Dr. Kissinger to see if I could get his help to retain it and he told me that he could not get involved in that question without revealing the fact that he was conducting these talks in Paris. Occasionally he would come from Germany, where he had left U. S. *Air Force One* for an Air Force plane with a crew sworn to secrecy.

Generally when he came Dr. Kissinger would bring with him two assistants, young Foreign Service officers. They would all stay at my apartment in Neuilly. This was a small apartment with two bedrooms, a living room and a dining room. It had a garage with two entrances, each one of which could be locked to prevent anyone from following immediately. It also had the advantage that I could drive out on two different streets. Dr. Kissinger would sleep in my bedroom and the two assistants in the guest room. I would myself either sleep on the couch in the living room or else ask my enlisted aide to stay with friends and stay at his apartment one block away. This latter fact added to my problems because one block from me there was a large apartment building belonging to the American Embassy in which a number of Americans were housed, and from this proximity I ran the constant danger of having Dr. Kissinger recognized. I had told my cook-housekeeper that he was an American general named Harold A. Kirschman. I felt it necessary to have the right initials. My enlisted aide, of course, knew who the visitor was. He maintained admirable discretion.

On one occasion Dr. Kissinger asked me to take him to see President Pompidou at the latter's private apartment on the quai overlooking the Seine. He told me not to mention this to the two assistants who had come with him. We left them in my apartment and I drove him to the Quai de Bourbon in my car. He discussed the negotiations with Pompidou and thanked him for his help. Several months later a newsmagazine published the fact that Kissinger had seen Pompidou at the latter's private apartment. I had not told the magazine; I was certain Pompidou had not; that left only one possibility.

Dr. Kissinger would generally arrive late in the evening. We would go to my house and he would spend the night there. Next morning they would have breakfast. He is not much given to praise but he once said that I served the best breakfasts he could remember. That is, my cook-housekeeper and enlisted aide did. Then we would go to the meeting with the North Vietnamese. For this purpose I had to use rented cars so that the diplomatic licenses on the cars outside the Vietnamese villa would not give the whole show away. After the meeting with the North Vietnamese I would generally take him to Orly Airport to the secluded parking area for aircraft and he would go to Germany or the UK to pick up *Air Force One* for his return to the United States. Later when the talks with the Chinese began he would see them first and the Vietnamese later. He did mention to the Chinese that he was talking to the Vietnamese. It was clear that the Chinese had already been told this by the North Vietnamese. Sometimes they would make oblique references to it by saying to Kissinger, "Are you seeing anyone else on this trip?" I do not know for sure but I very much doubt that the Chinese ever told the North Vietnamese that they too were talking to the Americans.

When Dr. Kissinger came we always saw them in a small house in Citoisy on Rue Darthe, never in the houses where I called on them alone. These talks would go on at varying degrees of intensity. Dr. Kissinger would come to meet with Le Duc Tho and Xuan Thuy. I would translate into French what Kissinger had said and the Vietnamese interpreter would then render it into Vietnamese. They would reply in Vietnamese and the interpreter would render this into English. Why we used three languages instead of two I never understood but that was the way they wanted it and that was the way it was done as long as I participated in the talks. After Kissinger's departure I relayed messages for both sides. I did not myself get into the substance of the negotiations at any time, but I would have long talks with them on occasion. When they gave me the letter from Ho Chi Minh to President Nixon, we discussed Ho and his life at considerable length. We talked about the war and it was clear to me that their real hope was not so much for victory on the battlefield but victory on the battlefield of American public opinion. They were right. They won in the United States, not in the central highlands of South Vietnam where they staged their final victorious offensive. Le Duc Tho and Xuan Thuy headed their side throughout. At the public talks, Ambassador Lodge was succeeded by Ambassador David Bruce and still later by Ambassador Porter. I was never authorized to brief Ambassador Lodge but I was allowed to tell Ambassadors Bruce and Porter. Generally after putting Kissinger on the plane I would see Bruce or Porter and tell him what had happened. These negotiations prevented me from making many of the normal attaché trips and also prevented me from making a number of trips with the Ambassador that I normally should have made as his attaché.

It was difficult for me to plan any vacation or trips as I knew that at any moment on short notice I might be required to bring Dr. Kissinger into France to meet with the North Vietnamese. In contrast with talks with the Chinese, the discussions with the North Vietnamese were filled with propaganda on their part. They were constantly accusing the United States of waging an aggressive and imperialistic war and of not showing "good will and serious intent." The latter expression was one of their favorite catch phrases. Sometimes Kissinger would get fed up with the propaganda and would say, "Why don't you save that stuff for the public talks at the Majestic?" They would grin and go right on.

At first they would demand as an absolute precondition that the United States "get rid of the Thieu, Ky, Khiem clique." Over a period of time when they saw that was getting nowhere they knocked out Khiem and demanded the ouster of Thieu and Ky. Still later they reduced the demand to the removal or elimination of Thieu. One day they were harping on this and Kissinger said that we could not do it. We had 200,000 men in Vietnam and Thieu had over a million. Le Duc Tho, who was later to share a Nobel Peace Prize with Kissinger, said, "You know what to do." Kissinger replied that he did not understand what Le Duc Tho was asking. Again Le Duc Tho said, "You know. Get rid of him." I was sure that Kissinger knew what the North Vietnamese was suggesting but he wanted to make him say it. Dr. Kissinger said, "I really don't understand what it is that you want. Do you mean that we should kill him?" Le Duc Tho replied immediately, "Yes, but you don't have to put that in the agreement." In this way he bluntly suggested that the United States assassinate its ally. He had no visible qualms about making such a suggestion. Henry replied sternly that this would be a dishonorable crime and that the United States would have no part of any such action. As always when embarrassed the North Vietnamese would giggle nervously.

On another occasion when Kissinger arrived expecting to meet Le Duc Tho he found only Xuan Thuy, who told him that Le Duc Tho was not well and would not attend. Henry said, "I am a very busy man. I am the Special Assistant to the President of the United States and when I come this far I expect to be met by someone of corresponding rank." Xuan Thuy then said, "I am an Ambassador Extraordinary and Plenipotentiary." Henry replied, "So is Bill Porter. Go talk to him." He then left and returned to his aircraft and flew back to the United States. Thereafter Le Duc Tho was present at all of the meetings. They had gotten the message. Every couple of months North Vietnamese intransigence would lead to a breakoff of the talks. Then after a few weeks one side or the other would suggest that the talks be resumed with a "new approach." The North Vietnamese had but one approach: the same constant demand for the elimination of Thieu. They clearly viewed him as a strong leader and the chief obstacle to their hopes of conquering the South. I worried about the effect of this incessant hammering on Kissinger, who was also under great pressure from Congress. I said to him, "If you ever intend to give them the head of Nguyen Van Thieu, don't expect me to carry the plate." He looked at me quite shocked and asked whatever gave me the idea that he might contemplate such a thing. I replied, "Nothing. I just want to make sure you get a good Nobel Peace Prize, not a bad one." Kissinger worried constantly about what Congress might do to force the Administration to make further concessions to the North Vietnamese. Time and again he would mutter to me in the car, "We'll never get through another session of Congress without their giving the farm away."

Throughout these wearying talks Kissinger showed admirable patience and forbearance. Only when they became arrogant would he neatly let the air out of them with some self-deprecating remark. At first this proclivity of his for self-deprecation had them puzzled. When he would say, "I am but a simple college professor," they would not know whether it was true, whether he was pulling their leg or attempting to deceive them. They suspected that there were elements of all three intentions present. The constant repetition of their propaganda themes reminded me of the talks with Mossadegh in 1951. Like him they believed that if they repeated something enough times the other side would finally accept it as the truth.

They clearly were very suspicious of the United States and did not believe that we could be trusted. They never admitted that they had any troops of their own in the South, nor any influence over the Provisional Revolutionary Government. It was an incredibly frustrating experience and Kissinger showed great patience, exploding only on one or two occasions when they had said something particularly offensive. All of this activity took place without anyone in my office outside of my secretary knowing. Talking to them at our meeting place was always a stilted and stiff business. Eventually Mai Van Bo, who was suspected in Hanoi of going native in France, was recalled and I dealt with his successor, Vo Van Sung, who is now the North Vietnamese Ambassador to France. He was much less urbane than Mai Van Bo. In my talks with them they were always probing about the state of public opinion in the United States and hoping that it would force the Administration to capitulate to their demands.

When we went into Cambodia they were truly shaken and for the first time seemed to me to be fearful. They kept repeating to me, "How could your President do a thing like this? He is absolutely unpredictable." I think it was then that I realized for the first time what a powerful weapon unpredictability could be. The uproar in the United States that followed the Cambodian incursion filled them with hope that these disorders would force the U.S. government to give them what they wanted. In the end, of course, they were right in this hope. The incredible stupidity of Watergate helped make their victory possible by so weakening the presidency that Ford was unable to continue on the course Eisenhower, Kennedy, Johnson and Nixon had tried to follow in Southeast Asia.

I can never forget the day in September 1971 when I walked up the steps of their villa with Kissinger and saw Le Duc Tho standing at the head of the steps. He smiled triumphantly down at Kissinger and said, "I really don't know why I am negotiating anything with you. I have just spent several hours with Senator McGovern and your opposition will force you to give me what I want." The note of triumph in his voice was grinding. This was one of Kissinger's great days. He looked at Le Duc Tho and said, "Mr. Special Adviser, you are a citizen of the most totalitarian nation on the surface of this planet. You know nothing about an opposition because you have always brutally destroyed any opposition that showed itself in your country. Leave the interpretation of an opposition to those who tolerate one and do not attempt to interpret things about which you know nothing." Le Duc Tho giggled nervously, realizing that his attempt to intimidate Kissinger had failed. Never again did they refer directly to U.S. internal affairs.

These were truly tedious and frustrating talks. One would have the impression of some progress and then they would go back behind the original starting point. In August I got a letter from Kissinger in which he said: "Thank you again for your invaluable contributions which have proved successful up to now. You will note that in his press conference yesterday the President may have inadvertently added to speculation that secret talks are being conducted. His comments will further complicate your already difficult task . . ." He was right; they did. The North Vietnamese suspected that we might leak the fact that there were secret talks to take the pressure off the Administration to negotiate with them. The day after that letter from Kissinger I had a most acrimonious meeting with them. Later on August 24, 1971, I transmitted to them a message that said the United States was prepared to renew the talks on the basis of new approaches.

The talks were renewed but the stalemate continued. They insistently demanded the removal of President Thieu as the head of the South Vietnamese government. This they made a sort of sine qua non of any substantial negotiations. In November I brought Kissinger in via England to talk to them again. I had to go to London to see people in the Air Ministry to ensure that his movement would be handled discreetly. It is a source of considerable pride to me that though the press suspected there might be secret negotiations going on somewhere, there was never any news about Henry's comings and goings from Paris. In January 1972 I was summoned by Vo Van Sung, who accused us of leaking the fact that there were talks. Later in February it was agreed that the talks would continue. My time in Paris, however, was running out and I was anxious to be rid of this difficult burden. Though the North Vietnamese were surly I maintained a relatively good personal relationship with them; they indicated that they were quite satisfied to be dealing through me. As I knew that I would soon be concluding my assignment to France I recommended to Dr. Kissinger and General Haig that my assistant, the Air Attaché to France, Colonel Georges Guay, would be the appropriate person to continue this relationship with the North Vietnamese. He was an extraordinarily personable officer, spoke perfect French and had Abenaki Indian ancestors which gave him a vaguely oriental look. He was extremely discreet and had showed me on many occasions that he had very good judgment. Kissinger agreed and I informed the North Vietnamese that he would be succeeding me in this contact position. I took him out to the villa in Vitry and introduced him to them.

Sometime before this when I would take Dr. Kissinger to meet with the North Vietnamese I would send my secretary Nancy Ouellette ahead in another rented car to cruise around the area and see if there were any press or suspicious bystanders around the North Vietnamese villa. She would then meet us nearby at a previously agreed-upon point and report that the coast was clear. I found the coding and decoding so tedious that I showed her how to do it and she saved me a great deal of time and labor by coding the incoming and outgoing messages. I cannot praise too highly the assistance she rendered to me during this difficult period. She alone in the Embassy in Paris knew of my activities with the North Vietnamese and Chinese Communists. Another source of constant concern to me during this period when I was seeing both the North Vietnamese and the Chinese Communists was that the CIA or FBI might pick up my activities and believe that I was defecting to or in treasonable contact with both of these Communist powers. Curiously they did not. After I left Paris a high-ranking CIA officer I had known there said to me, "Gee! All along I just thought you were a good linguist." An honest statement but not the most tactful to someone who was about to become his boss.

At my last meeting with the North Vietnamese they asked me how things had gone at the Azores meeting between Nixon and Pompidou, since they had seen me there in the news show on television. I then told them that I would be returning shortly to the United States to become the deputy director of the CIA. Vo Van Sung said to me rather sourly, "Well, let us hope that you will never do anything in that job that will give us cause to reproach you." I replied that my only concern would be to do nothing in that job that would give my own country cause to reproach me. He nodded without further comment.

When I left Georges Guay took over the job of dealing with them and did such an outstanding job that he was promoted to brigadier general in the Air Force. He conducted the discreet liaison with the North Vietnamese until the talks became public in 1972 and Kissinger would come quite openly to Paris to meet with them.

For nearly two and a half years I had been dealing with the North Vietnamese in Paris and there had never been a leak of any sort that might reveal what had been going on. Dr. Kissinger was well aware of the difficulties that this contact imposed upon me in the normal performance of my duties as attaché. More than once he sent me words of encouragement. General Haig, with whom I dealt most frequently in Kissinger's office, was also extraordinarily understanding and helpful to me.

Dealing with the North Vietnamese was nowhere near as interesting as dealing with the Chinese. I had to carry on both relationships simultaneously and maintain the fiction that neither knew about the other. Sometimes I felt like a juggler with three balls in the air, the attaché to France ball, the Chinese ball and the North Vietnamese ball. With a lack of modesty that is I hope pardonable, I did not drop any of them during this long and frustrating period. At least with the Chinese I could see some progress. The gradual thaw, Dr. Kissinger's visit to China followed by the President's. With the North Vietnamese there was no visible progress, only long recriminations and often acrimonious oratory. The Chinese were sophisticated and had an excellent sense of humor. The Vietnamese too may have had these qualities. All I can say is that if they did, they successfully concealed them from me during the whole of this two-and-a-half-year period. Going to see the Chinese was always stimulating and challenging, going to see the North Vietnamese was like going to the dentist. Besides, the North Vietnamese only gave me tea. The Chinese fed me well.

My own repugnance to dealing with the North Vietnamese had been overcome by the fact that it was my duty to obey orders and by the memory of the beautitude "Blessed are the peacemakers." I had failed but not because I had not sincerely tried. I marveled at Dr. Kissinger's patience and willingness to make these long and tiring trips in addition to his normal duties in Washington. He was amazingly skillful at repartee and they never got the best of him. His patience and forbearance at times seemed to me to be almost saintly, although that is not normally a word I would connect with the good doctor. He truly did his best under conditions few negotiators have ever had to face before.

For me it was an unusual and challenging experience. I had to talk to the other side and with very few resources organize one of the great secret missions of our time. I was helped by a long past spent in intelligence and with the accumulated experience of dealing with peoples of another culture and way of thinking. During these talks I had read more Vietnamese history and literature (in translation, of course) than in the whole rest of my life. These things enabled me to get myself accepted by them as a man with some knowledge of their country, its culture and its past.

My participation in these two sets of negotiations with the Chinese Communists and the North Vietnamese, together with a long career in intelligence, led to my appointment as deputy director of Central Intelligence and to the stormiest and most turbulent period of my government service. In the spring of 1972 my missions to the North Vietnamese and to the Chinese Communists came to an end.

25. THE CHINESE COMMUNISTS

On October 1, 1949, in Tien An Men Square in Peking, Mao Tse-tung proclaimed the Chinese People's Republic established by the Chinese Communists. This was the culmination of a long Chinese civil war interrupted by the struggle against Japan in World War II. In that civil war, the United States had supported Generalissimo Chiang Kai-shek and his Nationalist forces. There had been brief contact with the Communists during and for a short time after the war against Japan. Other than that, there had been only a great silence between the Chinese Communists and the United States. Some feeble attempts had been made to talk in Warsaw but they had amounted to nothing.

After Chiang Kai-shek was driven off the mainland, we continued to support his Nationalist government on the island of Taiwan and the U. S. Seventh Fleet was ordered to prevent a Communist invasion of Taiwan. As a result of this, the United States had in fact had no real diplomatic contacts with Chairman Mao since 1945.

The intervening quarter of a century had passed with little or no evidence of lessening hostility between the mainland Chinese and the United States. The Chinese were actively engaged against us during the Korean War and a son of Chairman Mao was killed in the fighting there as a "volunteer" with the North

Koreans. The Chinese Communists believed that the United States was responsible for their long exclusion from the United Nations and we had indeed voted on several occasions against their admittance. Bitterness between the two countries continued as the Chinese propaganda apparatus attacked us without letup. Even the break between China and the Soviet Union did not greatly change the situation. In the Vietnam War, China along with the Soviet Union furnished the food, money and weapons that enabled the North Vietnamese to continue their aggression in the South. Chinese air space provided sanctuary for their planes from U.S. attacks. They had shot down our aircraft and issued us hundreds of "serious warnings." Almost every international issue found us on opposite sides. At international gatherings whether formal or social where both sides were present they carefully ignored one another. As an attaché I myself had studiously avoided any contact with my Chinese Communist colleagues. They had reciprocated. Once at a Polish reception the Soviet attaché had said to me, "The North Vietnamese are right behind you." I had replied, "The Chinese are right behind you and there are a lot more of them." He had looked dismayed. Here was a situation in which the most populous nation on earth and the richest and most powerful nation on earth had absolutely no contact whatsoever with one another. In fact, they did not even have an effective channel of contact other than through third parties.

The whole issue of China had become a difficult one even within the United States, where there was widespread belief that someone or other had "sold out China to the Reds." This had been a burning issue in American politics, where the right charged the left with responsibility for the loss of a quarter of mankind to the Communists. Americans have always been drawn emotionally toward China, yet under the existing circumstances it would have been most difficult for a senior American government official to have advocated some change in the existing situation.

Nor was there any clear indication that the Chinese were desirous of further contact with the United States. Despite the break with the Soviet Union, their propaganda against the United States continued as bitterly and vitriolically as ever. It took courage of the highest order to move to break this log jam. Richard Nixon showed it. Henry Kissinger implemented this policy in a patient and tireless fashion. In a way both moved toward China because they perceived a possibility that China's good offices might be used to persuade the North Vietnamese to desist from their aggression. This particular hope was to be dashed and some 20 million South Vietnamese were to pass behind the Bamboo Curtain because of U.S. isolationism. In the larger area a door was opened to China which still remains open. The degree to which it will remain open will in large measure depend on the measure in which the Chinese Communists perceive the United States to be a strong and resolute nation. If, on the other hand, they believe that we are falling back into isolationism and a fortress American concept, they will lose interest in us. If we abandon Korea and Japan the way we have abandoned South Vietnam, Cambodia and Laos, they will draw the necessary conclusions for their policies from this. In my opinion, if we were to abandon Taiwan, the Communist Chinese would regard this more as a sign of unreliability on our part than as an act of friendship for them. It is vital that we remain able to talk to one another on this tiny planet. Neither of us really has any other alternative.

My mission to the Chinese Communists probably began almost without my recognizing it as such in January of 1969 when on a trip back from Paris, where I was Army Attaché, I called on President-elect Nixon at the Pierre Hotel in New York City. We had a short visit, and during this he told me that among the various things he hoped to do in office was to manage to open the door to the Chinese Communists and get in touch with them. He felt it was not good for the world to have the most populous nation on earth completely without contact with the most powerful nation on earth.

The idea at that time seemed quite farfetched to me and I did not understand how he could possibly do it. Shortly after I saw Mr. Nixon, I went to see at his suggestion Dr. Henry Kissinger, whom Mr. Nixon had selected as his Special Assistant for National Security Affairs. I had never met Dr. Kissinger before; he was in another room at the Pierre. I had read a number of his books, and he had obviously, somewhere or other, heard of me. He asked me to do three papers for him. I gave them to him within a few days. One on Brazil, one on NATO and one on Vietnam. President-elect Nixon had felt that part of the solution to the Vietnam problem might be reached through the Chinese. At the Pierre I saw something I was not to see again, an almost meek Henry Kissinger wondering why he had been chosen by the President-elect.

A year passed before there was any further follow-up on these thoughts about the Chinese. On one of my frequent trips back to the United States from Paris in connection with the negotiations going on with the North Vietnamese, I was told that Donald Rumsfeld might come through Paris and bring me a message for the Chinese. But he never came. On another trip to the United States, Dr. Kissinger handed me a letter which I was to deliver to the Chinese. It said, in effect, that the United States was prepared to hold secret talks if the People's Republic of China desired such talks. They could be held completely confidential, and the letter offered the channel of Major General Vernon A. Walters, the U. S. Military Attaché in Paris. The letter also indicated that President Nixon was prepared, if need be, to send a high-level representative to Paris to talk to the Chinese Communists there. I was authorized verbally to say that this would be Dr. Kissinger. I also saw the President, who told me that I was to report directly to him through Dr. Kissinger and that I should not reveal to anyone my part in this attempt to communicate with Peking.

On April 27, 1970, I attempted to deliver this message to the Chinese Military Attaché to France, Fang Wen. He was the Chinese official whom I saw more frequently than any other Chinese official. At this time, neither we nor the Chinese recognized or acknowledged one another's presence. We did not shake hands or talk to one another, and it was very hard for me to find an opportunity to see the Chinese Military Attaché alone. This opportunity, unexpectedly, occurred on the above-mentioned date. I was standing in the courtyard of the Polish Embassy in Paris after leaving a reception there when I suddenly realized that I was alone in the courtyard with Fang Wen. I walked up to him and I said in French, which I knew he understood, "I am General Walters, the American Military Attaché, and I have a message for your government from my President." He looked at me and his mouth dropped open. He tried to say something and he could hardly speak. Finally, he gasped in French, "I'll tell them; I'll tell them; I'll tell them," and jumped into his Mercedes-Benz and drove off. I reported this failure to Kissinger and was instructed to do nothing for the time being.

On June 16 I received a message which I was instructed to deliver on June 19 to Huang Chen, the Ambassador of the People's Republic of China in Paris. I decided at once that the way to do this was to go and see him at the residence in the Neuilly suburban district of Paris, rather than to attempt to go to the Chinese chancery downtown. This would draw a lot of attention. The following morning, the seventeenth, I went over on foot to the Chinese residence, not far from my own home, at about eight o'clock. At eight-thirty on the dot, the Ambassador drove out in his proletarian Mercedes-Benz car. On the eighteenth the same procedure was repeated, and it became apparent to me that he left the residence routinely at eight-thirty. Consequently, at eight-twenty on the morning of July 19, without any prior announcement, I pushed open the outer gate of the garden of the Chinese Embassy on Boulevard du Château in Neuilly. I had gone there on foot as I did not wish to park my car with its clearly recognizable diplomatic license plate in the immediate vicinity of the Chinese Embassy. Henry Kissinger's quick trip to Peking from Pakistan had just been announced. My instructions must be the result of this contact.

The Chinese Communists had two main buildings in Paris. One was the chancery of the Embassy on Avenue George V in the very heart of Paris and in an area where it attracted much attention. This was a large old office building which they had taken over from the Nationalists when France had recognized Mao Tse-tung's government as the legal government of China. Because this building was very well known and the center of much interest, I decided not to try and see the Chinese there. The Chinese residence was a large mansion in the elegant suburb of Neuilly, where I also lived but in far less elegant surroundings. The building was in the style of a Norman manor house and was set back from the street in the middle of a garden. It had a high wall around it and on the street side there was a high wrought-iron railing with sheets of metal backing it up to prevent passers-by from looking into the garden. In addition to the Ambassador, a large number of the people attached to the Chinese Embassy lived in the building in the compound fashion much favored by the Chinese for their diplomatic personnel abroad. The building had evidently been the property of a very wealthy French family. The problem of contact with them was aggravated by the fact that all vehicles belonging to foreign embassies or foreign diplomats individually are given license plates that reflect the country represented. These numbers are well known. CD 6 is the United States, CD 45 Great Britain, CD 26 Communist China and CD 115 the Soviet Union, and the presence of my CD 6 car in the immediate vicinity of the Chinese Embassy could not fail to draw attention. I had been told in no uncertain terms by both the President and Dr. Kissinger that discretion in these matters was absolutely essential and any indiscretion might compromise the whole project.

As I pushed open the gate a young Chinese was waiting and I identified myself to him and told him I had a message. He told me his name was Wei Tung and he was the Ambassador's assistant. He motioned for me to come with him, walked me across the garden to the main door of the residence, where I was received by another Chinese official who identified himself as Tsao Kuei-sheng. Tsao spoke English. Since they seemed to expect me, I concluded that Dr. Kissinger had gotten a message to them. They took me into the Embassy residence, to a large room whose walls were covered with red silk and had a distinctly Chinese appearance.

In a few moments the Ambassador came in and he complimented me on my discretion in coming to the residence rather than to the chancery downtown, where the police and newsmen would have easily picked up my presence. He said he was glad to talk to a colleague who was also a general and explained to me that he had been a general in the Chinese People's Liberation Army before he became an ambassador. He promised to transmit the message to Peking and was somewhat guarded in his reaction to the message itself. He spoke in Chinese and Wei Tung translated what he had said into French.

At a subsequent meeting, he indicated that the Chinese People's Republic would accept the principle of having these talks. They further agreed to the principle of using me as the channel between the two governments. He added that if Dr. Kissinger were to come to Paris, he would like to know the agenda of the questions that Dr. Kissinger would like to discuss with him.

On the following day, July 20, the Chinese accepted July 25 or 26 as dates to see Dr. Kissinger in Paris. I immediately reported this to Kissinger using a special code system held only by me and his office in the White House. I told Dr. Kissinger that I must tell my secretary, Nancy Ouellette, what I was doing since if I were to disappear into the Chinese Embassy and not come out, someone had to know where I was. He reluctantly agreed to let me do so.

With one or two exceptions, all of my meetings with the Chinese took place in this same living room. The furniture was Chinese, as were all of the paintings and light fixtures in the room. It was large and high-ceilinged. Generally, the Ambassador and I sat side by side on a low sofa facing a table on which food and drinks were served. On our right sat Wei, who translated in French, and on our left was Tsao, who translated into English. On every visit they would ply me with tea and Chinese flower wine and a stronger drink called mai tai. I was always careful to take the latter only in small quantities and never to become involved in Chinese "Gambehs" or "Bottoms up." They also provided lichee nuts, which I did not like, and extremely hot dates, from the tree of course—and finally some preserved apricots, which I found quite tasty. They soon noticed my preference for the apricots over the dates, which appeared to have been cooked in boiling water while wrapped in cellophane. After the first few meetings, the Ambassador would usually give me a box of these apricots. This presented somewhat of a problem for me because clearly written on each box was the name written in English, Peking Candy Factory No. 13. By the time I left Paris, I had an entire safe full of apricots. I could not, of course, leave them lying around either in my house or in my office. There would have been inevitable questions as to their origin. I did not wish to be outdone, so I began bringing them boxes of American candy or a fountain pen or pencil or something similar. We never exchanged any gifts of real value. As our relationship grew more relaxed, they plied me with questions about the United States and I answered the questions and then asked about China. Our relationship, stiff and formal at first, gradually became informal and friendly in a cautious way.

Bringing Dr. Kissinger discreetly into Paris was a major undertaking. I had discussed this with him and he had asked me whether it was necessary to tell the French and I told him there was no way out of this since France was a highly sophisticated country and would undoubtedly pick up the contact between the Chinese and myself and would certainly pick up any entry of his into France through the many sources of intelligence which they have. He seemed dismayed at this and wondered how this matter could be kept out of all levels of French intelligence channels. I said this could be done quite easily by going to President Pompidou and asking him to keep it at a very restricted level within the French intelligence establishment. This was in fact done. I took Dr. Kissinger to see President Pompidou at his personal apartment and the French President promised to help and keep the whole matter at the top level of French intelligence. He was as good as his word.

I began on July 25, 1970, to smuggle Dr. Kissinger into Paris to see the Chinese. I had, of course, been bringing him in for over a year to talk secretly to the North Vietnamese. Now on his visits to Paris he would usually see the Chinese first and then

the North Vietnamese. To avoid establishing a pattern, I varied the routes and methods by which I brought him into France. Basically, he traveled in U. S. *Air Force One*, the President's plane, which was ostensibly on a training flight. He would be seen in Washington, would come to Paris, do his negotiations, return to Washington and be seen again. Usually he came on a weekend. The reason for the use of the presidential plane is that at that time it was desired that these negotiations not be known to anyone else in the U.S. government except the President and some of Dr. Kissinger's immediate collaborators. I had on a trip to Washington been instructed by the President that I was not to tell either the State or Defense Department. So it was that on July 25 I brought Dr. Kissinger into Paris from a neighboring country with the co-operation of that country.

Dr. Kissinger stayed at my apartment in Neuilly and he brought with him two assistants. I gave him my bedroom. The two assistants had the guest room, and I slept in the living room on the sofa. I had a problem with my cook/housekeeper. I was concerned that she might recognize him. I identified him to her as a General Harold Kirschman. Experience had taught me that in this kind of operation it was better to use correct initials. If one used different initials for the pseudonym, this could attract undesirable attention. I also had an enlisted aide, Chuck Hall, and I identified Kissinger to him but did not disclose the purpose of his visits. Chuck Hall was very discreet.

The following morning after a hearty breakfast at my house, I took Dr. Kissinger to see the Chinese for the first time on July 26, 1971. As they had with me, they gave him tea and lichee nuts and preserved apricots. Dr. Kissinger and the Ambassador noted that they had seen one another at General de Gaulle's funeral. Dr. Kissinger said he had contemplated talking to the Ambassador at that time, but this would have caused a great furor. The Ambassador, getting down to business, said that Chou En-lai accepted the principle of a visit by Dr. Kissinger to be followed by a visit by President Nixon in the latter part of the month of October. If Kissinger wished to come to China, the Chinese suggested that he go to Alaska and fly from Alaska to Shanghai. Dr. Kissinger suggested that Ambassador Bruce, who was conducting the Vietnamese peace talks in Paris, come with him. The Chinese viewed this coolly and felt this was a bad idea for a number of reasons. Kissinger expressed regret at this, saying that Ambassador Bruce had the full confidence of the President. Dr. Kissinger then said that the United States would keep the Chinese informed of any talks we might have with other Socialist countries and this could be reported to Chou En-lai. This seemed to please and reassure the Chinese.

The meeting was somewhat stiffer than the previous meetings I had had with the Chinese. Dr. Kissinger felt that initially the Chinese in Paris were just messengers and had no part in the decision process. After Kissinger's visit, I continued to meet with the Chinese at regular intervals, and on August 16 Kissinger returned to Paris. This time he came into another neighboring country. There, discreetly, I picked him up and brought him into France. In all his visits he never saw a French immigration or customs officer. This took a lot of work and discreet organization on my part.

When I called on the Chinese, they were always extremely interested in talking to me quite apart from whatever message I might bring or whatever message they might give me. It was clear they were fascinated at meeting an American to whom they could talk after the quarter-of-a-century separation that had isolated the mainland Chinese and the Americans from one another. Our talks were somewhat cumbersome in that I spoke in either French or English. The Ambassador's secretary, Wei Tung, spoke French quite fluently and would translate easily for the Ambassador. Tsao spoke fluent English and could also translate for the Ambassador. Sometimes when there was some doubt about some question, they would ask me to say it in both French and English, and then the Ambassador would get the benefit of both translations, which seemed to give him a feeling of greater security as to the fact that he was getting exactly what I had said. The process of double translation was slow and our talks would often last several hours. Initially, they would give me a piece of paper to read and make notes on but would not let me keep it. As the relationship progressed, they gave me messages that I could keep, and I did likewise. I used only paper with a French watermark, not U.S. government paper. They were very concerned about using the telephone and we used it only to arrange for meetings, never to discuss any subjects whatever. Always we used agreed code names in speaking to one another. I was to communicate only with Tsao or Wei and in my case they were to talk only to me or my secretary Nancy Ouelette, since no one else in the American Embassy knew what was going on. This was in accordance with most explicit instructions that I had received in Washington. It was not easy for me to have to explain to the Ambassador why I could not accompany him to some military commemoration, but Dick Watson was a good friend and I think he may have sensed what was going on. He was as events turned out to take over the channel when I left Paris to become deputy director of the Central Intelligence Agency in March 1972. The Chinese evidently did some research on me because they were at pains to let me know that they knew that I had been in Vietnam, that I liked to ski and that I was interested in subways as a hobby. The Ambassador once said to me, "When you come to China we will take you in the Peking subway and you can also see the tunnels that we have built in our cities." At no time did they ever discuss Taiwan with me. It was one of the taboo subjects, fortunately, as their position and mine on this would have been quite far apart. Generally, we tended on both sides to stay away from controversial subjects. Once when I referred to the Soviets as left they corrected me and said that the Soviets were actually rightist social imperialists.

Dr. Kissinger's reception was somewhat different from mine. Generally, when I went to see the Chinese, I would be met at the gate by Wei, taken to the door of the building where I would be met by Tsao, then taken into what I called the Fu Manchu Room, decorated in red, and in a few minutes the Ambassador would come in, clasp his hands and say, "Ni hao," to which I would reply, "Ni hao." Then we would sit down and they would urge food—the preserved apricots or the lichee nuts

—and jasmine tea upon me, and sometimes something stronger like mai tai, or lukewarm pink wine which I did not particularly like. When Kissinger came the procedure was quite different. At the outer gate of the Embassy residence when I took him in, we were met by Wei and Tsao. As we walked up to the building, the Ambassador was standing at the entrance, and as we went into the building, there was faint background Chinese music and also a faint odor of incense wafting through the residence.

After the meeting was over, Kissinger asked me whether when I was received there it was in exactly the same way, and I said no, there was a difference. I was not met by two people at the outer gate and the Ambassador generally came in after I was seated in the red room, and furthermore, I did not get either incense or background music. I saw a quiet smile of satisfaction steal across Henry's face as he realized that even in a classless society, there was some recognition of the hierarchal difference between his position and mine.

My visits to the Chinese were frequent, passing messages back and forth from the White House, still relating to the visit in principle of the President to be preceded by a visit by Dr. Kissinger. The Ambassador, as we talked, became more and more relaxed, and on one occasion he commented that it was interesting that the channel for the messages passing between the two countries moved through the hands of soldiers, himself and me. He said that China was dedicated to peace. I replied that when he got to know the United States better, he would find that the United States also was dedicated to peace. He asked me whether my Soviet colleagues in the attaché organization had ever asked me about our relations with the Chinese, and I truthfully replied that they had not. He asked me if I thought the Soviets knew about Kissinger's trip. I said I did not know; the Soviets were very active in all forms of intelligence, but my experience with them had shown that they were not seven feet tall. The Ambassador roared with laughter and slapped me on the back.

He asked me many questions about the United States, such as, could a governor of a state be of a different party than the President; what did the governors do; did a Cabinet minister have to be a member of the Senate or the House. He asked me how many cars there were in the United States, and I told him there were over 100 million automobiles for a population slightly in excess of 200 million people, and this did seem to have some impact on him.

He did not seem to be able to get over the fact that although we both had a military background, we were now involved in diplomacy of a most sensitive type. As our meetings went on through the months of August and September, I found that the Ambassador was getting less stiff and more cordial and more forthcoming with me. He obviously could not make any major decisions without referring to Peking.

On August 31, 1971, I saw Mr. Michel Jobert, the assistant to President Pompidou, who was often referred to as Pompidou's Kissinger. He asked me how things were going in the negotiations and I said that the Chinese had accepted the principle of a visit by President Nixon to be preceded by a visit by Henry Kissinger. He asked me whether I thought the Chinese really ran Vietnam and I said they and the Soviets both did since they provided the weapons, food and money that kept North Vietnam afloat. He felt that the Chinese had far more influence than the Soviets and said that he had recently told the Soviet Ambassador, Valerian Zorin, that France and the U.S.S.R. had one thing in common in Vietnam, that neither of them had the slightest influence, but that the Soviets were expending vast sums of money in Vietnam. He said that Zorin appeared very unhappy at this. At this point, I suggested to the White House that I thought it would be a good idea if President Nixon were to write President Pompidou and thank him for his help and co-operation in the conduct of these negotiations; this was done and appreciated by Pompidou.

On September 3 I took the Chinese a message concerning our negotiations with the U.S.S.R. involving incidents at sea. The Chinese Ambassador digested this and with a grin said he hoped there would be no collisions at sea. I said that I hoped so too, but the Soviets often sailed very close to our ships, and I myself had seen them in the Mediterranean only a few hundred feet from our aircraft carriers.

The Ambassador would talk about many things, including China's population problem. He once recalled that Khrushchev had said that a Czechoslovakia was born in China every year, namely 13 to 15 million people. The Ambassador said the Chinese were trying to hold this down to 10 million a year. The Ambassador also commented, curiously, that the New York Times' James Reston had written a fairly objective article about China but that mostly it had been about his own operation there. The Chinese were backward in many areas. They would need help, but they did have knowledge in the acupuncture field that they would be glad to share along with other medical techniques with the Westerners.

Every time I met with them it was clear that they wanted to keep me and talk to me longer. They enjoyed talking and exchanging ideas and I spoke quite frankly to them. The Ambassador asked me a number of questions about myself—how I had gotten into the Army, how I had become an officer, where I had been during the war. They asked me whether I was married. I told them I was not. They asked me if I believed in God. I replied that of course I did. They asked me what religion I belonged to and I told them that I was a Catholic and they nodded, neither approvingly nor disapprovingly but simply acknowledging the fact that I had told them. Once the Ambassador said to me, "This Kissinger, is he Jewish?" I replied somewhat stiffly that I had never discussed religion with Dr. Kissinger. The important thing they should bear in mind was that he was an American. I later reported this exchange to Kissinger. He seemed pleased with my reply to the Chinese.

On September 21, I gave them the list of the crew for the aircraft that would be taking Dr. Kissinger to China. After this transaction, they asked me more questions, such as at what age did one retire in the United States Army. I told them that as a major general I would retire at fifty-eight, and if I were to be promoted to lieutenant general I could stay until age fifty-nine. The Ambassador seemed to think that this was a very young age at which to retire. He then asked me whether I was given a car and driver after I retired. I said no, I was given a substantial pension which enabled me to live very comfortably, but I was not given an automobile or driver. He grinned and said, "But I am in my country." I grinned back and said, "Well, Mr. Ambassador, I suppose that is one of the advantages of living in a completely egalitarian society like yours." He laughed again and slapped me on the back and did not seem irritated at the dig.

After Dr. Kissinger had called on the Chinese several times, the Ambassador commented to me that he liked to talk to Dr. Kissinger because he was always frank and direct and had an excellent sense of humor. He commented that when President Nixon came to China he would get a very good welcome. At one point, Ambassador Huang Chen asked me whether Kissinger had ever been in the Army. I said that he had. He asked me what his rank was and I thought it was better to tell him what Kissinger's last rank was rather than his earlier one of private during the war. I said Kissinger was a captain. "Oh," said the Ambassador, "in that case he has to salute us. We are generals." "Ah," I said, "Mr. Ambassador, he may still salute you. Unfortunately, he no longer salutes me." I enjoyed the humorous, relaxed nature of our conversations. It was as though we were from different planets and had finally established contact.

On September 22 I got a call from Tsao, saying that he must see me. I might add that in my negotiations with the Chinese, I used the code name of "Jean." With the North Vietnamese—many of my talks with the Chinese were being conducted simultaneously with the negotiations with the North Vietnamese—I used the code name "André." If I called the Chinese, I would say that I was Jean and that I wanted to talk to Wei or Tsao. If I were speaking to the North Vietnamese, I would say that it was André. I came to see Ambassador Huang Chen and we exchanged further information regarding the frequencies on which Kissinger's airplane would communicate with Hungjao tower at Shanghai. We discussed languages and I regretted my inability to speak Chinese. We explored one another's areas of knowledge, and, finally, we came up with one common language, which was Russian. We spoke Russian to one another. Mine was not good, but his was worse. He laughed and said that no one would ever believe that the Ambassador of the People's Republic of China in Paris and the American Military Attaché to France were speaking together in Russian. By this time, we had reached the stage where he would walk me to the door with his arm over my shoulder. I, of course, lived in constant concern that my visits would be picked up by the Soviets or even the CIA or the FBI, who would certainly wonder what a U. S. Army general was doing in the Chinese Communist Embassy. They never picked me up.

I saw them again on September 28 and told them that I would be returning to the United States to consult with Dr. Kissinger and President Nixon. The Ambassador commented they were talking to the French about the possibility of buying Concordes for their overseas routes; however, once relations with the United States were somewhat more normal, they would undoubtedly buy U.S. planes for their domestic routes. I said, "You will buy them until you can build your own." He laughed and said, "That's exactly what we intend to do." He then questioned me about the drug problem in the United States, and asked me what I thought should be done with drug peddlers. I said very bluntly that I thought drug peddlers who were selling hard drugs to teen-agers and minors should be executed. He fully agreed with this and said that no punishment could be too severe for them. They destroyed the fiber of a nation.

On October 2 I gave them a brief report on the talks between President Nixon and Soviet Foreign Minister Gromyko. I told the Ambassador that the Soviets had invited President Nixon to go to Moscow, that he had neither accepted nor refused yet and that we would keep the Chinese informed. Obviously, I did all of this on direction from Washington. Shortly after that on October 3, when I delivered another message, they asked me how much money Ambassador Watson earned, how much I earned, and I indicated to them that in the United States when you earned a million dollars, you paid 80 per cent of the million dollars in income tax. They seemed very surprised at this. The Ambassador commented that as a soldier he liked to do business with a soldier. We were not devious like diplomats. Wei and Tsao both looked uncomfortable as they translated this. At this meeting also, they agreed to the composition of Dr. Kissinger's party. They asked me to transmit their agreement. The Ambassador commented that he had known General and Mrs. Marshall in China in 1945 and he remembered Mrs. Marshall with great respect. I told him that she was still alive and in her nineties.

The discussions involving the airplane went into very great detail, with descriptions of the Shanghai airport, the ground power supply, the steps for the aircraft. They would have dry and wet ice available; they would have toilet service for the aircraft; they would provide security to guard the aircraft. All measurements were given in the metric system. They would notify Guam two hours prior to the departure of the aircraft from Hungjao; the U.S. crew were requested to wear civilian clothes at all times and not to carry any weapons openly.

Sometimes they would call me late at night. On October 9 they asked me to come over at ten o'clock at night. On each of these occasions I would either walk from my house or leave my car five or six blocks away and proceed on foot to the Embassy, verifying several times either with a small mirror or by turning around that I was not being followed by anybody. On October 9 they accepted the crew list and added a little jab that normally the Chinese banks would not accept U.S. dollars, but that they would do so on this occasion as a special favor to Dr. Kissinger. They provided me with details for the approach to Hungjao Airport, and I told them that President Nixon would shortly be visiting Moscow and that they were the first foreign country to be told of this. I then gave them a copy of Dr. Kissinger's press briefing, which they received with great interest.

On October 12 I saw them again. They gave me answers to many questions that I had asked. I told them what the call sign of the aircraft would be and that it would be coming from Guam. They asked me very warmly to tell Dr. Kissinger that they foresaw no problems with the trip and they were looking forward to his visit. They added that they were looking forward also to President Nixon's visit to China. The President had shown great courage in opening the door to them and would be warmly welcomed in China. The Ambassador felt that it was probable that the Chinese invitation to the President had provoked the Soviets into their invitation. The Ambassador then asked me who in the United States knew about the negotiations going on between the Chinese and us. I replied that to the best of my knowledge President Nixon, Dr. Kissinger, General Haig and a few of Dr. Kissinger's immediate entourage were the only ones who knew. The only person in Paris who knew about these negotiations, besides myself, was my secretary, Miss Nancy Ouellette. I gave them her name and phone number. If they ever had any urgent communications and it happened that I was out of Paris, they could get in touch with her and indeed they did on a later occasion. The Ambassador told me that on the Chinese side very, very few knew and that in his Embassy only Wei and Tsao knew. He told me Dr. Kissinger had proposed that these negotiations be conducted in Ottawa since the Chinese People's Republic now had an ambassador there, but the Chinese did not feel that this was an appropriate place and they preferred to deal through the Paris channel through him and through me.

During the chitchat that followed the official communication, the Ambassador asked me why the United States had decided not to build a supersonic transport. I said I thought this decision was wrong and we would have to build it in the future. He agreed. Once again, he expressed his satisfaction at our relationship as soldiers, saying that even though we had a different philosophy of life each of us could understand the motivation of the other in serving our respective countries.

I saw them again on October 14 and October 15. On these occasions I passed messages relating to the forthcoming trip and as usual we would discuss various things afterward. They asked me about the role of the U.S. military in American life. I said that we were the servants of the nation and not its guardians in an internal sense. We could not run for office. We had no political status. We could not attend political meetings in uniform, and we had a law which I found odd which said that no one who served in the armed services in the previous ten years could be Secretary of Defense. I thought this was rather discriminatory and presumed a danger from the military which was absolutely unjustified in American history. He seemed rather bewildered on hearing this and asked about General Marshall and General Eisenhower. I said that in the case of General Marshall the Congress had voted a special exception for him to the law and that General Eisenhower had resigned his five stars before running for President. I mentioned to them that the Soviets had once asked me whether I could run for offices, and I said no, I couldn't. And my Soviet colleague had said he could, and I said, "Yes, but I'm still one up on you because I can join the opposition and you can't." The Ambassador laughed heartily at this even though China was like the U.S.S.R. in this respect.

I saw them every few days at fairly regular intervals and on November 18 we agreed that the announcement of President Nixon's visit to China would be made at five o'clock in the morning on November 30, Peking time, and four o'clock in the afternoon on November 29, Washington time. It would be indicated that it would be a seven-day visit and the President, in addition to Peking, would also go to Hangchow. The Americans had at first suggested that the announcement take place on the twenty-third. The Chinese objected strenuously to this and when I pressed them for the reason, they sheepishly admitted that a high-ranking official of North Vietnam would be in Peking at that time and they did not want him there when the announcement was made.

They were constantly pressing me to drink some of their liquors and I always declined, saying that I had to drive my car and I did not want to be arrested for drunkenness. Finally, I decided to tell them a story that I had heard about the Russians. They always enjoyed stories about the Russians. I said that Khrushchev had gone to the United States, according to this story, and in talking to President Eisenhower had commented on the large number of drunks he saw in the United States. Eisenhower had been rather surprised and said he didn't think the United States had any more drunks than anyone else, but Khrushchev insisted that it did. So General Eisenhower had opened the drawer of his desk, taken out a pistol, given it to Khrushchev and said, "You have my permission to shoot any drunks you see." Khrushchev put the pistol in his pocket and went to New York, stayed overnight at the Soviet Embassy to the United Nations and the next morning went for a walk. At Park Avenue and Eightieth Street he saw a drunk and shot him. At Madison Avenue and Eighty-second he saw another drunk and shot him. At Lexington Avenue and Eighty-fourth Street he saw another drunk and shot him. Then I told the Chinese the punch line. The next morning the New York newspapers came out with giant headlines: THREE SOVIET DIPLOMATS MYSTERIOUSLY MURDERED. I have rarely seen them laugh as heartily as they did on this occasion.

The Ambassador asked me on this occasion whether I was going to China with Dr. Kissinger. I said I had not heard anything to that effect. The Ambassador told me he had told the Chinese government about me and how I had helped open a door that was closed for twenty-five years. I had very much hoped that Dr. Kissinger would take me on his trip to China; however, he decided not to do so.

On November 20 they asked me why Kissinger had canceled the visit to see the North Vietnamese. I said that after agreeing that Le Duc Tho would be present, the North Vietnamese had suddenly told us two days before the event that he would not be there, and in consequence, Dr. Kissinger would not go and see a lesser official. On this particular occasion, I was given incense for the first time, which indicated to me that I was growing in stature in their eyes.

On November 29 and 30 I saw them again and told them that I would be going to the Azores with President Nixon. On that same day I sent a message to Haig saying that on previous occasions when I had gone to Rome and Madrid with the President, my name was not on any list, there were no quarters reserved for me, nor was my transportation provided for, and that I hoped this would not be the case in the Azores this time. I got a warm note from Haig saying that the President's favorite interpreter would be properly taken care of on this occasion. I asked the Chinese on instructions from President Nixon to release Richard Fecteau and John Downey, two Americans they had been holding for more than twenty years on the charge of being CIA agents. The message I conveyed was that if they would see their way to make the gesture and release them, this would be very much appreciated in the United States. The Ambassador promised to transmit the message but did not give me an answer at that time. I left to go to the United States and depart for the Azores with President Nixon. While I was gone, they sent for my secretary, Nancy Ouellette, and told her that they would release Fecteau and Downey. Years later I was to see both men and introduce them to my secretary and tell them that I had asked for their release and my secretary had been told that they would be released.

On December 20 I went to see them again. The Ambassador had seen me on television in the Azores with President Nixon and President Pompidou and this had obviously boosted my prestige. They praised Nancy Ouellette, saying that she was very discreet and efficient in dealing with them. I said I knew this and this was why she was my secretary. They seemed very embarrassed about the progress of the Indian-Pakistani War, and my impression was that they had very much the feeling that after calling us paper tigers for a long time, they, after their strong support for Pakistan, had done practically nothing for Pakistan and had been shown up as somewhat of paper tigers themselves. This time as he saw me out, Wei said to me, "We will never forget the arrogance of the Soviets at the United Nations."

On Christmas Day they called me and wished me Merry Christmas and said they would like to see me the next day. When I went the next day, they expressed again warm greetings for me and for the American people for New Year's. The Ambassador commented that President Nixon had shown great courage in dealing with monetary matters at the Azores meeting as he had shown great courage in opening the door to China. He said that nearly everyone felt this except James Reston, who had told Prime Minister Chou En-lai that Nixon did not have courage when Chou En-lai had paid tribute to the President's courage. The Ambassador said that they supported the Prime Minister and felt that Mr. Nixon had shown great courage in making the approach to them. He also expressed warm thanks for the treatment that had been given to the Chinese in New York, where they had come to set up the PRC Embassy to the United Nations. They commented the Americans had been most helpful in helping them to get settled. The Ambassador commented on the United States' great production of food. I said that the Soviets had twice as much cultivable land as we did and it required thirty-two Soviets on the land to feed one hundred people in the Soviet population, while it required only two Americans on a farm to feed one hundred Americans. This was not simply a question of mechanization since the Soviets had more tractors than we did, it was simply that we were more efficiently organized for this.

On December 31 they agreed to the various methods of contact with the presidential aircraft. In a general philosophical discussion I said that I felt each people must work out their own way to govern themselves and run their own affairs and the United States would resent any foreigners attempting to tell us how to run our affairs.

On January 19 they seemed upset because it appeared that a drone aircraft from South Vietnam had flown into southern China and crashed. I explained to them what had happened, as I had been briefed on this matter. They once again praised President Nixon for his opening toward China, and I said that I was sure on their side it had not been easy either. They nodded rather solemnly at this and it was perfectly clear that they had had some explaining to do within the party as to why they had allowed President Nixon to come after denouncing him in the United States for so long. I said that I believed only a moderate President of the United States like Nixon could have successfully opened contacts with the Chinese People's Republic. If a liberal Democratic President had tried it, he would have been accused of selling out to the "Reds." They praised President Pompidou and said they did not understand why the French Communists were attacking him. The Ambassador said that the Soviets had long sought a master and servant relationship with the Chinese and that this was odious to the Chinese and they would not stand for it. He said that they had been deceived once by the Soviets but they would not be deceived again. He then said he felt President Nixon could probably understand aspects of the problems of the working class better than some of his critics since he came from the working class whereas many of his opponents were very rich.

On January 20 I gave them the list of the people who would sit in at the various meetings with the Chinese. I gave them the plan for the aircraft arrivals. I gave them a list of the administrative group who would be with the President. They gave me the room assignments in Hangchow. I gave them a copy of Ron Ziegler's press briefing and I gave them the special flags for the President's car. They fingered the flags and commented on the splendid quality of the silk and the embroidery. No mean compliment from the Chinese!

I saw them again on January 26, and they seemed overwhelmed at the number of aircraft that were going. As I was leaving the Embassy after this meeting, a Volkswagen bus drove into the courtyard of the Embassy. The Chinese practically grabbed me, pushed me into a side room and closed the door while a large number of Chinese who lived in the residence got out of the bus and went to various places in the Embassy residence. They were clearly very anxious that these people did not see me in the Embassy.

On January 30 after we had asked them to try and use some good offices to make the North Vietnamese more reasonable, they gave me a very harsh message, reiterating that the North Vietnamese were right and the United States was conducting an imperialistic, immoral war. It was clear as they read this to me that they were very embarrassed, but they did not comment upon it. On the following day I came back from Germany for another message, which was equally harsh. This time they gave it to me to read myself rather than read it aloud. I guessed what its content would be and I made a deliberate effort to show no expression or emotion of any sort on my face, and simply said, coolly, that I would transmit it. As soon as this particular formal part of the meeting was over, they were very cordial. After the harsh note, it was as though they were trying to make it up to me. We had asked them whether there would be any possibility of President Nixon seeing Le Duc Tho, who would be in Peking around that time. They said it was none of their business and they would not arrange the meeting. Any such contact was a matter between the United States and North Vietnam. I then gave them the text of President Nixon's toast at Chou En-lai's banquet. We then discussed the famous Chinese writer on the art of war, Sun-tzu, and the Ambassador told me that his writings were required reading in all Chinese military schools.

About this time, the Chinese gave me a report which they had without any confirmation. They said they had information to the effect that the Chiang Kai-shek "clique" would attempt to shoot down President Nixon's aircraft on its way to the People's Republic of China, and that they would have Chinese mainland markings on the aircraft. They added that it was difficult to judge reliably the validity of this report, but they were sending the message to us anyway so we would know. I told them I thanked them and that we would take appropriate measures.

On February 11 the Chinese again refused to take any part in arranging a meeting with Le Duc Tho in Peking, repeating that this was a matter between the United States and North Vietnam. Again, I could see that the Ambassador and his aides were embarrassed at the harsh tone of the message which they had to give to me. On February 15 they commented that it was the forty-second meeting, and said I was like a member of the family and they had gotten to know me very well. On February 17 the Chinese said that they would assure protection of the aircraft when it entered their territorial air space twelve nautical miles from the coast. They emphasized this was twelve nautical, not twelve miles.

President Nixon's trip went off very well and the Chinese were extremely pleased with it and expressed their satisfaction many times to me, feeling that this had opened new possibilities, and again repeating their praise for the President. I told them that the United States was a strange country and it was probably only a conservative President who could have taken such a step without being accused of having sold out to the Communists. By this time, I was close to leaving Paris and I had discussed the matter of passing on a channel to the Chinese and it had been agreed by Dr. Kissinger that this would be done through Ambassador Watson, who, by this time, had been told of my involvement. As a matter of fact, he found out on one occasion when he had driven Kissinger to meet me at a prearranged meeting on the Trocadéro Square. The Ambassador had been surprised to see me there and Kissinger had decided to tell the Ambassador the whole story and told him that I had been directed not to discuss this with anyone.

On March 5 I went down to have dinner with the Chinese. This was almost the last day I was in Paris. They knew this and they insisted that I come. We sat in a large dining room under a gigantic tapestry of Mao with the ethnic minorities. The artist was visibly inspired by the representations of the Last Supper. It was a fourteen-course meal washed down with Chinese flower wine and Château Haut-Brion. The Ambassador made a little speech and said that I had become an old friend, and whatever happened in the future, he and I at least had performed our mission successfully. We had put our chiefs in touch with one another and the fact that we were both soldiers had made this contact easier and made it possible for us to work together. At the dinner toast he said, "I know where you are going, to the CIA, and if I can give you one piece of advice, it is watch the Soviets. They are very dangerous people. We Chinese know." I replied thanking him for his courtesy to me in helping to make my task, which was an unprecedented one, easier, and I said that they should know that in my new job I would always serve my country faithfully but I would always remember the friendship they had shown me and the importance of the friendship between our peoples. The Ambassador replied that he would have thought less of me if I had not expressed my determination to serve my country loyally. Again, he repeated his amazement at the size of the press party that went with President Nixon to China. He said that no chief of state that had visited China had ever brought more than eight or ten people. The Ambassador then said that our negotiations had been successful because so few people had known about them. The Ambassador went back to the beginning of our relationship, saying that I had shown good judgment in coming to the residence and that I had been wise to watch and see what time he left. I noted that we could have gotten these negotiations under way at a much earlier date if his Military Attaché had accepted the message which I had attempted to give him in April. He smiled, shrugged and said, "Then the time was not ripe. Later it became ripe." The Ambassador then noted that we had met forty-five times, and he toasted our forty-sixth meeting, wherever it might be. He added that I would always be welcome in China for the part that I had played in bringing that country and the United States to a position where they could talk to one another without the hostility that had characterized their relationship for so many years.

This had been a fascinating exchange with the Chinese. It had been a matter of enormous difficulty for me to smuggle in Kissinger for these meetings. On one occasion I took him to see President Pompidou at his private home, and Kissinger cautioned me not to tell his two assistants, who were staying at my apartment, where we were going. I did not tell them, and a year or two later in a U.S. weekly magazine there had been a comment to the effect that Kissinger had visited Pompidou in his private apartment. Since I had not told the weekly magazine and I was quite sure that President Pompidou had not told the weekly magazine, only Dr. Kissinger could have told them. His staying at my apartment was always a problem in that someone who knew me might come to the apartment while they were there and see them. Fortunately, I had a garage in the basement of the house, and I could bring the car in, lock the door behind me, park and take him upstairs before anybody could get into the garage and follow us closely. I had succeeded in convincing my housekeeper that he was General Kirschman until he did an interview on French television with a French television girl reporter. The maid then told me that she knew who he was, and I told her that she thought it was Dr. Kissinger, but that Dr. Kissinger was a very important man, the special adviser to the President, and if he came to Paris, he would certainly stay at the Ambassador's sumptuous residence and not at my small apartment. I agreed that my friend General Kirschman did look a good deal like Henry Kissinger if you saw them apart, but if you saw them together, they really were quite unlike one another. This seemed to convince her. My enlisted aide, Sergeant Chuck Hall, knew about this. He served Kissinger breakfast when he came and maintained, for a very young man, extraordinary discretion throughout this whole episode. He left and was replaced by another aide, John Sawyer, who showed equal discretion in this matter. They were of great assistance to me.

It was a satisfying relationship in that we went, so to speak, from point zero to a triumphant and successful visit by the President to China. Several years later, after Mr. Nixon had resigned, he called me from San Clemente to tell me that he was going to China and said that since I had opened the door, he wanted me to be the first to know that he was going to visit Mao. He wanted to see Mao before he died and recalled that the first time he had seen him, Mao looked at him and said, "I am the greatest Communist in the world, and you are the greatest anti-Communist, and history has brought us together." It had been a long and interesting relationship. Many times the Ambassador and I had seen one another at various receptions around Paris and we always passed one another without any public sign of recognition, even though we might have spent two or three hours together earlier in the day. I believe the secret was well kept. I ascertained subsequently that President Pompidou, faithful to his word, had kept this at the highest levels of French intelligence. When the announcement was

made of the relationship, very few people had known. I felt a
certain pride in having been able to conduct these extensive negotiations with very little logistical support and very little base,
and with only my secretary knowing of these negotiations. It
had been a long, difficult time for me as I had to code and
decode many complex messages myself. I used to say that I was
the highest-paid code clerk in the United States government.
But it was a feeling of satisfaction to have had a small part to
play in this bold move by the President and by Dr. Kissinger to
put our relationship with China on a new base. I could not help
but admire the boldness and imagination of Henry Kissinger.
He was tireless and demanding, sometimes arrogant and unreasonable, but he truly understood power and its uses. Like President Nixon he had to contend with an unfriendly, often hostile
Congress. I watched him with admiration; not always agreeing
with him, but wondering who else could have done half as well.
And thus came to an end, at least for the time being, my mission to the Chinese Communists.

26. GENERAL FRANCO

In February 1971 I had returned from Paris to Washington for consultation with the President and Dr. Kissinger regarding the negotiations in Paris with the Chinese and North Vietnamese.

On February 15 I was told that the President would see me in his office the next morning at ten o'clock. I entered the Oval Office at the appointed time and was most cordially received by the President. He invited me to sit down. He then told me that he had been reflecting about the situation in Spain and what might happen after Franco's death. Spain was vital for the West and he did not want to see a chaotic or anarchic situation develop. He expressed the hope that Franco would enthrone the young Prince Juan Carlos on the throne. The Prince had made a most favorable impression on the President during a recent visit to Washington. The President felt that this would be an ideal situation in that it would ensure a peaceful and orderly transition which Franco himself could oversee. Failing this, President Nixon expressed the hope that General Franco would appoint a strong Prime Minister who could ensure the transition from Franco's regime to the monarchy. The President told me that he was just thinking out loud and had no desire to interfere in the internal affairs of Spain, nor did he wish to tell Spaniards what to do in their own country. He genuinely liked Spain and Spaniards and had been deeply impressed by the warm welcome they had given him on his two visits there. He said that his concern arose from the importance of a stable Spain.

The President then said that he wished me to go to Spain and see Franco alone, if I could, and find out what he had in mind concerning events after his own demise. To say that I was shaken by this instruction is to understate the case. First, there was the problem of getting to see Franco alone without the U. S. Embassy or the Spanish Foreign Ministry knowing. This was extremely difficult. Secondly, talking to a man about his own death is not an easy task. I asked the President what chance he thought a Spanish Army officer would have of getting to see him alone without the help of his own Embassy or the State Department. He replied, "None, but you have done it before, so go and do it now." The President then directed me to dictate my report upon my return to his own secretary, Rose Mary Woods, rather than to the girls in Henry Kissinger's office where I normally dictated my reports when I was in Washington. I deduced from this instruction that he had talked the idea over with Kissinger, who was unenthusiastic about it, but he had decided to go ahead and do it anyway. He then gave me a letter for General Franco and told me to deliver it personally. Finally, the President said that if I felt it was necessary I could tell Ambassador Robert Hill in Madrid about the matter but that I should not get him involved in it as it might sour his relations with the Spanish Foreign Office. He also gave me a letter for Ambassador Hill. I then flew back to Paris, still wondering how to handle this awkward and complex mission.

I flew to Madrid on February 23 and gave Ambassador Hill the letter addressed to him. Even though that letter did not refer to the purpose of my visit, Ambassador Hill, a shrewd and able diplomat, guessed at once what had brought me to Madrid. He was not like many of his colleagues who believe that there should be no contact with the chief of state in the country where they are accredited except through them. This parochial point of view has been a problem on many occasions. These men forget that they are the President's representative and he may conduct foreign policy through whatever channels he chooses. Ambassador Hill believed that it would be difficult to arrange a meeting with Franco as Foreign Minister Gregorio López Bravo was out of the country. I said that I felt confident I could arrange this through Chief of Government Admiral Luis Carrero Blanco. I knew him quite well and felt sure that he would help me. On the following day, I saw Admiral Carrero Blanco in his office alone and told him that I had been instructed by President Nixon to seek an audience with General Franco alone. I also told him that I had a letter from the President with instructions to hand it to the generalissimo. Carrero Blanco asked me if this matter had been taken up through any of the ministries and I said that I did not believe that it had. He then said that he would see Franco at 1 P.M. the following day and would discuss the matter with him.

Later that evening Ambassador Hill asked me to come over and see him. He said that on his return from Tunisia, López Bravo had been notified by Carrero Blanco of the request. At this time, López Bravo was reported to be involved in some difficulties. He was later exonerated but that evening he was quite agitated and had asked Ambassador Hill to come over and see him the next morning. I felt it was very important that Ambassador Hill's position be protected and suggested that he tell López Bravo that I had arrived in the country with a letter from the President. Since the Foreign Minister was out of the country and there was a certain urgency to the matter, I had not wished to go through the acting Foreign Minister and I had telephoned Admiral Carrero Blanco, whom I knew personally, and who was the next higher authority in the government. Ambassador Hill agreed to this and by the time he saw the Foreign Minister the next morning, López Bravo was quite relaxed but still very curious about the nature of my mission. The Foreign Minister asked if I would come over and see him, as he had known me since 1959. I agreed to see him and went to the Foreign Ministry, where he received me alone. I explained the circumstances of my visit, but did not discuss the nature of my message, nor did I tell him what I was attempting to ascertain from General Franco. He commented that General Franco never saw any foreigners alone, but that he would recommend to Franco that he do so in this case.

At one-thirty that afternoon I saw Carrero Blanco again at his office. He told me that I would be received by General Franco at El Pardo at 5 P.M. that afternoon. I asked the admiral if he would send a car for me, as I did not wish to use an Embassy car with its high-profile diplomatic license plate. He agreed to send a Spanish government car to take me to the *caudillo*. At four-fifteen a car came for me and I drove to General Franco's residence just outside Madrid. As I was well ahead of schedule, I had the driver pull off to the side of the road near the palace and waited to see who went by. López Bravo did and I presumed that he would be present at the interview with Franco. I was thus prepared for this contingency. Carrero Blanco had warned me that Franco was quite old and sometimes seemed feeble. Spaniards did not like him to see foreigners alone. He would try and arrange for me to see Franco alone, but if that were not possible, he hoped that I would understand. Fifteen minutes before my appointment I arrived at El Pardo. I was ushered by liveried footmen into a large waiting room on the second floor of the palace. The walls of this room were entirely covered with yellow silk. The silence of my wait was broken only by the clearly audible ticking of five clocks. Like Adenauer, another old man, Franco was fascinated with time. Spain's great King Emperor Charles V had died in a monastery at Yuste surrounded by clocks.

It was a lonely wait, but not a long one. At exactly five o'clock, I was ushered into Franco's private office. It was the same room where I had seen him once with Eisenhower and twice with Nixon. At his side stood the smiling Foreign Minister. General Franco was in civilian clothes and no one else was present. It was clear to me at this point that to insist on seeing him alone would have been a humiliating affront to the Foreign Minister and I decided not to do this. I opened by thanking General Franco for receiving me and held out the President's letter. He reached out for it but his hand trembled violently and he motioned for the Foreign Minister to take it. López Bravo took the letter and took out of the envelope the Spanish translation of Mr. Nixon's letter and read it to General Franco, who nodded and asked me to sit down. I then said that I brought greetings from President Nixon, who would never forget the extraordinarily moving welcome he had received in October 1970 from the generalissimo and the Spanish people. I recalled that on arriving at the Moncloa guest palace, the President had said to me, "These people are really our friends." General Franco nodded and said that this was indeed true. I then said that General Franco must know what tremendous burdens the President had to bear; not only did he manage the affairs of the United States but he also bore great world responsibilities. The President greatly valued General Franco's views on the future stability of Spain and the situation of its neighbors.

General Franco spoke first of all of the situation in the Middle East and felt that the death of Nasser had lessened the chances for a settlement in that part of the world. He said that in dealing with the Russians in the SALT talks whatever the Russians signed they would not respect. It was very difficult to get the better of them. I commented with a smile that he had. For an instant, a smile lit the old man's face and he nodded at the compliment. He then said that he felt that what the President was most interested in was what would happen in Spain after his own demise. I replied, "That is correct, General." He said that the succession would be orderly. There was no alternative to the Prince. Spain would move some distance along the road we favored but not all the way, as Spain was neither America nor England nor France. It was Spain. He indicated that the Armed Forces would never let things get out of hand, and expressed confidence in the Prince's ability to handle the situation after his death. He said that he had created a number of institutions to ensure an orderly succession. He smiled and said that many people doubted that these institutions would work. They were wrong; the transition would be peaceful. General Franco then stood up as though to indicate that the interview was over. He said to me, "Tell President Nixon that insofar as the order and stability of Spain are concerned, this will be guaranteed by the timely and orderly measures I am taking." He then asked me to convey to the President his warmest greetings and his gratitude for Mr. Nixon's kind words about the Prince, himself and Spain. We could await the future with full confidence in Spain. He had faith in God and the Spanish people.

I walked slowly downstairs wondering how many men in any walk of life could talk so dispassionately about their own death. I did not believe that this could be very far off. General Franco looked old and weak. His left hand trembled at times so violently that he would cover it with his other hand. At times he appeared far away and at others he came right to the point, as in the remark about his own death and the future stability of Spain. I felt more forgiving toward López Bravo for having worked himself into the interview. If Franco had been my chief of state I would not have wanted to leave him alone with a foreigner. As I drove back for Madrid, I could not but think that Franco had ruled Spain for more than thirty-five years. One way or the other he had given the country peace and a considerable degree of prosperity. Would these be sufficient to guarantee an orderly succession and change of regime? I felt that the President had given me a mission that really required me to do more than talk to General Franco. Ostensibly on leave in Spain, I saw a number of friends in the Spanish Armed Forces who were occupying key positions in the command structure. All of these made quite clear their support for the accession of Prince Juan Carlos on Franco's death and expressed their belief that there would be no disorder or political breakdown in the nation.

All of the senior officers to whom I talked doubted that Franco would place the Prince on the throne before his own death. They did, however, believe that he would appoint a Prime Minister. They did not believe that there would be any disturbances of consequence in the country when Franco died and said that the Armed Forces could easily handle such problems. It was a sobering and unique experience.

I flew back to Washington and there dictated a report to the President in his office. I also spoke to him personally and gave him my impression that the succession would go off in an orderly fashion when the time came. I expressed to him my amazement and the calm and unemotional way in which Franco had discussed the subject. Few men could.

Thus ended my mission to General Franco to discuss the events that would follow his demise. It was a mission unlike any other.

27. JOURNEYS WITH PRESIDENT
NIXON

I was still serving as Military Attaché to France in Paris when President Nixon was elected in November 1968. Not too long after his election, I was called upon to translate for him on his trips abroad as I had for several of his predecessors.

In early February 1969, a White House advance party composed of Robert Haldeman, John Ehrlichman and others arrived in Paris to arrange for a visit by the President. I was ordered to join them and was told that I would be translating for the President during his trip. I was a little surprised as I was by this time a major general and that was a little senior for an interpreter.

This was the first time I had ever met these men, and I accompanied them in their discussions with the French authorities who would be responsible for the President's schedule and safety in France. I knew many of them from trips by previous Presidents. Ambassador Shriver, who was President Kennedy's brother-in-law, worked closely with them. He had been appointed by Lyndon Johnson, but Nixon was to keep him on in Paris for a considerable time. I was interested to note that there did not seem to be an element of personal rivalry between Haldeman and Ehrlichman. Generally, in the other White House groups I had observed over the years, this sort of rivalry had been present. This group was firm in its dealings with the French but not overbearing. Ehrlichman in particular seemed quite relaxed. After Paris we went on to Brussels and London to make the same sort of arrangements there. Then we flew on to Bonn, Berlin and Rome. The advance party returned to Paris and then flew back to the United States.

Rome was a somewhat delicate stop in that it was the seat of two governments to be visited, Italy and the Vatican. The United States did not have diplomatic relations with the Holy See and this complicated matters a little. There were, however, the precedents of the visits of Presidents Eisenhower and Johnson to the Vatican to serve as a guide.

Europe was anxious to see the new President and in a sense to take his measure, so there were no real difficulties or complications anywhere in arranging the schedule. It was decided that the Rome visit would take place in two phases. First a visit to the Italian government, then a trip to France, followed by a visit to the Vatican. It was clearly understood that on completion of the trip, I would return to my assignment as Defense Attaché to France. I had had some experience with such groups under various different administrations. The people on them were different, but they all had one thing in common—a great desire to limit access to the President and to let as few outsiders as possible see him. They all seemed to regard the power and authority of the White House as a finite quantity, and if anyone else got in on this, they would lose a share of theirs. For this reason, I would always make clear to the local authorities that I was not a regular member of the party and would at the end of the presidential visit return to my normal assignment. This never failed to produce a visible feeling of relief from whatever advance party I happened to be with. I would always carefully point out that "they" were from the White House, but I was from the NATO Standing Group or the Embassy in Paris or wherever I happened to be serving at the time. In fact, the only time in my career that I ever served in the White House was with Mr. Harriman under President Truman. This tactic enabled me to avoid frictions. It had failed to work only with Salinger and O'Donnell during their visit to Paris to prepare for President Kennedy's visit. All they could see was the fact that I had worked for President Eisenhower, forgetting that I had also worked for President Truman and Mr. Harriman.

As always, one of the principal problems was the access of the Secret Service to the local chief of state's residence. With good will this too was worked out.

On February 15, 1969, I flew back to Washington to join the President's party. On February 17, I visited former President Dwight Eisenhower in Walter Reed Army Hospital. He was his usual warm and cheerful self, despite the fact that he was hooked up to a machine that was monitoring his heartbeat. On February 20, I saw Mr. Nixon at the White House and we talked about some of the personalities he was to see. I gave him my impressions of them and what they might be likely to take up with him. He was full of plans of what he was going to do in office: create an atmosphere that would make it possible to talk to the Soviets, take some initiative to bring the Chinese Communists in from the cold and find an honorable way to end the war in Vietnam without abandoning our allies. I was later to be involved in the latter two projects.

On February 23, 1969, I flew off the White House lawn in a helicopter to Andrews Air Force Base near Washington. There we boarded *Air Force One* for the trip to Brussels. We had a smooth and uneventful voyage to the Belgian capital. I had told Mr. Nixon that King Baudouin spoke excellent English and that he would have no need of my services in his talks with the Belgian monarch. On arrival in Brussels, King Baudouin made his welcoming speech in English, which relieved him from the obligation of having to deliver it in both French and Dutch, Belgium's two official languages.

Mr. Nixon and his party stayed at the Hilton Hotel. This was a marked departure from the practice of staying in quarters provided by the host country. Mr. Nixon had talks with Prime Minister Gaston Eyskens, who had been to college in the United States and spoke excellent English. I was present, however, and subsequently wrote the memorandum of conversation with the Belgian Premier. At the meeting with Foreign Minister Pierre Harmel, I did translate. Later King Baudouin and Queen

Fabiola gave a state luncheon for the President at the royal palace. I knew that the Queen was Spanish by birth and that she spoke both French and Dutch. I was quite unprepared for her superb command of English. She had great charm and grace and looked precisely the way one would expect a queen to look. Before the lunch we stood and talked in a large reception room. The King asked me where I had learned French and I told him that I had lived in France for ten years as a child from the age of six to sixteen. Then a receiving line was formed at the entrance to the dining room. The guests were formally presented to the Belgian sovereigns and to the President. Because of the bilingual character of Belgium, each guest was presented in his or her language. For instance, the Foreign Minister was introduced in French and I whispered the introduction into the President's ear, as I was standing directly behind him. The Secretary-General of the Foreign Ministry, on the other hand, was introduced in Dutch, and again I whispered a translation into Mr. Nixon's ear. King Baudouin looked at me in surprise and said to me in Dutch, "General, can you do this in Dutch too?" I replied in Dutch that I could not speak it as well as French, but my knowledge was adequate for this purpose. He commented to the President that he could not recall meeting a U.S. general officer who could speak Dutch. The lunch was magnificent and a very pleasant occasion as well. There were no problems or tensions with the Belgians. Mr. Nixon told the King that this was his first trip to Belgium. In the past he had always been sent where there were problems, and since we had no problems with Belgium, he had never been there previously.

The President laid a wreath on the tomb of the Belgian Unknown Soldier and visited both NATO and the European Economic Community, both of which organizations have their seat in Brussels. At both organizations, the President made a speech defining the policies of his administration toward them. We then left Brussels for England. The flight to London was uneventful and the welcome by the British very warm. In England I had little to do with the official program and in a sense had some time off to visit friends and do some shopping. On the next day we flew to Germany. Here too, the President received a warm welcome from the Germans, who were ever watchful for any sign of a lessening U.S. commitment to them and to the defense of the old German capital in Berlin. The inclusion of Berlin in his itinerary had been a great reassurance to them.

Up to this time, I had always tried to avoid high-level interpreting in German. I spoke the language quite fluently, but did not feel that I could catch and convey all the nuances of meaning as I could in the other languages I spoke. I had never lived or been stationed in Germany, and simply did not feel wholly comfortable translating for a very senior official where my lack of total fluency might cause a misunderstanding. I had never objected to translating small talk. Circumstances made me set aside this principle on this visit.

Germany at that time was governed by the so-called grand coalition of the Christian Democratic and Social Democratic parties. Dr. Kurt Kiesinger, a Christian Democrat, was Chancellor and Willy Brandt, a Social Democrat, was Vice-Chancellor. The President called on the German President and Foreign Minister and held a lengthy press conference at which I did not translate. These calls were followed by a lunch given by the Chancellor at his residence overlooking the Rhine. I noted that during this visit, insofar as he could, Henry Kissinger avoided speaking German except in two main conversations. After lunch the Chancellor made a long, humorous and sometimes emotional speech to the President in German. When he had finished, everyone looked around for the interpreter to render the speech into English, but he was not there. Then the German Ambassador to the United States, Rolf Pauls, said he would try and repeat what the Chancellor had said in English. He had not gone far before the Chancellor, who spoke some English, interrupted to say, "No, no, that is not what I said." There was some confusion. I then asked the Chancellor if he would allow me to try. He told me to go ahead and I proceeded with the translation into English. I watched the Chancellor carefully as I spoke and as he continued to nod approvingly, I presumed that I was on the right track. He said that Mr.

Nixon's performance in going from the No. 2 spot to the No. 1 spot gave him some concern. He was afraid it might be tried in Germany too. This with a glance at the Vice-Chancellor. All laughed including Brandt, who did in fact later become Chancellor. After the lunch, Mr. Nixon asked me why I had always said I would not translate in German. I explained that a slight mistake or slip of the tongue at that level could cause serious misunderstandings. There is nothing more painful than watching an interpreter try to handle something that he is not really qualified to do. I did not wish to find myself in that position.

On the way to Berlin Mr. Nixon was told that the weather was not good. The U. S. Army garrison of that city would be drawn up on Tempelhof Airfield for review and he would pass along the line in a jeep. He said that he would prefer to walk and was told that it might rain. "In that case, I'll get wet just like the soldiers," he replied. It did not rain and he walked the whole length of the line of troops. The Berliners, living under constant threat as they do, were most happy to see the American President and to hear him reaffirm the U.S. commitment to that city. We had lunch with the burgomaster at Charlottenburg Palace and the President visited the infamous Wall that splits the city in two. We then flew on to Italy that afternoon, leaving large, happy crowds of Berliners behind.

The flight to Rome was uneventful. The Swiss and Austrians had given exceptional permission for the U. S. Air Force plane carrying the President to overfly their neutral territory. On arrival in Rome, I translated welcoming speeches and replies by the President. Then we drove into Rome through small but friendly crowds. Near the Colosseum we did see a small Communist demonstration. We drove to the vast Quirinale Palace where we were to be housed. Once the residence of the Popes and later the kings of Italy, it is now the official residence of the President of the Republic. The building was so huge that I felt quite lost in it. I was present at all of the President's meetings with Italian government leaders and people from the private sector as well. I translated at all of these meetings. President Giuseppe Saragat at one point, in reply to a question by Mr.

Nixon concerning the question of the true loyalties of the Italian Communist party, expressed the view that the Communists were more devoted to the interests of Moscow and world communism than to purely Italian concerns. Saragat spoke strongly on behalf of the unity of Europe and hoped that the Europeans would find a friendly America supporting them. The President assured him that he would. Saragat then told a story about a pre-Hitler German trade union leader whom he had visited in Germany before Hitler came to power. Saragat was then an exile from Mussolini's Italy. The German had berated Saragat, saying that the Italians had not defended their freedoms against a dictatorship, but that this could never happen in Germany. Then, commented Saragat, "many years later as President of Italy on a visit to Paris I laid a wreath on the tomb of that German trade union leader in Père Lachaise Cemetery in Paris, where he had died an exile from Hitler." The President spoke to Saragat about the importance of strengthening NATO, building European unity, and asked for understanding of the fact that the United States might at times have to engage in bilateral negotiations to ensure peace. He assured the Italians that we would consult with them on a regular basis and that they would be kept informed.

We then flew to Paris to begin the visit to General de Gaulle. The White House press secretary's office had already distributed to the press the text of the remarks that Mr. Nixon intended to make upon his arrival at Orly Airport. When we landed we were met by General de Gaulle, looking as austere and historic as usual. In greeting the President, he went out of his way to be warm and friendly in his reference to Mr. Nixon. He said, "We rejoice at your trip and consider it an honor because of all the esteem which our people have for the statesman which the American people have just placed in charge of their affairs. Esteem to which I must for my part add my long and well-tested friendship for you." President Nixon was so moved by what de Gaulle had said that he whispered to me to disregard the distributed press remarks because he was going to say something else. He then spoke with great personal warmth and admiration of General de Gaulle. Later a member of the party who had received the distributed remarks said that I had changed what the President had said. I said that whatever might be on the piece of paper he had received, I had translated what the President had in fact said. While there were no sensational breakthroughs in the talks with General de Gaulle and his ministers, these went well and a new warmth crept into Franco-American relations. De Gaulle received Mr. Nixon at the Trianon at Versailles. Commenting on the surroundings he said, "If it had not been for our Kings, how could the Republic have received its guests?"

At the reception for General de Gaulle at the American Embassy, Mr. Nixon spoke warmly of the fact that the last time there had been such an occasion was when a popular young American President, John Kennedy, had given a similar reception for the French President. Mrs. Shriver, the Ambassador's wife and Kennedy's sister, seemed touched by the reference. While in Paris, Mr. Nixon met with many French political personalities and business leaders as well. He laid a wreath on the Tomb of the Unknown Soldier under the Arch of Triumph and on his way down the Champs Elysées stopped at a number of places to shake hands with the crowds that had gathered to cheer him. On arriving back at his quarters, he found that he had lost one of his cuff links. This set had been given to him by Mrs. Nixon for his birthday just before his inauguration and he seemed quite upset at the loss. The cuff links were later found and returned. While in Paris the President also met with Vice-President Nguyen Cao Ky of South Vietnam, who was leading his country's delegation to the peace talks then going on in Paris. As we left Paris to return to Rome to see the Pope, General de Gaulle saw Mr. Nixon off and said that the visit had been a success for both countries and for the President.

We arrived at Rome after a scenic flight across the Alps. On landing in Rome we flew at once in U.S. helicopters to the Vatican and landed in St. Peter's Square, almost at the very spot where I had stopped my jeep on the day of Rome's liberation in 1944. The President was received by high Vatican prelates and we were led to the Pope's office after honors by the Swiss guards dressed in uniforms designed by Michelangelo. It was the first time I had seen Pope Paul VI. He was a much smaller man than either of his predecessors. No Catholic ever enters the Pope's presence without a certain feeling of awe and I felt it on this occasion. The two leaders talked in the Pope's office overlooking the great square. Monsignor Carew, a Canadian prelate, translated for the Pope into English and I translated what Mr. Nixon had said into Italian.

The discussion covered many subjects, tensions between East and West, the hostilities in the Middle East and the need to ensure the inviolability of the holy places of the three great monotheistic religions. They spoke also of the problems of European unity and of the Far East and Vietnam in particular. The Pope expressed warm support for the U.S. efforts to save the South Vietnamese people from communism. He said to the President, "You are doing the right thing. You cannot abandon the Christian community or it will be destroyed." I have often wondered subsequently why he did not say something like this in public. The Pope then expressed concern about the situation in Spain and Portugal and noted the great importance for Europe of what happened in those two countries. He then spoke with some concern of events in Chile and the growing strength of communism in that country, which had infiltrated Christian Democratic movements and even the Catholic university in Santiago. He said that there were times when he thought that the Catholic university was Catholic in name only. He urged Mr. Nixon to watch the situation there closely. Presents were exchanged and the Pope gave me a small silver medal. We then left his office. The President then spoke briefly to the students of the North American College in Rome. This was a group of seminarians studying for the priesthood. They gave him a rousing cheer and he commented that it was probably the only college before which he could speak without problems. He was of course referring to the multiple college campus demonstrations against the Vietnam War.

President Nixon then flew to the airport and departed for the United States. I remained behind in Rome and prepared to return to my normal duty assignment in Paris. My brother Vincent had come over for the Columbia Broadcasting System to cover the visit and we had an opportunity to visit together and eat fettucine at Alfredo's. We flew back to Paris together and my brother then went on to New York.

Prior to leaving Rome, I wanted to call on three senior Italian officials with whom I had had contact during my time there as Military Attaché in 1960 and 1962. These were then Defense Minister Giulio Andreotti and General Giovanni de Lorenzo, who had been chief of Intelligence during my tour in Rome. Subsequent to my departure, de Lorenzo had become Chief of Staff and had become embroiled in various controversies. He had been fired as Chief of Staff, but had got himself elected as a member of Parliament. I asked the Embassy if it would be all right for me to make these calls and they had no objections. I called General de Lorenzo and he sent his car for me. We talked about old times and a little about current problems. I thanked him for his many courtesies to me during my service as attaché in Rome. He seemed to be his usual ebullient self. I then returned to my hotel, where I saw General Aloia Giuseppe, who had been Chief of Staff while I was stationed in Italy. He was now retired and a mortal enemy of de Lorenzo's. Thus, I played no favorites. All of these men had been courteous and friendly to me during my tour in Italy and it seemed to me to be the right thing to do to call on them. Shortly after I left Italian leftist papers trumpeted the fact that I had been to see de Lorenzo and interpreted it as some sort of plot, or that I was carrying a message from Nixon to him and other similar absurdities. There were even questions asked in Parliament. I had spoken to all of these men about my stay in Italy. There was no conspiracy but by selectively omitting the fact that I had seen Andreotti and Aloia, my visit was portrayed in a sinister light. The Embassy could not complain because they had approved my making these calls.

I then flew back to Paris and returned to my normal assignment. Shortly after I returned, I received a call from a Portuguese worker in Paris who had found Mr. Nixon's cuff link on the ground on the Champs Elysées. Since it showed the seal of the President, and there had been an article about the lost cuff link, he had contacted the American Embassy. As he spoke only Portuguese, they referred him to me. I met with him, retrieved the cuff link, gave him some tokens of appreciation. His name was Nobre, which means "noble" in Portuguese. I told him that his action in returning it showed that he was noble in fact as well as in name.

The next trip on which I translated for President Nixon took place a year and a half later in September and October of 1970. I had gone on a trip to the Far East from Paris. I had visited the Osaka World's Fair and had then gone on to Saigon, where I stayed for a few days with General Creighton Abrams, the commander in chief. While there I received a message telling me that I had to be in Paris on September 27 to meet Dr. Kissinger, who was going to talk to the North Vietnamese on that date. I would then continue to Rome with him and join the President's party there to translate for him in Italy and Spain. I would not be accompanying him on his trip to Yugoslavia, nor on his visit to the Sixth Fleet in the Mediterranean.

I then arrived in Paris on September 26 and on the following day saw the North Vietnamese with Dr. Kissinger. The talk as on previous occasions was unproductive and devoted largely to propagandistic recriminations by them against us. That afternoon I flew to Rome with Dr. Kissinger. As usual, I translated the President's speech on arrival. We then drove to the Quirinale and called on President Saragat. I could tell that he was not too happy to see me because of the furor of eighteen months earlier over my call on de Lorenzo. On one occasion, he tried to have me excluded from a meeting with the President. It was done discreetly, but I noticed it and it did not work. President Saragat gave the President a fine lunch at the Quirinale. There was a long meeting between the two chiefs of state. At the lunch, Mr. Nixon delivered a very long toast without pausing for translation. It must have been between seven to eight minutes long. I was able, however, to handle it even though I had not taken notes. After lunch the President asked me whether that had been too long and I replied, "No sir, but it shouldn't be any longer."

As the President was driving through the streets of Rome a man broke through the motorcycle escort and clutched the door of the car, running alongside it waving a piece of paper he obviously wanted to hand to the President. He stumbled and fell and I thought that he would go under the wheels, but he stood up and continued to run alongside the car as the motorcycle police tried to remove him. When this first happened, the President had tried to roll down his window to take the piece of paper, but it would not open. He then tried to open the door and that too was locked. He then said, "Someone take that man's paper before he falls under the car." The Secret Service men made no move to obey. They did not know whether this was an assassin or not. The President then said in a loud voice, "God damn it, I am the President of the United States. Stop this car and open that door!" The car stopped, the President opened the door and took the man's petition. The crowd gave a big cheer. It seemed to them that Mr. Nixon was not afraid of a possible assassin. Mr. Nixon then handed me the petition and said, "What does it say?" It was from a war veteran claiming that he was not getting all the benefits to which he thought he was entitled. The Defense Minister was riding in the car with us. After I told the President what was in the petition, he handed it to the Defense Minister and said, "It is really meant for you." The petitioner was in fact an Italian veteran and he wanted Mr. Nixon to bring pressure on the Italian Defense Ministry to give him what he wanted.

We then drove to the Vatican to call on Pope Paul VI. The President was taken to the Pope's private office and once again it was Monsignor Carew who served as the Pope's translator and I in turn translated the President's remarks into Italian. This time, also, the Pope expressed his concern over the situation in the Middle East and his hope that some arrangement could be made to make access to the holy places possible for the faithful of all religions. While he again expressed his support for the assistance we were giving the South Vietnamese government, he was more cautious than at the previous meeting. The President said that he intended to be firm in Vietnam. We would give the South Vietnamese the means to defend themselves and would not deliver them up to the tyranny of communism. The Pope praised this course. After further discussion of world problems, we left and the President went off to Naples to join the Sixth Fleet. I stayed in Rome for two days. This time prudence dictated that I not visit any old friends.

On October 1, 1971, I flew to Madrid on a commercial flight to await the arrival of the President. General Franco met him at the airport and there were the usual welcome and arrival speeches. I would whisper into the President's ear what General Franco was saying and then I would translate what the President had said over the public address system.

The President and General Franco then drove through large and enthusiastic crowds in downtown Madrid. It was not as big as the reception given General Eisenhower, but it was the largest crowd by far that had greeted President Nixon on either of his trips to Europe. We drove to the Moncloa guest palace where the President was to stay. On arrival he was met by a guard of honor commanded by a young Spanish captain. The captain was carrying a sword and after the President reviewed the guard, he held out his hand to the young captain, who was clearly embarrassed. He then told the President that he would be honored to shake his hand but that Spanish Army regulations would not allow him to do it when he was carrying a sword. The President complimented him on his courage in speaking up and for the fine appearance of the guard of honor. Inside the building the President mentioned how pleased he was by both the size and warmth of the welcome he had received in Madrid. He commented, "These people are really our friends." Later the young Prince of Spain, Don Juan Carlos, came by and talked to Mr. Nixon. As the Prince's English was excellent, I did not attend their meeting, but I greeted him on arrival and walked back to his car with him. Still later the chief of government, Admiral Carrero Blanco, called. I translated a long talk between the President and the admiral. Carrero Blanco, who was later assassinated by Basque terrorists, expressed the belief that the Communists were systematically undermining the will of the West to resist by propaganda to destroy our traditional values and by spreading pornography and drugs. He likened the moral laxness of our time to that prevailing in Rome at the time of the fall of the Empire. He said, "The barbarians are waiting at the walls." There were a number of social occasions that the Spaniards do so well, including a concert in which all of the violins used were Stradivariuses.

Next morning I rode out in the car with the President and Mrs. Nixon to the airport. While we were driving she asked me whether I had anything to do with the Paris peace talks. I had been instructed to keep this matter very secret and before I could answer, the President changed the conversation. I did not have to answer Mrs. Nixon's question. We then flew to London. I rode on the back-up plane, which was very comfortable. The President returned to the United States and I flew back to Paris to resume my job as attaché to France.

My next trip with Mr. Nixon was to attend General de Gaulle's funeral. We arrived in Paris to find the city strangely hushed and silent. Only solemn music was played on the radio and television. The President stayed at the Embassy residence and I stayed at the Crillon Hotel. As the President was ushered into President Pompidou's office at the Elysée Palace, the French President paid great tribute to General de Gaulle but also offered an interesting analysis of the man. Pompidou said that General de Gaulle never really trusted anyone and in the end this had brought him down. Pompidou himself had been a victim of that mistrust.

Pompidou himself was impressive. I never saw him give a snap answer and he always appeared very sure of himself. He seemed to me to have much the same lack of trust which he attributed to General de Gaulle. He did not really like Americans, but he understood what we represented in the world in terms of power. He had been greatly shaken by the hostile demonstrations which he had encountered on his trip to the United States and never understood why the federal government could not have stopped them if it had really wanted to do so. He was, however, very quick to take advantage of being the aggrieved party. He repeated to President Nixon that any society which would not defend itself would not survive and would not deserve to survive.

The President, along with many other world leaders, attended the memorial mass for General de Gaulle in Notre Dame Cathedral. It was a most impressive ceremony. In the evening, Pompidou had a small reception for the delegations that had come from other countries to attend the funeral. I met Prince Charles of Great Britain. Surrounded by four British Prime Ministers, he appeared very much at ease. The President then flew back to the United States and I resumed my functions in Paris.

I was also to go to the mid-Atlantic meeting in the Azores between Presidents Pompidou and Nixon from the twelfth to the fourteenth of December 1971. I accompanied the President to his several meetings with Pompidou and also took Dr. Kissinger several times to call on the French President. These were tough meetings on financial matters, which to the French often seemed more important than political matters. John Connally, the U. S. Secretary of the Treasury, and Valéry Giscard d'Estaing, who was later to succeed Pompidou, fenced fiercely and the United States finally agreed to devalue the dollar. Nixon in his talks with Pompidou was very interested in getting the French President's estimate of the Soviet's views and personalities. Pompidou felt that Podgorny, though theoretically the Soviet chief of state, had no real power. Kosygin was very articulate and particularly anti-German. Brezhnev was unquestionably the boss. He had boasted to Pompidou about his SS 9 missile, claiming that it was the largest and most powerful in the world. He felt that the U.S.S.R. was now dealing from a position of advantage in its discussions with the United States. Pompidou said that he did not necessarily share these opinions, but that was what Brezhnev felt. The Soviet leader spoke repeatedly to the French President about Soviet power. He said that the Soviet Union wanted peace, but it would never "draw back." Pompidou was not quite sure what that meant. The French President said that the Soviets were really deeply concerned about the problem of China. Podgorny had said that he did not think the death of Mao would make any difference in the Sino-Soviet relationship and that hostility between the two Communist powers would continue. The Russians faced not only the West but a hostile China as well.

During these talks at the Azores, Pompidou seemed more tense than at any of the previous meetings I had attended with him. Perhaps this was attributable to the onset of the disease that was to kill him. Nixon made several flattering references to Pompidou including stating that he greatly valued the French President's opinion. I do not recall Pompidou reciprocating once. Always with Pompidou was his superb trilingual interpreter Prince Andronikof, who not only had total command of English and Russian in addition to French, but complete understanding of the subject matter being discussed and an extraordinarily retentive memory.

I also took Kissinger on two occasions to see Pompidou and must admit that Henry seemed almost as much at home in complex economic affairs as in political matters. He had done his homework very thoroughly.

On the evening of December 13, Portuguese Premier Marcello Caetano as the host gave a splendid dinner at Angra do Heroísmo. Pompidou was surprised that I also spoke Portuguese and translated the toasts three ways, into Portuguese, French and English. He must have forgotten to look at the biographic card which the French Intelligence Services had surely given him on me. On the fourteenth the conference ended and I flew back to Washington to complete the various memoranda of conversations in which I had participated. While in Washington, I translated for the President in his meeting with Brazilian President Emílio Médici. It was at this conversation that I learned I was to be appointed deputy director of Central Intelligence. I then returned to Paris to wind up my affairs there prior to my return to Washington. I had been stationed outside the

United States for the previous twelve years. I had returned on many trips, but I had actually been assigned overseas since 1960.

I was to make one more trip overseas with President Nixon and this was to attend the funeral of President Pompidou. In many ways, this was almost a rerun of the de Gaulle funeral. Pompidou, showing extraordinary courage, had worked in his office right up to the morning of his death.

The Watergate matter was at its height and the strain showed to some degree on the President. He again stayed at the Embassy residence in Paris and walked the 150 yards to Elysée Palace to call on acting French President Alain Poher. He walked up the Faubourg St. Honoré through large and friendly crowds, and it clearly gave him a great boost. Later he attended a reception given by Poher for the chiefs of delegations to the funeral. He talked at length with many chiefs of states, and seeing the young Crown Prince of Morocco, he commented that he was the son of a great King and would be a great King himself someday. To say that the Moroccans were pleased would be understating the case. He also spoke to Mexican Foreign Minister Rabasa for a while and then Canadian Premier Trudeau broke in saying, "He is your southern neighbor." Later, Prime Minister Olof Palme worked his way toward the President. He had once compared Mr. Nixon's actions in Vietnam to those of Adolf Hitler. I told Mr. Nixon that he was moving toward him and the only reply I got was a growl. Then the Swedish Ambassador, whom I knew from my service in Paris, said to me that the Prime Minister wanted to meet the President. To my amazement, Mr. Nixon was positively cordial to him. The following day, April 7, 1974, Mr. Nixon flew back to Washington. It was to be his last foreign trip before his resignation.

President Nixon greatly enjoyed these trips aboard and the contact they gave him with foreign leaders. He believed that much could be done by such contacts and that leaders who knew one another personally were less likely to react rashly to what the other might do. He felt that his strongest suit was in foreign policy and he was right. Had his judgment in domestic affairs been as good, the nation would have been spared the trag-edy of Watergate.

One curious episode occurred in June of 1970. I had returned to Washington to see Dr. Kissinger. While in his office I was in-formed that Mr. Haldeman, the President's Chief of Staff, wanted to see me. I could not imagine what he wanted to dis-cuss with me. When I saw Haldeman in his office he told me that President Nixon had been greatly impressed by my ability to write extensive memoranda of conversations without taking any notes. He wanted to know if I would be interested in com-ing back to the White House and attending all of the Presi-dent's meetings, not just those with foreigners, and recording what had transpired and in a sense be the historian of the Ad-ministration. I replied that I was grateful for the offer but I was really not interested in such a job. If ordered to do it I would request retirement. He seemed surprised that I did not jump at the offer. I told Kissinger about this conversation but he just shook his head and made no comment.

I believe that not long after this conversation with Haldeman the tape recorder was installed in the White House.

28. THE MIDNIGHT RESCUE OF HENRY
KISSINGER

Bringing Henry Kissinger and his group of assistants into Paris, generally two in number, who came to conduct the negotiations with the Chinese and the North Vietnamese, was always a difficult and complex operation. It was necessary to use many different methods in order to keep the comings and goings of Dr. Kissinger from the ever curious press. My instructions were that it was absolutely essential that total secrecy be maintained concerning these negotiations or the other side would break them off. In Paris the only American aware of my maneuverings was my secretary Nancy Ouellette.

Generally, Kissinger would come in U. S. *Air Force One*, the President's plane. The passenger list did not go through normal channels. At this point neither Secretary of State William Rogers nor Secretary of Defense Melvin Laird knew of these talks. At the beginning of these clandestine trips, Kissinger asked me whether he could enter France unknown to the French. I replied that I did not think this was possible. The French had a highly sophisticated intelligence service and certainly from monitoring my movements or those of the Chinese or North Vietnamese they would pick up the knowledge that he was there. Kissinger then asked me how this could be prevented from being splattered all over the French intelligence system. I said that in my view, the way to do this was to go directly to

President Pompidou, inform him of the talks and ask him to keep these matters held at a very high level within the French intelligence community so that knowledge of them would not become widespread. Pompidou co-operated fully, and fortunately so, for on one occasion on April 3, 1970, I was informed that Dr. Kissinger would be coming to meet with the North Vietnamese. I arranged to bring Kissinger into a French airfield at Bourges in central France, from where I was going to bring him to Paris. The choice of Bourges was dictated by the fact that it was located within a reasonable distance of Paris. The airfield was inside a large French military complex. At this airfield the French kept their KC-135 tankers, which they used to refuel their nuclear strike force. These aircraft are very similar in appearance to the VC-137 in which Kissinger traveled, namely U. S. *Air Force One*. Now, the cover plan for the movement of this aircraft was generally that U. S. *Air Force One* was on a training mission for the crew with no passengers or VIPs aboard. Kissinger would often arrange to be seen in Washington at a cocktail party, and this was before he was married, generally with a very attractive girl. Immediately afterward he would go directly to Andrews Air Force Base and take off. When he returned from Paris, he would again arrange to be seen publicly. The interval of his absence from the United States was barely perceptible. Anyone who saw him in Washington on Friday night and again on Monday night would be unlikely to imagine that Kissinger had gone to Paris for negotiations and returned.

On this particular occasion, I was informed that he would be coming into Bourges in the late evening. I would meet him there and take him directly to Paris. About five o'clock in the afternoon I began to receive messages from Washington indicating that there was some technical complication aboard the aircraft which might require a change in its destination and that it might not be able to go to Bourges. I continued to receive somewhat agitated messages from the White House and it was not clear what the final destination would be. Obviously there was great concern that he would have to land at an airport where his presence would become known and thereby blow the cover for the whole program of the secret meetings. I received increasingly strident messages from Washington urging me to do something. Finally, in some irritation I replied that I simply could not cover every airport in Western Europe by myself and that if they would be good enough to let me know where the aircraft was going to land, I would then see what I could do to extricate him from a very awkward situation. About eight o'clock I received a phone call from Al Haig. General Haig was Kissinger's NATO commander. He is one of the most brilliant and able officers I have known in thirty-five years of military service. He informed me that the aircraft had difficulty with its hydraulic system and the brakes might not function effectively. It had therefore been decided that the aircraft would land at Rhine Main airport near Frankfurt, where there was an arresting barrier at the end of the runway to take care of just such situations as this. Haig added, however, that he could not think of a worse place for the aircraft to land because the possibility of Kissinger being recognized was probably greater there than anywhere else. He urgently pressed me to see what I could do to bail Kissinger out of this situation. I said that I would find a solution for the situation, although at the time I spoke to him, I did not know what I was going to do. After I hung up, I sat for a few moments—I was alone, the office was closed, my secretary had gone home—and finally I decided the only thing I could do was go to President Pompidou.

I walked from my office down to the Elysée Palace, walked in to the gendarme at the entrance and told him that I was General Walters, the American Military Attaché, that I had accompanied Mr. Pompidou on his recent trip to the United States. In fact, many French newsreels and much television coverage of Pompidou's trip in the United States had shown me. The gendarme appeared rather startled at my request, but he got on the telephone to Michel Jobert, who was in a sense Pompidou's Kissinger and who was aware of the negotiations going on in Paris. In a few moments I was walked up to Jobert's office and I described the situation to him. He left me for a moment, went into the President's office next door, came back and said, "The

President wants to speak to you." I walked into President Pompidou's office and expressed the usual greetings one expresses to a superior in French by saying, "I present you my respects, Mr. President," to which he rather graciously replied, "And I, my dear Walters, present you with my friendship." I then explained the situation to him. He reached for the telephone on his desk and he called his flight crew at Villacoublay Airport south of Paris, where the President's executive aircraft, a Mystère 20, was kept. After a brief conversation, he said to me, "Go out to Villacoublay. They will be waiting for you and they will take you to Frankfurt, where you can pick up Kissinger and bring him back here." I thanked the President for his gracious gesture which would help me solve this almost unsolvable problem, and as Jobert led me out, this normally rather quiet, rather restrained Frenchman wished me luck in this enterprise. I thanked him for his help, went back to the Embassy and got in my car, which I drove myself out to Villacoublay Airport. I did know where the VIP aircraft were kept at Villacoublay. I drove up there to the operations room. The French crew was waiting for me. The President's plane was ready to go. I boarded the aircraft. The pilot was Colonel Calderon of the French Air Force. We swung onto the runway and in a few moments we were airborne. I looked at my watch. It was an hour and six minutes after I had left President Pompidou's office. Extraordinarily good reaction time for a totally unexpected flight, even though the presidential crew presumably lived at Villacoublay.

We climbed rapidly out of the Paris area in fine weather and headed eastward. As we headed eastward, I began to have some misgivings. I thought to myself, "If this plane ever crashes, I will be not only dead but also dishonored. They will say I was defecting to the Soviet Union in a French military airplane." I doubted very much if Kissinger would say publicly that I had been about his business to extract him from an awkward situation in Frankfurt. Nevertheless, all went well. Soon we saw directly ahead of us the aircraft in which Kissinger was traveling. We followed it through the approach pattern and landed at Frankfurt directly behind it. Since our aircraft was much smaller and its roll was much shorter, we taxied off the main runway before the larger aircraft did and taxied over to an area on the military side of the airfield where they were obviously waiting for U. S. *Air Force One* with a large number of searchlights illuminating the area. I was in civilian clothes, but I got out of the aircraft and, in the most authoritative voice I could muster, I said, "I'm General Walters. Turn off those lights at once." It worked and the lights went off. Shortly afterward, U. S. *Air Force One* taxied up, the stairs were lowered and I climbed aboard the aircraft. I found Dr. Kissinger slouched in his seat. He looked up at me and said, "Jesus Christ, am I glad to see you. What are we going to do now?" I said, "Dr. Kissinger, take off your glasses, roll up your coat collar, go down the ladder, go up the ladder of the little French aircraft which is parked alongside and wait there while we transfer the baggage from this aircraft to the other." I was not concerned about the two assistants who were traveling with him as it was highly unlikely that they would be recognized, and if they were, this would be no indication that Dr. Kissinger was with them. Dr. Kissinger hastened to do what I said. He went down the steps, up the steps of the small French aircraft and sat there while we transferred his two assistants and his baggage to the Mystère 20. This was done with great speed and very shortly we swung back onto the runway, lifted off Rhine Main and headed back toward Paris.

As we were flying toward Paris, the French pilot asked me to come up front and said to me, "*Mon général*, what am I going to tell the Germans? They know that this is the President of France's airplane. They now know that in the middle of the night, without any clearance, without filing any flight plan, we penetrated German airspace, landed at Frankfurt airport, taxied over to the U.S. military side of the airport, remained nine minutes on the ground and took off again headed back for Paris. This is going to be a very awkward situation because they are certainly going to ask me what it is I was doing. What shall I tell them?" I was taken aback by this problem, which I had not even considered in my relief at getting the aircraft to extract Dr. Kissinger from Rhine Main. I thought about it for some minutes, and finally an idea came to me, and I said to Colonel Calderon, "tell them it involves a woman. They will believe it of the French and be discreet." "Ah," said Colonel Calderon, "but what if Madame Pompidou finds out? What will we tell her?" I said to him, "Colonel Calderon, if Madame Pompidou finds out, I give you my word of honor as a U. S. Army officer that I will tell her the truth." This seemed to satisfy Colonel Calderon, and we flew on back to Paris, landed at Villacoublay, where I escorted Kissinger and his two assistants to my car and drove them back through the Forest of Meudon and down toward the bridge at Sèvres and up to my apartment at Neuilly.

As we were driving in—it was about one o'clock in the morning—Dr. Kissinger said to me somewhat querulously, "Why are you bringing me in this way? Somebody will recognize me." It had been a long day. I was tired. I frankly thought I had already performed a miracle for him and was irritated that he would needle me in this way. I said to him, "Dr. Kissinger, why don't you run the world, and let me run the insertions and extractions. I know much more about them than you do." He exploded, "Nobody talks to me this way," then he caught himself and said, "I know, I know. Nobody does for me things that you do." I said, "Dr. Kissinger, you are so right." Needless to say, no one recognized him. I drove him to my apartment, opened the underground garage, drove him in, took him up in the elevator and installed him in the bedroom.

The epilogue to this story is somewhat amusing. I did not see Colonel Calderon of the French Air Force for a number of months, and when I did cross his path again, I could not forbear from asking him whether the Germans had ever pursued the matter as he had expected. He replied that indeed they had. Shortly after he got to the office the morning after the flight, he was informed that the German Air Attaché wanted to see him. The German Air Attaché came in and asked him what this flight was about. I said to Colonel Calderon, "What did you tell him?" Colonel Calderon smiled and said, "Oh, I told him what we had agreed upon." And I asked, "Did that satisfy him or did he ask any other questions?" Calderon smiled even more broadly and said, "He only asked one other question." And I said, "What was that?" He said, 'Is she German?' "

This was one of the many difficulties encountered in this multiple smuggling of Dr. Kissinger in and out of France. It was an indication of the type of thing that could unexpectedly arise and would require the use of all sorts of resources to bail him out. Not long after this episode, Dr. Kissinger wrote me a letter of thanks for my efforts in helping the negotiations in moving him in and out of France, but he added a paragraph to the effect that if he were to say that I had done this uncomplainingly, I would think he was either deaf or a liar. Then he went on in another paragraph to say, "But all kidding aside, I know that under that gruff exterior there beats a heart that is gruff."

Obviously, these operations were enormously disrupting my personal life as well as my official life. It was difficult for me to make any of the trips that an attaché normally makes in the country to which he is accredited. Sometimes the Ambassador would want me to go somewhere with him and this would be the time that Kissinger was coming and I would have to cook up some incredible excuse for the Ambassador as to why I could not go with him. On another occasion when Dr. Kissinger was coming, my sister was staying with me. I was informed of his arrival and I had to ask her to move out of my apartment for three days. She said, "Why do I have to move out of your apartment?" I said, "Don't ask me any questions. Just go somewhere for three days." She said, "What are you doing, bringing some woman in?" I said, "Laureen, it's none of your business. Just go away for the three days and then come back." Of course, these trips never lasted more than two days.

Another amusing incident occurred during these various trips of Dr. Kissinger because I had a very suspicious cook/housekeeper. She often wondered why I used to give up my bedroom to this visitor. One evening Kissinger arrived and his clothes were quite rumpled. He asked me if he could get some clothes pressed. I said certainly, that the cook/housekeeper would be glad to press them for him. At this time, I was having a problem with him because it was impossible for me to use my own private or official car in connection with these missions of Dr. Kissinger. All cars owned by foreign diplomats, whether they belong to the Embassy or to private individuals, have a distinctive marking that tells everyone what country they are from. I could not show up at the Chinese or North Vietnamese residences with such a telltale license plate. I therefore had to have my warrant officer rent a car which he would turn over to me. This was the car I would use to move Dr. Kissinger to and from his meetings with the Chinese or the North Vietnamese. However, I could not tell the Defense Intelligence Agency, for whom I worked, that I had rented a car or they would ask me why, when I had six official cars in my office, I needed to rent an additional car in Paris. On Dr. Kissinger's first two trips, I had been obliged to pay for the rental of these cars out of my own pocket. I attempted to discuss this matter with him, and he dismissed me airily, saying, "I am trying to restore peace to the world and you are burdening me with all these administrative details." I saw that this would do no good. On this night when he asked me to have his suit pressed, I took the jacket from him, and he said, "Oh, but I can't give it. My name is written in the label." I looked at it and the label was quite loose. I reached in and tore the label out. In so doing, I tore the lining. Dr. Kissinger said, "Oh, but you've torn the lining. Who is going to pay to repair it?" I said to him, "Pay for it out of the same fund from which I rent the cars." He got my message. On his very next trip, as he descended from the aircraft, he handed me a piece of paper and said, "There is your goddamned appropriation number to which you can charge the rental of the cars."

It was a difficult but rewarding task. I must at this point pay tribute to President Pompidou and to his assistant Mr. Jobert for their help and discretion. President Pompidou in particular never hesitated for an instant in placing aircraft at my disposal to rescue Kissinger. They maintained a most discreet and helpful silence throughout. And so, in the space of one night between eight o'clock in the evening and two o'clock in the morning, I concluded the midnight mission to rescue Henry Kissinger.

29. WATERGATE

Now I come to an episode that was to become one of the great political problems of modern American history. This incident was to touch me quite closely. Almost all of my Army career had been spent in intelligence assignments, but my knowledge of foreign languages was to lead me to translate for four American Presidents. Shortly after Mr. Nixon's election, I was called upon to translate for him as I had for his predecessors. As an Army officer I had served each commander in chief in turn. I do have strong political convictions, but up to this time I had avoided any political label. Until I was named deputy director of Central Intelligence by Mr. Nixon, I had received every promotion in the Army from corporal to major general under Democratic administrations, the only exception being my promotion to colonel, which occurred under General Eisenhower's administration.

Unlike many who had served for long periods in intelligence, this specialization had not harmed my career. I was the senior officer serving in intelligence continuously in the Armed Forces at the time of my appointment as deputy director. I had just completed a four-and-a-half-year tour of duty as Army and Defense Attaché to France.

I had never served with the CIA before being sworn in as deputy director on May 2, 1972. In a sense I had worked for a rival organization, the Defense Intelligence Agency. In all of my foreign posts, I had had good relations with the CIA chief of station. However, my more recent activities in Paris with the Chinese and the North Vietnamese had been conducted without the knowledge of the CIA. The President submitted my name for confirmation to the U. S. Senate and in March 1972 I returned from Paris to prepare for my confirmation hearings. I was aware that there was in the Congress at this time a considerable sentiment in favor of a civilian deputy director. I also knew from various sources that the director, Richard Helms, would probably have preferred someone from within the organization for this post.

When the time came for my confirmation hearing before the Armed Services Committee, my principal questioner was Chairman John Stennis. He asked me how long I intended to remain in this job. I replied that as far as I knew, I served at the pleasure of the President and it could be one day or the full duration of his term. The chairman pressed the question more closely and asked me what I intended to do after leaving this position. I think what he feared was that I might, as deputy director, do something to please the Defense Department and ensure myself a good post after my tour at the CIA was over. I told him that I had been so highly specialized in intelligence that I doubted if the Defense Department would have anything to offer me after I finished my tour at the CIA. Senator Stennis then asked me what my ambition was after I left the CIA. I replied that when I came into the Army as a private my ambition was to make major and if I were not confirmed as deputy director and retired as a major general, I would have had one of the most rewarding careers of any officer who ever wore the United States uniform. Senator Stennis commented that this was a good way to look at things. Some of the other members of the committee asked me a few questions. Senator Goldwater spoke in a friendly fashion, pointing out that I had entered the Army as a private and that my name was now before them for confirmation as a lieutenant general. This was somewhat of an American success story. I was in due course confirmed by the Senate without difficulty.

Throughout this whole period, I was being briefed at the CIA on various aspects of that organization and its activities.

I had met Director Helms some years before in Paris when he came there on his honeymoon. When I was introduced to him he asked me whether I was the "legendary General Walters." I replied that I did not know whether I was legendary or not, but I was indeed General Walters. When I made my first call on him he noted that he had, of course, heard of me but he wondered what my experience in intelligence was. Somewhat irked at this question, I replied that in 1942 I had led a special intelligence detachment ashore in an assault landing, had kidnapped some crane operators and had conducted extensive prisoner-of-war interrogation. More recently I had conducted secret negotiations with both the North Vietnamese and the Communist Chinese in Paris without anyone in the CIA knowing anything about it. I probably should not have replied so sharply but I was annoyed at the form of the question. He smiled and thereafter was most cordial to me.

I was sworn in at the White House in the Oval Office by President Nixon in the presence of my brothers Fred and Vincent and my sister Laureen and their families on May 2, 1972. During the next six weeks before the Watergate break-in took place, I saw President Nixon only once. I was called to the White House and I found that he was preparing a speech to be made before a joint session of the Canadian Parliament. He intended to say a few words in French in recognition of Canada's bilingual character and he wanted to make sure that his pronunciation would be understandable. We rehearsed what he intended to say in French and he did very well. Later on when he made the speech in Ottawa and after saying the part in French, he added, "If that's not right, it is not my fault. It is the fault of General Walters, who told me that I sounded like a French Canadian."

Apart from this, I spoke to the President once or twice on the phone regarding intelligence matters connected with the Soviet leaders. He did not at any time discuss my assignment with me

nor did he give me any particular instructions. I was not to see
him again until long after the Watergate affair took place.

On the day of the break-in at the Democratic National Committee, June 17, 1972, I had gone to Martha's Vineyard to attend the wedding of my niece Maleen Montamat. Late that afternoon I flew to Tarrytown, New York, to be present at a
dinner given by Governor Nelson Rockefeller of New York for
the Mexican President and Mrs. Alvarez Echeverría. Mrs. Alvarez
Echevarría was not very fond of Americans and the governor
the Mexican President and Mrs. Alvarez Echeverría. Mrs. Alvarez
asked me if I would sit next to her and talk to her in Spanish dur-
the meal. I had a most cordial conversation with Mrs. Echeverría
as we dined around the governor's enclosed pool. The first
knowledge that I had of the Watergate break-in was through
the media. I cannot recall whether I heard about it on radio or
television or whether I read about it in the paper on the following morning. On the following Monday, June 19, at the morning meeting at the CIA, Helms remarked that a number of the
people who had been arrested in connection with the break-in
had formerly been employees of the Central Intelligence Agency
and that we should co-operate with the FBI in the investigation,
but should not divulge any more identities of CIA officers than
was strictly necessary for the pursuit of the investigation, since
by disclosing the identity of officers it was difficult to use them
abroad and might even endanger their personal safety should
their identity become known. At several other morning meetings
there was some further discussion of the information that was
being passed to the FBI in connection with their investigation.

On the morning of June 22, 1972, I received a phone call telling me to be at Mr. Ehrlichman's office at the White House
with Director Helms at one-thirty that afternoon. I met Helms
downtown and we had lunch together at the Two Continents
restaurant. We had some speculative discussion concerning this
meeting and thought that it might have something to do with
the Watergate case because of the publicity that had been given
to the fact that a number of the people involved had worked
previously for the CIA. We then drove in Helms' car to the
White House and were shown into Ehrlichman's office. He was

alone at the time and we exchanged some small talk in the outer office. Later Haldeman came in and said that the FBI investigation was leading to a lot of important people. He asked Helms what connection the Watergate case might have with the CIA. Helms replied that there was no connection with the CIA on this case. Haldeman then expressed concern that the investigation of the Mexican leads in this case might compromise some CIA activity in Mexico that might be jeopardized by this, and he was most insistent that this could happen. He said that it had been decided that Walters should go to FBI director L. Patrick Gray and tell him that the pushing of this inquiry further in Mexico could lead to the exposure of some CIA assets and channels for moving money. Helms said that he had talked to Gray on the previous day and told him that the agency was not involved and that none of the suspects had worked for it in the last two years.

Haldeman said that nevertheless Walters should go and see Gray and tell him that he had talked to the White House and that to push the investigation in Mexico further could expose CIA operations in that country. I had been in Washington for six weeks at this point and it simply did not occur to me that the Chief of Staff to the President might be asking me to do something that was illegal or wrong. If one were to question every order from the White House, it would be almost impossible to conduct the daily business of the government. Had I been asked by Haldeman to stop the whole investigation, I might have become suspicious, but at this moment the Mexican aspects of the case had not even come to my attention. Likewise it seemed quite plausible to me that Haldeman might have some information to which I was not privy. There was no way in which either Helms or I could be fully aware of every facet of CIA activities in any particular country. I immediately remembered that I had conducted secret negotiations in Paris for two and a half years without the CIA knowing about it. I did transmit my messages to and from Kissinger through CIA communication channels, but since I encoded and decoded the messages myself, there was no way they could know what was going on. The thought occurred to me that there might be similar negotiations going on in Mexico with Fidel Castro concerning relationships with Cuba. I genuinely believed that Haldeman had some information that I did not have and agreed to go to Gray and convey the message as I had been directed. Helms offered no objection and suggested that I remind Gray of the agreement between the CIA and the FBI not to expose one another's sources. We left Ehrlichman's office and walked downstairs to the west executive entrance of the White House and talked for a moment. I do not recall whether I went straight to Gray's office, where an appointment had been made for me at two-thirty, or whether I simply killed time downtown. I am sure that I did not have time to go back to the agency at Langley. My car had followed Helms and me to the White House and was waiting for me. Helms returned to Langley and I went to see Gray at his office in the Department of Justice Building. I saw Gray and told him that I had come from the White House and that I was aware of his talk with Helms on the previous day, and while investigation of this matter in Mexico had not yet touched agency projects, continuation of it there might expose some assets. I reminded him of the agreement between the two agencies as Helms had suggested. Gray told me that he would have to talk to John Dean, at the White House. I then left Gray's office and returned to the CIA headquarters. I believed at that time that one of the reasons that might have led to my being sent to Gray rather than Helms was the fact that there had been some ill feeling between Helms and J. Edgar Hoover. Gray and I were both new on the job and it might be easier for us to handle matters between the two organizations without this background of ill feeling.

When I returned to the CIA that Friday afternoon after talking to Gray, I reported to Helms and looked into the matter to ascertain whether there were any CIA assets in Mexico that might be jeopardized. One of the questions that I asked in the light of my own experience in Paris was whether there was any coded traffic coming out of Mexico City which the CIA was not reading. I was told that there was no such traffic and no one seemed to know of any CIA assets that might be endangered. I do not know whether I got this information that Friday or on the following Monday morning.

The next development in this matter occurred on June 26. This was the first working day after I had talked to Haldeman, Ehrlichman and Gray. I received a phone call from the President's counsel, John Dean, asking me to meet him at his office in the Executive Office Building next to the White House. He told me that he wished to speak to me about the matter Helms and I had discussed with Haldeman and Enrlichman on the previous Friday. I replied that I did not know who he was and was somewhat reluctant to discuss this matter with him. He said that he was in charge of this matter and that I could check this out with Ehrlichman. I had some difficulty in reaching Ehrlichman, but he confirmed that Dean was in charge of the whole matter and confirmed that I could talk to him.

At 11:45 A.M. I went to Dean's office. I was shown into his large, plush office, where I introduced myself and was asked to sit down. In a few moments, I was shown into his private office. He was alone at the time. I had never met Mr. Dean before and I was somewhat surprised how youthful he was to be occupying that post. His straw blond hair did not seem to match his complexion and that seemed somewhat strange to me. Dean began by asking me what the CIA connection with the Watergate break-in was. I replied that there was none and that I had checked quite carefully to make sure that there were no CIA assets that might be endangered by a further pursuit of the investigation in Mexico. Dean had already told me that he was in touch with Gray and at that time I believed that he would pass on to Gray what I had told him. It did not occur to me that he might not. Dean then asked if the CIA might not be involved without my knowing about it. I said that this was not possible, I had talked with Helms about the matter and he shared my view. I knew that the agency had had no part in the Watergate break-in and therefore there was no way I could say that further investigation in Mexico would jeopardize agency assets. After some further discussion, an almost pleading note crept into his

conversation and it appeared to me that he might be looking
for help. He did not admit to me that these burglars might in
any way be connected with him or any of his friends. There
was an underlying implication that they needed help and perhaps there was some connection with the CIA. I knew that the
agency was not involved and I was determined that I would not
get connected with this matter. Dean said that the whole thing
was causing problems for the Administration. The opposition
was trying to maximize it. The FBI was working on three possible theories. One, that it had been organized by the Republican
National Committee; two, that it had been organized by the
CIA; three, that it had been organized by someone else. I repeated to Dean that I had discussed this matter with Helms and
we were quite sure that the agency was not in any way involved.
I knew on the contrary that the director wished to distance
himself from the whole matter. Dean again pressed me that
the agency might be involved. He said he believed that Barker,
one of those arrested, had been involved in a clandestine entry
into the Chilean Embassy. I said that I was sure that none of
the suspects had been on the agency payroll for the last two
years. I was wrong—one of them, Martínez, had been receiving
$100 a month as an informer on Cuban matters. I then told
Dean again that I was sure that there was no agency involvement in this matter, that any attempt to involve it would be
a grave disservice to the President, to the Congress and to the
nation. The value of the CIA to the nation arose from the fact
that it was a non-partisan organization. It did not support either
of the parties. It served the United States government regardless of the personal opinions of those who served there. If it
were to become involved in any partisan political activity, it
would lose all value to the President and to the nation. These
arguments seemed to make some impression on him. I pressed
home the fact that there was no way I could see the agency
becoming in any way involved in this matter. There was no
agency involvement and I could not see any way in which it
could be of assistance. I knew that the personnel in the agency
broadly reflected the political divisions in the United States.

There were probably more Democrats there than Republicans, and it would be absolutely impossible to use the agency for partisan political purposes without it flying apart at the seams. My interview with Dean lasted about ten or fifteen minutes. I was firm, he seemed convinced and I thought that I was through with Mr. Dean. I did not then know that he was to summon me twice again. I returned to the CIA and reported in great detail to Helms on my talk with Dean. He assured me that I had acted exactly right and supported me fully in what I had told Dean.

On the following day I was again summoned to Dean's office. I went this time knowing what the meeting would be about. I was prepared to be firm in the light of my own convictions and my conversation with Helms. Dean again received me in the same office. He began by saying that some of the accused were "wobbling." I said that even if they were "wobbling" they could not implicate the agency since it was not involved. Dean then said that these men were looking for help and he wondered if there was any way in which the CIA could pay bail for them (they had been unable to raise bail) and added that it was not just bail that was needed. If these men went to jail could the agency find some way to pay their salaries while they were in jail out of secret funds. I told Dean in no uncertain terms that this was not possible. I was the deputy director and the only authority I had was that delegated to me by the director and I knew that he would not tolerate such a thing. The strength of the agency and its value to the President and the nation lay in the fact that it was non-political and did not get itself involved in partisan political disputes. I had been with the agency only a short time, but I knew that Director Helms felt very strongly about this. I said that whatever the present difficulties of the Watergate affair might be, if the agency were to do what he wanted, this would become known in the present leaking atmosphere of Washington and the matter would be far worse. The scandal would be ten times greater and such action could only be envisaged upon direction "at the highest level." If that were to take place it would be a disaster. Dean then looked at me with an almost pleading look and said in a whisper, "What shall we do? What shall we do?" I looked him right in the eye and said, "Fire everyone connected with this." He was startled and then he said in a low voice, "No one is going to be fired." I then replied, "Then, Mr. Dean, what is now a small conventional painful explosion will become a multi-megaton hydrogen bomb and those who are not now touched by the matter certainly will be." I meant the President. I believed at this time that he could not possibly be in on such a stupid and inept operation. Dean at first seemed taken aback but then seemed impressed by this argument. I repeated that it was an unacceptable risk. The agency would be completely discredited before the public. I did not know of any way in which we could be of help to him with his problem. If I were asked to do this, I would resign. I told him that on the day I went to work at the CIA I had hung on the wall of my office a color photograph showing the view through the window of my home in Florida. It was a beautiful view showing the trees and the ocean at Palm Beach. When people asked me what it was, I told them that was what was waiting if anyone squeezed me too hard. Dean seemed to understand that I was not going to do what he wanted and I left his office.

I returned to the CIA at Langley and talked to Helms about what had happened. He seemed surprised that Dean had made such a suggestion. I told him I had told Dean that any such expenditures out of secret funds had to be reported to the congressional oversight committees and this had greatly lessened his enthusiasm for pressing the matter further. I thought that this would be the last I would hear of this matter, but I was wrong. It was after this suggestion that I decided to jot down brief memoranda for my own use about what had happened. I do not recall whether I decided to do this by myself or whether Helms suggested it. These memoranda were to refresh my memory. I showed them to Helms but they received no other circulation and I kept them in my safe.

On the following morning, June 28, I was again summoned to Dean's office. I went there and saw him alone as on the two previous occasions. He then told me that the director's meeting with Gray that day was canceled (this was the first I had heard of it). John Ehrlichman had suggested that he deal with me instead. Dean said that his problem now was how to stop the FBI investigation beyond the five suspects. He mentioned Ken Dahlberg and a Mexican named Guena and spoke of some $89,000 that was unrelated to the bugging case. He said that Dahlberg was refusing to answer questions. These names and the reference to the money meant nothing to me as I had never heard them before. Dean asked hopefully whether I had any suggestions or could do anything. I said that I realized he had a tough problem, but if there was any agency involvement, it could only be as a result of directive from the President himself. The political risks that were concomitant with this were unacceptable. The present chapter might be awkward and unpleasant but directed intervention by the agency could be electorally mortal if it became known. The chances of keeping a thing like this secret were almost nil. I noticed that many scandals in Washington were short-lived and were often replaced by spicier ones. Dean was obviously very concerned with this whole matter and groping around for help like a drowning man. He did not seem to grasp the enormity of what he was suggesting.

Subsequently, some members of various committees were understandably concerned as to why I did not tell Dean that what he was asking was illegal. First of all, Mr. Dean was a lawyer and I was not. Presumably he knew the law better than I did. Secondly, I was not completely sure that it was illegal since I did not know the exact extent of the President's powers in such matters. Third, I did not feel that an appeal to Mr. Dean's sense of ethics would have much effect. I saw him hellbent on trying to involve the agency in this affair and I used the arguments that were most likely to dissuade him from this course. I knew that what he was suggesting would not work and would be a complete disaster for the agency, the nation and the President himself. I told Dean that it was natural for anyone with my long military background to seek to protect the presidency, but what he wanted was nonsense and would not protect the President. It would make things very difficult for him.

Dean then wondered who might be behind this whole affair. At no time did he admit to me that he knew anything about the origin of this burglary attempt. He asked again who might be behind it. I said that I had read a newspaper editorial that morning suggesting that anti-Castro Cuban exiles, fearful that the Democratic party might restore diplomatic relations with Cuba if it came to power, might have some interest in trying to find out whether this was true. Dean nodded thoughtfully and said that it might cost a half a million dollars. What he meant was not really clear to me. Whether he meant that it would cost this much to ascertain whether the Cuban exiles had done it or whether it would cost this much to bribe the Cubans to say that they had done it, I was not sure. In retrospect, I should have told him that this was a wrong course. At this point, I felt he had given up the idea of trying to involve the agency and I was so relieved that I did not set him straight on this hypothesis.

Naïve as it may seem in hindsight, it had not occurred to me at this time that everything I told Dean was not relayed to Gray, in particular that there was no agency involvement and that the pursuit of the investigation in Mexico would in no way bother us. I had been told that Dean was in charge of this matter and that he was by his own statements to me in daily touch with Gray. I did not then think that Dean would deliberately fail to inform Gray of what I had told him. This was a considerable mistake by me.

At this last meeting I told Dean that if I were directed to pay bail and salaries for those arrested, even by the President, I would resign and would ask to see the President to tell him why I was resigning. That seemed to convince Dean and have the effect on him that I hoped it would. I was not to see him for eight months. In February of 1973, I was to tell him no once again.

It is interesting to note that in the book he has written about these events, *Blind Ambition*, Dean has not mentioned these three meetings with me. In fact, in his testimony before the Senate select committee he spoke of only two meetings—there were actually three. He testified about these matters before the

United States Senate Select Committee on Presidential Campaign Activities. In describing these events to that committee this is what he said, and I quote:

"On Monday morning, June 26, I spoke with Ehrlichman regarding this suggestion. [That is, the suggestion he had made to have Ehrlichman and Haldeman contact the CIA for possible assistance in this matter.] He thought it a good idea and worth exploring. He told me to call the CIA and explore it with them. I told him that I had never dealt with anyone at the CIA and did not know Director Helms. He told me that I should not call Helms but rather General Walters. I told him that I did not know General Walters either. He then told me that he and Haldeman had just had a little chat with Helms and General Walters a few days earlier about their dealings with the FBI in relationship to the investigation. He was not specific. He then told me that I should deal with General Walters because he was a good friend of the White House and the White House had put him in as deputy director so that they might have some influence over the agency. He told me that I should call General Walters and tell him that I was calling because he, Ehrlichman, had requested that I follow up on the earlier meeting and if there were any problems General Walters should call him. After my meeting with Ehrlichman, I telephoned General Walters. I told him that I was calling at Ehrlichman's request on a matter relating to his previous discussions with Ehrlichman and Haldeman and I would like to have him visit with me if possible. He seemed somewhat surprised and uncertain about my call, so I told him he might like to check with Mr. Ehrlichman. He said he would get back to me later and he called me back to set up a meeting about noon on that date. When General Walters came to my office I told him again that I was meeting with him at Ehrlichman's request. I made some general comments about the Watergate case. It was from my discussions as a result of general comments with Walters that I became aware of the fact that Ehrlichman and Haldeman had discussed the Dahlberg and Mexican money. We then discussed the fact that some of the leads that the FBI were pursuing were to my understanding unrelated to the Watergate but could result in persons totally uninvolved being embarrassed. I would just like to note to counsel for the record that some of this is different from the original pagination of my draft that may have been lost through the transcribing of it here. I told him that I understood that the FBI had developed three possible theories in the case which I explained and asked if in fact any of the men arrested were persons who were working for the CIA. General Walters assured me that they were not. I then told him that I had been asked to explore every possible means of dealing with this rather embarrassing and troublesome situation because some of the men involved were looking for assistance. I asked him if there was any possible way that the CIA could be of assistance in providing support for the individuals involved. General Walters told me that while of course it could be done, he told me he knew the director's feeling about such a matter and that the director would do it only on a direct order from the President. He then went on to say that to do anything to compound the situation would be most unwise, that to involve the CIA could only compound the problem because it would require the President to become directly involved. While I cannot recall in detail everything that General Walters told me, I do recall that his argument was most sound and very persuasive. I told him that I agreed with his position fully and I had merely been asked to explore the potential which he rightly stated was too great a risk. As the discussion ended I asked him if he had any further ideas and told him I would appreciate the benefit of his thoughts. I thanked him for coming over and for his candid answers and he departed. Subsequent to my meeting with General Walters, I reported back to Ehrlichman that Walters had informed me that any involvement by the CIA in this matter was impossible. I recall that when I reported this to Ehrlichman, he very cynically said, 'Very interesting.' He told me that I should talk with General Walters further and push him a little harder to see if the CIA couldn't help out, particularly with regard to the necessary pursuit of investigative leads. I also recall Ehrlichman saying something to the effect that General Walters seems to have forgotten how he got where he is today."

Dean then went on to say that on the morning of the twenty-eighth, he arranged to meet with me, and he stated,

"I was first embarrassed about requesting the meeting, because he [General Walters] had been most explicit and convincing to me at the first meeting."

There is considerable confusion in some of this testimony inasmuch as he refers only to two meetings and there were three, on June 26, 27 and 28. Actually he did not make the bail suggestion to me until our second meeting on June 27. It was following that suggestion that I decided to make the memoranda. Dean noted also in his testimony before the Senate committee:

"Before Walters departed, I assured him that I agreed that it would be most unwise to involve the CIA and I thanked him almost apologetically for coming by again. At no time did I push him as I had been instructed."

Dean then went on to say that he subsequently informed Haldeman and Ehrlichman that unless the the President directly ordered the CIA to provide support for those involved, the CIA was not going to get involved. He added, "I told them that I agreed with Walters that this would be a terrible mistake and they both told me that they agreed."

Dean's testimony and mine do not coincide in several respects. I am prepared to stand on my recollection of my talks with him based on memoranda. He made none. Within two or three days of my first talk with him, I started preparing the memoranda on our discussions. He was testifying from his recollection a year later.

I do believe that it is quite clear from Dean's testimony that he got my message that I was not prepared to have the CIA involved in this matter in any way. I did not hear from John Dean again. I felt that I had made the point that there was no CIA involvement in this whole matter and that the agency was not going to put up any money for bail or anything else for those who had been arrested in connection with this case.

Since I had told Dean on three separate occasions that there was no CIA involvement in this matter, I was somewhat surprised to receive a phone call from FBI Acting Director Pat Gray late in the afternoon of July 5, telling me that he could no longer hold up the investigation in Mexico unless he received an indication from me in writing that this would jeopardize CIA sources. I obviously did not wish to discuss this matter with him over the phone and told him that I would come to see him next morning.

On the morning of July 6, I saw him at ten o'clock in his office. We were alone and had a cordial conversation. I handed him a memorandum which covered the relationship between the Watergate suspects and the agency; that is, covering the period of their employment and so forth. This had been prepared for the FBI by our personnel and security people. I told him that I could not tell him to cease further investigations in Mexico on the ground that this would compromise the security interests of the United States or the CIA. Even less could I write him a letter to that effect. He said he fully understood this. He himself had told Ehrlichman and Haldeman that he could not possibly suppress the investigation of this matter. Even within the FBI itself there were leaks. He had called in the components of his field office in Washington and "chewed them out" because information had leaked into the press concerning the Watergate case and they were the only ones who had this information. In the light of the past poor relations between the FBI and the CIA I told him that I thought the only basis on which he and I could deal was one of absolute frankness. I wished to recount my actions in this matter to him.

I had been called to the White House with Director Helms and had seen two senior staff assistants. I did not name Ehrlichman and Haldeman. I said that we had been told if this case were investigated further in Mexico it could lead to some awkward places and I had been directed (the implication being that the President had directed this, although it was not so specifically stated) to go to Acting Director Gray and tell him that if this investigation were to be pursued further in Mexico it could uncover some ongoing covert operations of the agency. I had believed what they told me and had done this. Subsequently, I had investigated this matter and had seen Mr. Dean, the White House counsel, and told him that there was no CIA involvement in this matter and that whatever the current unpleasant implications of the Watergate case were, to implicate the agency would not serve the President and would enormously increase the risk for him. I did not believe at this time that the President knew about this matter. The whole operation seemed so incredibly stupid and ill conceived that I thought it had been dreamed up at some middle-level meeting of overzealous political amateurs. All of my background led me to wish to protect my superiors, but I did not believe that a letter from me to the FBI telling them to lay off this investigation on the spurious grounds that it would uncover covert operations would serve the President. Such a letter in the current atmosphere of Washington would become known prior to Election Day and what was now a minor wound could become a mortal wound. I said that I would write such a letter only if personally directed by the President to do so and only after I had an opportunity of explaining to him how dangerous I thought such an action would be to him. I said to Gray that if I were really pushed on this matter, I was prepared to resign. Gray thanked me for my frankness and said that this opened the way to fruitful co-operation between us. He would be frank with me too. He could not stop the pursuit of this investigation. He had told Kleindienst this. He had told both Ehrlichman and Haldeman that he would prefer to resign. But his resignation would raise many questions that could be detrimental to the President's interest. Like me, he could not see why he or I should jeopardize the integrity of our organizations to protect some middle-level White House figure who had acted imprudently. He was prepared to let this go to Ehrlichman, Haldeman or Attorney General Mitchell for that matter. He felt that it was important that the President be protected from his would-be protectors. This was very similar to my own views. Gray said that he had explained this to Ehrlichman, Haldeman and Dean. He said that he was not anxious to talk to Mitchell because he was afraid that at his confirmation hearings he would be asked whether he had talked to Mitchell about the Watergate case and he wished to be in a position to reply negatively. He said that he would like to talk to the President about it but he feared that a request from him to see the President would be misinterpreted by the media. I said that I felt we should strongly resist any and all pressures to become involved in this incredible mess. I then repeated that if I were directed to write a letter to him saying that further investigation into this matter in Mexico would jeopardize ongoing operations of the agency, I would ask to see the President and explain to him the disservice I thought this would do him. The potential danger to the President of such a course would far outweigh any protective aspect it might have for other figures in the White House. I was quite prepared to resign on this issue. I told Pat Gray that I had recently inherited a considerable sum of money and I did not need my pension. I was not prepared to let myself "be pushed around by these kids." By kids I meant Dean and those like him. I must confess that I did feel a certain resentment at being peremptorily summoned three days in a row by Dean, who was little more than half my age. Gray said he understood this fully and hoped I would stick to my guns.

On July 12 the Office of Security at CIA gave me some additional data on the assistance that had been given to Howard Hunt and which was terminated in August 1971—long before I came to the agency—when his demands escalated to an inappropriate level. We had assisted him following a request from the White House and it was our understanding that it was for the purpose of tracking down security leaks in the government. I went to see Gray with this information. We then discussed the Watergate case and he told me that it could not be snuffed out and it would lead quite high politically. Gray said that the President had called him to congratulate him on the FBI action which had frustrated an airplane hijacking in San Francisco. Toward the end of the conversation, the President had asked Gray whether he had talked to me about the Watergate case. Gray replied that he had. The President then asked him what his recommendation was in this matter. Gray replied that the case could not be covered up, that it would lead quite high. He felt that the President should get rid of the people who were involved. Any attempt to involve the CIA or the FBI in this case could only prove a mortal wound and would achieve nothing. The President had then said, "Then I should get rid of whoever is involved no matter how high?" Gray replied that that was his recommendation. The President then asked Gray what I thought and Gray replied that that was my view also. I felt the same way about it as he did. The President, according to Gray, took this well and thanked him.

Later that day Gray had talked to Dean and had repeated the conversation to him. Dean's only comment was "Okay." Gray then asked me whether the President had spoken to me about this case and I replied that he had not. I had had one phone call from him about an intelligence matter involving the Soviet Union, but that was all. The President had at no time mentioned the Watergate case to me.

Gray then said that the U. S. Attorney had subpoenaed the financial records of the Committee to Reelect the President and it had been suggested to him that he stop this. He had replied that he could not. Whoever wanted this done should talk to the Attorney General to see if there was a legal way to get it done. He could not. He said that he had told the President in 1968 that he should beware of subordinates trying to wear his commander in chief stripes. I agreed, saying that in my view the President should be protected from his would-be protectors, who would harm him while trying to cover up their own mistakes. Even at this point, I could not conceive that the President might have been aware of what was going on. Gray said that our views coincided on this matter. He, too, would resign on this issue if necessary. I said that by maintaining the integrity of our services, we were rendering the President the best possible service.

On July 28, I again saw Acting Director Gray in his office. As on previous occasions we were alone. I gave him some additional information regarding the assistance which had been rendered to Howard Hunt. He had been given some disguises and personal documents. We had also loaned him a clandestine camera which was returned. We had developed one roll of film for Mr. Hunt, of which we had copies showing some unidentified building, possibly the Rand Corporation. This information had been given to me by the Office of Security in the CIA. The events had taken place nearly a year before I came to the agency. We had had no contact with Hunt since September 1971. Gray thanked me for this information and asked whether the President had called me on the Watergate matter. I replied that he had not. Gray then commented that a lot of pressure had been brought on him on this matter but he had not yielded. I said that to destroy the integrity and reputation of our service would be the worst disservice we could do to the President and I would not be a party to it. Gray said that he would not either. He commented as I left, "This is a hell of a thing to happen to us at the outset of our tenure in our respective offices." I agreed heartily with this. There were no further developments on this matter involving me. Further information was passed directly to the FBI without passing through me.

On the evening of February 9, 1973, John Dean telephoned the new director of Central Intelligence, Dr. James Schlesinger, and referred to a package of material that had been sent to the Department of Justice in connection with the Watergate investigation by the CIA. Dean suggested to Dr. Schlesinger that the department be requested to return this packet to the agency. Then the only information that would be left at Justice would be a card in the files indicating that the package had been returned to the agency. As soon as Dr. Schlesinger had been sworn in as director, I had briefed him in a general way on the Watergate matter and my knowledge of the events connected with it. Thus, he was generally aware of what had taken place. This was fortunate since he was thus able to judge Dean's request accurately. Dr. Schlesinger called me in and asked me what I thought of this request. I replied that we should not do what Dean wanted. The only result would be to leave an arrow in the Department of Justice files pointing directly at the CIA. It was interesting to me that Dean had not called me in this connection. I could only presume that he was tired of getting no for an answer from me and that he had called Dr. Schlesinger instead. The director, to whom I had reported my three conversations with Dean, then said, "Well, you've said no to him before, go down and say no to him again." I then attempted to reach Dean, but he was in Florida and it was not until February 21 that I was able to reach him and get an appointment. I went to his office in the Old Executive Building at 2:30 P.M. on the twenty-first. I explained to him that in connection with his request that we ask the Department of Justice to return this package, this was quite impossible. We had been asked not to destroy any material connected with Watergate. I repeated that there was no agency connection at all with this matter and to attempt to get us in any way involved would be harmful to the United States. He seemed disappointed and I left.

Eight months had passed since the Watergate break-in. The matter was still making considerable news in the papers. The election had taken place and Mr. Nixon had been easily reelected. At the time of the election, I had suggested to Helms that I submit my resignation, as was customary after an election. This would give the President the opportunity to replace me if he wished to do so. Helms replied that he did not want me to do this. He felt that such resignations should be submitted only for normal political posts. He did not wish the CIA to be in this category. He did not intend to submit his own resignation and he did not wish me to submit mine. I deferred to his wishes. Sometime after this he was called to Camp David to talk to the President. Upon his return it was quite clear to me that he would be leaving. He did not tell me this, but I could see it from his face. Not long afterward, the nomination of Dr. James R. Schlesinger was announced as the new director. During the period between Helms' departure to the State Department for briefings on Iran and the swearing in of Dr. Schlesinger, I was the acting director of Central Intelligence. During this period I went to the Far East. I went to Laos and flew into the beleaguered fortress of Long Tien. Here a small garrison under the able leadership of General Vang Pao had held out against the Communist Pathet Lao for many, many months. I also visited other installations in that area.

It was while I was in the Far East that the full publicity of the Watergate case began. I was in Taipei on my way home when I received a telegram from Dr. Schlesinger asking me to return at once. I rose at 4 A.M. and caught a plane and flew straight through to Washington, after changing planes in Tokyo. I was met at the airport by a helicopter and flew straight to CIA headquarteers at Langley. I returned from the Far East on May 10, 1973.

The investigation was in full swing and the press in full cry. Dr. Schlesinger asked me to prepare an affidavit recounting my whole connection with this matter and I did so. I was asked on May 11 to stop by the White House and see General Haig and Mr. J. Fred Buzhardt, President Nixon's counsel, inasmuch as they wanted to see whether there were any secret matters covered in my affidavit on which they might want to claim privilege. I left a copy of the affidavit with them on May 12. On May 14 I went down with Dr. Schlesinger to a briefing for the full Senate Armed Services Committee. This was chaired temporarily by Senator Stuart Symington in the absence of Senator Stennis, who had been shot in a holdup.

Toward the end of the hearing after I had testified fully, Senator Symington asked me whether I had made any memoranda concerning the discussions with Dean and Gray. I replied affirmatively. Senator Symington then asked me to bring these memoranda down to him and I replied that I would do so. The attitude of the Senate Armed Services Committee was curious and interested but not hostile. Later that afternoon I saw General Haig and Mr. Buzhardt and they said that there were no parts of my affidavit on which they wished to claim privilege.

Later that afternoon I also saw David Dorsen, who was the assistant chief counsel of the Senate Select Committee on Presidential Campaign Activities. I discussed the matter further with him. The following day, May 15, I saw Federal Prosecutor Earl Silbert in the U. S. Attorney's office. He was much taken by the fact that in Howard Hunt's papers they had found a copy of a letter from him congratulating me on my nomination as deputy director of Central Intelligence and a reply from me. They asked me when I had last seen Hunt and I replied that I had last seen him in Uruguay eleven years before. They asked me whether he was a close friend and I pointed out that in his letter he had addressed me as "dear Vernon." All of my friends call me by my nickname, which is "Dick." This seemed to satisfy them. I described again in great detail to the federal prosecutors all of the events in this case starting with the conversation in Ehrlichman's office. I testified also before other committees. On May 16 I testified before the House Armed Services Subcommittee on Intelligence, which was chaired by Congressman Lucien Nedzi. Congressman Nedzi, a troubled little man, was greatly agitated when I told him that I did not believe the President knew about these matters. At one point, he expressed doubt that I was telling the truth and I expressed my willingness to answer these questions in a lie detector test. He waved this offer aside angrily and did not pursue it further. I also gave him copies of my memoranda, as I had to Senator Symington.

In giving these copies of the memoranda to the committees of the House and Senate, I pointed out that these were simply memoranda I had made to refresh my own recollection. They did not purport to be full accounts of the conversations that they covered. They were a record of the salient points in my talks with Dean and Gray. On May 17 I testified again before the Senate Armed Services Committee. By this time, as might be expected, my memoranda had been leaked to the New York Times and were published on its front page. Senator Symington badgered me a little on this and asked if I had given them to the House Subcommittee. I replied that I had and he said, "Well, if you are going to give them to everybody, you must expect them to leak." The House Subcommittee and Mr. Nedzi had exactly the same right to them that Senator Symington did.

On May 18 I again saw the prosecutor, Mr. Silbert, at his office. On the twenty-first I testified for the third time before the House Armed Services Subcommittee and the Senate Armed Services Committee. On August 3, I had my "longest day." I testified for three hours before the Senate Select Committee on Presidential Campaign Activities, from 9:30 A.M. until 12:45 P.M. This Testimony was broadcast live on television. I had watched the testimony of previous witnesses closely and had learned from this. Some of them smoked furiously, others drummed their fingers on the table. Others crossed and uncrossed their legs and most of them were accompanied by lawyers. I made it plain that I did not wish to be accompanied by a lawyer. At the conclusion of my testimony, Senator Ervin said that I had testified so clearly he had no questions to ask me.

In the course of my testimony, I was asked about my relationship with Mr. Nixon. I said I had met him for the first time on the trip to South America in 1958. On two occasions during this trip, great violence had been encountered. I had been in the car with him when all of the windows were broken by angry mobs seeking to get at him, and if I did not tell the committee of the admiration I had for Mr. Nixon's courage and calm, I would be hiding part of the truth from them. Senator Ervin said that he wished to associate himself with my tribute to the President's courage.

On one occasion, I was told that there were some minor discrepancies in my testimony. I said that this was possible since I was being asked about events that had taken place over a year before, but I said that there were no substantial discrepancies. I noted that three of the four evangelists had been present at the crucifixion. They were all good and holy men, yet we have four separate versions of what was written on the scroll over His head on the cross. I simply happened to be a lesser man than Matthew, Mark, Luke or John.

I welcomed this opportunity to testify, live over television. It enabled me for the first time to give publicly my side of the story. There had been some innuendo by part of the press to the effect that I was Nixon's man, put there to oversee the whole thing. This in spite of the fact that I had served many Presidents and had reached the rank of major general before Mr. Nixon was elected.

In reporting on Dean's testimony concerning his talks with me, many newspapers in the United States had stopped their stories at the point where Dean testified that Ehrlichman had said to him, "Walters won't play ball. Go back and lean on him." Almost none of them reported the next sentence of Dean's testimony, "I was first embarrassed about requesting the meeting, because he had been most explicit and convincing to me at the first meeting."

Pat Gray testified immediately after I did. His recollection of what had transpired between us differed in some detail. Certain phrases he could not recall, but there was no basic contradiction between us on substance. Pat Gray was one of the real victims of Watergate. He was basically a fine and decent man.

My appearance before the Senate committee was not the last of such inquiries. On June 3, 1974, I had a long session with House Judiciary Committee investigators Messrs. Evan Davis, Bernard Nusbaum and Bob Traynor at CIA. None of these investigators would use previous testimony and asked me to describe the events again. Whether they hoped that if I were to testify enough times they would surely come up with some contradictions or not I do not know.

On August 27, 1974, I went again to the Special Prosecutor's office to testify anew on these matters. On November 11, 1974, I testified once more at the Ehrlichman and Haldeman trial before Judge Sirica. Prior to that I had also testified before the Watergate Grand Jury in August of 1974. This was an extremely brief matter. In all, I testified under oath on these matters nearly twenty times.

My own view during this long and harrowing period was that this idea was cooked up at a mid level in the White House entourage. When those who thought it up found that their men had been arrested and jailed, they started reaching up for help and cover. The President apparently out of loyalty tried to help them and this was a major mistake.

Watergate was an American tragedy in every sense of the word. Because of a basic mistake by the President, the presidency itself was crippled and has not yet fully recovered. The nation was shaken by a convulsion that has no parallel in our history. This at a time when we needed unity and consensus as never before. I saw a President who I thought was unusually able in foreign affairs and who projected to friends and enemies an image of strength brought down by his own lack of understanding of what the American people would tolerate. To this day, I believe Mr. Nixon harbors the idea that someone in the CIA tried to do him in, or acted in some way against him. He is wrong in this belief. The CIA simply could not act against any President. The people in the organization simply would not tolerate it.

Years later, after my retirement, I visited Mr. Nixon at San Clemente, as I had visited Mr. Truman at Independence and General Eisenhower at Gettysburg. Mr. Nixon asked me what he had done wrong. I replied, "Mr. President, there is no way in which what you did can be presented as right, but you can put it in some perspective." He was not the first President to do things that broke the law. Lincoln suspended habeas corpus, closed the Maryland State Legislature when he thought it would vote Maryland out of the Union. He used great force against the Copperheads, his war protesters. When Mr. Nixon came to power he found a war going on which he had not started. Leading members of the opposition were in touch with the enemy. I cannot forget Le Duc Tho's triumphant statement to Kissinger in Paris: "Your opposition will force you to give me what I want." Subsequent events tragically showed that Le Duc Tho was right. The Administration was eventually forced to abandon South Vietnam to the Communists. When Mr. Nixon came to power, the secrets of the United States were being spilled across the newspapers of the world, and unlike other nations, we had no law to prevent this. Had some of the "leakers" been citizens of democratic and socialist Sweden or of democratic and neutral

Switzerland, they would have spent twenty or thirty years in jail, as those countries prize their democratic freedoms as much as we do. Mr. Nixon understood that an unfriendly Congress was not about to give him such legislation and he took the law into his own hands in an attempt to stop this sort of thing. This was a major mistake in judgment and in the American framework it was wrong. I repeat that there is no way in which what Mr. Nixon did can be portrayed as right, but it seems to me that there should be some understanding of the circumstances in which he acted. There was tremendous opposition to the war. The bipartisan support for foreign policy had collapsed. The majority of the Congress was not in the President's hands. He himself believed that he was being persecuted and harassed.

In San Clemente when he asked me what he should have done, I said that if I could have reached him after the Watergate break-in, I would have told him what I told John Dean, "Fire everyone connected with this." I told him that he had been completely isolated either through his own action or that of his entourage. He nodded thoughtfully.

In the midst of an otherwise somber panorama, I had a few better moments. One of these was at a morning meeting at the CIA. Dr. Schlesinger in the spring of 1973 told me that a single misstep by me could have destroyed the agency and I did not make it. He then conferred upon me the Distinguished Intelligence Medal. The citation recognized that I had resisted great pressures on me and by so doing had avoided even more serious consequences for the agency. The simple fact is that the CIA was almost the only government organization not to do what was asked. This was obscured by many elements in the media which placed all the emphasis on the fact that I did go to Gray on July 23 as directed by Haldeman. I did this because I had no reason then to doubt the word of the President's Chief of Staff. The idea that he was asking me to do something illegal or wrong seemed preposterous at the time. He did not ask me to talk to Gray about stopping the whole investigation, *only* that part of it in Mexico. No emphasis was given to the fact that I refused Dean's appeal for help, and would not use secret funds to bail out the Watergate burglars. His own testimony to this effect is clear. Those who wanted to weaken or destroy the CIA had to cover up the fact that it had refused to participate in the cover-up. The impact of all this on the CIA was great. In the course of this investigation every opportunity was taken by the enemies of the intelligence process to drag out as much intelligence as possible and to try and discredit the agency and the use of intelligence by our government.

Americans have always had an ambivalent attitude toward intelligence. When they feel threatened they want a lot of it, and when they don't, they tend to regard the whole thing as somewhat immoral.

As I reflect on this tragic episode I recall the words of Winston Churchill, spoken in November 1940: "The only guide to a man is his conscience; the only shield to his memory is the rectitude and sincerity of his actions. It is very imprudent to walk through life without this shield, because we are so often mocked by the failure of our hopes and the upsetting of our calculations; but with this shield, however the fates may play, we march always in the ranks of honor."

30. LOOKING BACKWARD AND LOOKING FORWARD

As I look back across the more than one third of a century of my military service, I am grateful to my country and to its Army for a fascinating and rewarding career and for unimagined opportunities.

So much occurred during those eventful years that it is at times difficult for me to analyze what has seemed most important. The overwhelming impression I retain is of the importance of people. Great men shape events. They channel the currents of history and are not swept along by them.

As the United States moves into the last quarter of this century, we must bear in mind a number of factors that will decide whether we shall survive as a free and democratic society. Three factors strike me as particularly important.

First: The strength of a nation depends as much on its will, sense of direction and common purpose as it does on material power. The way we are compels us to search for something more than purely material gratification. We must find anew a consensus of our people that will give us once again the basis of a foreign policy that will guarantee our security and earn us respect.

Secondly: We must recognize the importance for us of an effective American intelligence organization that can shed some light on the dark and troubled waters that lie ahead. Our position of strength in the world is changing, not necessarily for the better. This calls for more vigilance on our part than ever before. Those who know that they cannot successfully surprise us will not be led into this temptation if we maintain the capability to pick up any preparations for a surprise attack against us. We must guard too against the efforts of some to make us feel so guilty that we will be unwilling to defend our freedoms and those of our allies.

Third: We must as a people maintain our ability to communicate with other peoples, not only through knowledge of their language, history and culture, but also by understanding the values that stir and inspire them and have made them what they are.

For the first time since Valley Forge we face a global power with the capability of inflicting grievous damage upon us. Tomorrow with China we may face still another. Germany and Japan at the height of their power were simply regional European or Asiatic powers. They were not global powers in the accepted sense of the word. Our own values have come under such attack at home that a certain uncertainty is felt in the land, both as to what is right and what we should do.

It is vital that we remember that what must be preserved is not just the physical integrity of our nation, but also those values that have made us what we are. With all of our shortcomings we have still produced the most equitable society that man has created since he came out of the caves. It gives a higher percentage of our people a chance at the good things of life than any other form of government that has evolved. Our system contains all of the mechanisms for orderly change when a majority desires such change.

We must find again a spirit that many of us have lost. We must rekindle our faith in our way of life and renew our commitment to justice for all of our people.

We must always remember that a certain innocence is to be respected and admired, not derided and scorned. The cynic and the skeptic would lead us down the drab road to decline and self-abasement.

With faith and courage our tomorrows will yet be brighter than all our yesterdays.

Day by day the world in which we live grows smaller. New countries, new forms of government are constantly emerging. We live in closer contact with them than at any time in our past. We can no longer afford the isolation we knew in the past when wide oceans and vast distances insulated us in a sense from others. A mighty struggle is under way between different conceptions of life and human dignity. Our example of affluence and well-being is not enough. Today we are the target of a vast but subtle attack. We must find the way to explain our side of the story to others, or our enemies will win the struggle for the minds and hopes of men. We must not lose this struggle through our own default or an excessive sense of guilt for our imperfections.

Since World War II our enemies have focused upon our innate moral sense and encouraged us to blame ourselves for matters in which we played no part or had little ability to influence the outcome. Our own shortcomings have been emphasized, our mistakes and omissions trumpeted. Only a few years ago we felt that we had a country and a way of life that offered new hope to all mankind. We had built a society in which a larger percentage of people enjoyed the good things of life than in any previous society. Opportunities for change and social betterment were increasingly in evidence. Now many of our people are haunted by a sense of anxious guilt for the shortcomings and sins of commission and omission of our past. Many feel guilty because we are rich and prosperous, because we have not always treated all of our fellow citizens fairly, because we are responsible for so much of the progress of our time. The United States developed and employed nuclear weapons solely to end the war. President Truman decided to use the weapon to prevent the loss of millions of lives, military and civilian, American and Japanese, the inevitable price of an invasion of the Japanese islands. These feelings are hammered into us by those who believe that small is good, humiliation is salutary, progress is evil, and by those who yearn to return to the womb. Of course we are not without sin;

clearly there have been episodes in our national life of which we are not proud. We have not come this far as a nation in the last two hundred years without our share of injustice, arrogance and omission. We must not allow these flaws to destroy our sense of perspective. We have fought several great wars in this century. We have annexed no territory, we have forced no one to become an American who did not want to do so. We have deprived no other people of their freedom. After these wars in a gesture that is without parallel in all human history, we have stretched out our hands to those who were our enemies and helped them to rise from the ashes of defeat. More than that, we have financed them back into competition with us. At the end of the Second World War almost all of the factories in the world lay either in ruins or filled with worn-out antiquated machinery. If today Volkswagen, Fiat or Renault sell thousands of cars in the United States it is because in those early years after the war we put machine tools in their factories through the Marshall Plan. Our generosity made it possible for them to compete with us, not just in world markets but in the United States itself. We helped them to become productive, self-supporting and confident again. In all human history of which we have record I know of no similar gesture from victor to vanquished. Churchill described it as "the single most unselfish act."

Twenty-five centuries ago a Chinese author wrote *The Art of War*. Sun-tzu relies upon the historical constancy of human nature to bring about the downfall of an enemy. He describes the techniques to be used to humble a hostile power. Fighting is the crudest form of making war upon an enemy. Break the will of the enemy to fight and you accomplish the true objective of war. Sun-tzu tells us to cover with ridicule the enemy's traditions, involve his leaders in criminal enterprises and then turn them over to the scorn of their fellow countrymen. Exploit and aggravate the inherent frictions within the enemy country. Agitate the young against the old. Prevail if possible without armed conflict. "The supreme excellence," states Sun-tzu, "is not to win a hundred victories in a hundred battles. The supreme excellence is to subjugate the armies of your enemies without ever having to fight them." Our constitutional democracy is an ideal crucible in which to test the theories of Sun-tzu. Our society offers all of the mechanisms for orderly change. Communist societies seek only to preserve the status quo. Today Sun-tzu remains required reading in the military and political schools of those who would humble and destroy us.

Experience leads me to believe that the greatest danger to our way of life and freedoms does not come from the Communist parties of the world. They are not an overwhelming danger to us. They are so easily recognized that they cannot be fully effective. Their unwillingness to fault Marxism invalidates in great part what they say. In some measure they are aware of this and are working hard, especially in Europe, to build a new image of the human face of communism. For my part I fear far more the pious dupes of the New Left who condemn equally, in words at least, the United States and the Soviet Union. If we examine their deeds, however, we find a different pattern. Against the Soviet Union they use only words. Against the United States they use murder, vilification and violence. They kill American diplomats and representatives abroad. They attack U.S. installations. They hijack U.S. aircraft. They peddle as gospel every lie about us. The overwhelming majority of this New Left sincerely think of themselves as truly independent and opposed to Soviet as well as American imperialism. Yet the result of their activities redounds to the benefit of the Soviet imperial web. The unrelenting worldwide campaign of the New Left preaches American principles to undermine the institutions that secure American democracy. Fidelity to our Constitution requires toleration of the denial or denunciation of God, country, family and flag. We must tolerate the slanders against those who defend our country; the denigration of the virtues that brought our nation into being. These are manna from heaven for those who wish to replace our way of life with a harsh tyranny masquerading as a progressive ideal. There is no corresponding denigration of the values of Marxism within the Communist world. Only one side suffers: ours.

Communism has now been in control of the largest country

in the world for six decades. The Russians control a crop-grow-ing area far larger than ours, yet they are still unable to feed ade-quately a population only slightly larger than ours. It takes thirty-two Russians on the farm to feed one hundred Russians. It takes only two Americans on the farm to feed one hundred Americans, and we export great quantities of food as well. There is an apocryphal story to the effect that at the Missouri-Kansas border there is a large billboard which says "Welcome to Kan-sas, the breadbasket of the Soviet Union." If the sign is not there it ought to be. Any society that after sixty years is still una-ble to feed its population is not the wave of the future.

History shows us that America cannot be stopped from the outside. If our enemies are to win then America must be stopped from within. Vietnam, Cambodia, Laos, Angola and to a lesser extent the Dominican Republic are there to show what can be done if Americans can be made to feel that what they are doing is wrong and immoral. In the last few years some 40 mil-lion human beings have passed under Communist rule because this tactic has been successful. Those peoples may not have en-joyed all of the liberties to which we may have thought them en-titled, but today they have far less and their voices of protest are now silenced by the total tyranny of communism. If we look at history we can see at once the parallel of the reoccupation of the Rhineland by Hitler. Then followed the annexation of the Saar, Austria, the Sudetenland, all of Czechoslovakia, Danzig and Memel. Because Britain and France were paralyzed from within there followed the attack on Poland and World War II. Nations can seek to postpone resisting the assaults of tyranny but history is a harsh teacher and it haunts those who sought to avoid un-pleasant tasks. We cannot be the policeman of the whole world but we do not have the right to ask like Cain, "Am I my brother's keeper?" Those who point to our failures and say, "We are as bad as the Communists, look at the things we have done," are either naïve, ignorant or willing servants of tyranny. In our concern for the rights of our citizens, and this is a vital concern, we sometimes forget that we require those who defend us to take an oath to defend the United States against all enemies, foreign and domestic. America cannot survive abroad if it is rendered helpless at home. Any society that cannot or will not defend itself will perish.

In the unending struggle for freedom we must be able to communicate with all those who wish to remain free. Too long have we expected all of our friends to speak English. Too long have we relied upon our immigrants and their children for language ability. The grandchildren of the immigrants rarely speak the language of the old country. In the years ahead we shall be faced with acute shortages of qualified people to communicate with our friends and enemies. Yet in the American educational system today we see decreasing emphasis given to the study of foreign languages. Many are convinced that a technical education offers far greater rewards than one which builds the skills for communication with other peoples. We have greater need for these skills than at any time in our national life. Our ability to get our side before the peoples of the world may well depend on our finding those who can speak articulately for us. It is not just ability to speak foreign languages that we need. This skill must go hand in hand with knowledge and understanding of other peoples' history, literature, culture and even poetry; in a word, all the things that make them what they are.

On one occasion the U.S. government sent me to talk to a most hostile group of terrorists. I saw them alone and unarmed in a part of the world sympathetic to their cause. My position made me a major target. I had studied their past, their hopes, their dreams, even their poetry. I was able to convey to them the message that I had been ordered to deliver. We were able to communicate and there were no further acts of blood between us.

The actions which we take as a people are in large measure determined by the policy we have for that particular subject. We often believe that this is also the way other peoples act. Some do but most do not. The vast majority of the peoples of the world are moved by human relationships and by personal feelings of friendship or hostility. If people like you they will not always do what you want. It has been my experience that if they do not like you they will invariably not do what you want.

During the great investigations into the United States intelligence community I had occasion to talk to many chiefs of foreign intelligence services, friendly and otherwise. Damage was being done to us not by the enemy, but by a distorted sense of national guilt cleverly exploited by those hostile to us. Many of these chiefs of foreign services were appalled at the spectacle of the United States dragging into public view not just dubious actions, but many of the sources and methods by which we worked. The United States seemed to them to have gone on an orgy of self-denigration. No one believes that secrecy should be used to cover up wrongdoing. Improper actions can and should be thoroughly investigated and appropriate punitive action should be taken. The circus-like atmosphere, however, is unnecessary and actually tends to undermine the credibility of the investigation while doing serious harm to the national intelligence services. In many democratic countries there have been investigations into the actions of the intelligence services. In nearly every case these investigations were conducted in a thorough, responsible and discreet manner but were not allowed to offer certain politicians prime TV time to advance their political ambitions.

During these difficult times I did what I could to reassure our friends that the United States would soon return to more sensible behavior and would once again act like a reasonable and rational nation, willing to defend its way of life.

I do not by any means believe that we should use the same methods as the dictatorial and tyrannical regimes who oppose us; but if we use kid gloves when they use brass knuckles then our way of life and with it human freedom will stand in very great danger.

Important to the defense of our cause is the knowledge of history. This enables us to rebut falsehoods and place truths in proper perspective. An awareness of the culture and literature of other peoples makes them more accessible to us. The ability of our friends to hear us in their own language makes us more effective and credible. We cannot disregard the need for such abilities and understanding at a time when the spoken or written word leaps across distances with the speed of light. If we know and understand our own history this enables us to comprehend our own present. By remembering the antics of Joe McCarthy yesterday we can understand better the Frank Church and Otis Pike of our own time. Our own history speaks to us of our tomorrows. It tells us what is transitory and what is lasting. Many of the things that seem strange to us have happened before. A new phenomenon, I believe, is the thirst for notoriety that leads some to paint the defenders of their country as the worst threats to its freedoms. The men and women who serve America on the silent battlefield of intelligence have neither the forum nor the means to rebut these slanders.

On one occasion at the height of the attack on the intelligence services I spoke at the National Press Club in Washington. I spoke for thirty-five minutes and then answered questions for a similar period. I tried to dispel some of the falsehoods that had been circulating about American intelligence. At that time I was the second highest official in the Central Intelligence Agency. On the following day both of the Washington newspapers reported only that there had been a meeting and that new officers had been elected. An organization devoted to fairness in the media took these papers to task for their silence. They explained that I had "not said anything new." When asked what "anything new" might be they had replied that further derogatory revelations about the CIA would fit into that category. In short, these papers were interested only in an attack on the intelligence organizations, not in anything that might be said in their defense.

People are the ultimate goal of those who believe in majority government. We must be able to reach and convince them. We must have access to them through a knowledge of their language, culture and values. We must know what are the things that stir their souls. I regret that in some of our service schools there persists the illusion that all a graduate requires is technical and specialized training. If we are to survive we must have defenders who know more than small-unit tactics, nuclear propulsion plants and delta wing structures.

Much has been made of the alleged threats to American liberties from our own intelligence agencies. Some cases of stupidity and overzealousness have been distorted into a broad pattern of dangers to our liberties. I speak only of the Central Intelligence Agency in this connection. In the past thirty years some 76,000 men and women have passed through its ranks. None has been convicted or even indicted for threatening the freedoms of his fellow citizens. I submit that the record of the intelligence organizations compares favorably to that of most other government organizations. Biased reporting and propagandistic journalism have sometimes hidden this fact.

I come now to the question of intelligence itself. What is it, why do we need it, how do we get it and what do we do with it when we get it?

Intelligence is information, not always available in the public domain, relating to the strength, resources, capabilities and intentions of a foreign country that can affect our lives and the safety and future of our people. By far the most difficult type of information to obtain is that which relates to the intentions of other governments or leaders. Normally this can only be obtained from human sources, that is to say, by espionage.

Why do we need intelligence? We need it because our leaders are required to make their decisions in an entirely new framework of time and speed. We no longer can deliberate at great length about what we ought to do. Shrinking distances and time factors compel decision-making at a far faster rate than we have known in the past. The decisions are more complex and have more far-reaching consequences. Such decisions must be made on the basis of maximum knowledge of all the factors involved. Right decisions can only be made on the basis of the best possible information. We were able to survive Pearl Harbor because we had two great oceans and time and distance to protect us. The Japanese did not press home their advantage, our aircraft carriers were not in port when the attack came. Most of all we survived and won because the attack itself united our peo-

ple and unleashed the staggering industrial capacity of the
United States. I doubt that any future enemy will ever again
give us such a nation-unifying provocation. Nonetheless, thinking Americans must ask themselves whether we could survive a
nulear Pearl Harbor. If the answer is no, then we must understand that the greatest deterrent to such an attack is the perception by a potential enemy that the United States has the capability of detecting the preparations for such action and the means
for massive retaliation. We must have both an effective intelligence community and the forces sufficient to discourage any
country from contemplating aggression against the United
States.

The intelligence community in the United States is made up
of a number of organizations. Some of them are civilian, such as
the Central Intelligence Agency and the intelligence components of the State, Treasury and Justice departments. Others are
military, such as the Defense Intelligence Agency, the National
Security Agency and the intelligence components of the armed
services. The director of Central Intelligence is by statute the
head of this community. He must approve the budgetary requests of each of the components before they can go forward to
the Congress. He co-ordinates and directs the efforts of the various components but he does not have command authority over
any of them. He does of course have command authority over
the Central Intelligence Agency. Its primary mission is to provide national intelligence to the President, the Secretaries of
State, Defense and Treasury and other interested government
departments. The National Security Agency is headed by a senior officer of the Armed Forces and deals with communications. The Defense Intelligence Agency is likewise headed
by an officer of the Armed Forces and is charged with providing the information required by the Secretary of Defense
and the Joint Chiefs of Staff. It also co-ordinates the activities of
the several intelligence components of the armed services in
areas beyond their immediate responsibility to their own service.
In all of these military intelligence organizations there are large
numbers of civilians. In many cases they occupy senior positions,

sometimes they hold the No. 2 spot. The intelligence components of State and Treasury are responsible to their own departments and share in the intelligence collected by the community
as a whole. The Justice Department and through it the FBI is
responsible for counterintelligence activities in the United
States.

The intelligence community does not operate in watertight
compartments. They share collected data and are all working on
the basis of the same information. The analysts are in touch
with one another on subjects of common interest. All of the
major areas of intelligence, whether in forces or in geographic
areas, have a national intelligence officer who is in continual
touch with everyone in the community who has knowledge of
this particular area or subject. He acts as a sort of co-ordinator
and when a study is requested he designates a drafter and follows the study to completion. This national intelligence officer
is not in the chain of command. Many wonder if there is not
some duplication within the community. There is. What is essential is that this duplication not reach wasteful or destructive
proportions. A certain amount of duplication held within reasonable limits can provide additional perspective. I have always
been able to get a far better picture by looking through binocu-
lars than through a telescope.

Often the analysts of the various organizations do not agree.
The military generally take a less optimistic view than the CIA
does. They feel that they are nearer to military realities than the
civilian agency. The CIA in turn often is tempted to feel that
the military are simply offering conclusions to support the budgetary requests of the Secretary of Defense. Neither of these
views is wholly correct. The decision makers generally have to
understand that they will get some variation in views between
the civilian and military intelligence organizations. In recent
years Congress has tended to place more emphasis on the CIA
view since it enables them to vote in good conscience somewhat
smaller defense appropriations. Historically both organizations
have been right on occasions where they had basically divergent
views. There is no strong evidence to show that one is right

more often than the other. In a very human way each organization tends to remember rather well the times when it was right. Often because of new intelligence or acquisition of a reliable human source estimates have had to be changed, sometimes very substantially, as was the case not long ago on Soviet defense expenditures.

Fortunately the decision makers in our government receive the divergent points of view. Estimates and studies reflect the majority view of the community, but there are footnotes that reflect dissents and the reasons for them. When these studies go to the President and Secretary of State or Defense they are aware of the differences of view, if any, between the members of the community. The CIA sometimes tends to take a more hopeful view of differences in the Socialist camp, whereas the military services tend to view such things as Eurocommunism or the human face of socialism with considerable skepticism. Thus Congress sometimes hears two voices, the CIA which says, "Beware, but it is not that bad," and the military who simply say, "Beware." Only the years that lie ahead will tell us who was right more often. The great problem of our time is that Communist takeovers tend to be permanent and irreversible, in contrast to the rightist dictatorships, which have never solved the problem of perpetuating themselves beyond the life of a particular dictator. The Communists are durable. Once in power they do not leave.

We collect intelligence in many ways: from open and published sources; through the great technical systems that American genius had adapted to the world's oldest profession—intelligence, not prostitution—and finally through human sources.

Open collection probably accounts for by far the largest percentage of intelligence, but it is the most easily gathered. Next in volume comes the intelligence from the technical systems. While second in volume it is very much more sensitive and useful. The human sources collect the smallest volume of intelligence but generally it is the most difficult to obtain and the most useful when we do get it. It is in this area that the best information is acquired on the all-important subject of intentions.

It is not enough to know a great deal about a potential enemy's strength, deployment and resources. It is vital to know what his intentions are, as this is the key to our own decisions.

An essential requirement for the proper use of intelligence is access to the decision makers and knowledge of their requirements. We cannot collect everything that it would be nice to know. We may be rich but our resources are not unlimited. Our leaders must tell us what their priority requirements are and we can then apply the available resources to satisfy them. We must know our own agencies well enough to know who has the ability to collect against certain targets and who does not. In this way we can avoid frittering away the assets of those who are not in a position to collect successfully against a particular target.

Vital also to the proper use of intelligence is objective and unprejudiced analysis. Even the best intelligence improperly analyzed can be misleading. Those who work in analysis generally come from the academic world and reflect this somewhat placid environment. Those who collect generally live in contact with a harsher and more realistic world. The problem arises from the fact that the collectors do not analyze and the analysts do not live in contact with this harsher world. To men from Academia it often seems illogical that the Soviet Union intends to dominate the world and spread communism to every country. Their study of history tells them that no one has been successful in doing this, therefore it is not logical for the Soviet Union to attempt it. The intellectual inclination to seek Utopia has a great deal to do with wishful thinking about the Soviets. During my time at the CIA I had several extensive discussions with some of these analysts. We disagreed profoundly on certain studies about Italy, Cuba and other areas. Their academic credentials were far greater than mine, but I had lived in Italy and spoke the language well. In early 1962 I had accompanied Fidel Castro around Washington and had taken him to call on Vice-President Nixon and the Secretary of State. To me he was not a statistic, he was a person, and I thought, perhaps mistakenly, that I knew something about him. Subsequent events have not changed my views. Those who believe that Italian Communists are not genuine Communists any more are deceiving themselves as much as those who believe that Fidel Castro no longer wants to export the revolution. While I disagreed with them I did not attempt to force my views on them. This is a sensitive area because there is a tendency in some analysts to regard disagreement from above as an attempt to coerce their thinking or limit their freedom. Perhaps I should pay a little more attention to academic credentials and they should set a little more store by practical experience. In the past nearly all of our analysts had some form of military experience in their background. Today a new generation enters without such experience.

Whether we like it or not almost half of mankind is ruled by some form of military government—rightist or leftist, but military. The hard facts are that no one can talk to a soldier like another soldier. We must recognize this fact and use it where it can be of service to our nation.

Intelligence demands immense patience. An operation may be undertaken that will produce almost nothing for a long time. Then suddenly it will yield enormous results that amortize the project many times over. Another will yield nothing. The application of the principles of cost effectiveness to intelligence demands a very special kind of skill and judgment. We must select our priorities for intelligence carefully and then devote the appropriate amount of resources to those priorities. It is clear that intelligence is not really an exact science. Good judgment in dealing with it is as always the most important element.

Many sensationalist writers have on occasion given the American public the image of a vast threatening intelligence apparatus that is really making the key decisions in the U.S. government. I learned how false this was early in my tenure as deputy director of Central Intelligence. The director was away and as acting director I was attending a meeting at the White House chaired by Henry Kissinger. I briefed the group and then presented the intelligence views of the consequences of several options that were being considered. Following this Kissinger went around the table asking for the point of view of the various government departments represented at the meeting. Each expressed his preference for a particular option. As Kissinger came to me he pointed his finger questioningly and I instinctively replied with the option I favored. He wagged his finger at me and said, "You in intelligence don't have a vote." He then went on to the man sitting next to me, who did. Intelligence of course can exercise some, even considerable, influence by the form in which it presents the possible consequences of the several options. The decisions are made without the vote of the intelligence agencies.

In the military services intelligence had long been regarded as a side show and not an area that would lead to promotion and influence. In recent years this has changed. The Armed Forces have produced many outstanding intelligence officers. The Army has given us men like Danny Graham, who resigned as director of Defense Intelligence when Jim Schlesinger was fired as Secretary of Defense; and Sam Wilson, an outstanding linguist and intelligence officer. The Air Force has given us men with the integrity of Gene Tighe and the tenacity of George Keegan. The Navy has given us men with the perseverance of Rex Rectanus and the brilliance of Bobby Inman. I was fortunate enough to become one of the first general officers from the arm of military intelligence and the second reserve officer in American history to reach the rank of lieutenant general in the United States Army.

Perhaps the most fascinating aspect of my career has been meeting the people who fight for us on the invisible battlefield of intelligence, a battlefield that is quiet but never still. My own experience with those I met in the intelligence services of the Armed Forces was a truly rewarding one. These were splendid men and women serving with devotion and integrity. I count myself lucky to have worked with such people for nearly thirty years. Their love of our country and the high motivation with which they served it will always remain before me as a superb example. I have no words adequate to express my pride in having served among them.

I would speak too of the men and women who served in the Central Intelligence Agency during my tenure as deputy director or acting director. I have never known a finer group of Americans. They live by the same principles and beliefs as their fellow countrymen. I am as proud of my association with them as I am of my service in the Army. They stood steadfast as a rock under a barrage of lies, slander and innuendo without parallel in American history. Their sturdy courage helped bring the agency through the almost mortal storm that rocked it. It survived because of them and because the American people understand that without effective intelligence the United States would be a blind and deaf giant, helpless before its enemies. This our people will not tolerate.

On many occasions it was my proud privilege to present medals to men and women who had served well and often heroically on the invisible battlefield and on the battlefields of Southeast Asia. On not a few occasions as I awarded medals that would win no publicity for those who had earned them, I found tears in my eyes as the citations were read. I was not ashamed of them, for they were not tears of weakness, they were tears of pride.

When Bill Colby left the CIA in December 1975 I announced that I would remain only for the transition until the new director was firmly in place. This transition lasted longer than I had expected, more than six months. On the day George Bush arrived as director I handed him an undated letter of resignation. I told him he could date it and send it to the President whenever he wished. On July 7 my successor was confirmed by the Senate. A few days before my departure I was given a heartwarming farewell dinner by my friends and colleagues at the CIA. One can only retire from the Army on the last day of the month so my resignation from the Army took effect on July 31, 1976. The Army gave me my third Distinguished Service Medal and a retirement parade at Fort Myer. Several days before my retirement President Ford approved the award to me of the National Security Medal. This is the highest award for service in intelligence. The medal has been awarded only some twenty times in the nearly thirty years of its existence. I was the first deputy director of Central Intelligence to receive it. I was naturally pleased and honored. President Ford personally awarded me the medal in the Oval Office in the White House. The presentation of the medal took place in the presence of Vice-President Rockefeller; Secretary of State Kissinger, Secretary of Defense Rumsfeld; the chairman of the Joint Chiefs of Staff, General George Brown; the director of Central Intelligence, George Bush; the Chief of Staff of the United States Army, General Fred Weyand; and members of my family. Other senior members of the intelligence community were also present. Once again I felt that my country had been inordinately generous with me.

On the day I left the Central Intelligence Agency I walked down into the great marble lobby of the headquarters and stood silently for a few minutes in front of the stars carved into the marble on the right side of the lobby to commemorate those of the agency who have laid down their lives that we might live free. Their sacrifice was made on an invisible battlefield and their glory is known but to a few. They will live forever in the hearts of those who know what they did. I reflected on how much they had given in comparison to me and felt humbly thankful for their sacrifice.

As I stood there I thought that in the stormy years ahead our country will need dedication, hard work and skill. Most of all we will need courage, not just physical courage but true courage. True courage swims against the tide. True courage begins when everyone else has either given in or stopped fighting. True courage is never being swept along by what everyone else is doing. True courage is often lonely. On our journey I pray that we will have as our companions Faith to light the road ahead, for dark is the path of the nation that walks without faith; Enthusiasm that has made us great and will keep us a force for good in the world; and finally Courage, greatest of all human virtues since it guarantees all of the others.

I look forward to the years ahead with unbounded faith in our great destiny. It is not, as the pessimists would have us believe, twilight. It is daybreak. The American dream has only just begun.

As I look back gratefully across the thirty-five years in which I had the honor of serving the American people, the thought occurs to me that to each man it is given to live one life on this earth. A great part of mine was spent in the service of my country and its Army. They have rewarded me beyond the wildest dreams of the young private who entered their service in 1941. I have loved them both more than the written or spoken word can say.

INDEX

Marshall Plan and, 171, 177–79;
and NATO, 211, 225
Green, Julian, 18–19
Green, William, 8
"Green and Gold Hour," 132
Green Berets Special Forces
(Vietnam), 443, 444, 451
Grées du Loup, Colonel des, 501
Gremlin's Castle (plane), 81
Gromyko, Andrei, 287, 288, 538
Gronchi, Giovanni, 298
Gross, Ernest, 260–61
Gruenther, Alfred M., 108, 220,
226, 230–31, 233, 281, 282–83;
described, 230–31, 283
Gruenther, Grace, 230–31
Guay, Georges, 520, 521

Haakon VII, King (Norway), 216
Habib, Philip, 508
Hagerty, Jim, 294, 304
Hague, The, 259
Haig, Alexander M., Jr., 501, 520,
521, 540, 543, 578, 605
Haldeman, H. Robert, 558, 575,
588–89, 590, 596, 598, 599,
600–1, 608, 610
Hall, Chuck, 531, 549
Halsey, Admiral William F., Jr.,
143
Hamblen, General, 203
Hamilton, Colonel, 14
Hanoi, 507 (*see also* North
Vietnam); Hilton, 506; and
Paris peace talks, 509–22 *passim*
"Hardtack" (U.S. nuclear tests),
284
Harmel, Pierre, 560
Harmon, General Ernest N.,
39–40, 42–43, 45, 46, 47, 48–49
Harriman, Marie (Mrs. W.
Averell Harriman), 245, 246,
257, 269, 274

Harriman, W. Averell, 149, 151,
152, 156, 157, 161–62, 163–64,
168–69, 324, 354, 400, 560; and
De Gaulle, 497; described,
163–64, 176–77, 188, 242, 246;
and Marshall Plan, 172, 173,
176, 177, 178, 179, 180–81,
188–89; and Mossadegh and
British-Iranian oil dispute,
242–63 *passim*; and Tito and
Yugoslavia, 266–74 *passim*; and
Truman and MacArthur,
190–98, 202, 203, 204, 207; and
Vietnam peace talks, 507–8;
Walters as assistant to, 149, 168,
169, 172, 173, 176–77, 178–79,
180–81, 188–89, 190–201, 208,
213, 217, 219–20, 223, 242–63
passim, 266ff., 559–60
Hassan, Crown Prince (later King
Hassan II, Morocco), 52, 308
Hawaii, 207. *See also* Honolulu
Hay, John H., 43
Helena, Princess (Romania), 147
Helms, Richard, 585, 586, 587–89,
590–93 *passim*, 596, 599, 604–5
Herter, Christian, 299
Hill, Robert, 552, 553
Hill 881 (Vietnam), 419
History, knowledge of, 619–20
Hitler, Adolf, 5, 54, 91, 197, 478,
564, 574, 617
Ho Chi Minh, 512, 515
Hochmuth, Bruno, 419–20
Hoffman, Paul, 183, 185
Holland. *See* Netherlands
Hong Kong, 76, 410
Honolulu, Hawaii, 203, 207
Hoover, J. Edgar, 589
Horsey, Outerbridge, 362
House Armed Services
Subcommittee on Intelligence,
606, 607